THE MESSIANIC THEOLOGY OF
THE NEW TESTAMENT

The
MESSIANIC THEOLOGY
of the
NEW TESTAMENT

Joshua W. Jipp

WILLIAM B. EERDMANS PUBLISHING COMPANY

GRAND RAPIDS, MICHIGAN

Wm. B. Eerdmans Publishing Co.
4035 Park East Court SE, Grand Rapids, Michigan 49546
www.eerdmans.com

26 25 24 23 22 21 20   1 2 3 4 5 6 7

ISBN 978-0-8028-7717-8

Library of Congress Cataloging-in-Publication Data

Names: Jipp, Joshua W., 1979– author.
Title: The Messianic theology of the New Testament / Joshua W. Jipp.
Description: Grand Rapids, Michigan : William. B. Eerdmans Publishing Com-
    pany, 2020. | Includes bibliographical references and index. | Summary: "An
    overview of the New Testament as a collection of texts that proclaims Jesus
    as the messiah"—Provided by publisher.
Identifiers: LCCN 2020020634 | ISBN 9780802877178
Subjects: LCSH: Messiah—Biblical teaching. | Bible. New Testament—Criticism,
    interpretation, etc.
Classification: LCC BT230 .J56 2020 | DDC 225.6—dc23
LC record available at https://lccn.loc.gov/2020020634

Contents

PART TWO

THE MESSIANIC THEOLOGY OF THE NEW TESTAMENT

Abbreviations

AcBib	Academia Biblica
AnBib	Analecta Biblica
ANTC	Abingdon New Testament Commentaries
ANRW	*Aufstieg und Niedergang der römischen Welt*
ASE	*Annali di storia dell' esegesi*
AThR	*Anglican Theological Review*
ATR	*Australasian Theological Review*
AYB	Anchor Yale Bible
AYBRL	Anchor Yale Bible Reference Library
BBR	*Bulletin for Biblical Research*
BDAG	W. Bauer, F. W. Danker, W. F. Arndt, and F. W. Gingrich, *Greek English Lexicon of the New Testament and Other Early Christian Literature,* 3rd ed. (Chicago: University of Chicago Press, 2000)
BECNT	Baker Exegetical Commentary on the New Testament
BETL	Bibliotheca Ephemeridum Theologicarum Lovaniensium
Bib	*Biblica*
BibInt	Biblical Interpretation Series
BTB	*Biblical Theology Bulletin*
BZNW	Beihefte zur Zeitschrift für die Neutestamentliche Wissenschaft
CBQ	*Catholic Biblical Quarterly*
ConBOT	Coneictanea Biblica: Old Testament Series
CQ	*Church Quarterly*
CurBS	*Currents in Biblical Studies*
EC	*Early Christianity*
ET	English translation
ExpTim	*Expository Times*
FAT	Forschungen zum Alten Testament
ICC	International Critical Commentary
HBT	*Horizons in Biblical Theology*
HTR	*Harvard Theological Review*

HTS	Harvard Theological Studies
Int	*Interpretation*
JBL	*Journal of Biblical Literature*
JETS	*Journal of the Evangelical Theological Society*
JRS	*Journal of Roman Studies*
JSJ	*Journal for the Study of Judaism in the Persian, Hellenistic, and Roman Periods*
JSNT	*Journal for the Study of the New Testament*
JSNTSup	Journal for the Study of the New Testament Supplement Series
JSOT	*Journal for the Study of the Old Testament*
JSOTSup	Journal for the Study of the Old Testament Supplement Series
JSPL	*Journal for the Study of Paul and His Letters*
JSPSup	Journal for the Study of the Pseudepigrapha Supplements
JSS	*Journal of Semitic Studies*
JTI	*Journal of Theological Interpretation*
JTS	*Journal of Theological Studies*
LNTS	Library of New Testament Studies
MT	Masoretic Text
NICNT	New International Commentary on the New Testament
NIGTC	New International Greek Testament Commentary
NKZ	*Neue kirchliche Zeitschrift*
NovT	*Novum Testamentum*
NovTSup	Supplements to Novum Testamentum
NSBT	New Studies in Biblical Theology
NTL	New Testament Library
NTS	*New Testament Studies*
RB	*Revue biblique*
SBLDS	Society of Biblical Literature Dissertation Series
SBLEJL	Society of Biblical Literature Early Judaism and Its Literature
SBLMS	Society of Biblical Literature Monograph Series
SBT	Studies in Biblical Theology
SJT	*Scottish Journal of Theology*
SNTSMS	Society for New Testament Studies Monograph Series
SNTW	Studies of the New Testament and Its World
SP	Sacra Pagina
SSEJC	Studies in Scripture in Early Judaism and Christianity
ST	*Studia Theologica*
StBibLit	Studies in Biblical Literature
STDJ	Studies on the Texts of the Desert of Judah

SZNT	Studien zum Neuen Testament
THNTC	Two Horizons New Testament Commentary
TJ	*Trinity Journal*
TS	*Theological Studies*
TynBul	*Tyndale Bulletin*
VCSup	Supplements to Vigiliae Christianae
WBC	Word Biblical Commentary
WUNT	Wissenschaftliche Untersuchungen zum Neuen Testament
ZNW	Zeitschrift für die Neutestamentliche Wissenschaft und die Kunde der älteren Kirche

Jesus Is the Messiah of God

The Messianic Theology of the New Testament

In the fall of 2016, I received the news that I was scheduled to teach a seminar on New Testament Theology (hereafter "NTT"). Though I knew the course was regularly offered at my divinity school, I confess that I was unsure as to *why* our faculty considered the seminar worth having in our regular curriculum. A course on Lukan theology or the theology of Revelation I could understand, but does anyone—scholar, student, or pastor—engage in a theology of the entire New Testament?[1] Is NTT still a live discipline, or is it an interesting chapter in the history of modern biblical interpretation? While the discipline of NTT has a rich and valuable legacy—one cannot help, for example, but think of the signal contributions of Rudolf Bultmann, Adolf Schlatter, G. B. Caird, and George Eldon Ladd among many others—for some time now the discipline has fallen a bit out of vogue. Many of the recent NTTs lack the rigor and theological creativity of the earlier classic works. While they can provide useful summary and synthesis of the biblical texts, they rarely offer fresh and creative proposals regarding the unity amid the diversity of the texts, the relationship between history and theology, or a hermeneutically fresh engagement of the texts and our current contemporary situation. Furthermore, as Luke Timothy Johnson has noted, rather than opening up vigorous theological discussion and debate, they now often seem to produce an inappropriate sense of closure.[2]

1. My question should not be taken to imply that there are no significant recent and valuable works on NTT. See, for example, the recent and very different works of Dale B. Martin, *Biblical Truths: The Meaning of Scripture in the Twenty-First Century* (New Haven: Yale University Press, 2017); Craig L. Blomberg, *A New Testament Theology* (Waco, TX: Baylor University Press, 2018); Peter Stuhlmacher, *Biblical Theology of the New Testament* (Grand Rapids: Eerdmans, 2018).

2. Luke Timothy Johnson, "Does a Theology of the Canonical Gospels Make Sense?," in

Whereas writing an NTT used to be seen as an opportunity for a scholar to produce a crowning scholarly achievement which crystallized decades of research, this is no longer the case. And there are powerful undercurrents within biblical scholarship that work against the grain of the discipline. Many of these objections center upon our contemporary preference for plurality and diversity over synthesis and unity.[3] I myself have voiced (and continue to do so) some of these concerns: Doesn't a theology of the NT result in a reductionistic account of the biblical texts? Aren't we better off simply affirming the plurality of images, theologies, christological portraits, and multifaceted concerns of the biblical texts rather than searching for synthesis? Won't the end product simply be an abstraction that is of little use to the scholar, student, or pastor?

Perhaps with a sense of irony (or maybe it was divine providence), within the same year I was scheduled to teach NTT, I was also given the opportunity to choose the topic for a doctoral seminar I would lead. The title I came up with for the seminar was "Messianism and New Testament Christology." This seemed to me a natural choice, given that I had recently published a book on Jewish messianism and ancient kingship discourse informing Paul's Christology.[4] One of my arguments in *Christ Is King*—soteriology conceptualized as participating in Christ's kingship and kingdom—seemed to be worthy of further exploration for other NT depictions of salvation.[5] Furthermore, I had long been interested in how deeply the NT authors drew from the well of the Psalter, especially in their depiction of Jesus's messianic sufferings, death, resurrection, and royal enthronement.[6] Knowing just a little about how some

---

The Nature of New Testament Theology: Essays in Honour of Robert Morgan, ed. Christopher Rowland and Christopher Tuckett (Malden, MA: Blackwell, 2006), 94–95.

3. This is only one objection to the discipline of NTT. See further Heikki Räisänen, *Beyond New Testament Theology: A Story and a Programme* (London: SCM, 1990). These concerns were in many ways given classical expression by William Wrede, *Über Aufgabe und Methode der sogenannten Neutestamentlichen Theologie* (Göttingen: Vandenhoeck & Ruprecht, 1897); ET: "The Task and Methods of 'New Testament Theology,'" in *The Nature of New Testament Theology: The Contribution of William Wrede and Adolf Schlatter*, ed. Robert Morgan (Naperville, IL: Alec R. Allenson, 1973), 68–116. Wrede's project is clearly delineated and critiqued by Hendrikus Boers, *What Is New Testament Theology: The Rise of Criticism and the Problem of a Theology of the New Testament* (Philadelphia: Fortress, 1979), 45–60.

4. Joshua W. Jipp, *Christ Is King: Paul's Royal Ideology* (Minneapolis: Fortress, 2015).

5. I had argued something similar regarding Hebrews in Joshua W. Jipp, "The Son's Entrance into the Heavenly World: The Soteriological Necessity of the Scriptural Catena in Hebrews 1:5–14," *NTS* 56 (2010): 557–75.

6. See Joshua W. Jipp, "'For David Did Not Ascend into Heaven . . .' (Acts 2:34a): Reprogramming Royal Psalms to Proclaim the Enthroned-in-Heaven King," in *Ascent into Heaven in Luke-Acts*, ed. David K. Bryan and David W. Pao (Minneapolis: Fortress, 2016),

early church fathers engaged in messianic readings of Israel's Scriptures and Jewish traditions in order to depict Christ's identity and saving work, I was excited to further explore the possibility that Jewish messianism had an afterlife within patristic biblical interpretation and, more broadly, Christian theology. In other words, while I did not want to argue that Christ's messianic kingship was the singular and all-encompassing theme within the NT texts, the confession of Jesus as the Messiah of Israel did seem to be worthy of exploration as a foundational center point of the NT texts. I still emphatically agree that we should avoid offering hegemonic interpretations of the NT which effectively reduce the texts to one theme, motif, or image. And yet despite the contemporary climate which values plurality, difference, and multiplicity, I think it is still worth asking: Why read these particular twenty-seven NT compositions together? What generated the particular ideas and discourses in these texts? Diversity and plurality are a given, and it takes no great courage or skill for the contemporary scholar to demonstrate this. And while unity need not imply sameness (and for the NT writings cannot), how might one go about offering an account of the canonical unity and coherence of these texts?[7]

The central argument of this book is that the messianic identity of Jesus of Nazareth is not only the presupposition for, but is also the primary (though certainly not exclusive) content of, New Testament theology.[8] I invite the reader to explore with me the question: How much of the NT's Christology can be understood as messianic discourse? Certainly not all of it, and yet, I want to propose that Jesus's messianic kingship is something of a root metaphor, a primary designation and driving image for making sense of NT Christology. That is to say, not only do the major NT compositions presuppose Jesus as the Davidic messianic king but they are also creative expansions upon the earliest Christian confession that Jesus is the Messiah of God.[9] And, as we will see, this has significant implications for the NT's construal of the role and activity of the Father and

---

41–59; "Luke's Scriptural Suffering Messiah: A Search for Precedent, a Search for Identity," *CBQ* 72 (2010): 255–74; "Messiah Language and *Gospel Writing*," in *Writing the Gospels: A Dialogue with Francis Watson*, ed. Catherine Sider Hamilton, LNTS 606 (London: T&T Clark, 2019), 126–44.

7. See here, with respect to the canonical Gospels, Richard B. Hays, "Can Narrative Criticism Recover the Theological Unity of Scripture?," *JTI* 2 (2008): 193–211.

8. On the messianic identity of Jesus as the presupposition but not the content of the NT, see Donald Juel, *Messianic Exegesis: Christological Interpretation of the Old Testament in Early Christianity* (Philadelphia: Fortress, 1988), 175–77.

9. With respect to the canonical Gospels, see Michael F. Bird, *Jesus Is the Christ: The Messianic Testimony of the Gospels* (Downers Grove, IL: InterVarsity Press, 2012), 4: "It is the contention of this study that the messianic identity of Jesus is the earliest and most basic

the Holy Spirit.[10] If Jesus's messianic kingship is one center point for NTT, then theological reflection upon how his messianic kingship informs our dogmatic and practical theology is worthy of consideration for each generation.

Jesus's Messianic Kingship as the Content of New Testament Theology

Most would agree that the confession "Jesus is the Christ" is assumed by (at least many of) the NT authors, but many would see the NT authors as moving from this conviction to something bigger, better, and more profound. For example, Mark's Jesus, some would say, seeks to move his disciples from the christological affirmation of Jesus as the Messiah to Jesus as the Son of Man. John's Gospel assumes Jesus is the Christ, but this designation is, it is suggested, unhelpful for understanding Jesus's divine identity as the preexistent *Logos*. Paul's favorite designation for Jesus is, of course, "Christ," but many have thought that this designation is now simply a name (rather than a title) for Jesus. After all, would gentiles care or even understand the meaning of Christ as the anointed king of Yahweh? Paul only rarely mentions Jesus's Davidic ancestry, after all. And Hebrews is dominated by the image of Jesus as a Melchizedekian high priest; certainly, his Davidic messiahship, if important at all, is overshadowed by his priestly identity.

But does this make sense of even a cursory examination of how much weight the NT texts place upon Jesus as the Christ? Is Jesus's messianic identity only the presupposition and not the content of the NT writings? Consider the following. The simple claims "Jesus is the Messiah" (e.g., John 20:31; Acts 17:3; 18:5, 28; 1 John 2:22; 3:23; 5:1) and "Jesus is Lord" (e.g., Acts 10:36; 1 Cor 12:3; Phil 2:10–11) are amply attested as the earliest Christian confessions, and both have explicit royal connotations in presenting Christ as messianic ruler.[11]

---

claim of early Christology. What is more, it is precisely the testimony to Jesus as the Messiah that is arguably the most defining Christological affirmation of the canonical Gospels."

10. While he makes many important correctives and rightly emphasizes the diversity of messianic figures in Second Temple Judaism, I think Charlesworth's following conclusion is strongly overstated: "Suffice it to be stated now that Jewish messianology does not flow majestically into Christian Christology." See James H. Charlesworth, "From Jewish Messianology to Christian Christology: Some Caveats and Perspectives," in *Judaisms and Their Messiahs at the Turn of the Christian Era*, ed. Jacob Neusner, William S. Green, and Ernest Frerichs (Cambridge: Cambridge University Press, 1987), 255.

11. See further Oscar Cullmann, "The Kingship of Christ and the Church in the New

Paul's Epistle to the Romans begins with the creedal confession affirming that the content of the gospel centers upon the identity of Jesus of Nazareth as the messianic Son of David and resurrected powerful Son of God (Rom 1:1–5), and the letter's discursive argument concludes with the affirmation that he is the Christ, the son of Jesse, the one who rules the nations (Rom 15:7, 12). The author of 2 Timothy invokes the centrality of Jesus's Davidic sonship as he reminds his audience of "Messiah Jesus raised from the dead, from the seed of David, according to my gospel" (2 Tim 2:8). Paul refers to Christ as having his own kingdom and as one who will act as the eschatological judge (e.g., 1 Cor 6:9–11; 15:23–28; 2 Cor 5:10; Col 1:13; Rom 2:16; 14:17; 1 Thess 2:12). While it is a matter of some dispute as to whether Paul retains the titular meaning of Χριστός, we can note that this term is far and away his favorite for Jesus of Nazareth, as it occurs close to 270 times in the Pauline letters. The Synoptic Gospels cohere in their depiction of Jesus as one who proclaimed God's kingdom (e.g., Matt 13; 25; Mark 1:14–15; Luke 4:43–44), whose ancestry can be traced to the royal family of David (Matt 1:18–25; Luke 1:31–35, 68–69; 2:1–8; cf. Mark 12:35–37), and who inspired a significant amount of messianic speculation (e.g., Mark 8:27–33; John 7:25–44). All four Gospels preserve the memory of Jesus as one who was crucified by Rome as a messianic pretender (Mark 14:55–64; 15:1–38; John 18:33–19:22).[12] All four canonical Gospels apply generous quotations and allusions from the Davidic psalms to explain how Jesus's sufferings, death, and vindication correspond to the pattern of the righteous royal sufferer in the Psalter. A remarkable amount of NT compositions apply Ps 110:1 to Jesus to describe him as the enthroned messianic lord who reigns over his people and has subjected his enemies to himself (e.g., Acts 2:30–36; 5:31; 1 Cor 15:23–28; Rom 8:33–34; Heb 1:3, 13; 12:2; 1 Pet 3:22). The author of Revelation engages in a reinterpretation of major Davidic messianic images and titles, reworking the notion of victory and conquest around the death and resurrection of Jesus (esp. Rev 5:5–6; 12:1–17).

It hardly needs stating that the twenty-seven writings that constitute the New Testament utilize a remarkable amount of rich and diverse images to describe Jesus of Nazareth. Jesus is remembered as an authoritative teacher (Mark 1:23–28; Luke 4:16–30), a revealer of divine insight and wisdom (Matt 5:20–48;

Testament," in *The Early Church: Studies in Early Christian History and Theology*, ed. A. J. B. Higgins (Philadelphia: Westminster, 1956), 105–37.

12. See here Nils A. Dahl, "The Crucified Messiah," in *Jesus the Christ: The Historical Origins of a Christological Doctrine*, ed. Donald H. Juel (Minneapolis: Fortress, 1991), 27–47; Martin Hengel, "Jesus, the Messiah of Israel," in his *Studies in Early Christology* (Edinburgh: T&T Clark, 1995), 41–58.

7:21–28; 11:25–30), a powerful healer and exorcist (Mark 3:23–30), a martyr (Luke 23), the powerful Son of Man (Acts 7:55–60; Rev 1:12–20), one who shared table fellowship and hospitality with all people including sinners and tax collectors (Luke 7:36–50; 15:1–2; 19:1–10), the "prophet like Moses" (Acts 3:22–23; 7:17–37), the divine *Logos* (John 1:1–3, 14), the second Adam (Luke 3:38; Rom 5:12–21; 1 Cor 15:20–22), the sacrificial Lamb of God (1 Cor 5:7; Rev 5:5–6), and the heavenly high priest (Heb 4:14–16). One could continue to multiply the list with christological image after image, but here my simple aim is the rather obvious one—namely, to establish the point that the NT writings draw upon an array of titles, historical precedents, and conceptual categories to articulate the meaning and significance of Jesus of Nazareth. While this study does argue for the centrality of Jesus's messianic kingship, I have no intention to sideline or minimize the vast display of diverse non-messianic images, categories, titles, and conceptual precedents drawn upon by the NT authors to understand the significance of Jesus. I am emphatically *not* arguing that everything in the New Testament is explained by messianic discourse.

The primary argument of this book, then, might seem to fly in the face of the largely obvious claim that the NT is composed of a plethora of robust christological images. Thus, while the NT cannot be reduced to one single theme or even a cluster of themes, and while the texts contain a remarkable amount of diversity, I want to suggest that one primary and unifying thread of the NT consists in their being creative expansions upon the earliest "Christian" confessions: "Jesus is the Messiah" and "Jesus is Lord." That is to say, one of the central and defining features of the NT writings is their articulation of Jesus as the singular messianic king. The NT texts articulate Jesus's identity and activities as messianic by means of drawing upon messianic scenarios and motifs, applying messianic honorifics and titles to Jesus, and interpreting his life through royal-messianic Scriptures. Stated differently, and in an explicitly theological and synthetic study (part 2), through an examination of the major NT compositions, I argue that there is a significant amount of unity among these texts as it pertains to the Messiah and

1. Scriptural exegesis (messianic honorifics and the appropriation of the Scriptures of Israel),
2. Christology (the messianic articulation of the life, narrative, and acts of Jesus),
3. Soteriology (the inauguration of the saving reign of the messianic king),

4. Ecclesiology and sanctification (the people of God as sharing in the very person, character, and mission of their messianic ruler), and

5. Politics and eschatology (how Christ's people relate to the worldly powers and institutions and wait for his final enactment of his just rule over creation).

The book is divided into two major parts. In part 1 ("The Messianic Testimony of the New Testament"), I examine most of the compositions of the New Testament in order to illuminate how each of them is a creative articulation of the confession that Jesus is God's Spirit-anointed messianic ruler. Each NT text sets this forth in its own distinctive manner; the unity here is not a simplistic synthetic summary of common themes, nor is it to be found in the texts conforming to a preformed messianic pattern or idea. While I will engage in some level of synthesis, noting common motifs, images, messianic exegesis, and so forth, I will attempt to allow each NT text to have its own unique say in its depiction of Christ as the Messiah. My hope is that it will be possible to engage in some level of synthesis that illuminates the NT while simultaneously honoring the particular diverse voices of each NT composition or author. I have no peculiar or creative method here other than the normal practices and assumptions of NT exegesis. While I have learned much and draw richly from the historical and exegetical works of William Horbury, Matthew Novenson, and Adela Yarbo Collins and John Collins, among others, my interests here center primarily upon exegesis and the theological texture of the writings. Having examined the messianic logic of each NT composition, in part 2 ("The Messianic Theology of the New Testament") I set forth the way in which the New Testament's central theological convictions and practices are rooted in the earliest Christian confession: Jesus is the Messiah.

SHIFTING SANDS IN EVALUATING THE SIGNIFICANCE OF MESSIANISM FOR NT CHRISTOLOGY

Before moving on into the heart of my study, it might be worth asking the question: Why has Jesus's Davidic messianic identity not seemed to most to be a particularly helpful category for understanding NT Christology? Without any pretense of telling this story in a comprehensive manner, I want to very briefly suggest four reasons why Jewish messianic traditions and texts have been minimized or seen as somewhat insignificant for NT Christology. First, one should not underestimate the remarkable influence of Wilhelm Bousset's

Kyrios Christos. His division between Palestinian and Hellenistic Christianity, where the former focused upon the heavenly transcendent Son of Man and the latter emphasized the title "Lord," set forth a model of evolutionary Christology whereby Davidic messianic traditions were devalued and left behind as belonging to a bygone era.[13] A Jewish-Christian emphasis on Jesus as the so-called nationalistic Davidic Messiah, so it was thought, was insignificant and perhaps even incomprehensible for Hellenistic Jews and gentiles who, instead of a nationalistic Messiah, valued Jesus as the exalted Lord.[14] One of the consequences of this historical paradigm of christological development has been the belief that Χριστός within Paul's letters has lost its titular, messianic significance and is now simply a proper name.[15] But this history of religions historical construct has crumbled in the past few decades. It can no longer be assumed that "the Palestinian church" was not in some ways hellenized, nor do the typical assumptions about the beliefs of these communities stand up well to historical scrutiny.[16] It is by no means obvious, then, that Jesus's Davidic descent was valued only in the earliest Jewish-Christian circles.

Second, and very closely related, there has been a strong strand of scholarship that holds that the earthly/historical Jesus did not make any messianic claims, but rather was retrospectively proclaimed as the Messiah as a result of his resurrection from the dead. It is supposed that Rom 1:4 and Acts 2:36 preserve the early adoptionist Christology whereby Jesus is made the messianic Lord at his resurrection.[17] And this belief has often had negative consequences for the significance of Jesus's Davidic messianic identity, which has been qualified, transcended, and/or left behind.[18] Some have also pointed to Jesus's reticence to use the title for himself and suggest that the places where it does occur as a positive description of Jesus's identity may stem from early

13. Wilhelm Bousset, *Kyrios Christos: A History of the Belief in Christ from the Beginnings of Christianity to Irenaeus*, trans. John E. Steely (Nashville: Abingdon, 1970).

14. See further, Rudolf Bultmann, *Theology of the New Testament*, 2 vols. (New York: Scribner's Sons, 1951), 1:49–50, 237.

15. I have discussed this in more detail in my *Christ Is King*, 3–11.

16. See here the classic study of Martin Hengel, *Judaism and Hellenism*, 2 vols. (Philadelphia: Fortress, 1974); see also Larry W. Hurtado, "New Testament Christology: A Critique of Bousset's Influence," *TS* 40 (1979): 306–17.

17. For a recent and popular articulation, see Bart D. Ehrman, *How Jesus Became God: The Exaltation of a Jewish Preacher from Galilee* (San Francisco: HarperOne, 2014), 211–46. Ehrman prefers the language of "exaltation Christology."

18. I discuss and evaluate these scholarly claims in much more detail in my "Ancient, Modern, and Future Interpretations of Romans 1:3–4: Reception History and Biblical Interpretation," *JTI* 3 (2009): 243–48.

Christian confessions (e.g., Mark 8:27-29; John 4:25-26). Thus, it was the belief in Jesus's resurrection from the dead that led the earliest Christians to view Jesus as Messiah and further resulted in the post-Easter creation of messianic traditions about the historical Jesus. The so-called messianic secret in Mark's Gospel, in fact, was explained as a pre-Markan literary construct to show why the earliest church did *not* claim Jesus as the Messiah (again, since this only began with belief in his resurrection).[19] While I cannot argue the point in detail here, I should state that I find the idea of a non-messianic Jesus implausible and the view that Christology underwent an evolutionary development from a "lower" to "higher" form based on Christ's adoption at the resurrection to rest on slender evidence. Perhaps I can be permitted here to draw upon some of the conclusions of Martin Hengel's lengthy and persuasive argument that Jesus both saw himself as, and was remembered from the earliest days by his followers as, the Messiah of Israel.

> If Jesus never possessed a messianic claim of divine mission, rather sternly rejected every third-hand question in this regard, if he neither spoke of the coming, or present, "Son of Man," nor was executed as a messianic pretender and alleged king of the Jews—as is maintained with astonishing certainty by radical criticism unencumbered by historical arguments—then the emergence of christology, indeed, the entire early history of primitive Christianity, is completely baffling, nay, incomprehensible.[20]

Third, there has been an appropriate backlash among many scholars against overstated (and often "Christianizing") claims regarding both the meaning and importance of Jewish messianic traditions. For example, it is simply and quite obviously not the case that all Jews during the time of Jesus (or during the Second Temple period) were waiting, praying, and hoping for a Davidic Messiah. The most egregious examples of Christianizing claims often uncritically "use" and co-opt Jewish texts as mere preparations for the coming of Christ. Furthermore, it is well known that the postexilic prophets (other than Haggai and Zechariah), Josephus, Philo, and most of the texts in the Apocrypha contain very little by way of Jewish messianic expectation.[21] Furthermore,

---

19. See here the foundational work of William Wrede, *Das Messiasgeheimnis in den Evangelien: Zugleich ein Beitrag zum Verständnis des Markusevangeliums* (Göttingen: Vandenhoeck & Ruprecht, 1901); ET, *The Messianic Secret*, trans. J. C. G. Greig, Library of Theological Translations (Cambridge: James Clarke, 1971).

20. Hengel, "Jesus, the Messiah of Israel," 14.

21. This has led some to speak of a "messianic vacuum" hypothesis. For the ongoing

it is almost certainly not the case that there was anything near a unified or coherent understanding of Israel's messianic traditions.[22] One of the great culprits here, leading to vast confusion, has been the notion that ancient messiah texts belong to the world-historical notion of the "messianic idea." On this view, there is an independent supra-historical messianic idea about the ideal utopian eschatological age, of which all of the messiah texts provide evidence (e.g., Zech 6; Pss. Sol. 17; 4 Ezra 7). One can see the reaction against the idea of a single, unified notion of a messiah in works which emphasize diversity and plurality.[23] Thus, as Matthew Novenson notes, the study of Jewish messianism has often been "organized around an artificial concept, not a corpus of texts, and the result has been a kind of interpretive anarchy."[24] The consequences here are significant, for it results in messiah texts being prejudged to see if they conform to a prior model or definition of the messiah. Rather than beginning, however, with a predetermined notion of the messiah as an idealized, transcendent figure (or whatever definition one might proffer), Novenson argues convincingly that exegetes and historians should instead simply "describe the various ancient uses of the word 'messiah' and the pertinent differences among them without artificially privileging one as the ostensibly real, proper, strict, fully evolved definition."[25] Thus, rather than arguing for a messianic idea to which the NT messiah texts conform, or appealing to the prevalence of messianic hopes and expectation in the first century, a better way forward—and one I will seek to implement in my study—is to recognize that messiah discourse is an exegetical project; that is, it uses ancient scriptural texts in order to talk about an anointed Jewish ruler.[26]

---

importance, however, of God's promises to Israel to be ruled through the Davidic monarchy, a hope that was powerfully alive even after the Babylonian exile well into the first century, see Joseph Blenkinsopp, *David Remembered: Kingship and National Identity in Ancient Israel* (Grand Rapids: Eerdmans, 2013).

22. William Horbury, *Jewish Messianism and the Cult of Christ* (London: SCM, 1998) has argued for both the prevalence and coherence of messianic expectations during early Judaism. While his work is, in my view, groundbreaking and deserving of more attention, many have questioned his emphasis on coherence (arguing instead for diversity) and prevalence (i.e., no dominant expectation). See, for example, Kenneth Pomykala, *The Davidic Dynasty Tradition in Early Judaism: Its History and Significance for Messianism*, SBLEJL 7 (Atlanta: Scholars Press, 1995).

23. See, for example, James H. Charlesworth, William Scott Green, and Ernest Frerichs, eds., *Judaisms and Their Messiahs at the Turn of the Christian Era* (Cambridge: Cambridge University Press, 1987).

24. Matthew V. Novenson, *The Grammar of Messianism: An Ancient Jewish Political Idiom and Its Users* (Oxford: Oxford University Press, 2017), 8.

25. Novenson, *The Grammar of Messianism*, 63.

26. This is one of the central arguments of Novenson, *The Grammar of Messianism*, 11–33.

Fourth, one should not underestimate the ideologically motivated antipathy some have for notions of monarchy, kingship, and messianic traditions. Kings and monarchs, whether human or divine, operate through power, manipulation, and subjugation; therefore, construing the divine in terms of a king is inherently bad and exploitative and should be rejected in favor of other models or metaphors for the divine. Construing the divine in terms of kingship is problematic for many for the way in which it portrays God as a transcendent figure who is distant from the world and who powerfully controls and manipulates the world through force.[27] Feminist interpreters of the NT have explicitly argued that "kyriocentric" traditions—discourses that justify domination and subjugation often through conceptions of the divine—have had disastrous ramifications for women. For Elisabeth Schüssler Fiorenza, for example, contemporary interpreters must privilege the liberating potential of women's experience and deconstruct hegemonic kyriocentric christological discourses which oppress and subjugate women.[28] Others reject messianic discourse due to its potential to be exploited for violent and nationalist agendas. Davidic messianic texts which promise worldwide victory to the king and the subjugation of the gentile nations through expansionist wars are offensive and deeply problematic if drawn upon to legitimize the goals and agendas of modern nation-states or other groups. Messianic royal discourse not only can be, but often has been, co-opted as a means of legitimating violence, revolution, and harm against those without power.[29] We will see that the NT texts witness to a potential (mis-)understanding of Jewish messianism as calling for power and freedom through violence and force. In other words, already within the NT texts themselves we see a similar concern that many (conventional) understandings of kingship and messianism have the potential to lead to violence, subjugation, and oppression. I argue in what follows that the NT texts consistently read the Davidic kingship texts through the lens of the particular history of Jesus the Messiah, a history that the earliest Christians believed initiated God's kingdom through the particular life of one man's peace, justice, enemy-love, and crucifixion. In fact, one of the primary themes we will

---

27. See here especially Sallie McFague, *Models of God: Theology for an Ecological, Nuclear Age* (Philadelphia: Fortress, 1987), 65.

28. See here, for example, Elisabeth Schüssler Fiorenza, *Jesus: Miriam's Child, Sophia's Prophet: Critical Issues in Feminist Christology*, 2nd ed. (London: T&T Clark, 2015), esp. chapters 1 and 2.

29. For one example, see Matthias Riedl, "Apocalyptic Violence and Revolutionary Action: Thomas Müntzer's *Sermon to the Princes*," in *A Companion to the Premodern Apocalypse*, ed. Michael A. Ryan, Brill's Companions to the Christian Tradition 64 (Leiden: Brill, 2016), 260–96.

encounter in our study of messianism and kingship in the NT is the critique and displacement of the ungodly uses of power wielded through human rulers and kingdoms. Nevertheless, while the NT texts reject a notion of God's kingdom coming through violence, the possibility that messianic discourse may be appropriated in contemporary contexts is certainly still with us. One thinks of the appropriation of numerous facets of kingship discourse by Constantine as a means of legitimating his sovereignty and use of military violence to accomplish his ends. And this has led many to reject or minimize the importance of messianic christological discourse in favor of more contemporaneously palatable ways of speaking of God.

Nevertheless, multiple strands of recent scholarship are calling for a reassessment of the centrality of Jesus's messianic identity for understanding the NT writings. Novenson has shown that Paul's use of Χριστός to speak of Jesus conforms to ancient honorifics and suggests that Paul's Christ language is messianic discourse.[30] Douglas Campbell has argued that Paul's argument in Romans 8 presumes a narrative of Christ as the resurrected, ascended, and glorified messianic King of Israel.[31] An abundance of recent scholarship on Paul's Christology has sought to understand Paul's argumentation in light of his conviction that Jesus Christ is the Davidic Messiah of Israel.[32] Horbury has argued that the rise of the worship of Christ (the "Christ cult") is best explained in light of Jesus's messianic and kingly identity.[33] N. T. Wright, among others of the so-called third quest for the historical Jesus, has made a powerful argument that Jesus's aims, intentions, and activities are best understood in light of Jesus's messianic self-consciousness.[34] Michael Bird has argued forcefully for the centrality of messianism for understanding the fourfold gospel:

---

30. Matthew V. Novenson, *Christ among the Messiahs: Christ Language in Paul and Messiah Language in Ancient Judaism* (Oxford: Oxford University Press, 2012).

31. Douglas A. Campbell, "The Story of Jesus in Romans and Galatians," in *Narrative Dynamics in Paul: A Critical Assessment*, ed. Bruce W. Longenecker (Louisville: Westminster John Knox, 2002), 97–124.

32. For example, Paula Fredriksen, *Paul: The Pagans' Apostle* (New Haven: Yale University Press, 2017); Matthew Thiessen, *Paul and the Gentile Problem* (Oxford: Oxford University Press, 2016); Haley Goranson Jacob, *Conformed to the Image of His Son: Reconsidering Paul's Theology of Glory in Romans* (Downers Grove, IL: InterVarsity Press, 2018); Larry W. Hurtado, "Paul's Messianic Christology," in *Paul the Jew: Rereading the Apostle as a Figure of Second Temple Judaism*, ed. Gabriele Boccaccini and Carlos A. Segovia (Minneapolis: Fortress, 2016), 107–31.

33. See Horbury, *Jewish Messianism and the Cult of Christ*.

34. See N. T. Wright, *Jesus and the Victory of God*, vol. 4 of *Christian Origins and the Question of God* (Minneapolis: Fortress, 1996).

"The messiahship of Jesus comprises the primary framework in which the sum of all christological affirmation in the Gospels are to be understood, that is, all Christology is a subset of messianology."[35] A host of scholarship has focused upon the NT's use of the Davidic psalms and has noted places where Christ himself prays the prayers of David or where his life, especially his sufferings and death, is patterned after King David in the Psalms.[36] Yarbro Collins and Collins have argued that the "early Christian proclamation of Jesus as son of God must be seen in [the] context of Jewish messianic expectation."[37] For the Collinses, Israelite and Jewish messianism is an indispensable context for understanding the emergence and growth of Christian theology.

Both Scot McKnight and Matthew Bates have produced slightly more popular but strongly textual arguments that the heart of the gospel and message of the NT centers upon the conviction that Jesus is King.[38] McKnight critiques contemporary versions of the gospel message which equate the gospel with salvation or justification and unwittingly minimize the heart of the NT—namely, the fact that the gospel is the proclamation that Jesus's entire life brings Israel's story to its climax and centers upon Jesus's messianic lordship. The gospel of Jesus is, in other words, "anchored in an exalted view of Jesus. Jesus is seen as suffering, saving, ruling, and judging because he is the Messiah and the Lord and the Davidic Savior. He is now exalted at the right hand of God."[39] Bates argues that the gospel is the full narrative of what God has done in the person of the messianic king: his incarnation, his life and teachings, his death, resurrection, and enthronement.[40] Paul's explicit definitions of what the gospel is come in the little proto-creeds of Romans 1:3–4 and 1 Corinthians 15:3–5, as well as Pauline

---

35. Bird, *Jesus Is the Christ*, 4.

36. To state only a few, see Richard B. Hays, "Christ Prays the Psalms: Paul's Use of an Early Christian Convention," in *The Future of Christology: Essays in Honor of Leander E. Keck*, ed. Abraham J. Malherbe and Wayne A. Meeks (Minneapolis: Fortress, 1993), 122–36; Peter Doble, "Luke 24.26, 44—Songs of God's Servant: David His Psalms in Luke-Acts," *JSNT* 28 (2006): 267–83; Margaret Daly-Denton, *David in the Fourth Gospel: The Johannine Reception of the Psalms* (Leiden: Brill, 2000).

37. Adela Yarbro Collins and John J. Collins, *King and Messiah as Son of God: Divine, Human, and Angelic Messianic Figures in Biblical and Related Literature* (Grand Rapids: Eerdmans, 2008), 207.

38. See also Sigurd Grindheim, *Living in the Kingdom of God: A Biblical Theology for the Life of the Church* (Grand Rapids: Baker Academic, 2018).

39. Scot McKnight, *The King Jesus Gospel: The Original Good News Revisited* (Grand Rapids: Zondervan, 2011), 132.

40. Matthew W. Bates, *Salvation by Allegiance Alone: Rethinking Faith, Works, and the Gospel of Jesus the King* (Grand Rapids: Baker Academic, 2017), esp. chapters 2 and 3.

christological hymns and narratives such as Phil 2:5–11 and Rom 10:1–13. Given that the Pauline gospel climaxes in God's enthronement of the messianic king, the right response to this king is one of allegiance and fidelity.

With respect to the Apocalypse of John, Richard Bauckham has argued for the importance of the christological image of Jesus as a conquering Davidic Messiah whose triumph takes place through his sacrificial death. The Messiah is depicted as the leader of a messianic holy war of, ironically, martyrs.[41] Similarly, Justin Jeffcoat Schedtler has demonstrated that Revelation draws from kingship discourses to paint a picture of the crucified and resurrected Jesus as Israel's last and greatest King.[42] The relevance of messianism and Jesus's kingship does not fade in the writings of the early church in the second through the fourth centuries. For example, Per Beskow has argued that the New Testament's depiction of Christ in royal and messianic categories continued "during the pre-Constantinian period" and "became enriched by its confrontation with Hellenistic culture; and how this development, in the course of doctrinal disputes of the fourth century, gave rise to that conception of Christ as King which dominated the theology of the Byzantine period and the Middle Ages in the West."[43] More recently, Novenson has also argued against the misguided opinion that Messiah texts and language did not continue well into late antiquity. In his words: "The ghost of the messianic movement surrounding Jesus of Nazareth haunted early Christian Christology, both orthodox and heterodox, for centuries to follow."[44]

Finding an appropriate ending point in highlighting recent work on messianism in the New Testament would take another chapter or two, but fortunately my simple point here is only that there are a variety of scholars who have argued that the NT texts are often best understood in light of Jewish messianism and the depiction of Jesus of Nazareth as the messianic king. In what follows, I attempt to demonstrate not that Jesus's messianic identity is the only christological image in the NT but that it is one of the unifying, central threads of the witness and theology of the NT writings.

---

41. Richard Bauckham, *The Climax of Prophecy: Studies on the Book of Revelation* (London: T&T Clark, 1993).

42. Justin Jeffcoat Schedtler, *The Last King: Royal Ideologies in the Book of Revelation* (forthcoming).

43. Per Beskow, *Rex Gloriae: The Kingship of Christ in the Early Church*, trans. Eric J. Sharpe (Uppsala: Almqvist & Wiksells, 1962, trans. Eugene, OR: Wipf & Stock, 2014), 9. Citation refers to the Wipf & Stock edition.

44. Novenson, *The Grammar of Messianism*, 262.

A Brief Word on Method and Scope

Given that my central argument centers upon demonstrating the significance of Jesus's messianic life and identity, it is appropriate to give a brief word on how I define and discern the presence of messianism in the NT writings. On the one hand, I want to avoid establishing a unified portrait or idea of the Messiah to which the NT texts must conform. I have noted some of the problems in too strictly predetermining the coherence of messianism or beginning with a "messianic idea" above. The Scriptures of Israel and Second Temple Jewish writings can interpret messianic texts and deploy messianic images in a variety of ways. On the other hand, and again this is stated well by Novenson, one can say at minimum that messiah-language "could be used meaningfully in antiquity because it was deployed in the context of a linguistic community whose members shared a stock of common linguistic resources."[45] These "linguistic resources" are, primarily, the Scriptures of Israel which reflect upon God's anointed Davidic king. While by no means comprehensive, foremost are texts such as Genesis 49:8–12; Numbers 24:17–19; 2 Samuel 7:12–14; Psalms 2, 89, and 132; Isaiah 9 and 11; Jeremiah 23:1–5; Ezekiel 34; and Daniel 7.[46] The NT authors' conviction that God's anointed Messiah has come enables them to engage and work with royal motifs and Scriptures regardless of whether they were originally understood as messianic. Thus, once the belief that Jesus is the Messiah arises, all kinds of scriptural reflections upon the ideal king become susceptible to a messianic interpretation (whether they are messianic in their original contexts, or not).[47] While some define messianism more broadly so as to include angels, semi-divine intermediary agents, prophets like Moses, and priestly figures, my focus is on an anointed royal king and one most frequently associated with the house and lineage of David. I suggest that in addition to these "messianic" texts, one should also be open to the presence of biblical texts which engage in reflection upon Israel's ideal king (e.g., Deut 17:14–20; 2 Kgs 22:2–23:3; Ps 72). I should also note here that I do not make as sharp of a division between Davidic and non-Davidic types of messianism given that, in the words of Horbury, many of the Jewish texts connect the coming messiah "not just with David, but with the whole series of Jewish kings and rulers, including the judges."[48] Also, given the NT authors' starting point that Jesus is

---

45. Novenson, *Christ among the Messiahs*, 47.

46. I present a lengthier sketch of messianic and kingship discourse in ancient Israel and Jewish traditions in Jipp, *Christ Is King*, 31–42.

47. I have also written more on this in my *Christ Is King*, 29–31.

48. William Horbury, "Messianism in the Old Testament Apocrypha and Pseudepi-

the Messiah of Israel, texts that in their original context may have only spoken of the ideal king (rather than an eschatological messiah) may also function as the linguistic and conceptual resources for the depictions of the Messiah in the NT. Thus, I am less interested in modern historical classifications of texts as messianic versus ideal kingship, superhuman/angelic versus human, Davidic ruler versus Son of Man ruler, and so forth, as I am in how messianic expectation and exegesis is on display in the NT texts.[49] This also means that my primary emphasis in what follows is upon how the NT texts develop messianic readings of Scripture. Once Jesus of Nazareth is identified as Israel's Messiah, this conviction functions as the key for fuller illumination of the meanings of the Old Testament and Second Temple Jewish messianic traditions.[50]

Others have engaged in close analyses of Israelite royal ideology, and so here I only very briefly note that these texts frequently portray the messianic king as a descendant of David; the elected Son of God; one committed to the establishment of justice and righteousness for his people; a triumphant military ruler who fights God's battles; a conduit for the Spirit of God; one who takes the lead in observance of the laws; a shepherd who cares for God's people; one who is uniquely related to God's presence and holiness; the one who establishes God's peaceful and prosperous dominion; and one who reigns over and receives honor from the gentile nations.[51] Thus, I suggest that one can often safely conclude that an NT author is engaging in messianic discourse when he: (a) refers to Jesus using a royal honorific such as Christ, Son of David, Branch, the Lion of Judah, shepherd, King, and so on; (b) cites or

---

grapha," in *Messianism Among Jews and Christians: Biblical and Historical Studies*, 3rd ed. (London: T&T Clark, 2016), 81.

49. Again, Horbury, "Messianism in the Old Testament Apocrypha," 83, is worth quoting here: "Messianic expectation was linked with the royal line, the Jewish constitution, and the relevant biblical figures not as they *were* according to modern historical reconstruction, but as they were *envisaged* from time to time in the Graeco-Roman world. This means that material which now looks multifarious, for it includes messianic treatment of priests, judges and patriarchs, in the Greek and Roman periods would have naturally associated itself with the single succession of legitimate Jewish rulers."

50. While my discussions could undoubtedly benefit from even lengthier engagement with the original context of the OT, my exegetical analysis of each NT text is focused upon how the NT develops a messianic theology through a retrospective reading of the Old Testament. On the meaning of retrospective readings of the OT, see Richard B. Hays, *Reading Backwards: Figural Christology and the Fourfold Gospel Witness* (Waco, TX: Baylor University Press, 2014).

51. See my sketch of some of the ways of speaking of the ideal king and messianic ruler in ancient Israel and the Jewish writings in Jipp, *Christ Is King*, 29–42.

alludes to common and well-known scriptural texts which involve a messianic king or the good/ideal ruler; and/or (c) activates a messianic image, motif, or scenario such as a king engaging in military battles, one who rules his people with justice and righteousness, or one who protects his people from threats to their safety and well-being.[52]

As noted already, the first part of my study is strictly exegetical. I set forth readings of most of the primary compositions of the New Testament in some level of detail. While some repetition has been unavoidable, I have tried to minimize too much repetition; so, for example, I do not engage in as detailed a reading of Matthew's passion narrative given my more extensive treatment of Mark and Luke. I have also engaged in more synthesis in the three chapters on Paul, rather than testing the reader's patience by working through each of the thirteen canonical Pauline letters.

In part 2, I will suggest that the NT authors' conviction that Jesus is the Spirit-anointed Messiah of Israel illuminates: (1) their scriptural exegesis of Israel's Scriptures (chapter 10), (2) the specific identity and shape of the narrative of the life of Jesus of Nazareth and the conviction that he is to receive worship alongside the God of Israel (chapter 11), (3) the manner in which they conceptualize God's provision of salvation through the incarnation, death, resurrection, and ascension of the Messiah (chapter 12), (4) their emphasis on the ecclesiological union between the Messiah and his people and the resulting call to embody his character (chapter 13), and (5) what it means to live as citizens of Christ's kingdom in a world ruled through power, violence, and coercion (chapter 14). Though I try to avoid preaching, I make no attempt to hide the fact that this is a specifically theological engagement of the messianic convictions of the NT authors. While the days of writing full-scale theologies of the New Testament seems to be waning, my hope is that this study will offer a creative, illuminating, and integrative theological vision of the New Testament.

Note that unless otherwise indicated, all translations of Scripture passages quoted are my own.

---

52. Similarly, and with respect to Paul, see Novenson, *Christ among the Messiahs*, 172.

Part One

The MESSIANIC TESTIMONY
of the NEW TESTAMENT

CHAPTER 1

The Son of David Who Saves His People from Their Sins

The Gospel of Matthew

Jesus's identity as "the Son of David" and God's "Messiah" within the Gospel of Matthew is indisputable. Whereas Mark has three references to Jesus as the "Son of David" (Mark 10:47, 48; 12:35), Matthew includes nine (Matt 1:1; 9:27; 12:23; 15:22; 20:30, 31; 21:9, 15; 22:42).[1] Peter's confession that Jesus is "the Messiah, the Son of the Living God" is met with Jesus's affirmation of the confession as revealed by the Father from heaven (16:13–17). Jesus is referred to as "King of the Jews" and receives obeisance from foreign dignitaries even as a child (2:1–12). Further, Matthew's opening genealogy redounds with echoes of Davidic kingship as it begins with the words: "the record of the genealogy of Jesus the Messiah, the Son of David, the Son of Abraham" (1:1). The Davidic messianic aspect of Jesus's identity is highlighted in the way Matthew structures his genealogy, neatly moving in three periods of fourteen generations—from Abraham to "King David" (1:2–6a), from David and the period of the kings to the Babylonian exile (1:6b–11), and from the Babylonian exile to the birth of Jesus "who is called the Messiah" (1:12–16; cf. 1:16b).[2]

As the messianic Son of David and the Son of God, Jesus is tasked with

---

1. A host of studies have been devoted to establishing the importance of Jesus's Davidic ancestry for the Gospel of Matthew. See, for example, Lidija Novakovic, "Jesus as the Davidic Messiah in Matthew," *HBT* 19 (1997): 148–91; Joel Willitts, "Matthew and Psalms of Solomon's Messianism: A Comparative Study in First-Century Messianology," *BBR* 22 (2012): 27–50; H. Daniel Zacharias, *Matthew's Presentation of the Son of David: Davidic Tradition and Typology in the Gospel of Matthew* (London: T&T Clark, 2016).

2. Most scholars agree that the number fourteen is a veiled reference to the name of "David" by way of gematria (the numerical sum of the Hebrew letters in David's name). See Stephen C. Carlson, "The Davidic Key for Counting the Generations in Matthew 1:17," *CBQ* 76 (2014): 665–83.

saving his people from their sins as his primary mission (1:21). Jesus's identity and mission are inextricably linked. Patrick Schreiner gets to the point: "Monarchy is the chief metaphor Matthew employs to illuminate Jesus."[3] In what follows, I argue that Matthew presents Jesus as God's royal Son who enacts God's rule and saves his people by means of: (1) delivering his people from their sins; (2) authoritatively teaching, interpreting, and obeying God's Torah; (3) enacting merciful and compassionate royal justice through his deeds; and (4) inviting and enabling his disciples to share in his messianic rule and pattern of life. Jesus is the Christ who, as God's final Davidic king, enacts God's kingdom by saving his people from their sins; rightly teaching, interpreting, and embodying God's law; and enacting mercy, compassion, and justice for God's people. In what follows I will explore these four messianic themes through a literary and thematic study of the Gospel of Matthew.

The Messianic Son of God Pays the Debt for His Peoples' Sins

Matthew's genealogy retells a condensed version of the biblical story of God's history with his covenant people that situates the birth of the Messiah within God's election of Abraham and the people of Israel, the rise of the Davidic monarchy, and the tragedy of Israel's deportation to Babylon. The threefold pivot in the genealogy between Abraham, David, and the Babylonian deportation is striking for the way in which the latter event acts as the seemingly insurmountable obstacle to the fulfillment of God's promises to Abraham and David.[4] Richard Hays rightly notes that the genealogy tells Israel's story as structured around "promise, kingship, exile, and return" and culminating in Jesus as the messianic Savior.[5] Jesus's Davidic, royal ancestry is of obvious importance as the genealogy refers to Jesus as "the Son of David" (1:1), traces his lineage through "King David" (1:6), and gives the title of "Messiah" to Jesus (1:16, 17). Thus, Israel's hopes for a righteous ruler from the line of David are activated in an obvious manner.

---

3. Patrick Schreiner, *Matthew, Disciple and Scribe: The First Gospel and Its Portrait of Jesus* (Grand Rapids: Baker Academic, 2019), 101.

4. See Nicholas G. Piotrowski, "'After the Deportation': Observations in Matthew's Apocalyptic Genealogy," *BBR* 25 (2015): 189–203.

5. Richard B. Hays, *Echoes of Scripture in the Gospels* (Waco, TX: Baylor University Press, 2016), 111.

Babylonian Deportation, Sin, and the Failure of Davidic Kingship

But despite the importance of Jesus's Davidic ancestry, seen clearly in that David alone receives the moniker of "king" (τὸν Δαυὶδ τὸν βασιλέα, 1:6), the genealogy leaves us in no doubt that sin and evil have taken root within Israel's kings.[6] Judah, from whose tribe comes the line of David, is the one who fathers Perez and Zerah by Tamar; Tamar plays the part of the prostitute and deceives Judah as a means of procuring justice for herself (1:3; see Gen 38; 49:8–12). The attentive reader will note that it is Judah, not Tamar, who acts sinfully (see Gen 38:26), thereby further highlighting the sinfulness of Judah.[7] Matthew's inclusion of Judah's sin toward Tamar likely previews King David's own sinful history with Bathsheba. Rather than directly naming Bathsheba, Matthew reminds the reader that "David begot Solomon by the wife of Uriah" (1:6b). The compact phrase calls to mind David's wicked acts of greedy lust, adultery, and murder of an innocent man (2 Sam 11–12). Matthew's recounting of the lineage of David, especially in 1:6–11, recalls the stories of Judah's kings from the canonical books of 1 and 2 Kings—stories which, despite some glimmers of hope (e.g., Hezekiah and Josiah), include sad remembrances of sons of David who did evil in the sight of the Lord (e.g., 1 Kgs 11:6; 14:22), who exploited their own people (e.g., Ahab in 1 Kgs 21), and who committed gross acts of idolatry (e.g., 2 Kgs 21:1–16). Jeconiah, fathered by Josiah, is listed as the final king of Judah; taken into Babylonian captivity, he is even given the title "Jeconiah the captive" by the Chronicler (1 Chr 3:17). Four times, Matthew refers to the deportation to Babylon (1:11, 12, and twice in 1:17). Thus, in a highly condensed form, Matthew retells Israel's history in such a way that God's scriptural promises for a just and righteous Davidic ruler over God's people appear frustrated as a result of the wickedness and sin of Israel's kings. For Matthew's Gospel, exile marks the failure and end of kingship in Israel. While Israel's Scriptures do indeed portray an end to the exile and celebrate God's faithfulness to return the people to the land (e.g., Jer 29:10–32; also Ezra, Nehemiah; Isa 45; Haggai), the postexilic writings still consistently portray Israel as a people marked by

---

6. The only other figure in the genealogy who receives an explicit honorific or title is, of course, Jesus, who is referred to as "the Messiah." See, further, Matthias Konradt, *Israel, Church, and the Gentiles in the Gospel of Matthew*, trans. Kathleen Ess, Baylor–Mohr Siebeck Studies in Early Christianity (Waco, TX: Baylor University Press, 2014), 25.

7. See further Esther Marie Menn, *Judah and Tamar (Genesis 38) in Ancient Jewish Exegesis: Studies in Literary Form and Hermeneutics*, Supplements to the Journal for the Study of Judaism 51 (Leiden: Brill, 1997).

sin and lacking a righteous Davidic king.[8] And, therefore, despite a (limited) real return to the land, God's chastisements of his people have not ended and his promises are not yet fulfilled.

One is reminded of Ps 89 and the people's hopes for God to be faithful to the promises and the covenant he made with David and his house: "I have made a covenant with my chosen one; I have sworn an oath to David my servant: 'I will establish your offspring forever and build up your throne for all generations'" (Ps 89:3–4). And yet the psalmist laments that God's promises to the house of David have not been fulfilled, as he laments their condition of shame, humiliation, and the apparent absence of God (89:38–51). Matthew retells Israel's history by juxtaposing God's covenantal promises for a righteous Davidic son with the sin and faithlessness of David (and the Judean kings in his lineage).[9] Israel's sin and resulting punishment of deportation, where there is no Davidic king, appear to have frustrated God's people who are in need of rescue and deliverance. One of the many echoes of Matthew's reminder of Israel's deportation to Babylon is the vacancy of the throne of David as a result of the sin of the kings. Francis Watson states this point with clarity: "This people is a sinful people, and its sin is pervasive, spreading down through the generations."[10] Israel's Scriptures repeatedly portray the event of Israel's exile as a consequence of sin, idolatry, and failure to obey God's Torah. N. T. Wright has emphasized the biblical link between sin and the Babylonian deportation. He notes that Israel's "prophets of the time of the exile (in particular Jeremiah, Ezekiel, and Isaiah 40–55) saw Israel's exile precisely as the result of, or the punishment for, her sins."[11] Given the conceptualization of sin as a debt in the Old Testament, the prophets can speak of the end of Israel's exile coming through the payment of a debt or wage (e.g., Isa 40:1–2; Jer 31:15–16; cf. Neh 9:29–35; Lam 4:22; Dan 9:16).[12] But Matthew 1:17, which presents Jesus as the climax of the genealogy ("fourteen generations from the deportation to Babylon until the Messiah"), indicates that Messiah Jesus is the one who will,

---

8. I have learned much here from my colleague Steven Bryan. See, for example, Steven M. Bryan, "The End of Exile: The Reception of Jeremiah's Prediction of a Seventy-Year Exile," *JBL* 137 (2018): 107–26.

9. Hays, *Echoes of Scripture in the Gospels*, 110–11.

10. Francis Watson, *The Fourfold Gospel: A Theological Reading of the New Testament Portraits of Jesus* (Grand Rapids: Baker Academic, 2016), 41.

11. N. T. Wright, *Jesus and the Victory of God*, vol. 4 of *Christian Origins and the Question of God* (Minneapolis: Fortress, 1996), 268.

12. See especially Gary A. Anderson, *Sin: A History* (New Haven: Yale University Press, 2009).

once and for all, deal with his people's sins, restore the Davidic kingdom, and usher in God's prophetic restoration blessings.

The Restoration of the Davidic Kingdom and Salvation from Sins

Matthew is emphatic that Jesus is born within a situation bearing the effects of Israel's exile—namely, the failure and end of Davidic kingship. Jesus is born, in other words, within a prior story of God's promises to rescue and rule his people through a son of David, and of a people plagued by idolatry, injustice, and sexual infidelity. Again, Watson puts it well: "This history cannot deliver itself from the burden of its past. The coming of the Messiah must be the act of God."[13] On the one hand, Jesus shares the same flesh and the same ancestry as Abraham, David, and the other human figures of the genealogy. And yet, Matthew is clear that the birth of the Messiah is an unprecedented and climactic act of God that takes place through the Holy Spirit (1:18, 20).[14] The genealogy identifies thirty-nine (by my count) male figures who beget another male figure until the birth of Messiah Jesus, where the reader is surprised to find that it is not Joseph who begets Jesus; rather, "Jacob fathered Joseph the husband of Mary, who gave birth to Jesus who is called the Messiah" (1:16b).[15] Joseph, the "son of David" (1:20), does indeed adopt Jesus, so to speak, into the line of David. But as Dorothy Jean Weaver has noted: "Jesus Messiah is indeed the Son of David. But he is so not through ordinary and respectable channels, as the biological son of Joseph. Rather Jesus Messiah is born through the extraordinary agency of the Holy Spirit."[16] As a result, within the infancy narrative Jesus is given the name "Immanuel, which is translated as God with us" (1:23), and as a child he receives the worship or obeisance of the foreign magi who have come "to worship him" (2:2). It is within this context that the angel declares to Joseph that Mary "will give birth to a son, and you are to name him Jesus, because he will save his people from their sins" (1:21). Within the Matthean context, "his people" must refer to Israel, that is, God's

---

13. Watson, *The Fourfold Gospel*, 41.

14. One need not pit Jesus's divine conception as the Son of God and his Davidic messianic sonship against each other. See Konradt, *Israel, Church, and the Gentiles*, 28.

15. However, the four women in the genealogy (Tamar, Rahab, Ruth, and Bathsheba, the wife of Uriah)—all of whom are remembered as righteous figures despite surprising sexual encounters—foreshadow Mary as the mother of the Messiah.

16. Dorothy Jean Weaver, "Rewriting the Messianic Script: Matthew's Account of the Birth of Jesus," in *The Irony of Power: The Politics of God within Matthew's Narrative* (Eugene, OR: Pickwick, 2017), 128.

covenant people in need of salvation due to their suffering the consequences of sin, injustice, and idolatry, as hinted at in the genealogy. The gentile women in the genealogy, the presence of the magi in Matthew 2, and the extension of the gospel to the nations (Matt 28:16–20) foreshadow the Messiah's people as later including the gentiles, but here the emphasis is primarily upon the descendants of Abraham.[17] Further, it should be noted that Jesus's salvation of his people is explicitly predicated upon his identity as the messianic Davidic Son and as the Son of God.[18]

Matthew's well-known OT citations in Matthew 1–2 function to establish Jesus's identity as the Davidic king who restores God's kingdom. We could spend a great deal of time examining Matthew's literary artistry and the riches of his engagement of the OT here. But for my purposes, my primary point is to establish that Matthew's OT citations situate Jesus as the singular agent, the final Davidic Messiah, who enacts God's restoration promises as found in Israel's prophets. Considering that each quotation centers upon the restoration of the Davidic kingdom and subsequent blessings, Matthew is obviously concerned to establish Jesus's Davidic messianic identity as deeply related to how he accomplishes the salvation of his people.

First, the citation of Isaiah 7:14 in Matthew 1:23 ("See, the virgin will become pregnant and give birth to a son, and they will name him Immanuel, which is translated 'God with us'") evokes the broader context of Isaiah 7–9, where God promises to be with his people (Immanuel) by means of his ongoing faithfulness to the house of David. The child to be born, named Immanuel, will function as "a symbol of God's faithfulness to the line of David."[19] Israel's response to this promise will determine whether they experience judgment or salvation. Isaiah forecasts this as a prophetic event,[20] and Matthew draws upon it to argue that the birth of Jesus, in the words of Nicholas Piotrowski, means

17. On the four women in the genealogy as praiseworthy gentiles, see Jason B. Hood, *The Messiah, His Brothers, and the Nations: Matthew 1.1–17*, LNTS 441 (London: T&T Clark, 2011), 119–38.

18. Konradt, *Israel, Church, and the Gentiles*, 48: "In the context of Matt 1, the statement of 1.21 is connected with the double presentation of Jesus' identity as the Son of God and Son of David."

19. Andrew T. Abernethy, *The Book of Isaiah and God's Kingdom: A Thematic-Theological Approach*, NSBTS 40 (Downers Grove, IL: InterVarsity Press, 2016), 122.

20. The original context of Isa 7:14 and whether it anticipates an imminent or a farther off eschatological fulfillment is a matter of controversy we need not engage here, given our focus on Matthew's messianic reading of Isaiah. On the original context, see Abernethy, *The Book of Isaiah and God's Kingdom*, 121–25.

that "David's throne is reestablished, and the people can know that Yahweh is covenantally with them through his faithfulness to David's house."[21]

Second, the response of the chief priests and scribes to Herod's inquiry regarding the birth of the Messiah draws upon Micah 5:1, 3 and 2 Samuel 5:2: "And you Bethlehem, in the land of Judah, are by no means least among the rulers of Judah: because out of you will come a ruler who will shepherd my people" (Matt 2:6). The text introduces the theme of the ruling classes' opposition to Jesus, who will function as the ruler of his people as their shepherd-king. The context of Micah 5 is, unsurprisingly, one of prophetic expectation of the end of Israel's exile (Mic 4:9–13). The supplementation of Micah 5 with 2 Samuel 5:2 establishes Micah's good shepherd-king explicitly as a Davidic ruler who will restore the Davidic kingdom and usher in God's full restoration promises.[22] However, given the Jewish messianic script of the complementary relationship between the Davidic king and the Jerusalem priesthood, the collaboration between the Jerusalem authorities and Herod strikes an ominous note.[23]

Third, though Matthew does not explicitly cite any OT texts here, the account of the foreign magi from the east who bring their gifts and treasures to worship the "the King of the Jews" (Matt 2:1–11) almost certainly alludes to the expectation that God's enthronement of his Davidic king would result in the gentile nations offering gifts and worship to God's Messiah in Zion (e.g., Ps 45:7–9; 72:15; Isa 60:1–17). The scene further recalls the story recounted in 1 Kings 10 when the Queen of Sheba came to visit King Solomon in Jerusalem and, recognizing his great wisdom and wealth, bowed before him and gave gifts.

Fourth, in his famous reference to Hosea 11:1 in 2:15b ("Out of Egypt I called my son"), as well as Jeremiah 31:15 in 2:18 ("A voice was heard in Ramah, weeping, and great lamentation, Rachel weeping for her children; and she refused to be comforted because they are no more"), Matthew shows that Israel, with its opposition to the Davidic king from Herod and Israel's religious leaders, is functioning like Egypt as a place of captivity whereas Egypt itself ironically becomes a place of refuge. But more importantly, the larger contexts of Ho-

---

21. Nicholas G. Piotrowski, *Matthew's New David at the End of Exile: A Socio-rhetorical Study of Scriptural Quotations*, NovTSup 170 (Leiden: Brill, 2016), 53–54. I am deeply indebted to Piotrowski's broader argument for my analysis of Matthew's OT citations in his infancy narrative.

22. See here especially Joel Willitts, *Matthew's Messianic Shepherd-King: In Search of "The Lost Sheep of the House of Israel,"* BZNW 147 (Berlin: de Gruyter, 2007), 51–92; Konradt, *Israel, Church, and the Gentiles*, 32–33.

23. On this script, see Bernardo Cho, *Royal Messianism and the Jerusalem Priesthood in the Gospel of Mark*, LNTS 607 (London: T&T Clark, 2019), 25–77.

sea 11 and Jeremiah 30–31 function as prophetic anticipations for the future of God's restoration of his relationship with his people, and both do so by reflecting upon the past events of the exodus (Hosea) and exile (Jeremiah). Jesus, here, is not only the messianic leader of Israel, but as God's Son (τὸν υἱόν μου) he recapitulates corporate Israel, whom God led out of Egypt (cf. Exod 4:22–23).[24] Jesus embodies within himself the role of "his people" whom he will save from their sins as God's beloved son (2:15; 3:17; 17:5). "Jesus fulfills both Jeremiah 31:15 and Hosea 11:1 as a representative figure in whom the suffering and salvation of all Israel is recapitulated. He, like the people of Israel, was exiled amidst wailing and death, and he is the 'beloved Son' called out of exile."[25] The reader of Matthew is thereby able to follow the events of the child Jesus as calling for the child to be the one who will inaugurate the promises of Hosea and Jeremiah for a new temple, new covenant, and forgiveness of sins through a new Davidic rule.[26]

Finally, the difficult and ambiguous quotation in Matthew 2:23 ("he will be called a Nazarene [Ναζωραῖος]"), where no explicit citation is provided, may draw upon the MT of Isa 11:1, where the Hebrew text refers to the coming Messiah as a "shoot" or "branch" (נצר) which will come from the family of David.[27] Matthew employs the plural "prophets" here precisely because this horticultural image is found across a wide spectrum of prophetic texts which "*forecast the house of David reemerging from the ashes of the exile* (Jer 23:1–8; 33:14–18; Zech 3:6–10; 6:9–15; 4QFlor III, 10–13)" (the Hebrew language here is not נצר but צמח).[28] In Isaiah 11 the "shoot" and "branch" from Jesse forecast a Davidic king who, by means of the powerful presence of the Spirit, executes justice, righteousness, and peace for his people (Isa 11:2–9). Again, Matthew hints that God's salvation and blessings for his people is dependent upon the reestablishment of the Davidic monarchy.

While Matthew's OT citations in the infancy narrative could be examined in much greater detail, my primary concern is to establish that they preview Jesus's identity as the Davidic Messiah who, as the locus of God's presence in Zion and as the messianic shepherd-king, will save his people and usher in God's restoration blessings.

---

24. Hays, *Echoes of Scripture in the Gospels*, 113.

25. Nathan Eubank, *Wages of Cross-Bearing and the Debt of Sin: The Economy of Heaven in Matthew's Gospel*, BZNW 196 (Berlin: de Gruyter, 2013), 118.

26. In much more detail, see Piotrowski, *Matthew's New David*, 114–49.

27. Ulrich Luz, *Matthew 1–7: A Commentary*, trans. Wilhelm C. Linss (Minneapolis: Augsburg, 1989), 149–50.

28. Piotrowski, *Matthew's New David*, 160.

Matthew's thesis statement for Jesus's mission in 1:21—"he will save his people from their sins (αὐτὸς γὰρ σώσει τὸν λαὸν αὐτοῦ ἀπὸ τῶν ἁμαρτιῶν αὐτῶν)"—must be interpreted within the broader context of Jesus as the Davidic Messiah who brings an end to the plight of his people by delivering them and forgiving their sins. We have already noted that Israel's deportation to Babylon was a consequence of her sin and idolatry. And there are a variety of Jewish texts which refer to Israel's exile in Babylon as the result of their debt of sin. Isaiah 50:1, for example, states: "Where is your mother's certificate of divorce that I used to send her away? Or to which of my creditors did I sell you? Look, you were sold because of your sins and your mother was sent away because of your transgressions." Similarly, Jeremiah 31:16 and Isaiah 40:2 further establish the relationship between Israel's Babylonian deportation and repayment of a debt.[29] I suggest that one significant aspect of Jesus's saving his people from their sins consists in Jesus's death providing the payment that ransoms Israel out of their debt-bondage to sin. Jesus saves his people from their sins/debts by offering true obedience to God the Father and by laying down his life to deliver his people.

The Son of God's Solidarity with His Sinful People

Matthew's depiction of both Jesus's anointing at his baptism (3:13–17) and his temptations in the wilderness (4:1–11) center upon his messianic vocation as the Son of God to identify with and take on the plight of sinful Israel, his people, and to offer faithfulness and obedience to his Father. As such, they preview Jesus's climactic act of saving his people from their sins when he lays down his life on the cross in obedience to the Father.

Jesus's solidarity with Israel is seen in his submission to John's baptism, a ritual explicitly intended to symbolize Israel's repentance for the forgiveness of sins (3:1–2, 6, 11). John is enacting the script of Isaiah 40 and thereby preparing Israel for a new day when Israel's sin and debt captivity would be ended: "Speak tenderly to Jerusalem and announce to her that her time of forced labor is over, her iniquity has been pardoned, and she has received from the Lord's hand double for all her sins" (Isa 40:2). Thus, John's baptism is offered to "prepare" the people for the coming of God in the wilderness, the one who will enact Israel's restoration. Within this context of John's baptism of repentance for the forgiveness of sins, John's surprise that "the stronger one" (3:11) would come and seek baptism is entirely understandable (3:14), given that Jesus has

29. See the helpful discussion by Eubank, *Wages of Cross-Bearing*, 112–14.

been characterized as Israel's messianic shepherd, the divinely conceived Son of God, and the Davidic Messiah who will restore the Davidic kingship over his people. Jesus's response—"allow it to be so, for in this way it is fitting to fulfill all righteousness (πληρῶσαι πᾶσαν δικαιοσύνην)" (3:15)—indicates that his baptism for repentance is a righteous requirement and expresses his identification with the sinful people he has come to save (1:21). He is the one who will end Israel's time of debt captivity which has resulted from her sins (Isa 40:2). Jesus's baptism "is an expression of solidarity with [his people] in their sinfulness, in their standing under the looming judgment of God, and in God's deliverance of them."[30]

Jesus's fulfillment of this righteous requirement of standing in solidarity with sinful Israel elicits the descent of the Spirit of God from heaven and the Father's approving response as he declares from heaven: "This is my beloved Son (οὗτός ἐστιν ὁ υἱός μου ὁ ἀγαπητός). I am well pleased with him" (3:17). We will have occasion to examine parallel accounts of the baptism scene in the following chapters, but here I just note the following. First, Matthew has presented Jesus as the singular Davidic messianic king *and* the one who recapitulates Israel's own history. We have seen, for example, that he is, like Israel, "God's Son" called out of Egypt (Matt 2:15). But, of course, the title "son of God" is an honorific granted to the Lord's anointed, commissioned to rule on God's behalf (e.g., 2 Sam 7:12–14; Ps 2:7). Jesus's baptism evokes the Davidic traditions whereby David's anointing results in the Spirit's descent upon him (see 1 Sam 16:13).[31] Thus, Jesus is designated here as God's messianic agent commissioned to enact God's righteousness both *for the sake* of Israel and identified fully *with* Israel. Second, Jesus's messianic vocation as the Spirit-anointed Son of God (3:16–17) will consist in his obedience to the Father to save his people from their sins in fully identifying with their plight (3:13–15). Jesus is anointed as the royal Son of God, but as he stands in solidarity with his sinful people, his anointing previews a messianic vocation that will lead to his death. Nathan Eubank states it well when he notes that Jesus's baptism "presages the whole of Jesus' identity and mission. While there is nothing in the baptism itself that leads inexorably to crucifixion, Jesus' submission to baptism indicates the nature of his mission, a mission which ends in Jesus giving his life."[32]

Jesus's testing in the wilderness by the devil centers upon his messianic

30. J. R. Daniel Kirk, *A Man Attested by God: The Human Jesus of the Synoptic Gospels* (Grand Rapids: Eerdmans, 2016), 238.

31. See also Michael Patrick Barber, "Jesus as the Davidic Temple Builder and Peter's Priestly Role in Matthew 16:16–19," *JBL* 132 (2013): 938.

32. Eubank, *Wages of Cross-Bearing*, 130.

vocation as the Son of God (Matt 4:1–11). The scene presents a typological depiction of Israel in the wilderness with Moses (e.g., wilderness, temptations, Son of God, the number forty), and Jesus as God's Son again recapitulates and identifies with Israel, who was unfaithful and disobedient in the wilderness.[33] Jesus is the faithful Son who responds to each one of Satan's tests through quoting portions of Deuteronomy 6–8. The devil tests Jesus by questioning precisely this identity marked out for Jesus at his baptism: "If you are the Son of God . . ." (εἰ υἱὸς εἶ τοῦ θεοῦ, 4:3, 6). At stake here is the nature and character of Jesus's messiahship. Will his power and authority be used for personal aggrandizement such as miraculous breadmaking (cf. 4:3–4; cf. Deut 8:2–3) and displays of power from the pinnacle of the temple (4:5–7; cf. Ps 91:11–12), or will his messianic vocation be found in humble obedience to his Father? Perhaps most striking is the devil's offer in the third temptation, where he shows Jesus "all the kingdoms of the world and their glory" and declares: "I will give to you all these things if you fall down and give worship to me" (4:8b–9; cf. Deut 6:13).[34] Given Jesus's identity as God's own Son, the messianic Davidic King of Israel, he has indeed been promised authority, power, and a kingdom (cf. Matt 28:16–20); however, Jesus's messianic vocation consists in an alternative route to the glory of the kingdom that involves suffering the plight of his people and offering the obedience to God that they had failed to give in the wilderness. Jesus is indeed the Son of God, the messianic ruler who shares in God's authority, but "strict adherence to God's will is just as much a part of divine Sonship—even when it comes to utilizing divine authority."[35] Jesus's commitment to "fulfill all righteousness" (3:13–15) and to offer obedience and faithfulness to his Father (4:1–11) instead of using power for his own purposes previews the way in which Jesus's messianic vocation finds its climax on the cross. Furthermore, Jesus's three quotations from Deuteronomy in response to Satan previews his role as Israel's pious king who observes God's Torah faithfully (Deut. 17:14–20).

The Messiah's Death Provides the Ransom for Israel's Sins

Jesus provides an explicit interpretation of his death as the event that will save his people by providing the payment or ransom that delivers them from

33. The classic study here is Birger Gerhardsson, *The Testing of God's Son (Matt. 4:1–11 & Par): An Analysis of an Early Christian Midrash* (Eugene, OR: Wipf & Stock, 2009).

34. The resonances and interplay of the Old Testament texts in Matthew 4:1–11 are examined in detail by Hays, *Echoes of Scripture in the Gospels*, 117–20.

35. Konradt, *Israel, Church, and the Gentiles*, 289.

bondage to sin. Thus, in Matthew 20:28, Jesus declares that "the Son of Man did not come to be served, but to serve and to give his life as a ransom for many (λύτρον ἀντὶ πολλῶν)." Eubank has shown that the Septuagint always uses λύτρον to refer to a price or payment offered as a means of redemption, payment, or some kind of exchange (e.g., Exod 21:30; 30:12; Lev 19:20; 25:51–52; 27:31; Num 3:46–49). Frequently this payment is offered as a means of delivering persons from some kind of debt-bondage or captivity.[36] Within Matthew's context, which has emphasized Israel as a sinful people, lacking a righteous Davidic king, the OT texts which speak of God "providing a ransom" to deliver his people from Egypt and/or from exile are almost certainly relevant to Jesus's interpretation of his own death (Exod 6:6; Mic 4:10; 6:4; Jer 31:11). In other words, as the humble and obedient messianic Son, Jesus identifies with Israel's sinful plight and offers his own life as the payment or ransom that will rescue Israel from captivity and save them from their sins.

While the focus of the so-called parable of the unmerciful slave centers upon how disciples of Jesus must embody a similar ethic of mercy and forgiveness with each other (18:21–35), Jesus similarly compares the kingdom of heaven with a king (ὡμοιώθη ἡ βασιλεία τῶν οὐρανῶν ἀνθρώπῳ βασιλεῖ, 18:23a) who wanted to settle accounts with his servants.[37] But when one of his servants so impossibly lacks the amount of money needed to pay back his debts and is on the verge, along with his entire family, of being sold into debtor's prison (18:25), the king, out of gratuitous mercy, "had compassion on the servant, released him (ἀπέλυσεν), and forgave him (ἀφῆκεν αὐτῷ) of his loan" (18:27). Again, later, the king recounts how he embodied mercy by forgiving (ἀφῆκά) the slave of all his debt (πᾶσαν τὴν ὀφειλήν) that he owed to the master (18:32–33). It takes little imagination to see the king of the parable as playing the role of Messiah Jesus who, despite being the sinless and obedient Israelite, out of sheer mercy gives up his life and so pays the debt of his sinful people, thereby ransoming them out of captivity.

Jesus's primary interpretation of his death occurs at the Last Supper, where he anticipates his impending death and interprets the Passover wine as "the blood of my covenant which is poured out for many for the forgiveness of sins (εἰς ἄφεσιν ἁμαρτιῶν)" (26:28).[38] The language "blood of the covenant" recalls the covenant God made with Israel at Sinai (Exod 24:8), which was

36. Eubank, *Wages of Cross-Bearing*, 149–54.

37. On the relationship between the parable and Jesus's death as the act which procures forgiveness for Israel, see Boris Repschinski, "'For He Will Save His People from Their Sins' (Matthew 1:21): A Christology for Christian Jews," *CBQ* 68 (2006): 260.

38. Anders Runesson, *Divine Wrath and Salvation in Matthew: The Narrative World of*

also ratified with a meal (Exod 24:9–11). While the people of Israel promise obedience to the Lord's laws and statutes at Sinai (Exod 24:7), Matthew's reader knows that Messiah Jesus alone, the one who has stood in solidarity with Israel, has offered perfect obedience and righteousness to God.[39] Thus, the theme of obedience of God's covenant people along with the language of "covenant" and "forgiveness of sins" calls to mind Jeremiah's expectation for a new covenant. Jeremiah anticipates a day when God will bring Israel's exile to an end, write his law on his people's hearts, and bring an end to their sin (Jer 31:31–34).[40] This new covenant, however, is directed to Jesus's people (Matt 1:21), that is, captive Israel waiting for their messianic and Davidic shepherd.[41]

The phrase "for the forgiveness of sins" obviously echoes the angel's prophecy that Jesus would save his people from their sins (1:21), as well as Jesus's submission to John's baptism of repentance for the forgiveness of sins (3:2, 6), and Jesus's interpretation of his death as a payment of ransom for those in captivity (20:28). Matthew's interaction with the prophet Zechariah to interpret Jesus's final days leading to his death in Jerusalem further confirms that Jesus's death is the payment for Israel's sins and thereby ransoms them out of their debt-bondage. Matthew's engagement with Zechariah is significant for the latter's depiction of a humble, messianic Davidic shepherd who is rejected by Israel's leaders but also inaugurates a new covenant with God's restored people and is enthroned to a position of rule over his faithful people in Mt. Zion.[42] Jesus's language of "my blood of the covenant" (Matt 26:28) alludes to Zechariah 9:11 (itself almost certainly an allusion to Exod 24:8), a text Matthew cites explicitly to describe Jesus's entrance into Jerusalem as a fulfillment of Zechariah 9:9: "Say to Daughter Zion, behold your king comes to you; he is gentle and riding on a donkey even on a colt, the foal of a donkey" (Matt 21:5). This humble messianic king makes his way into Jerusalem to save his people from their sins by offering his own body and blood as the wages for Israel's ransom.[43] In this surprising way, through his rejection and death, the humble messianic king will "proclaim peace to the nations" and will establish a "dominion from sea

---

the First Gospel (Minneapolis: Fortress, 2016), 126–30, argues that Jesus's death is the place of atonement for the people given that the temple is defiled.

39. See also Hays, *Echoes of Scripture in the Gospels*, 134.

40. Piotrowski, *Matthew's New David*, 146–49.

41. See Konradt, *Israel, Church, and the Gentiles*, 340–45.

42. The influence of Zech 9–14 on Matthew's Gospel could be examined here with profit in much more detail. See, for example, Charlene McAfee Moss, *The Zechariah Tradition and the Gospel of Matthew*, BZNW 156 (Berlin: de Gruyter, 2008).

43. See Wright, *Jesus and the Victory of God*, 560–61.

to sea" (Zech 9:10). Thus, Zechariah 9:11, echoed in Jesus's own interpretation of his death, acts as the critical context for making sense of the meaning of the messianic king's death: "By the blood of the covenant (ἐν αἵματι διαθήκης), I will release your prisoners from the waterless cistern." Jesus's offer of his own life, his blood, inaugurates a covenant which redeems and releases his people from the debtor's prison, from the sin that has resulted in their exile. Tragic irony is present, however, in Matthew's recounting of Jesus's death, where "all the people" (πᾶς ὁ λαός) plead with Pilate to crucify Jesus and declare: "His blood be upon us and upon our children" (27:25; cf. 23:35). While the reception history of this verse is reprehensible, and it cannot be denied that Matthew sees "the people" as a whole as responsible for Jesus's death, there is another layer of meaning that has not always been recognized or emphasized.[44] The people's cry for the blood of Jesus to be upon them and their children almost certainly functions as an ironic echo and counterpart to the people of Israel in the wilderness who are splattered with the blood of the covenant (Exod 24:7–8). The call for Jesus's blood thereby affirms both Israel's culpability for Jesus's death *and* the people's salvation by means of offering his blood to effect redemption and a new covenant that cleanses God's people from sin.[45]

Matthew's addition of the name "Jesus" to the *titulus* (Mark lacks the name "Jesus," having only "king of the Jews"), making for the written charge "this is Jesus (οὗτός ἐστιν Ἰησοῦς), the King of the Jews," reminds the reader of the meaning of Jesus's name in 1:21, the one who will save his people from their sins (cf. Matt 26:28).[46] This further heightens the irony of those mocking Jesus, who suppose that his identity as "the Son of God" and "Israel's King" is manifestly false, given his inability to save himself by coming down from the cross. Three times the mockers use the language of "save" or "salvation" in their taunts of Jesus. Thus, "Save yourself (σῶσον σεαυτόν)! If you are the Son of God, come down from the cross!" (Matt 27:40b); "He saved others (ἄλλους ἔσωσεν), but he cannot save (δύναται σῶσαι) himself! He is Israel's King! Let him come down now from the cross and we will believe in him" (27:42). The mockery of "if you are the Son of God" reminds the reader quite clearly of the devil's threefold temptation of Jesus and Jesus's demonstration of his true messianic vocation in humble obedience to God rather than self-aggrandizement. As in the time of his temptations, "Jesus as the Son of God, in obedience to the

44. See, for example, Catherine Sider Hamilton, "'His Blood Be upon Us': Innocent Blood and the Death of Jesus in Matthew," *CBQ* 70 (2008): 82n1.

45. So Repschinski, "'For He Will Save His People,'" 263.

46. See Repschinski, "'For He Will Save His People,'" 264.

will of the Father, does not make use of the power he possesses but instead fulfills the will of God."[47] Here Jesus's identity as Israel's King and the Son of God is revealed in him refusing to save himself, but instead saving his people from their sins through his death on the Roman cross. Furthermore, little do the mockers know that Jesus's crucifixion will function as the means of his enthronement, as he is soon to be exalted as the resurrected Lord (see further Matt 26:61–64). While we will examine this theme in more detail in following chapters, here we can briefly note that the emphasis in Matthew's passion narrative upon the Davidic Psalter as a means of explaining Jesus's suffering and death (e.g., Matt 27:46); the apocalyptic signs of the tearing of the temple veil, the earthquake, and the opening of the tombs (27:50–53); and the centurion's confession of Jesus as the Son of God (27:54) function to portray Jesus as the true Son of God and portend his ultimate vindication and enthronement. Patrick Schreiner nicely summarizes Matthew's portrait of Jesus as the suffering and wise Davidic king: "Matthew skillfully positions Jesus on the cross as the new David, who suffers at the hands of his enemies. Not only the words of Jesus carry the melodies of the Psalms, but even the actions of those who crucify Jesus point back to David."[48]

MESSIAH JESUS TEACHES, INTERPRETS, AND OBEYS GOD'S TORAH

If Jesus is the messianic king who has delivered his sinful people by paying the debt of their sins through the cross, then it would not be surprising if the Messiah also provided a remedy for the cause of their exile, namely—Israel's sins and transgressions. We have already seen the causal connection between sin and exile in the previous section. Here I note the connection between the king of Israel's disobedience to Torah and the ensuing exile, seen clearly in King Solomon's prayer which Israel will recite in a future time of exile: "We have sinned and done wrong; we have been wicked. . . . May you forgive your people who sinned against you and all their rebellions against you, and may you grant them compassion before their captors so they may be treated with compassion" (1 Kgs 8:47b, 50). Israel's return from exile will not be apart from their commitment to eradicate their sins of disobedience to the Torah. And within Matthew's sym-

---

47. Konradt, *Israel, Church, and the Gentiles*, 301. See also Michael F. Bird, *Jesus Is the Christ: The Messianic Testimony of the Gospels* (Downers Grove, IL: InterVarsity Press, 2012), 76–77.

48. Schreiner, *Matthew, Disciple and Scribe*, 92.

bolic universe, sin is not defined as general wrongdoing, nor is it a state or power (cf. Rom 5:14–21), but it is, rather, disobedience to the Torah.[49]

The Davidic King Loves God's Torah

As the one who "fulfills all righteousness" (3:15) and teaches his disciples about a "superior righteousness," it makes sense that Jesus consistently upholds Torah obedience throughout the Gospel of Matthew. Thus, all of the law and the prophets remain in effect and those who relax even the smallest commandments are "least in the kingdom of heaven" (Matt 5:18–19; cf. 23:2, 23). In Matthew's Gospel, Jesus saves his people from their sins not only through his death on the cross but also in his taking the lead in teaching, interpreting, and embodying God's Torah.[50]

Furthermore, within Israel's Scriptures the primary task of Israel's king is to take the lead in observing the Torah. In fact, the Old Testament's only law concerning kingship is found in Deuteronomy 17:14–20 ("the Law of the King"), where the king is tasked with writing, reading, and obeying Torah.[51] Israel's king is to "diligently observe all the words of this law and these statutes, neither exalting himself above other members of the community nor turning aside from the commandment, either to the right or to the left so that he and his descendants may reign over his kingdom in Israel" (17:19–20). Deuteronomy's "Law of the King" functions as the primary guide for evaluating Israel's kings and whether they take the lead in modeling the Torah-obedience God demands of all his people.[52] Thus, God promises to give the land to Joshua, presuming he does "not turn from [the law] to the right or the left" (Josh 1:7; cf. Deut 17:20). Josiah is the only king who, like Joshua, is described as not "turning to

---

49. Runesson, *Divine Wrath and Salvation*, 54–57.

50. While I have placed much more emphasis on Jesus saving his people from their sins by means of the cross, I am in large agreement with Blanton who suggests that Matthew's Gospel provides a variegated approach to how Jesus accomplishes his mission in Matthew 1:21—one of them related to obeying the Torah. See Thomas R. Blanton IV, "Saved by Obedience: Matthew 1:21 in Light of Jesus's Teaching on the Torah," *JBL* 132 (2013): 393–413.

51. I have written more on this in Joshua W. Jipp, *Christ Is King: Paul's Royal Ideology* (Minneapolis: Fortress, 2015), 54–60.

52. On this point, see the excellent book by Gerald Eddie Gerbrandt, *Kingship according to the Deuteronomistic History*, SBLDS 87 (Atlanta: Scholars Press, 1986). See further James L. Mays, *The Lord Reigns: A Theological Handbook to the Psalms* (Louisville: Westminster John Knox, 1994), 132–34; Patrick D. Miller, "The Beginning of the Psalter," in *The Shape and Shaping of the Psalter*, ed. J. Clinton McCann, JSOTSup 159 (Sheffield: JSOT Press, 1993), 83–92.

the right or the left" from the law; for this reason, he is spoken of as "walking in all the ways of his father David" (2 Kgs 22:2). Josiah's positive evaluation is based upon his renewal of the covenant and his implementation of Israel's turn toward obeying the law (2 Kgs 23:1–3). Josiah is given high praise for following God's Torah, and the narrator declares that "before him there was no king like him, who turned to the Lord with all his heart, with all his soul, and with all his might, according to all the law of Moses" (2 Kgs 23:25; cf. 1 Kgs 2:3; 3:6; 8:58; 9:4–5). Throughout 1–2 Kings, to follow in the ways of David is to love God by means of following the Torah; alternatively, to depart from the ways of David is to disregard obligations to God's covenant—the end result being exile.[53] Similarly, the editing of the Psalter, which places Torah psalms next to royal Davidic psalms, has the literary consequence of portraying the king as the lover and exemplary follower of God's Torah (see Pss 1–2; 18–19; 118–119).[54] Thus, David is the preeminent lover of God's law: "I delight to do your will, O my God, your law is within my heart" (Ps 40:8; cf. Ps 1:2). In the Psalter, David gives voice to the righteous ones within Israel who seek to walk blamelessly in loving God's statues and laws (Pss 15, 24). Within Israel's Scriptures, then, the combination of Davidic kingship and Torah-obedience testifies to God's plan to rule his people through a righteous lover and observer of God's law, even by means of a king who has internalized the Torah within himself. Thus, a non-Torah-observant Davidic Messiah makes little sense within either the context of Israel's Scriptures or the symbolic world of Matthew's Gospel.

Messiah Jesus Interprets and Embodies Torah

We have seen that Jesus has inaugurated a new covenant through his death. But one of the promises of Jeremiah's new covenant was that God's law would be written on the hearts of God's people; thus, there is the expectation that true repentance and obedience to the Torah would be a profound mark of the messianic age (see Deut 30:11–14; Jer. 31:31–34).[55] Within Matthew's Gospel we see Jesus as the wise king who authoritatively interprets Torah and proclaims proper obedience to God's laws. Matthew portrays Jesus as the righteous Da-

53. On this dynamic for evaluating kings in 1–2 Kings, see Alison L. Joseph, *Portrait of the Kings: The Davidic Prototype in Deuteronomist Poetics* (Minneapolis: Fortress, 2015).

54. Excellent here is Jamie A. Grant, *The King as Exemplar: The Function of Deuteronomy's Kingship Law in the Shaping of the Book of Psalms*, Academia Biblical 17 (Atlanta: Society of Biblical Literature, 2004).

55. See the short study by W. D. Davies, *Torah in the Messianic Age and/or the Age to Come*, SBLMS 7 (Atlanta: Scholars Press, 1952).

vidic King who loves, teaches, and embodies God's Torah. W. D. Davies refers to Jesus's teachings in Matthew as "the Torah of the Messiah."[56] One aspect of Matthew's portrait of Jesus as the Son of David is that he is the wise and Torah-observant king.[57] While echoes of Jesus as a new Moses are certainly present, one should not underestimate Matthew's portrait of Jesus as a royal figure.[58] Bracketing Jesus's teachings (chs. 5–7) and merciful healings (chs. 8–9) is the narrator's description of Jesus as "proclaiming the gospel of the kingdom and healing every disease and every sickness among the people" (4:23; cf. 9:35). Two of Jesus's Beatitudes center upon the promise of sharing in the kingdom of heaven (5:3, 10), and Jesus teaches his disciples to pray for the coming kingdom (6:9–10). Further, it would be highly unusual for Matthew to set forth Jesus's messianic Davidic identity so strongly only to drop it in the following chapters.[59] Jesus's sage-like teaching and revelation of the hidden mysteries center, especially in chapter 13, upon his intimate knowledge of the kingdom of heaven and his insight that the kingdom is present in history despite its "hidden, unexpected presence in the world" (e.g., 13:11, 19, 24, 31, 33, 44, 45, 47, 52).[60]

Any interpretation of Jesus and Torah that suggests he overturns or abrogates the law runs aground on Jesus's central teaching in 5:17: "Do not suppose

56. Davies, *Torah in the Messianic Age*, 92. However, my reading obviously parts ways with his argument that a new Torah will be present in the messianic age. A further unpacking of my argument would involve more thorough engagement with the work of Roland Deines. See especially the summary of his larger argument in Roland Deines, "Not the Law but the Messiah: Law and Righteousness in the Gospel of Matthew—An Ongoing Debate," in *Built upon the Rock: Studies in the Gospel of Matthew*, ed. Daniel M. Gurtner and John Nolland (Grand Rapids: Eerdmans, 2008), 53–84. While Deines does not believe that Jesus dispenses with or abrogates the Torah, he does argue that the eschatological righteousness of Matthew makes, to some extent, concrete observation of the Torah something superfluous for Jesus's followers.

57. Ben Witherington III, *Jesus the Sage: The Pilgrimage of Wisdom* (Minneapolis: Fortress, 1994), 352, states that "Matthew set out to show that Jesus was *the* Son of David, like unto but wiser even than Solomon because Jesus was Wisdom in the flesh. There is thus a major stress on showing Jesus as the perfect king manifesting all the qualities of self-control, prudence, good judgment, wise speech, and righteousness expected of a Solomonic royal figure."

58. On Jesus as a Moses-like figure, see Dale C. Allison Jr., *The New Moses: A Matthean Typology* (Minneapolis: Fortress, 1993, repr., Eugene, OR: Wipf & Stock, 2013).

59. Schreiner, *Matthew, Disciple and Scribe*, 102.

60. George Eldon Ladd, *A Theology of the New Testament*, 2nd ed. (Grand Rapids: Eerdmans, 1998), 94. Ladd's entire chapter 7 (89–102) presents an excellent interpretation of the "mystery of the kingdom."

that I have come to destroy the Law and the Prophets; I have not come to destroy but to fulfill (πληρῶσαι)."[61] The meaning of *fulfill* is disputed, but it cannot mean anything less than to observe the teachings of the Law and the Prophets as is made clear in 5:18–19, where Jesus declares that the law remains in effect until the end of history and that if one should break, and teach others to break, "one of the least of these commandments," that one will be least in the kingdom of heaven.[62] Jesus, in fact, calls his community to a "righteousness (ἡ δικαιοσύνην) that exceeds that of the scribes and Pharisees" if they would enter into the kingdom of heaven (5:20). And those who fail to understand and obey Jesus's interpretation of the Torah and his call for a better righteousness will find themselves as eschatological lawbreakers, excluded from the kingdom of God (7:21–27). Jesus's messianic task to save his people consists, in part, of teaching his disciples how to embody the better righteousness found in his interpretation of God's Torah.[63]

Jesus sets forth some kind of abundant righteousness as necessary for participation in God's kingdom. Jesus's six "but I say to you" sayings all present the divine intention, often focusing upon the deeper principles or inner motivations of God's laws. Jesus interprets the Torah under the belief that God's laws have been written upon the hearts of his kingdom people and that the law has been interiorized, just as Jeremiah 31 and Ezekiel 36 prophesied.[64] This is explained in detail in 5:21–48, where Jesus calls his disciples to obey the true intent of God's law and to do so from the heart. The divine intention of the Torah's prohibition against adultery (Exod 20:14; Deut 5:18), for example, is ultimately to be found in the inner eradication of illicit desire and lust for what belongs to someone else (5:27–30). The divine intention of the command "do not murder" (Exod 20:13; Deut 5:17) is to refrain from the inner propensity to anger and bitterness (5:21–26). Jesus is not overturning the Torah but is rather interpreting the divine intention of God's commandments.[65] Jesus makes it

---

61. Dale C. Allison Jr., *The Sermon on the Mount: Inspiring the Moral Imagination* (New York: Crossroad, 1999), 58–61.

62. R. T. France, *Matthew: Evangelist and Teacher* (Downers Grove, IL: InterVarsity Press, 1995), 195–96, rightly notes that 5:18 "does expect Jesus' disciples to continue to observe the law. . . . [The commandments] remain the word of God, and none of them is to be discarded or disparaged." See also Runesson, *Divine Wrath and Salvation*, 61–68.

63. Similarly, see Blanton, "Saved by Obedience," 405–6.

64. See here Jonathan T. Pennington, *The Sermon on the Mount and Human Flourishing: A Theological Commentary* (Grand Rapids: Baker Academic, 2017), 170–79.

65. Note Pennington, *The Sermon on the Mount*, 181: "These six examples, then, are not antitheses but exegeses. They are illustrations that interpret, or exegete, both the Old Tes-

clear that his starting point for understanding the correct interpretation of Torah is rooted in his knowledge of the character of God and the goal of the Torah is conformity to God's holy character (5:48; cf. Lev 19:2). In other words, Jesus agrees with the scribes and the Pharisees that the Torah is holy, given by God, and reveals his will and righteousness; but Jesus is the authoritative interpreter of the Torah who understands and can interpret its meaning in a way that rightly aligns with God's perspective.

Thus, in Matthew 22:34–40, when Jesus is put to the test by an expert in the law who asks which commandment is the greatest, Jesus responds with two texts from the Torah which call for love for God (Deut 6:5) and love for neighbor (Lev 19:18). Jesus twice declares that the Law and the Prophets find their meaning in these two commands (22:40; cf. 7:12). In chapter 23 Jesus denounces the scribes and the Pharisees for interpreting the Torah in such a way that exalts themselves as religious experts but places impossible burdens upon those they teach (23:2–12). The Torah rightly interpreted is not a burdensome or impossible yoke; neither is it something that is rightly used as a means of exalting oneself above one's neighbor (23:11–12). But Jesus does not, as a result, argue for dispensing with the Torah; rather, his disciples are to continue to listen to and observe the laws of Moses (23:3). They are to continue to observe the entirety of the Torah, even continuing to tithe mint, cumin, and dill, but they are to understand that the weightier matters of the Torah are found in its call for "justice, mercy, and faithfulness" (τὴν κρίσιν καὶ τὸ ἔλεος καὶ τὴν πίστιν, 23:23). One can hardly overstate the importance of this text for Jesus's engagement of Torah: the weightier matters of the Torah—justice, mercy, and faith—take precedence over the lesser commandments.[66]

Given that God is merciful and kind to everyone (Matt 5:43–48), Jesus believes that God's Torah is rightly interpreted from a standpoint of mercy and justice. This makes good sense of many of Jesus's interpretations of Torah in the Sermon on the Mount. Disciples of Jesus are called to be persons who refuse vengeance, retaliation, covetousness, and greed, and instead embrace honesty and love for neighbors and enemies (5:21–48). Jesus's "hermeneutic of mercy" as it relates to his ministry and interpretation of Torah is seen clearly in 12:1–14. When Jesus and his disciples are questioned about breaking the law by picking and eating grain on the Sabbath, Jesus responds with a quotation from Hosea 6:6: "If you had known what this means, 'I desire mercy and not

---

tament teachings and Jesus's words together, showing how the fulfillment-not-abolishment of 5:17–20 is worked out."

66. Runesson, *Divine Wrath and Salvation*, 72–73.

sacrifice,' you would not have condemned the innocent" (12:7). Mercy and sacrifice here "stand for, respectively, a form of piety that focuses on God's compassion toward human needs and a form of piety that focuses on ritual observances."[67] And Jesus declares that God's law itself prioritizes mercy and compassion as the proper means of interpreting the commandments of the Torah. For this reason, Jesus declares that the Sabbath day is the appropriate day to demonstrate mercy and compassion in healing the sick (12:9–12). Jesus's interpretation of the Torah does not dispense with any commandment, but it does require the proper evaluation and ranking of commandments when they conflict with one another.[68]

Jesus consistently turns to the Torah as a means of articulating God's will for merciful and loving relations among his people. So, for example, in his dispute with the Pharisees who wonder why he and his disciples do not follow the traditions of the elders, Jesus accuses them of "breaking God's commandment because of your tradition" (15:3). Specifically, their tradition of dedicating their possessions to the temple instead of using it to care for their mother and father results in them breaking the commandment to honor their parents (Exod 20:12; Deut 5:16). The point here is that Jesus accuses the scribes of failing to obey God's Torah and invokes Torah as a means of understanding what God demands as righteous behavior for his disciples. In another episode, Jesus responds to the rich young man's question about how to obtain eternal life by listing the second table of the Ten Commandments, along with the summary commandment of Leviticus 19:18 (cf. Matt 7:12; 22:24–30): "Do not murder; do not commit adultery; do not steal; do not bear false testimony; honor your father and mother, and you shall love your neighbor as yourself" (Matt 19:18–19). There is nothing facetious or ironic here in Jesus responding to the man's desire for life by invoking God's commandments which promised life to those who observed them (Lev 18:5; Deut 30:1–14). The man believes that he has kept these laws, but his refusal to give his possessions to the poor (19:20–21) likely indicates he has not given himself to the "better righteousness" (5:20) as found in Jesus's central interpretation of the divine law as demanding mercy, compassion, and love for neighbor.

But Jesus not only interprets the Torah, he also follows it himself and can be seen as the premier example of one who interiorizes God's law. We have seen that one of the primary tasks of Israel's kings was precisely taking the

67. See here the excellent discussion of Jesus's "hermeneutic of mercy" in Hays, *Echoes of Scripture in the Gospels*, 123–28 (quotation from 126).

68. Blanton, "Saved by Obedience," 407–8.

lead in obeying the law. This is also true of the rabbis whose lives offered a visible model of emulation for their disciples. Robert Kirschner has shown how the rabbis' "most intimate habits and activities were subjected to careful scrutiny."[69] Unlike the Pharisees and scribes, who are repeatedly referred to as "hypocrites" (23:13, 15, 28) and do not "practice what they teach" (e.g., 23:3), Jesus is the one who "fulfills all righteousness" (3:15) and is himself a "righteous man" (27:19).[70] And, in fact, in Matthew 11:27–30, Jesus declares that his own life is a visible display of Torah obedience: "All things have been handed over to me by my Father, and no one knows the Son except the Father, nor does anyone know the Father except the Son and the one to whom the Son desires to reveal. Come to me all who labor and are heavily burdened and I will give you rest. Take my yoke upon you, and learn from me, for I am gentle and lowly in heart (ὅτι πραΰς εἰμι καὶ ταπεινὸς τῇ καρδίᾳ), and you will find rest for your souls; for my yoke is easy and my burden light." Jesus's claim that he and his teaching manifest "meekness" or "gentleness" resonates with Matthew's depiction of Jesus as the "meek" (πραΰς) and humble "King" (ὁ βασιλεύς) entering into Jerusalem during the triumphal entry (Matt 21:5). King Jesus's calmness, rejection of anger, and care for his subjects presents a powerful contrast with the angry and tyrannical King Herod (again, Matt 2:1–2, 19).[71] Jesus's life and his teaching embody this rejection of anger, aggression, and violence (see Matt 5:21–26).[72]

Scholars have also long noted the similarities between Jesus's words and Jewish depictions of wisdom where wisdom is often identified with Torah or God's commandments (see Prov 8; Sir 24; Wis 7:22–27; 1 En. 42).[73] The most strikingly similar Jewish wisdom text, and one that explicitly identifies wisdom with Torah (24:23), is Sirach 51:23–27:

> Draw near to me, you who are uneducated. . . . Why do you delay in these matters, when your souls thirst so much? . . . Place your neck under the yoke, and let your soul accept training—she is near if you wish to find her.

---

69. I am dependent here upon Robert Kirschner, "Imitatio Rabbini," *JSJ* 17 (1986): 70–79.

70. See also Pennington, *The Sermon on the Mount*, 91.

71. See especially Deirdre J. Good, *Jesus the Meek King* (Harrisburg, PA: Trinity Press International, 1999).

72. Good, *Jesus the Meek King*, 82–88.

73. On these echoes, see Witherington, *Jesus the Sage*, 360–61; Hays, *Echoes of Scripture in the Gospels*, 153–59; M. Jack Suggs, *Wisdom, Christology and Law in Matthew's Gospel* (Cambridge, MA: Harvard University Press, 1970). On the messianic precedents for Jesus as a teacher of wisdom and justice, see Schreiner, *Matthew, Disciple and Scribe*, ch. 1.

Witness with your own eyes that I have labored little yet have found much rest for myself. . . . Come to me, you who desire me, and eat your fill of my fruits. For the memory of me is sweeter than honey, and the possession of me sweeter than the honeycomb. Those who eat of me will hunger for more, and those who drink of me will thirst for me.

Jesus seems to be identifying himself and his yoke of instruction with the wisdom of the Torah. To take Jesus's "easy yoke" upon oneself is not less than committing oneself to his interpretation of the Torah which calls for mercy, justice, and ultimately love for one another. And Matthew presents Jesus as embodying his own interpretation of the Torah precisely by portraying Jesus as doing what he says. Jesus acts, then, as an exemplary model for embodying God's righteousness in one's deeds. Dale Allison Jr., among others, has noted this feature of Matthew's Gospel and compiled an extensive list of how Jesus's character conforms to his own teachings. For example, Jesus's blessing upon the meek (5:5) is embodied in his character as one who is meek and lowly of heart (11:29; 21:5). His blessing upon the merciful (5:7) is seen in his healings and exorcisms which enact mercy to the oppressed (9:7; 15:22; 22:30). Jesus is persecuted for the sake of righteousness in his trial and crucifixion (5:10; 27:23). He turns his other cheek to those who mock and beat him (5:39; 26:67; 27:30). He prays in private places (6:6; 14:23). One could find plenty more examples, but the point should stand that Jesus's teaching, often encapsulated in his interpretation of the Torah, is embodied in his own deeds.[74]

THE MERCIFUL MESSIANIC SHEPHERD-KING

The primary proclamation of Jesus and perhaps the central theme throughout Matthew's Gospel is, of course, the kingdom of heaven/God (e.g., 4:17, 23; 5:3, 10, 19, 20; 6:10, 13, 33). One aspect of Matthew's use of the phrase kingdom of heaven is its contrast with all of the rest of the kingdoms of the earth.[75] The manner and nature of God's rule is, throughout the Gospel of Matthew,

74. I am dependent for my insights upon Dale C. Allison Jr., "The Embodiment of God's Will: Jesus in Matthew," in *Seeking the Identity of Jesus: A Pilgrimage*, ed. Beverly Roberts Gaventa and Richard B. Hays (Grand Rapids: Eerdmans, 2008), 117–32; Dale C. Allison Jr., "Structure, Biographical Impulse, and the *Imitatio Christi*," in *Studies in Matthew: Interpretation Past and Present* (Grand Rapids: Baker Academic, 2005), 135–55.

75. See throughout Jonathan T. Pennington, *Heaven and Earth in the Gospel of Matthew*, NovTSup 126 (Leiden: Brill, 2007), esp. 321–23.

different from human assumptions regarding the meaning and purpose of power, authority, and kingship. This should be no great surprise, as Jesus's temptation by the devil indicates his rejection of the devil's gift of "all the kingdoms of the world and their glory" (4:8) and the trappings of the evil use of power advanced by earthly kingdoms. This offer from the devil stands as the counterpart or antithesis to the reference to the "kingdom of heaven" in Matthew 3:2 and 4:17. As Jesus proclaims the kingdom of heaven, so Matthew frequently depicts him as the King, the Messiah, and the Son of David (e.g., 1:1, 20; 2:2, 6; 9:27; 21:9, 15). And yet Matthew is frequently concerned with emphasizing the contrast between Jesus's wielding of power and authority as the agent of the kingdom of heaven and the wielding of power in earthly kingdoms. We will examine this theme as one aspect of Jesus's enactment of God's saving reign over his people.

The Shepherd-King and the Clash of the Kingdoms in Matthew 2

The Son of David enacts God's rule by saving his people from their sins and rightly teaching and interpreting the Torah; now we will see that the Davidic Messiah enacts God's rule as Israel's messianic shepherd who inaugurates a rule of mercy and compassion over his people. And this merciful rule is one that challenges and exposes as corrupt and counterfeit the earthly kings and leaders who wield their power in ways that harm God's people.

The contrast between two kings and their kingdoms is presented immediately in Matthew's infancy narrative, where the child Jesus, the one "born the King of the Jews" (ὁ τεχθεὶς βασιλεὺς τῶν Ἰουδαίων, 2:2a), provokes conflict for King Herod and "all of Jerusalem with him" (2:3).[76] The child Jesus receives royal homage from eastern wise men and rulers (ἤλθομεν προσκυνῆσαι αὐτῷ, 2:2; cf. 2:8, 11). The "star in the east," which guides the gentile wise men, resonates both with messianic promises of "a star which will come forth from Jacob, and a scepter which will arise from Israel" (Num 24:17), as well as with messianic hopes that the gentile nations and rulers would one day come bringing gifts to Israel's king (e.g., Ps 45:7-9; 72:15; Isa 60:1-6; Pss. Sol. 17).[77] The royal child is even ironically spoken of as the fulfillment of Scripture when King Herod seeks counsel from the chief priests and scribes as to the origins

---

76. See here the excellent study of David R. Bauer, "The Kingship of Jesus in the Matthean Infancy Narrative: A Literary Analysis," *CBQ* 57 (1995): 306-23.

77. See further Dale C. Allison Jr., "The Magi's Angel (Matt. 2:2, 9-10)," in *Studies in Matthew: Interpretation Past and Present* (Grand Rapids: Baker Academic, 2005), 17-41.

of the Messiah. They speak to Herod the words of Micah 5:1, 3 and 2 Samuel 5:2: "and you Bethlehem, land of Judah, are by no means the least among the rulers of Judah; for from you will come a ruler who will shepherd my people Israel" (Matt 2:6). This previews one of Jesus's central messianic titles and tasks, namely, the shepherd-king who will act as the merciful shepherd over God's flock.[78] The resonances of "will shepherd my people Israel" (ποιμανεῖ τὸν λαόν μου τὸν Ἰσραήλ, 2:6) with the angel's promise that Jesus will "save his people (τὸν λαὸν αὐτοῦ) from their sins" (1:21) draws further attention to Jesus's messianic task to redeem Israel.[79]

The Davidic Messiah's ministry to shepherd God's flock recalls significant prophetic promises which foretell a day when God will raise up a faithful king from the house of David who will accomplish justice, peace, and mercy for God's scattered and exploited flock: "I will establish over them one shepherd, my servant David, and he will shepherd them. He will tend them himself and will be their shepherd" (Ezek 34:23). God's raising up a Davidic shepherd, however, will result in judgment against the current shepherds, or faithless leaders of Israel, who have exploited God's sheep for their own benefit such that God's flock is scattered, oppressed, and prey for their enemies (Ezek 34:1-21). Micah further refers to the messianic king who will shepherd God's people "in the Lord's strength and in the majestic name of the Lord his God" (Mic 5:4). The king will lead God's people in peace and security and will protect God's flock from their enemies (4:9-13; 5:4-6; cf. Jer 23:1-6; Ezek 37:24; Zech 9:16; 10:2-3; Pss. Sol. 17:40).

The contrast between King Herod and Messiah Jesus in Matthew 2 contains "an explicit emphasis on the fact that Jesus as king stands in opposition to all other false kings and kingdoms."[80] Within Matthew 2, Herod plays the role of the tyrannical ruler or false shepherd who rules over God's people/flock for his own benefit. Three times Herod is referred to as "king" (2:1, 3, 9), though the reader knows that the child Jesus is the true Davidic king of God's people. King Herod engages in all of the stereotypical tyrannical means of wielding power. Described as "troubled" by one who might challenge his throne (2:3), he colludes with the religious aristocracy to determine the birth and origins of the Messiah (2:4), employs deception and trickery to protect his throne (2:7-8),

---

78. There are many good studies of Matthew's depiction of Jesus as Israel's messianic Shepherd. See, for example, Willitts, *Matthew's Messianic Shepherd-King*; Young S. Chae, *Jesus as the Eschatological Davidic Shepherd: Studies in the Old Testament, Second Temple Judaism, and in the Gospel of Matthew*, WUNT 2.216 (Tübingen: Mohr Siebeck, 2006).

79. Konradt, *Israel, Church, and the Gentiles*, 38.

80. Pennington, *Heaven and Earth*, 315.

and exhibits rage and grotesque violence against the vulnerable (2:16–21). Herod's collusion with the scribes and priests against the Messiah in 2:4–6 foreshadows the collusion between Rome and Israel's temple leaders. Matthew portrays King Herod as engaging in all the trappings of royal power and authority—yet, ironically—also as pathetic and despicable in that he is terrified of a child (2:3–4) and outfoxed by the magi (2:16). Later, he is described as dead (2:19–20). Matthew presents Jesus as the Davidic king, but as a king who will wield power differently from human rulers and authorities. The King of the Jews is described throughout the scene as a "child" (2:8, 9, 11, 13, 14, 20, 21). He must flee as a refugee to Egypt (2:13–15). And the prophecy of his origins from Micah 5 indicates that he will shepherd God's people with justice and peace (2:6). Jesus's kingship, then, is revealed in the paradox of powerlessness and vulnerability, a kingship that foreshadows the shepherd-king's consistent wielding of power for mercy rather than violent force.[81]

The Lost Flock of the House of Israel

Numerous OT and Second Temple Jewish texts portray Israel as God's flock of sheep (e.g., Isa 40:10–11; Jer 13:17; 23:1–6; Pss 74:1; 77:21; 78:52), thereby emphasizing Israel's dependence, for good or for bad, upon their shepherds. Matthew presents a portrait of "the people," that is Israel, as the exploited, scattered, hapless flock of God in need of salvation—in part, from their own leaders. Jesus refers to the object of his mission as Israel—the lost and scattered flock of God. In his sending of the seventy-two, Jesus commands his disciples to go only "to the lost flock of the house of Israel" (πρὸς τὰ πρόβατα τὰ ἀπολωλότα οἴκου Ἰσραήλ, 10:6). Again, in his conversation with the Syro-Phoenician woman, he declares: "I have only been sent for the lost flock of the house of Israel" (οὐκ ἀπεστάλην εἰ μὴ εἰς τὰ πρόβατα τὰ ἀπολωλότα οἴκου Ἰσραήλ, 15:24).[82] The language of "the lost sheep" echoes Ezekiel 34, which speaks a word of judgment against Israel's shepherds: "You have not strengthened the weak,

---

81. See especially Weaver, "Rewriting the Messianic Script," 125–36. Bauer, "The Kingship of Jesus," 323: "The contrast between Herod and Jesus points to the essential character of Jesus' kingship as legitimate, effective, humble (dependent upon God), righteous, and committed to the salvation of the people from their sins, even to the point of sacrificing the self. In the process, Matthew also describes the essential character of Herod's kingship, which represents God-opposing systems and persons who orient behavior to the goal of maintaining their own power, even to the point of destroying others."

82. Willitts, *Matthew's Messianic Shepherd-King*, 203–20, argues that the lost sheep refers to northern Israel.

healed the sick, bandaged the injured, brought back the strays, or sought the lost. Instead, you have ruled them with violence and cruelty." Likewise, Jesus's description of Israel as the lost flock echoes Jeremiah 50:6–7: "My people have been lost sheep; their shepherds have led them astray, leading them away on the mountains; they have wandered from mountain to hill having forgotten their fold. All who have found them have devoured them, and their enemies have said, 'We are not guilty, for they have sinned against the Lord, the true pasture, the hope of their ancestors, the Lord.'"[83]

Matthew's portrait of those in positions of power and leadership over the people of Israel is unrelentingly negative, and this theme further contributes to the opposition between the kingdom of heaven and Jesus as the singular King of Israel versus every other earthly kingdom and ruler. That is to say, Matthew's depiction of Jesus as the shepherd-king has as its counterpart a strong critique of Israel's current rulers.[84] Matthew's genealogy, as we have seen, depicts Israel as a "sinful people" in need of salvation (1:21), in large part as a result of Israel's kings, whose wickedness, idolatry, and failure to obey the law of Moses are responsible for their current state of exile (1:7–12). We have already seen Herod the Great characterized as an angry tyrant who uses deception and violence to accomplish his purposes (2:1–16). Herod Antipas, the "tetrarch" (14:1), is another ruler who is marked by excessive fear and superstition (14:2), sexual improprieties (14:3–4, 6), and foolishness (14:7), culminating in his violent and grotesque execution of the righteous prophet John the Baptist (14:4–5, 10–11). Pilate, the Roman "governor" (27:2, 11, 14, 15, 21), knows that Jesus has been delivered to death because of envy (27:18), hears from his wife that Jesus is a "righteous man" (27:19), makes a mockery of the Jewish leaders in washing his hands of responsibility for the fate of Jesus (27:24), and, nevertheless, hands Jesus over to the Roman soldiers to be crucified (27:27–31).[85] The scribes and the Pharisees, likewise, do not rule over the people with justice and integrity; instead, Jesus criticizes them for interpreting the Torah in such a way that it places impossible demands upon the people (23:3–4). Their ultimate commitments and interpretation of the Torah demonstrate that they love status and honor (23:5–8). They evade God's purpose and divine will for human life by insisting upon their traditions and human commandments (23:16–24; cf.

---

83. For this reference I am dependent upon Hays, *Echoes of Scripture in the Gospels*, 128.
84. Konradt, *Israel, Church, and the Gentiles*, 36.
85. On Pilate as a figure of power and Matthew's ironic critique of Pilate and Roman power, see Warren Carter, "Pilate and Jesus: Roman Justice All Washed Up (Matt 27:11–26)," in *Matthew and Empire: Initial Explorations* (Harrisburg, PA: Trinity Press International, 2001), 145–68.

15:1–9). The scribes and priests are often portrayed as wanting to destroy and kill Jesus (12:14; 16:21; 17:23; 21:38–39; 27:20). The temple has become a "den of thieves," given their violent intentions for Jesus (21:13). The priests' use of wealth is for the corrupt purpose of destroying Jesus, and they are portrayed as engaging in a stealthy conspiracy (26:4–14; 27:7–10; 28:11–15).[86]

The Merciful and Compassionate Shepherd-King

In contrast to the earthly kingdoms, Roman rulers, and Jewish scribes, priests, and Pharisees, Matthew portrays Jesus as the merciful shepherd-king who establishes and enacts the rule of his heavenly Father over his people. We have already seen that Jesus's interpretation of the Torah takes as its starting point the call for mercy, love, and justice as an imitation of the heavenly Father (e.g., 5:43–48; 11:25–12:14; 23:23). In addition to his call for mercy in his reading of the Torah, one of the primary ways in which Jesus enacts his rule as the merciful messianic shepherd is through his compassionate healings of those on the margins of society. Scholars have long noted that Matthew positions many of Jesus's healings within the context of his merciful activities as the Son of David. "The deeds of the Messiah" (τα ἔργα τοῦ Χριστοῦ, 11:2) consist of his healings of the oppressed: "The blind receive their sight, the lame walk, the lepers are cleansed, the deaf hear, the dead are raised, and the poor hear the good news" (11:5). For example, in 9:27–31 Jesus touches and heals two blind men who cry out: "Have mercy upon us, Son of David!" (ἐλέησον ἡμᾶς, υἱὸς Δαυίδ, 9:27). Jesus's mercy, exemplified primarily in healings and inclusion of outsiders in chapters 8–9, is the context not only for the blind men's invocation of Jesus as the Son of David but also Matthew's description of Jesus who "upon seeing the crowds, had compassion for them because they were harassed and distressed like sheep without a shepherd" (9:36).[87] Matthew is echoing here Numbers 27:17 and Moses's leadership of Israel during the wilderness generation, but the quotation is situated within Matthew's emphasis on Jesus as the messianic Davidic shepherd of Israel (cf. 10:6; 15:24). The rulers of Israel, the current shepherds, have failed to attend to the needs of the flock and have thereby abdicated their role as Israel's leaders. Jesus's compassion on the "harassed and distressed" flock of God is the context for his sending out the twelve disciples

86. See further Dorothy Jean Weaver, "'What Is That to Us? See to It Yourself': Making Atonement and the Matthean Portrait of the Jewish Chief Priests," in *The Irony of Power*, 66–84.
87. Kirk, *A Man Attested by God*, 466–67.

48

to "the lost sheep of the house of Israel" (10:6a) to cast out demons, heal the sick, and proclaim the kingdom of heaven (10:1–8). The disciples are called to continue the compassionate ministry of Jesus the messianic shepherd.[88]

Immediately preceding Jesus's healing of a demon-possessed man, Matthew invokes a lengthy quotation from Isaiah 42:1–4 as coming to fulfillment in Jesus's healings (12:15–21): "Behold my servant whom I have chosen, my beloved upon whom my soul is well-pleased; I will put my spirit upon him and he will proclaim judgment to the nations; he will not argue or cry out, and no one will hear his voice in the streets. He will not break a bruised reed and he will not put out a smoldering wick until he has brought justice to victory. And the nations will hope in his name" (12:18–21). The quotation serves to further portray Jesus as the messianic, spirit-anointed servant who has been elected by the Father to carry out his righteousness (cf. Matt 3:15–17). The quotation serves a dual function in that it portrays Jesus's healings as one means of establishing justice and righteousness—a central characteristic of the Messiah and messianic age—over God's people.[89] But it also portends a future time in which the bruised reed will be broken.[90] Within the context of Matthew, this can only recall Jesus's reference to the kingdom of Herod Antipas, described as a "reed swaying in the wind" and a man dressed in "soft clothes" living "in royal palaces" (11:7–9). Jesus's contrast between John the Baptist and Herod Antipas in 11:1–15 portends 14:1–12, where Herod kills John the Baptist. But the reader knows that Herod, this "bruised reed" and "smoldering wick," will be brought to nothing, and Jesus, the Spirit-empowered agent of justice, is the one called "to replace the ineffective rule of earthly kings with God's just reign."[91] This makes good sense of the literary placement of Matthew's summary statement in 14:14 ("he saw a large crowd and had compassion on them

---

88. On the importance of compassion in Jesus's task as the messianic Shepherd, see Wayne Baxter, *Israel's Only Shepherd: Matthew's Shepherd Motif and His Social Setting*, LNTS 457 (London: T&T Clark, 2012), 137–42.

89. On the contribution of Isa 42 in Matthew's depiction of Jesus as an ideal king who establishes God's compassionate justice for the oppressed, see Richard Beaton, *Isaiah's Christ in Matthew's Gospel*, SNTSMS 123 (Cambridge: Cambridge University Press, 2002), 164–72; also Beaton, "Messiah and Justice: A Key to Matthew's Use of Isaiah 42.1–4," *JSNT* 75 (1999): 5–23.

90. Note the temporal phrase ἕως ἂν in 11:20.

91. See here the entire illuminating study of Alicia D. Myers, "Isaiah 42 and the Characterization of Jesus in Matthew 12:17–21," in *The Synoptic Gospels*, vol. 1 of *'What Does the Scripture Say'? Studies in the Function of Scripture in Early Judaism and Christianity*, ed. Craig A. Evans and H. Daniel Zacharias (London: T&T Clark, 2012), 70–89, quotation here is from 85.

and healed the sick"), which continues the contrast between Jesus's royal rule of mercy and compassion and the earthly kingdom of Herod. As we have seen, the ineffectiveness of Herod Antipas's actions is seen in the ironic way in which his power cannot combat his grief and fear. Jesus alone is God's servant and messianic Son who obeys the Father, is anointed by the Spirit to bring liberation and healing to the oppressed, and even has "compassion upon the crowd," providing food for the hungry (e.g., 15:32; also 14:15–21).

This contrast between kingdoms is further expanded upon in Jesus's ensuing interpretation of his healings and exorcisms, where he asks: "If I drive out demons by the Spirit of God, then the kingdom of God has come upon you" (12:28). Jesus's mercy and compassion on the distressed and needy continues to be seen in his healing of the man possessed by a demon, who is unable to see or speak (12:22). The healing elicits the question from the crowds: "Could this be the Son of David?" (12:23). Despite his call to go only to the lost sheep of Israel (15:24), Jesus finally responds by healing the gentile woman who cried: "Have mercy on me, Lord, Son of David!" (15:22). In Matthew 20:29–34, two blind men twice cry out: "Lord, have mercy on us, Son of David" (20:30–31). Jesus, filled with compassion, touches their eyes and heals them (20:34). As Jesus makes his entrance into Jerusalem and the temple, the crowd confesses that he is "the Son of David" (21:9). Jesus heals the blind and the lame in the temple (21:14), but Matthew notes that the chief priests and scribes were furious when they saw the miracles and heard children shouting, "Hosanna to the Son of David" (21:15). In response to the anger of the priests and scribes, Jesus quotes Psalm 8:3, "Out of the mouths of babies and infants you have prepared praise for yourself" (Matt 21:16), indicating that the children rightly understand Jesus's identity when they call him the Son of David. Matthew's connection of Jesus with the Son of David may find its religious-historical precedent in the Jewish traditions which portrayed both David and Solomon, David's son, as healers and exorcists (e.g., Josephus, *Jewish Antiquities* 6.166–68; 8.45–47; T. Sol. 1.5–7; Wis 7:17–21; cf. 1 Sam 16:14–23).[92] Regardless of the exact tradition, Matthew is

---

92. Konradt, *Israel, Church, and the Gentiles*, 44, commenting on Jesus as the Davidic Shepherd of Ezek 34: "This presentation of Jesus as the healing Son of David is well-suited to the caretaking aspect of the shepherd imagery: a good shepherd is concerned about the well-being of his flock." There are many excellent studies examining Matthew's portrait of Jesus as Son of David and healer. For example, see Anthony Le Donne, *The Historiographical Jesus: Memory, Typology, and the Son of David* (Waco, TX: Baylor University Press, 2009), 137–183; Dennis C. Duling, "The Therapeutic Son of David: An Element in Matthew's Christological Apologetic," *NTS* 24 (1977–78): 392–410; Dennis C. Duling, "The Eleazar Miracle and Solomon's Magical Wisdom in Flavius Josephus's *Antiquitates Judaicae* 8.42–49," *HTR*

clear that Jesus's identity as the Davidic messianic shepherd is embodied in the merciful and compassionate care he provides—signified powerfully in healings and exorcisms—for the distressed and harassed lost sheep of Israel.

Given that Jesus enacts his Davidic rule through mercy and compassion, and has called his followers to forgo revenge in imitation of their heavenly Father who is kind to the righteous and unrighteous alike (e.g., 5:38–48), we should note here that Matthew portrays Jesus as embodying his Davidic messianic task even in his sufferings from the hands of his enemies.[93] Jesus has, after all, drawn the deepest connection between his messianic kingship and his sufferings (e.g., 16:12; 17:21; 20:18–19). Immediately after Jesus's final meal with his disciples, where he interprets his impending death as a payment for sins (26:26–29), at the Mount of Olives Jesus brings the shepherd motif to a conclusion: "'I will strike the shepherd and the sheep of the flock will be scattered.' And after I have been raised I will go before you into Galilee" (Matt 26:31b–32). Jesus's works of healing have embodied his mercy and compassion for the sheep, but Matthew portrays the climactic act of the messianic shepherd's mercy as coming in Jesus's death at the hands of the wicked shepherds.[94] Drawing upon Zechariah 13:7 (and possibly Ezek 34:31), Jesus speaks of himself as the Davidic shepherd who is struck down in judgment with the result that the flock (i.e., the disciples) is scattered; but, ironically, it is through this very act of the shepherd's death that the flock is forgiven, restored, and purified. Jesus's embodiment of his messianic task is seen, finally, in his rejection of violence and force in his arrest and ensuing death. Recently, Nathan Johnson has demonstrated that Matthew's account of Jesus's prayer in Gethsemane and his arrest (Matt 26:36–56) have been typologically modeled on David's sufferings and trials during Absalom's revolt (2 Sam 13–18).[95] For example, after Absalom rebels, King David and his followers leave Jerusalem and go to the Mount of Olives just as Jesus, the Davidic Messiah, leaves Jerusalem and goes to the same Mount (2 Sam 15:15–30; Matt 26:30–31). David and his followers are described as mourning and weeping, just as Jesus, accompanied by his disciples, is in emotional distress and praying to God with the lament Psalms

---

78 (1985): 1–25; Lidija Novakovic, *Messiah, the Healer of the Sick: A Study of Jesus as the Son of David in the Gospel of Matthew*, WUNT 2.170 (Tübingen: Mohr Siebeck, 2003).

93. Jesus's messianic task is quite obviously not a simple recapitulation of the life and character of David who was prevented from building a temple for God since he was "a man of war" (1 Chr 28:3).

94. See further Baxter, *Israel's Only Shepherd*, 154–55.

95. Nathan C. Johnson, "The Passion according to David: Matthew's Arrest Narrative, the Absalom Revolt, and Militant Messianism," *CBQ* 80 (2018): 247–72.

of David (2 Sam 15:23, 30; Matt 26:36–44; cf. Ps 41:6, 12; 42:5 LXX). As David is betrayed by Ahithophel, who leads a group of the king's enemies against David during the night while he is tired (2 Sam 17:1–4), so does Jesus's "friend" Judas betray him while he is in distress during the night (Matt 26:47–50; cf. Ps 55:12–21). Both Ahithophel and Judas die by hanging (2 Sam 17:23; Matt 27:5). These are just a few of the many parallels one can adduce, but the function of Matthew's portrait of Jesus as typologically undergoing David's sufferings is precisely to depict Jesus's kingship as embodied in the rejection of violence and force, a refusal to seek retribution against his enemies, and a faithful reliance upon God for his vindication.[96] And this is, as we have seen, precisely why Matthew's flurry of references to Jesus as Messiah, Son of God, and King of Israel are, in a deeply ironic manner, found in the mouths of Jesus's enemies as the Son of David is on the cross (27:36–44).

The Messiah's People Share in His Messianic Activities

Matthew's messianic Christology is one of the principal foundations for his advocacy of the particular manner of life he expects from followers of Jesus. In other words, for Matthew, discipleship is a participation in the kingdom of heaven as embodied in the Son of David. Let me exemplify how this is so, briefly, with three examples—all of which follow from Jesus's messianic identity as the Son of David who saves his people.

Disciples Share in Cross-Bearing

In Peter's climactic confession of Jesus's identity as "the Messiah, the Son of the Living God" (16:16), Jesus declares that Peter, and the rest of the messianic community, will only grasp the meaning of this confession in light of Jesus's impending rejection, suffering, and death in Jerusalem, and his resurrection from the dead (16:21). In response to Peter's shock and rejection of this path for the Messiah, Jesus declares that those who would wish to be his disciples must also "take up their cross and follow me" (16:24). Just as the Messiah receives resurrection after taking up his cross, so also his disciples will only save and find their lives by taking up the Messiah's cross (16:25–26).[97] At the glorious return

96. See the conclusion of Johnson, "The Passion according to David," 271–72.
97. The following discussion is indebted to the important work of Eubank, *Wages of Cross-Bearing*, 134–48.

of the Messiah, Jesus will "pay back each one according to their deeds" (16:27; cf. 6:19–21). Eschatological life is contingent, then, upon cross-bearing.

In response to the rich young man who refuses to engage in cross-bearing and self-denial by giving up his possessions for the poor (19:16–22) and Jesus's teaching on the difficulty of salvation for the rich (19:23–26), Peter declares that he and the disciples have "left behind everything and followed you. What will there be for us?" (19:27). Peter's language echoes Jesus's promise of life for those who take up their crosses (16:24–27). Here again, Jesus promises that Peter and the disciples will share in Jesus's messianic rule: "Truly, I tell you in the renewal of all things, when the Son of Man sits on his glorious throne, so also you who have followed me will sit on twelve thrones and will judge the twelve tribes of Israel" (19:28). Jesus extends the promise of sharing in his messianic rule to all of his followers by then declaring that everyone who has left behind houses, family, land, and business pursuits "for the sake of my name will receive a hundred times more and will inherit life eternal" (19:29).

Finally, in Matthew 20:20–27, when the mother of the sons of Zebedee asks Jesus for her sons to "sit—one on your right and one on your left—in your kingdom" (20:21b), it is clear she is asking that they be privileged participants in Jesus's messianic kingdom. The irony of her request, obvious to the reader, is that Jesus's kingdom rule will come by means of the cross, where there are two criminals on his right and his left (cf. 26:39). Thus, drinking the cup with Jesus functions as a metaphor for sharing in Jesus's death (20:22–23), and their sitting on thrones in the messianic kingdom will only come by taking up their crosses in imitation, not of the gentile rulers and kings of the earth (20:25), but by taking the posture of a servant and slave in imitation of the Son of Man (20:26–27). These three texts indicate that there is indeed a promise of life, resurrection, and enthronement for disciples but that sharing in the rule of the Messiah is only granted to those who take up their crosses, engage in renunciation of their status, and follow the pattern of the Messiah who gave his life for his disciples on the cross.

Disciples Share in the Messianic Shepherd's Ministry of Mercy and Forgiveness

We have seen already that Jesus's messianic shepherding ministry of extending mercy to the "distressed and harassed" flock of God (9:36) is extended to his disciples, who share in the shepherd's ministry to "the lost sheep of the house of Israel" (10:6). The disciples do this by means of healings, exorcisms, and the proclamation of the kingdom of heaven (10:1, 7–8). One of the primary ways the messianic community continues to embody Jesus's shepherding ministry is through forgiveness, reconciliation, and extending mercy to the needy. Disciples pray to the Father: "Forgive us from our debts, even as we forgive those who have debts to us" (6:12). We have seen that Jesus pays the debt of Israel's sin by giving his own life as a ransom (1:21; 20:28; 26:28). Those who have had their debts paid are obligated, according to the Messiah, to engage in the cancellation and forgiveness of the debts of others. This makes sense of the otherwise challenging statement: "If you forgive people their trespasses, so will your heavenly Father forgive you too; and if you do not forgive people, then neither will your Father forgive you of your trespasses" (6:14). God's mercy, forgiveness, and debt-cancellation for those who were in captivity and bondage to sin must have as its logical outcome disciples who continue to forgive and extend mercy to their debtors. We have seen this theme already in the parable of the unmerciful slave in 18:21–35, which functions as an interpretative commentary on Matthew 6:12, 14–15. In response to Peter's question regarding the extent of forgiveness, Jesus's parable positions disciples as those who have experienced the incredible mercy and compassion of the one who has paid their incredible debt, and who are thereby obligated to continue the practice of mercy and debt-cancellation for their neighbors (18:33–35). Matthew's redactional note in the conclusion of Jesus's healing and forgiveness of the paralytic ("they gave glory to God who had given such authority to people," 9:8b) may hint at Matthew's conception of the messianic community as a people who forgive and cancel each other's debts and transgressions (cf. 18:18–19).

Disciples continue Jesus's ministry as the messianic shepherd when they embody the humility or downward mobility of children (18:1–4), when they give no offense (18:6–7), and when they do not look down upon any of God's "little ones" (18:10). Jesus calls his disciples to restore any of God's "lost sheep" who have gone astray (18:12–13) and reconcile with and forgive any brothers or sisters who have sinned (18:15–20). In Jesus's parable of the sheep and the goats (Matt 25:31–46), the glorious and enthroned Son of Man declares as the eschatological judge that his disciples will be publicly vindicated as his sheep at the final judgment based on whether they have extended mercy, hospitality, food, drink, and clothes for "the least of these brothers and sisters of mine" (25:40, 45). Jesus's promises in the Beatitudes are fulfilled in the scene envisioned by this parable, as those who pursue peace, mercy, righteousness, poverty of spirit, meekness, and so forth in the name of Jesus (5:3–12) receive their eschatological inheritance. The one who has embodied mercy as the compassionate shepherd will, then, judge and evaluate people upon whether they, too, have demonstrated mercy and compassion in their care for fellow disciples (also 10:40–42).

Disciples Share in the Risen Jesus's Authority to Make Disciples of All the Nations

Matthew's final scene of the risen and enthroned Jesus's commission to his disciples on the mountain is explicit in its call to the church to continue Jesus's task of making disciples, but now with the authority and presence of the enthroned Messiah *and* for all the nations of the earth (28:16–20). On the mountain, Jesus draws upon the language of Daniel 7:13–14 to declare that "all authority on heaven and earth has been given to me" (28:18b). Perhaps echoing Psalm 2:8 and the promise of the messianic king receiving the nations as his inheritance, Matthew portrays Jesus as the resurrected and enthroned Messiah who has entered into his worldwide dominion—something that has been gifted to him from the Father (rather than Satan's promise of authority in 4:8–10).[98] Jesus's resurrection from the dead is the necessary messianic event whereby he enters into God's power and authority ("on heaven and earth") and acts as the eschatological royal judge over all the nations (e.g., 25:31–46).[99] Thus, the risen Jesus tasks his disciples to "go and make disciples of all the nations" (28:19a). While Jesus's ministry centered upon the "lost sheep of the house of Israel" (10:6; 15:24; cf. 9:35–36; 26:31), Matthew has repeatedly foreshadowed that the gentile nations will be brought to worship the Messiah and will "place their hope in his name" (12:21; cf. 2:1–12; 4:15–16; 8:5–13; 15:20–28).[100] "The hints that the blessings of Abraham would overflow from the lost sheep of the house of Israel to all the gentile nations will be fulfilled as the disciples extend the story of Jesus's ministry, superintended by his continuing presence."[101] Their task of making disciples of the nations and teaching everything Jesus commanded them (διδάσκοντες αὐτοὺς τηρεῖν πάντα ὅσα ἐνετειλάμην ὑμῖν, 28:20a) is an explicit call to continue Jesus's mission by means of passing on his commandments, not least of which is Jesus's merciful interpretation of the commandments of the Torah (e.g., 5:17–48; 11:25–12:14; 23:23). And just as Jesus promised that Peter, as the representative of the Messiah, would be the "rock"

98. On the echo of Ps 2:7–8, see Trent Rogers, "The Great Commission as the Climax of Matthew's Mountain Scenes," *BBR* 22 (2012): 394–95; also, Kirk, *A Man Attested by God*, 381.

99. Kirk, *A Man Attested by God*, 385.

100. See Hays, *Echoes of Scripture in the Gospels*, 175–185; Konradt, *Israel, Church, and the Gentiles*, 265–81.

101. Kirk, *A Man Attested by God*, 382.

upon which he would build (οἰκοδομήσω) his church (thereby foreshadowing that the messianic community would be the new temple [16:16–19] built upon Christ the rejected and vindicated cornerstone [21:42; cf. Ps 118:22]), so Jesus promises his risen presence as Emmanuel to be with the disciples until the end of the age to empower them for their mission (28:20b; cf. 1:23; 18:20).[102] Jesus's promise to give Peter the "keys of the kingdom of heaven" likely echoes Isaiah 22:21–22 ("the key of the house of David"), thereby positioning the disciples as priests of the Messiah's eschatological temple who, through their teaching, judging (cf. Matt 19:28), and dispensing of Jesus's forgiveness (i.e., "binding" and "loosing"), continue the Messiah's ministry. This authority is explicitly grounded in the Messiah's ongoing presence and authority.[103] So close, in fact, is the relationship between the enthroned Messiah's presence and his people that he has promised to vindicate or condemn people based upon the hospitality and mercy they extend to Jesus's brothers and sisters (25:31–46; cf. 10:40–42).[104]

CONCLUSION

The Gospel of Matthew portrays Jesus as the messianic Son of David and Son of God who is Israel's true and final king. His messianic role is executed in his delivering Israel from their sins, authoritatively teaching and obeying God's Torah, providing mercy and compassion through his acts, and enabling his disciples to share in his messianic ministry and activities.

---

102. Note God's promises to the Son of David (i.e., the Son of God) in 2 Sam 7:12–13 and 1 Chr 17:7–10 (also Zech 4:7–9) that he would build a house for God's name. See further Barber, "Jesus as the Davidic Temple Builder," 940–42. On the risen Jesus's ongoing powerful presence with his people, see Kirk, *A Man Attested by God*, 385.

103. Again, Barber, "Jesus as the Davidic Temple Builder," 947–51.

104. On the relationship between Matt 25:31–46 and 28:18–20 as it pertains to the risen Jesus's continuing presence to empower mission, see Beaton, *Isaiah's Christ*, 186–89.

CHAPTER 2

The Powerful, Humiliated Son of God and the Kingdom of God

The Gospel of Mark

The incipit of Mark's Gospel designates the writing as a messianic text given that Jesus is right away referred to as Χριστός: "The beginning of the gospel of Jesus, the Messiah" (1:1).[1] The proclamation of the "gospel" (εὐαγγέλιον) draws upon Isaiah's prophetic anticipations of the establishment of God's saving rule over his people (Isa 40:1-11; 52:7-10; 61:1-4).[2] The "gospel" (1:1, 14) and "the kingdom of God" are inaugurated by the one Mark refers to as "Messiah," and the messianic connotations of the opening are increased if one regards υἱοῦ θεοῦ as original.[3] In fact, some have argued that "Messiah" and messianism might be the central title and category within which to understand Mark's story.[4] At a critical juncture in the Gospel, Peter designates Jesus as "the Messiah" (8:29); Jesus himself finally responds to the high priest's question, "Are you the Messiah, the Son of the Blessed One" with the affirmation "I am" (14:61-62); and Jesus quotes the royal psalms of David during his sufferings and crucifixion while—ironically—mocked as "the Messiah the King of Israel" (15:32). At critical junctures Jesus is referred to as the messianic Son of God

---

1. On the Isaianic overtones of *gospel* in Mark and the establishment of God's triumphant, apocalyptic rule over his people, see Suzanne Watts Henderson, *Christology and Discipleship in the Gospel of Mark*, SNTSMS 135 (Cambridge: Cambridge University Press, 2006), 40-43.

2. Rikki E. Watts, *Isaiah's New Exodus in Mark* (Grand Rapids: Baker, 1997), 96-102.

3. On this see, Tommy Wasserman, "The 'Son of God' Was in the Beginning (Mark 1:1)," *JTS* 62 (2011): 20-50.

4. See, for example, Donald Juel, "The Origin of Mark's Christology," in *The Messiah: Developments in Earliest Judaism and Christianity; The First Princeton Symposium on Judaism and Christian Origins*, ed. James H. Charlesworth et al. (Minneapolis: Fortress, 1992), 450-51.

(Mark 1:10–11; 9:7; 15:39) and positions himself as God's beloved Son (12:6; 14:36). Thus, there are good reasons for insisting upon understanding Χριστός as a royal honorific and emphasizing the importance of Jesus's messiahship as a critical factor in making sense of Mark's Gospel (see further 12:35; 13:21).[5]

Is Mark's Gospel a Messianic Text?

And yet, Mark's designation of Jesus as Messiah has proved difficult and coun- terintuitive for many readers of the Gospel. Jesus often seems to redirect attention away from speculation upon his messianic identity by referring to himself as the Son of Man (e.g., 8:29–33); his earthly career and vocation have not seemed to conform to messianic, royal traditions such as what we find in Psalms of Solomon 17–18; those who confess Jesus as God's Son and/or the Holy One are frequently silenced by Jesus (e.g., 1:24–25; 3:11–12; 5:7–9; 8:27–31; 9:7–9);[6] and Jesus seems reticent at best to apply to himself the designation of "Son of David" in his controversy with his opponents in the temple (Mark 12:35–37).[7]

Central to the Gospel of Mark is the paradox or tension between Mark's understanding of the meaning of Jesus's royal, messianic identity and contem- porary or traditional messianic reflection.[8] Fundamental to Jesus's royal task is his vocation of sacrificial service culminating in his humiliating crucifixion on a Roman cross. Jesus is not a King in spite of but because of his sacrificial leadership, faithful sufferings, and crucifixion. Thus, any understanding of king, messiah, kingdom, power, and authority is reworked by Mark's Gospel around "the history of Jesus of Nazareth, principally in the events that brought his career to an end and offered a whole new beginning. [Mark's] Christology is firmly anchored there, in the cross of the one who died as 'the king of the

---

5. See further Adela Yarbro Collins and John J. Collins, *King and Messiah as Son of God: Divine, Human, and Angelic Messianic Figures in Biblical and Related Literature* (Grand Rapids: Eerdmans, 2008), 162–63.

6. On the so-called Markan messianic secret and the speculation that it developed, in part, out of Jesus's nonroyal earthly life, see William Wrede, *The Messianic Secret*, trans. J. C. C. Grieg (Cambridge: James Clarke, 1971).

7. On Jesus's frequent deflection of honor and attention away from himself, see Elizabeth Struthers Malbon, *Mark's Jesus: Characterization as Narrative Christology* (Waco, TX: Baylor University Press, 2009), 129–194.

8. Juel, "The Origin of Mark's Christology," 457–58.

Jews.'"[9] Readers of Mark must not stop by simply noting that Jesus is the royal messianic Son of God; they must further ask, In what way and how is Jesus God's Messiah? And what is the nature of the royal kingdom he announces and enacts?[10] In what follows, I will take an extended look at: (1) Jesus's messianic mission to inaugurate the kingdom of God; (2) Mark's contrast between Jesus's kingship versus other royal pretenders; (3) the revelation of Jesus's messianic kingship through his sufferings and death; and (4) how Mark conceptualizes discipleship as sharing in Christ's rule.

THE TRIUMPHANT, POWERFUL SON OF GOD

In Mark 1:9–15 Jesus is designated as God's messianic king who, by means of his endowment by the Spirit of God, will enact God's kingdom by executing judgment upon the evil and demonic rulers of the realm of Satan. Jesus's reception of the Holy Spirit and God's designation of him as his beloved Son mark Jesus out as God's royal, messianic king responsible for inaugurating God's kingdom.

The Beloved Son of God and the Kingdom of God

Jesus first appears on the scene during his baptism by John the Baptist: "when he came up out from the waters he saw the heavens split open and the Spirit as a dove descending upon him; and a voice came from the heavens: 'You are my beloved Son, I am well pleased in you'" (Mark 1:10–11). Mark narrates three divine events which occur at Jesus's baptism: (1) the opened heavens; (2) the descent of the Spirit upon Messiah Jesus; and (3) the divine voice designating Jesus as God's beloved Son. Mark's narration casts this scene as something of a private vision, discernable only to Jesus himself and to those reading Mark's Gospel. And the scene conforms to Mark's original designation of Jesus in his opening as "Messiah" (1:1), thereby confirming to the reader that this is

9. Juel, "The Origin of Mark's Christology," 459.

10. This is stated well by Nicholas Perrin, *The Kingdom of God: A Biblical Theology* (Grand Rapids: Zondervan, 2019), 100: "Yet Mark is not just interested in the fact of Jesus's kingship but also in—the much more involved question of—*what kind* of king Jesus might be. In other words, for Mark it is not merely a question of identity (Is Jesus the king or not?), but also a question of modality (If he is, what kind of king is he?) and functionality (If he is, what will he do?)." See also Bernardo Cho, *Royal Messianism and the Jerusalem Priesthood in the Gospel of Mark*, LNTS 607 (London: T&T Clark, 2019), 78–105.

a messianic, royal anointing. As was the case with Israel's kings, so Messiah Jesus is anointed and empowered for his ministry by means of the Spirit of God (1 Sam 16:13–26; Isa 11:1–5). John's reference to the coming one as "the stronger one" (ὁ ἰσχυρότερος, 1:7) may, in fact, allude to Isaiah's promise of "a spirit of strength" (ἰσχύς, Isa 11:2) empowering the Davidic king. Mark will again have the Father enter into the narrative to designate Jesus as his "beloved Son" at the transfiguration (9:7), and Jesus will refer to God as "Abba Father" (14:36) during his prayers in the midst of suffering in Gethsemane.[11] Given that Jesus's prayer draws upon David's words of lament in Psalm 41:6, 12, and 42:5 ("my soul is grieved to the point of death," Mark 14:34), Jesus's prayer in the garden makes good sense within the context of the Psalter's depiction of Yahweh as the Father to the Davidic king (e.g., "He will cry to me, 'You are my Father!'" Ps 89:26).[12] Here, Mark is leading the reader to see that divine sonship, the royal anointing of Jesus as the Son of God, will be revealed in his suffering, sacrificial death on the Roman cross.

Most decisive, however, for seeing Jesus's baptism as his messianic commission and anointing is the fact that the voice from heaven in 1:11 echoes the words of Isaiah 42:1 and Psalm 2:7—"you are my son." Psalm 2 represents something of an expansion and development of 2 Samuel 7:12–14, where God promises David a royal son whose kingdom will be established forever by God. God further promises: "I will be a Father to him, and he will be a son to me" (2 Sam 7:12). Psalm 2 can be divided into three parts. In verses 1–3, the kings, people, and rulers of the earth rebel against God and God's anointed one. In vv. 4–9, God responds against his enemies by installing his son as king who will rule from Zion. Significant for our purposes are verses 6–7, where God declares to the nations that he has enthroned his son in Zion, and the king responds: "He said to me, 'You are my son. Today I have begotten you'" (Ps 2:7). And finally, in verses 10–12, the rulers and kings are exhorted to recognize the reign of God and his anointed son and cease their opposition to his kingdom. Within the Psalter, the royal king, the son of God, is gifted and commissioned as the earthly representative of God's rule. He reigns underneath and in service to God, the true King, and it is his task to establish or manifest the kingdom of God on earth.[13] The unity of purpose and mission between God and the desig-

11. See Robert D. Rowe, *God's Kingdom and God's Son: The Background to Mark's Christology from Concepts of Kingship in the Psalms* (Leiden: Brill, 2002), 257–58.

12. For much more detail on this point, see Stephen P. Ahearne-Kroll, *The Psalms of Lament in Mark's Passion: Jesus' Davidic Suffering*, SNTSMS 142 (Cambridge: Cambridge University Press, 2007), 179–91.

13. See, for example, Rowe, *God's Kingdom*, 242–43.

nated king are central to the royal ideology of the Psalter, such that James Mays notes that when "the king was named 'son of God,' the title was a confession of faith that the king was the representative and agent of the deity in such unity and coherence that only the term 'son' could display the correspondence and claims between the two."[14] Jesus is the royal Son of God, then, who is gifted by God with a share in his power, rule, and kingdom. If Mark portrays Jesus as the messianic king of the Psalter who is elected by God and tasked with establishing God's kingdom, then it is not surprising in the least that Mark would portray Jesus as one who deflects honor and attention away from himself to God and whose sole purpose it is to enact *God's* reign on earth.

Joel Marcus has shown that the reception of Psalm 2 in Second Temple Jewish writings is united in drawing upon the psalm to depict the way in which "this joint kingship of God and his Messiah is opposed by an unholy alliance of the kings of the earth with the demonic ruler or rulers from whom they derive their power."[15] Thus, it is no surprise that after Jesus's messianic commission and anointing by the Spirit, he triumphs over Satan's attacks and temptations in the wilderness (1:12–13). Just as God's messianic Son receives the opposition and attacks of the rebellious rulers and kings of the earth but is enthroned to a position of powerful rule over them in Psalm 2, so here God's Son withstands the opposition of the realm of the demonic. Mark's note that "he was with the wild beasts and the angels were serving him" may allude to Isaiah 11:1–9, which foretells God's coming Davidic ruler (11:1) who will be marked by God's Spirit (11:2), will enact justice and righteousness for God's people (11:3–5), and will initiate a period of peaceful rule between God's people and the wild animals (11:6–9).[16] While Mark does not narrate the details of Jesus's battle against Satan in the wilderness, he clearly suggests that Jesus was successful, as he declares that Jesus immediately makes his public appearance in Galilee proclaiming "the gospel of God" (1:14) and that "the time has been filled up and the kingdom of God (ἡ βασιλεία τοῦ θεοῦ) has come near" (1:15).[17] Jesus—as God's faithful,

14. James L. Mays, *The Lord Reigns: A Theological Handbook to the Psalms* (Louisville: Westminster John Knox, 1994), 112.

15. Marcus examines 4QFlor 1:18–2:3; Pss. Sol. 17:21–46; Acts 4:25–26; Rev 11 and 17–19. See Joel Marcus, *The Way of the Lord: Christological Exegesis of the Old Testament in the Gospel of Mark* (Louisville: Westminster John Knox, 1992), 66. See further, Sam Janse, *"You are my Son": The Reception History of Psalm 2 in Early Judaism and the Early Church* (Leuven: Peeters, 2009).

16. See Joel Marcus, *Mark 1–8*, AYB 27 (New York: Doubleday, 2000), 169–70.

17. On the centrality of the kingdom of God in the Synoptic Gospels, see George Eldon Ladd, *A Theology of the New Testament*, 2nd ed. (Grand Rapids: Eerdmans, 1998), 54–67.

Spirit-anointed, divine Son—has the authority to announce the establishment of God's royal reign and to call people to "repent" or turn away from the dominion of Satan and to believe in the gospel.[18] Again, like the figure of Psalm 2, God's Son is portrayed as establishing God's royal rule in opposition to the hostile kings and rulers of the earth who oppose God and his Messiah.[19]

The Son of God Establishes the Kingdom of God against Its Enemies

If Mark 1:9–15 portrays Jesus as the Son of God, anointed by the Spirit, triumphant over Satan, and proclaiming the gospel and kingdom of God, then it makes sense to read the following scenes in Mark's Gospel as showing us what the kingdom of God is. In Mark 1:16–3:35 Jesus calls disciples to himself (1:16–20; 2:13–17; 3:7–19), forgives sins (2:1–12), heals the sick (1:29–34, 40–45; 2:1–12), and teaches and proclaims the gospel (1:21–22, 38–39; 2:18–28; 3:20–35). But here I want to focus primarily on the conflict between the demons and Jesus, the messianic king. In our study of Matthew's Gospel we have noted the messianic traditions which portray David and David's son Solomon as Spirit-endowed exorcists and healers: the relationship between Jesus's royal anointing by the Spirit as the Son of God (1:9–11) and his powerful triumph and successful holy war against Satan is evident in Mark as well (1:12–13; 3:23–30). As Kirk states: "Jesus can exorcise demons because he is God's king, anointed by the spirit, exercising God's reign with full divine authority on the earth."[20] The demons recognize that Jesus is God's messianic Son commissioned to establish God's kingdom over and against all who oppose him. In Mark 1:23–28 Jesus encounters a man with "an unclean spirit" who cries out, "What do you want with us, Jesus of Nazareth? Have you come to destroy us? I know who you are—the Holy One of God!" (ὁ ἅγιος τοῦ θεοῦ, 1:24). The demon's reference to Jesus as "the Holy One of God" is likely a messianic title which originated out of the practice of sanctifying and anointing the Davidic king with holy oil (see here, for example, LXX Ps 88:19–21).[21] Israel's kings, among

---

18. I agree with Joel Marcus that 1:15a refers to "filling up" or the end of the reign of Satan. See Joel Marcus, "'The Time Has Been Fulfilled!' (Mark 1:15)," in *Apocalyptic and the New Testament: Essays in Honor of J. Louis Martyn*, ed. Joel Marcus and Marion L. Soards, JSNTSup 24 (Sheffield: Sheffield Academic Press, 1989), 49–68. See also Perrin, *The Kingdom of God*, 104–5.

19. Marcus, *The Way of the Lord*, 66.

20. J. R. Daniel Kirk, *A Man Attested by God: The Human Jesus of the Synoptic Gospels* (Grand Rapids: Eerdmans, 2016), 424.

21. This has been argued convincingly by Max Botner, "The Messiah is 'the Holy One': ὁ ἅγιος τοῦ θεοῦ as a Messianic Title in Mark 1:24," *JBL* 136 (2017): 417–33.

other ancient rulers, were often anointed with holy oil, thereby conferring power, authority, and holiness upon the ruler.[22] Thus, the "unclean spirit" recognizes Jesus as one marked by a "holy spirit" (1:11–12) and thereby having the strength (1:7) and holiness to make war against the demons.[23] Likewise, in Mark 3:10–11 we are told that whenever Jesus approached those afflicted by diseases, the unclean spirits would fall down before Jesus and cry out, "You are God's Son!" (σὺ εἶ ὁ υἱὸς τοῦ θεοῦ, 3:11); similarly, the legion of unclean spirits within the Gerasene demoniac refers to Jesus as "Son of the Most High God" (5:7). Thus, the demons have secret knowledge of what occurred privately at Jesus's baptism and are aware that he is God's messianic ruler tasked with the mission and granted the authority to establish God's kingdom. And, indeed, Jesus silences the demon and casts it out of the man, thereby further inducing the people's amazement at Jesus's power and authority (1:25–28). Jesus's parable of the binding of the strong man provides his interpretation of the meaning of his exorcisms (3:23–30). Jesus is "the stronger man" who, by means of God's Holy Spirit (1:7–8, 11), establishes God's kingdom by making war against the kingdom (βασιλεία) of Satan and his demons (3:24), thereby liberating people from his lordship and evil dominion.[24]

TWO KINDS OF KINGSHIP

The language of "gospel" and "Son of God" in Mark's prologues has suggested to many that Mark's portrait of Jesus may challenge Roman imperial ideology (Mark 1:1, 15).[25] Jesus is a royal figure who inaugurates God's kingdom through powerful displays of exorcisms, healings, and benefactions.[26] Recently Michael Peppard has argued that Mark's account of Jesus's baptism would resonate with those influenced by Roman imperial ideology and suggests that many would thereby interpret the dove, a symbol of Roman power and rule, as a "counter-

---

22. On this practice see Sigmund Mowinckel, *He That Cometh: The Messiah Concept in the Old Testament and Later Judaism*, trans. G. W. Anderson (Grand Rapids: Eerdmans, 2005), 4–5.

23. See further, Botner, "The Messiah is 'the Holy One,'" 431.

24. On the apocalyptic depiction of the Messiah's holy war in Mark 3, see Elizabeth E. Shively, *Apocalyptic Imagination in the Gospel of Mark: The Literary and Theological Role of Mark 3:22–30*, BZNW 189 (Berlin: de Gruyter, 2012); see also Watts, *Isaiah's New Exodus*, 140–56.

25. See more broadly Adam Winn, *The Purpose of Mark's Gospel: An Early Christian Response to Roman Imperial Propaganda*, WUNT 2.245 (Tübingen: Mohr Siebeck, 2008).

26. See Winn, *The Purpose of Mark's Gospel*, 183–94.

symbol to the Roman eagle." These readers would hear God's declaration "as an adoption, the beginning of Jesus' accession as a counter-emperor."[27] The descent of the dove indicates that this Son of God, Jesus, "will rule not in the spirit of the bellicose eagle, but in the spirit of the pure, gentle, peaceful, and even sacrificial dove."[28] Mark's christological title "Son of God" could not but call to mind comparisons and contrasts with Augustus and the Roman emperor as self-proclaimed sons of God.[29] Peppard argues that ancient Roman adoption practices show us how Mark conceptualized Jesus's divine sonship—namely, that Jesus is also adopted as a powerful Son of God.[30] Peppard argues, however, that this is a remarkably high Christology, given Mark's cultural and historical context: "The Roman emperor, the most powerful person in the world, gained his sonship by adoption. If Mark was crafting a narrative that presents Jesus to Roman listeners as a counter-emperor, the authoritative son of God, then adoption was the most effective method of portraying his divine sonship."[31]

Adoption

While Peppard unnecessarily minimizes the importance of the influence of Israel's Scriptures, and while I remain unpersuaded that Mark intends for his readers to understand the baptism as Jesus's *adoption* as God's Son,[32] Mark's explicit contrast between Jesus's messianic vocation and that of Roman and gentile rulers in 10:41–45 lends support to the view that Mark depicts Jesus as a counter-imperial figure. Mark's contrast between the nature and character of Jesus's messianic rule and that of the kings and rulers of the nations is highlighted most clearly in Mark 6:14–44 and 10:35–45.

Two Kinds of Royal Banquets

One of the primary ways in which ancient rulers fulfilled their royal task and legitimated their rule was through the provision of gifts or benefactions.[33] Among a variety of possible benefactions, these gifts often included the provi-

---

27. Michael Peppard, *The Son of God in the Roman World: Divine Sonship in Its Social and Political Context* (Oxford: Oxford University Press, 2011), 87.

28. Peppard, *The Son of God*, 123.

29. Peppard, *The Son of God*, 28. See also Adela Yarbro Collins, "Mark and His Readers: The Son of God among Greeks and Romans," *HTR* 93 (2000): 85–100.

30. Peppard, *The Son of God*, 123.

31. Peppard, *The Son of God*, 131.

32. See the critique of Peppard, primarily as it pertains to reading Mark's Christology as adoptionist, by Michael F. Bird, *Jesus the Eternal Son: Answering Adoptionist Christology* (Grand Rapids: Eerdmans, 2017), 64–81.

33. See M. P. Charlesworth, "The Virtues of a Roman Emperor: Propaganda and the Creation of Belief," *Proceedings of the British Academy* 23 (1937): 105–33.

sion of food, banquets, and safety and/or rescue from one's enemies.[34] In Mark 6:14–44 we find the seemingly unrelated stories of Herod Antipas's execution of John the Baptist (6:14–29), a decision made by the tetrarch during a banquet, and Jesus's compassionate provision of food for the hungry crowd of people in the wilderness (6:30–44). The banquets and gifts of these two royal figures display the way in which Jesus is presented by Mark as embodying "a different kind of kingship over a different kind of kingdom."[35]

Mark's literary placement of Herod's decision to kill John the Baptist is striking as it represents a flashback to Mark 1:14 ("after John was handed over, Jesus came into Galilee proclaiming the gospel of God") as well as seeming to interrupt Mark's account of the sending out of the Twelve (Mark 6:7–13) and their return (6:30).[36] In this way, Mark indicates that both Herod's (6:14–29) and Jesus's (6:30–44) banquets should be read together, with an eye to their implications for discipleship (6:7–13, 30). Despite Herod Antipas's official title as "tetrarch" (Matt 14:1; Luke 3:19; 9:17; Acts 13:1), Mark goes out of his way to refer to Herod as "king" (βασιλεύς), repeating the title four times in a span of six verses (6:22, 25, 26, 27). The reader knows, of course, that Jesus alone embodies true royalty as God's beloved Son (Mark 1:9–11), whereas Herod's struggles to procure the kingship and his fraught relationship with his father were well known.[37] Dining together with the king at his banquet are "the great ones (τοῖς μεγιστᾶσιν), commanders, and the first ones (τοῖς πρώτοις) of Galilee" (6:21b; cf. 10:42, 44). Given Jesus's later teaching on "greatness" and "firstness" (see Mark 10:41–45), we are primed here to view this scene as an ironic and wrongheaded use of royal power. And, indeed, Mark's portrait of "King" Herod is hardly flattering, as Mark applies to him well-known literary traits of despised, tragic tyrants.[38] He is superstitious and emotionally unstable; his hearing of the reports of the miraculous healings and exorcisms of Jesus and

---

34. See, for example, Julien Smith, *Christ the Ideal King: Cultural Context, Rhetorical Strategy, and the Power of Divine Monarchy in Ephesians*, WUNT 2.313 (Tübingen: Mohr Siebeck, 2011), 37–47. See also Joshua W. Jipp, *Christ Is King: Paul's Royal Ideology* (Minneapolis: Fortress, 2015), 18–29.

35. Kirk, *A Man Attested by God*, 451.

36. On Markan intercalation and the way in which the technique highlights the most important themes of the Gospel, see James R. Edwards, "Markan Sandwiches: The Significance of Interpolations in Markan Narratives," *NovT* 31 (1989): 193–216.

37. See Gabriella Gelardini, "The Contest for a Royal Title: Herod versus Jesus in the *Gospel according to Mark* (6,14–29; 15, 6–15)," *ASE* 28 (2011): 103–6.

38. On Mark's ironic and anti-kingly depiction of Herod, see Gelardini, "The Contest for a Royal Title," 99–101. More broadly, see Tessa Rajak et al., eds., *Jewish Perspectives on Hellenistic Rulers* (Berkeley: University of California Press, 2007).

the Twelve causes him to cry out: "John, the one I beheaded, has been raised!" (6:16). Herod is unstable, divided in his own mind, and unable to control his will as he puts John to death despite his desire to protect him (6:20). The king is tricked and manipulated by two women into putting John to death (6:24–28), ultimately as a result of his inability to control his sexual passions when the young girl dances in the company of his friends (6:22). The king foolishly offers the girl whatever she wants, even up to "half of my kingdom" (6:23). And despite being "greatly depressed" (6:26a), he follows through on her request lest he—the king!—lose face in front of his banqueting guests (6:26b).

The banquet scene comes to an end with Herod's command to kill John and bring his head to the girl *on a dinner platter* (ἐπὶ πίνακι, 6:28). The irony is thick and the feast truly grotesque, as the serving platter with the head is passed from the executioner, to the young girl, and then to the mother (6:28). The characteristics of instability of emotions, enslavement to sexual passions, arbitrary and grotesque use of violence against the innocent, manipulation by women, and superstition function to portray the so-called king and ruler as a foolish tyrant, as one who "merely *appears* to rule (cf. 10:42), whereas his strings are pulled by others."[39]

The contrast between King Herod's banquet and Jesus's benefaction of food for the hungry could not be greater (6:30–44). The setting for Jesus's banquet is the desolate wilderness, not the royal palace; the characters are "the many" who are pressing in upon Jesus and his disciples, instead of "great" and "first" ones of Galilee; and the situation is one of hunger, as they had scarcely had any time to eat (6:31). Upon seeing that the crowd was "like sheep without a shepherd," Jesus is characterized as having compassion upon the crowd (6:34). Jesus involves his disciples in the feeding of the crowd by commanding them, "you give them something to eat" (6:37) and by ordering them to have the crowd sit in symposia-like banqueting groups (6:39). The disciples do participate in distributing the food to the great crowd, but only after they have received the provision of food from Jesus.[40] The result is that all of the people eat and are satisfied at the messianic feast (6:42–44). Mark is drawing upon Numbers 27:16–17 in his depiction of Jesus as a Moses-like shepherd of the people who both teaches and feeds the people (6:34b, 40–44). But without denying the Mosaic typology here—Moses was also frequently understood as a good king or ruler over God's people (e.g., Philo's *Moses* 1, 2)—the reader is justified in seeing this as a fulfillment of God's promise to raise up a good shepherd from

39. Marcus, *Mark 1–8*, 398.
40. So Marcus, *Mark 1– 8*, 420.

66

the house of David who will lead, nourish, feed, and save the lost sheep who had been scattered and exploited by Israel's corrupt leaders (Ezek 34).[41] The messianic Mosaic shepherd and his compassionate benefactions for his people could not offer a greater contrast against the so-called "King" Herod. After Jesus's second miraculous and compassionate provision of food for the crowd (8:1–10), he warns his disciples to "beware of the leaven of the Pharisees and the leaven of Herod" (8:15; cf. 3:1–6). Kirk summarizes the literary effect of this well: "The feeding narratives, then, are displaying a means of shepherding the people of God that stands in sharp contrast to the would-be 'king' and Israel's religious guardians."[42]

Messianic Rule as Service and Greco-Roman Theories of Royal Rule

Jesus explicitly contrasts the rule of the Messiah and all who would follow after him with that of Roman and gentile rulers in 10:42–45. Jesus's teaching is given within the context of correcting James and John, who want to share in Jesus's messianic rule, as they make their way into Jerusalem (10:35–40). Their desire to share in the messianic kingdom is indicated clearly in their request that they sit at the right and left of Jesus when he enters into his glory (10:37b). Jesus responds by asking them if they are able to "drink the cup which I drink" and "be baptized with the baptism I am baptized with" (10:38). Their desire to share in Jesus's messianic rule is not wrongheaded but entirely understandable within the contours of Mark's Gospel, as Jesus has frequently commanded his disciples to share in his life, character, and glorious destiny with the promise of reward (e.g., 8:34–9:1). In fact, there are a plethora of allusions in Mark 10:35–45 to the Danielic Son of Man who receives from the Ancient of Days "dominion, and glory, and a kingdom, so that those of every people, nation, and language should serve him. His dominion is an everlasting dominion that will not pass away and his kingdom is one that will not be destroyed" (Dan 7:14).[43] So John and James hope to share in the Son of Man's glory (10:37, 45), but where they go wrong is their failure to understand that sharing in Jesus's

---

41. So Kirk, *A Man Attested by God*, 451.

42. Kirk, *A Man Attested by God*, 454.

43. The most obvious allusion to Dan 7:13–14 in Mark 10:35–45 is, of course, the title "Son of Man." But see also the common references to glory, authority, and service/worship. See the helpful chart given by Marcus, *Mark 1–8*, 753. On the "Son of Man" language as having messianic resonances both in Daniel (see Dan 9:24–27) and more broadly in the first century, see William Horbury, "The Messianic Associations of 'The Son of Man,'" in

glory entails suffering, sacrifice, denying oneself, and taking up one's cross as a disciple of Jesus (e.g., 8:34–38). Drinking Jesus's "cup" and undergoing "baptism" with him point forward to Jesus's baptism unto death (note the parallels between Mark 1:9–11 and 15:36–39) and his drinking the cup which symbolizes his new-covenant-inaugurating death (14:23, 36).

As a result of their request, the rest of the disciples are indignant with James and John (10:41). Jesus's teaching in 10:42–45 clarifies once and for all for the disciples the nature of true discipleship, which contrasts greatly with contemporary notions of power, rule, and kingship. Jesus says: "you know that those who seem to rule (οἱ δοκοῦντες ἄρχειν) among the nations lord (κατακυριεύ-ουσιν) it over them and the great ones (οἱ μεγάλοι) act as authoritative tyrants (κατεξουσιάζουσιν) over them" (10:42).[44] Jesus declares, in other words, that Roman and Hellenistic rulers wield power and authority in a tyrannical way to increase their power and ability to lord their authority over their subjects. This may have been offered as a critique of Greco-Roman kingship discourse, which often depicted the good ruler as a servant who even risks his own life for the good of his people.

Numerous Greco-Roman texts portray the ideal for the good ruler as one who serves the people even to the point of risking his own life. To give just one example, Dio Cassius notes that Otho goes to his death such that the people might learn that "you chose for your emperor one who would *not give you for himself, but rather himself for you*" (64.13).[45] Jesus draws upon this kingship propaganda and subverts it by claiming that these rulers fail to live up to their own standards as servants who pursue the good of their subjects. They wield authority for their own benefit instead of serving their people even to the point of giving up their own lives if necessary. As Matthew Thiessen has noted, Jesus draws upon popular Hellenistic and Roman kingship discourse "in order both to call into question the type of authority these rulers exercise and to contrast them with his own rule, which truly fulfills this flattering portrait of the servant king. While those who rule the gentiles claim to serve them, they in fact rule and exercise authority over them in a way that contrasts with the

---

Messianism among Jews and Christians: Biblical and Historical Studies, 2nd ed. (London: T&T Clark, 2016), 153–85.

44. I understand both Mark's "*seem* to rule," as well as the κατά prefixes to the verb, as emphasizing Jesus's pejorative understanding of Roman imperial rule. See further Adam Winn, "Tyrant or Servant: Roman Political Ideology and Mark 10.42–45," *JSNT* 36 (2014): 342–43.

45. As suggested by Matthew Thiessen, "The Many for One or the One for Many: Reading Mark 10:45 in the Roman Empire," *HTR* 109 (2016): 447–66, esp. 454–56.

rulership of the Son of Man, who came in order to die for the many."[46] It is difficult not to see in Jesus's statement a biting critique of the common "divine honors in exchange for benefactions" that led to the worship and divinization of Hellenistic kings and Roman rulers.[47] The language of "great ones" and "first ones" was used in Mark 6:21 to describe the noble elite in the king's palace, but Jesus instead advances greatness and first-ness as coming, instead, through sacrificial service of others: "Whoever wants to be great (μέγας) among you will be your servant, and whoever wants to be first (πρῶτος) must be a slave to everyone" (10:43–44). Jesus's claim that greatness and true leadership are embodied in the socially degraded identity of a slave radically reorients one's understanding of power, authority, and kingly rule.[48] And this form of greatness, leadership, and rule is such because it follows the pattern of the messianic Son of Man who "did not come to be served but to serve and to give his life as a ransom for many people" (10:45).[49] Jesus's disciples will not be able to rule or share in his messianic kingdom unless they recognize that his kingdom will be inaugurated by means of—and his kingship is fully enacted in—his suffering for the world on a Roman cross (cf. also Mark 14:22–25).

THE CRUCIFIXION OF THE MESSIAH AND THE SCRIPTURES OF ISRAEL

In this section I want to take a look at Mark 11–15 in order to suggest that the Scriptures of Israel provided mnemonic aids for the remembrance of Jesus as the crucified King of Israel and that these remembrances are of utmost significance for Mark's articulation of Jesus's identity.[50] While I fully affirm that the

---

46. Thiessen, "The Many for One," 463.

47. On this "honors for benefactions structure," see Ittai Gradel, *Emperor Worship and Roman Religion*, Oxford Classical Monographs (Oxford: Clarendon, 2002); S. R. F. Price, *Rituals and Power: The Roman Imperial Cult in Asia Minor* (Cambridge: Cambridge University Press, 1984).

48. I find this to be underemphasized in Winn, "Tyrant or Servant," 343–45, who sees Jesus's remarks in 10:42–45 as conforming to Roman political ideals. However, he rightly notes that Mark's combination of "slave" with "first" is a surprising departure from these ideals, though in my view his claim that this radicalizes "Roman political ideals by taking them to their extreme but logical conclusion" does not go far enough.

49. Despite lacking obvious lexical parallels, many have seen Isa 53 as the context for Jesus's giving his life as a ransom for many. See further Adela Yarbro Collins, "The Significance of Mark 10:45 among Gentile Christians," *HTR* 90 (1997): 371–82.

50. What follows is a revision of my "Messiah Language and *Gospel Writing*," in *Writing*

Gospel of Mark is already a creative interpretation of earlier gospel tradition, I am less confident than many others in my ability to reconstruct a pre-Markan passion narrative.[51] I take it for granted, however, as do most, that Jesus was indeed crucified by Rome and mocked by Pilate with the inscription "King of the Jews."[52] As Dale Allison Jr. has stated: "perhaps the strongest argument for Jesus having been in fact crucified as 'king of the Jews' is the lack of a better suggestion regarding his alleged crime. . . . Somebody must have represented Jesus, despite his lack of an army, to be a potential threat to the political order."[53] Again, the task before me is to demonstrate that the Scriptures of Israel, particularly those concepts and texts capable of being read as offering a window into the identity of Israel's Messiah, function as a means of remembrance for Mark's Gospel and that Mark uses these scriptural resources in order to interpret the death of Jesus—the crucified Messiah—as the climactic moment in the story of Jesus. The titles or honorifics of "King" and "Messiah" are contested and capable of all kinds of different interpretations,[54] and Mark invokes messianic scriptural texts, concepts, and traditions as means of interpreting the meaning and significance of Jesus the crucified King.

Is Jesus the Son of David? (Mark 11–12)

One of the themes that dominates Jesus's entrance into Jerusalem in Mark is the question of Jesus's relation to David. Is Jesus or is he not the Son of David?[55] As Jesus journeys to Jerusalem he encounters blind Bartimaeus "seated alongside the way" (10:46) who twice calls out to Jesus: "Son of David show

---

the Gospels: A Dialogue with Francis Watson, ed. Catherine Sider Hamilton, LNTS 606 (London: T&T Clark, 2019), 131–42.

51. On a pre-Markan passion narrative, see Joel Marcus, Mark 8–16, AYB 27A (New Haven: Yale University Press, 2009), 924–27.

52. Nils A. Dahl, "The Crucified Messiah," in Jesus the Christ: The Historical Origins of a Christological Doctrine, ed. Donald H. Juel (Minneapolis: Fortress, 1991), 36–37; Martin Hengel, "Jesus, the Messiah of Israel," in his Studies in Early Christology (Edinburgh: T&T Clark, 1995), 41–58.

53. Dale C. Allison Jr., Constructing Jesus: Memory, Imagination, and History (Grand Rapids: Baker Academic, 2010), 235–36.

54. I am indebted here to the groundbreaking work of Matthew V. Novenson, Christ among the Messiahs: Christ Language in Paul and Messiah Language in Ancient Judaism (Oxford: Oxford University Press, 2012).

55. See especially John P. Meier, "From Elijah-Like Prophet to Royal Davidic Messiah," in Jesus: A Colloquium in the Holy Land, ed. Doris Donnelly (London: Continuum, 2001), 54–56.

mercy to me" (10:47, 48). Jesus does not explicitly praise the man for his use of the title, but Jesus does interpret the man's request for healing (and perhaps his act of leaving behind his cloak) as an act of faith that has resulted in his salvation (10:50, 52). After Jesus heals the blind man, the narrator tells us that "he followed him on the way" (10:52).[56] This is the second blind man Jesus heals in Mark's Gospel, and the healing episodes provide bookends for Mark's "way" section (8:22–10:52). The healing of the first blind man, which takes place in two stages, functions, most recognize, as a metaphor for discipleship and the difficult paradox of holding together Messiah and crucifixion. Thus, the two-stage healing functions as a metaphor for discipleship as the disciples travel with Jesus "on the way" (8:27). Yes, Peter and the disciples have seen that Jesus is "the Messiah" (8:29), but they will need to take a harder second look to see that Jesus's messiahship means he will experience shame, suffering, and even death as a result of his obedience to his Father (8:3–34). Jesus's divine sonship, power, and kingdom on display in the transfiguration account come by means of, not apart from, Jesus's suffering unto death (9:2–9).[57] Thus, Jesus does not reject or confirm Bartimaeus's designation of him as "Son of David," but rather in his following Jesus on the way to Jerusalem and ultimately to the cross, Bartimaeus is invited to rethink the meaning and significance of his confession of Jesus as Son of David.[58]

This healing provides a window into our interpretation of Jesus's so-called triumphal entry into Jerusalem (Mark 11:1–11). The scene of a royal claimant seated on a horse and entering into Jerusalem and receiving praise and acclamations before he makes his way to the temple evokes, of course, all sorts of biblical and post-biblical scenes and prophecies of a coming warrior-like Israelite king (2 Sam 16:2; 1 Kgs 1:32–40; 2 Kgs 9:13; Zech 9:9–15; 1 Macc 13:51).[59] Mark's description of Jesus entering into Jerusalem on "a colt on which no one

---

56. Thus, Bartimaeus fits the Markan pattern of those minor characters who rightly respond to Jesus with faith (e.g., 1:40–44; 5:25–34; 7:24–30; 9:14–29). See further Richard B. Hays, *Echoes of Scripture in the Gospels* (Waco, TX: Baylor University Press, 2016), 50–51.

57. See Rowe, *God's Kingdom*, 259–60.

58. Ahearne-Kroll, *The Psalms of Lament*, 143–44, argues that Mark presents Bartimaeus as a reliable character who rightly recognizes Jesus as the Son of David. But Mark intentionally associates this title with healing and not militaristic or political notions of rule. On the association of healing with the Son of David designation, see Lidija Novakovic, *Messiah, the Healer of the Sick: A Study of Jesus as the Son of David in the Gospel of Matthew*, WUNT 2.170 (Tübingen: Mohr Siebeck, 2003).

59. On the resonances with the processions of rulers, generals, and emperors in Greco-Roman texts, see Paul Brooks Duff, "The March of the Divine Warrior and the Advent of the Greco-Roman King: Mark's Account of Jesus' Entry into Jerusalem," *JBL* 111 (1992): 55–71.

has ever sat" (11:2b) seems to echo Genesis 49:11 and Zechariah 9:9—two texts which, taken together, anticipate a royal figure riding on a colt and making his way to Jerusalem.[60] The deep association between Messiah and temple undoubtedly helps explain the cry of the crowds: "Hosanna! Blessed is he who comes in the name of the Lord. Blessed is the coming kingdom of our father David! Hosanna in the highest!" (Mark 11:9b–10). Thus, just like Bartimaeus, the crowds give voice to the hope that Jesus is the Davidic king, namely, the referent of the warrior figure in Psalm 118 who comes to Jerusalem to save Israel and to "cut down" the pagan enemies of Israel. Joel Marcus notes that the imagery from this psalm is "ideally suited to ignite the sort of apocalyptic fervor that characterized the Jewish revolt against the Romans."[61] But, of course, nothing of the sort takes place. Jesus enters into Jerusalem and into the temple, and after having a look around he retreats with his disciples to Bethany (11:11). Jesus's journey to the temple, in other words, is remarkably anticlimactic; there is no revolutionary activity or warfare, no royal enthronement, and no welcome from the Jerusalem priests.[62] Thus, the acclamation of the crowds that Jesus has come to bring the kingdom of "our father David," the echoes of Genesis 49 and Zechariah 9, and the activation of the scriptural associations between Messiah and temple remain ambiguous as to whether they tell the reader anything meaningful about the identity of Jesus.[63]

So far we have seen the narrator activating resonances of Jesus as a royal Davidic figure (Mark 11:1–11)—Peter referring to Jesus as "the Messiah" (8:27–31), Bartimaeus calling him the "Son of David" (10:47–48), and the crowd acclaiming him the coming one who brings "the kingdom of our father David" (11:9b–10). We have not seen Jesus openly welcome these designations or identify himself as the royal Son of David. But in Mark 12:1–12, in the parable of the vineyard, Jesus tells a parable about an owner of a vineyard who sent his servants to the tenants in order to receive some of the produce from the vineyard. The tenants shame, reject, and even kill the servants of the landowner. And so, the landowner devises another course of action. Jesus tells the audience that the owner "still had one beloved son; and finally, he sent him to them, saying, 'They will respect my son'" (12:6). We should pause here to note that while the language of a father and a "beloved son" has a deep resonance with the story

---

60. On the association between temple and messiah, see Marcus, *Mark 8–16*, 776.

61. Marcus, *Mark 8–16*, 780.

62. On the silence of the Jerusalem priests and their refusal to pronounce the benediction of Ps 117:25–26 (LXX), see Cho, *Royal Messianism*, 136–39.

63. See the discussion in Timothy C. Gray, *The Temple in the Gospel of Mark: A Study in Its Narrative Role* (Grand Rapids: Baker Academic, 2010), 20–22.

of the beloved son in Genesis 22,[64] Jesus's explicit citation of the royal Psalm 118:22 in 12:10–11, among other indicators, suggests that an important context for the language of the beloved son is Psalm 2:7.[65] Jesus concludes the parable with an explicit quotation of Psalm 118:22: "The stone which the builders rejected, this has become the chief cornerstone; this has come about from the Lord and it is marvelous in our eyes" (Mark 12:10–11).[66] This is the same Psalm 118 which provided the language for the crowd's acclamation of Jesus as the Davidic king (11:9–10), but Jesus has appealed to the most cryptic element of the psalm—that which speaks of the rejection (and ensuing vindication) of the speaker of the psalm. Ahearne-Kroll states the dynamic well when he notes that Jesus "chooses a psalm that can be read as articulating the difficulties that David experienced as king . . . [and] chooses a place in the psalm that is not focused on the military triumph of the king, but rather articulates a quality of royalty that does not leap to mind immediately when thinking of a king."[67] In other words, Jesus *is* related to the coming Davidic king spoken of by the psalmist, but the relationship is not an uncomplicated one of triumph, victory, and power—but, rather, one of rejection, murder, and divine vindication.

Perhaps, then, the notoriously difficult riddle posed by Jesus in Mark 12:35–37 cannot be so easily answered by scholarly claims that Jesus either polemicizes against/rejects *or* that he embraces/affirms a Davidic Christology as central to his identity.[68] In this riddle Jesus confounds the temple leaders with the question: "How can the scribes say that the Messiah is the Son of David?" Jesus then appeals to Psalm 110:1 and notes that David himself states: "The Lord

---

64. On the role of Gen 22 in Mark's portrait of the relationship between God and Jesus, see Matthew S. Rindge, "Reconfiguring the Akedah and Recasting God: Lament and Divine Abandonment in Mark," *JBL* 130 (2011): 755–74. See also Perrin, *The Kingdom of God*, 102–4.

65. On the importance of Ps 2:7 for the language of "beloved son" in the Synoptics Gospels, see Frank J. Matera, *The Kingship of Jesus: Composition and Theology in Mark 15*, SBLSDS 66 (Chico, CA: Scholars Press, 1982), 77–79. On the parable's depiction of the wicked tenants as playing the role of the rebellious rulers and nations of Ps 2:1–3, see Rowe, *God's Kingdom*, 261–62.

66. As is often noted, the word Jesus uses for "rejected" is the same word he uses to predict his impending death in Mark 8:31. On the significance of the overlap between Mark 8:31–34 and 12:10–11, see Hays, *Echoes of Scripture in the Gospels*, 80–81.

67. Ahearne-Kroll, *The Psalms of Lament*, 160.

68. For rejection, see Francis Moloney, *The Gospel of Mark: A Commentary* (Grand Rapids: Baker Academic, 2002), 243; Paul J. Achtemeier, "And He Followed Him: Miracles and Discipleship in Mark 10:46–52," *Semeia* 11 (1978): 126–30. For affirmation, see Michael F. Bird, *Jesus Is the Christ: The Messianic Testimony of the Gospels* (Downers Grove, IL: InterVarsity Press, 2012), 32–56.

said to my Lord, 'Sit at my right hand until I put your enemies under your feet.'" So, then, Jesus asks: "Since David calls him Lord, how can he be his son?" In other words, if a father (David) is greater than his son (the son of David), how can it be that David refers to his son as Lord? Jesus gives no answer to the question; the scribes are left in a state of perplexed silence, and so it would seem fair to say that any interpretation of this pericope should retain a level of ambiguity and complexity.[69] Perhaps Mark is presenting a challenge to his readers to rethink the meaning of the titles "Messiah" and "Son of David."[70] Nevertheless, given Peter's designation of Jesus as the Messiah in 8:29, Jesus's explicit appeal to Psalm 118 in 12:10–11, and Jesus's explicit messianic claim in 14:61–62, where he again draws upon Psalm 110:1, Mark certainly intends for the reader to understand his riddle as centering upon Jesus's own identity.[71] Marcus again strikes the right balance when he says that Mark "means both to affirm and to qualify the idea of Davidic messianism."[72] Again, the honorifics of "Son of David" and "the Messiah" are capable of a variety of interpretations, and Mark has no intention of portraying Jesus as the kind of "Son of David" and "Messiah" hoped for by the author of Psalm of Solomon 17, who would purge the gentiles from Jerusalem and destroy the unlawful nations. Jesus is indeed *more* than David, as indicated by his quotation of the part of the psalm which portrays him seated next to the right hand of God and thus in a position of heavenly co-rule with Yahweh. That is to say, Jesus interprets Psalm 110:1 in such a way that he is the one addressed by David as "my Lord" and is thereby invited by Yahweh to share in his rule.[73] Jesus, then, does not outright reject the notion that he is the messianic Son of David, but he does problematize one popular notion of what the messianic identity entails.[74]

---

69. See Robert M. Fowler, *Let the Reader Understand: Reader-Response Criticism and the Gospel of Mark* (Minneapolis: Fortress, 1991); R. T. France, *The Gospel of Mark*, NIGTC (Grand Rapids: Eerdmans, 2002), 483, notes that Jesus's question is "remarkably enigmatic, the more so since it is unanswered and is left hanging tantalizingly in the air."

70. So Hays, *Echoes of Scripture in the Gospels*, 54.

71. France, *The Gospel of Mark*, 484, is right to note that it was "an unquestioned conviction in first-century Christianity that the title 'Son of David,' even though not much emphasized especially in the Gentile church, was appropriate for Jesus. . . . If it had been Mark's intention to supplant this belief he would have needed a far more direct approach than these three verses offer, and he would have had to rewrite 10:47–48 and 11:10."

72. Marcus, *Mark 8–16*, 850.

73. See Matthew W. Bates, *The Birth of the Trinity: Jesus, God, and Spirit in New Testament & Early Christian Interpretations of the Old Testament* (Oxford: Oxford University Press, 2015), 48–50.

74. Again, Hays, *Echoes of Scripture in the Gospels*, 55: "Jesus *is* the Son of David, the

So, within Mark 10–12 we have seen a host of royal tropes as well as echoes and allusions to expectations for a coming Davidic king from Israel's Scriptures. It is remarkable, then, that answering whether Mark presents Jesus as the Son of David is more difficult than giving an unequivocal yes or no. I think Daniel Kirk is close to the mark when he states: "Like the term 'Christ' itself, Davidic messiahship is not a sufficient category for interpreting Jesus' ministry. It needs reframing and reinterpretation by Jesus' own ministry. . . . [I] suggest that son of David is not a wholly inappropriate title for Jesus within Mark, but that it demands a radical reorientation around the fate of Jesus that includes not only authority, suffering, and death, but also resurrection and enthronement."[75] And given, of course, that there is no single meaning to *messiah* or messiah language, this should not occasion great surprise.[76]

Messiah and Temple

The only charge brought against Jesus in his trial before the Sanhedrin was the testimony that he said: "I will destroy this temple made with human hands and in three days I will build another one not made with human hands" (Mark 14:58). As Jesus was hanging from the cross, Mark tells the reader that others were passing by and mocking Jesus saying, "Ha! You who would destroy the temple and rebuild it in three days, save yourself and come down from the cross" (15:29).[77] Mark presents the first accusation as "false testimony" (14:57), and yet scholars have rightly noted there is some ironic truth in the charge. While Mark has not presented Jesus as claiming to be the agent of the temple's destruction, Jesus did declare that the temple would be destroyed (13:2), did perform a prophetic act of judgment within the temple (11:15–17), did say that his body would be raised after three days (8:31), and did identify himself as the rejected but vindicated cornerstone of the temple (12:10–11).[78] Thus, there

---

Messiah, as Bartimaeus had perceived and as the title *Christos* asserts. But the meaning of *Christos* is transposed to a new key and subjected to inversion. The Messiah is more than a new military leader and pretender to the throne; he is the Son of God who is to be enthroned in the heavens and recognized as David's Lord."

75. Kirk, *A Man Attested by God*, 497.

76. See further Matthew V. Novenson, *The Grammar of Messianism: An Ancient Jewish Political Idiom and Its Users* (Oxford: Oxford University Press, 2017).

77. The language used by Jesus's enemies to mock him resonates with what is found in Ps 22:7–8. See Hays, *Echoes of Scripture in the Gospels*, 84–85.

78. See Gray, *The Temple in the Gospel of Mark*, 174: "Thus, it is consistent with Mark's style to show that the testimony regarding Jesus' comments about the temple is false on

is a level of truth in the accusation brought against Jesus as evidenced by his symbolic act of judgment against the temple (11:15–19), his word of judgment against the temple leadership (12:12), and his prediction that "there will surely not be one stone upon a stone here that won't be destroyed" (13:2b). Further, Jesus's allusive claim to be the new "chief cornerstone" (12:10–11; Ps 118:22), his claim that, as Lord in heaven, he will be more exalted than David (12:36; cf. Ps 110:1), and his inauguration of a new sacrificial Passover meal (14:22–25)[79] can be interpreted as evidence for the claim that he is inaugurating a new temple "not made with human hands." After Jesus's prophetic act within the temple, he had spoken of his disciples as embodying the functions of the temple (e.g., prayer, faith, and forgiveness) in their own community (11:20–25).[80] There is a convergence here between the themes of the resurrection of the Messiah and a new temple, which suggests that "Jesus' resurrection in some way brings about the eschatological temple foretold in the restoration oracles of Israel's Scriptures."[81]

It is well known that Jewish Scriptures and traditions often connected royal-messianic figures with temple building, and for most Jews this tradition was based on God's promise to David: "I will raise up your seed after you, who will come forth from your body, and I will establish his kingdom; he will build a house for my name, and I will establish the throne of his kingdom forever" (2 Sam 7:12–13; cf. 2 Chr 36:22–23; Zech 6:12; Pss. Sol. 17:21–23; Sib. Or. 5:422; 4QFlor. 1:10–13; 1 En. 90:29; 4 Ezra 9:38–10:27). In other words, the Son of David would be associated with temple building.[82] Allison suggests that the implications of the charge brought against Jesus in Mark 14:58 (and John 2:19) are obvious: "Opponents could readily have moved from 'He claims he will destroy and rebuild the temple' to 'He claims to be king.'"[83] This explains perfectly why the high priest moves from questioning Jesus about these temple-building charges to asking him: "Are you the Messiah, the Son of the Blessed?"

---

one level, but nevertheless true in a way that escapes the grasp and the intentions of Jesus' perjurers: the old temple is to be destroyed and replaced by another."

79. On the importance of the temple context for Jesus's sacrificial Passover meal with his disciples, see Brant Pitre, *Jesus and the Last Supper* (Grand Rapids: Eerdmans, 2015), 389–403.

80. See here John Paul Heil, "The Narrative Strategy and Pragmatics of the Temple Theme in Mark," *CBQ* 59 (1997): 76–100.

81. Gray, *The Temple in the Gospel of Mark*, 179. See also Jens Schröter, *Jesus of Nazareth: Jew from Galilee, Savior of the World*, trans. Wayne Coppins (Waco, TX: Baylor University Press, 2015), 187–90.

82. See Nicholas Perrin, *Jesus the Temple* (Grand Rapids: Baker Academic, 2010), 101–102.

83. Allison, *Constructing Jesus*, 238.

(14:61b).[84] If there was any truth that Jesus had claimed to rebuild a temple, then the implication would seem to be that he was indeed the Messiah, the Son of David. Thus, the chief priest is asking Jesus whether he is Israel's King, the Messiah, the one authorized to rebuild God's temple. It is worth repeating the point that "Son of God" language stems from 2 Sam 7:10–14 and is messianic kingship language which associates "Son of David" with "Son of God" (cf. Ps 2:6–8; Ps 89).[85] For a non-Jewish audience, of course, the honorific "son of God" would also have royal connotations, as the language was used for the Roman emperor.[86]

Jesus responds, at first, with the simple affirmation, "I am" (14:62a). In other words, as Marcus has stated, Jesus's opponents have once again "spoken the very Christological truths they abhor" (cf. 14:2, 65; 15:2, 18, 26, 29–32).[87] But Jesus combines this simple and explicit messianic affirmation with a claim to be the Son of Man: "You will see the Son of Man seated at the right hand of power and coming with the clouds of heaven" (14:62b). Jesus's response to the chief priest, which combines Daniel 7:13–14 with Psalm 110:1, points forward to his vindication by way of resurrection and enthronement.[88] But the narrative has made it clear that Jesus's vindication and enthronement will not come apart from suffering, and specifically apart from crucifixion (8:31; 9:31; 10:33–34).[89] And, ironically, while the Jerusalem priests were supposed to offer a welcome to God's eschatological Messiah, they are the ones who hand

84. Marcus, *Mark 8–16*, 1015–16, states rightly that "the high priest's question about Jesus' messianic identity (14:61b) . . . is a balder form of his question about the Temple charge (14:60)."

85. Jipp, *Christ Is King*, 32–36.

86. See, for example, Peppard, *The Son of God*.

87. Marcus, *Mark 8–16*, 1016.

88. Gray, *The Temple in the Gospel of Mark*, 179.

89. John Donahue, "Temple, Trial, and Royal Christology (Mark 14:53–65)," in *The Passion in Mark: Studies on Mark 14–16*, ed. Werner Kelber (Philadelphia: Fortress, 1976), 71. There is not enough space, nor is it necessary to do justice to the exegetical conundrums posed in Jesus's response, but readers of Mark will be familiar with Jesus's use of the Danielic Son of Man language as a means of refracting (but not rejecting!) the messianic honorific (e.g., 8:29–33; 9:31–32; 10:41–45). On this Markan literary technique and the notion of "refracted" Christology, see Malbon, *Mark's Jesus*, 195–217. Mark's Jesus has consistently reinterpreted Christ-language in tandem with the depiction of the Danielic Son of Man who suffers and is then vindicated by God. Readers have recognized that Jesus's response combines Dan 7:13 with Ps 110:1. Thus, Kirk is right to note that this returns our attention to Mark 12:35–37 and indicates that Mark shows the referent of Ps 110:1 "is none other than this Christ whom Jesus says is so much greater than David as to be called David's 'Lord'" (*A Man Attested by God*, 328).

Jesus over to suffering and death. Cho states this well: "Fundamental to Jesus's stance towards the temple and the fate of the Jerusalem institution in Mark, therefore, is the way the priests respond to Jesus as the end-time king. Who is Israel's rightful ruler? To Mark it is Jesus the messiah, who, albeit rejected, will soon be enthroned in heaven at the right hand of God."[90]

The primary point for our purposes is that Mark preserves and interprets the memory of Jesus as Israel's Messiah who, precisely as the Son of God and Son of David, was remembered as speaking and acting in ways only appropriate for someone who was the King of Israel. The preserved memories of Jesus acting critically and authoritatively about Israel's temple (11:12–26), the belief that he had claimed to destroy and rebuild the temple (14:58; 15:29), and his citations of the royal theology encapsulated in Psalm 110:1 and Daniel 7:13 as a means of articulating his identity to the high priest (14:61–62) add further weight to the claim that Mark is drawing upon messianic texts, concepts, and traditions in order to interpret Jesus's life and death as Israel's crucified King.

The Psalter, Irony, and the Crucified King (Mark 15)

John Donahue has made the suggestion that since Mark has made a "definitive christological statement" in 14:62, "the titles which dominate the latter part of the Passion Narrative, King and Son of God (Mk 15), are to be seen as already having been given a meaning in the trial narrative."[91] And this seems to be good common sense. I would only add to this that, in addition to the titles in Mark 14:61–62, most readers will activate the numerous messianic and royal tropes and texts (which we have examined) that have dominated Mark 11–15.[92] Thus, the *Roman* Pilate's question to Jesus—"Are you the King of the Jews?" (Mark 15:2; cf. vv. 9, 12, 26)—is not surprising in the least and is perfectly in line with the *Jewish* high priest's question "Are you the Messiah, the Son of the Blessed One?" (14:61).[93] I want to make two simple but important points about

90. Cho, *Royal Messianism*, 203.

91. Donahue, "Temple, Trial," 71.

92. This statement coheres with one of the broad points argued by Matera, *The Kingship of Jesus*—namely, that Pilate's threefold question to Jesus and the placard naming Jesus as the King of the Jews has been anticipated by Mark in other sections of his Gospel.

93. Donald Juel, *Messianic Exegesis: Christological Interpretation of the Old Testament in Early Christianity* (Philadelphia: Fortress, 1988), 93: "To the Romans, the royal claim is understood in political terms: Jesus is tried, mocked, and crucified as King of the Jews. Jew is what Gentiles called Israelites; 'King of the Jews' and 'Christ, the King of Israel' are appropriate to the speakers."

Mark's depiction of Jesus as the crucified King of the Jews in his passion narrative. First, as many have recognized, Mark portrays Jesus's death as a mock parody of a kingly coronation. Six times Mark uses the term *king* (βασιλεύς) to speak of the ironic mockery of Jesus's crucifixion (15:2, 9, 12, 18, 26, 32).[94] The soldiers, who clothe Jesus in purple, place a crown of thorns on his head and make mocking gestures of obeisance to "the King of the Jews" (Mark 15:17–20), are engaging in a mock ritual of a king's accession to his throne.[95] Jesus then takes his kingly position seated upon the cross (15:24–25) under the inscription "The King of the Jews" (15:26). From the cross Jesus is mocked explicitly for his royal messianic pretensions—namely, for his plan to build another temple "in three days" (15:29) and his belief that he is "the Messiah, the King of Israel" (15:32). The irony here is evident, for Jesus is indeed the Messiah, the King of Israel, the Son of God. Donald Juel states that it is "the enemies of Jesus who provide for his investiture and enthronement, contrary to their intentions and beyond their understanding."[96] Marcus states it well: "From the point of view of the soldiers, of course, the 'King of the Jews' inscription is a mockery; Jesus' crucifixion shows that he is certainly *not* royal, as he claims to be. For the Christian reader, however, the opposite conclusion would emerge: the mocking inscription unwittingly expresses the truth."[97] Readers of Mark have learned from Jesus that his ambivalent reticence to accept the royal designation "Messiah" or "Son of David" is due to the human inability to see Jesus's renunciation of rights and his suffering and crucifixion as the primary revelation of Jesus's kingship.

Second, Mark laces his passion narrative with Davidic psalms where the King is depicted as suffering and lamenting. We could not ask for a better mnemonic aid for remembering and interpreting Jesus's death than these Davidic psalms.[98] Mark's appropriation of these Davidic psalms is not surprising, given his use of a David typology in his depictions of Jesus's trials and sufferings in Mark 14. For example, both David and Jesus make a sorrowful trip to the Mount of Olives (Mark 14:26–31; 2 Sam 15:30–31); both receive an oath of loyalty unto death from one of their followers (Mark 14:27–31; 2 Sam

---

94. See Matera, *The Kingship of Jesus*, 121.

95. On the soldiers' activity as mimicking a Roman triumph for a victorious general or ruler, see T. E. Schmidt, "Mark 15.16–32: The Crucifixion Narrative and the Roman Triumphal Procession," *NTS* 41 (1995): 1–18.

96. Juel, *Messianic Exegesis*, 94; also, Kirk, *A Man Attested by God*, 200–201. Also helpful here is Juel, "The Origin of Mark's Christology," 449–60.

97. Marcus, *Mark 8–16*, 1050. Similarly, see France, *The Gospel of Mark*, 648–49.

98. The tradition that connected David with all of the Psalms is well known. See, for example, Ahearne-Kroll, *The Psalms of Lament*, 51–56.

15:19–24); and both are betrayed by trusted friends (Mark 14:42; 2 Sam 15:31).[99] While there are a variety of allusions to the Psalter in Mark's passion narrative, there are five citations or allusions that seem particularly clear:[100] Jesus gives voice to Psalm 41:10 when he predicts that "the one who is eating with me will betray me" (Mark 14:18b); Jesus appropriates the language of Psalms 42:6, 11, and 43:5 when in the Garden of Gethsemane he cries out, "my soul is grieved to the point of death" (Mark 14:34); Mark uses the language of Psalm 69:21 and 22:18 to describe the crucifiers' acts of offering sour wine to Jesus and casting lots for his garment (Mark 15:23–24); and climactically, Jesus gives voice to the words of David from Psalm 22:1—"'Eloi, Eloi, lama sabachtani?' which means, 'My God, my God, why have you forsaken me?'" (Mark 15:34). The typological echoes of David's sufferings and trials and the voice of David as expressed in the Psalter portray Jesus as a King, but a very particular kind of King—namely, a King "who experiences the realities of human rejection and suffering, expresses the horrors of his suffering, and cries out to God in the midst of that suffering."[101] Thus, when the Roman centurion declares Jesus to be the Son of God, he ironically testifies that Jesus's kingship is revealed through suffering and crucifixion (Mark 15:39; cf. 1:10–11). Now the reader can see that Jesus's messianic anointing as the Son of God (1:9–11) and the vision of the Son of God's glorious splendor at the transfiguration (9:2–9) were surprisingly pointing toward the Son of God's crucifixion as the ultimate display of his royalty and sonship. Jesus is the Messiah "who reigns from the cross . . . [and] his glorious kingship is paradoxically hidden in his gruesome death. The radiance of his glory is seen as darkness, his power as weakness, and his kingship as servanthood."[102]

DISCIPLESHIP AS SHARING IN CHRIST'S RULE

While Mark's Gospel is dominated by Christology and poses the question of the nature and character of Jesus's messiahship as pointedly as any text, the Messiah's inauguration of the kingdom of God is deeply intertwined with his

99. I am dependent here upon Donahue, "Temple, Trial," 76; see also Allison, *Constructing Jesus*, 283, 387; Ahearne-Kroll, *The Psalms of Lament*, 167.

100. For a maximalist approach to discerning allusions to the suffering righteous king in the Psalter, see Marcus, *The Way of the Lord*, 172–86.

101. Ahearne-Kroll, *The Psalms of Lament*, 219; see also, Juel, *Messianic Exegesis*, 93–103; Kirk, *A Man Attested by God*, 509–15.

102. Jeremy Treat, *The Crucified King: Atonement and Kingdom in Biblical and Systematic Theology* (Grand Rapids: Zondervan, 2014), 99.

commission and authorization of the disciples as "collective participants in the Christological mission that characterizes his own purpose and destiny."[103] Thus, the implication of the messianic community's confession that "Jesus is the Son of God" (1:11; 9:7; 15:39) who rules over God's kingdom is a call to actively participate in and extend his messianic rule. As Kirk has rightly noted, the Gospel of Mark makes it clear that "discipleship is inherently connected with Jesus's messiahship."[104]

Discipleship and the Kingdom of God

We have seen that Mark's prologue positions Jesus as God's uniquely anointed, Spirit-empowered Son who is victorious against the attacks of Satan and who proclaims the inauguration of God's rule (1:9–15). And almost immediately Mark depicts Jesus as enacting God's rule by making war against the demonic (1:21–28). But Jesus's very first act, after the prologue's introduction, depicts Jesus calling Andrew and Simon (1:16) and then James and John (1:19) to participate in his ministry. The language of discipleship permeates the passage as they are called by Jesus to "come after me" (1:20), are commissioned as "fishers of people" (1:17b), and in each instance they leave their fishing nets in order to "follow him" (1:18). Coming immediately after the description of Jesus as proclaiming "the gospel of God" and "the kingdom of God" (1:14–15), Mark depicts discipleship as an active participation in the Son of God's inauguration of his kingdom reign.[105]

Exorcisms and Teaching

We have seen that one of the major facets of Jesus's enactment of the reign of God is his war against the demonic through exorcisms and healings, as well as his proclaiming the kingdom of God (1:21–45). Mark's Jesus calls and commissions the twelve apostles to enact the kingdom through these very same acts of exorcising demons and healing those who are afflicted, as well as proclaiming God's kingdom. Thus, Mark's portrait of Jesus's commission of the Twelve shows that Jesus called them "to be with him and to be sent out to preach and he gave them authority to cast out demons" (3:14b–15). Again, in Mark 6:7–13 Jesus commissions the Twelve by granting them "authority over the unclean

---

103. See here Henderson, *Christology and Discipleship*, 4. The entire study here is an excellent demonstration of this point.

104. Kirk, *A Man Attested by God*, 215.

105. See also Henderson, *Christology and Discipleship*, 52–53, 64–65.

spirits" (6:7) and calling them to "preach that people may repent" (6:12; cf. 1:15). Mark's summary statement of their mission is that "they cast out many demons and anointed many who were sick and healed them" (6:13). Mark's so-called parable of the soils in Mark 4:1–20 is almost certainly given by Jesus in order to provide the disciples a lens for understanding why both Jesus's and their own proclamation of the kingdom of God is characterized by both success (the good soil) and various forms of rejection (the bad soils).[106] The disciples have already been commissioned as "fishers of people" (1:17) and tasked with being "sent out in order to preach" (3:14); thus, Jesus here further reminds them that they have been gifted with "the mystery of the kingdom of God" (4:11). Ladd notes that this mystery "is the coming of the Kingdom into history in advance of its apocalyptic manifestation."[107] As a result, the disciples, along with Jesus, are called to sow the seeds of God's kingdom and to trust God's power to bring about a fruitful harvest even in the midst of enemy territory.[108] While we will examine the relationship established between Jesus and the messianic community as it pertains to hospitality and table fellowship in much more detail in our next chapter on Luke-Acts, I briefly note here that Mark, too, portrays the disciples as sharing in Jesus's compassionate and shepherding gifts of food for the hungry in Mark 6:31–44. When the disciples rightly diagnose the need for food, Jesus commands them: "You give them something to eat" (6:37a). Jesus exhorts them to make the groups recline in banqueting groups in "the green grass" (6:39; cf. Ps 23). And Jesus has the disciples act as hosts as they distribute the food to the people (6:42). Luke will make explicit what is implicit here in Mark—namely, Jesus's call to the disciples to actively participate in shepherding God's people through the hospitable provision of food.

Mark could not be any clearer about the connection between Jesus's messianic power and identity and the call to discipleship for Jesus's community as Jesus extends his messianic authority to the disciples and calls them to actively participate in the kingdom of God. Suzanne Watts Henderson rightly notes that interpreters have recognized the high Christology in Mark whereby Jesus shares in the power and authority of the God of Israel, but many have failed to recognize Mark's similarly high view of discipleship as Jesus calls his community to participate in and enact the very same kingdom that characterizes the mission of Jesus.[109]

---

106. See here especially, Marcus, *Mark 1–8*, 291–313.
107. Ladd, *A Theology of the New Testament*, 91.
108. See Perrin, *The Kingdom of God*, 94–97.
109. Henderson, *Christology and Discipleship*, 79.

The Messianic Community as the New Temple

In an earlier section ("Messiah and Temple") I noted that Jesus's seemingly unrelated exhortation in 11:22–25 to Peter and the disciples to have faith in God when they pray and to forgive one another is actually deeply related to the larger Markan context centering upon Jesus and the temple. We have already examined the theme of the Messiah as temple builder, as well as Mark's depiction of the temple leadership's rejection of the Messiah and, as a result, the temple's fruitlessness and lack of preparation for the messianic age. Within this context, Jesus's call to the disciples to embody faith, prayer, and forgiveness indicates that the Messiah is commissioning them "to be the fulfillment of the temple's purpose of being a house of prayer for all people, in the wake of Jesus's judgment and condemnation of it. They will be the place, also, where forgiveness is found."[110] If Jesus is the once rejected, but now vindicated cornerstone of God's eschatological temple (see Ps 118:22 in Mark 12:10–11), then the messianic community is God's new temple, embodying the tasks of faith, prayer, and forgiveness in the messianic age.

Sharing in the Reign of the Son of Man through Service, Sacrifice, and Cross-Bearing

Disciples of the Messiah share in his rule by embodying his character of service, sacrifice, and humility in service to God. Given that the Messiah's family are those who do "the will of God" (3:31–35), as Jesus's divine sonship is marked by obedience and submission to Abba Father's will (Mark 14:36), so also the sons and daughters of the Messiah are called to the same pattern of cruciform lifestyle in obedience to the Father. Mark's "way" section contains a powerful literary dynamic whereby: (1) Jesus presents the necessity of giving up of his life unto death (8:31; 9:31; 10:32–34); (2) the disciples respond with a failure to understand the congruence between the kingdom of God and the necessity of Jesus's death on the cross (8:32–33; 9:32–34; 10:35–41); and (3) Jesus subsequently corrects the disciples and calls them to follow his example of service, sacrifice, and cross-bearing (8:34–9:1; 9:35–50; 10:42–45). The simple point I wish to draw attention to here is that the pattern of the Messiah, the crucified Son of God, which we have examined in detail in Mark's passion narrative sets the same pattern for the character and discipleship of *all of the children of God*. Disciples are those who take up the cross of Jesus and willingly sacrifice their lives for

---

110. Kirk, *A Man Attested by God*, 214.

Jesus's sake and the gospel (8:34–35). Disciples embody a form of leadership that dispenses with pursuits of power and greatness and instead become "a slave of all" (9:35; 10:44). Just as the Messiah lays down his life in sacrifice with the expectation of vindication and participation as God's glorious Son of Man (cf. 9:2–8; 12:10–11; 13:26; 14:61–62), so the messianic community is offered the same hope of sharing in the glorious consummation of the kingdom of God—but only by means of following the pattern of the Messiah (see, for example, 9:1). We have seen that Jesus uses the images of drinking the cup and undergoing Jesus's baptism as metaphors for sharing in Jesus's suffering unto death on the cross before one shares in his glory (10:37–39). These two images resonate powerfully with the way Christians "drink the Lord's cup at communion and thus proclaim his death until he comes" (cf. 1 Cor 11:26) and their sharing "in that death in a deep sacramental sense through baptism" (cf. Rom 6:3).[111] Thus, the sacraments of baptism and the Lord's Supper symbolize the reality of sharing in the glorious messianic rule through bearing one's cross with the Messiah.

CONCLUSION

Mark's Gospel depicts the Messiah as God's Son who inaugurates and establishes God's reign through his life, suffering, and death on the cross. Jesus is triumphant in his war against the realm of the demonic, provides compassionate benefactions for the people, and not only serves the good of his people but even willingly lays down his life to rescue his subjects. On the Roman cross, the place of humiliation, weakness, and shame, Mark declares that Jesus's messianic commission, divine sonship, and embodiment of the attributes of the truly "good ruler" are revealed and thereby establish God's kingdom. The Messiah's family are both exhorted and promised to share in the Messiah's rule through proclaiming the kingdom of God, making war against the realm of evil, and embodying the sacrifice, service, and cross-bearing of their messianic king.

---

111. Marcus, *Mark 8–16*, 754.

CHAPTER 3

The Messianic King and the Hope of Israel

Luke-Acts

In Luke-Acts Jesus is the Davidic Messiah who fulfills the covenantal promises made to David, brings God's salvation to his people, suffers and dies as
the righteous and faithful messianic king, and is enthroned to a position of
heavenly rule whereby he continues to mediate God's salvific blessings and
establish his reign on earth by means of the Spirit and his witnesses.[1] For Luke,
Jesus is, of course, also the Son of Man, the Isaianic servant, and the prophet
like Moses; but there can be little doubt that for Luke the centrality of Jesus as
the promised Davidic Messiah who enacts the kingdom of God occupies the
most critical role.[2] In what follows, I will set forth Jesus's messianic identity and
vocation by means of examining: (1) Jesus's birth in Luke's infancy narrative;
(2) Luke's depiction of Jesus as the Spirit-anointed Messiah who enacts God's
kingdom through healing and table fellowship; (3) Luke's use of the psalms
of David to portray Jesus as the righteous suffering Messiah; and (4) Jesus's
resurrection as his heavenly enthronement, whereby he continues to act to
establish and expand the kingdom of God.

---

1. The Gospel of Luke and the Acts of the Apostles certainly have their own literary
integrity and can be (and have been) read on their own terms with great profit. However,
I understand the book of Acts as a second volume that continues Luke's story of Jesus in
the Gospel of Luke.

2. See also Graham Stanton, "Messianism and Christology: Mark, Matthew, Luke and
Acts," in *Studies in Matthew and Early Christianity*, ed. Markus Bockmuehl and David
Lincicum, WUNT 309 (Tübingen: Mohr Siebeck, 2013), 247–56.

The Birth of the Messiah and the Hope of Israel

Jesus's Davidic messianic identity is established immediately in Luke's infancy narrative. Jesus is the agent who fulfills God's promises made to David for an everlasting kingdom; his earthly father and birthplace emphasize his Davidic lineage; he receives messianic honorifics such as Son of God, Messiah, Branch, Savior, and Lord; and he is tasked with establishing God's kingdom and delivering and saving his people from their enemies.

The Fulfillment of the Davidic Promises

The incredible amount of parallels between Luke's infancy narrative and 1 Samuel 1–2, centering especially upon the stories of the barren women and their messianic hymns (1 Sam 2:1–10; Luke 1:46–55), draw the reader's attention to both God's promises to Abraham (Gen 12–21), and the origins of the Davidic monarchy (1 Sam 1–2), thereby hinting at God's prophetic plan to finally restore the Davidic kingdom.[3] The establishment and renewal of this monarchy will take place against the backdrop of imperial Rome, as Luke ironically describes the lowly birth of the Messiah against the backdrop of Augustus's assertion of total sovereignty as exemplified in his census or registration of "the entire inhabited world" (repeated four times within Luke 2:1–7). Luke's repeated language throughout Luke 1:5–2:52 of Savior, Son of God, peace, gospel, and Lord to describe Jesus draws a contrast between Jesus the Davidic king and the rule of Augustus and Rome.[4]

Jesus will fulfill the promises God made to David through establishing an everlasting kingdom. This means that the kingdom of God, in Luke's Gospel, is the fulfillment of God's royal promises made to David. Mark Strauss highlights the significance of this point when he notes that "the first thing the narrator tells the reader about Jesus . . . is that *through him God will fulfill his promises to David.*"[5] In Gabriel's announcement of Jesus's birth to Mary, the angel declares: "he will be great, and he will be called a Son of the Most High (υἱὸς ὑψίστου), and the Lord God will give to him the throne (τὸν θρόνον) of David his father, and he will rule (βασιλεύσει) over the house of Jacob forever, and his kingdom

---

3. On the parallels between Luke 1–2 and 1 Samuel, see Sarah Harris, *The Davidic Shepherd King in the Lukan Narrative*, LNTS 558 (London: T&T Clark, 2016), 41–43; Joel B. Green, "The Problem of a Beginning: Israel's Scriptures in Luke 1–2," *BBR* 4 (1994): 61–85.

4. Harris, *The Davidic Shepherd King*, 69–79.

5. Mark L. Strauss, *The Davidic Messiah in Luke-Acts: The Promise and Its Fulfillment in Lukan Christology*, JSNTSup 110 (Sheffield: Sheffield Academic Press, 1995), 89.

(τῆς βασιλείας) will have no end" (Luke 1:32–33). As Raymond Brown has noted, there is nothing distinctively Christian in Gabriel's words except for the fact that the Davidic promises have been identified as in the process of being fulfilled through Jesus.[6] The terms *throne, reign,* and *kingdom* indicate that the central feature of Jesus's identity is that of Davidic kingship.[7] The promise that Jesus will receive the throne of David his father, his designation as God's Son, and the promise that Jesus will have an everlasting kingdom and rule echo God's covenant made with David in 2 Samuel 7:12–14. Here, God makes a promise to David that he will "raise up after you your seed, who will come from your body, and I will establish his kingdom" (7:12), that this kingdom will be established forever (7:13, 16), and that God will be a Father to him and he will be God's son (7:14).[8] When Mary asks how Gabriel's words will come to pass, the angel responds by promising her: "the Holy Spirit will come upon you and the power of the Most High will overshadow you, such that the begotten holy one will be called God's Son" (Luke 1:35). Jesus's divine sonship is thereby grounded in the work of the Spirit of God.[9] Despite the surprising relationship between the Spirit of God and Jesus's conception, the royal messianic connotations of Jesus's sonship could not be clearer. Richard Hays states it well: "The effect, then, of Gabriel's words is to kindle the reader's expectation that God's ancient promise to David will now find its fulfillment, despite the intervening years of exile, in an everlasting kingdom ruled by a king who is both son of David and son of the One who gave the promise."[10]

Jesus Born in the City of David

Luke emphasizes Jesus's Davidic lineage by noting that Mary is engaged to a man named Joseph, who is "from the house of David" (1:27). Furthermore,

---

6. Raymond Brown, *The Birth of the Messiah: A Commentary on the Infancy Narratives in the Gospels of Matthew and Luke,* AYBRL (New Haven: Yale University Press, 1999), 311.

7. See further Michael Wolter, *The Gospel according to Luke: Volume 1 (Luke 1–9:50),* trans. Wayne Coppins and Christoph Heilig (Waco, TX: Baylor University Press 2016), 80–81; Scott W. Hahn, *Kinship by Covenant: A Canonical Approach to the Fulfillment of God's Saving Promises,* AYBRL (New Haven: Yale University Press, 2009), 218.

8. The resonances with 2 Sam 7, 1 Chr 17, and Ps 2 are recognized by most interpreters. See J. R. Daniel Kirk, *A Man Attested by God: The Human Jesus of the Synoptic Gospels* (Grand Rapids: Eerdmans, 2016), 219.

9. Strauss, *The Davidic Messiah,* 93.

10. Richard B. Hays, *Echoes of Scripture in the Gospels* (Waco, TX: Baylor University Press, 2016), 195.

Luke notes twice that Jesus's birthplace of Bethlehem is "the city of David" (2:4, 11). While Matthew's Gospel makes this point explicit (Matt 2:6), Luke's twofold reference to Bethlehem as the city of David likely draws upon the prophetic promise of Micah 5:1, which foretells of Bethlehem as the location of the birth of Israel's messianic ruler.[11]

Messianic Titles

Luke draws upon well-known and scriptural messianic titles to portray Jesus as the Davidic king. Zechariah interprets the miraculous births of John the Baptist and Jesus the Messiah as the means whereby God has "raised up for us a horn of salvation in the house of David his servant, just as he spoke through the mouth of his holy prophets from of old" (1:69–70). The Davidic Messiah is the mighty warrior, the one who will deliver and redeem God's people from their enemies (1:71, 75).[12] The connection between God's promises to Abraham and David are clear in Zechariah's hymn, as he immediately proceeds to praise God for remembering the oath he made "to Abraham our father" (1:73; cf. 1:5–25). His song builds upon Mary's hymn which praises God for his merciful remembrance of his promises to Abraham (1:54–55) and creates a further link between Abraham and David.

Zechariah refers to Jesus as the "ἀνατολή from on high (ἐξ ὕψους) who will give light to those who sit in darkness and in the shadow of death, to guide our feet into the path of peace" (1:78–79). The term ἀνατολή has been translated in a variety of ways (e.g., "dayspring," "rising sun," "morning star"), but it almost certainly connotes the early Jewish title "Branch" for the coming Davidic messianic ruler.[13] Jeremiah, for example, declares God's promise to "raise up a righteous Branch for David. He will rule wisely as king and execute justice and righteousness in the land" (Jer 23:5; cf. Isa 11:1–5; Jer 33:15; Zech 3:8; 6:12; 4QFlor 1, 1:11). While the term echoes the messianic title "Branch," its connection to the messianic expectations for light and peace indicate that it should probably be translated as "light" or "rising sun."

When the angels appear to the shepherds to announce Jesus's birth as "good news for all the people" (2:10), they refer to him as the "Savior who is the

---

11. See Yuzuru Miura, *David in Luke-Acts: His Portrayal in the Light of Early Judaism*, WUNT 2.232 (Tübingen: Mohr Siebeck, 2007), 203.

12. In much more detail, see Strauss, *The Davidic Messiah*, 98–101.

13. Strauss, *The Davidic Messiah*, 102–3; Simon J. Gathercole, "The Heavenly ἀνατολή," *JTS* 56 (2005): 471–88.

Messiah, the Lord" (σωτὴρ ὅς ἐστιν χριστὸς κύριος, 2:11).[14] The language has a royal pedigree in the Old Testament (e.g., 1 Sam 16:6). Zechariah has already established a relationship between Jesus's Davidic identity and his task to provide salvation for God's people (1:69, 74). Here again we see that Jesus's saving activity for his people is a function of his Davidic kingship.[15] The connection here between "Messiah" and "Lord" indicates that the latter functions as a royal title for Jesus (cf. Luke 20:41–44; Acts 2:36). Yet as C. Kavin Rowe has noted, there is an intentional overlap in Luke's narrative between the God of Israel as Lord and Jesus as Lord, thereby creating a remarkably close relationship between the God of Israel and Jesus (see Luke 1:41–45; 2:11).[16] One might say that Jesus's messianic lordship embodies and implements the rule and lordship of the God of Israel. Luke uses the language again when he refers to the elder Simeon, described as one "waiting for the consolation of Israel" (2:25b), who had been promised that he would not die before he saw "the Messiah of the Lord" (τὸν χριστὸν κυρίου, 2:26). Simeon again identifies Jesus's messianic lordship as consisting in God's salvation (τὸ σωτήριόν σου, 2:30) for Israel and the nations (2:31–32).

THE SPIRIT-ANOINTED MESSIAH ENACTS THE KINGDOM OF GOD

John's baptism of the people in the Jordan River and his call to the people to prepare themselves for God's coming (3:1–14) elicit messianic speculation as to whether John himself "might be the Messiah" (μήποτε αὐτὸς εἴη ὁ χριστός, 3:15). John emphatically denies that he is the Messiah and redirects the attention of the people to a coming messianic figure who will act as the eschatological judge and will baptize them "by the Holy Spirit and fire" (3:16).

Messiah and Spirit

The divine voice from heaven at Jesus's baptism which declares "you are my beloved Son, in whom I am well-pleased" (3:22b) echoes the words of Gabriel to Mary who twice declared that her son would be called the Son of God (1:32, 35) in fulfillment of the promises made to David. Thus, we rightly hear the word-

14. The association of shepherds and Bethlehem may function to subtly draw the reader's attention to the story of David. See Harris, *The Davidic Shepherd King*, 64–67.

15. So Kirk, *A Man Attested by God*, 395–96.

16. C. Kavin Rowe, *Early Narrative Christology: The Lord in the Gospel of Luke* (Grand Rapids: Baker Academic, 2009), 39–45.

ing of the divine pronouncement as drawing upon the language of Psalm 2:7: "you are my son (υἱός μου εἶ σύ); today I have become your Father."[17] Both Psalm 2 and Luke 3:21–22 depict scenes of messianic anointing whereby the royal Son of God is commissioned as God's ruler to enact his kingdom and rule on earth. This is not to deny that the voice from heaven also alludes to Isaiah 42:1 ("with you I am pleased"). Luke draws upon Isaiah's Servant Songs to provide something of a blueprint for his Gospel, not least for his articulation of Jesus's identity, and yet Luke's primary category for articulating Jesus's identity stems from his understanding of Jesus as the royal Messiah.[18]

The anointing of the Messiah takes place by means of the Holy Spirit, who descends upon Jesus while he is praying (3:21–22a). Thus, both John's prophetic anticipation (3:16–17) and the Father's commission of the Son for messianic service at his baptism (3:21–22) anticipate a flurry of references to Jesus's empowerment by the Spirit to withstand the temptations of the devil (4:1–14). Thus, Jesus is "full of the Holy Spirit" (4:1a), "led into the wilderness by the Spirit" (4:1b), and returns from the wilderness to Galilee "in the power of the Spirit" (4:14). The Spirit empowers Jesus in each of the devil's attempts to tempt Jesus by appealing to his identity as the Son of God ("if you are the Son of God," 4:3, 9) as the basis for using power for personal gratification and self-exaltation. In the second temptation, the devil shows Jesus "all the kingdoms of the inhabited world" and promises to give "all this authority to you along with their glory" if Jesus will offer worship to him (4:5–7). One can see here the devil parodying the offer of authority, the royal throne of David, and the kingship promised to Jesus by his own Father from Psalm 2 (cf. Luke 1:32–35). Through the power of the Spirit, however, Jesus remains obedient to his Father as he embodies faithfulness to his Father in using his power and authority only for the purpose of his messianic commission.

After his successful battle against the devil, Jesus enters a synagogue in his hometown of Nazareth and reads from the scroll of Isaiah, particularly Isaiah 61:1 and 58:6: "The Spirit of the Lord is upon me, because he has anointed me to proclaim good news to the poor; he has sent me to preach release for the captives and to open the eyes of the blind, to give release to the oppressed, and to proclaim the year of the Lord's welcome" (4:18–19). While a variety of figures and individuals are anointed in Israel's Scriptures, including priests and prophets, in the context of Luke's Gospel, where the Spirit anoints Jesus as the Son of God (3:21–22) and is responsible for the conception of Jesus as the one

17. See Joel B. Green, *The Gospel of Luke*, NIGTC (Grand Rapids: Eerdmans, 1997), 186; Wolter, *The Gospel according to Luke*, 177.

18. See especially David W. Pao, *Acts and the Isaianic New Exodus*, WUNT 2.130 (Tübingen: Mohr Siebeck, 2000).

who will sit on the throne of David ruling over the house of Jacob (1:31–35), Jesus's declaration of Spirit-anointment must be seen as a messianic claim. Outside of Isaiah 61, it is only the king (not priests or prophets) who is spoken of as both anointed and bearing the Spirit.[19] Israel's Scriptures often portray Israel's king as sacred and holy as a result of bearing God's Spirit (e.g., 1 Sam 24:6; LXX Ps 88:21–29). The human king enacts God's rule on earth precisely by means of his anointment and empowerment with the Holy Spirit (1 Sam 10:1–13; 16:13; Isa 11:1–2; Pss. Sol. 17:22, 37; 18:5–7).[20]

One of the primary tasks of Israel's kings was enacting justice and righteousness for his people, and this justice was to reflect God's righteous rule over the entire world (e.g., 2 Sam 8:15; 1 Kgs 3:16–28; 10:9; Isa 11:1–5; Jer 23:5–6; 33:14–16).[21] Jesus's messianic vocation, empowered as it is by means of God's Spirit, will take place through the concrete actions of proclamation of good news to the poor, liberation and release for the oppressed, and opening the eyes of the blind (4:18–19). This vocation has obvious similarities to the task set forth for Jesus in the infancy narrative where he is referred to as Savior, providing liberation and rescue and enacting peace for God's people. All of these activities bear close resemblances to royal attributes of good kings.[22] Luke merges what scholars have often separated in discussing Luke's Christology; in other words, Luke does not shift back and forth between a royal and prophetic Christology. Rather, he understands Jesus as the royal, Davidic Messiah who, as the Lord's anointed, fulfills the role of the Isaianic servant.[23]

Messiah and Healing

As in Mark's Gospel, so in Luke's Gospel Jesus is portrayed as enacting the kingdom of God through battle against Satan and the demonic (e.g., 4:31–37, 40–41; 8:26–39), healing the sick and the diseased (e.g., 4:38–39; 5:12–26;

19. Strauss, *The Davidic Messiah*, 230.

20. See further Aubrey Johnson, *Sacral Kingship in Ancient Israel* (Cardiff: University of Wales Press, 1967), 114–15.

21. See the classic works of Moshe Weinfeld, *Social Justice in Ancient Israel and in the Ancient Near East* (Minneapolis: Fortress, 1995); Keith W. Whitelam, *The Just King: Monarchical Judicial Authority in Ancient Israel*, JSOTSup 12 (Sheffield: Sheffield Academic Press, 1979).

22. Stated well by Strauss, *The Davidic Messiah*, 233: "While some of these features are not exclusively royal, they are all qualities associated with kingship."

23. The similarities between the Davidic ruler in Isa 1–39 and the Servant of the Lord in Isa 40–55 are extensive. For a helpful analysis of the relationship, see Andrew T. Abernethy, *The Book of Isaiah and God's Kingdom: A Thematic-Theological Approach*, NSBT 40 (Downers Grove, IL: InterVarsity Press, 2016), 138–42. See further Strauss, *The Davidic Messiah*, 244–49.

10:9–11; 13:11–17), and proclaiming the good news of the kingdom of God (4:42–44; 6:20–23). Luke's healing narratives exemplify how Jesus's healings are enactments of release and liberation from satanic/demonic oppression and into *shalom*—peace, freedom, and life as intended by God. Jesus's messianic vocation is enacted, then, through his life-giving healings and exorcisms.

For example, in the story of the Gerasene demoniac (Luke 8), the man is initially described as "one who had demons" (v. 27) and later as "the man from whom the demons had gone" (vv. 28, 33, 36, 38). The man's fundamental characteristic is one who is in bondage and oppression to demonic power (4:18–19). The picture is that of a totally dehumanized person, driven out of society (house and city) and forced to live in the abode of the dead. He is literally "shackled in chains and bonds" (v. 29) and lives among the tombs as one who is essentially dead (v. 27). Jesus's healing of the man results in a point-by-point overturning of the man's prior condition: (1) he had many demons (v. 27)//demons gone from the man (v. 35); (2) he had worn no clothes (v. 27)//he was clothed (v. 35); (3) he did not live in a house but among tombs (v. 27)//told to return to his own home (v. 39); (4) he was out of control (v. 29)//he was in his right mind (v. 35).

The story of the healing of the bent woman demonstrates most obviously that Jesus's healings are enactments of liberating release from the power of Satan (13:10–17). This is why the story is filled with language of "binding and loosing" (You have been set free, v. 12; each of you frees his cow/donkey, v. 15; the woman is set free from the bonds of Satan, v. 16.) Her affliction is due to "having an unclean spirit" (v. 11). Jesus asks, "ought not this daughter of Abraham, whom Satan has oppressed for eighteen years, must she not be set free from this bondage on the Sabbath?" (v. 16). Her healing, then, is a form of release which signifies wholeness and freedom from diabolic and social oppression. Further, note Jesus's word of inclusion to her when he refers to her as "this daughter of Abraham."

The healing ministry of Jesus continues in the early church, as evidenced by the book of Acts. Peter's Pentecost speech is significant here, as it both provides explicit evidence that Jesus was remembered as one "attested by God among you through powerful acts, wonders, and signs which God did among you" (2:22) and indicates that God's Spirit will continue to act among the church with signs and wonders (2:19; cf. 2:43).[24] Peter's healing of the lame man at the temple gate (Acts 3:1–10) and Paul's healing of the lame man in Lystra (14:8–10)

---

24. The apostles are portrayed as engaging in healing in 3:1–8; 5:12–16; 6:8; 8:6–7; 9:17–18, 32–54; 14:3, 8–10; 15:12; 16:16–18; 19:11–12; 20:7–12; 28:7–9.

are clearly patterned after Jesus's healings (esp. Luke 5:17–26). Furthermore, they are performed through praying to Jesus, and in the name of Jesus. The obvious conclusion is that Jesus's apostles continue what Jesus himself had done, but now through the power of the risen and heavenly enthroned king (this is explicit in 3:12–16).[25] The Messiah's healings, then, are a form of release and welcome that liberates humans from bondage and oppression, restores them to proper physical and social engagement, and flows from Jesus's compassion for human suffering and vulnerability.

Messiah and Table Fellowship

Jesus further enacts the justice and peace of the kingdom of God through shared hospitality and table fellowship with the poor, the lost, and the outcast.[26] Israel's Scriptures often refer to a coming time when God and/or God's Messiah will inaugurate the kingdom and will make known God's presence in full measure to his people. For example, Isaiah speaks of God preparing "for all peoples a feast of rich food, a feast of well-aged wines, of rich food filled with marrow, of well-aged wines strained clear" (Isa 25:6). God will defeat death and remove the pain and disgrace of his people, with the result that the people declare: "This is our God. We have waited for him that he might save us. This is the Lord for whom we have waited. Let us be glad and rejoice in his salvation" (Isa 25:9). Later, Isaiah invites God's people to come and drink God's provisions of good wine and milk, and to eat God's provisions of choice food, as manifestations of God's fulfillment of the promises he made to David (Isa 55:1–3).[27] The prophet Ezekiel anticipates a day when God will act to save his people by raising up a Davidic king who will save God's people and shepherd them with justice and righteousness (Ezek 34). This Davidic shepherd will provide the nourishment, food, and peace that God's flock needs to live well (Ezek 34:23–31). In Psalm 23 David himself testifies to God's extension of hospitality to him and his life-giving sustenance (esp. Ps 23:5–6).

God's promise to provide peace, salvation, and his own presence to his people through food and banqueting is the critical context for understanding Jesus's messianic vocation of sharing God's saving hospitality with his people in the Gospel of Luke. Jesus's frequent meals are all anticipations of the

---

25. See Jan-Olav Henriksen and Karl Olav Sandnes, *Jesus as Healer: A Gospel for the Body* (Grand Rapids: Eerdmans, 2016), 86–91.

26. I have written on this in more detail in *Saved by Faith and Hospitality* (Grand Rapids: Eerdmans, 2017), 19–31.

27. See further Isa 49:9–10; 62:8–9; 65:13–18; Amos 9:13–15; Zech 8:19–23.

final messianic banquet (most obviously Luke 9:11–17; 22:14–30; 24:28–35).[28] Thus, the tax collector Levi's response of throwing a great banquet for Jesus is interpreted as a sign that Levi's relationship with God has been restored (Luke 5:29, 31–32). The so-called sinful woman shows great hospitality to Jesus, interpreted as a sign of her great love for Jesus, in response to Jesus's offer of forgiveness of sins, peace, and welcome into the people of God (7:36–50). Jesus exhorts Zacchaeus the tax collector: "I must receive hospitality in your house today" (19:5). And this shared hospitality between the Messiah and Zacchaeus results in the latter's salvation: "Today salvation has come to this house" (19:9). The recipients of Jesus's table fellowship are surprising. Jesus extends God's saving welcome to tax collectors (Luke 5:27–32; 19:1–10), women (7:36–50; 10:38–42), the poor crowds (9:11–17), and his disciples (22:15–20). Jesus's famous parables of the lost sheep, lost coin, and lost son (15:3–32) are told in response to the Pharisees and scribes who are grumbling and complaining that Jesus eats with and extends hospitality to sinners (15:1–2). The recovery of the lost sheep, coin, and son symbolize Jesus's ministry of table fellowship with sinners as his form of seeking and saving the lost (19:10; cf. 15:4–7, 24, 32).[29] Jesus is enacting the role of the Davidic shepherd in Ezekiel who searches for his lost sheep, saves them, and shepherds the flock with justice and peace (see Ezek 34:11–16).[30]

Peter's confession of Jesus as the Messiah of the Lord occurs, in fact, within the context of his having witnessed Jesus enacting his role as the divine host to the crowd of five thousand near Bethsaida (9:10–17). Luke notes that Jesus "welcomed" the crowd, proclaimed to them "the kingdom of God," and "healed those in need of healing" (9:11). He then made them recline (9:14–15) and "took the five loaves and two fish; he looked into heaven and blessed them and broke and distributed the food to his disciples to set before the crowd" (9:16). And "all of them ate and were satisfied" (9:17a). Again, the context for Jesus's extension of hospitality to the crowd occurs within Jesus's proclamation of God's kingdom (9:11) and Peter's recognition that Jesus is "the Messiah of God" (τὸν χριστὸν τοῦ θεοῦ, 9:20). Jesus's ominous warning concerning his impending death, however, hints that Jesus's hospitality and provision of meals

---

28. See especially Eugene LaVerdiere, *Dining in the Kingdom of God: The Origins of the Eucharist in the Gospel of Luke* (Chicago: Liturgy Training, 1994).

29. On Luke 15 and Jesus as embodying the qualities of the Davidic shepherd-king in Ezek 34, see Harris, *The Davidic Shepherd King*, 92–105.

30. In the immediately preceding pericope the blind man confesses Jesus to be "the son of David" (Luke 18:38–39), further highlighting Jesus here as the Davidic messianic shepherd. See, Harris, *The Davidic Shepherd King*, 119–20.

anticipate both present feasting *upon* and eschatological feasting *with* Jesus in the kingdom of God. Jesus's feeding of the five thousand in Luke 9:11–17 obviously anticipates Jesus's final meal with his disciples right before his death in Luke 22:15–20. Jesus again is the host who reclines together with his apostles (22:14b) and acts as the host who "gives to them" the bread which is "my body given for you" (22:19; cf. 9:16). He serves them the wine "of the new covenant in my blood poured out for you" (22:20b).

Jesus then confers upon his disciples the very kingdom that he had enacted through his hospitality and table fellowship practices: "I confer upon you [the kingdom] just as my Father has conferred the kingdom (βασιλείαν) upon me, so that you may eat and drink at my table in my kingdom (ἐπὶ τῆς τραπέζης μου ἐν τῇ βασιλείᾳ μου) and you will sit on the thrones (ἐπὶ θρόνων) of the twelve tribes ruling Israel" (22:29–30; see also 12:32). The language of "kingdom," "thrones," and "ruling" recalls Gabriel's prophecy that God would fulfill the promises made to David through Jesus the Messiah. In association with the emphasis on the number twelve, Jesus's commission resonates with Jewish associations of the twelve princes of the tribes of Israel who are often connected to well-known Israelite rulers (e.g., Moses, David, and Solomon).[31] Further, the context of Passover and the scriptural associations between Israel's kings and the celebration of the (eschatological) Passover function to portray Jesus and his messianic community as celebrating God's restoration of the Davidic kingdom (see 2 Chr 30:1–8; 35:16–18; Ezek 45:21–23).[32] Jesus's kingdom has been enacted by means of his shared hospitality and table fellowship, and now the apostles are called upon to continue to extend God's kingdom by eating and drinking at the Messiah's "table." Jesus provides the disciples with a reminder of the specific character of these messianic meals as opportunities for embodying Jesus's specific practices of service, humility, and inclusion rather than, as Scott Hahn says, the "hierarchy of domination and pride characteristic of the kingdoms of this world" (see Luke 22:24–27). The continuation of the presence of the risen Messiah through food, hospitality, and fellowship is made clear in Luke 24:28–35, where Jesus is "made known in the breaking of the bread" (24:30, 35). As Hahn has said, Jesus "establishes the Apostles as vice-regents of the Davidic kingdom . . . , empowering them to rule over the church in the opening chapters of Acts."[33]

---

31. For more detail, see William Horbury, "The Twelve and the Phylarchs," in *Messianism among Jews and Christians: Biblical and Historical Studies*, 2nd ed. (London: T&T Clark, 2016), 212–16.

32. Brant Pitre, *Jesus and the Last Supper* (Grand Rapids: Eerdmans, 2015), 382–84.

33. Hahn, *Kinship by Covenant*, 226.

And this is exactly what we see in Acts 1–6, where the messianic kingdom and the presence of the risen Messiah continue through the sharing of meals, provisions of food, and imitation of Jesus's hospitality practices.[34] One should not underestimate the significance of the opening of Acts where Luke portrays Jesus as proclaiming "the kingdom of God" and "eating together" (συναλιζόμενος) with the disciples as they are instructed to wait in Jerusalem for the promise from the Father (1:4). Here we have the constellation of the themes so central to Luke's depiction of Jesus's messianic identity—namely, the kingdom, the Spirit, and table fellowship. Thus, it is no surprise that one of the core practices of the early church is breaking bread and enjoying table fellowship in each other's homes (2:42, 46). The practice recalls Jesus's meals and hospitality as the means of extending his revelatory presence with his people, and the tangible presence of the Messiah is noted by Luke in that the people are rejoicing, praising God, and having a sense of awe (2:46–47). Further, the sharing of food and possessions with one another mirrors Jesus's activities as host to the hungry (Luke 9:11–17) who provides hospitality to all people (15:1–2). The indiscriminate sharing of food and rejection of possessions as a means of pursuing power and status, seen for example in Barnabas's selling his field for the church (Acts 4:36–37), implements Jesus's commands to share wealth and extend hospitality to all people (e.g., Luke 6:27–38; 14:12–24; 22:24–47). Further, the frequent language of "fellowship" (2:42), "sharing all things in common" (2:44; 4:32), and "one heart and soul" portray the church as a community of friends that has implemented the ethics of the Messiah in their extension of hospitality to one another.[35]

The Suffering Righteous King

We have already seen briefly that Jesus's messiahship, gifted to him by God, is of a different order than the authority and kingdoms of the world offered to Jesus by Satan (4:1–13). Jesus's response of obedience and faithfulness as the true Son of God (4:3, 9) fends off the attacks of the devil, who leaves Jesus "for a time" (4:13). In his moment of temptation to turn his back on his messianic vocation, Jesus offers his own body as the Passover offering (22:14–20),

---

34. Hahn, *Kinship by Covenant*, 221.

35. See here especially Douglas A. Hume, *The Early Christian Community: A Narrative Analysis of Acts 2:41–47 and 4:32–35*, WUNT 2.298 (Tübingen: Mohr Siebeck, 2011); Alan C. Mitchell, "The Social Function of Friendship in Acts 2:44–47 and 4:32–37," *JBL* 111 (1992): 255–72.

prays for Peter's faith (22:31–34), and remains faithful and steadfast in prayer (22:39–46). But in the scribes and priests' quests to destroy Jesus (22:1), Satan comes onto the scene again as he enters into Judas who, in collaboration with the priests and temple officials, begins to look "for a good time" to betray Jesus (22:3–6). Jesus interprets their murderous actions as the embodiment of the kingdom of Satan against the innocent and righteous: "This is your hour and the dominion of darkness" (22:53). Thus, Luke positions the ensuing death of Jesus as a conflict between the faithful, righteous messianic king and the satanic kingdom of darkness. Luke is able to show Jesus following the script and pattern of the righteous king as he consistently draws upon royal messianic psalms to interpret Jesus's conflict with his enemies.

The Rejected but Vindicated Stone of Psalm 118

As we have briefly noted already, however, Jesus's messianic vocation is not welcomed by many of Israel's religious leaders, and Jesus warns them of the consequences of rejecting his mission and person. Jesus frequently draws upon the royal Psalm 118 to warn Israel's leaders of the massive consequences and futility of failing to welcome Jesus as the King of Israel.[36] Psalm 118 depicts Israel gathered together as a sacred assembly celebrating God's faithfulness to the king (vv. 1–4). God has answered the king's prayer for salvation and rescue from his enemies (vv. 5–6, 10–18), and he thereby calls upon Israel to trust in and take refuge in the Lord (vv. 7–9). The speaker of the psalm proclaims: "I will not die, but I will live" (v. 17a), thereby testifying to God's accomplishment of salvation on the king's behalf. As a result, the king makes his way into the sanctuary: "Open the gates of righteousness for me; I will enter through them and give thanks to the Lord. This is the Lord's gate; the righteous will enter through it. I will give thanks to you because you have answered me and have become my salvation" (vv. 19–21). The king is the stone, seemingly rejected but now enthroned and "glorified as the main stone in the structure of God's society."[37] This enthroned king, recipient of God's salvation, is now established and identified with the very name of the Lord, and he receives the praise of the people from the Lord's house (v. 26).

Luke portrays Jesus as engaging in a similar but surprising experience,

---

36. I have learned much and been influenced by J. Ross Wagner, "Psalm 118 in Luke-Acts: Tracing a Narrative Thread," in *Early Christian Interpretation of the Scriptures of Israel: Investigations and Proposals*, ed. C. A. Evans and J. A. Sanders, SSEJC (Sheffield: Sheffield Academic Press, 1997), 154–78.

37. John H. Eaton, *Kingship and the Psalms*, SBT 32 (London: SCM, 1976), 62.

acting the part of the king in Psalm 118. Thus, in Luke 13:31–35 Jesus, on his journey to Jerusalem (e.g., 9:51–56), laments over Jerusalem as the city that stones and rejects the prophets (13:34). He warns the leaders of the consequences of rejecting him: "Behold, your house is left to you. I say to you that you will not see me until you say, 'blessed is he who comes in the name of the Lord'" (13:35). Here Jesus warns the people that if they reject their messianic king, the so-called "Lord of the house," if they refuse to bless him as he makes his way to the temple in Jerusalem, then God's presence will in turn abandon the temple (e.g., Jer 7:8–15; 22:5). Jesus's warning is fulfilled in 19:28–40 as Jesus enters Jerusalem as Israel's messianic Lord (19:31, 33; cf. 2:11). It is significant that some in the crowd rejoice and praise God, drawing upon Psalm 118:26: "Blessed is the one who comes, the King (ὁ βασιλεύς), in the name of the Lord" (Luke 19:38). The language of kingship and lordship draws the reader back again to the messianic destiny and vocation marked out for Jesus in Luke 1–2, particularly the promise that Jesus would reign forever as the Davidic king.[38] And Luke's addition of "the King" makes it clear that "the coming one" (see also Luke 7:19–20; cf. 4:18–19) is a messianic term. The people's cry draws upon Jesus's promise in 13:35 ("you will not see me until you say 'blessed is he who comes in the name of the Lord'") and marks them as those who rightly see Jesus's entrance into Jerusalem as the messianic Lord's coming to his city. But, of course, it is notable that within the scene there are no priests, scribes, or temple leaders; the Pharisees, in fact, demand that the Messiah silence those who recognize him to be the Messiah (19:39).[39] Thus, as Jesus enters the city he weeps and laments that the people have not welcomed him as its Messiah and Lord; his offer of peace, a peace which is part and parcel of his messianic vocation (e.g., Luke 1:79; 2:14; 7:50; 8:48; 10:5–8), will be traded for violence, ultimately culminating in the destruction of the temple (19:41–44). Jesus is indeed the messianic king of Psalm 118, the king who comes in the name of the Lord, and God's chief cornerstone. But the ominous note of Psalm 118—that the builders will reject God's stone—is played out as the temple leaders reject his vocation of peace and the temple itself is found to be "a den of robbers" (19:46). In Jesus's telling of the parable of the vineyard (20:8–18), he makes it clear to all who listen that the temple leaders are the usurpers who are playing the role of "the builders" who reject God's beloved Son (20:13), the now rejected stone, who will be vindicated by God and made to be the chief cornerstone of God's

38. Strauss, *The Davidic Messiah*, 316.
39. See especially Brent Kinman, "Parousia, Jesus' 'A-Triumphal' Entry, and the Fate of Jerusalem (Luke 19:28–44)," *JBL* 118 (1999): 279–94.

temple and kingdom (20:17). Jesus warns that those who stumble and fall over this stone will be broken and shattered (20:18); as a result, the scribes and the chief priests begin to look for opportunities to kill him (20:19).

The Psalms of David and the Suffering and Death of the Messianic King

In Luke's account of the death of Jesus, the Messiah's sufferings and death are the very means whereby Jesus enters into his messianic coronation.[40] Thus, Jesus's opponents ironically give voice to the connection between Jesus's messiahship and his sufferings when they say: (1) "Let him save himself if he is the Messiah, the chosen one of God" (23:35b); (2) "Save yourself if you are the King of the Jews" (23:37); and (3) "Are you not the Messiah? Save yourself and us" (23:39b). The epitaph on Pilate's placard likewise reads: "this one is the King of the Jews" (23:38b). The mockery of the Jewish leaders, the Roman soldiers, and the criminal all find their home in the reviling words of the enemies of the Davidic king of the Psalter. Luke's patterning Jesus's crucifixion against the background of these psalms of David demonstrates that Jesus's messianic vocation is not simply compatible with his sufferings and crucifixion, but is actually at the heart of his kingship.[41]

It is striking that within the span of thirteen verses (Luke 23:34–46) Luke peppers his passion narrative not only with an abundance of royal imagery but also with frequent quotations of and allusions to explicit Davidic psalms.[42] The psalms function as Luke's premier intertext whereby the voice of David is transposed onto the suffering Messiah.

1. Psalm 22. In Luke 23:34b, Luke draws upon Psalm 22:18 (LXX 21:19) to describe the persecutors' mockery of Jesus as they "distributed his garments and cast lots." Luke further uses a rare word (ἐξεμυκτήριζον)

---

40. I have written on this in more detail in "Luke's Scriptural Suffering Messiah: A Search for Precedent, a Search for Identity," *CBQ* 72 (2010): 255–74.

41. Helpful here is John T. Carroll, "Luke's Crucifixion Scene," in *Reimagining the Death of the Lukan Jesus,* ed. Dennis D. Sylva, Athenäums Monografien, Theologie 73 (Frankfurt am Main: Anton Hain, 1990), 114–15.

42. See also the helpful set of essays by Peter Doble: "The Psalms in Luke-Acts," in *The Psalms in the New Testament,* ed. Steve Moyise and Maarten J. J. Menken, The New Testament and the Scriptures of Israel (London: T&T Clark, 2004), 83–119; Doble, "Luke 24.26, 44—Songs of God's Servant: David and His Psalms in Luke-Acts," *JSNT* 28 (2006): 267–83.

to describe the mocking speech of the persecutors, a word likely drawn from Psalm 22:7 (LXX 21:8).

2. Psalm 89. In Luke 23:35 the rulers say, "He saved others, let him save himself if indeed he is the Messiah of God, the chosen one." This evokes Psalm 89:19–20 (LXX 88:20–21), where the Messiah is referred to as "my chosen one from the people" and "David my servant . . . I have anointed him."

3. Psalm 69. In Luke 23:36 the soldiers mock Jesus's kingship as they offer him sour wine, just as King David had experienced: "They gave me gall for my food, and for my thirst they gave me vinegar to drink" (Ps 69:21; LXX 68:22).

4. Psalm 31. Jesus's last breath gives voice to the very words of David, a near direct quotation of Psalm 31:5 (LXX 30:6): "Into your hands I commit my spirit" (Luke 23:46). One could not ask for a clearer indication that Jesus's crucifixion is being made to conform to the sufferings of the righteous king in the Psalter. The psalm on which Jesus draws is a paradigmatic psalm of hope and confidence in God that despite his sufferings he will be rescued by God.

5. Psalm 38. Luke notes that after Jesus's final breath, his friends and companions were far from him at his death (Luke 23:49a), and this resonates with Psalm 38:11 (LXX 37:12), where the king laments: "my companions stood at a distance."

When the reader reaches the statement of the Roman centurion—"truly this man was righteous (δίκαιος)," Luke 23:47b—the conclusion becomes inescapable that Luke is portraying Jesus as the psalms' righteous, royal sufferer. Given the fact that Luke has just quoted Psalm 31, the psalm that portrays the sufferer as δίκαιος (31:18; LXX 30:19), it becomes increasingly likely that the centurion is unwittingly identifying Jesus as the righteous, royal sufferer of the psalms. The sufferings of the righteous king in Psalm 31 match well the sufferings of Jesus: both figures are verbally mocked and persecuted, the friends of both stand at a distance, and each one's murder is premeditated by his enemies. Luke emphasizes throughout both volumes that Jesus is righteous and without fault (see Luke 23:4, 14–15, 41, 47; Acts 3:14; 7:52; 22:14). Luke's decision to delete Mark's "truly this man was the Son of God" (Mark 15:39b) and replace it with δίκαιος suggests that the Davidic psalms are Luke's intertext. It is the Psalter, after all, that begins with an *inclusio* whereby the "righteous" are blessed in opposition to the wicked scoffers who persecute God's anointed (compare Ps 1:5–6 with Ps 2:11). Scholars have long noted that Psalms 1–2 function as a preface to the Psalter, thereby introducing a hermeneutic to the whole work.[43] As Psalm 1 indicates, one of the major motifs of the Psalter is the opposition between the righteous and the wicked. The word "righteous" (δίκαιος) itself appears over fifty times throughout the Psalter. Psalm 2 attaches a royal messianic interpretation to the righteous/wicked contrast. Thus, in Luke 23:46, Jesus, the Anointed One, speaks the words of David, the anointed one from Psalm 31:5 (LXX 30:6), entrusting himself in hope to his Father. One verse later (v. 47), the royal centurion testifies from the language of the Psalter that this Jesus is the messianic righteous sufferer.

The Resurrected and Enthroned Messiah in the Acts of the Apostles

The Acts of the Apostles narrates how Jesus the Messiah continues to establish his saving reign over his people, but now as the resurrected king enthroned in heaven. His kingdom is mediated through the Spirit, who is poured out upon his kingdom people from his new heavenly location and through his witnesses who participate in the expansion of his rule. The messianic identity and vocation of Jesus continues in the Acts of the Apostles, where the basic early confession of the movement is "Jesus is the Messiah" (Acts 2:36; 5:42; 9:22; 17:3; 18:5, 28) and/ or "Jesus is the Son of God" (Acts 9:20). God's saving activities are mediated through the *name* of the Messiah. Thus, Peter calls people to be baptized "in the name of Jesus the Messiah" (2:38); the Holy Spirit is mediated through the name of Jesus Christ (Acts 2:28–39; 10:46–48); Philip proclaims the good news concerning the kingdom of God and the name of Jesus the Messiah (8:12); healing occurs through the name of Jesus the Messiah (Acts 3:6; 9:34); and the power of the demonic is defeated through the name of Jesus the Messiah (16:18).[44]

The Kingdom of God and the Messiah's Resurrection and Ascension in Acts

Luke summarizes the content of the risen Jesus's forty-day proclamation to his disciples with the familiar language of "the kingdom of God" (1:3b).[45] The

43. For example, see James L. Mays, "'In a Vision': The Portrayal of the Messiah in the Psalms," *Ex auditu* 7 (1991): 2–3.

44. See here Michael F. Bird, *Jesus Is the Christ: The Messianic Testimony of the Gospels* (Downers Grove, IL: InterVarsity Press, 2012), 90.

45. I have written on this in more detail in my *Reading Acts*, Cascade Companions (Eu-

disciples, too, question Jesus about the timing of the restoration of "the kingdom to Israel" (1:6b). And the language of God's kingdom occurs at important moments within the narrative in order to summarize the content of the proclamation of Christ's witnesses (see Acts 8:12; 14:22; 19:8, 20:25; 28:23, 31). We have seen, of course, that Luke's Jesus—the one who had received the promise that he would sit on David's throne and rule God's people forever—repeatedly spoke of God's kingdom (Luke 1:31–35; also 4:43; 6:20; 8:10; 9:2, 11, 27). This suggests that readers of Acts are intended to understand the content of the book as narrating "what the kingdom of God looks like now that Jesus has come, announced the arrival of the kingdom, died, risen and ascended to the right hand of the Father."[46] Luke connects Jesus's proclamation of God's kingdom (Acts 1:3b) to his command to stay in Jerusalem and "to wait for the promise of the Father which you heard from me" (1:4b). The language recalls Luke 24:49 where Jesus declares that *he* will send the promise of the Father in order to clothe his witnesses with heavenly power. What Jesus sends and what the Father has promised is explicitly spoken of in 1:5b and 1:8a—namely, the Holy Spirit who will empower the witnesses for their mission.

In Acts 1:9–11 Luke depicts Jesus's ascension, and the fourfold repetition of the phrase "into heaven" (εἰς τὸν οὐρανόν) emphasizes Jesus's spatial location from which he rules. Luke's frequent and programmatic use of royal psalms presents Jesus's ascension as the event whereby Israel's Messiah is enthroned in heaven and enters into a more powerful rule through which he inaugurates and establishes the kingdom of God.[47] At the ascension, God completes the process of exalting his Son by enthroning him to a position of heavenly rule from where the messianic king reigns over his people, judges his enemies, and extends the sphere of his dominion. As such, Luke's depiction of Jesus's ascension as the event whereby the Messiah enters into his heavenly rule has literary significance beyond the description of the actual event, as Jesus is seen as continuing to enact his kingship and establish God's kingdom from heaven. While Luke is clear that from Jesus's birth he is Messiah, Son of God, and Lord, it is not until Jesus's resurrection and ascension in Acts 1:9–11 that

---

gene, OR: Cascade, 2018); also in "'For David Did Not Ascend into Heaven . . .' (Acts 2:34a): Reprogramming Royal Psalms to Proclaim the Enthroned-in-Heaven King," in *Ascent into Heaven in Luke-Acts: New Explorations of Luke's Narrative Hinge*, ed. David K. Bryan and David W. Pao (Minneapolis: Fortress, 2016), 41–59.

46. Alan J. Thompson, *The Acts of the Risen Lord Jesus: Luke's Account of God's Unfolding Plan*, NSBT 27 (Downers Grove, IL: InterVarsity Press, 2011), 47.

47. Similarly, see Luke Timothy Johnson, *The Acts of the Apostles*, SP 5 (Collegeville, MN: Liturgical Press, 1992), 30.

he is enthroned to a position of universal power and actively establishes God's kingdom (cf. 1:8). The meaning and central significance of Jesus's ascension to heaven is articulated in three major speeches in Acts.

The Resurrected Davidic King Reigns from Heaven Forever: Peter in Acts 2:22–36

Peter's speech immediately draws upon the Psalter to demonstrate the inability of death to keep Jesus underneath its power, when it refers to God as the one who "raised [Jesus] by loosing <u>the birth pangs of death</u>" (2:24). The underlined phrase almost certainly stems from Psalm 17:5 (LXX), where "David" cries to God and trusts God to rescue him out of the pangs of death and exalt him over his enemies (17:49–50).[48] The psalm concludes with the summary: "[God] gives great victories to his king. He shows loyalty to his Messiah, to David and his seed forever" (Ps 17:51 LXX).

In Acts 2:22–36, however, Peter declares that while David is the speaker of the Psalms, David is not their referent or subject matter; rather, David spoke in the Psalms as a prophet (2:30) who looked forward to the Messiah's resurrection and exaltation into heaven (2:31–33).[49] More precisely, as Matthew Bates has argued, "David was not merely speaking *about* him, but rather this yet-to-be-revealed Jesus was making an in-character speech at the time of David *through David*."[50] Peter justifies this reading by exploiting the fact that David is dead and buried and his tomb is accessible to the public in Jerusalem (2:29), but the Psalms (specifically Ps 15 LXX) speak of a figure who is always joyfully living in God's presence, whose body will not experience decay, who will never be abandoned to Hades, and who continues to experience the ways of life.[51] Thus, in Acts 2:31b Peter declares that it is the resurrected Messiah who is the referent of Psalm 15:9–10 (LXX) and who "has neither been abandoned into Hades nor has his flesh seen corruption."

Peter's most creative interpretive move in his sermon—though one that is

---

48. Strauss, *The Davidic Messiah*, 136–37.

49. For the way in which Acts and other Second Temple Jewish sources depict David as a prophetic figure, see Joseph A. Fitzmyer, "David 'Being Therefore a Prophet . . .' (Acts 2:30)," *CBQ* 34 (1972): 332–39.

50. Matthew W. Bates, *The Birth of the Trinity: Jesus, God, and Spirit in New Testament and Early Christian Interpretations of the Old Testament* (Oxford: Oxford University Press, 2015), 153.

51. See especially, Donald Juel, "The Social Dimensions of Exegesis: The Use of Psalm 16 in Acts 2," *CBQ* 43 (1981): 543–56.

common in early Christian discourse—is his interpretation of the Messiah's resurrection from the dead as the event that fulfills God's promise to David: "God swore an oath to him [i.e., David] to seat on his throne one from the fruit of his loins" (Acts 2:30; cf. Ps 132:11). Standing behind Psalm 131:11 (LXX) is obviously God's promise to David in 2 Samuel 7:12: "I will raise up after you your seed, who will come from your body, and I will establish his kingdom."[52] Jesus's resurrection, then, must be more than a return to mortal existence, given Peter's declaration that the Davidic Messiah now reigns over God's kingdom and shares God's heavenly throne.[53]

Psalm 15 (LXX) suits Peter's purposes nicely as it also speaks of this royal figure as one who is located at God's right hand (2:25b). The spatial placement of God's throne next to the Messiah is what protects the referent of Psalm 15 from being shaken, and within the context of Acts 2:22–36 this almost certainly refers to God's assistance to sovereignly rescue his messianic Son from death (cf. Acts 7:54–60).[54] Again, given that the Father has invited a second Lord to "sit at my right hand" (κάθου ἐκ δεξιῶν μου) until God has triumphed over all their enemies and placed them under the Lord's feet (2:35), this, too, cannot refer to David, who "did not ascend into heaven" (2:34). Obviously, Peter's scriptural interpretation assumes the premise that God has raised Jesus from the dead and located him in a position of heavenly and royal power.[55] And Peter's threefold mention of the Messiah at God's right hand emphasizes the heavenly location of the Messiah's powerful rule.

Peter's use of the Davidic psalms establishes Jesus's resurrection and ascension as the means whereby God enthrones his Davidic king to a position of heavenly rule. Peter brings together Psalms 15:11 (LXX) and 109:1 (LXX), in part because of their shared phrase "at the right hand" (ἐκ δεξιῶν, Acts 2:25b and 2:34b), in order to demonstrate that the resurrected Messiah is currently enthroned in heaven and shares in God's powerful rule at his right hand (τῇ δεξιᾷ ... τοῦ θεοῦ ὑψωθείς, Acts 2:33).[56] This is why David himself cannot

---

52. Timo Eskola, *Messiah and the Throne: Jewish Merkabah Mysticism and Early Christian Exaltation Discourse*, WUNT 2.142 (Tübingen: Mohr Siebeck, 2001) 164–65.

53. Robert F. O'Toole, "Acts 2:30 and the Davidic Covenant of Pentecost," *JBL* 102 (1983): 251.

54. Bates, *Birth of the Trinity*, 155.

55. Luke Timothy Johnson, *Septuagintal Midrash in the Speeches of Acts* (Milwaukee: Marquette University Press, 2002), 40.

56. Lidija Novakovic, *Raised from the Dead according to Scripture: The Role of Israel's Scripture in the Early Christian Interpretations of Jesus' Resurrection*, Jewish and Christian Texts Series 12 (London: T&T Clark, 2012), 205–7.

be the referent or subject matter of his own speech—David's death makes it certain that David is not the one who "ascended into heaven" (2:34b). This statement about David, however, reminds the reader of another figure who has ascended "into heaven" (1:10–11). Psalms 15 and 109 enable Peter to explain the meaning of Jesus's resurrection as not simply a temporary return to embodied existence, but rather as a heavenly royal enthronement.[57] Peter uses the language of the Psalter to make precisely this point in Acts 2:33: the Messiah "who has been exalted to God's right hand" is the agent and the cause of the outpouring of the Spirit. The first act of the enthroned king, in other words, is to send God's powerful πνεῦμα as the means for the expansion of God's kingdom (cf. Acts 1:6–11). Peter's use of Psalm 109:1 and its designation of the Messiah also as Lord further enables him to interpret the resurrection as Jesus's heavenly enthronement to a position of absolute lordship: "God has made him both Lord and Messiah" (Acts 2:36).

The Fulfillment of God's Faithful Promises to David: Paul in Acts 13:32–37

Paul's sermon begins by presenting a mini-history of God's people, whereby Paul emphasizes God as beneficently electing and caring for his people Israel. Paul's election theology is explicit in his first sentence: "The God of this people Israel chose our fathers and exalted the people" (13:16). Throughout the sermon, God is the subject who cares for his people Israel: he compassionately leads them out of Egypt (13:17), provides for them in the wilderness (13:18), gives them land for an inheritance (13:19), and grants them judges and prophets (13:20). It is important to note, however, that Paul orients God's climactic actions for Israel in relation to King David (13:21–22). God has "raised up David" as the king who will do that which God desires (22b). As God elected Israel as his people, so God elected David as the monarch of his people. The pinnacle of the argument comes in verse 23, where Paul roots his message about Jesus in Israel's traditions about David: "From this person's seed, according to the promise, God has brought to Israel the Savior Jesus." This language of "promise" and "seed" alludes to the promises made to David in 2 Samuel 7:12–14, where God declares that one of David's "seed" will have his kingdom established forever (7:12; cf. 2 Sam 22:51; 1 Chr 17:4–14; Ps 89:20–38).

The most striking component of the speech's first stage is that it situates Jesus within Israel's election history, not only as the promised heir of David's

---

57. Similarly, see Eskola, *Messiah and the Throne*, 163.

throne, but also as the long-awaited Savior of Israel (13:23b). One might expect, based on the emphasis on the Davidic promises, that Paul would, instead, use a royal designation such as "Messiah" or "Son of God." "Savior" is a distinctively Lukan title for Jesus, and it comports well with Luke's overall concern to narrate how the message of Israel's Davidic king will be good news for the gentiles. Thus, Paul's thesis is given in verse 26: "Men, brothers, sons of the family of Abraham, and those among you who fear God, the word of this salvation has been sent forth to us."

The event whereby God accomplishes salvation for his people reaches its high point in Paul's claim that the Messiah's resurrection is the fulfillment of God's promises to Israel (13:32–33a). And as does Peter, so also Paul uses biblical enthronement texts to interpret the meaning of Jesus's resurrection as the Messiah's heavenly enthronement (Ps 2:7; Isa 55:3; Ps 15:10).[58] The fulfillment of the promise for the children comes through "the raising up of Jesus" (ἀναστήσας Ἰησοῦν, 13:33). Some have argued that this phrase refers to God bringing Jesus into the world.[59] These arguments are not persuasive, however, and the phrase should be interpreted, as most rightly do, as a direct reference to the resurrection.[60] While it is correct that not every occurrence of ἀνίστημι ("to raise up") in Acts refers to the resurrection, the fact that the verb occurs again just a few words later as an explicit reference to the resurrection is significant (ἀνέστησεν αὐτὸν ἐκ νεκρῶν, 13:34). Most important, however, is the simple fact that the entire discussion of 13:33–37 focuses upon a scriptural demonstration of Jesus's resurrection as his enthronement as Israel's King. Further confirmation that the "raising up of Jesus" should be interpreted as a reference to Jesus's resurrection can be demonstrated on the basis of its connection to Psalm 2:7 in Acts 13:33b. Specifically, the "raising up of Jesus" is said to be according to what "has been written in the second psalm" (13:33b). Psalm 2 is a Davidic psalm that portrays the victory of God's people through the installation of God's anointed king on Zion. Given that Luke explicitly reads Psalm 2:1–2 in Acts 4:25–27 as a reference to the enemies of the Messiah

---

58. A. W. Zwiep, *Ascension of the Messiah in Lukan Christology* (Leiden : Brill, 1997), 158–59; Simon David Butticaz, *L'identité de l'Eglise dans les Actes des apôtres: De la restauration d'Israël à la conquête universelle*, BZNW 174 (Berlin: de Gruyter, 2011), 286–88.

59. The most comprehensive argument for this position that I am aware of is Martin Rese, *Alttestamentliche Motive in der Christologie des Lukas*, SZNT 1 (Gütersloh: Mohn, 1969), 83–84; see also F. F. Bruce, *Commentary on the Book of Acts* (Grand Rapids: Eerdmans, 1970), 275–76.

60. Darrell L. Bock, *Proclamation from Prophecy and Pattern: Lucan Old Testament Christology*, JSNTSup 12 (Sheffield: JSOT Press, 1987), 244–56.

who rage against God and his Christ, it makes good sense that Psalm 2:7 would be adduced to indicate God's act of vindicating the Messiah by means of resurrection. Thus, what was originally a declaration of God's election of the Davidic dynasty is now fulfilled in the messianic Son of God's resurrection and enthronement.[61]

The most difficult part of Paul's speech is found in the citations of Isaiah 55:3 and Psalm 15:10 (LXX) in Acts 13:34–35. Paul argues that Jesus's resurrection from the dead is not a mere resuscitation but is, rather, a promise that Jesus shall "never turn back to decay" (13:34a; cf. Acts 2:25–29). It is important to note the relationship between 13:34a and the quotation of Isaiah 55:3 in 13:34b: "*because* (ὅτι) he [God] has raised him [Jesus] from the dead . . . *so he has spoken*" the words of Isaiah 55:3. In other words, it is Jesus's resurrection that activates the gift of "the holy and reliable things of David to you." Paul invokes Isaiah 55:3 as a reference to God's covenantal promises made to David for the benefit of future generations.[62] The genitive Δαυίδ should be viewed, then, as an objective genitive—"the faithful and sure things [promises made] to David."[63] The citation of Isaiah 55:3 recalls the broader context of Isaiah 55: "I will make an everlasting covenant with you." In this view, the "holy things of David" could refer either to the promised blessings associated with the Davidic covenant (e.g., an heir, a kingdom, and protection from enemies)[64] or to the divine oracles promised to David (cf. 2 Sam 7:12–14).[65] Thus, the relationship between Acts 13:34a and 13:34b would be as follows: *because* God has raised Jesus from the dead (v. 34a) as the fulfillment of his promise to the fathers, *so now* he has bestowed the Davidic covenantal blessings upon the recipients (v. 35). It is a characteristic of the Davidic covenant that it promised salvific blessings to its recipients (2 Sam 7:10–14; Jer 23:5–6; Ezek 34:22–31; 37:24–28; also Luke 1:68–73). The promises are certain, trustworthy, and "faithful" (τὰ

---

61. Johnson, *Septuagintal Midrash*, 42.

62. See Strauss, *The Davidic Messiah*, 170–74; Bates, *Birth of the Trinity*, 74–76.

63. That "Δαυίδ (David)" is to be understood as an objective and not a subjective genitive is also strongly suggested by its Old Testament background. God is the one who demonstrates his "lovingkindness" and "faithfulness" on behalf of David and his dynasty. This is the case in Isa 55:3 as well as in the Davidic covenantal texts of 2 Sam 7:15; Ps 89:30–34; 89:49–51; 1 Kgs 3:6; and 2 Chr 6:42. On this, see H. G. M. Williamson, "'The Sure Mercies of David': Subjective or Objective Genitive?," *JSS* 23 (1978): 31–49.

64. So Joseph A. Fitzmyer, *The Acts of the Apostles*, AYB 31 (New York: Doubleday, 1998), 517.

65. So Johnson, *Septuagintal Midrash*, 44–45.

πιστά) because they depend for their efficacy upon the resurrected king who "shall not see corruption" (13:34–35).

Paul again invokes Psalm 15:10 (LXX) to support his claim that his audience is the recipient of the blessings of the Davidic covenant. The psalm's promise—that the holy one would not see corruption (13:35)—does not refer to David because David "fell asleep," "was added to his fathers," and "he *did* see corruption." The meaning of "he served the will of God in his own generation" is not unlike Peter's claim in his Pentecost speech that David functioned as a prophet to his own generation by making predictions about the coming Messiah. So, when Paul refers to David as a servant to his own generation, it is David's role as a prophet to his own generation that is in mind. David's "seeing ahead" (2:31) corresponds neatly with his "serving the will of God" (13:36). David is dead and his body has seen corruption, but Jesus—the object of David's psalms, "the one whom God has raised—this one has not seen corruption" (13:37).

Paul Is on Trial for the Hope of Israel—The Messiah's Resurrection of the Dead

When Paul is given the opportunity to speak in his defense speeches, he essentially has three basic claims. Paul has nothing against his people; he is a faithful Torah-observant Jew; and he believes everything written in the Law and the Prophets—his loyalty to his Jewish ancestral customs cannot be questioned.

Paul claims that the real reason he is on trial and in chains is due to his proclamation of the hope of Israel. And this hope of Israel is defined by Paul as God's resurrection of Messiah Jesus from the dead. God has visited his people by resurrecting the Messiah and has offered repentance and salvation in his name. And this is all in fulfillment of Jewish Scriptures. Thus, it is not simply "resurrection" that Paul proclaims, it is God's resurrection of the Messiah—Jesus of Nazareth.[66] Paul states to Felix that he "believes everything laid down according to the Law or written in the Prophets" (24:14). But in the next breath Paul defines the content of the Law and the Prophets as centering upon a future resurrection from the dead for both the just and the unjust (24:15). Paul declares to Herod Agrippa II that he is "saying nothing beyond what the Prophets and Moses said would take place" (26:22b). And Paul is absolutely convinced

---

66. See here Alexandru Neagoe, *The Trial of the Gospel: An Apologetic Reading of Luke's Trial Narratives*, SNTSMS 116 (Cambridge: Cambridge University Press, 2002), 195–218; Robert F. O'Toole, *Acts 26, The Christological Climax of Paul's Defense (Ac 22:1–26:32)*, AnBib 78 (Rome: Pontifical Biblical Institutes Press, 1978).

that the content of their writings is "that the Messiah would suffer, and would be the first to be resurrected from the dead, and would proclaim the message of light to both the people and the gentiles" (εἰ παθητὸς ὁ χριστός, εἰ πρῶτος ἐξ ἀναστάσεως νεκρῶν φῶς μέλλει καταγγέλλειν τῷ τε λαῷ καὶ τοῖς ἔθνεσιν, 26:23). This is why Paul believes he is on trial "on account of my hope in the promise made by God to our ancestors, a promise that our twelve tribes hope to attain. . . . Why is it thought incredible by you that God raises the dead?" (26:6–8). And again, in Luke's summary of Paul's speech to the Jews in Rome, Paul declares: "I am bound in chains because of the hope of Israel (28:20b).[67] Predictably, Paul's explanation of this hope centers upon the kingdom of God and the relationship between Jesus as the context of the Law and the Prophets (28:23). In other words, Paul's Jewish ancestral traditions center upon and demand a positive response to God's resurrection of the Messiah, and this event, for Paul, has taken place. When Paul says that he is simply proclaiming that the fulfillment of Moses and the Prophets has taken place in the Messiah's suffering and resurrection, he is claiming that God has now begun to fulfill and complete the promises he made to his people in their Scriptures.

Third, Paul is emphatic that God's resurrection of the Messiah from the dead is the prior event which gives rise to his mission to the gentiles. The Lukan Paul sees God's welcoming of the nations into his people as something that was also foretold in the Law and the Prophets. Once God acted to restore Israel, the way was open for Paul to take God's light and salvation to the gentiles (Acts 13:47 quoting Isa 49:6; cf. Luke 2:30–32).[68] And Paul declares that his gentile mission is rooted in his obedience to the risen Messiah who appeared to him and called him to take the message of salvation to the gentiles (22:21; 26:18–19).

THE RESURRECTED AND ENTHRONED MESSIAH ESTABLISHES HIS KINGDOM

The risen and ascended Jesus actively exerts his rule and enacts God's kingdom as the enthroned heavenly king. There is no justification for speaking

67. The phrase "the hope of Israel" functions within Paul's defense speeches as a pithy summary of the content of Paul's proclamation about Jesus. See Klaus Haacker, "Das Bekenntnis des Paulus zur Hoffnung Israels," *NTS* 31 (1985): 437–51.

68. For the Lukan Paul (and the other Jesus-believing characters in Acts), the gentile mission is also rooted in Israel's Scriptures (e.g., Isa 49:6 in Acts 13:47; Amos 9:11–13 in Acts 15:16–17). This is a point frequently emphasized by Jervell. For example, Jacob Jervell, *Luke and the People of God: A New Look at Luke-Acts* (Minneapolis: Augsburg, 1972), 44–64.

of an absentee Christology in Acts; rather, the king enthroned in heaven actively establishes God's kingdom through pouring out God's Spirit, vindicating his witnesses, defeating his enemies, and procuring Israel's repentance and salvation.

The Enthroned King Pours Out the Holy Spirit

Peter interprets the first act of the ascended and enthroned Messiah as making good on his promise (Luke 24:49; Acts 1:4, 8) to pour out the Holy Spirit (2:14–36). Peter's speech, using the exaltation language of Psalm 110:1 (Ps 109:1 LXX), makes a precise connection between the Messiah's heavenly exaltation to God's right hand (2:33) and the Spirit's descent. That the sending of the Spirit should be viewed as a royal act of the enthroned Davidic king is demonstrated in a variety of ways. First, as we have already seen, Peter draws upon four royal psalms (Pss 16, 18, 110, and 132) in order to justify his claim that God has fulfilled his promises to David to seat one of his descendants on God's throne in the resurrection and ascension of Jesus. Second, we have also seen that the Lord's anointed Davidic ruler was often viewed as an agent of God's Spirit and, therefore, there was a traditional association between Messiah and Spirit (1 Sam 16:13; Isa 11:1–2; 61:1–3). Third, while the prophets do not use the language of "the kingdom of God," they do frequently associate the sending of God's Spirit with the time when God would restore his people, forgive their sins, dwell among them, and ingather the nations (Joel 3:1–5 in Acts 2:16–21; cf. Isa 32:15; 44:1–4; Ezek 36:26–27; 37:14).[69] Finally, in Acts 1:4–8 the risen Jesus closely associates his sending of the Spirit, which will empower the disciples in their missionary task (1:4b, 5, 8), and the kingdom (1:3b, 6). While Jesus redirects the disciples from concerns with timing (1:6), he does go on to "describe the means by which the kingdom will be restored—namely, through the Spirit-inspired witness of the Apostles throughout the earth (v. 8)."[70] Thus, it is significant that the very next event Luke narrates is Jesus's ascension into heaven (1:9–11), and in this way, Luke establishes the closest possible connection between Jesus's royal enthronement, the outpouring of the Spirit, and the inauguration and expansion of God's kingdom.

---

69. Pao, *Acts and the Isaianic New Exodus*, 115–16.

70. Hahn, *Kinship by Covenant*, 231. See also Thompson, *Acts of the Risen Lord Jesus*, 126–31.

The Enthroned King Defeats His Enemies and Vindicates His Witnesses

The enthroned messianic king continues to act from heaven to establish his witnesses and to protect them from their enemies. I will discuss three instances of this dynamic here.

We have already seen, for example, that Luke characterizes Judas as an enemy of the Messiah who is taken over by Satan's kingdom (Luke 22:3, 53). In Acts, Peter continues to characterize Judas as an enemy of the Messiah as he reads two Davidic psalms as anticipating Judas's treachery (Ps 69:26 in Acts 1:20a; Ps 109:8 in Acts 1:20b). Peter's claim that Judas's act was in some way "a necessity" (1:21), without providing reason or motive for his act of betrayal, points to the psalms' depiction of the suffering righteous king. Luke melds together Psalm 69:25 (LXX 68:26) and Psalm 109:8 (LXX 108:8) to describe Judas's fate as an enemy of the suffering king. Psalm 69 portrays a suffering righteous king, God's own servant, (v. 17), unjustly persecuted by his own enemies (vv. 1–4, 19–29), and crying out to God for vindication (vv. 1–2, 30–36). Likewise, the Davidic psalm 109 describes the persecution of the righteous king wherein he prays for curses against his enemies. The psalm ends with David's words of praise to God as the one who vindicates his "servant" (LXX 108:28), who stands at the "right hand" (v. 31) of those unjustly persecuted and gives retribution to the wicked (vv. 28–31).[71] Thus, given that Judas is an enemy of Jesus, the Lord's Anointed, one can better understand Peter's descriptive and graphic retelling of Judas's death not for the purpose of gloating in the downfall of his enemies but, rather, as an encouragement and warning that God will protect the church. Peter announces that Judas's death "became known to everyone who lived in Jerusalem" (1:19a) as an implicit warning about how God responds to those who threaten the messianic movement. While Gamaliel has not yet voiced his warning to the Sanhedrin to leave the community alone "lest you be found to be a God-fighter" (5:40), Judas is the first of a handful of figures who receive divine retribution for their violence against the Messiah and his people—an act that Luke's narrative holds to be fighting against God.[72]

In Acts 4:23–28, the apostles come together in prayer after their harassment

---

71. I have written on this in more detail in Jipp, "Luke's Scriptural Suffering Messiah," 266–69.

72. Scott Shauf, *The Divine in Acts and in Ancient Historiography* (Minneapolis: Fortress, 2015), 238.

from the Jerusalem priests and elders. In Peter's prayer, they use the language of Psalm 2 to interpret Jesus as the anointed Davidic king who is persecuted by the agents of Psalm 2:1–2, namely, Israel's rulers, Herod, and Pilate. In 4:29–30, their prayer demonstrates that the early Christians are enacting the role and pattern of the Anointed One as they, too, are now suffering at the hands of Israel's leaders. Their prayer, however, demonstrates their belief that the vindicated Anointed One of Psalm 2 is still alive and is able to empower them to perform healings, signs, and wonders through the name of Jesus (4:30). And as God vindicated his messianic Son (Acts 13:32–36), so he answers their prayer by sending forth the Spirit to further empower their mission (4:31).

One sees a similar dynamic in Acts 7:54–60, where Stephen is martyred as a result of his vision of the ascended and enthroned Christ: "Being filled with the Holy Spirit, and gazing into heaven, he saw God's glory and Jesus standing at God's right hand. And he said: 'Behold I see heaven opened up and the Son of Man standing at God's right hand'" (7:55–56). The vocabulary of the "Holy Spirit," "heaven," "divine glory," and the Psalm 110 language of "God's right hand" converge to indicate that Stephen has encountered a proleptic vision of the full glory of the enthroned Messiah (cf. Luke 9:22; 21:27).[73] While the risen Lord does not save Stephen from death, he does (1) receive Stephen's spirit (7:59) and (2) use Stephen's death to expand the kingdom into the rest of Judea and Samaria (8:1–4; cf. Acts 1:8).[74] Thus, both Acts 4:23–31 and 7:54–60 use the language of the Psalter to show how, from his throne in heaven, the Messiah of Acts 1:6–11 answers the prayers of his people and establishes God's kingdom through empowering the testimony of his witnesses. In addition to these examples, we might take a further look at other hubristic tyrants who persecute the church (12:20–23), as well as miracle-working competitors (8:14–24; 13:4–12; 19:11–20), to see how the superior power of the risen Messiah protects and vindicates his people and overthrows the power of those who seek to harm the church.

The Enthroned King Provides Blessings for His People

In Acts 3:1–10, Peter and John heal the lame man sitting at the gate of the temple. The obvious parallels between this account and Jesus's healing of the

73. Eskola, *Messiah and the Throne*, 180–81.

74. Especially insightful for relating the spatial location of the heavenly Messiah and the geographical expansion of the Messiah's witnesses is Matthew Sleeman, *Geography and the Ascensions Narrative in Acts*, SNTSMS 146 (Cambridge: Cambridge University Press, 2009), 163–71.

paralytic suggest that the healing ministry of Jesus continues through his witnesses (see Luke 5:17–26). But Peter is emphatic that the healing derives not from his own abilities (3:12), but rather takes place "by *the name* of Messiah Jesus of Nazareth" (Acts 3:6b; cf. 4:9–10). Peter's speech declares that it is the resurrection power of the God of Israel (3:13a) which "glorified his servant Jesus" (3:13b) that is responsible for the healing of the lame man. The language of God glorifying Jesus probably draws upon the Psalter's frequent promise that God would exalt his anointed Davidic servant (e.g., Ps 89:20–21; cf. Isa 52:13).[75] Thus, the enthroned king is able to continue his healing ministry on earth by means of his witnesses. This is further emphasized by the notoriously difficult statement in 3:19–21, where Peter exhorts the people to repent so that they might experience "times of refreshment from the face of the Lord" (3:19–20). These times of refreshment come from the glorified heavenly figure (3:21) who grants signs of his favor, presence, and healing to those who turn to him as a foretaste of his "time of universal restoration" (3:21a). The parallels between 3:20–21 and 1:6–11 (times and seasons, restoration, heaven, Jesus's return, Spirit/refreshment) suggest that the heavenly enthroned king is actively responsible for pouring out blessings upon his repentant people in anticipation of his return.[76]

In Acts 5:30–31, Peter uses the language of Psalm 110:1 (109:1 LXX) to ground Israel's repentance in God's exaltation of Jesus: "God has exalted this one to his right hand (ὕψωσεν τῇ δεξιᾷ αὐτοῦ) as prince and Savior in order to provide repentance to Israel and the forgiveness of sins."[77] Thus, Acts 3:19–21 and 5:30–31 indicate that God's enthronement of Jesus to his right hand stands behind the mass conversions of the Jews in Jerusalem who turn to God and experience divine forgiveness (2:41; 4:4; cf. 13:38–39).

In Acts 4:10, Peter declares that the rejected but now resurrected Messiah is the one who has healed the lame man (4:10b), and Peter quotes Psalm 117:22 (LXX) to identify him as "the stone that was despised by your builders, this one has become the head stone" (4:11). The claim that "there is no other name under heaven" that can procure humanity's salvation links Jesus's ascended, enthroned status with his ability to continue his healing ministry. Given Peter's direct quotation of the psalm, it is also likely that the frequent invocation of the name of Jesus as the powerful agent of healing (3:6, 16; 4:7, 10, 12, 17, 30)

---

75. Jipp, "Luke's Scriptural Suffering Messiah," 264–65.
76. Kevin L. Anderson, *"But God Raised Him from the Dead": The Theology of Jesus's Resurrection in Luke-Acts* (Eugene, OR: Wipf & Stock, 2007), 228.
77. Eskola, *Messiah and the Throne*, 177–78.

stems from Psalm 117, where the king embodies "the name of the Lord" (Ps 117:26a) and triumphs as the result of "the name of the Lord" (Ps 117:10, 11, 12). Thus, in Acts 3–4, Luke continues to use the Psalter (Ps 117 directly and Ps 88 and the language of royal enthronement indirectly) to show how the resurrected, ascended, and enthroned Messiah sends forth healing (3:1–10; 4:10–11), forgiveness of sins and times of restoration (3:20–21), and salvation (4:12) to those who turn to the Lord (3:19).

The Enthroned King and the Expansion of the Kingdom

Acts also makes it clear that the enthroned king acts from heaven to expand the kingdom to new people and new places. Luke portrays the expansion of the kingdom to new people and new geographical territories as a direct result of God's fulfillment of the promises made to David. Thus, when Paul's mission to the gentiles draws the ire of some in Jerusalem, James suggests that "the words of the prophets are in harmony" (15:15a) with how "God has intervened to take from the gentiles a people for his name" (15:14). James appeals to just one prophetic text—namely, Amos 9:11–12: "After these things I will return and rebuild David's fallen tent. I will rebuild its ruins and set it up again, so the rest of humanity may seek the Lord—even all the gentiles who are called by my name—declares the Lord who makes these things known from long ago" (15:16–18).[78] How does this seemingly obscure prophetic text contribute to James's desire to affirm the gentile mission apart from circumcision?[79] The language of *rebuilding* and *restoring* anticipates a day when the Davidic kingdom and kingship would be restored. And while James only draws upon the prophet Amos to make his point, he is likely alluding to the prophetic expectation that the gentiles would submit to God when he restored the Davidic monarchy (e.g., Num 24:17–18; Isa 11:11–14; Pss. Sol. 17:21–26).[80] Un-

---

78. It is well known that James's argument is only possible from the Old Greek version of Amos which reads "so that the rest of humanity might seek the Lord" instead of the Hebrew's "so that they might inherit the remnant of Edom" (Amos 9:12). See further Carl R. Holladay, *Acts: A Commentary*, NTL (Louisville: Westminster John Knox, 2016), 300–302.

79. Though note that Amos 9:11 ("I will raise up the fallen tent of David") is associated with 2 Sam 7:10–14 in 4Q174. See, further, John J. Collins, *The Scepter and the Star: The Messiahs of the Dead Sea Scrolls and Other Ancient Literature* (New York: Doubleday, 1995), 60–61.

80. Amos 9:11 is interpreted by 4Q174 as a rebuilding of the Davidic monarchy. See the helpful discussion in Esau McCaulley, *Sharing in the Son's Inheritance: Davidic Messianism*

like the time in exile when there was no Davidic king and no united people under the Davidic king's reign, the prophet Amos looks forward to a time when the people are united under the reign of a Davidic ruler. Alan Thompson helpfully summarizes the implications: "The reference to 'the dwelling of David' is a reference to the restoration of the Davidic kingdom under Davidic rule and therefore anticipates the restoration of Davidic kingship *as well as* the restoration of the eschatological people of God under the rule of the Davidic King."[81]

What Amos anticipated has been fulfilled in that the Son of David has been placed on the throne, as the Messiah reigns from heaven over God's people (Luke 1:32–33, 68–69; Acts 2:30–31; 13:32–37). We have seen a plethora of evidence that God has established the Davidic kingdom. But it is the next part of the quotation that is critical for the direct argument. For Amos prophesies that once the promises made to David have been fulfilled, then the rest of humanity will seek the Lord and "all the Gentiles" will call upon the name of the Lord (15:17). In other words, first restoration/salvation comes to Israel through the Davidic king, and then promises go to the gentiles. This is the foundation for Luke's unrelenting emphasis on the geographical expansion of the message of the kingdom of God to all peoples. And the risen Messiah plays an active role in accomplishing this expansion.

Thus, the risen Lord encounters Saul in a Christophany and calls him to take the message of the gospel to "the nations, kings, and the sons of Israel" (9:15). The risen Messiah initiates the salvation of Cornelius and the attendant inclusion of the gentiles within the people of God by giving Peter a *heavenly* vision (10:9–11). God directs Paul's travels in another surprising way in Acts 16, where the plans of Paul and his team are at first frustrated when the Holy Spirit forbids them to work in Asia (16:6) and then again when the Spirit of Jesus prevents them from missionary work in Mysia (16:7). While they are waiting in Troas, Paul receives a vision of a Macedonian man who is pleading with Paul to "cross over into Macedonia and help us!" (16:9b). Paul and his team draw the conclusion that "God had called us to preach the gospel to them" (16:10). In this way, the message of Jesus Christ moves further westward as it goes across the Bosphorus and into Greece.

---

and Paul's Worldwide Interpretation of the Abrahamic Land Promise in Galatians, LNTS 608 (New York: T&T Clark, 2019), 80–82.

81. Thompson, *The Acts of the Risen Lord Jesus*, 122.

CONCLUSION

For Luke and Acts, Jesus's Davidic messiahship is critical for his articulation of how God is faithful to the promises he made to his people. God had promised Israel that it would have a king who would establish God's people in justice, righteousness, and peace. God had promised that this king would shepherd God's people, providing them with food and nourishment, and would rescue them from their enemies. This Messiah would rule over God's people by means of the empowerment of God's own Spirit. And in Luke-Acts, we see a picture of a Davidic king who is anointed by God's Spirit and who enacts God's rule and salvation by means of extending compassionate healings and divine hospitality and table fellowship to the lost. This righteous king offers faithfulness and obedience to his Father even in the midst of violent opposition to his rule among his enemies. As a result, this king is resurrected and enthroned to a position of heavenly rule whereby he continues to establish God's kingdom by pouring out God's Spirit upon all flesh, vindicating his witnesses amid their enemies, continuing to offer the experience of his saving blessings, and expanding his rule into new geographical territories and peoples.

CHAPTER 4

The Kingdom and the Glory of the Messiah

The Gospel of John

If one approaches the Gospel of John with a predetermined and fixed understanding of the shape and pattern of Jewish (or Christian) messianism, or a conviction that it reveals a "high" divine Son of God Christology that is actually correcting or reinterpreting messianic beliefs about Jesus, one might mistakenly conclude that the Fourth Gospel is uninterested in portraying Jesus as God's messianic king. John's portrait of Jesus does not readily cohere with either Matthew's vision of Jesus as the Son of David who ends Israel's exile, nor does it look similar to the Psalms of Solomon's expectations of a Davidic figure who will liberate Israel from its foreign oppressors. And, in fact, John's prologue demonstrates no interest in Jesus's Davidic messianic origins (cf. Matt 1–2; Luke 1:31–35; 2:1–11) and hardly even mentions Jesus as Messiah (see John 1:17). Instead, John asserts that Jesus is the *Logos* who has existed from eternity together with God and is even responsible for the origins of the created world (John 1:1–3). John's prologue ends with the assertation that Jesus is the "only and unique God" (John 1:18).[1] Further, John often has Jesus emphasizing his identity as the heavenly Son of Man who is a type of heavenly revealer of mysteries to humanity (e.g., John 3:13–4; 8:25–9). This has seemed to many readers of the Gospel to indicate that John has moved on from, and has larger

---

1. Note here the sage comments of James F. McGrath, "The Gospel of John as Jewish Messianism: Formative Influences and Neglected Avenues in the History of Scholarship," in *Reading the Gospel of John's Christology as Jewish Messianism: Royal, Prophetic, and Divine Messiahs*, ed. Benjamin E. Reynolds and Gabriele Boccaccini, Ancient Judaism and Early Christianity 106 (Leiden: Brill, 2018), 55: "That it has taken so long for us to reach the point of treating the Gospel of John as giving expression to a form of Jewish messianism is due to concerns that have more to do with Christian theological commitments (and their influence even on some who may not hold to them), than with historical-critical exegesis."

concerns than, the earlier versions of messianic Christology of the Synoptic Gospels. As Benjamin Reynolds has said: "The Gospel of John's Christology is understood to be removed not merely from Jewish messianic beliefs but from messianic belief in early Christianity."[2]

Nevertheless, it would be a mistake to minimize the centrality and importance of Jewish messianic motifs, language, and titles as a resource for John's christological portrait of Jesus of Nazareth.[3] Nils Dahl notes correctly that it is a remarkable and surprising "fact that the title *Christos* in the Fourth Gospel has not been made obsolete by predicates like '*Logos*', 'Son of God', 'Savior of the World.'"[4] A variety of characters in John's Gospel are searching for the Messiah and asking questions as to whether or not Jesus might be Israel's Messiah (e.g., 1:20–25; 4:29; 7:26–42). John's Gospel is infused with the Davidic psalms as a means of explaining Jesus's royal identity, and within John's passion narrative there are twelve references to Jesus as "King" (18:33, 37 [2x], 39; 19:3, 12, 14, 15 [2x], 19, 21 [2x]; cf. 1:51; 12:13) and three to Jesus's "kingdom" (John 18:36 three times). Three times John notes that those who confess Jesus as the Messiah will be thrown out of the synagogue (9:22; 12:42; 16:2). Jesus is proclaimed King of Israel with the messianic exegesis of Psalm 118:26 and Zechariah 9:9 in the triumphal entry (John 12:13–15),[5] and the stated purpose of the Gospel is to persuade people that Jesus is "the Messiah, the Son of God" (20:31). The key points at which the language of Messiah is used—namely, in the prologue (1:17), the confession near the end of Jesus's ministry (11:27), and the conclusion (20:31)—suggest that the title "Messiah" is a deeply significant

2. Benjamin E. Reynolds, "The Gospel of John's Christology as Evidence for Early Jewish Messianic Expectations: Challenges and Possibilities," in *Reading the Gospel of John's Christology as Jewish Messianism*, ed. Benjamin E. Reynolds and Gabrielle Boccaccini (Leiden: Brill, 2018), 23.

3. See, for example, John Lierman, "The Mosaic Pattern of John's Christology," in *Challenging Perspectives on the Gospel of John*, ed. John Lierman, WUNT 2.219 (Tübingen: Mohr Siebeck, 2006), 233, who notes that David is barely mentioned in John's Gospel. If one is looking for David's name, then this is obviously true; but there are, of course, other ways of indicating Jesus's messianic significance.

4. Nils A. Dahl, "The Johannine Church and History," in *The Interpretation of John*, ed. John Ashton (London: T&T Clark, 2000), 127. Quoted from John Ashton, *Understanding the Fourth Gospel*, 2nd ed. (Oxford: Claerndon, 2007), 147. See also the helpful comments in Jörg Frey, *The Glory of the Crucified One: Christology and Theology in the Gospel of John*, trans. Wayne Coppins and Christoph Heilig (Waco, TX: Baylor University Press, 2018), 285–312.

5. Jocelyn McWhirter, "Messianic Exegesis in the Fourth Gospel," in *Reading the Gospel of John's Christology as Jewish Messianism*, ed. Benjamin Reynolds and Gabriele Boccaccini (Leiden: Brill, 2018), 124–48, demonstrates how John's messianic exegesis stands behind many of his most important christological claims.

part of John's Christology.[6] John's Christology may not be messianic in the same sense as the Christology of Matthew or Luke-Acts, but there are prima facie good reasons for considering John's Christology as another creative version of Jewish messianism shaped around the remembrances of Jesus of Nazareth. Furthermore, there are no good reasons why John's depiction of Jesus as messianic king cannot be developed through a depiction of the Son's unique and personal relationship with God, the Father of Israel.[7] My study of messianism's influence upon John's Christology will proceed by: (1) taking an extended look at the theme of the quest for the Messiah (especially in chapter 1); (2) a study of three messianic themes in John—namely, Spirit, temple, and shepherd; and (3) examining John's paradoxical depiction of Christ's crucifixion as his royal enthronement.

Come, See, and Believe in Jesus the Messiah of Israel!

While not everyone in Israel was looking for the Messiah, John 1–12 provides numerous examples of Jews—and even some Samaritans—who were. The quest to find the Messiah was alive and well. While speculation about the Messiah was common during feast times, it was heightened when a man called Jesus began healing the sick and feeding the hungry by miraculous means. John uses all these stories to build a convincing case that Jesus is the Messiah.

The Quest for the Messiah in John 1:19–51

John 1:19–51 contains a series of vignettes describing people's initial encounters of the Messiah as a prelude to Jesus's revelatory signs (John 2–12), which heighten an eschatological messianic hope that Jesus might be the Son of God, the Messiah and King of Israel. Within this stretch of text, Jesus is referred to as the Messiah, the Son of God (or Elect One), the Lamb of God, the one spoken of in the Law and the Prophets, the King of Israel, and the Son of Man. [8]

In 1:19–21 John the Baptist responds to the question of the priestly delegates

---

6. Similarly, see the argument of Warren Carter, *John and Empire: Initial Explorations* (London: T&T Clark, 2008), 177–82.

7. Again, McGrath, "The Gospel of John," 55: "The Gospel of John is unique in certain respects, but so too are all expressions of Jewish messianism that are known to us."

8. The language for the subtitle comes from the appropriately named title by John Painter, *The Quest for the Messiah: The History, Literature and Theology of the Johannine Community*, 2nd ed. (Nashville: Abingdon, 1993).

from Jerusalem: "I am not the Messiah" (ἐγὼ οὐκ εἰμὶ ὁ χριστός, 1:20).[9] The honorific "the Messiah" can have a variety of connotations but, at minimum, it refers to something like a royal Davidic king (e.g., 2 Sam 7:12–14; Ps 2:6–8; Isa 9:6–7; 11:1–5). John's messianic denial leads the priests to ask if he is Elijah or the prophet (1:21). The reference to "*the* prophet" draws upon the "prophet like Moses" of Deuteronomy 18:15–18, and Elijah redivivus may recall Malachi 4:5–6 (also Sir 48:10–12; cf. Mark 9:10–13; Luke 1:16–17). While John's ministry of baptism with water would seemingly signify a task of cleansing and purification, John's significance for the Fourth Gospel lies in his testimony (ἡ μαρτυρία τοῦ Ἰωάννου, 1:19; cf. 1:6–8, 15)—namely, "in order to reveal to Israel" (1:31; cf. 1:33) that Jesus is the "Lamb of God who takes away the sin of the world" (1:29; cf. 1:36) and the greater and superior "coming one" (ὁ ὀπίσω μου ἐρχόμενος, 1:27; ὀπίσω μου ἔρχεται ἀνήρ, 1:30). Jesus as God's Lamb likely draws upon the language from Jewish messianic portraits of a figure who will cleanse God's people from sin (e.g., 1 En. 90).[10] Jesus's identity as the Lamb of God and as "the coming one" will take on greater messianic significance as the narrative proceeds, but the pinnacle of John's testimony is found in 1:32–34, where John testifies that he saw "the Spirit descending like a dove from heaven and it remained upon him" (1:32). We will look at this scene in more detail shortly, but for now we can briefly note that John's vision of the Spirit descending upon Jesus like a dove signals that Jesus is the Spirit-anointed Messiah.

In the next scene, the Baptist sees Jesus walking by and declares "Behold, the Lamb of God," and this results in two of the Baptist's disciples leaving John in order to "follow" Jesus (1:35–37). The audience is invited to join the disciples in their quest to see and understand the meaning of Jesus's messianic identity, as Jesus asks, "What do you seek?" (τί ζητεῖτε, 1:38) and invites the disciples to "come and see" (ἔρχεσθε καὶ ὄψεσθε, 1:39) where the teacher "abides" or "stays" (ποῦ μένεις, 1:38). Andrew, one of the unnamed disciples of John, searches for and "finds" (εὑρίσκει) his brother Simon Peter and brings him to Jesus, declaring to his brother: "We have found the Messiah (εὑρήκαμεν τὸν Μεσσίαν), which is translated as the Christ (χριστός)" (1:41).

The encounters are not finished, however, for the next day Jesus "finds" (εὑρίσκει) Philip and says, "follow me" (1:43). Having been found by Jesus, Philip then "finds" (εὑρίσκει) Nathanael and declares: "We have found the one about whom Moses wrote in the Law and the Prophets" (1:45). Nathanael's

---

9. John the Baptist repeats the phrase again in 3:28: "I am not the Messiah."

10. See further C. H. Dodd, *The Interpretation of the Fourth Gospel* (Cambridge: Cambridge University Press, 1953), 232–38.

location under a fig tree (1:48) may allude to the oracle in Zechariah 3:8–10 which declares that in the eschatological age, on the day when God brings forth his servant, the Davidic Branch (Zech 3:8b; cf. Zech 6:12; Jer 23:5; 33:15), each Israelite "will invite his neighbor to sit under his vine and fig tree" (Zech 3:10).[11] Nathanael's suspicion concerning the Messiah coming from Nazareth is transformed in his initial encounter with Jesus, such that he declares: "Rabbi, you are the Son of God (σὺ εἶ ὁ υἱὸς τοῦ θεοῦ); you are the King of Israel (σὺ βασιλεὺς εἶ τοῦ Ἰσραήλ)" (1:49).[12] John does not indicate exactly which Scriptures or figure Nathanael has in mind, but the emphasis upon Jesus as Son of God, Messiah, and King of Israel may indicate that the reader is expected to think of those oracles centering upon a royal Davidic ruler (e.g., Gen 49:8–12; Num 24:17; Ps 2; Isa 9, 11; Ezek 34).[13] Jesus declares that Nathanael will "see greater things than these" (1:50b), as he will "see the heaven opened up and the angels of God ascending and descending upon the Son of Man" (1:51). Jesus's statement echoes Genesis 28:12–17, where Jacob has his vision of the ladder into the opened heaven; at minimum we can say here that John presents Jesus, the Son of Man, as the revelatory link between heaven and earth. Jesus does not reject or even correct Nathanael's confession, but his response indicates the difficulty of understanding Jesus's identity apart from Jesus's own revelation.[14]

11. Craig R. Koester, *Symbolism in the Fourth Gospel: Meaning, Mystery, Community*, 2nd ed. (Minneapolis: Fortress, 2003), 39–40.

12. I have argued in detail in the preceding chapters that "the Son of God" is a messianic honorific. See further Mavis M. Leung, *The Kingship-Cross Interplay in the Gospel of John: Jesus' Death as Corroboration of His Royal Messiahship* (Eugene, OR: Wipf & Stock, 2011), 59–63. Frey, *The Glory of the Crucified One*, 297–98, is close to the mark, though he unnecessarily moves to situating John's language of the "Son of God" within Hellenistic and Roman religious understandings of the honorific, when he states: "While Jesus is, of course, 'the Messiah' and 'the king of Israel' (1.49) for John, Messiah or Χριστός is no longer the decisive Christological predicate. Rather, it is interpreted through the title 'Son of God' with which Χριστός is connected in multiple places (11.27; 20.31) and which—although it likewise comes from the Messiah tradition—is much more generally understandable, not least in the framework of the frequent talk of 'sons of god' in the Hellenistic-Roman world."

13. See Matthew V. Novenson, "Jesus the Messiah: Conservativism and Radicalism in Johannine Christology," in *Portraits of Jesus in the Gospel of John: A Christological Spectrum*, ed. Craig Koester, LNTS 589 (London: T&T Clark, 2018), 112. See further Richard Bauckham, "Jewish Messianism according to the Gospel of John," in *The Testimony of the Beloved Disciple: Narrative, History, and Theology in the Gospel of John* (Grand Rapids: Baker Academic, 2007), 230–31.

14. Benjamin E. Reynolds, *The Apocalyptic Son of Man in the Gospel of John*, WUNT 2.249 (Tübingen: Mohr Siebeck, 2008), 92, rightly notes that John uses "Son of Man" in a messianic sense and that there is no indication that Jesus corrects or revises "the disciples'

These initial encounters with Jesus have been appropriately described as *quest stories*, as they center upon individuals' attempts to find the Messiah.[15] Within these initial encounters, Jesus is described as the coming one (1:27, 30), the Messiah (1:41), the Lamb of God (1:29, 36), the Spirit-anointed one (1:32–33), the Son of God (1:34, 49), the one prophesied by Moses and the prophets (1:45), the King of Israel (1:49), and the Son of Man (1:51). John uses the language of "find" five times within John 1:41–45 to describe the process of finding the Messiah and then finding others with whom to share the news. In addition to the language of finding, John uses a variety of verbs to describe this quest for the Messiah, including that of coming (1:29, 30, 39, 47), knowing and revealing (1:31, 33), testifying (1:19, 32, 34), seeing (1:36, 39, 48, 50), hearing (1:37), following (1:38, 40, 43), seeking (1:38), and staying or abiding (1:38, 39). These active terms are metaphors for "faith" or "belief." The emphasis on the active search for the messianic identity of Jesus further foreshadows that, for the Fourth Gospel, the meaning of the confession "Jesus is the Messiah (or Son of God, or King of Israel)" is not self-evident; rather, understanding the messiahship of Jesus requires an active and difficult quest into the paradoxical and strange nature of Jesus's royal rule. Marida Nicolaci states the dynamic well: "The *Jewish question about the Messiah*, therefore, forms the background against which the question about and consequently the *search for Jesus* in the rest of the Gospel is placed both narratively and theologically. Far from dissolving the Jewish messianism in his Christology, then, the evangelist is creating a shrewd and fundamental tension between the Jewish question about the Messiah and the *form* of response offered to it by/in Jesus of Nazareth."[16]

Jesus's responses are typical for John's Jesus in that they are cryptic and elusive. He asks the disciples: "What are you seeking?" (1:38); he does not give a straightforward answer to their question as to his abode but says "come and see" (1:39); he renames Simon (1:42); he commands Philip to follow him (1:43); and he tells Nathanael that he will see greater things than he can anticipate (1:50). The readers of John's Gospel, together with the earliest disciples of Jesus, are invited to seek after Jesus in their quest to see and understand the meaning of his messianic identity.[17]

---

messianic understanding. 'Son of Man' is one more title that is merely added to the 'bouquet' of titles in John 1."

15. Painter, *The Quest for the Messiah*, 163–88.

16. Marida Nicolaci, "Divine Kingship and Jesus's Identity in Johannine Messianism," in *Reading the Gospel of John's Christology as Jewish Messianism*, ed. Benjamin Reynolds and Gabriele Boccaccini (Leiden: Brill, 2018), 184.

17. So also, Michael F. Bird, *Jesus Is the Christ: The Messianic Testimony of the Gospels* (Downers Grove, IL: InterVarsity Press, 2012), 111–12.

Johannine Messianic Speculation

Speculation as to Jesus's messianic and kingly identity and credentials does not end in John 1 but pervades numerous episodes in John 2–12. Jesus instructs Nicodemus the Pharisee on the necessity of new birth for seeing and entering into "the kingdom of God" (3:3, 5). Jesus's mysterious teaching to the Samaritan woman at the well leads her to state: "I know that Messiah is coming (Μεσσίας ἔρχεται), the one who is called the Christ (ὁ λεγόμενος χριστός); when that one comes (ἔλθῃ), he will declare all things to us" (4:25). This elicits Jesus's positive response: "I am he, the one who is speaking to you" (4:26). This is as clear a confession to Jesus's messianic identity as one could hope for. The woman leaves the well and finds her fellow Samaritans in the city and announces: "Come and see a man who told me all the things I have done; could this perhaps be the Messiah?" (4:29). Jesus's self-revelation moves the woman from speculation that he may be a prophet (4:19) to the belief that he is the Messiah (4:25–26, 29). Her language again associates the messianic agent with a "coming one" who is a revealer of hidden wisdom and knowledge.[18] Speculation as to the identity of Jesus continues in John 6, where a large crowd follows Jesus because they are seeing his miraculous signs (6:1–2). This is the context for the Johannine Jesus's feeding of the five thousand, and the response of the people seeing the abundance of bread is: "This must surely be the prophet who comes into the world" (6:14). We notice again the language of "coming into the world" to describe Jesus, but here the crowd draws the conclusion that Jesus is "the prophet"—presumably the prophet like Moses prophesied in Deuteronomy 18 and 34. John's note that Jesus departed from the crowd because he knows that the crowd wanted to make him "King" (βασιλέα, 6:15) may draw upon the depiction of a Mosaic prophet-king.[19] Jesus's retreat from the crowd does not indicate his rejection of the title "King," but rather it previews his conversation with Pilate where he clarifies a true and false notion of his kingship (John 18:33–40).

Messianic speculation concerning Jesus's origins reaches a high point during the Jewish Festival of Tabernacles where Jesus teaches in the temple (7:2, 14–24, 37–39). The people are confused because they think they know Jesus's origins and that this disqualifies Jesus from fulfilling the role of Mes-

---

18. So also Novenson, "Jesus the Messiah," 113.

19. The classic study here is Wayne A. Meeks, *The Prophet-King: Moses Traditions and the Johannine Christology*, NovTSup 14 (Leiden: Brill, 1967). On Philo's depiction of Moses as a king, see briefly Joshua W. Jipp, *Christ Is King: Paul's Royal Ideology* (Minneapolis: Fortress, 2015), 52.

siah. Some of the people from Jerusalem who are listening to Jesus's teaching wonder: "Do the rulers truly know that this is the Messiah? But we know from where this man has come. When the Messiah comes, no one will know where he is from" (7:26–27). The crowd here may demonstrate awareness of a Jewish "hidden Messiah" tradition which supposes that the origins of the Messiah will be unknown and his identity will remain concealed from the masses and revealed to only a few (e.g., 1 En. 62:7; 4 Ezra 7:28–32; 13:32; Justin Martyr, *Dialogue with Trypho* 8; 110).[20] Some have also pointed to Micah 5:2 and its description of a Judean king "whose origin is from of old, from ancient of days" as a possibility for explaining the supposition that "no one will know where he [i.e., the Messiah] is from."[21] One thinks, for example, of God's revelation to John the Baptist that Jesus is the Messiah by means of the anointing of the Spirit upon Jesus (1:32–33). But the Jerusalem people supposedly know Jesus's origins, and likely the reader is meant to infer here the common knowledge that Jesus is from Nazareth of Galilee (e.g., 1:46; 7:41).

Jesus's response surprisingly meets their messianic expectation, though not in a way that they understand and accept, for in fact, his origins are indeed mysterious and heavenly. He declares: "I have not come on my own. But the one who sent me is true, and you do not know him. I know him, because I am from him and have been sent by that one" (7:28b–29). The reader knows that Jesus's origins are otherworldly—the one who has come "from heaven" (e.g., 3:13, 31; 6:32–38).[22] As a result of his teaching, some try to arrest Jesus (7:30), while others in the crowd "believed in him and said, 'When the Messiah comes, will he do more signs than what he has done?'" (7:31). Bauckham makes the reasonable suggestion that their expectation for signs performed by a Spirit-anointed Davidic Messiah may have been made by a link between Isaiah 11:1–2 and Isaiah 61:1 (see also 4Q521 2.2.7–14).[23] After Jesus's invitation to believe in him and receive the Spirit, the speculation begins once again in earnest (7:37–39). Some suppose he is a Moses-like prophet-king: "this one is truly the prophet" (7:40; cf. 1:21; 6:14–15); others claim, "this one is the Messiah," while still others suppose that "the Messiah cannot come out of Galilee"

---

20. Adele Reinhartz, "The Lyin' King? Deception and Christology in the Gospel of John," in *Johannine Ethics: The Moral Word of the Gospel and Epistles of John*, ed. Sherri Brown and Christopher W. Skinner (Minneapolis: Fortress, 2018), 130–32.

21. So Richard B. Hays, *Echoes of Scripture in the Gospels* (Waco, TX: Baylor University Press, 2016), 293–94.

22. Bird, *Jesus Is the Christ*, 119–20.

23. Bauckham, "Jewish Messianism," 234–35.

(7:41).[24] The justification for their belief is the testimony of Scripture which indicates that the Messiah will be born from the line of David and in the village of Bethlehem (7:42; cf. Mic 5:1–3). It seems quite likely that John assumes some level of familiarity with the traditions (or even accounts) of the Synoptic Gospels, and likely expects his audience to know that Jesus is indeed from "the seed of David" and was born in Bethlehem (see Luke 1–2; Matt 1:18–2:13; Rom 1:1–4; 2 Tim 2:8). Richard Hays states the irony well: "So those who fail to accept Jesus as Messiah are ignorant of both his human Davidic lineage and his heavenly origin."[25]

In the story of Jesus's healing of the blind man, John emphasizes the social consequences for those who believe that Jesus is the Messiah. The blind man's parents refuse to continue engaging the Pharisees and the Jews out of fear: "for the Jews had already agreed that anyone who confessed Jesus to be the Messiah would be put out of the synagogue" (ἵνα ἐάν τις αὐτὸν ὁμολογήσῃ χριστόν, ἀποσυνάγωγος γένηται, 9:22). This is the first of three instances where John uses the language of ἀποσυνάγωγος to describe excommunication of Jews from the synagogue based on the confession "Jesus is the Messiah" (see also 12:42; 16:2). Whether expulsion from the synagogue makes better sense within Jesus's own lifetime, or as scholarly consensus has it, as stemming from a later first-century conflict, the passages seem to indicate the genesis of a split between formative Judaism and those Jews confessing Jesus to be Israel's Messiah.[26]

After Jesus's good shepherd discourse (John 10:1–18), Jesus is walking in the temple during the Feast of the Dedication (10:22–23) and is asked by the Jews: "How long will you keep us in suspense? If you are the Messiah, tell it to us plainly" (10:24). Before Jesus raises Lazarus from the dead, Martha confesses to Jesus: "Yes, Lord, I believe that you are the Messiah, the Son of God who comes into the world" (ὁ χριστὸς ὁ υἱὸς τοῦ θεοῦ ὁ εἰς τὸν κόσμον ἐρχόμενος, 11:27). Here the title "Son of God" along with "the one who comes

---

24. This seems to indicate, among other evidence within the Fourth Gospel, that John distinguishes between the categories of "Messiah" and "the prophet." See further Bauckham, "Jewish Messianism," 225–34.

25. Hays, *Echoes of Scripture in the Gospels*, 294. Similarly Bird, *Jesus Is the Christ*, 122: "The objectors misunderstand Jesus's true origins—both his heavenly origins and the circumstances of his earthly birth—since if they knew from where Jesus hailed, they would have grounds, not grievance, for Jesus' messianic claim."

26. See the classic work of J. Louis Martyn, *History and Theology in the Fourth Gospel*, 3rd ed. (Louisville: Westminster John Knox, 2003). I have written on this debate in much more detail in Joshua W. Jipp, "Raymond E. Brown and the Fourth Gospel: Composition and Community," in *The Gospel of John in Modern Interpretation*, ed. Stanley Porter and Ron Fay (Grand Rapids: Kregel, 2018).

into the world" further defines and clarifies the meaning of Jesus's messiahship. Martha's confession of Jesus as the "Messiah, the Son of God" is precisely what John will later declare to be the purpose of his narrative (20:31). When Jesus speaks of his impending enthronement and victory over Satan, the crowd questions Jesus: "We have heard from the law that the Messiah will remain forever. How can you say that the Son of Man must be lifted up? Who is this Son of Man?" (12:34). The crowd here identifies "Messiah" and "Son of Man."[27] Their reference to the Messiah remaining forever likely alludes to those oracles that promised an everlasting reign to David and his offspring (e.g., Gen 49:8–12; 2 Sam 7:12–17; Ps 89:28–29, 35–37; Pss. Sol. 17:4). Isaiah 9 and Ezekiel 37 both anticipate God sending a final Davidic ruler whose reign would have no end.[28] Whatever the precise scriptural antecedent, once again John portrays the crowds and Jewish leaders working to understand the peculiar identity of Jesus in light of current messianic traditions.

The emphasis on Jesus's kingship is the major topic under discussion between Pilate and Jesus during his trial in chapter 18–19. Pilate asks Jesus whether he is the King of the Jews (18:33), and Jesus, in a roundabout way, affirms that he has a kingdom that is not of this world (18:36). Pilate makes the logical response, "So then you are a king?" and Jesus responds with the cryptic, "You say that I am" (18:37). Jesus is crucified, then, as "the King of the Jews" (19:3, 14, 15, 19) and as one who "claimed to be the Son of God" (19:7).

So You May Believe Jesus Is the Messiah, the Son of God (John 20:30–31)

What can be said about our survey of the messianic quest stories in John 1 and the consistent thread of messianic speculation that pervades John 1–12? First, it is worth stating the obvious: Messiah language and traditions pervade the Fourth Gospel. John's Christology is constructed and articulated by means of affirming Jesus's messiahship. John's high Christology, seen for example in

27. Novenson, "Jesus the Messiah," 118. This is not in itself all that surprising, as the Danielic Son of Man and Davidic Messiah were not interpreted as distinct figures in Second Temple Judaism, as noted by Bauckham, "Jewish Messianism," 236. Bauckham points to 2 Bar. 39–40; 4 Ezra 13; Sib. Or. 5:414–27. See also the arguments of Reynolds, *The Apocalyptic Son of Man*, esp. 37, 46, 52, 57; William Horbury, "The Messianic Associations of 'The Son of Man,'" in *Messianism among Jews and Christians: Biblical and Historical Studies*, 2nd ed. (London: T&T Clark, 2016), 156–59.

28. See further Bauckham, "Jewish Messianism," 235–37; for Isa 9:5–6 and its expansion in the Targum, see Brian McNeil, "The Quotation at John XII.34," *NovT* 19 (1977): 22–33.

his emphasis on Jesus as the preexistent *Logos* (1:1–5, 14–18), as the heavenly Son of Man who uniquely reveals God (3:13–14; 8:21–30), and as the one who frequently claims to be "I Am" (e.g., 6:20; 10:1–16; 11:25–27), is not at all at odds with his depiction of Jesus as the Messiah (or King of Israel). Second, we have seen that many of the other titles for Jesus are used together in contexts where Jesus's messiahship is affirmed. As Michael Bird notes: "The titles Prophet, Son of God, Son of Man, and King of Israel are all glued together with reference to Jesus as the Messiah."[29] We have seen, for example, the crowds identify the Son of Man with the Messiah (12:34) and Jesus's messiahship frequently invoked in contexts where he is also referred to as the "coming one" or the "one who comes into the world" (e.g., 1:32–34; 4:25–26; 7:26–47; 11:25–27). This is not to say that these titles are synonymous or that John does not distinguish between them. The honorifics have their own particular connotations and activate distinct scriptural traditions, and yet they all work together to depict Jesus as the Messiah. Third, John's concern to articulate his Christology through messiah language and traditions indicates that the question of Jesus's messiahship was an important matter for John's audience.[30] Thus, the purpose statement of John's Gospel, found in John 20:30–31, fits neatly with the quest stories and messianic speculation we have surveyed. There John writes: "These have been written so that you may believe that Jesus is the Messiah, the Son of God, and that by believing you may have life in his name."[31] One of John's primary goals, then, may have been to invite the audience to consider Jesus as the Messiah of Israel by drawing upon diverse messiah traditions, which he has creatively shaped around the life, death, and glorification of Jesus as a means of defining the surprising meaning of Jesus's messiahship and kingship.

Three Messianic Themes in John—Spirit, Temple, and Shepherd

The previous section has argued that John's Christology has not dispensed with Jesus's messiahship but rather that Jesus's messianic identity is a critical

---

29. Bird, *Jesus Is the Christ*, 138.

30. So Novenson, "Jesus the Messiah," 122.

31. For a discussion of the syntactical and grammatical issues involved in interpreting this verse and their significance for understanding the audience of the Gospel of John, see D. A. Carson, "The Purpose of the Fourth Gospel: John 20:30–31 Reconsidered," *JBL* 108 (1987): 639–51; D. A. Carson, "Syntactical Text-Critical Observations on John 20:30–31: One More Round on the Purpose of the Fourth Gospel," *JBL* 124 (2005): 693–714.

concern of the characters within John's Gospel and that the Gospel has been written to invite others to see and believe that Jesus is, indeed, the Messiah of Israel. In this section, I show how three themes of John's Gospel are creative Johannine expansions of Messiah traditions, namely, (1) the connection between Jesus's messiahship and his role as dispenser of the Holy Spirit; (2) Jesus as the messianic temple builder; and (3) Jesus as the messianic good shepherd.

Messiah and Spirit

We have seen that Israel's messianic traditions often depict the Lord's anointed as endowed with God's authority to enact his rule and that this relationship between God and messiah enabled the king to operate as an agent for God's Holy Spirit (e.g., 1 Sam 16:13; Isa 11:1–4; 61:1–3; Pss. Sol. 17:22, 37; 18:5–7).[32] In John, Jesus's reception of the Spirit is also situated within the broader context of his presentation as Israel's Messiah and Son of God (see throughout 1:19–51). The vision of a descending dove signals to the Baptist that Jesus is the Spirit-anointed Messiah who will baptize others with the Spirit: "I saw the Spirit descending like a dove from heaven and it remained upon him" (1:32). This vision enables John to know that Jesus is "the one baptizing by the Holy Spirit" (1:33). John concludes with further messianic testimony: "I have seen and I have testified that this one is the Son of God" (1:34; or possibly "the elect one," cf. Ps 88:4, 19 LXX). Sandwiched within the account of Jesus's reception of the Spirit are two messianic titles ("Lamb of God," 1:29; "Son of God," 1:34), and many have rightly seen the account as resonating with Isaiah 11 and its depiction of a Davidic king upon whom "rests" (ἀναπαύσεται ἐπ᾽ αὐτὸν πνεῦμα τοῦ θεοῦ, Isa. 11:2) a Spirit of wisdom, strength, and insight which will empower the Davidic ruler to use his speech for justice and revelation (Isa 11:2–4).[33] One sees a similar tradition of the Messiah as engaging in Spirit-empowered teaching and cleansing in Psalms of Solomon 17. Here we see the Messiah as a Davidic king who is "powerful in the Holy Spirit and wise in the counsel of understanding with strength and righteousness" (17:37; cf. Isa 11:2). He is one who is "taught by God" (17:32) and thereby leads God's people in righteousness.

Similarly, in John, one of the primary functions of Jesus's endowment by the Spirit is his ability to reveal divine truth and thereby act as the true judge

32. See further Aubrey Johnson, *Sacral Kingship in Ancient Israel* (Cardiff: University of Wales Press, 1967), 15–19.

33. See further Gary M. Burge, *The Anointed Community: The Holy Spirit in Johannine Tradition* (Grand Rapids: Eerdmans, 1987), 54–62; also Cornelis Bennema, "Spirit-Baptism in the Fourth Gospel: A Messianic Reading of John 1,33," *Biblica* 84 (2003): 41.

of God's people: "The one whom God has sent speaks God's words, for he gives the Spirit without measure. The Father loves the Son and has given all things into his hands" (3:34–35). Jesus's teaching is Spirit-endowed and therefore life-giving: "The words I have spoken to you are Spirit and life" (6:63). Thus, Jesus's ministry as the Spirit-anointed Messiah who baptizes with the Spirit may portend his rule as the heavenly revealer of truth and wisdom.[34] The goal of Jesus's teaching, then, is to reveal God and thereby bring salvation to humanity, but the consequence of his divine revelation is that those who reject his teaching stand under divine judgment (e.g., John 3:17–21; 5:24–30). Jesus's Spirit-empowered word provides freedom and liberation (8:21–47), sanctification and purification (15:3; 17:17–18), and judgment (12:48–49).[35]

In Jesus's first miraculous sign at the wedding feast in Cana (2:1–11), immediately after Jesus has been confessed as "the Son of God" and "the King of Israel" (1:49), Jesus turns the water into wine—and it seems likely that this wine symbolizes the newness and glory of the messianic age. John notes that there were six stone water pots used for "the Jewish rites of purification" (2:6), and Jesus uses these pots to contain the water transformed into wine (2:7). The wedding host responds to the bridegroom with amazement that he had "kept the good wine until now" (2:10). The water used for the rites of purification (2:6) is surpassed by the better wine of the new covenant which Jesus provides. Jesus will later speak of himself as the one who provides cleansing and washing for his people by means of the cross (13:10) and by his spoken word (15:3). Many have noted the many Jewish traditions which associate the coming of the Messiah and the messianic age with the symbol of an abundance of wine. Amos 9:11–14 declares that when God restores the fallen Davidic dynasty "the mountains shall drip sweet wine, and all the hills shall flow with it" (9:13). The author of 2 Baruch notes that the Messiah's revelation will result in one cluster of grapes producing a thousand grapes and each grape producing 120 gallons of wine (2 Bar. 29:5; cf. Isa 25:6; Jer 31:12; Joel 3:18).[36] Wine is associated with the coming of the Messiah also in Jacob's blessing of Judah, the ancestor of the Messiah, in Genesis 49:9–12.[37] John notes that this was Jesus's first sign whereby "he revealed his glory" to his disciples (2:11). One should not miss the cryptic ways in which this scene, like so many in the Fourth Gospel, anticipates

34. Bennema, "Spirit-Baptism," 39, argues that it refers to revelation and cleansing.

35. See here Cornelis Bennema, "The Sword of the Messiah and the Concept of Liberation in the Fourth Gospel," *Biblica* 86 (2005): 35–58.

36. See here Koester, *Symbolism in the Fourth Gospel*, 83–84.

37. See Jane S. Webster, *Ingesting Jesus: Eating and Drinking in the Gospel of John*, AcBib 6 (Atlanta: Society of Biblical Literature, 2003), 40–41.

Jesus's full revelation of his glory on the cross. The brief exchange between Jesus and his mother wherein Jesus notes "my hour has not come" (2:4; cf. 7:30; 8:20; 16:32), the presence of his mother at the cross (19:25–27), and the reference to cleansing and purifying his disciples (see John 13:1–10) indicate that Jesus's glory and his provision of the messianic wine of the new covenant are only given for those who understand that Jesus's messiahship and glory take place on the cross.[38] This messianic wine, which cleanses and purifies God's people and is fully given to people when the Messiah is crucified, is associated with the giving of the Spirit to God's people. John notes that Jesus's invitation on the Feast of Tabernacles to the thirsty to come to him and drink living water refers to the promise of the Spirit which believers would receive after Jesus's glorification (7:37–39). The context for Jesus's promise to give this life-giving Spirit is one of messianic speculation, thereby further connecting Jesus's dispensing of the Spirit with his messiahship.

Given that Jesus is the Spirit-anointed Messiah who "baptizes with the Holy Spirit" (John 1:33), the rest of the Fourth Gospel portrays Jesus's messianic task as dispensing God's Spirit to others. Thus, Jesus declares to Nicodemus that "unless one is born from water and Spirit one cannot enter into God's kingdom" (ἐὰν μή τις γεννηθῇ ἐξ ὕδατος καὶ πνεύματος, οὐ δύναται εἰσελθεῖν εἰς τὴν βασιλείαν τοῦ θεοῦ, 3:5b).[39] Again, note the connection between the language of kingdom and Spirit. Jesus's cryptic statement likely alludes to Ezekiel 36:23–27 which promises that God will, with the advent of his Davidic messianic king, sanctify and cleanse the people of God through the Spirit. In his conversation with the Samaritan woman, Jesus promises a day when true worshippers will worship God "in Spirit and truth" (4:23) since "God is Spirit and those who worship him must worship him in Spirit and truth" (4:24). The woman does not divert the conversation when she replies, "'I know that Messiah is coming' (who is called the Christ)" (4:25; cf; 4:29); rather, she *rightly* connects Jesus's promise of the coming Spirit with his role as Messiah.[40] The "Spirit" here is to be understood as the Holy Spirit and anticipates Jesus's promise of the coming gift of "the Spirit of truth" (14:17; 15:26; 16:13), which will be granted to true worshippers upon Jesus's glorification. Jesus refers to himself as the one who will dispense the Spirit (e.g., 15:26), perhaps further unpacking what the Baptist meant when he referred to Jesus as "baptizing in the

38. So Koester, *Symbolism in the Fourth Gospel*, 86.

39. On the importance of the conception "the kingdom of God" to John's Gospel, see Nicholas Perrin, *The Kingdom of God: A Biblical Theology* (Grand Rapids: Zondervan, 2019), 117–32.

40. Bird, *Jesus Is the Christ*, 116–17.

Holy Spirit" (1:33). The Spirit will continue to aid the disciples in remembering the revelatory teachings of Jesus (16:12–15) and will cleanse and judge the people with respect to sin and unrighteousness (16:8–11). The glorified Jesus fulfills this promise in John 20:19–23, where he gives the Spirit to his disciples (20:22). Jesus commissions the Spirit-empowered disciples now to continue the mission of the Father and the Son and to continue Jesus's task of providing freedom and forgiveness of sins and judgment to the unrepentant (20:21–23). The Spirit of the Messiah will enable the disciples to continue Jesus's ministry of teaching, salvation, and judgment.[41] Jesus's breathing upon (ἐνεφύσησεν) his disciples is an act of new creation (cf. Gen 2:7), but as Michael Gorman has noted, it is an act of new creation "parallel to new birth from the Spirit (1:12; 3:1–8; cf. Ezek 37) rooted in the promise of the life-giving Spirit" as seen in Ezekiel 37:9–10: "Prophesy to the breath/spirit, prophesy human one. Say to the breath/spirit, 'The Lord God proclaims: "Come from the four winds, breath/spirit. Breathe into (ἐμφύσησον) these dead bodies, and let them live."' I prophesied as he commanded me. When the breath/spirit entered them, they came to life and stood on their feet, a very large assembly."[42] This oracle, as we have seen, further speaks of a Davidic king who will shepherd God's people, one of the primary contexts for Jesus's good shepherd discourse in John 10. The Baptist's vision of Jesus as the messianic Son of God who baptizes by the Holy Spirit finds its fulfillment here in the disciples who receive the Spirit to continue the mission of the Father and the Son.[43]

Finally, I briefly note that 1 John 2 also presupposes that Jesus is the Spirit-anointed Christ who dispenses the same gift of anointing to his people. John makes a contrast between "the many anti-christs" (ἀντίχριστοι, 2:18) who deny that "Jesus is the Messiah" (Ἰησοῦς οὐκ ἔστιν ὁ Χριστός, 2:22) and those who know the truth because they have "an anointing (χρῖσμα) from the holy one" (2:20). Note that John says that the church's anointing is dependent upon the Messiah's own Spirit-anointing: "And for you, the anointing (τὸ χρῖσμα) you have received from him abides upon you (μένει ἐν ὑμῖν)" (2:27a). And John further notes, "you have no need for anyone to teach you, since his anointing teaches you about all things" (2:27b). Standing behind John's claims here is the notion of the Messiah as one who has received the divine anointing of the Holy Spirit (e.g., 1 Sam 16:13; Isa 61:1; Luke 4:18; Acts 4:27; cf. 2 Cor 1:21), and

41. See Bennema, "Spirit-Baptism," 54–55.

42. Michael J. Gorman, *Abide and Go: Missional Theosis in the Gospel of John* (Eugene, OR: Cascade, 2018), 140.

43. Gorman, *Abide and Go*, 140–43.

more specifically the Gospel of John's depiction of Jesus as the Spirit-anointed Messiah who shares the "Spirit of truth" who indwells his people and leads them into the truth (John 14:17; 15:26; 16:13).[44] Thus, 1 John provides further evidence for the belief that Jesus's people share in his anointing by the Spirit, and that one of the Spirit's tasks is to lead Christ's people into truth by continuing to lead them in the testimony that Jesus is the Messiah who has come from God and in the flesh as a human (also 1 John 4:2, 3).[45]

Messiah and Temple

Jewish texts and traditions also often make a close connection between Messiah and temple, with some of them even portraying the Messiah as the builder of the eschatological temple. Nicholas Perrin notes that for "at least a sizable swathe of Second-Temple Judaism, it was the messiah who would rebuild the temple."[46] The origins of this association are God's covenant with David, where God promises David that "your offspring . . . will build a house for my name (αὐτὸς οἰκοδομήσει μοι οἶκον τῷ ὀνόματί μου), and I will establish the throne of his kingdom forever" (2 Sam 7:12b, 13; cf. 1 Chr 17:1–15). Zechariah refers to a Davidic king whose name is "Branch" who "will branch out in his place, and he will build the temple of the Lord. It is he who will build the temple of the Lord; he will bear royal honor, and will sit upon his throne and rule" (Zech 6:12–13a; cf. 3:8–10). Isaiah even speaks of Cyrus as God's shepherd, his anointed one who will rebuild Jerusalem and lay the foundations of the temple (Isa 44:28–45:1). In Sibylline Oracle 5, there is a heavenly ruler who eradicates evil and makes a holy, beautiful temple in the city of God (5.414–433). In 4 Ezra 13, there is a vision of a man who comes up out of the sea (13:2) and who "carved out for himself a great mountain" (13:6). Later a great multitude of people flock to the man and his temple on Mount Zion (13:35) and the restored Zion and the eschatological temple built by the Messiah will be revealed to all people (13:36). More Jewish traditions which associate temple and messianic kingship could be adduced (e.g., Ezek 45–47; 1 En. 53, 71; 4Q174), but these texts should prove sufficient to make the point that there was a close connec-

44. See further Timothy Wiarda, *Spirit and Word: Dual Testimony in Paul, John and Luke*, LNTS 565 (London: T&T Clark, 2017), 172–78.

45. See especially Stephen S. Smalley, *1, 2, 3 John*, WBC 51 (Waco, TX: Word, 1984), 104–8.

46. Nicholas Perrin, *Jesus the Temple* (Grand Rapids: Baker Academic, 2010), 101.

tion between messianic king and temple and that some texts even portray the messiah as building the eschatological temple.[47]

The connection between messiah and the building of the eschatological temple is found also in the Fourth Gospel. John's prologue has already set forth Jesus's body as the tabernacle where the glory of God is displayed (1:14), and we have seen that in John 1:51 Jesus refers to himself as the Son of Man, the new ladder connecting earth with the divine glory in heaven.[48] Now, in John 2:13–22, the Fourth Gospel presents the crucified and risen Messiah as both builder and locus of the eschatological temple.[49] The setting for the temple scene in John is bracketed with the language of Passover (2:13, 23), which foreshadows the timing of Jesus's crucifixion (see 11:55; 12:1; 13:1; 18:28, 39). Jesus enters the temple and drives out the money changers and sellers, along with their animals, and overturns the money tables (2:14–15). Jesus's words of judgment are: "Get these things out of here! Stop making the house of my Father a house for markets (μὴ ποιεῖτε τὸν οἶκον τοῦ πατρός μου οἶκον ἐμπορίου)" (2:16).

Jesus's actions and words in the temple raise a host of important matters, most of which we cannot enter into here. I simply note the following. First, Jesus's authority to engage in this symbolic act of judgment against the temple and its leaders presumes the authority of a messianic king. In other words, Jesus's temple act is an implicit declaration that he, as the messianic king, has authority over the temple.[50] Jesus's reference to "the house of my Father" (2:16b) echoes the language of 2 Samuel 7:12–14, where God promises the seed of David that, *as* God's own Son, he will build a house for God's name. Second, Jesus's action is directed primarily against the money changers and

47. See here especially, Leung, *The Kingship-Cross Interplay*, 72–81; Steven M. Bryan, "The Eschatological Temple in John 14," *BBR* 15 (2005): 187–98, here, 192–93; Koester, *Symbolism in the Fourth Gospel*, 87; Perrin, *Jesus the Temple*, 102–5.

48. On the links between the Davidic Messiah, the Son of God, and notions of divine presence in the temple, see Beth M. Stovell, "Son of God as Anointed One? Johannine Davidic Christology and Second Temple Messianism," in *Reading the Gospel of John's Christology as Jewish Messianism*, ed. Benjamin E. Reynolds and Gabriele Boccaccini (Leiden: Brill, 2018), 168–71.

49. There are many helpful studies on John's temple imagery. I have benefited especially from Alan R. Kerr, *The Temple of Jesus' Body: The Temple Theme in the Gospel of John*, JSNTSup 220 (Sheffield: Sheffield Academic Press, 2002); Mary L. Coloe, *God Dwells with Us: Temple Symbolism in the Fourth Gospel* (Collegeville, MN: Liturgical Press, 2001); Joseph R. Greene, "Jesus as the Heavenly Temple in the Fourth Gospel," *BBR* 28 (2018): 425–46.

50. This point is emphasized convincingly by N. T. Wright, *Jesus and the Victory of God*, vol. 4 of *Christian Origins and the Questions of God* (Minneapolis: Fortress, 1996).

the sellers (2:14–15), and even his word of judgment emphasizes his critique of the merchants (2:16). This almost certainly echoes the expectation for the eradication of merchants from the eschatological temple as found in Zechariah 14:21: "and there will no longer be traders in the house of the Lord of hosts on that day." Zechariah 14 envisions an eschatological temple where "living waters will flow out" from the temple (14:8), where the Lord will reign as king (14:9), and everything will be sanctified and consecrated to the Lord (14:20–21). Thus, Steve Bryan has noted that when the Messiah comes to Herod's temple and finds the traders still present in the temple, and presumably the continuation of defilement, sin, and economic exploitation, Jesus indicts "the temple for failing to be the eschatological temple."[51] Third, John's quotation from Psalm 69:9 (68:10 LXX)—where he notes that "the disciples remembered that it was written, 'Zeal for your house will consume me'" (2:18)—is probably best understood as a reference to the temple leadership's zeal for the temple, which is directed against the righteous messianic king.[52] Thus, Jesus is "consumed" by the Jewish leaders' zeal for the temple. This is suggested by the fact that Jesus is arrested within John's Gospel for the threat he poses to the temple (see esp. 11:48–50; 18:13–14). Further, John draws upon Psalm 69, a Davidic psalm which speaks of the persecutions and sufferings of the royal figure, on two other occasions to describe the Messiah's sufferings from the Jewish leaders which culminate in his crucifixion (see Ps 69:5 in John 15:25; Ps 69:22 in John 19:29).[53] The use of Psalm 69 in John's passion narrative (John 19:29), along with the dual references to the Passover, adds further weight to the connection between Jesus's act in the temple and his crucifixion.[54] When Jesus is asked by what authority or what credentials he has to enact such authority over the temple, Jesus responds with a riddle: "Destroy this temple and in three days I will raise it back up" (2:19). The Jews mistakenly think Jesus is talking about Herod's temple which took forty-six years to build (2:20), but John notes that Jesus "was speaking about the temple of his body (περὶ τοῦ ναοῦ τοῦ σώματος αὐτοῦ)" (2:21). The reference to the post-resurrection remembrances of the

51. Steven M. Bryan, "Consumed by Zeal: John's Use of Psalm 69:9 and the Action in the Temple," *BBR* 21 (2011): 492. For prophetic critiques of priestly economic exploitation and defilement of the temple, see Jer 7; Zeph 3:1–8; Mal 3.

52. Thus, the reference to zeal does *not* refer to "Jesus' consuming commitment" to the temple, contra, among many others, Margaret Daly-Denton, *David in the Fourth Gospel: The Johannine Reception of the Psalms* (Leiden: Brill, 2000), 126.

53. On Ps 69 in the Fourth Gospel, see the excellent analysis of Daly-Denton, *David in the Fourth Gospel*, 118–31, 201–8, 219–29.

54. So Leung, *The Kingship-Cross Interplay*, 88.

disciples (2:17, 22) suggests that the disciples' reflection upon Psalm 69, Jesus's conflict with the temple establishment which culminated in his death, and his resurrection led them to believe that Jesus's crucified and resurrected body instantiates the eschatological temple. The Messiah's crucified and resurrected body becomes the means whereby Messiah Jesus builds the eschatological temple. Again, Bryan states the dynamic well: "Together, the citation and the riddle indicate that only as Jesus is consumed by his enemies' zeal for the temple will the true temple, the eschatological dwelling of God with his people be established through Jesus' death and resurrection."[55]

The Johannine theme of Jesus as the eschatological temple continues throughout the Fourth Gospel. All of these episodes could be expanded upon in much greater detail, but allow me to mention four ways John continues to portray Jesus as the temple. First, Jesus's conversation with the Samaritan woman where he promises her a time "when true worshippers will worship the Father in Spirit and truth" anticipates a time when Jesus the Messiah will receive worship from worshippers who have the Spirit of the Messiah.[56] Second, Jesus's declaration during the Feast of Tabernacles, again occurring within the context of speculation as to his messianic identity (7:25–36, 41–52), resonates powerfully with Zechariah 14 (and Ezek 47:1–14), which speaks of "living waters" flowing forth out of the eschatological temple (Zech 14:8).[57] Here Jesus gives the invitation: "If anyone is thirsty, let that one come to me and let the one who believes in me drink. For as the Scripture has said, 'Out of his belly (ἐκ τῆς κοιλίας αὐτοῦ) will flow rivers of living water.' Now he said this about the Spirit, which those believing in him were about to receive; for up to this point there was no Spirit since Jesus had not been glorified" (7:37b–39).[58] The reference to what "the Scripture has said" likely refers to Israel's Scriptures, such as Zechariah 14 and Ezekiel 47, which anticipated an eschatological temple and an abundance of life-giving waters. As Hays notes, "the source of the superabundant eschatological outpouring of water that Jesus offers is . . . *Jesus himself as the symbolic temple prefigured in the prophetic texts*."[59]

---

55. Bryan, "Consumed by Zeal," 487.

56. See further, Coloe, *God Dwells with Us*, 99–108.

57. One might also add Zech 13:1, which anticipates a "fountain opened for David's house."

58. I think this translation, which takes the pronoun αὐτοῦ as referring to Jesus, is more likely than the one which speaks of rivers flowing out of *the believers'* belly. For a robust defense of this interpretation, see Kerr, *The Temple of Jesus' Body*, 236–37.

59. Hays, *Echoes of Scripture in the Gospels*, 316. On the symbolism associated with the Feast of Tabernacles and John 7:37–39, see Koester, *Symbolism in the Fourth Gospel*, 192–200.

Third, Jesus refers to his role in building the eschatological temple in John 14:2–3 when he says: "in my Father's house (ἐν τῇ οἰκίᾳ τοῦ πατρός μου) are many rooms. If not, would I have told you that I am going to prepare a place for you? And if I go and I prepare a place for you, I will come again and I will take you to myself, so that where I am, you may also be." Numerous considerations suggest that Jesus's words most likely refer to his role in building and preparing the eschatological temple. To begin with, the only other occurrence of "my father's house" refers to the temple in John 2:16. In addition, the term "place" is often used in contexts where God speaks of preparing a place (i.e., the temple) where his name will dwell (e.g., Exod. 15:17 LXX), and John himself has already used it in this way in 11:48.[60] Finally, Jesus's washing of his disciples' feet in John 13 is undertaken, in part, so that they might be cleansed and thereby pure to enter into the eschatological temple (see John 13:5, 10–11).[61]

Fourth, rather than the temple, now it is Jesus who is the supreme embodiment of holiness and the one who can sanctify and consecrate his disciples. Margaret Daly-Denton has noted that "Jesus thus ushers in the final age when the holiness proper to the Temple and its officiants will be accessible to all in the Temple, which, according to the Johannine author, is Jesus' body."[62] Richard Bauckham has argued that John's reference to the "sanctification" (ὃν ὁ πατὴρ ἡγίασεν) of Jesus by the Father in John 10:36 is analogous to the consecration of the temple which would have taken place before Hanukkah (John 10:22). This depiction of Jesus's consecration in the context of Hanukkah is, Bauckham argues, deeply connected to "the theme of Jesus as the new temple, fulfilling the meaning of the Jerusalem temple with eschatological newness."[63] Jesus's holiness as the consecrated temple is the basis, then, for his ability to sanctify the disciples. In his prayer, Jesus states: "Sanctify them in the truth. Your word is truth. Just as you have sent me into the world, so I have sent them into the world. And for their sakes I sanctify myself, so that they also may be sanctified in truth" (17:17–19). Thus, Jesus as both priest

---

60. Perrin, *Jesus the Temple*, 54; Bryan, "The Eschatological Temple," 194.

61. On the relationship between John 13 and John 14 as preparation and cleansing for entering into God's household and/or temple, see Joshua W. Jipp, *Saved by Faith and Hospitality* (Grand Rapids: Eerdmans, 2017), 89–92; Mary L. Coloe, *Dwelling in the Household of God: Johannine Ecclesiology and Spirituality* (Collegeville, MN: Liturgical Press, 2007), 123–48.

62. Daly-Denton, *David in the Fourth Gospel*, 123.

63. Richard Bauckham, "The Holiness of Jesus and His Disciples in the Gospel of John," in *The Testimony of the Beloved Disciple: Narrative, History, and Theology in the Gospel of John* (Grand Rapids: Baker Academic, 2007), 263.

and eschatological temple consecrates the disciples and shares his holiness with them such that they are set apart from the profane world (17:14–16). This consecration prepares them for mission in the world and is likely fulfilled in 20:19–23, where the disciples receive the Holy Spirit and the commission to continue Jesus's ministry.[64]

Messiah and Shepherd

In John 10 Jesus declares himself to be the good shepherd, the gatekeeper, and the gate for the sheep (John 10:1–18). John's good shepherd discourse is situated within the context of controversial speculation over Jesus's messianic identity. We have seen that the drama of John 9 centers upon the expulsion from the synagogue of those who confess that Jesus is the Messiah (John 9:22). Thus, when Jesus claims that he is the gate to the sheepfold, this "provides a commentary on the story of the expulsion of the man born blind from the synagogue."[65] Confession of Jesus as the Messiah is the means whereby one enters into God's messianic flock. And in John 10:24, the Jews grow frustrated with Jesus and ask him to declare to them plainly whether or not he is the Messiah. The literary context suggests that Jesus's discourse is a parabolic claim to be Israel's promised messianic shepherd (John 10:5–6). The statement, "I am the good shepherd" is, then, a "royal and even messianic claim."[66] Israel's Scriptures and Greco-Roman texts frequently employ the title of "Shepherd" to describe good kings and rulers.[67] And Jesus emphasizes that he is uniquely qualified to provide care, compassion, and life for God's people. Jesus's care for his sheep is exemplified in his knowing his sheep by name (John 10:3), leading and calling them (10:4–5), giving the sheep pasture (10:9), providing salvation and life abundant (10:9–10), and laying down his own life for the sheep (10:11–18).

---

64. Bauckham, "The Holiness of Jesus," 268–69.

65. Koester, *Symbolism in the Fourth Gospel*, 110.

66. See Stefan Schreiber, "Rätsel um den König: Zur religionsgeschichtlichen Herkunft des König-Titels im Johannesevangelium," in *Johannes Aenigmaticus: Studien zum Johannesevangelium für Herbert Leroy*, Biblische Untersuchungen 29 (Regensburg: Friedrich Pustet), 61–62; Bird, *Jesus Is the Christ*, 127. On the parabolic nature and metaphorical figure of speech employed by Jesus in John 10, see Christopher W. Skinner, "'The Good Shepherd Lays Down His Life for the Sheep' (John 10:11, 15, 17): Questioning the Limits of a Johannine Metaphor," *CBQ* 80 (2018): 97–113.

67. On good kings as shepherds, see Dio Chrysostom, *Or.* 2.6; 2.72; Pliny, *Panegyricus* 2.3; 7.4. Warren Carter argues that Jesus's claim to be the "good shepherd" is set "in contrast to imperial and allied leaders [and] forms part of the Gospel's rhetoric of resistance." See Carter, *John and Empire*, 188.

In our examination of Matthew's portrait of Jesus as the Davidic shepherd who extends God's mercy and compassion to the lost sheep of Israel, we saw shepherding imagery applied to King David to describe his service, care, and protection of God's people (e.g., 1 Sam 17:34–35; 2 Sam 5:2). And we saw that Israel's prophets anticipated another Davidic messiah-shepherd who would rule God's people with justice and compassion (e.g., Jer 23:1–5; Mic 5; Zech 9–14; Pss. Sol. 17:40). John 10, however, draws primarily upon the oracles of Ezekiel 34 and 37.[68] In Ezekiel 34:1–10, the prophet declares God's judgment against Israel's shepherds who have served as wicked leaders over God's people. They have exploited the sheep, not healed the sick or cared for the injured, and have scattered them such that the lost sheep have become food for wild animals. Within John's narrative and Jesus's speech, these false shepherds are the Pharisees and Jewish leaders who attempt to prevent the people from confessing Jesus as the Messiah (cf. 9:18–41; 10:1–5). They are those described by Jesus as "thieves and bandits, but the sheep did not listen to them" (10:8). As a result, Ezekiel declares that God himself will come to search for his sheep, will rescue them, and will care for them with justice and mercy (Ezek 34:11–16). God accomplishes this, however, by means of raising up a Davidic shepherd: "I will set up over them one shepherd, my servant David, and he will feed them: he will feed them and be their shepherd. And I, the Lord, will be their God, and my servant David will be prince among them; I, the Lord, have spoken" (34:23–24). Again, in Ezekiel 37:24 the Lord declares: "My servant David will be king over them; and they will all have one shepherd." Thus, Jesus's reference to himself as "the one shepherd" (εἷς ποιμήν, 10:16) and God's restored people as "the one flock" (μία ποίμην) stems from Ezekiel's anticipation of God's unified people gathered together under the reign of the messianic shepherd-king (esp. Ezek 34:23 and 37:24).[69] Ezekiel is not alone in portraying a coming Davidic king as deeply connected to a hope for the reunification of all Israel (e.g., Hos 3:5; Isa 11; Jer 30:9). Gorman notes that Ezekiel 34 presents a portrait of the "abundant life" that Jesus the messianic shepherd promises to give to his sheep. This life involves rescue, good pasture, care of injuries, being strengthened, justice, security and peace, satisfaction of hunger, liberation from slavery, eradica-

---

68. This has long been recognized by scholarship. For example, Bruce Vawter, "Ezekiel and John," *CBQ* 26 (1964): 450–58. See also Andreas J. Köstenberger, "Jesus the Good Shepherd Who Will Also Bring Other Sheep (John 10:16): The Old Testament Background of a Familiar Metaphor," *BBR* 12 (2002): 67–96, esp. 76–78; Koester, *Symbolism in the Fourth Gospel*, 112–13.

69. See further Leung, *The Kingship-Cross Interplay*, 140.

tion of fear, and a right relationship with God.[70] But Jesus's promise to be the "one shepherd" for the "one flock" anticipates his act of gathering the *other* sheep into the sheepfold (10:16). Whether this refers to diaspora Jews or gentiles (or something else), Jesus clearly accomplishes this act of gathering more sheep into the "one flock" by means of his crucifixion. Four times within John 10:11–18 Jesus refers to laying down his life for the sheep as the proof that he alone is the true good shepherd (vv. 15, 17, and twice in v. 18).[71] Further, the ironic statement of the high priest Caiaphas clearly connects Jesus's death to the gathering of the scattered people of Israel: "He prophesied that Jesus was about to die for the nation, and not only for the nation but also to gather into one the scattered people of God" (11:51–52; cf. 18:14).[72] This is of one piece with Jesus's promise that it will be through his crucifixion (when he is "lifted up") that he will draw all people to himself (12:31–32). Thus, Jesus's identity as the messianic shepherd who lays down his life for his sheep anticipates Jesus's enthronement and glorification at the cross. As Leung has said: "Jesus as the royal Messiah fulfills his shepherding mission *by means of* his death," and it is the allusions to Jesus's death "in the shepherd discourse [which] corroborates the royal-messianic identity of the crucified Jesus by asserting that the shepherd's death is essential and instrumental to the assembly of 'other sheep' and the establishment of 'one flock'—a flock that recognizes the voice of Jesus as the messianic shepherd-king."[73]

THE GLORIOUS ENTHRONEMENT OF THE KING

John's extensive concern to present Jesus's surprising messianic identity, along with the speculation of the Johannine characters as to whether Jesus could be the Messiah, is seemingly left behind in the passion narrative as John now uses the language of kingship instead of messiahship. And yet, there are good reasons for seeing the language of kingship as continuing the theme of the nature of the Messiah and the nature of his kingship and rule. The full revelation of Jesus's glorious kingship is revealed in the enthronement of the Messiah which, paradoxically, takes place in his crucifixion. So Frey: "The crucified one is the

70. Gorman, *Abide and Go*, 52–55.

71. See Hays, *Echoes of Scripture in the Gospels*, 341.

72. See in more detail John A. Dennis, *Jesus' Death and the Gathering of True Israel: The Johannine Appropriation of Restoration Theology in the Light of John 11.47–52*, WUNT 2.217 (Tübingen: Mohr Siebeck, 2006).

73. Leung, *The Kingship-Cross Interplay*, 144.

glorified one, and at the same time the glorified one is enduringly the crucified one."[74] In fact, we have already had occasion to see John foreshadow how messianic and royal images will be reworked by interpreting them through the Messiah's crucifixion. For example, Jesus will build the eschatological temple through his death and departure to the heavenly Father, and Jesus's crucified and risen body will be the locus for God's new temple (John 2:13–22; 7:37–39; 14:1–6). The Spirit-anointed Jesus will baptize people with the Holy Spirit, thereby providing cleansing, sanctification, and revelation ultimately through his death and resurrection (e.g., 2:1–11; 7:37–39). And Jesus is the Davidic messianic shepherd who gives abundant life and unites the scattered children of God into one people through laying down his life for the sheep (John 10:11–18). Jane Heath rightly notes that John's frequent references to "sovereignty repeatedly point to the passion and glorification."[75]

John 12 and the Nature of Jesus's Kingship

In John 12:1–8 Mary anoints Jesus, and Jesus interprets the act of anointing as preparing him for his burial (12:8). Given John's strong connection between Jesus's kingship and the cross and the ensuing triumphal entry in 12:9–19, it is likely that John portrays Mary as anointing Jesus as Israel's messianic king (e.g., 1 Sam 10:1). It is within the triumphal entry that Jesus is explicitly hailed as King. The crowd greets Jesus with their palm branches and goes out to "meet him" (εἰς ὑπάντησιν αὐτῷ) and proclaim: "Hosanna! Blessed is the one who comes (ὁ ἐρχόμενος) in the name of the Lord, the King of Israel (ὁ βασιλεὺς τοῦ Ἰσραήλ)" (12:13). And John notes that Jesus riding on a young donkey fulfills the oracle of Zechariah 9:9: "Do not be afraid, daughter of Zion. Look, your King is coming (ὁ βασιλεύς σου ἔρχεται), sitting on the colt of a donkey" (12:15). John here explicitly connects Jesus's kingship to the specific scriptural texts of Psalm 118 and Zechariah 9.[76] Thus, Nathaniel's earlier acclamation to Jesus—"you are the Son of God, the King of Israel" (John 1:49)—is indeed correct, but John's references to Jesus's kingship (12:13, 15) are capable of being interpreted by the crowds along the same lines as their earlier mistaken assumption in John 6:14–15—that Jesus's kingship would inaugurate Judean political sovereignty. The reference to the palm branches is reminiscent of

---

74. Frey, *The Glory of the Crucified One*, 175.

75. Jane Heath, "'You Say that I Am a King' (John 18.37)," *JSNT* 34 (2012): 243.

76. See Daly-Denton, *David in the Fourth Gospel*, 177; Hays, *Echoes of Scripture in the Gospels*, 325.

episodes during the Hasmonean dynasty when the Israelites celebrated the victory of Simon Maccabeus (1 Macc 13:51) and the rededication of the temple (1 Macc 1:59; 2 Macc 10:7). Commentators often note that coins produced by those who revolted against Rome during the rebellions of 66–70 and 135 CE had images of palm trees and the words, "For the redemption of Zion." Thus, the crowd may be greeting Jesus as the one who will provide royal liberation for Israel.[77] But for John, Jesus's kingship is rightly interpreted as pointing to the cross as the event where the Messiah is enthroned and glorified. It is striking that both Psalm 118:26 and Zechariah 9:9 contain the language of "kingship" and "coming."[78] The title of "the coming one" has been used in a messianic sense already by the Samaritan woman (John 4:24–26) and the people in Jerusalem speculating about Jesus's messianic identity (7:25–31). Whether the crowd understands it or not, their praise of their king as the one who comes in the name of the Lord (John 12:13; Psalm 118:26) rightly—even if unknowingly so on their lips—confesses Jesus to be the coming one who has been sent from the Father/above into the world and who will soon return to the Father through his glorification (John 1:9; 3:31; 5:42–43; 12:44–46; 13:16; 17:6).[79] Jesus's kingship, then, as he is the one who comes from heaven, is of an altogether different order than what the crowds anticipate.

John notes that Jesus's disciples did not understand "these things" until "Jesus was glorified (ὅτε ἐδοξάσθη Ἰησοῦς), and then they remembered that these things had been written of him and had been done to him" (John 12:16). In other words, the disciples did not understand the meaning of their confession of Jesus's kingship and their application of Psalm 118 and Zechariah 9 to Jesus until the Messiah's passion and glorification revealed the true meaning of his kingship. John's statement about the retrospective understanding of the disciples highlights Jesus's promise to send forth the Spirit/paraclete after his glorification and resurrection (2:22; 7:39; cf. also 14:16–17; 15:26; 16:13). Thus, the Messiah's dispensation of the Spirit enables his disciples to read and understand the relationship between Israel's Scriptures and their fulfillment in Jesus as the crucified and glorified messianic king.

The scenes that ensue in John 12 continue to explain and redefine the meaning of Jesus's kingship. First, Jesus declares that his glorification and enthronement will take place by means of his death (John 12:23–29). We have seen, albeit briefly, that the revelation of Jesus's glory (2:11) at the wedding in

---

77. See the helpful discussion in Leung, *The Kingship-Cross Interplay*, 155–56.

78. Daly-Denton, *David in the Fourth Gospel*, 178.

79. See further Daly-Denton, *David in the Fourth Gospel*, 182–88.

Cana foreshadowed Jesus's "hour" (2:4) of crucifixion. And here, when Jesus hears of some Greeks at the Passover festival who are searching for him, Jesus interprets this as an indication that "the hour has come for the Son of Man to be glorified" (ἐλήλυθεν ἡ ὥρα ἵνα δοξασθῇ ὁ υἱὸς τοῦ ἀνθρώπου, 12:23). Jesus interprets this glorification as encompassing his death (12:23–24). The event of which Jesus speaks "is the hour of Jesus's exaltation, when he is exalted on the cross in order to be exalted to heaven."[80] Jesus's death on the cross is simultaneously the glorification of the Son of Man *and* the revelation of the glory of the Father as seen in Jesus's prayer: "'Father, glorify (δόξασόν) your name.' Then a voice came from heaven, 'I have glorified it, and I will glorify it again' (ἐδόξασα καὶ πάλιν δοξάσω)" (12:28). While glory can mean honor or praise (e.g., 5:41, 44; 8:50–54), it can also mean the revelation of the splendor and majesty of God's presence (e.g., 1:14).[81] The Father's glory is revealed in Jesus's death, which is the completion and fulfillment of the work given to him by the Father; thus, the cross simultaneously glorifies the Father and the Son (John 13:31–32, 17:1–5). God's promise to glorify the Son refers at minimum to giving him honor and vindication at his resurrection and his return to the Father, but it paradoxically also refers to the humiliation of the cross as the enthronement of the Son and the very revelation of the glory of God.

Second, and deeply connected to the glorification of the Son at the cross, Jesus's kingship is revealed in his victorious battle against the evil one: "Now is the judgment of this world, and now the ruler of this world will be cast out. And when I am lifted up (ὑψωθῶ) from the earth, I will draw all people to myself" (12:31–32). Again, Jesus accomplishes this victory in a surprising way, for the battle will not be accomplished through a sword such as is wielded by Peter during Jesus's arrest (18:10, 36); rather, Jesus interprets his death on the cross and ensuing glorification as the means whereby "the ruler of the world" comes under judgment and is defeated (see also John 14:30–31 and 16:8–11).[82] The ruler of the world wields a dominion of hatred and violence against Christ and his disciples (3:20–21; 15:26; cf. 13:1–2, 27), but Christ's cross overcomes the world through its revelation of divine love (3:16).[83] As Craig Koester notes:

80. Richard Bauckham, *Gospel of Glory: Major Themes in Johannine Theology* (Grand Rapids: Baker Academic, 2015), 58.

81. See further G. B. Caird, "The Glory of God in the Fourth Gospel: An Exercise in Biblical Semantics," *NTS* 15 (1968/69): 265–77.

82. See the helpful discussion by Judith L. Kovacs, "'Now Shall the Ruler of This World Be Driven Out': Jesus' Death as Cosmic Battle in John 12:20–36," *JBL* 114 (1995): 227–47.

83. Though his emphasis is upon the cross as a defeat of "the ruler of the world" in terms

"The one 'exorcism' in John's Gospel is the crucifixion itself."[84] Throughout the Fourth Gospel, Jesus has frequently spoken of the cosmic conflict between God and evil (e.g., 1:5; 3:18–21; 8:23–28); here in 12:31–33 Jesus sees his ensuing crucifixion and glorification as the means whereby the battle against the "ruler of this world" is won. Jesus's farewell discourse in chapters 14–17 in part enables the disciples to understand that Jesus's arrest, trials, and crucifixion are the means whereby he accomplishes this victory: "I have spoken these things to you so that you may have peace. In the world you have tribulation, but take heart; *I have conquered the world* (ἐγὼ νενίκηκα τὸν κόσμον)" (16:33). The flurry of references to Jesus's glorification (12:23, 28; 13:31–32; 17:1–5) make sense as depicting Jesus's accession to his glorious throne upon defeating his enemies, not unlike the description of the Son of Man/Chosen One in the Similitudes, who after defeating his enemies is seated on his "throne of glory" and judges evil (1 En. 51:3; 69:29; cf. Matt 19:28; 25:31–46).[85]

Third, Jesus famously refers to his crucifixion as being "lifted up" (12:33). This is the third occurrence of ὑψόω to describe Jesus's death (3:14–15; 8:28). John's gloss on the meaning of Jesus being "lifted up" as "signifying the kind of death he was to die" makes it clear that the term refers to the physical act of Jesus being lifted up on the cross. Jesus's earlier teaching of Nicodemus about the kingdom of God (3:3–5) led Jesus to speak of his impending act of being lifted up on the cross and the judgment of the world (3:13–21). This "lifting up" thereby simultaneously refers to Jesus's death on the cross *and* his enthronement and exaltation whereby he returns to the Father to share in his glory.[86] Jesus's enthronement on the cross is the means whereby God's eschatological kingdom is established (3:3, 5), Jesus's divine identity is revealed ("you will know that I am," 8:28; cf. 13:19), and God's love is revealed, thereby drawing all people to Jesus (12:32b). The "lifting up" of Jesus results in his ability to extend eternal life to everyone who believes (3:15–16; cf. 20:30–31).

---

of Roman rulers and authorities, see Tom Thatcher, *Greater than Caesar: Christology and Empire in the Fourth Gospel* (Minneapolis: Fortress, 2009), 116–22.

84. Koester, *Symbolism in the Fourth Gospel*, 230.

85. Kovacs, "'Now Shall the Ruler,'" 244–45.

86. See further Bauckham, *The Gospel of Glory*, 72–74; Godfrey C. Nicholson, *Death as Departure: The Johannine Descent-Ascent Schema*, SBLDS (Chico, CA: Scholars Press, 1983), 141–44; on Isa 52:13–14 and its reference to the servant's exaltation and glorification as the source of John's way of speaking about Jesus's exaltation and enthronement, see Richard Bauckham, *Jesus and the God of Israel: God Crucified and Other Studies on the New Testament's Christology of Divine Identity* (Grand Rapids: Eerdmans, 2008), 1–59. Reynolds, *The Apocalyptic Son*, 122–27, helpfully notes that the cross is critical to the "lifting up" of the Son of Man, but that it is also inclusive of his ascent and heavenly enthronement.

Cross and Kingship

In Jesus's trial before the Jewish high priest he is not asked, as he is in all three Synoptic accounts, whether he is the Messiah (Matt 26:63; Mark 14:61; Luke 22:67); rather, in John, the chief priest only questions Jesus about his disciples and his teaching (John 18:19). John's account, in contrast to the Synoptics, contains a lengthy trial scene that includes a dialogue between Jesus and Pilate concerning the nature of Jesus's kingship (18:33–19:16). Martin Hengel has noted that the "kingship of Jesus weaves through this text like a red thread. The title βασιλεύς appears twelve times as the keyword of the charge [John 18:33, 37 twice, 39; 19:3, 12, 14, 15 twice, 19, 21 twice] and the reference to his βασιλεία occurs three times [all in John 18:36] in Jesus' answers."[87] The discussion begins with Pilate's initial question to Jesus: "are you the King of the Jews?" (18:33b). Pilate uses the language of "king" here in its ordinary sense, not unlike the crowds who hoped to make Jesus "king" after his miraculous feeding of the crowd (6:14) and the crowds during Passover who greet Jesus in his entrance into Jerusalem as a king who will bring freedom and liberation to Judea (12:13, 15). Jesus has already explicitly rejected this type of political kingly identity for himself (6:15). And he does so again in his response to Pilate: "My kingdom is not from this world; if my kingdom were from this world, my servants would be fighting so that I would not be handed over to the Jews; but now my kingdom is not from here." Both Pilate and the Jews belong to the same political order (hence Pilate's ironic question: "I am not a Jew, am I?" in 18:35). Jesus is the one who has come from above and does not belong to this world (3:31; 8:23). As a result, Jesus's kingship rejects the normal trappings of military power and violence. "It has nothing do with the kingdoms of this world, completely ruled as they are by calculating political powers."[88]

Pilate responds with a repetition of his earlier question: "So then you are a king?" (18:37a). Jesus's response does not deny Pilate the truth of his statement: "You say I AM a king" (σὺ λέγεις ὅτι βασιλεὺς εἰμι ἐγώ, 18:37b). While the punctuation here is disputed, I agree with Jane Heath that the underlined phrase in the previous sentence should be taken as one of Jesus's "I AM" sayings (e.g., 4:26; 6:20; 8:24, 28, 58).[89] Thus, Jesus's response to Pilate, βασιλεὺς εἰμι ἐγώ, brings the theme of Jesus's kingship to a climax. Jesus's kingship is

---

87. Martin Hengel, "The Kingdom of Christ in John," in *Studies in Early Christology* (London: T&T Clark, 2004), 335.

88. Hengel, "The Kingdom of Christ," 338.

89. Heath, "'You Say that I Am a King,'" 233–39.

revealed, however, not in political power but in his reign of truth and manifestation of the Father to humanity, as Jesus explicitly connects his kingship to his task of testifying to the truth (18:37).[90] Jesus's kingship is revealed in that he alone, as the "coming one" sent from the Father, is the true judge (3:19; 5:30; 8:16; 9:39; 12:31, 47). Pilate, however, as the representative of imperial Rome, is portrayed as entirely oblivious to and uninterested in the truth as he dismisses any commitment to justice and truth in his treatment of Jesus.[91] The irony is thick throughout the mock trial as Pilate judges Jesus from the bench of justice (19:8–16). As Andrew T. Lincoln notes, "there is the irony that the one on trial is the real judge while the judge is himself put on trial."[92]

Jesus's kingship is revealed and God's kingdom is inaugurated, as we have already noted, in the crucifixion of Jesus. Jörg Frey states this well: "The cross is, in truth, the kingly throne, and in his death the king accedes to his βασιλεία, which he speaks of before Pilate (18.36–37). This is, at the same time, the dawning of the reign of *God*, the eschatological event in which the victory over the world and its ruler takes place (16.11, 33)."[93] Jesus is the messianic ruler who lays down his life for his sheep in order to gather them into one flock (10:11–18). Jesus's glorification and exaltation takes place by means of his crucifixion and his return to the Father (3:13–14; 8:28; 12:31–34; 13:31–32; 17:1–6). Jesus's kingship is evident in his sufferings as he undergoes an ironic and mock royal enthronement by his persecutors before he is publicly rejected by the Jews as the King of the Jews (19:1–7) and as he fulfills the laments of David as seen in John's application of the Davidic psalms to Jesus during his sufferings and death (Ps 22:18 in John 19:24; Ps 69:21 in John 19:28–29; cf. Ps 69:9 in John 2:17).[94] Jesus receives the mock acclamations from Pilate—"Behold, the Man!" (19:5) and "Behold, your King!" (19:14)—and the reader knows by now the ironic truth of both of these claims. Pilate's decision to write the *titulus* over Jesus as "Jesus of Nazareth, the King of the Jews" in Hebrew, Latin, and Greek (19:19–20) calls to mind Jesus's promise that his glorification and enthronement through the cross would be the means of drawing "all people" to himself

---

90. See Schreiber, "Rätsel um den König," 63–65; Andrew T. Lincoln, *Truth on Trial: The Lawsuit Motif in the Fourth Gospel* (Peabody, MA: Hendrickson, 2000), 127.

91. See especially Helen K. Bond, *Pontius Pilate in History and Interpretation*, SNTSMS 100 (Cambridge: Cambridge University Press, 1998), 180–92; Hengel, "The Kingdom of Christ," 342; Lincoln, *Truth on Trial*, 129–30; Carter, *John and Empire*, 289–314.

92. Lincoln, *Truth on Trial*, 134.

93. Frey, *The Glory of the Crucified One*, 175.

94. On which, see Hays, *Echoes of Scripture in the Gospels*, 326–27; Daly-Denton, *David in the Fourth Gospel*, 208–29.

(12:32) and his expectation that this death would unite the scattered children of God into one people (10:16; cf. 11:48–52). Frey again states the paradox well when he notes that the combination of the event of the crucifixion and the royal motifs "give the text an ironic ambiguity, in which the christological truth hidden beneath its opposite is mediated to the readers of the passion narrative—namely, that in Jesus's way to death his true majesty, his kingship, is simultaneously shown in a paradoxical manner in his way of death."[95] Jesus's kingship is revealed, then, in its power to draw all people to the truth of God as revealed in the Son's salvation of the world through his death on the cross. Jesus is a king, but not the kind of king that Pilate (or anyone else) anticipated; rather, Jesus's kingship can only be interpreted in light of Jesus as the heavenly revealer of truth *and* as the crucified one. Hengel's concluding comments bring the theme of Jesus's kingship in John to a fitting close: "The kingdom of Christ is completely identical with the kingdom of God, and is realized in deepest humiliation and powerlessness in the death of Jesus on the cross. Here the new Creation happens, here he comes into his kingdom. The place of the tortured death of the Crucified One and the enthronement coincide."[96]

CONCLUSION

Despite the remarkable christological designations of Jesus as the *Logos*, the heavenly Son of Man, the preexistent one who shares the Father's glory, and the one who is I AM, the Fourth Gospel has not abandoned or, when compared to the Synoptic Gospels, even minimized the importance of designating Jesus as the Messiah.[97] In fact, one of the primary purposes of John's Gospel is to elicit faith in Jesus as the messianic king and to clarify the very meaning of this confession. The Gospel invites the reader, then, to join Philip, Andrew, Nicodemus, the Samaritan woman, and many other Johannine characters in this quest for the Messiah and the meaning of his kingdom and kingship, but along the way John redefines and reworks the expectations of his readers

95. Frey, *The Glory of the Crucified One*, 253–54.

96. Hengel, "The Kingdom of Christ," 355.

97. McGrath, "The Gospel of John," 62 notes that John's "messianism is distinctive . . . because of two factors which were characteristic of the broader Christian movement. The first is the fact that Christianity is a form of messianism expressed in relation to a historical person that had been encountered, and not just an individual that it was hoped would appear in the future. The second is the fact that Christian messianism had to adapt to the reality of Jesus's crucifixion."

as a means of persuading them that Jesus's messianic kingship is revealed through his crucifixion. Thus, for the Fourth Gospel, Jesus is indeed the Spirit-anointed dispenser of the Holy Spirit, the eschatological builder of the temple, the shepherd-king who unites the scattered people of God, the true judge, and the glorious and enthroned king, but each one of these messianic tasks is accomplished by the way of the cross. The disciples' own mission is rooted in Jesus's messianic role as the Spirit-anointed giver of the Spirit to empower them to continue the mission of the Father and the Son in giving liberation, forgiveness of sins, and judgment and conviction to the unrepentant. As we have seen, the Spirit, which comes to the disciples upon the Messiah's enthronement and return to the Father, empowers them to do the "greater works" (14:12) in continuing Jesus's ministry of teaching, judgment, and salvation.

CHAPTER 5

The Messianic Christology of the Apostle Paul

The State of the Discussion and a Few Themes

This chapter is the first of three wherein I argue that Jesus's messiahship is one significant aspect of Paul's Christology.[1] In this chapter, I review the long-standing assumption to the contrary and draw upon recent scholarship which seems to be building to a consensus that Paul's frequent references to Χριστός should be understood as a royal honorific. And I examine four broad themes that provide further evidence for Paul's messianic Christology: the crucified Messiah, the Messiah's inheritance of the nations, Messiah and law, and Messiah and justice. In the next two chapters, I make an extended argument that Paul conceptualizes believers' union with Christ as sharing in the rule and reign of the Messiah.

MESSIAH AS NAME, TITLE, OR HONORIFIC?

Paul frequently refers to Jesus as "Jesus Christ," "Christ Jesus," and simply "Christ." But what is the significance of "Christ" to Paul? Is it just a name, or is he making a theological point with regard to Jesus's identity?

---

1. In these three chapters (chs. 5–7) I am moving from a reading of individual compositions to a synthetic analysis of a group of writings associated with the apostle Paul. There are obvious and well-known challenges here. In this chapter (ch. 5) and the next I make my arguments primarily with respect to Paul's *Hauptbriefe*. In chapter 7 I focus upon Ephesians, Colossians, and 2 Timothy. Given that Paul's authorship of all thirteen letters associated with him in our New Testament is highly disputed, I have tried to present my argument in a way that allows for as minimal distraction from my argument as possible while knowing my arrangement will not please everyone.

The Supposed Insignificance of Jesus's Messiahship for the Apostle Paul

Despite a few notable exceptions, Paul's Christology has not seemed to many to be particularly indebted to Jewish messianism, and thus Jesus's messianic status has often played a fairly minimal role in examinations of Paul's theology.[2] The roots of this neglect are likely due in part to the long-standing scholarly consensus that within Paul's letters Χριστός is a proper name that had lost its titular connotations.[3] After all, as many have noted, Paul's statements where he uses the language of "Christ" are all explicable for those who assume that "Christ" is simply a name.[4] And Paul's use of messiah language certainly does not resemble what we have seen, for example, in texts like the Gospel of John or the Acts of the Apostles where early Christian leaders announce and seek to persuade others that Jesus is the Messiah (e.g., John 20:30–31; Acts 17:2–3). It can be stated with little exaggeration that Wilhelm Bousset's influential *Kyrios Christos* and its positing of a division between Palestinian and Hellenistic Christianity, with the latter valuing the title of "Lord" but devaluing Jewish Davidic traditions, has provided the historical foundations for Paul's supposed lack of interest in Jesus's Davidic descent.[5] Thus, many have argued or assumed that early Christian statements regarding Jesus's Davidic descent stem from an early Jewish-Christian Christology that saw Jesus as a "nationalist" Messiah

---

2. A notable exception regarding the positive relationship between messianism and kingship discourse and the rise of early Christian Christology is William Horbury, *Jewish Messianism and the Cult of Christ* (London: SCM, 1998).

3. Nils A. Dahl, "The Messiahship of Jesus in Paul," in *Jesus the Christ: The Historical Origins of Christological Doctrine*, ed. Donald H. Juel (Minneapolis: Fortress, 1991), 15–25; Rudolf Bultmann, *Theology of the New Testament*, 2 vols. (New York: Scribner's Sons, 1951), 1:49–50, 237; Magnus Zetterholm, "Paul and the Missing Messiah," in *The Messiah in Early Judaism and Christianity*, ed. Magnus Zetterholm (Minneapolis: Fortress, 2007), 33–55.

4. This argument is advanced forcefully by Martin Hengel, "'Christos' in Paul," in *Between Jesus and Paul: Studies in the Earliest History of Christianity* (Philadelphia: Fortress, 1983), 65–77.

5. Wilhelm Bousset, *Kyrios Christos: A History of the Belief in Christ from the Beginnings of Christianity to Irenaeus*, trans. John E. Steely (Nashville: Abingdon, 1970). Preceding Bousset, however, in the division between Palestinian and Hellenistic Christianity was Wilhelm Heitmüller, "Zum Problem Paulus und Jesus," *ZNW* 13 (1912): 320–37. On the role of Bousset on historical investigations of the origins of Paul's Christology, see Leander E. Keck, "Christology of the New Testament: What, Then, Is New Testament Christology?," in *Who Do You Say That I Am? Essays on Christology*, ed. Mark Allan Powell and David R. Bauer (Louisville: Westminster John Knox, 1999), 187–91.

for the people of Israel (e.g., Matt 9:27; Luke 1:27, 31–35; Rev 5:5).[6] In describing the meaning of *Christ* within the Hellenistic church setting, Reginald Fuller states without argument that it is "widely recognized, Χριστός ('Christ') lost its distinctive titular force, and sank to the level of a proper name, both when standing alone, and also in combination with 'Jesus.'"[7] Further, it is supposed, gentile Christians would have had little interest or understanding of a figure titled "Messiah."[8] Many thereby suggest that Paul indeed assumes the confession that Jesus is the Messiah as traditional, and hence the frequency of the use of the second surname to refer to him, but that Jesus's messiahship plays a marginal role in Paul's theological discourse.[9]

Challenging the Consensus

But there have always been outliers to the supposed consensus, and many have simply drawn attention to simple places in Paul's letters where Jesus's messianic status seems to be of great significance for Paul. For example, N. T. Wright (among others) has drawn attention to the importance of Jesus's Davidic messiahship for his argument in Romans.[10] Romans contains an *inclusio* that affirms Jesus's Davidic lineage (Rom 1:3–4; 15:7–12), and it is against this scriptural Davidic-sonship framework that Paul makes sense of Jesus's resurrection and enthronement (see 2 Sam 7:12–14; Pss 2:7; 89:26–27).[11] Adela Collins provides a brief but convincing sketch that Paul's abundant use of the

6. See, for example, Ferdinand Hahn, *The Titles of Jesus in Christology: Their History in Early Christianity* (New York: World, 1969), 240–46.

7. Reginald H. Fuller, *The Foundations of New Testament Christology* (New York: Charles Scribner's Sons, 1965), 230.

8. This supposition is found frequently, but see most strongly the arguments of Werner Kramer, *Christ, Lord, Son of God*, Studies in Biblical Theology 50 (London: SCM, 1966).

9. See, for example, Andrew Chester, "Christ of Paul," in *Redemption and Resistance: The Messianic Hopes of Jews and Christians in Antiquity*, ed. Markus Bockmuehl and James Carleton Paget (London: T&T Clark, 2008), 109–21.

10. See N. T. Wright, *Paul and the Faithfulness of God*, vol. 4 of *Christian Origins and the Question of God* (Minneapolis: Fortress, 2013), 818–21; Christopher G. Whitsett, "Son of God, Seed of David: Paul's Messianic Exegesis in Romans 1:3–4," *JBL* 119 (2000): 661–81. Also, see my "Ancient, Modern, and Future Interpretations of Romans 1:3–4: Reception History and Biblical Interpretation," *JTI* 3 (2009): 258–59.

11. On Paul's messianic exegesis, see Lidija Novakovic, *Raised from the Dead according to Scripture: The Role of Israel's Scripture in the Early Christian Interpretations of Jesus' Resurrection*, Jewish and Christian Texts Series 12 (London: T&T Clark, 2012); Donald Juel, *Messianic Exegesis: Christological Interpretation of the Old Testament in Early Christianity* (Philadelphia: Fortress, 1988).

honorific "indicates that the proclamation of Jesus as the Messiah of Israel was a fundamental part of his announcement of the good news to those who formed the core membership of the communities that he founded."[12] Further, as emphasized by Richard Hays, Paul's appropriation of royal psalms to Jesus—Psalm 68:23–24 in Romans 11:9; Psalm 68:10 in 15:3; Psalm 17:50 in 15:9; Psalm 117:1 in 15:11; and Ps 115:1 in 2 Cor 4:13–14—is only intelligible because of Paul's belief that Jesus was the messianic descendant of the Davidic king.[13] Moreover, Douglas Campbell has argued persuasively that Paul's argument in Romans 8 is indebted to "a story of ascent through resurrection to glorification and heavenly enthronement" and that this story is "explained by royal messianic theology, and in particular by the Old Testament's enthronement texts, among which Psalm 89 is outstanding."[14] Similarly, Haley Goranson Jacob has argued that Paul echoes two messianic psalms (Pss 89 and 110) to speak of the messianic Son of God (Rom 8:29 and 34). She further argues that Paul portrays his audience as sharing in the messianic Son of God's rule over creation.[15] Further, numerous continental philosophers have seen Paul's apocalyptic messianism displaying a politics of an alternative sovereignty based on the crucified Messiah.[16] And William Horbury's important *Jewish Messianism and the Cult of Christ*, while broader in scope than the Pauline letters, argues

---

12. Adela Yarbro Collins and John J. Collins, *King and Messiah as Son of God: Divine, Human, and Angelic Messianic Figures in Biblical and Related Literature* (Grand Rapids: Eerdmans, 2008), 122. See also Stefan Schreiber, *Gesalbter und König: Titel und Konzeptionen der königlichen Gesalbtenerwartung in frühjüdischen und urchristlichen Schriften*, BZNW 105 (Berlin: de Gruyter, 2000), 405–24.

13. Richard B. Hays, "Paul's Use of an Early Christian Convention," in *The Future of Christology: Essays in Honor of Leander E. Keck*, ed. Abraham J. Malherbe and Wayne A. Meeks (Minneapolis: Fortress, 1993), 122–36; Matthew V. Novenson, *Christ among the Messiahs: Christ Language in Paul and Messiah Language in Ancient Judaism* (Oxford: Oxford University Press, 2012), 151–56.

14. Douglas A. Campbell, "The Story of Jesus in Romans and Galatians," in *Narrative Dynamics in Paul: A Critical Assessment*, ed. Bruce W. Longenecker (Louisville: Westminster John Knox, 2002), 116.

15. Haley Goranson Jacob, *Conformed to the Image of His Son: Reconsidering Paul's Theology of Glory in Romans* (Downers Grove, IL: InterVarsity Press, 2018).

16. See, for example, Jacob Taubes, *The Political Theology of Paul*, trans. Dana Hollander (Stanford: Stanford University Press, 2004); Giorgio Agamben, *The Time That Remains: A Commentary on the Letter to the Romans*, trans. Patricia Dailey (Stanford: Stanford University Press, 2005); Alain Badiou, *Saint Paul: The Foundation of Universalism* (Stanford: Stanford University Press, 2003); on the philosophical turn to Paul for contemporary matters, see Ward Blanton and Hent de Vries, eds., *Paul and the Philosophers* (New York: Fordham University Press, 2013).

that Jewish messianism and Greco-Roman notions of kingship provide the context for the origination of the Christ cult, evidenced particularly in the similarities with which Christ receives acclamations, hymns, and titles.[17] Recently, Larry Hurtado has argued that "Paul's Christology reflects a particular and distinctive 'variant-form' of the Jewish messianism of his time."[18] While Hurtado points to a variety of distinctives in Paul's messianic Christology, he finds most striking the way in which "the exalted Jesus is programmatically treated as the rightful co-recipient of devotional practice (including corporate worship), along with God."[19]

Χριστός as a Royal Honorific

In my *Christ Is King* (2015),[20] I noted that the former consensus that "Messiah" functions as a name in Paul shows signs, however, of being overturned, as many voices have marshaled evidence that indicates that the term means "Messiah" and retains its royal connotations.[21] And I argued that traditions of the good king, both in Jewish and Greco-Roman texts, had influenced Paul's portrait of the Messiah as the singular messianic king. As far as I have been able to tell, no one has provided a serious counter-argument to Matthew Novenson's monograph *Christ among the Messiahs*, in which he demonstrates that Paul's use of Χριστός conforms quite closely to common uses of honorifics in the ancient world.[22] Thus, for Paul, Χριστός is not a proper name (or, strictly speaking, a title), but is rather an honorific such as Seleucus *the Victor*, Alexander *the Great*, or Judah *Maccabee*. Honorifics can be used in combination with the individual's proper name or can stand in for the proper name. In this view, such honorifics are honorable names granted to the individual, usually

17. William Horbury, *Jewish Messianism and the Cult of Christ* (London: SCM, 1998).

18. Larry W. Hurtado, "Paul's Messianic Christology," in *Paul the Jew: Rereading the Apostle as a Figure of Second Temple Judaism*, ed. Gabriele Boccaccini and Carlos A. Segovia (Minneapolis: Fortress, 2016), 107.

19. Hurtado, "Paul's Messianic Christology," 118.

20. Joshua W. Jipp, *Christ Is King: Paul's Royal Ideology* (Minneapolis: Fortress, 2015). Kind thanks to Fortress Press for the permission to reuse abbreviated and revised portions of my earlier work in this chapter and the next.

21. N. T. Wright, *The Climax of the Covenant: Christ and the Law in Pauline Theology* (Minneapolis: Fortress, 1991); Wright, *Paul and the Faithfulness of God*, 815–36; Collins and Collins, *King and Messiah*, 101–22.

22. Novenson, *Christ among the Messiahs*. He has further expanded and strengthened his arguments now in his second monograph *The Grammar of Messianism: An Ancient Jewish Political Idiom and Its Users* (Oxford: Oxford University Press, 2017).

kings and rulers, to signify their unique identity and significance, often as a result of a military victory, accession to power, or benefaction.[23] In sum, Paul's variegated usage of "Christ", "Jesus Christ," and "Christ Jesus" makes sense, Novenson argues, within the conventions of Greek honorifics. Novenson examines a handful of Pauline texts and concludes that "Paul does all that we normally expect any ancient Jewish or Christian text to do to count as a messiah text and that in no case does he ever disclaim the category of messiahship."[24] Paul's Christ language is messiah language not as a result of its conformity to a Jewish messianic ideal or to the possible psychological messianic expectation of Paul's hearers, but rather because the language "could be used meaningfully in antiquity because it was deployed in the context of a linguistic community whose members shared a stock of common linguistic resources."[25] In other words, Israel's Scriptures provided the linguistic and conceptual resources whereby Paul, as an example of one Jewish writer, could use scriptural messiah language with the expectation of communicating successfully with those who shared the same Scriptures. We should further note that Paul's letters are all circumstantial texts written to communities to whom Paul had already explained the gospel. In other words, both Paul and the churches to whom he writes are already convinced of the messiahship of Jesus; therefore, we should not prejudge the matter by assuming Paul's messianic Christology will look like that of the Synoptic Gospels, the Gospel of John, or the Apocalypse.[26] In what follows, I will examine four messianic motifs and images in Paul: (1) the faithful suffering crucified Messiah, (2) the inheritance of the Messiah, (3) Messiah and law, and (4) Messiah and justice.

THE DEATH OF THE MESSIAH

Jesus's crucifixion raises difficult issues for his messiahship that the apostles had to resolve, not only for themselves, but for those to whom they proclaimed the gospel as well. Paul's extensive use of the Psalms helps him make his case.

---

23. Novenson, *Christ among the Messiahs*, 64–97.

24. Novenson, *Christ among the Messiahs*, 138.

25. Novenson, *Christ among the Messiahs*, 47. Thus, Nils Dahl, *Jesus the Christ: The Historical Origins of Christological Doctrine* (Minneapolis: Fortress, 1991), 17–19, is right to argue that the honorific "Christ" does not have fixed content which Paul takes over but, rather, that the meaning of *Messiah* is determined through the particular identity and work of Jesus Christ.

26. So Novenson, *Christ among the Messiahs*, 103.

A Crucified Messiah

In my earlier chapters on the Gospels, we have seen a distinct concern to explain how it is that Israel's Scriptures could make sense of a Messiah who suffered and died on a Roman cross. Luke's Jesus, for example, draws upon the psalms of the suffering Davidic king as one way of explaining how Israel's Scriptures testify to a suffering Messiah. John's Gospel wrestles with the death of the Messiah and ironically turns Jesus's death on the cross into the central moment of his glorification and exaltation, and hence the revelation of his sovereign kingship. These Gospel texts are undoubtedly narratival testimonies of early Christian reflection upon how and why the Messiah was crucified. It is quite obvious that the death of the Messiah was a standard, traditional component of the early Christian kerygma (also 1 Cor 11:23–26; 15:3–5; Gal 3:1).[27] And when Paul speaks of the significance of Jesus's death and resurrection, he repeatedly uses the title Χριστός to do so (e.g., Rom 5:5–6, 8; 14:9, 15; 1 Cor 5:7; 8:11; 15:20; Gal 2:21; 3:13). Hurtado has noted that this "seems to reflect an emphasis on Jesus' death and resurrection in particular as *messianic* acts/events—an emphasis that likely originated in circles of Aramaic-speaking and Greek-speaking Jews and was then echoed and developed by Paul."[28] The surprising combination of "Messiah" and "crucifixion" (or death) is testified to by the NT texts in a variety of ways as we have seen, not least by Paul's almost formulaic statement in 1 Corinthians 1:23: "we proclaim a crucified Messiah (Χριστὸν ἐσταυρωμένον)—a stumbling block for the Jews and foolishness for the gentiles." And again, a bit later Paul declares that his message among the Corinthians was simply that of "Jesus the Messiah and this one crucified" (Ἰησοῦν Χριστὸν καὶ τοῦτον ἐσταυρωμένον, 1 Cor 2:2). While the Messiah's death on a cross does not break the bounds of Jewish messianism, it certainly "unsettled more familiar Jewish messianic traditions," as evidenced by Paul's paradoxical reevaluation of God's power, wisdom, and strength in 1 Corinthians 1–2.[29]

---

27. See especially C. H. Dodd, *The Apostolic Preaching and Its Developments* (New York: Harper & Row, 1964). With respect to Rom 1:1–6 and 1 Cor 15:1–11, see Matthew W. Bates, *The Hermeneutics of the Apostolic Proclamation: The Center of Paul's Method of Scriptural Interpretation* (Waco, TX: Baylor University Press, 2012), 59–106.

28. Hurtado, "Paul's Messianic Christology," 111. See also Larry W. Hurtado, *Lord Jesus Christ: Devotion to Jesus in Earliest Christianity* (Grand Rapids: Eerdmans, 2003), 100–101.

29. See Paula Fredriksen, *Paul: The Pagans' Apostle* (New Haven: Yale University Press, 2017), 141, who rightly emphasizes throughout that Paul's language does not break the

The Psalter and the Death of the Messiah

Paul provides further evidence that the early Christians read the Psalter as a prophetic sourcebook of the sufferings, death, and vindication of Messiah Jesus. Paul draws upon the language of the Davidic psalms and its depiction of a righteous royal sufferer as setting a pattern for God's resurrection and deliverance of Messiah Jesus out of his sufferings and death (e.g., Ps 43:23 in Rom 8:36; Ps 68:10 in Rom 15:3; Ps 68:23 in Rom 11:9–10; Ps 115:1 in 2 Cor 4:13; and Ps 2:1–3 in Eph 1:20–2:3).

For example, in 2 Corinthians 4:13 Paul cites LXX Psalm 115:1 (ἐπίστευσα, διὸ ἐλάλησα) to explain or illustrate his claim that he and his apostolic team "have the same spirit of faith" (or of the faithful one).[30] This citation functions as a justification for Paul's *same* activity as the psalmist: "and so we also believe, and therefore we also speak" (καὶ ἡμεῖς πιστεύομεν, διὸ καὶ λαλοῦμεν, 2 Cor. 4:13b).[31] In other words, Paul's believing and speaking is rooted or based upon the prior activity of the believing and speaking of the psalmist. There are a handful of exegetical challenges in this text, but here I simply want to make a few observations. First, the broader narrative of Psalm 115 (LXX Ps 114 and 115) is that of one who is experiencing great suffering and is close to death. But the psalmist maintains his faith and confidence in God, and God rescues him from death. The result is that the psalmist speaks words of thanksgiving and praise to God.[32] Second, 2 Corinthians 4:7–15 contains Paul's argument that he and his apostolic team embody "the death of Jesus" and "the life of Jesus" in their bodies (4:10–11). In other words, the background for Paul's argument here is the death of Jesus and God's resurrection of him from the dead. Third, this suggests that Paul's application of Psalm 115, a psalm of a righteous sufferer, has been interpreted as, in the first instance, a psalm about the sufferings, faithfulness, death, and resurrection of Jesus the Messiah. Thus, Paul is able to declare that he, too, undergoes this same dynamic of faith and loyalty to God in the midst of suffering and being handed over to death (4:11), as well as

---

boundaries of Jewish messianism even if it was surprising and unsettling to his Jewish contemporaries. Also, Novenson, *Christ among the Messiahs*, 160–64.

30. This is Psalm 116:10 in the Hebrew.

31. On this text, I have learned much from Douglas A. Campbell, "2 Corinthians 4:13: Evidence in Paul That Christ Believes," *JBL* 128 (2009): 337–56; Thomas D. Stegman, "Ἐπίστευσα, διὸ ἐλάλησα (2 Corinthians 4:13): Paul's Christological Reading of Psalm 115:1a LXX," *CBQ* 69 (2007): 725–45.

32. The resonances between 2 Cor 4:7–15 and Ps 115 are nicely set out by Frank J. Matera, *II Corinthians: A Commentary*, NTL (Louisville: Westminster Knox, 2003), 112–13.

confidence in God's continuing deliverance whereby he speaks thanksgiving to God. The primary point is that Paul has understood Psalm 115 as containing the narrative of the suffering, faithful, and vindicated Messiah. And, in fact, as Frances Young and David Ford have argued, Paul's frequent autobiographical references to his sufferings, confidence in God, and faith that God will rescue and deliver him out of his trials are likely indebted to his belief in and reflections upon Messiah Jesus's perfect embodiment of the same pattern.[33]

We see a similar reading of the Psalter in Romans 15:1–12, where Paul portrays Christ as the messianic king by placing portions of two Davidic psalms on the lips of Jesus. In order to justify his claim that the Roman Christians should seek to please their neighbors, Paul writes: "for even the Christ (ὁ Χριστός) did not please himself, but as it has been written, 'the insults of those insulting you have fallen upon me'" (Rom 15:3).[34] The quotation derives from Psalm 69:9 (LXX 68:10), a royal psalm of David.[35] The speaker of Psalm 69, however, is not David but the subject of the previous sentence—"the Christ."[36] And again in Romans 15:9, the subject, the one speaking the words of the Davidic Psalm 18—"I will confess you among the gentiles, and I will praise your name" (Ps 18:50 [LXX 17:50])—is "the Christ" of the preceding verses (Rom 15:7, 8). This identification of "the Christ" with the anointed king of biblical tradition is no surprise for an epistle whose body begins by identifying Christ Jesus as God's "son . . . who was born from the seed of David according to the flesh" (Rom 1:3) and concludes by identifying him, in the words of Isa 11:10, as "the root of Jesse and the one who has been raised up to rule over the gentiles" (Rom 15:12). These descriptions of a ruler who is referred to as "the Christ" (15:3, 7, 8), who speaks David's psalms (15:3, 9), and who is described as "Jesse's son" (15:12) who rules

33. For more detail, see Frances Young and David F. Ford, *Meaning and Truth in 2 Corinthians* (Grand Rapids: Eerdmans, 1987), 63–69.

34. Bates, *The Hermeneutics of the Apostolic Proclamation*, 240–55, argues that this is a case of prosopological exegesis in that Paul portrays Christ as speaking the words of David from the standpoint of Christ's heavenly enthronement and reflection upon the event of the passion.

35. On Pss 69 and 18 as royal psalms, see John H. Eaton, *Kingship and the Psalms*, SBT 32 (London: SCM, 1976), 51–53, 113–16.

36. On Christ as the speaker of the psalm (in Rom 15:3, 9), see Richard B. Hays, "Christ Prays the Psalms: Paul's Use of an Early Christian Convention," in *The Future of Christology: Essays in Honor of Leander E. Keck*, ed. Abraham J. Malherbe and Wayne A. Meeks (Minneapolis: Fortress, 1993), 122–36. On a narrative of Christ grounding Paul's exhortations in Rom 15:1–7, see Douglas A. Campbell, "Participation and Faith in Paul," in *"In Christ" in Paul: Explorations in Paul's Theology of Union and Participation*, ed. Michael J. Thate et al. (Grand Rapids: Eerdmans, 2018), 49–50.

over the nations (15:7–12) justifies the claim that within the stretch of Romans 13:8–15:13, Paul characterizes Christ as Israel's messianic king.[37]

The primary activity of Christ is indicated in 15:3, where Paul's statement "even the Christ did not please himself" (καὶ γὰρ ὁ Χριστὸς οὐκ ἑαυτῷ ἤρεσεν) is presented as the self-giving, cruciform model to imitate for the Romans, specifically for the strong (15:1). Christ's not pleasing himself, undoubtedly a reference to his sufferings and death (in light of Ps 69),[38] justifies the appeal to the strong: "we who are strong ought to bear the weakness of the weak and to not please ourselves (μὴ ἑαυτοῖς ἀρέσκειν). Let each of us please one's neighbor (ἕκαστος ἡμῶν τῷ πλησίον ἀρεσκέτω) for the good of building up the neighbor" (15:1b–2). The reference here to "neighbor" suggests that Paul is paraphrasing Leviticus 19:18.[39] Christ functions as the supreme example of the one who bore his neighbors' burdens, as called for by Leviticus 19:18, and pursued his neighbor's good even at the cost of pleasing himself (Rom 15:3b). Earlier in the epistle Paul has spoken of Christ as the one who even died for "we who were weak" (5:6; also 15:1). The Messiah's embodiment of sacrificial love for his people as seen in his sufferings and death is the foundation for the church having "the same mind toward one another according to the standard of Messiah Jesus" (Rom 15:5–6), and this leads to a church that praises God together with one voice—with the Messiah himself leading the choir in praise to God (Rom 15:9–12).

The Messiah's sacrificial death to rescue his people accounts for what Hurtado has described as Paul's "striking intensity in expressing his relationship and that of other believers to Christ."[40] Thus, the messianic Son of God is "the one who loved me and gave himself up for me" (Gal 2:20b). The "Messiah's love" is a powerful force that Paul says constrains him and others such that they now live "for the one who died and was raised for them" (2 Cor 5:14–15). Paul celebrates the fact that the Messiah's death and resurrection ensures that nothing in creation will be able to separate believers from God's love which is in Messiah Jesus our Lord" (Rom 8:39). The Messiah's loving death is also the basis for Paul's demand that believers love one another. Thus, the Messiah's

---

37. Horbury, *Jewish Messianism*, 142–43.

38. Psalm 69 is quoted and alluded to in the passion narratives of all four Gospels (see Matt 27:34; Mark 15:32, 36; Luke 23:36; John 2:17; 15:25; 19:28–29). On the relationship between Paul's use of Ps 69 in Rom 15 and the Jesus-tradition, see Dale C. Allison Jr., *Constructing Jesus: Memory, Imagination, and History* (Grand Rapids: Baker Academic, 2010), 406–11.

39. James W. Thompson, *Moral Formation according to Paul: The Context and Coherence of Pauline Ethics* (Grand Rapids: Baker Academic, 2011), 125.

40. Hurtado, "Paul's Messianic Christology," 115. In more detail, see especially Chris Tilling, *Paul's Divine Christology*, WUNT 2.323 (Tübingen: Mohr-Siebeck, 2012), 105–37.

death "while we were still weak" (Rom 5:6) and "still sinners" (5:8) has revealed "God's love" (5:5, 8). Christ is "the one who loved us" (τοῦ ἀγαπήσαντος ἡμᾶς), thereby enabling his subjects to "conquer in all things" (8:37). The vicarious death of the Messiah for the weak is the basis for Paul's exhortation that believers walk "according to love" (Rom 14:15).

The Inheritance of the Messiah

Through his application of the Jewish Scriptures, Paul illuminates Messiah Jesus's inheritance as consisting of four main elements: rule over all the nations, a worldwide kingdom, a team of apostles securing the nations for his rule, and a renewed cosmos.

The Messianic Ruler of the Nations in Israel's Scriptures

One of the frequent refrains in Israel's messianic ideology is the promise that the king will rule peacefully over the non-Jewish nations (and in some texts even over a worldwide kingdom!).[41] This may go back all the way to some of the poetic seams in the Torah which look forward to a coming ruler, a royal descendant of Judah, who "is the expectation of the nations" (Gen 49:8–12, here, v. 10). This kingly figure's rule over his people and the nations will result in a return to Eden-like fertility in the land (49:8, 9b, 11–12). Similarly, in Numbers 24 Balaam prophesies of a coming king "who will rule over many nations, and his kingdom will be exalted above Gog, and his kingdom will be increased" (Num 24:7 LXX). As a result of his pacification of his enemies, the nations will be the "inheritance" of the king (24:17b–18), and they will give praise and honors to the Israelite king (Num 23:21). The Psalter is filled with royal hymns and promises that the coming Davidic king will establish a righteous rule over the entire cosmos and the foreign nations who will come to worship the king (e.g., Pss 72:1–18; 89:1–28). In fact, Psalm 72:17–18 envisions the rule of the messianic king as fulfilling the promise made to Abraham that he and his family would be a blessing to the nations (Gen 12:1–3). We have seen that God's response to the rebellious nations in Psalm 2 is that of

---

41. On the depiction of Israel's kings and messiahs as ruling over Israel's land, as well as even a worldwide rule, see Esau McCaulley, *Sharing in the Son's Inheritance: Davidic Messianism and Paul's Worldwide Interpretation of the Abrahamic Land Promise in Galatians*, LNTS 608 (London: T&T Clark, 2019), 47–75.

enthroning his Davidic king on Mount Zion and that God promises to give him the nations as his inheritance (Ps 2:6–8). In Psalm 18 the king declares that God has made him "the head over many nations" who come to the king in obedience to him (see Ps 18:39–45). The prophet Isaiah also anticipates a day when a Davidic king will rule the nations and subject them in obedience to the Messiah (Isa 11:1–15). While this royal ideology is capable of being employed for violence, force, and exploitation we will see that Paul employs this discourse to portray Christ as establishing a peaceful rule over the nations and the renewed cosmos.

The Messianic Seed of Abraham Who Blesses the Nations

God's promise to bless the nations through Abraham and his seed is repeated throughout the patriarchal narratives in Genesis (Gen 12:1–4; 17:9–21; 22:15–19), but Paul interprets the fulfillment of the Abrahamic promises as taking place through the Davidic Messiah.[42] The potential for connecting the Abrahamic promises with David predates Paul. For example, Genesis 17 and 2 Samuel can be understood as mutually illuminating one another, given that the covenant of Genesis 17 speaks of kings coming from Abraham's seed.[43] Furthermore, Psalm 72 clearly marks out the son of David as the seed of Abraham who will bless the nations. Compare, for example, Psalm 72:17 with Genesis 22:18.

> "May all the tribes of the earth be blessed in him, all the nations will bless him" (εὐλογηθήσονται ἐν αὐτῷ πᾶσαι αἱ φυλαὶ τῆς γῆς, πάντα τὰ ἔθνη μακαριοῦσιν αὐτόν). (Ps 71[72]:17)

> "All the nations of the earth will be blessed by/in your seed" (καὶ ἐνευλογηθήσονται ἐν τῷ σπέρματί σου πάντα τὰ ἔθνη τῆς γῆς). (Gen 22:18)

In Galatians 3:14–19 Paul presents a complex argument whereby he argues that the Davidic Messiah is the promised seed of Abraham who enables the blessing of Abraham to go to the gentiles. In Galatians 3:13–14 Paul states that Christ's death on the cross has provided a redemption from the curse of the law "in order that the blessing of Abraham may go to the gentiles in Messiah

---

42. Similarly, Novenson, *Christ Among the Messiahs*, 138–42; James M. Scott, *Adoption as Sons of God: An Exegetical Investigation into the Background of ΥΙΟΘΕΣΙΑ in the Pauline Corpus*, WUNT 2.48 (Tübingen: Mohr Siebeck, 1992), 254–56.

43. See McCaulley, *Sharing in the Son's Inheritance*, 145.

Jesus, in order that we might receive the promise of the Spirit through faith [or: "through the faithful one"]." Paul's language of "the blessing of Abraham" (ἡ εὐλογία τοῦ Ἀβραάμ) comes from Genesis 28:4, where Isaac grants the blessing to Jacob: "May he give to you the blessing of Abraham my father, even to you and *your seed* (τῷ σπέρματί σου) after you."[44] There is a further echo of Genesis 22:18 LXX, where God promises Abraham: "and in your seed all the nations of the earth will be blessed (ἐνευλογηθήσονται ἐν τῷ σπέρματί σου πάντα ἔθνη τῆς γῆς)."[45] The echo of Genesis 22:18 is not surprising given Paul's recent quotation of the same text in Galatians 3:8b. In Galatians 3:14 Paul has, then, interpreted God's promise to bless all the nations of the earth *in Abraham's seed* as taking place "in Messiah Jesus" (ἐν Χριστῷ Ἰησοῦ).[46] As is well known, Paul later identifies Abraham's seed with "Christ." In 3:16 Paul says that God's promises were made to Abraham and to his singular *seed*; and Abraham's seed "is the Messiah." Throughout the patriarchal narratives, God's promise to give something to Abraham *and his seed* is repeated four times (Gen 13:15; 17:8; 22:18; 24:7).[47] Paul's interpretation of Messiah Jesus as Abraham's seed is almost certainly due, in part, to his linkage of the Abrahamic covenant to God's promise to David in 2 Samuel 7:12–14 where God says to David: "I will raise up your seed after you; he will come from your loins, and I will prepare his kingdom" (2 Sam 7:12).[48] Within the context of 2 Samuel 7:12, it is clear that the seed refers to David's descendants who will have their own kingdom (also LXX Pss 17:49–51; 88:1–4). One sees this tradition as well in 4QFlorilegium where David's seed is explicitly said to be "the branch of David" (4Q174 1 I.10–12; also Zech 3:8; 6:12; Jer. 23:5).[49] Paul engages in further messianic interpretation when he draws upon the oracles of Genesis 49:8–12 (particularly Gen. 49:10 LXX) in speaking of the coming of the seed (ἄχρις οὗ ἔλθῃ τὸ σπέρμα, Gal 3:19).[50] The Messiah's promised inheritance is nothing less than his worldwide kingdom which, of

44. Juel, *Messianic Exegesis*, 85.

45. See here Nils A. Dahl, "Promise and Fulfillment," in *Studies in Paul: Theology for the Early Christian Mission* (Minneapolis: Ausburg, 1977) 130.

46. See here J. Thomas Hewitt and Matthew V. Noveson, "Participationism and Messiah Christology in Paul," in *God and the Faithfulness of Paul: A Critical Examination of the Pauline Theology of N. T. Wright*, ed. Christoph Heileg et al., WUNT 2.413 (Tübingen: Mohr Siebeck, 2016), 403.

47. See Novenson, *Christ among the Messiahs*, 140n11.

48. See Richard B. Hays, *Echoes of Scripture in the Letters of Paul* (New Haven: Yale University Press, 1989), 85.

49. See also Matthew Thiessen, *Paul and the Gentile Problem* (Oxford: Oxford University Press, 2016), 123.

50. See further J. Thomas Hewitt, "Ancient Messiah Discourse and Paul's Expression

course, includes Jews *and* gentiles.[51] Thus, for Paul, Abraham's seed is David's seed, namely, the Davidic Messiah. Even before God gave the law at Sinai, God had promised to Abraham that the Christ would come from his own offspring and would be the means whereby God would save the gentiles. If the gentiles have the Spirit of the Messiah (i.e., the seed of David), then they belong by definition to the family of Abraham and are recipients of his blessing (Gal 3:14, 26–29; 4:4–6). The gentile Christians are, then, those who share in the inheritance of the Messiah's worldwide kingdom (Gal 4:4–7; 5:21).[52]

Paul's Apostolic Task of Securing the Nations as the Messiah's Inheritance

The Davidic messianic *inclusio* in the opening of Romans (1:3–4) and the closing of the discursive argument (15:9–12) indicates that Paul conceptualized his apostolic task as "bringing gentiles to the worship of the true god" through "his proclamation of Jesus as the scion of David's house."[53] In Romans 1:3–4 Paul echoes Psalm 2:7–8 and God's promise to his Davidic king that he will give him the nations for his inheritance. And he refers to the Messiah as "our Lord" (τοῦ κυρίου ἡμῶν, Rom 1:4b), a title that seems to have made its way into Paul's vocabulary through LXX Psalm 109:1 and its promise of authority over the Lord's enemies. As Nils Dahl has rightly noted: "*Kurios* is to some extent an appropriate rendering of *Christos*, because it has a royal connotation that 'Christos' would not have had in Greek."[54] Psalms 2 and 110 are some of the most important linguistic resources Paul uses to speak of the enthroned Lord's cosmic lordship, a lordship that is, remarkably, exerted over the entire cosmos and includes Jews and the nations. In fact, Paul conceives of his apostolic task as working to secure the Messiah's "Psalm 2 inheritance" through bringing about "the obedience of faith among all the nations" (Rom 1:5). This is further confirmed by the allusion to Genesis 49:8–12—a royal oracle that looks forward to a king from Judah who will receive "the obedience of the nations" (MT Gen 49:10b; cf. Num 24:17–19; Isa 11:10).[55] Finally, Paul situates his apostolic

---

ἄχρις οὗ ἔλθῃ τὸ σπέρμα in Galatians 3.19," *NTS* 65 (2019): 398–411; McCaulley, *Sharing in the Son's Inheritance*, 154–59.

51. McCaulley, *Sharing in the Son's Inheritance*, 157.

52. For further argumentation, see McCaulley, *Sharing in the Son's Inheritance*, 171–87.

53. Fredriksen, *Paul: The Pagans' Apostle*, 136–37.

54. Dahl, "The Messiahship of Jesus," 20.

55. The LXX has "he is the expectation of the nations (προσδοκία ἐθνῶν)." The only interpreter I have found who argues similarly is Don Garlington, who says that the setting

task, and the entire ministry of his missionary team (note the first-person plural in 1:5), within this royal christological narrative in his statement that "we have received grace and apostleship for the obedience of faith among the nations (ἐν πᾶσιν τοῖς ἔθνεσιν) on behalf of his name" (Rom 1:5; cf. 15:7–12).[56] Remembering that God's decree in Psalm 2, echoed in Romans 1:4, has promised the "nations as an inheritance for you" (ἔθνη τὴν κληρονομίαν σου, Ps 2:8) to the enthroned Son, it seems likely that Paul views his apostolic task as securing the inheritance of God's Son through his apostolic ministry.[57]

Two further elements point in this direction. The exalted Messiah's speech in Romans 15:9–12, functioning as something of a Davidic messianic *inclusio* for Romans, concludes with the words of Isaiah 11:10: "the root of Jesse will come [cf. the seed of David in Rom 1:3], the one who rises to rule the nations (ὁ ἀνιστάμενος ἄρχειν ἐθνῶν)[58] [installed as God's Son by the resurrection from the dead, Rom 1:4a], the nations will hope in him (ἐπ' αὐτῷ ἔθνη ἐλπιοῦσιν) [the obedience of faith among the nations, Rom 1:5]" (Rom 15:12). The resurrected and enthroned Lord is exalted to a position of rule over the nations, and Paul "himself is the unnamed executor of the inheritance granted to God's Christ in Ps 2:7b–8//Rom 1:4–6."[59] That Paul sees his task as situated within the fulfillment of the scriptural promises that look forward to a coming Davidic king who would receive the obedience of the nations is further indicated by the catena of scriptural quotations in Romans 15:9–12, quotations which are best taken as the enthroned Lord's celebration of his eschatological receipt of his royal inheritance

---

of Rom 1:5 "is provided by a number of passages from Tanakh that anticipate a king/son who would take the peoples in captive obedience to himself." See Don Garlington, "Israel's Triumphant King: Romans 1:5 and the Scriptures of Israel," in *Jesus and Paul: Global Perspectives in Honor of Jams D. G. Dunn for His 70th Birthday*, ed. B. J. Oropeza, C. K. Robertson, and Douglas C. Mohrmann, LNTS 414 (London: T&T Clark, 2010), 173–83.

56. My focus upon Paul's messianic discourse should not be interpreted as a denial of the well-known and obvious priestly metaphors drawn upon by Paul in Rom 15:15–16.

57. Similarly, see Marie Emile Boismard, "Constitué Fils de Dieu (Rom. 1.4)," *RB* 60 (1953): 15.

58. While inconclusive, the remarkable parallels with Rom 1:3–5, the fact that Rom 15:9–12 presents the speech of the enthroned and resurrected Messiah, and the frequent association of "hope" with resurrection and eschatological realities suggest that ὁ ἀνιστάμενος should be read as a reference to the Messiah's resurrected rule over the nations. See also, J. R. Daniel Kirk, *Unlocking Romans: Resurrection and the Justification of God* (Grand Rapids: Eerdmans, 2008), 51–53.

59. Whitsett, "Son of God, Seed of David," 677. On the relationship between Rom 1:3–4 and 15:12, see also Donald Dale Walker, *Paul's Offer of Leniency (2 Cor 10:1): Populist Ideology and Rhetoric in a Pauline Letter Fragment*, WUNT 2.152 (Tübingen: Mohr Siebeck, 2002), 172–73.

and entrance into his rule over the nations.[60] In both Romans 1:3-4 and 15:9-12 Paul "interprets the Davidic heritage and kingship of Jesus on the basis of Jesus's resurrection and with reference to Christ's reign over Gentiles."[61]

The Restored Cosmos as the Messiah's Inheritance

In Romans 8 Paul speaks of the eschatologically renewed cosmos as the inheritance of the Messiah and his people. Corresponding to the full revelation of humanity's adoptive sonship (8:19, 21, 23) is the restoration of the entire world. Earlier, Paul had made the surprising comment that Abraham and his seed (ἢ τῷ σπέρματι αὐτοῦ) had been promised the entire world as an inheritance (τὸ κληρονόμον αὐτὸν εἶναι κόσμου, 4:13). The promises to the patriarchs for land in Genesis have been taken by Paul to mean that Abraham and his seed would inherit and rule the entire world.[62] Paul further states that this inheritance comes to Abraham and his seed through an eschatological act of "God giving life to the dead" (4:17b), and, in fact, God's act of raising Jesus from the dead and enthroning him to cosmic rule is the act that enables the Messiah, the seed of Abraham, to inherit the world as its rightful ruler. Paul's interpretation of the promises to Abraham in Genesis as messianic promises of a cosmic inheritance are expounded upon in Romans 8:18-39. Here Paul declares that the renewed creation will experience the reversal of God's curses in Genesis 3:17-19 as it will be marked by glory (8:18, 21); freedom (8:21); incorruption (8:21); the presence of the Spirit (now anticipated, 8:23); redeemed, glorified, filled human bodies (8:18, 23); and the fulfillment of humanity's hopeful longings for its inheritance (8:18-19, 23-25).[63] That the Messiah's dominion would be marked by something like a return to the garden of Eden and its peaceful and fertile conditions is frequently attested, as we have seen, as one of Israel's messianic expectations (e.g., Ps 71 LXX; Isa 11). Paul's citation of Isaiah 11:10 ("the root of Jesse will come, and one will rise to rule the nations, the nations will hope in him") in Romans 15:12 thereby explicitly connects the resurrected Messiah's rule with the oracle's expectation for a Spirit-empowered ruler who brings

---

60. Each of the four Septuagintal quotations in Rom 15:9-12 share the language of τὰ ἔθνη.

61. Whitsett, "Son of God, Seed of David," 673.

62. See also Jacob, *Conformed to the Image*, 213-14.

63. There are numerous interesting matters raised in Rom 8:18-30 that, due to my limited purposes, cannot be entered into here. See further Edward Adams, "Paul's Story of God and Creation," in *Narrative Dynamics in Paul*, ed. Bruce W. Longenecker (Louisville: Westminster John Knox, 2002), 19-43.

peace to all of creation.[64] As we have frequently seen, Paul reads the Davidic messianic texts of Israel's Scriptures through the lens of the crucified Messiah who establishes God's kingdom through peace, justice, and nonviolence. Just as David and his seed are recipients of the promises to Abraham for worldwide dominion and rule/blessing of the nations (e.g., Gen 15:18; Ps 71:21–22 LXX; Jer 33:14–26), so Paul sees the Messiah as the singular heir of God's promise for globalized sovereignty over creation and all the nations.[65] It is likely, then, that the Messiah's inheritance (Ps 2:7–8; Rom 4:13; 8:17) is his rule over the entire world and its eschatological renewal (Rom 8:18–25).[66]

The Law of the Messiah

Paul's most positive statement regarding law—the opaque phrase "the law of Christ" (Gal 6:2 and 1 Cor. 9:22)—has perplexed interpreters and remains without a convincing linguistic or conceptual background.[67] Unable to find a meaningful background for the phrase, scholars thereby often describe it as ironic, playful, and haphazard. Many are surprised to find Paul speaking positively of Christ in relation to Israel's law, especially in epistles where he constructs an antithesis between Christ and law (e.g., Gal 2:16; 3:13; Rom 6:14; 8:7). What, then, accounts for Paul's coining of the phrase "the law of Christ" (Gal 6:2), his depiction of Christ bringing Israel's law to completion (Gal 5:14; Rom 8:3–4; 13:8b), and his exhortation to followers of Christ to follow him in fulfilling the law (Rom 13:8–10; Gal 6:2)? It is within the context of discussions devoted to the relationship between king and law that these questions, and Paul's opaque phrase "the law of Christ," should be understood. One role of the ideal king in antiquity is to embody the law internally and to produce good legislation that transforms the people and leads them in obedience to the law. This ancient discourse suggests that the best governance is not the one where

---

64. Wright, *Paul and the Faithfulness of God*, 820.

65. See also the promise to the seed in Gen 13:15; 17:8; 24:7. See Juel, *Messianic Exegesis*, 87; Whitsett, "Son of God, Son of David," 671–72.

66. So Wright, *Paul and the Faithfulness of God*, 819.

67. Todd A. Wilson, "The Law of Christ and the Law of Moses: Reflections on a Recent Trend in Interpretation," *CurBS* 5 (2006): 123–44; David G. Horrell, *Solidarity and Difference: A Contemporary Reading of Paul's Ethics*, 2nd ed. (London: T&T Clark, 2015), 222–31; Andrew Chester, "The 'Law of Christ' and the 'Law of the Spirit,'" in *Messiah and Exaltation: Jewish Messianic and Visionary Traditions and New Testament Christology* (Tübingen: Mohr Siebeck, 2007), 537–69.

the laws rule supreme, but the one where the virtuous king submits himself to the laws and thereby internalizes them such that he himself becomes an embodiment of law—a "living law." It is only through this royal "living law," whereby they imitate the king who provides the perfect pattern for their own character, that the king's subjects can fulfill the demands of the law. Some brief reflections on this ancient motif will help us situate Paul's language within its appropriate context.

The Good King and Law in Greco-Roman Thought

In Plato's *Statesman*, one of Socrates's dialogue partners argues that "law-making belongs to the science of kingship . . . but the best thing is not the laws be in power, but that the man who is of wise and a kingly nature be ruler" (*Statesman* 294A; cf. 267C; 293C). The rule and legislation of the best man offers flexibility for individual situations that the written laws do not (294B–C; 297A–B).[68] This requires that only the best man should rule, meaning that the ruler must be a philosopher-king (*Republic* 473D; 6.484A–502C), that is, a ruler who possesses "expert knowledge" (*Statesman* 293C). Thus, the best constitution is the one where "the supreme power in man coincides with the greatest wisdom and temperance" (*Laws* 712A). Aristotle claims that if there is one who "is so outstanding by reason of his superior virtue" then such people "themselves are law" (*Politics* 1284a), like the good judge who "is so to speak justice embodied" (εἶναι οἷον δίκαιον ἔμψυχον, *Nicomachean Ethics* 1132a). If such a person exists, it is right that "this one individual be king" and that "everyone obey such a person" (*Politics* 1288a; cf. 1310b). In Philo's introduction to *On Abraham*, Philo divides the Torah into the particular written laws and the original unwritten laws (3–4). The latter are Israel's patriarchs: "for in these men we have laws endowed with life and reason (ἔμψυχοι καὶ λογικοὶ νόμοι)" (5). The patriarchs are incarnated laws, and they thereby have a mimetic pedagogical function to show that "those who wish to live in accordance with the laws . . . have no difficult task" (5). Philo narrates Abraham's life as one who was "himself a law and an unwritten statute" (275–76). But for Philo it is Moses who is the ideal king, indeed the perfect example of the philosopher-king and "truly perfect ruler" (*Life of Moses* 2.2–3, 187).[69] It is Moses's embodiment of

68. On king and law in *The Statesman*, see Christopher Rowe, "The *Politicus* and Other Dialogues," in *The Cambridge History of Greek and Roman Political Thought*, ed. Christopher Rowe and Malcolm Schofield (Cambridge: Cambridge University Press, 2005), 254–61.

69. See Wayne A. Meeks, "Moses as God and King," in *Religions in Antiquity*, ed. Jacob Neusner (Leiden: Brill, 1968), 354–71.

the law—"the reasonable and living impersonation of the law" (νόμος ἔμψυ-χός τε καὶ λογικός)—that enables him to function as God's legislator through the giving of written laws to Israel (1.162; cf. 2.10–11). Thus, the king as living law must be able to perform the main function of the law through righteous legislation.[70] Again, Moses is a living law precisely so that others may imitate him and implant his image in their souls (1.158–159).

The Good King and Law in Israelite and Jewish Writings

Numerous texts speak of the good ruler as central to God's purposes for Israel and as one who submits himself to the law, takes the lead in administering the covenant, and functions as the model Israelite for the people to imitate.[71] This aspect of Israel's ideal king is expressed most clearly in Deuteronomy's "law of the king" (17:14–20), the Old Testament's only law concerning kingship, where the task for Israel's ruler is that he write out, read, and obey the Torah (vv. 18–20). While the king is chosen by God, must be an Israelite, and must not acquire many horses, wives, silver and gold (vv. 15–17), the only proactive stipulation laid upon the king is diligent reading *and* observing of the law.[72] The king is not exalted above the law but is, rather, an intensified version of the Torah-obedience expected of all Israelites (e.g., Deut 6:4–9; 31:11–12).[73] The king takes the lead in modeling and internalizing the Torah-obedience God demands from his people, a notion not far off from the concept of the king as a living law.[74]

The OT writings often evaluate Israel's kings and rulers according to Deuteronomy's standard of internalization of the Torah. For example, Joshua's task is the same as that found in Deuteronomy 17:18–20, namely, to meditate upon and observe the Torah.[75] In Joshua 1:1–9, God promises to be with Joshua and

---

70. So Bruno Centrone, "Platonism and Pythagoreanism in the Early Empire," in *The Cambridge History of Greek and Roman Political Thought*, ed. Christopher Rowe and Malcolm Schofield (Cambridge: Cambridge University Press, 2005), 566.

71. Helpful here is Gerald Eddie Gerbrandt, *Kingship according to the Deuteronomistic History*, SBLDS 87 (Atlanta: Scholars Press, 1986), esp. 108–13.

72. For detailed analyses of the "law of the king," see Gerbrandt, *Kingship*, 103–16; Jamie A. Grant, *The King as Exemplar: The Function of Deuteronomy's Kingship Law in the Shaping of the Book of Psalms*, AcBib 17 (Atlanta: Society of Biblical Literature, 2004), 189–222.

73. Nowhere does Deuteronomy speak of the people as writing out the Torah.

74. Patrick D. Miller, "Kingship, Torah Obedience and Prayer," in *Neue Wege der Psalmenforschung*, ed. K. Seybold and E. Zenger (Freiburg: Herder, 1995), 130. S. Dean McBride, "Polity of the Covenant People: The Book of Deuteronomy," *Int* 41 (1987): 241.

75. On Joshua as a prototype of Israel's ideal king, see Richard D. Nelson, "Josiah in

to give the land to the people, provided that he "not turn from [the law] to the right or the left" (1:7; cf. Deut 17:20) and that he "meditate on it day and night" (1:8).[76] The only king who is described, like Joshua, as not "turning aside to the right or the left" (Deut 17:20) from the law is Josiah. For this reason, it is difficult to deny that Josiah is Israel's paradigmatic ideal king. Josiah's walking "in all the ways of his father David" (2 Kgs 22:2) indicates that King David is associated with obedience to the law.[77] That Josiah's positive evaluation is due to his regard for the law is evident in that it occurs within the context of his discovery and implementation of the law (2 Kgs 22:3-20).[78] Josiah's implementation of obedience to the Torah is what results in the narrator declaring that, "before him there was no king like him, who turned to the Lord with all his heart, with all his soul, and with all his might, according to all the law of Moses; nor did any like him arise after him" (2 Kgs 23:25; cf. 1 Kgs 2:3; 3:6; 8:58; 9:4-5).[79]

The depiction of Israel's king as one who loves the Torah and has established it within himself is set forth in the Psalter, where Torah psalms follow kingship psalms (Pss 1-2; 18-21; 118-119).[80] The editorial placement of the Torah psalms after kingship psalms has the effect of portraying the king as the exemplary follower of Torah. The links between Psalms 1 and 2 and their function as an introduction to the Psalter are well known.[81] The combination of Psalm 1, which speaks of God's blessing upon those whose "delight is in the law of the Lord and on his law they meditate day and night" (Ps 1:2), and Psalm 2, which speaks of God's anointed (2:2, 6-7), is reminiscent of the king in Deuteronomy 17, whose task is to meditate upon the Torah. It is no surprise, then, that the king is the speaker of the Torah psalms, the model of the Psalm 1 figure who delights in the law.[82] The king is the model Israelite who delights

the Book of Joshua," *JBL* 100 (1981): 531-40; J. R. Porter, "The Succession of Joshua," in *Proclamation and Presence: Old Testament Essays in Honour of Gwynne Henton Davies*, ed. J. R. Porter and J. I. Durham (London: SCM, 1970), 102-32; Geo Widengren, "King and Covenant," *Journal of Semitic Studies* 2 (1957): 13-16.

76. Widengren, "King and Covenant," 14.

77. Nelson, "Josiah in the Book of Joshua," 534.

78. So Gerbrandt, *Kingship*, 49-50.

79. This is stated simply by Gerbrandt, *Kingship*, 194.

80. Grant, *The King as Exemplar*; Miller, "Kingship, Torah Obedience and Prayer," 127-42.

81. James L. Mays, *The Lord Reigns: A Theological Handbook to the Psalms* (Louisville: Westminster John Knox, 1994), 132-34.

82. Patrick D. Miller, "The Beginning of the Psalter," in *The Shape and Shaping of the Psalter*, ed. J. Clinton McCann, JSOTSup 159 (Sheffield: JSOT Press, 1993), 91.

in, teaches, and internalizes the Torah.[83] Thus, the king of Psalm 118 gives voice in Psalm 119 to his "delight" in the law (119:35, 47 [LXX 118:14, 35]), his "meditation" upon the law (119:15, 23, 27 [LXX 118:15, 23, 27]), and his Torah-blamelessness (119:1, 80 [LXX 118:1, 80]). The king's declarations of love for the law show that he has internalized the law within himself (119:47–48, 97, 113, 119, 127 [LXX 118:47–48, 97, 113, 119, 127]).[84] King David declares: "I delight to do your will, O my God, *your law is within my heart*" (Ps 40:8 [LXX 39:9]; cf. Ps 1:2). Throughout the Psalter, this combination of kingship with Torah-obedience testifies to God's intent to rule his people through a righteous lover of his law, through one who has, as Israel's representative, internalized the Torah within himself.[85]

The Messiah and the Law in Paul

Our preceding foray into ancient kingship discourse prepares us for Paul's royal messianic figure who: (1) functions as Israel's ideal king and, like a "living law," embodies the Torah, reconfigured around Leviticus 19:18, within his own life and self-giving death on the cross and thereby brings the law to its surprising completion; (2) implements and interprets the Torah for his subjects through his authoritative teaching; and (3) secures the internal harmony of the community through providing a royal pattern for his subjects to imitate. For Paul the Torah is refracted through the lens of the Jesus-tradition and the narrative configuration of the king who embodied Leviticus 19:18—"you shall love your neighbor as yourself." There is no doubt that Leviticus 19 exerted enormous influence upon the ethical reflection of both Second Temple Jews and early Christians (and, I would add, Jesus of Nazareth).[86] There is, then, as we will see, both continuity and discontinuity between "the law of Christ" and "the law of Moses."[87] Paul sees the Messiah's loving death on the cross as supremely embodying the love of neighbor called for by Torah, and thereby bringing Torah to its completion, but the Messiah does so in a surprising cru-

---

83. So Miller, "The Beginning of the Psalter," 86–88.

84. Mays, *The Lord Reigns*, 125.

85. Eaton, *Kingship and the Psalms*, 141–42.

86. Dale C. Allison Jr., *Constructing Jesus: Memory, Imagination, and History* (Grand Rapids: Baker Academic, 2010), 352–53.

87. For a nuanced discussion of "the law of Christ" that suggests Paul sees the phrase as continuous with the law of Moses, in part due to the relationship between Gal 6:2 and 5:13–14, but with some significant qualifications and distinctions, see E. P. Sanders, *Paul, the Law, and the Jewish People* (Minneapolis: Fortress, 1983), 93–105.

ciform manner that both reconfigures the Torah and sets forth Christ now as the supreme focal point of imitation for Christians.[88]

Galatians

Paul's messianic interpretation of Scripture in Galatians 3:10–18, which trades upon Paul's assumption that Jesus is the Davidic Messiah and the recipient of the promises made to Abraham's seed, lends plausibility to his activation of kingship discourse when he combines "law" and "Christ" in his command: "bear one another's burdens and thereby fulfill the law of Christ" (ἀναπλη-ρώσετε τὸν νόμον τοῦ Χριστοῦ, Gal 6:2).[89] Many have supposed that because of the antithetical opposition between "Christ" and "Torah" that permeates Galatians, the phrase must either exclude a reference to the Mosaic law or was coined in an ironic, polemical manner and can have little importance for Paul's theology.[90] But the reader who is familiar with the ancient script of the good king as the preeminent Torah-lover may question whether the combination of "law" and "Christ" is so strange.

Crucial to understanding "the law of Christ" is Galatiahns 5:14: "for the entire law has been fulfilled in this one word, 'you shall love your neighbor as yourself'" (ὁ γὰρ πᾶς ἐν ἑνὶ λόγῳ πεπλήρωται, ἐν τῷ ἀγαπήσεις τὸν πλη-σίον σου ὡς σεαυτόν). The similarities between Galataians 5:14 and 6:2 are readily discernible and establish that the referent of "the law of the Messiah" (τὸν νόμον τοῦ Χριστοῦ) cannot entirely exclude the Torah, even if Christ reconfigures Torah and the love commandment through his cruciform death.[91] Paul's claim that the whole law "has been fulfilled" or "brought to completion" (πεπλήρωται) is routinely assimilated to his statement in Romans 13:9 that all the commandments "are summed up" in Leviticus 19:18.[92] Scholars often

---

88. While a full discussion of Paul's view of the law is not possible here, I want to emphasize that Paul's language of fulfillment or completion with respect to the Torah by no means necessitates its abolition or obsolescence as Paul continues to draw upon the Torah as a source of ethical reflection and wisdom.

89. See, for example, N. T. Wright, "Messiahship in Galatians?," in *Galatians and Christian Theology*, ed. Mark W. Elliott (Grand Rapids: Eerdmans, 2014), 3–23.

90. For example, Sam K. Williams, *Galatians*, ANTC (Nashville: Abingdon, 1997), 155; Hans Dieter Betz, *Galatians*, Hermeneia (Philadelphia: Fortress, 1979), 300–301.

91. See John Barclay, *Obeying the Truth: Paul's Ethics in Galatians*, SNTW (Edinburgh: T&T Clark, 1988), 131–32. Sanders, *Paul, the Law, and the Jewish People*, 96–98; Thompson, *Moral Formation*, 126–27.

92. There is no parallel in Paul for πληρόω meaning "to summarize" or "sum up." So

assume that Galatians 5:14 functions gnomically as a timeless maxim for the Galatians' behavior.[93] But the semantic weight of πληρόω in Paul is decidedly filled with concepts of "fulfilling completely" or "bringing to completion,"[94] and Paul often has eschatological overtones of carrying out God's covenantal purposes (see Gal 4:4).[95] Further, in Paul's most explicit comment on the law's fulfillment, where he speaks positively of "the law of the Spirit of life in Messiah Jesus" (Rom 8:2), he declares that the law is brought to completion through the agency of "his own son" (8:3)—"so that the requirement of the law might be brought to completion in us" (ἵνα τὸ δικαίωμα τοῦ νόμου πληρωθῇ ἐν ἡμῖν, 8:4a; cf. 13:9, 11; Gal 6:2). In other words, in Romans 8:2-4 the law is brought to completion for humanity through the agency and activity of the Son.[96] It may be that here Paul is also referring to what Christ did to bring the Torah to completion through his embodiment of the Torah's demand to love one's neighbor as oneself, and that this act of bringing the Torah to completion is the foundation for the Galatians to "through love, serve one another" (5:13b).[97] If this is the case, then Paul depicts Christ as conforming his character in the closest possible manner to the law, thereby transforming himself into a "living law." It is for this reason, I suggest, that Paul uses the genitive qualifier τοῦ Χριστοῦ with τὸν νόμον in order to draw attention to Christ as the focal point of Torah, in that he embodies Israel's law even as he reconfigures it through his cruciform pattern of love for neighbor.

Paul then uses the perfect passive form of πληρόω in Galatians 5:14 in order to foreground a past event—namely, an event that has occurred with respect to the law. One observes, for example, that Paul's statement regarding the fulfillment of the law in 5:14 functions as the ground for the exhortation to the Galatians to "serve one another through love" (5:13b). Paul's typical method is to ground the church's ethical capacity, including loving one another, in the work of Christ and the Spirit. One sees this directly in that Paul's statement

---

Michael Thompson, *Clothed with Christ: The Example and Teaching of Jesus in Romans 12.1–15.13*, JSNTSup 59 (Sheffield: JSOT Press, 1991), 128.

93. For example, Betz, *Galatians*, 275.

94. For example, Rom 15:19; 2 Cor 10:6; Phil 2:2; 4:19.

95. With respect to Gal 5:14, Barclay, *Obeying the Truth*, 140, states that πεπλήρωται bears the sense of "the total realization of God's will in line with the eschatological fullness of time in the coming of Christ." More broadly, see C. F. D. Moule, "Fulfilment Words in the New Testament: Use and Abuse," *NTS* 14 (1967–1968): 293–320.

96. On the importance of Rom 8:3–4 for understanding Gal 5:14 and 6:2, see Chester, "The 'Law of Christ,'" 582–89.

97. See also Richard N. Longenecker, *Galatians*, WBC 41 (Grand Rapids: Zondervan, 1990), 243; J. Louis Martyn, *Galatians*, AYB 33A (New York: Doubleday, 1997), 486–91.

that the Galatians "have been called for freedom" (5:13a) is the prior result of the liberating act of Christ: "Christ has set us free for freedom" (5:1a).[98] Christ's liberation of his people functions as the ground, then, for his peoples' loving service of each other. Thus, in 5:14 Paul refers to what Christ has done to fulfill the law—namely, to provide the perfect pattern of love for neighbor as demanded by Leviticus 19:18.

This is borne out through the epistle where Paul characterizes Christ as the exemplar and embodiment of the "one word" of Leviticus 19:18: "you shall love your neighbor as yourself." Christ is portrayed as a living law whose very nature is a reflection of Leviticus 19:18. In Galatians 2:19–20 Paul refers to the Christ as "the Son of God, the one who loved me and handed himself over on my behalf" (2:20b).[99] Paul indicates the prominence of this theme of the Messiah's self-giving love for his entire epistle in his initial statement about Christ "who gave himself for our sins, so that he might rescue us from this present evil age" (1:4a). Both statements refer to Christ's self-giving death on the cross for the rescue of humanity. The primary activity of Christ in Galatians, in fact, is obedience to God expressed in his vicarious giving of himself over to death for the redemption and liberation of humanity (see also 3:1, 13–14; 4:4–5; 5:1).[100] If Paul thinks of Christ as the embodiment of the love called for by Leviticus 19:18, then the implied subject of the perfect-passive πεπλήρωται is almost certainly Christ. Through his life and self-giving death, Christ perfectly embodies the one word of Leviticus 19:18 and thereby brings the Torah to completion.[101] Thus, it is now the pattern of this Messiah that functions as the authoritative focal point for the Messiah's people such that they conform themselves to his character and so fulfill the Messiah's law.

Christ's bringing the Torah to completion through the embodiment of love for neighbor is the foundation for Paul's command to "bear one another's burdens, and thereby fulfill (ἀναπληρώσετε) the law of Christ" (Gal 6:2). In other words, Christ's act of embodying the Torah provides the empowerment for the Galatians to fulfill the law of Christ.[102] As Christ has brought the law to

98. See Martyn, *Galatians*, 489–90.

99. Christ's redemptive love for his people and its relationship to ethics in Galatians is nicely set out by Richard B. Hays, "Christology and Ethics in Galatians: The Law of Christ," *CBQ* 49 (1987): 268–90.

100. See Hays, "Christology and Ethics in Galatians," 277; Richard B. Hays, *The Faith of Jesus Christ: The Narrative Substructure of Galatians 3:1–4:11*, 2nd ed. (Grand Rapids: Eerdmans, 2002), 163–83.

101. Similar here is Martyn, *Galatians*, 489.

102. Martyn, *Galatians*, 547.

fulfillment in his self-giving death, so the Galatians are to recapitulate Christ's act through neighbor-love and bearing others' burdens. The construction τὸν νόμον τοῦ Χριστοῦ may, then, be a rhetorical shorthand way of saying "the Torah as it has been embodied by Christ.[103]

But if Christ is a living law who conforms his character to the law and internalizes it, we are still left to ask: How does the royal living law *enable* the peoples' obedience and law-observance? Israel's prophets had looked forward to a time when God himself would plant his law *within* the heart of his people, thereby enabling them to obey the Torah (e.g., Jer 31:31–34; Ezek 36:24–28; cf. Deut 30:6, 8). What is needed is the *very presence of God* to effect a transformation of the people so that they can obey the law. We have seen that the task of Israel's ideal king, who is related to YHWH as God's son and God's anointed one (e.g., 1 Sam 16:13; 2 Sam 7:12–14; Pss 2:6–8; 89:20–38 [LXX 88:21–29]), is to internalize Torah within himself as the ideal Israelite; thus the king's presence somehow stimulates and enables the peoples' obedience. And here we immediately note how Paul speaks of the Galatians' transformed behavior, including love for others, as deriving from their union with Christ, whose very presence, now shared intrinsically and internally with his people, transforms the behavior of his subjects and enables them to obey the law of Christ. For those who are "in Christ Jesus" (ἐν γὰρ Χριστῷ Ἰησοῦ) it is "faith empowered (ἐνεργουμένη) through love" that "has strength" (ἰσχύει) to empower the Galatians' behavior (5:6). The language of power in this statement draws attention to the Galatians' ethical transformation to love by virtue of their incorporation "in Christ Jesus." The Galatians are to use the freedom bestowed upon them by Christ (5:1) not for their own benefit but to "serve one another through love" (5:13b). Love (5:22) is the first "fruit of the Spirit" listed that characterizes "those who belong to Christ" (οἱ δὲ τοῦ Χριστοῦ, 5:24a). Paul declares that they have been "clothed with Christ" (3:27), "are one in Christ Jesus" (3:28b), "belong to Christ" (3:29a), and that they saw "Jesus Christ publicly portrayed as crucified before their eyes" (3:1b). Paul states that he is in labor "until Christ be formed in you" (4:19b). He speaks of himself as "crucified with Christ" (2:19) and that "Christ lives in me" (2:20). Participation in the person and pattern of Christ supports the notion that to "fulfill the law of Christ" (6:2) is to reenact the same pattern of Christ's fulfillment of Torah in his self-giving love for others (5:14). The empowerment to do so derives not only from Christ's providing the perfect paradigm and embodiment of neighbor-love but also by means of uniting his people to

---

103. Barclay, *Obeying the Truth*, 134, defines it as "the law as redefined and fulfilled by Christ in love."

himself and sharing his transformative presence with them such that they are incorporated into his cruciform pattern of love for the other.

1 Corinthians

While Paul does not define the meaning of "in the law of Christ" (ἔννομος Χριστοῦ) in 1 Corinthians 9:21, several brief observations upon his characterization of Christ and his ethical significance for Christians will help confirm the argument that he views Christ as a living law whose embodiment of Leviticus 19:18 brings the Torah to completion even as it reconfigures it around Christ's self-giving death. First, the self-giving character of Jesus, particularly his death on the cross, functions throughout 1 Corinthians 8–10 as the primary ethical exemplar that shapes, or should shape, the behavior of the Corinthians.[104] The Corinthian must restrict his authority for the so-called weaker brother "for whom the Messiah died" (δι᾽ ὃν Χριστὸς ἀπέθανεν, 8:11). Christ so identifies with the weak that to sin against a weaker brother is to "sin against Christ" (εἰς Χριστὸν ἁμαρτάνετε, 8:12). Paul's apostolic exemplum in 1 Corinthians 9, as interpreters have emphasized, centers upon his refusal to make use of his rights, thereby embracing social shame (and perhaps even poverty through economic self-abasement), so that he might offer the gospel free of charge (9:18; cf. 4:8–13).[105] This self-lowering and embracing of social shame holds up to the Corinthians a model of imitating Christ, who did not seek to please himself (10:33–11:1), and thereby calls them to restrict their freedom and rights for the good of their weaker brothers and sisters. This is of one accord with the context within which one finds the phrase "in the law of Christ" (9:22), as Paul declares, "even though I am free from all, I enslave myself to all so that I may win many" (9:19). Seyoon Kim, among others, has rightly noted the resonances with Jesus's own teaching about his impending death: "whoever desires to be first among you, let him become slave of all" (Mark 10:44).[106] Paul's missionary adaptability most likely refers to Paul as an ideal guest who refuses his rights in order to share open commensality with all people—in imitation of Christ's table fellowship.[107] Just as he gives up his rights for financial recompense from

104. David G. Horrell, "Theological Principle or Christological Praxis? Pauline Ethics in 1 Corinthians 8–11:1," *JSNT* 67 (1997): 83–114.

105. See here especially Dale B. Martin, *Slavery as Salvation: The Metaphor of Slavery in Pauline Christianity* (New Haven: Yale University Press, 1990).

106. Seyoon Kim, "Imitatio Christi (1 Corinthians 11:1): How Paul Imitates Jesus Christ in Dealing with Idol Food," *BBR* 13 (2003): 197.

107. David Rudolph, *A Jew to the Jews: Jewish Contours of Pauline Flexibility in 1 Corin-*

the Corinthians so that he might offer the gospel free of charge, so Paul adapts himself to his hosts, forgoing his rights and preferences so that he might win all people to the gospel, even if this means lowering himself on the social status scale: "I have become weak to the weak so that I might win the weak" (1 Cor 9:22a).[108] That Leviticus 19:18 as it has been embodied in the loving cruciform character of Jesus stands behind Paul's exhortations can be seen in the echoes of Leviticus 19 throughout 1 Corinthians 8–10, many of which echo sayings of Jesus. Thus, Paul's language of not causing any weaker brother to stumble (πρό-σκομμα, 8:11; σκανδαλίζει, σκανδαλίσω, 8:13; ἀπρόσκοποι, 10:32) implements and adapts Jesus's own understanding of the call of Leviticus 19 to not "place a stumbling block" (οὐ προσθήσεις σκάνδαλον, Lev 19:14) before a blind or mute person (Mark 9:42–50).[109] Most significant, however, are those statements that resonate with Leviticus 19:18 and Jesus's teaching to love neighbor (Mark 12:28–31): "let no one seek his own but rather let him seek the good of the other" (1 Cor 10:24), "just as I also please all people in all things, not seeking my own things but rather the edification of the many so that they might be saved" (10:33). Standing behind these statements, as well as behind 1 Corinthians 9:19–23, is almost certainly Jesus's legislation to love neighbor, itself derived from Leviticus 19:18. Finally, Paul sets himself as one who imitates Christ and thereby provides a pattern for the Corinthians to imitate. Just as imitating the character of virtuous kings as living laws was thought to result in harmony and the eradication of strife and dissension, so also Paul's discourse has as its goal the creation of a unified community that has inculcated "the mind of Christ" (1 Cor 2:16) among its members and thereby serves, sacrifices, and loves each individual member of the community (1:10–11; cf. Phil 2:1–11). Thus, while the reference to the law of Christ in 1 Corinthians 9:22 is even more opaque than Galatians 6:2, I find nothing that calls into question my observations on Galatians 6:2. The significant overlap between the two texts suggests that Paul sees the law of Christ as that royal and living law brought into existence by Israel's Messiah, who both demanded love for neighbor in his teachings and conformed his own character to Leviticus 19:18. And in this way the Messiah has brought Israel's Torah to completion even as he reconfigures it around his loving and self-giving death.

---

thians 9:19–23, WUNT 2.304 (Tübingen: Mohr Siebeck, 2011), 173–208. Also Kim, "Imitatio Christi," 202–7.

108. Note resonances with Christ's pattern of interchange in Phil. 2:5–8; 2 Cor. 5:21; 8:9; Rom. 8:3–4.

109. Kim, "Imitatio Christi," 198–99.

Messiah and Justice

One of the primary tasks of Israel's king is that of administering justice. This can take the form of giving wise and equitable verdicts in disputes, establishing his people as having the moral qualities of justice and righteousness, providing judgment over one's enemies, and providing safety from one's enemies.[110] Israel's Scriptures look forward to a messianic Davidic king who executes and embodies justice. For example, Jeremiah anticipates a time when God "will raise up for David a righteous Branch, and he will reign as king and deal wisely, and he will execute justice and righteousness in the land. . . . And this is the name by which he will be called: 'The Lord is our righteousness'" (Jer 23:5–6; cf. Jer 33:14–16). Isaiah 9 speaks of a coming Davidic ruler who will "establish and uphold [his kingdom] with justice and righteousness" (Isa 9:7). And Isaiah 11 likewise declares that this Davidic king "will not judge by what his eyes see, or decide by what his ears hear; but with righteousness he will judge the poor and decide with equity for the meek of the earth; he will strike the earth with the rod of his mouth, and with the breath of his lips he will kill the wicked. Righteousness will be the belt around his waist, and faithfulness the belt around his loins" (Isa 11:1, 3–5). Throughout Isaiah there is a deep association between the king (and messianic age) and the establishment of God's righteous rule (e.g., 16:5; 32:1; 45:1, 8, 22–25; 59:14–21; 61:1–11). Paul's depiction of Christ's judicial tasks of establishing his people as righteous and secure and acting as God's agent of eschatological judgment are further evidence of Paul's messianic Christology.

The Messiah as God's Agent of Eschatological Judgment

Jesus's heavenly enthronement by God further functions as the basis for the Messiah's task of eschatological judgment (e.g., 1 Cor 15:23–28; Phil 2:9–11). For example, in 2 Corinthians 5:10 Paul says that we "must all appear before the judgment seat of the Messiah" (τοῦ βήματος τοῦ Χριστοῦ) in order to receive recompense for our actions. Paul's coinage of the phrase "judgment seat of the Messiah" may allude to Psalm 110:1, where the king is invited to sit next to God's right hand and to execute judgment.[111] Paul's statement is reminiscent of his

---

110. See the helpful book by Moshe Weinfeld, *Social Justice in Ancient Israel and the Ancient Near East* (Minneapolis: Fortress, 1995).

111. See James A. Waddell, *The Messiah: A Comparative Study of the Enochic Son of Man and the Pauline Kyrios*, Jewish and Christian Texts Series 10 (London: T&T Clark, 2011), 166.

claim in Romans 2:16 that "God will judge the secrets of people according to my gospel *by means of Messiah Jesus*." And while Romans 14:10 refers to everyone appearing before the "judgment seat of *God* (τῷ βήματι τοῦ θεοῦ)," the preceding verse has spoken of Christ's death and resurrection in association with his role as Lord and eschatological judge (ἵνα καὶ νεκρῶν καὶ ζώντων κυριεύσῃ, Rom 14:9).[112] Even Paul himself expects that "the Lord" will judge him on the last day when all the secrets will be brought to the light (1 Cor 4:3–5).[113] Many have noted that Paul speaks of the Messiah as acting as God's singular agent to accomplish justice and salvation such that "the Day of the Lord Yahweh has become the Day of the Lord Jesus Christ" (e.g., 1 Cor 5:5; Phil 1:6, 10; 2:16).[114] Paul expects that the Messiah will have a future coming or παρουσία where he will be accompanied by all of God's holy angels (1 Thess 3:13). On this day, the Messiah will rescue his people from wrath and will give resurrection life to those who have died in Christ (1 Thess 1:10; 4:15–18). In his complicated portrait of the eschatological scenario in 2 Thessalonians 1–2, Paul uses the words of Isaiah 11:4 to depict the Messiah as one who will destroy his enemies "by the breath of his mouth" (2 Thess 2:8). William Horbury has shown how "messianic expectations . . . included a judgment scene in which the messiah condemned and executed his great adversary."[115] Often, the Messiah's victory against his enemies is associated with messianic exegesis of Isaiah 11:4: "with righteousness, he will judge the poor, and reprove with equity for the meek of the earth. And he will smite the earth with the rod of his mouth, and with the breath of his lips he will slay the wicked." In addition to 2 Thessalonians 2:8, Christ's destruction of an adversarial figure, in connection with the messianic reading of Isaiah 11:4, seems to be on display in Revelation 11–12 (cf. 1 John 2:18; 4:3).

The Pastoral Epistles frequently speak of Jesus Christ's ἐπιφάνεια as the day of his (and God's) eschatological judgment (e.g., 1 Tim 6:14–15; 2 Tim 4:1, 8; Titus 2:13). Jesus is referred to in these contexts in ways which emphasize his role as eschatological judge: he is "Christ" (1 Tim 6:14), "King of kings and

---

112. See further L. Joseph Kreitzer, *Jesus and God in Paul's Eschatology*, JSNTS 19 (Sheffield: JSOT Press, 1987), 108.

113. Note Polycarp's *Letter to the Philippians* 6.2, which contains allusions to 2 Cor 5:10 and Rom 14:9–10: "If we pray to the Lord to forgive us, we ourselves must be forgiving, we are all under the eyes of our Lord and God, and every one of us must stand before the judgment-seat (βῆμα) of Christ, where each will have to give an account of himself." Quote taken from Kreitzer, *Jesus and God*, 111.

114. The quotation here is again from Kreitzer, *Jesus and God*, 129.

115. William Horbury, "Antichrist among Jews and Gentiles," in *Messianism among Jews and Christians: Biblical and Historical Studies*, 2nd ed. (London: T&T Clark, 2016), 371.

Lord of Lords" (6:15), "the one who will judge the living and the dead" (2 Tim 4:1), and "the righteous judge" (2 Tim 4:8).[116] Harry Maier, among others, has noted the impressive similarities between the depiction of Christ's final appearance and "imperial notions of παρουσία/*adventus*."[117] The mimicry of this imperial language works to portray Christ as the supreme king who alone is the eschatological judge and Savior.

The Righteous Messiah Establishes a Just Rule over His People

But Paul also speaks of the righteous Messiah as a good king who establishes his subjects within a dominion of righteousness and life by virtue of their participation in his justification.[118] Throughout Romans 5–8 Paul unpacks the soteriological significance of the Messiah's righteousness for his subjects. Romans 5:1–11 marks a transition in the letter, as it both summarizes Romans 1–4 and previews elements of Romans 5–8, a section of Romans that highlights humanity's participation in the rule of the Messiah. Royal motifs are signaled by Paul as he speaks of the royal access (τὴν προσαγωγήν) that results from humanity's justification (5:1–2), reconciliation as the overcoming of hostilities between warring parties through Christ (5:10–11), and the scriptural allusions to the pattern whereby the king's vindication results in shame for his persecutors. Thus, in 5:1 Paul's linkage of humanity's "justification" with "peace with God" has rightly reminded interpreters of Isaiah 32:17, where the rule of the righteous king (cf. v. 1) leads to a situation where "the deeds of righteousness will result in peace" (v. 17a; cf. king and justice/peace in Isa 9:6–7; Ezek 37:26).[119] This characteristic of peace with God as the absence of fear at

116. See Linda L. Belleville, "Christology, Greco-Roman Religious Piety, and the Pseudonymity of the Pastoral Epistles," in *Paul and Pseudepigraphy*, ed. Stanley E. Porter and Gregory P. Fewster, Pauline Studies 8 (Leiden: Brill, 2013), 227–29.

117. Harry O. Maier, *Picturing Paul in Empire: Imperial Image, Text and Persuasion in Colossians, Ephesians and the Pastoral Letters* (London: Bloomsbury T&T Clark, 2013), 154.

118. Similarly, Don Garlington, "The Obedience of Faith in the Letter to the Romans: Part I: The Meaning of ὑπακοὴ πίστεως (Rom 1:5; 16:26)," *WTJ* 52 (1990): 211: "Therefore the eschatological revelation of the righteousness of God (1:17; 3:21) can hardly be divorced from the formation of a righteous community modeled on the obedience of Jesus Christ, the Last Adam (5:12f.)."

119. On Isa 32:17–18 in Rom 5:1, see Don Garlington, "The Obedience of Faith in the Letter to the Romans: Part III: The Obedience of Christ and the Obedience of the Christian," *WTJ* 55 (1993): 90–91. The presence of the allusion to the righteous king's rule in Isa 32 is strengthened if Paul has just alluded to God's "justification of the righteous one" from Isa 53:11 in Rom 4:25.

the judgment runs throughout Romans 5–8 and is the result of the Messiah's extension of his righteousness to his people.

Paul's Adam-Christ contrast in 5:12–21 continues in 6:12–23 as it now centers upon two Lords who rule over humanity, but here the two Lords are "Sin" and "Righteousness." Paul's use of the language of "righteousness" to speak of the sphere within which humanity-in-Christ now participates fits nicely with how kings were tasked with establishing a righteous and peaceful dominion for their people. Christ, as a good ruler, creates and establishes a dominion of righteousness for his people. The predominant conceptual metaphor employed by Paul in 6:12–23, that of enslavement to royal masters and the use of "kingship-ruling language of sin and death and powers," is continued from 5:12–21.[120] Thus, "Sin" and "Righteousness" are the subjects of the verbal forms of the political language of βασιλεύω (6:12), κυριεύω (6:14), and ἐλευθερέω (6:18, 20, 22)—and this provides the major argument for seeing Sin and Righteousness as personified entities with their own dominion that exert power over humanity. Paul uses the language of δικαιοσύνη here to speak of Christ's rule on behalf of God, and this seems evident, not only due to the personification of Righteousness and the continuation of the themes in 5:12–21, but also since Christ is spoken of as the Lord in 5:21 and 6:23 (see also 6:14).[121] Righteousness is, therefore, tightly connected with the powerful lordship of Christ. The personification of δικαιοσύνη in 6:18–23 is clear: Christ's people are liberated from the dominion of Sin and "enslaved to Righteousness" (6:18b); this results in the ability to offer their bodies as "slaves to Righteousness resulting in holiness" (6:19b). But when humanity was enslaved to Sin they were "free with respect to Righteousness" (6:20b).[122]

If in Romans 5:12–21 and 6:6–7 Paul has spoken of Christ's righteousness as the foundation for humanity's justification and life, in 6:12–23 he calls them to behave in a way that is congruent with Christ's dominion of righteousness. Paul associates righteousness with resurrection as he conceptualizes the church's obedience to righteousness as a present participation in Christ's resurrection.[123] Thus, bodily enslavement to δικαιοσύνη is living out one's identity

120. Kirk, *Unlocking Romans*, 117. On the slavery metaphor in Rom 6, see Martin, *Slavery as Salvation*.

121. Many interpreters have noted that Paul personifies righteousness or speaks of it as a power, but see especially David J. Southall, *Rediscovering Righteousness in Romans: Personified dikaiosyne within Metaphoric and Narratorial Settings*, WUNT 2.240 (Tübingen: Mohr Siebeck, 2008), 83–112.

122. Southall, *Rediscovering Righteousness*, 118–19.

123. Brendan Byrne, "Living out the Righteousness of God: The Contribution of Rom 6:1–8:13 to an Understanding of Paul's Ethical Presuppositions," *CBQ* 43 (1981): 563.

"as those who are alive from the dead" instead of using one's body as "weapons of unrighteousness" (6:13).[124] Living in obedience and enslavement to unrighteousness and sin results in death (6:16, 21, 23), whereas those who share in the realm of "Christ Jesus our Lord" have "eternal life" (6:23; also 6:22b). Paul's claim that "you are slaves of the one you obey—either sin resulting in death or obedience resulting in righteousness" (6:16b)—is similar to 5:18–19, where Christ's obedience and righteousness leads to righteousness for his people. Christ's people follow the trajectory he has set in that their obedience (6:16) follows Christ's obedience (5:19) and thereby results in righteousness.

Christ further executes his judicial responsibilities with complete benevolence as he keeps his people from "condemnation" (κατάκριμα, 8:1) or accusations of judgment (τίς ἐγκαλέσει, 8:33)—an *enacted verdict* that would result in death (8:2b; also 5:16, 18). The impossibility of any enemy of Christ's people enacting a verdict of condemnation (τίς ὁ κατακρινῶν, 8:34a) is rooted in God's own enactment of acquittal and rescue for his people—"God is the one who justifies" (θεὸς ὁ δικαιῶν, 8:33b).[125] Since God has justified and resurrected the Messiah out of the dominion of death, this very Messiah—"Christ Jesus who died, and even more, has been raised" (Χριστὸς Ἰησοῦς ὁ ἀποθανών, μᾶλλον δὲ ἐγερθείς, 8:34b)—in whom Christ's people participate, stands as definitive proof that God is the justifier.[126] And the echo of LXX Psalm 109:1 in Romans 8:34 portrays Christ clearly as one invested with royal and judicial power. Christ is the powerful eschatological judge whose resurrection and enthronement enables him to protect his people from every other power (8:38–39; also 1:4; 2:16; 14:10). While the focus is on the security and life that belongs to those who are in Christ, it is the resurrected Messiah's justification that secures life, resurrection, and no condemnation for the people. Christ stands in the role of eschatological judge and vindicator as a result of his acquittal and enthronement. The themes are readily discernible throughout Romans 5–8 and especially 8:29–34: God's justification of his Messiah *is* the granting of life, resurrection, and deliverance from shame for the Messiah.

124. Morna D. Hooker, "Raised for Our Acquittal (Rom. 4,25)," in *Resurrection in the New Testament: Festschrift J. Lambrecht*, ed. R. Bieringer et al., BETL 165 (Leuven: Leuven University Press, 2002), 334; See also Kirk, *Unlocking Romans*, 117.

125. Kirk, *Unlocking Romans*, 153.

126. The allusion here to LXX Ps 109:1, a text that is consistently associated with Jesus's resurrection as his vindication and enthronement, further suggests that Christ's justification/acquittal is the means through which God justifies his people. On the allusion to LXX Ps 109:1 in Rom 8:34, see Martin Hengel, "'Sit at My Right Hand!': The Enthronement of Christ at the Right Hand of God and Psalm 110:1," in *Studies in Early Christology* (Edinburgh: T&T Clark, 1995), 137–43.

And so it is humanity's participation in this Messiah's destiny that ensures that they share in the same realities: hope in protection from eschatological shame (5:5; also 1:16), life that comes from justification (8:10–11), and protection from condemnation at the final judgment (8:37–39).

Conclusion

Paul's frequent use of the word Χριστός to refer to Jesus makes good sense as referring to Jesus as Israel's Messiah. Paul himself explicitly refers to Jesus as the Davidic Messiah (Rom 1:3–4; 15:7–12; 2 Tim 2:8). Paul's so-called messianic Christology is evident in the way in which his exegesis of Israel's Scriptures is explicitly dependent upon his conviction that Jesus is the Messiah. Since Jesus is David's seed, he is also the seed of Abraham who will bless the nations (Gal 3:13–16). Paul conceptualizes his apostolic ministry to the nations as making good on the Messiah's promised inheritance (Gen 49:8–12; Ps 2:7–8). Paul's conviction that Jesus is the Davidic Messiah provides the ground for his application of Davidic psalms to describe Jesus's sufferings and death (Rom 15:1–3; 2 Cor 4:13) as well as his resurrection and enthronement (1 Cor 15:23–28). And Paul draws upon themes associated with Israel's ideal king in his description of Jesus, thereby presenting him as the one who enables his people to obey God's law and the one who establishes his people in justice and righteousness. In the next chapters I will present further evidence, coalescing around Paul's participatory soteriology as *sharing in the rule and reign of the Messiah*, for Paul's messianic Christology.

CHAPTER 6

Participating in the Rule of the Messianic King (Part I)

Romans, 1-2 Corinthians, and Philippians

In the preceding chapter I argued and reviewed recent scholarship which suggests that Paul's favorite term for Jesus, Χριστός, is best understood as an honorific and as designating Jesus as the Davidic Messiah. Paul's emphasis upon Jesus as an agent of judgment and justice, his depiction of Jesus as ruler over the nations who fulfills the promises made to Abraham, and his portrayal of Jesus's relationship to God's Torah are indebted to his understanding of Jesus as the messianic king. In this chapter and the next I argue that Paul's messianic Christology is powerfully seen in the construction of his participatory soteriology—namely, as centering upon sharing in Jesus's messianic rule. Royal messianism, that is, the linguistic and conceptual resources rooted in reflections upon Israel's messianic king, best explains Paul's articulation of the narrative of Messiah Jesus, as well as his mapping of the same narrative identity onto the Messiah's people. Paul conceptualizes the relationship between Christ and his people as the relationship between king and subjects, with the Messiah's people, however, sharing in the rule and the benefits of the resurrected and enthroned Messiah's rule. In the first section, I take an extended look at Romans 1 and Philippians 2 to argue that Paul's gospel centers upon God's accomplishment of the salvation of humanity by means of the royal narrative of his messianic king. In the second section, I suggest, in 1 Corinthians, Philippians, and Romans 5–8, that Paul's participatory soteriology is often conceptualized as sharing in the identity and reign of the messianic king. Paul's creative innovation is on display in his taking shared christological confessions and hymns (Rom 1:3–4; 1 Cor 15:1–5; Phil 2:6–11) and expanding them into the pattern for Christ's sharing of his saving rule with his people (Rom 5–8; 1 Cor 15:20–28; Phil 3:20–21).

Paul's Gospel of the Messianic King

One of Paul's favorite and most important terms used to describe his message is "the gospel" or variants thereof (e.g., Rom 1:1, 9; 2:16; 10:16; 15:16). The word is most simply translated as "the good news." Within Israel's Scriptures, "gospel" is often used to describe the royal announcement that God has been faithful to his promises to Israel and has acted to establish himself as the king of Israel, a kingship which has the consequences of salvation, liberation, justice, and freedom for the oppressed (Isa 40:1–11; 52:7–12; 61:1–4).[1] It is also well known that the term "gospel" was employed to celebrate significant Roman imperial events such as the birthday of Caesar Augustus, imperial triumphs, and entrances of rulers and imperial dignitaries into cities.[2] We can see that while Paul is capable of using the language of gospel in a variety of ways, he speaks of the "gospel" as something that is defined by "Messiah." One can see this in the way that Paul often uses the genitive modifier Χριστοῦ ("Messiah") to describe or delimit τὸ εὐαγγέλιον ("the gospel").[3] In this section, I will suggest that Paul's gospel is best understood as the proclamation of the saving identity and narrative of the Messiah, and one which is centered upon the Messiah's incarnation, death, resurrection, and enthronement as cosmic king.[4]

Paul expounds upon the meaning of the relationship between Messiah and gospel in a handful of places in his letters, many of which appear to be traditional.[5] For example, in 1 Corinthians 15:1–5 Paul declares that the gospel he proclaims centers upon the following narrative about the Messiah: the Messiah's saving death in accordance with the Scriptures (15:3b), his burial (15:4a), and his resurrection on the third day according to the Scriptures (15:5). As we will see, this compact confession about the saving significance of the Messiah's death and resurrection is expanded upon by Paul throughout the rest of the chapter, where he argues that Jesus's resurrection from the dead

---

1. For a popular and helpful articulation of the meaning of the gospel, see N. T. Wright, *How God Became King: The Forgotten Story of the Gospels* (San Francisco: HarperOne, 2016).

2. For much more detail, see Neil Elliott, "Paul and the Politics of Empire," in *Paul and Politics: Ekklesia, Israel, Imperium, Interpretation*, ed. Richard A. Horsley (Harrisburg, PA: Trinity International, 2000), 17–39.

3. See Rom 15:19; 1 Cor 9:12; 2 Cor 2:12; 4:4; 9:13; 10:14; Gal 1:7; Phil 1:27; 1 Thess 3:2.

4. See Scot McKnight, *The King Jesus Gospel: The Original Good News Revisited* (Grand Rapids: Zondervan, 2011).

5. For a popular and helpful articulation of the relationship between Paul's gospel and the Messiah, see Matthew W. Bates, *Salvation by Allegiance Alone: Rethinking Faith, Works, and the Gospel of Jesus the King* (Grand Rapids: Baker Academic, 2017), 27–45.

functions as his royal enthronement to a position of powerful rule over the cosmos (15:20–28). Similarly, in 2 Timothy 2:8, "Paul" (or a Paulinist) exhorts Timothy: "Remember Messiah Jesus, who was raised from the dead, from the seed of David, according to my gospel." While the emphasis here is placed upon the Davidic Messiah's resurrection, the context presumes the Messiah's two-stage narrative of death and resurrection. We will return later to both 1 Corinthians 15 and 2 Timothy 2 in more detail; the simple point I am trying to make is that Paul's gospel sets forth Jesus's identity as *Messiah* and presents his narrative as centering upon two central events—the Messiah's death and resurrection. Paul's gospel is a story of the descent and ascent of the Messiah, and one can find variants of this pattern of the Messiah's narrative in a variety of Pauline texts (e.g., Rom 10:5–13; 2 Cor 8:9; Gal 4:4–6). In the words of Matthew Bates: "Initially Jesus preexisted as Son of God . . . taking on human flesh and then reaching the very bottom—the abode of the dead. But once he reached bottom, the ascent began—he was raised from the dead and then installed in the heavenly sphere as Son-of-God-in-Power."[6] In what follows, I want to look in some detail at two Pauline texts where Paul articulates his gospel as centering upon the royal narrative of the messianic king and his incarnation, death, and resurrection. This narrative is the foundation and pattern for humanity's enablement to participate in the rule of the Messiah.[7]

Romans 1:3–4

Paul begins his letter to the Romans by reminding his auditors that he is an apostle set apart for "God's gospel" (εὐαγγέλιον θεοῦ, Rom 1:1b), a phrase that, whether it is situated in a Roman imperial, an early Christian, or a Jewish biblical context, has regal connotations of divine kingship and rule. God's gospel is established, according to Paul, by the royal identity and narrative of Israel's Davidic, resurrected, and enthroned Messiah (Rom 1:3–4). In light of his claim in Romans 1:2, this narrative of God's resurrection and enthronement of the Davidic Messiah by the Spirit *is* the content of the holy Scriptures.[8] The intertextual and allusive echoes of 2 Samuel 7:12–14 and Psalms 2:7–8, 110:1, along with the themes of God's gospel—Davidic messiahship and seed, divine

---

6. Bates, *Salvation by Allegiance Alone*, 35.

7. Much of what follows originally appeared in my *Christ Is King: Paul's Royal Ideology* (Minneapolis: Fortress, 2015), ch. 4. Thanks to Fortress for the kind permission to reuse portions of my previously published work.

8. Rightly J. R. Daniel Kirk, *Unlocking Romans: Resurrection and the Justification of God* (Grand Rapids: Eerdmans, 2008), 44–45.

sonship, resurrection, enthronement, the Spirit of consecration, power, and lordship—set forth a narrative of Messiah Jesus as God's royal Son and kingly representative of his people.[9] Romans 1:3–4 states:

> [The gospel] about his son who was born from the seed of David according to the flesh, who was installed as God's Son in power according to the Spirit of holiness by means of the resurrection of the dead, Jesus Messiah our Lord (περὶ τοῦ υἱοῦ αὐτοῦ τοῦ γενομένου ἐκ σπέρματος Δαυὶδ κατὰ σάρκα τοῦ ὁρισθέντος υἱοῦ θεοῦ ἐν δυνάμει κατὰ πνεῦμα ἁγιωσύνης ἐξ ἀναστάσεως νεκρῶν, Ἰησοῦ Χριστοῦ τοῦ κυρίου ἡμῶν).

Paul uses this confession to establish the identity of Christ as the Davidic Messiah spoken of by Israel's royal ideology as God's Son who participates in God's kingship and is the embodied representative of God's people. While there are multiple components and subplots to the story, this christological narrative about God's Son has two primary trajectories that correspond to the two attributive participles which modify "his son" (τοῦ υἱοῦ αὐτοῦ):[10] (1) the Son's necessary participation in fleshly human existence as the promised one "who was born" (τοῦ γενομένου) from the seed of David (ἐκ σπέρματος Δαυίδ, 1:3), and (2) the Son's participation in God's kingship by means of his "installation" (τοῦ ὁρισθέντος) by the Spirit as the powerful, resurrected, and enthroned Lord (1:4). Both of these events in the life of the Son—his sharing in human flesh from the seed of David and his installation as the resurrected and powerful Son of God—make up the content of God's gospel (1:1) and the promise of Israel's Scriptures (1:2).

While Paul does not dwell upon Christ's preexistence, the figure in 1:3–4 is spoken of as "God's Son" (1:3a) *before* his birth (cf. 8:3; Gal 4:4–5).[11] The first stage of the Son's trajectory is described in 1:3, where Paul declares that God's Son "was born from the seed of David according to the flesh." The emphasis

9. So Douglas A. Campbell, *The Deliverance of God: An Apocalyptic Rereading of Justification in Paul* (Grand Rapids: Eerdmans, 2009), 696.

10. Thus Rom 1:3–4 provides no evidence for an adoptionist Christology as preceding a high Christology. Rightly, Timo Eskola, *Messiah and Throne: Jewish Merkabah Mysticism and Early Christian Exaltation Discourse*, WUNT 2.142 (Tübingen: Mohr Siebeck, 2001), 225–26.

11. On Paul's presupposition that God's Son is the preexistent one who becomes human, see Matthew W. Bates, *The Hermeneutics of the Apostolic Proclamation: The Center of Paul's Method of Scriptural Interpretation* (Waco, TX: Baylor University Press, 2012), 80–94; see also, C. E. B. Cranfield, *Romans 1–8*, ICC (London: T&T Clark, 2004), 58.

on Jesus's Davidic descent alludes to God's covenant with David wherein God promises to secure David's *seed* after him (ἀναστήσω τὸ σπέρμα σου μετὰ σέ, 2 Sam 7:12); ensures that David's seed will have an eternal kingdom (ἀνορθώσω τὸν θρόνον αὐτοῦ ἕως υἱόν εἰς τὸν αἰῶνα, 7:14); and enters into a Father-Son relationship with David and his dynasty (ἐγὼ ἔσομαι αὐτῷ εἰς πατέρα, καὶ αὐτὸς ἔσται μοι εἰς 7:14; cf. 1 Chr 17:11–14). As Matthew Novenson has pointed out, Romans 1:3 draws from the pattern of speech seen in 2 Kingdoms 22:51/ LXX Psalm 17:51, the one place in the LXX where "Christ," "David," and "seed" occur in close proximity.[12] The psalm proclaims David's praise to God for ensuring his faithfulness to David's dynasty by saving him from his enemies (see esp. 17:43–49). This promise that God would secure perpetual seed in the line of the royal Davidic family stands behind biblical and Second Temple Jewish expectations for an eschatological Davidic king (e.g., LXX Ps 88:2–5, 20–21; Isa 11:1–10; Jer 23:5; 33:14–26; Ezek 33:14–18; 34:23–24; 37:24–25; Zech 6:12; Pss. Sol. 17–18; 4QpIsaᵃ; 4QFlor), such that God's scriptural promises to rule the world through a Davidic monarch could in no way come about except through a descendant of David.[13] Thus, Paul's description of the Son as the seed of David born "according to the flesh" (Rom 1:3) functions in no way to devalue Jesus's Davidic ancestry,[14] but rather, marks out Jesus the Messiah as the fulfillment of God's covenant promises to the seed of David.[15] For the early Christians familiar with Israel's Davidic royal ideology and specifically the promise for a messianic king from the line of David, Romans 1:3 would almost

12. Matthew V. Novenson, *Christ among the Messiahs: Christ Language in Paul and Messiah Language in Ancient Judaism* (Oxford: Oxford University Press, 2012), 168.

13. Donald Juel, *Messianic Exegesis: Christological Interpretation of the Old Testament in Early Christianity* (Philadelphia: Fortress, 1988), 61–77; Lidija Novakovic, *Raised from the Dead according to Scripture: The Role of Israel's Scripture in the Early Christian Interpretations of Jesus' Resurrection*, Jewish and Christian Texts Series 12 (London: T&T Clark, 2012), 138; James M. Scott, *Adoption as Sons of God: An Exegetical Investigation into the Background of ΥΙΟΘΕΣΙΑ in the Pauline Corpus*, WUNT 2.48 (Tübingen: Mohr Siebeck, 1992), 237–39; Christopher G. Whitsett, "Son of God, Seed of David: Paul's Messianic Exegesis in Romans 1:3–4," *JBL* 119 (2000): 675–76.

14. For interpreters who think the prepositional phrases function to devalue Jesus's Davidic ancestry, see Joshua W. Jipp, "Ancient, Modern, and Future Interpretations of Romans 1:3–4," *JTI* 3 (2009): 243–45. See, however, the convincing argument of Nathan C. Johnson, who notes that Davidic sonship is not antithetical to (and is in fact, necessary for) divine sonship in "Romans 1:3–4: Beyond Antithetical Parallelism," *JBL* 136 (2017): 467–490. See also Paula Fredriksen, *Paul: The Pagans' Apostle* (New Haven: Yale University Press, 2017), 144, who rightly states about the titles "Son of God," "Son of David," and "Lord"—"They are synonyms."

15. Whitsett, "Son of God, Seed of David," 671.

certainly activate rereadings of the Davidic royal tradition around Messiah Jesus and would suggest that God had fulfilled his promises for a messianic Davidic ruler for Israel.[16]

In order to function as Israel's royal representative, as the true seed of David, it is necessary that God's Son share in human, Davidic flesh.[17] Thus, Paul's description of the Son's birth "according to the flesh" qualifies "the Son" to truly participate in humanity's fleshly existence (cf. Rom 4:1; 9:3, 5).[18] Paul's use of the noun σάρξ is, of course, incredibly flexible, but here it primarily speaks of the Son, the seed of David, as an actual man who shares in human existence and all the trappings that go with it. The Son's identification with fleshly human existence accords with Paul's claims elsewhere:[19]

"God sent his own Son in the likeness of sinful flesh" (ὁ θεὸς τὸν ἑαυτοῦ υἱὸν πέμψας ἐν ὁμοιώματι σαρκὸς ἁμαρτίας) (Rom 8:3).

"He took the form of a slave; he became the likeness of humanity; he was found in the appearance of a man" (μορφὴν δούλου λαβών, ἐν ὁμοιώματι ἀνθρώπων γενόμενος, καὶ σχήματι εὑρεθεὶς ὡς ἄνθρωπος) (Phil 2:7).

"God sent his son, born from a woman" (ἐξαπέστειλεν ὁ θεὸς τὸν υἱὸν αὐτοῦ, γενόμενον ἐκ γυναικός) (Gal 4:4).

In these depictions of the Son taking on human flesh, Paul does emphasize, however, fleshly human existence as marked by weakness, suffering, and death (cf. 1 Cor 15:42–43).[20] Human existence in the sphere of the flesh, throughout

---

16. Whitsett, "Son of God, Seed of David," 676.

17. Adolf Schlatter, *Romans: The Righteousness of God* (Peabody, MA: Hendrickson, 1995), 9.

18. The phrase "according to the flesh" must be read in the first instance as simply indicative of physical descent and not within the flesh/Spirit contrast found in Rom 5–8. See my comments on Rom 4:1 in Joshua W. Jipp, "Rereading the Story of Abraham, Isaac, and 'Us' in Romans 4," *JSNT* 32 (2009): 227–28; so Novenson, *Christ among the Messiahs*, 169.

19. Mehrdad Fatehi, *The Spirit's Relation to the Risen Lord in Paul: An Examination of Its Christological Implications*, WUNT 2.128 (Tübingen: Mohr Siebeck, 2000), 258. Aquila H. I. Lee, *From Messiah to Preexistent Son: Jesus' Self-Consciousness and Early Christian Exegesis of Messianic Psalms*, WUNT 2.192 (Tübingen: Mohr Siebeck, 2005), 311–13.

20. On the preexistent Christ's identification with human flesh, see Gordon D. Fee, *Pauline Christology: An Exegetical-Theological Study* (Peabody, MA: Hendrickson, 2007), 500–512; Vincent P. Branick, "The Sinful Flesh of the Son of God (Rom 8:3): A Key Image of Pauline Theology," *CBQ* 47 (1985): 246–62.

Paul's letters, "is associated with physically oriented human existence, especially human fragility, bodily appetites, and material decay."[21] Given that the Davidic king served as an embodied representative of his people, Paul's inclusion of the qualification "according to the flesh" serves as an indication that God's Son enters into the very anthropological, fleshly existence of Israel, taking on himself all of the physical weakness and decay that goes along with corporeal existence (cf. Rom 7:17–25).[22]

While Paul does not speak directly of the Son's sufferings here, nevertheless, his humiliation and death are implied within this stage of the Son's career, namely, the experience common to all fleshly humanity of being among "the corpses" (νεκρῶν, Rom 1:4a). The resurrection and heavenly enthronement described in 1:4 presumes that the situation of fleshly human existence has given way to a situation of existence among the dead. The Messiah's fleshly human existence has obviously given way to his death, which is logically prior to his resurrection.[23]

The second stage of the Messiah's trajectory is marked by the second attributive participle that Paul uses to describe the christological trajectory of the Son: here the Son is "installed" (τοῦ ὁρισθέντος) as "Son of God in power" (1:4a). While the first stage of the Son's narrative is marked by sharing in human flesh as Israel's royal representative (1:3), the second stage is marked by an elevation to divine kingship by means of his royal enthronement and sharing in God's Spirit. The depiction of Jesus as "appointed" as "the Son of God" has rightly reminded Paul's readers of Israel's royal enthronement discourse, particularly Psalm 2:7: "I will tell of the decree of the Lord: He said to me, 'You are my son; today I have begotten you.'"[24] As we have seen, within the context of Psalm 2, God's adoption of the Davidic king as his son and enthronement to share in God's rule is in response to the violent raging of the enemies of God and the king (2:1–3). Part of the son's rule, according to 2:8, includes God's granting to the king "the nations as an inheritance" (δώσω σοι ἔθνη τὴν κληρονομίαν σου). Four components of the Son's enthronement, difficult to neatly separate, are significant for understanding Paul's depiction of the ascent trajectory of the Messiah in Romans 1:4.

---

21. Bates, *The Hermeneutics of the Apostolic Proclamation*, 91; N. T. Wright, "The Letter to the Romans," in *The New Interpreter's Bible: A Commentary in Twelve Volumes* (Nashville: Abingdon, 2002), 10:417–18.

22. So also Bates, *The Hermeneutics of the Apostolic Proclamation*, 92.

23. Fatehi, *The Spirit's Relation*, 258.

24. Whitsett, "Son of God, Seed of David," 676; Kirk, *Unlocking Romans*, 41–42; Juel, *Messianic Exegesis*, 80–81.

First, given the early Christian association between the royal enthronement described in Psalm 2 and the Messiah's sonship and resurrection (e.g., Acts 2:22–36; 13:33; 1 Cor 15:23–26; Heb 1:5; 5:5), it is understandable that Paul sees Jesus's installation as "God's Son" taking place "from the resurrection from the dead" (Rom 1:4a).[25] The promise that God would "raise up your seed after you" (2 Sam 7:12) is, for Paul and many of the earliest Christians, seen as a reality in God's resurrection of Christ, born of the seed of David, from the dead. Thus, the claims made in Romans 1:3–4 are inextricably related to one another. Just as God responded to the machinations of the Davidic king's enemies by rescuing him and enthroning him to a position of rule, so God's resurrection of his Son from the dead functions as the means by which he installs his "Son of God in power" in a position of rule. Based on Paul's christological statements elsewhere (e.g., Rom 8:3; Phil 2:6–11) and other occurrences of ὁρίζω in the NT—where it refers to God enthroning the Messiah in power to rule and judge (e.g., 1 Cor 2:7; Acts 10:42; 17:31)—ὁρισθέντος here almost certainly means "installs" or "designates" to a position of rule.

Second, the sonship to which Jesus is installed as God's Son is a divine sonship characterized by power (ἐν δυνάμει). Paul frequently speaks of "power" as an attribute of God that is on display particularly in God's act of raising Jesus from the dead (1 Cor 6:14; 15:24, 43; 2 Cor 13:4; Eph 1:19–20; Phil 3:10, 21). The allusions to LXX Psalm 109 in Ephesians 1:19–23, 1 Corinthians 15:24–25, and Philippians 3:21 indicate that the Son's resurrection is a royal enthronement that entails the Messiah's deliverance from death and entrance into incorruptible life, a life that includes power and rule over his enemies.[26]

Third, the Son of God's resurrection and participation in divine power is the result of the "the Spirit of holiness" now marking his new resurrection existence. Just as Yahweh elected his anointed one by consecrating him with the Spirit, so the "Son of God in power" is installed as God's resurrected, enthroned son by the life-giving activity of the Spirit.[27] The expectation that Israel's ideal messianic king would have the Spirit of God in full to empower his mission and rule over his people (e.g., Isa 11:1–4; 61:1–4) also provides an important context for understanding the resurrected Christ as now marked by God's powerful Spirit. The Jewish Scriptures frequently associate God's

25. Kirk, *Unlocking Romans*, 42.

26. See Dennis Duling, "The Promises to David and Their Entrance into Christianity: Nailing Down a Likely Hypothesis," *NTS* 20 (1973): 70; Novakovic, *Raised form the Dead*, 144–45; Eskola, *Messiah and Throne*, 217–50.

27. Kirk, *Unlocking Romans*, 42–43. On the Spirit's association with life, see Ezek 37:1–14; Rom 8:9–11.

Spirit with life and with the power to create an intimate relationship with God (e.g., Ezek 36:26–28; Jub. 1:23–24; T. Jud. 24:3).[28] Thus, we can see that Jesus's messianic status "according to the flesh" (Rom 1:3) stands in parallel with the "according to the Spirit of holiness" qualifying his divine sonship (1:4; cf. 1 Cor 15:43–45). Thus, the resurrected, enthroned Son of God's existence is now marked by the qualities and attributes of the Spirit, foremost of which are, as we will see shortly, the power to bring the eschatological life associated with resurrection (Rom 8:9–11), familial relation to God (8:14–17), and liberation from hostile lords that allows humanity to please and worship God (7:5–6; 8:5–8).

Fourth, the Son participates in God's rule by virtue of his sharing in divine lordship. Paul further describes "Messiah Jesus" as "our Lord" (Rom 1:4b). Paul's application of this honorific to the Messiah makes sense in light of his application of LXX Psalm 109:1 to describe the relationship between God and the resurrected Messiah Jesus: "The Lord said to my lord (εἶπεν ὁ κύριος τῷ κυρίῳ μου), 'Sit at my right hand until I make your enemies a footstool under your feet.'"[29] Later, Paul draws upon LXX Psalm 109 to describe the enthroned Son as seated at God's right hand and interceding for his people (Rom 8:33–34). Paul's understanding of the Messiah's resurrection and enthronement to lordship is indicated by the association he makes elsewhere between Jesus's resurrection, his divine lordship, and his judicial powers (Rom 2:16; 8:33–34; 10:5–13; 14:8–12).[30]

Philippians 2:6–11

In his letter to the Philippians, Paul speaks frequently of "the gospel" (1:7, 12, 16, 27 [2X]; 2:22; 4:3, 15). Given Paul's assumption that he and the church in Philippi are in peaceful and harmonious fellowship with one another, Paul seems to assume that he and the church are in shared agreement about the content and meaning of the gospel. Nevertheless, although he does not use the term *gospel* here, Paul does set forth his "master story" about "Messiah Jesus" (2:5) in 2:6–11.[31] Furthermore, the basic trajectory of descent and ascent or incarnation, death, and enthronement parallels the movement of the gospel

---

28. Rightly noted by Caroline Johnson Hodge, *If Sons, Then Heirs: A Study of Kinship and Ethnicity in the Letters of Paul* (Oxford: Oxford University Press, 2007), 73–74.

29. Eskola, *Messiah and Throne*, 247–48.

30. Bates, *The Hermeneutics of the Apostolic Proclamation*, 94.

31. For example, Michael J. Gorman, *Inhabiting the Cruciform God: Kenosis, Justification, and Theosis in Paul's Narrative Soteriology* (Grand Rapids: Eerdmans, 2009), 9–39.

in Romans 1:3–4.[32] Philippians 2 depicts the Messiah as a royal figure who, through his refusal to exploit his equality with God, *redefines* royal power and is thereby worthy to rule the universe and receive divine honors.[33] Whether Paul composed the hymn I do not pretend to know, but it is clear that the hymn is tightly integrated within the letter's broader argument and should thereby be seen as representative of his christological discourse (esp. Phil 1:27–2:4 and 3:20–21). The hymn describes "Messiah Jesus" (2:5) as separate and distinguishable from God, but also as simultaneously sharing in "God's form" (2:6a); worthy of honors equal to God (2:6c); exalted by God over everything else (2:9); bearing the title of the divine κύριος (2:11); and the eschatological agent who will receive the worship of the entire world (2:10–11).

But how is it even possible that a monotheistic Jew could make these exalted claims about a recently crucified human?[34] The linguistic and conceptual resources that provide Paul with the discourse to present Christ as simultaneously distinguishable from God as his agent *and* as sharing in God's status and functions are ancient royal discourses of the good ruler or messianic king. This insight has been confirmed by many studies, and yet it often goes unrecognized due to the fact that many proposals have attempted to find too precise or specific precedents.[35] Throughout Philippians, and the hymn in particular, the Messiah is portrayed as a royal, imperial figure who is simultaneously worthy of divine honors and worship and one who redefines royal authority and rule. Thus, Paul is probably not attempting to draw a parallel between Christ and one specific ruler or emperor, but rather provides, as Mikael Tellbe

---

32. So Bates, *Salvation by Allegiance Alone*, 35.

33. The authorship and genre of Phil 2:6–11 is disputed. John Reuman, *Philippians: A New Translation with Introduction and Commentary,* AYB 33B (New Haven: Yale University Press, 2008), 361, refers to it as an encomium. Adela Yarbro Collins, "The Psalms and the Origins of Christology," in *Psalms in Community: Jewish and Christian Textual, Liturgical, and Artistic Traditions,* ed. Harold W. Attridge and Margot E. Fassler (Atlanta: Society of Biblical Literature, 2003), sees it as a prose hymn. Given the text's *hapax legomena*, the obvious elevated language, the early Christian penchant for singing hymns to Christ as if he were a god (Pliny, *Epistle* 10.96.7), and the presence of kingship motifs, I think the text should be classified as a hymn.

34. Similarly, see M. David Litwa, *IEUS DEUS: The Early Christian Depiction of Jesus as a Mediterranean God* (Minneapolis: Fortress, 2014), 210.

35. For example, K. Bornhäuser, "Zum Verständnis von Philipper 2,5–11," *NKZ* 44 (1033): 428–34, 453–62; K. Bornhäuser, *Jesus Imperator Mundi (Phil 3,17–1 und 2,5–12)* (Gütersloh: Bertelsmann, 1938), who suggests that the hymn was written in order to counter Caligula's grasping after divine honors. Similarly, see David Seeley, "The Background of the Philippians Hymn (2:6–11)," *Journal of Higher Criticism* 1 (1994): 49–72.

has argued, "a general contrast between Christ's exaltation and the pursuit of power among earthly rulers."[36]

In Philippians 2:6 Paul speaks of the Messiah as existing in "God's form" (ἐν μορφῇ θεοῦ, 2:6), a claim that is clarified by the articular infinitival expression τὸ εἶναι ἴσα θεῷ ("to be equal with God") and, understanding ἁρπαγμόν as "something to be exploited" rather than "something to be grasped,"[37] portrays the preexistent Christ as equal with God.[38] We have already seen numerous texts that associate rulers, kings, and messiahs with deities (or Yahweh) in the closest possible manner as they are seen to be functioning as the earthly representatives of the divine.[39] Here I simply add to my earlier comments some of the many references to kings and emperors as god-equal and appearing in the same visible appearance/form of a god.[40] For example, a second-century-CE papyrus provides an incredible parallel: "What is a god? The use of power. What is a king? One who is equal with a god (τὶ θεός; τὸ κρατοῦν. τὶ βασιλεύς; ἰσόθεος)."[41] Philo refers to Caligula as attempting to clothe himself with "the form of a god" (θεοῦ μορφή, *Legum allegoriae* 110; cf. Josephus, *Jewish Antiquities* 18.257–309). According to Suetonius, Caligula established a temple for his *numen* and then wore the same clothes with which his divine statue was garbed. As argued above, the bestowal of godlike honors was typically reserved for those royal figures who provided the most exceptional benefactions to their

---

36. Mikael Tellbe, *Paul between Synagogue and State: Christians, Jews, and Civic Authorities in 1 Thessalonians, Romans, and Philippians* (Stockholm: Almqvist & Wiksell International, 2001), 256; Peter Oakes, *Philippians: From People to Letter*, SNTSMS 110 (Cambridge: Cambridge University Press, 2001), 129–74. See also Stefan Schreiber, *Gesalbter und König: Titel and Konzeptionen der königlichen Gesalbtenerwartung in frijüdischen und urchristlichen Schriften*, BZNW 105 (Berlin: de Gruyter, 2000), 412–14.

37. There would appear to be something *close* to a consensus on this point. See especially N. T. Wright, *The Climax of the Covenant: Christ and the Law in Pauline Theology* (Minneapolis: Fortress, 1992), 56–98; Roy Hoover, "The HARPAGMOS Enigma: A Philological Solution," *HTR* 64 (1971): 95–119.

38. See here Fee, *Pauline Christology*, 376–83.

39. So Adela Yarbro Collins, "The Worship of Jesus and the Imperial Cult," in *The Jewish Roots of Christological Monotheism: Papers from the St. Andrews Conference on the Historical Origins of the Worship of Jesus*, ed. Carey C. Newman et al., Supplements to the Journal for the Study of Judaism 63 (Leiden: Brill, 1999), 249–50; Litwa, *IEUS DEUS*, 187–210.

40. One cannot escape the fact that μορφή signifies visible appearance. See here Markus Bockmuehl, "'The Form of God' (Phil. 2:6): Variations on a Theme of Jewish Mysticism," *JTS* 48 (1997): 1–23.

41. Quoted from Simon R. F. Price, "Gods and Emperors: The Greek Language of the Roman Imperial Cult," *JHS* 104 (1984): 95.

subjects.[42] Diodorus Siculus declares that great men and demi-gods, "because of the benefits they conferred which have been shared by all men, have been honored by succeeding generations with sacrifices which in some cases are like those offered to the gods" (4.1.4). Dio Cassius declares of Augustus "that his name should be included in their hymns equally with those of the gods (τοὺς ὕμνους αὐτὸν ἐξ ἴσου τοῖς θεοῖς)" (*Roman History* 51.20.1). Nicolaus of Damascus says that after the divinization and public funeral of Julius Caesar, everyone wept as they "saw him who had recently been honored equal to a god" (FGrH 90). Augustus's official granting of divine honors for his adoptive father thereby sets the precedent, says Appian, for following Roman emperors to receive honors "equal to the gods" (ἰσόθεοι; *Civil Wars* 2.148).

Not everyone saw this process of bestowing divine honors upon rulers for great benefactions as appropriate. For example, Erik Heen points to an edict of Germanicus in 19 CE in which he rejects these divine honors: "your acclamations, which are for me invidious and such as are addressed to gods (*isotheos*), I altogether deprecate."[43] Jewish texts frequently refer to the desire of rulers to attain godlike status as an act of hubris that seeks to usurp something that belongs only to God.[44] For example, the author of 2 Maccabees places these words in the mouth of the Hellenistic monarch Antiochus IV: "It is right to submit oneself to God and not to think that one who is mortal is equal to God (δίκαιον ὑποτάσσεσθαι τῷ θεῷ καὶ μὴ θνητὸν ὄντα ἰσόθεα φρονεῖν)" (9:12). Antiochus IV is brought to this realization as a result of God's punishment for the king's hubristic attempt to usurp power and authority reserved only for God (see 2 Macc 9:8–11).[45] When Jesus declares that both he and his Father are working, the Fourth Gospel has the Jews attempt to kill him since "he was calling God his own Father and thereby making himself equal to God (ἴσον ἑαυτὸν ποῖων τῷ θεῷ)" (John 5:18). Samuel Vollenweider has shown that it was a common trope to criticize the hubris of rulers for seeking after divine honors

42. Helpful here is Erik M. Heen, "Phil 2:6–11 and Resistance to Local Timocratic Rule: *Isa theō* and the Cult of the Emperor in the East," in *Paul and the Roman Imperial Order*, ed. Richard A. Horsley (Harrisburg, PA: Trinity Press International, 2004), 125–53; S. R. F. Price, "Between Man and God," *JRS* (1980): 28–30. I am dependent upon these works for many of the primary sources listed in this paragraph.

43. Quoted from Heen, "Phil 2:6–11 and Resistance," 145.

44. See Samuel Vollenweider, "Der 'Raub' Der Gottgleichheit: Ein Religionsgeschicht-licher Vorschlag zu Phil 2.6(–11)," *NTS* 45 (1999): 413–33.

45. Heen, "Phil 2:6–11 and Resistance," 146; Joseph H. Hellerman, "ΜΟΡΦΗ ΘΕΟΥ as a Signifier of Social Status in Philippians 2:6," *JETS* 52 (2009): 789.

and attempting to exploit their supposed equality with the deity.[46] The restored remnant of Israel will mock "the king of Babylon" (Isa 14:4) who boasted: "I will ascend to heaven; I will set my throne above the stars of God; I will sit on an exalted mountain, upon the exalted mountains toward the north; I will ascend to the tops of the clouds, I will be like the Most High" (Isa 14:13–14). Similarly, the prophet Ezekiel declares judgment upon the "prince of Tyre" for his hubristic attempt to make himself like God: "Because your heart is proud and you have said, 'I am a god. I have inhabited the dwelling place of a god in the heart of the seas'" (28:1–2). The author of Acts preserves an account of Agrippa I, who received God's judgment for his acceptance of the crowds' divine acclamation: "the voice of a God and not a mortal" (12:22).[47] Tyrants and wicked kings are often described as greedy, hubristic, and arrogant. Thus, Dio Chrysostom declares that "not every king derives his scepter or this royal office from Zeus, but only the good king," and this means he will not become filled "with hubris and arrogance" (ὕβρεως καὶ ὑπερηφανίας, *First Discourse on Kingship* 1.12–13; cf. 1.84).

The ancient royal ideology that would link rulers with gods and that would often present the former as deserving of godlike honors due to their shared power is easily observable in many of these examples, though the claims by these kings (often tyrants) is contested and shown to be acts of hubris by the fact that their thrones, kingdoms, and very lives are subject to mortality and, in the examples from the biblical texts, are subject to God's judgment.

Paul taps into similar royal discourse, as Philippians 2:6 presents the Messiah as a royal ruler who exists *alongside* the God of Israel as he shares God's form and is worthy of equal honors. Paul is emphatic that the Messiah's power is not revealed in hubristically usurping the honors that belong to God.[48] Unlike the other rulers, however, the Messiah neither exploits nor takes advantage of his divine status (2:7–8), but rather, by means of taking the form of a slave and submitting to death on the cross, embraces "the most dishonorable public *status* and the most dishonorable public *humiliation* imaginable in the world of Roman antiquity."[49] True divine rule and power is revealed, then, in the Messiah's refusing to exploit equality with God, and instead, in a total reversal

---

46. Vollenweider, "Der 'Raub' Der Gottgleichheit," 420–25; Tellbe, *Paul between Synagogue and State*, 255–57.

47. See also Heen, "Phil. 2:6–11 and Resistance," 147n81.

48. Vollenweider, "Der 'Raub' Der Gottgleichheit," 432.

49. Joseph H. Hellerman, *Reconstructing Honor in Roman Philippi: Carmen Christi as Cursus Pudorum*, SNTSMS 132 (Cambridge: Cambridge University Press, 2005), 131.

of the pattern of those usurping kings who seek to ascend to the heavens, obeying YHWH and refusing to make use of divine honors and prerogatives.[50]

It is precisely as a result of the Messiah's refusal to exploit his divine status that God exalts him as Lord of the universe. Peter Oakes, among others, has made a convincing case that Paul draws a comparison between Christ and the Roman Emperor in Philippians 2:9–11. Both Christ and the emperor are spoken of as receiving authority over the entire world. Just as Christ receives the highest name and worship from all creation, so the emperor, albeit often with highly poetic and mythological imagery, is spoken of as ruling the land, sea, and the entire cosmos.[51] The name that Jesus receives from God, namely "the name that is above every name" (2:9b), resonates with the depiction of the king in LXX Psalm 117, whose identity and actions embody "the name of the Lord" (117:10, 11, 26). The Messiah is, therefore, promised the universal confession of κύριος Ἰησοῦς Χριστός (Phil 2:11), since both honorifics bracketing his proper name have distinctly royal connotations.[52] The honorific κύριος alongside God's exaltation (ὁ θεὸς αὐτὸν ὑπερύψωσεν, Phil 2:9a; cf. Acts 2:33; 5:31) of the Messiah resonates with LXX Psalm 109:1, in which YHWH enthrones and shares his divine name with another royal figure.[53] Given that the Messiah receives the divine name, he also shares in God's rule as his vicegerent as he rules over the cosmos (2:10–11). Christ's receiving the royal acclamation in 2:10–11 fits perfectly within the context of divine honors bestowed upon kings and great figures who performed noble tasks and distributed great benefactions.[54]

50. Hellerman, *Reconstructing Honor*, 135.

51. Oakes, *Philippians*, 149.

52. On the royal connotations of κύριος, see Joseph D. Fantin, *The Lord of the Entire World: Lord Jesus, a Challenge to Lord Caesar* (Sheffield: Sheffield Phoenix Press, 2011); Hellerman, *Reconstructing Honor*, 152–53.

53. See Martin Hengel, "'Sit at My Right Hand!' The Enthronement of Christ at the Right Hand of God and Psalm 110:1," in *Studies in Early Christology* (Edinburgh: T&T Clark, 1995), 155–56: "The τὸ ὄνομα τὸ ὑπὲρ πᾶν ὄνομα is the tetragramm YHWH, for which κύριος was already being substituted in the reading of the LXX: God gave his unspeakable name to the Crucified and Exalted One." Cf. Fee, *Pauline Christology*, 396–98; Richard Bauckham, "The Worship of Jesus in Philippians 2:9–11," in *Where Christology Began*, ed. Ralph P. Martin and Brian Dodd (Louisville: Westminster John Knox, 1998), 131; N. T. Wright, "Jesus Christ Is Lord: Philippians 2.5–11," in *The Climax of the Covenant: Christ and the Law in Pauline Theology* (Minneapolis: Fortress, 1991), 94.

54. For royal acclamations within the NT, see Matt 21:9; Mark 11:9–10; Luke 19:37; John 12:13; Acts 19:34. On royal acclamations, see Charlotte Roueche, "Acclamations in the Later Roman Empire: New Evidence from Aphrodisias," *JRS* 74 (1984): 181–99; on acclamations and benefactions in the Roman Empire, see Clifford Ando, *Imperial Ideology and Provincial Loyalty in the Roman Empire* (Berkeley: University of California Press, 2000), 199–205.

The royal notions of this acclamation are seen already within the context of Philippians, as the precise parallel in 3:20 (κύριον Ἰησοῦν Χριστόν) is situated within a context using the language of citizenship, imperial power, and royal enthronement (esp. 3:21).[55] It is precisely the Messiah's refusal to exploit his relationship with YHWH, his willingness to accept the form of a slave, and his humiliation on the cross that results in (διὸ καὶ ὁ θεὸς αὐτὸν ὑπερύψωσεν, 2:9) his exaltation to a public status where he receives divine honors coequal with God.[56] Rulers were seen as having godlike status precisely due to the benefactions they provided their subjects, and here in Philippians 2:6–11 the logic would seem to be that, while the preexistent Christ *already shared* in God's status, his obedience to God and willing humiliation on the cross—the greatest of all benefactions to humanity—is *the act* that legitimates his rule, grants him universal authority, and qualifies him to receive divine worship.[57] Paul redefines true royal rule as exemplified through Christ's pattern of refusal to grasp or exploit power, obedience to God, and sacrificial service even to the point of death.[58]

PARTICIPATING IN THE RULE OF THE MESSIANIC KING

Paul often speaks of Christ's people as sharing in the rule and royal benefits of the Messiah. Paul makes the closest possible connection between the identity and narrative of the Messiah and that of the Messiah's subjects. To give one small example of how Paul portrays believers as sharing or participating in the Messiah's narrative and identity, note his statement in 2 Corinthians 1:21–22: "God is the one establishing us with you *into the Anointed One and has anointed us* (εἰς Χριστὸν καὶ χρίσας ἡμᾶς) by placing his seal on us and giving us his Spirit (τοῦ πνεύματος) in our hearts as a pledge" (2 Cor 1:21–22). Paul provides no explicit or detailed interpretation of the statement, but it seems likely that he is punning on the meaning of God's consecration of the Messiah as king and the church's consecration *into* the same royal identity.

---

55. Peter Oakes, "Re-mapping the Universe: Paul and the Emperor in 1 Thessalonians and Philippians," *JSNT* 27 (2005): 318–19.

56. Wright, *The Climax of the Covenant*, 86, translates the inferential conjunction as "*that* is why."

57. For expansion of these claims and for the specific acts and virtues of emperors that were seen as qualifying them to rule, though he does not see 2:6–8 as resonating with royal discourse, see Oakes, *Philippians*, 151–60.

58. Similarly, see Tellbe, *Paul between Synagogue and State*, 257–58.

God's consecration or anointing of the Messiah by God's Spirit is shared with the Corinthians who, by virtue of their own anointing (χρίσας), participate in the Messiah's royal consecration.[59] Margaret Thrall states this well: "The Christ whom God consecrates as messianic king has with him his own community to reign with him. Believers are themselves 'christed' to share in the messianic kingdom."[60] Thus, it would seem to be the case that the Corinthian church shares in the Messiah's royal rule and kingdom, and as Paul goes on to say, this takes place by sharing the Spirit of the resurrected Messiah. That the Corinthians would have heard 2 Corinthians 1:21–22 as indicating their incorporation into Christ's royal identity and the promise that they would reign with the Messiah in his kingdom by virtue of sharing the Spirit of the resurrected Messiah gains plausibility when we remember that Paul had already, in a previous letter to the church, conceptualized their salvation as sharing in Christ's sovereign rule (1 Cor 3:21–23; 4:8–9; 6:2–3, 9–11; 15:20–28, 50–58). I suggest that this text provides a useful point of entry into the royal and messianic roots of Paul's participatory soteriology and Paul's frequent conceptualization of participation as sharing in the Messiah's rule.

1 Corinthians

In his opening thanksgiving prayer in 1 Corinthians, Paul states that God has called the Corinthian church into existence "for the purpose of fellowship with his Son Jesus Christ our Lord" (1 Cor 1:9), and one of the ways Paul conceptualizes the church's fellowship with the Son is through sharing in the Messiah's sovereign lordship over all things by virtue of sharing Christ's Spirit. Paul reminds them of this when he chastises the Corinthians for losing sight of their cosmic inheritance when they boast about their favorite apostle, for "all things" belong to them (3:21). This includes not merely Christian leaders like Paul and Apollos, but even "the world, or life, or death, or things present, or things to come—all things are yours" (3:22; cf. Rom. 8:32).[61] The submission of these cosmic powers

---

59. See Novenson, *Christ among the Messiahs*, 147.

60. Margaret Thrall, *2 Corinthians 1–7*, ICC (London: T&T Clark, 1994), 155. See also Martin Hengel, *Studies in Early Christology* (Edinburgh: T&T Clark, 1995), 5–6.

61. Many of the disagreements between Paul and the Corinthians appear to stem from an ideological conflict between Paul's Jewish apocalyptic and eschatological thinking and the Corinthians' influence by Hellenistic philosophy and rhetoric. See Dale B. Martin, *The Corinthian Body* (New Haven: Yale University Press, 1995). On Paul's attempt to get the Corinthians to think eschatologically, see Richard B. Hays, "The Conversion of the Imagination: Scripture and Eschatologically in 1 Corinthians," *NTS* 45 (1999): 391–412.

to the Corinthians stems, however, from *their belonging to the Messiah*: "you belong to the Messiah, and the Messiah to God" (1 Cor 3:23). The weight of Paul's sarcasm, then, in 1 Corinthians 4:8-9 is *not* on the Corinthian expectation that they will be kings, but that they are already kings apart from and without Paul (χωρὶς ἡμῶν ἐβασιλεύσατε). Paul's hope, in fact, is that the Corinthians "might reign, so that we might reign with you" (4:8b; cf. Rom 5:17-19; 2 Tim 2:8-11a).[62] In 1 Corinthians 6:1-11 Paul twice appeals to the Corinthians' hope of sharing in Christ's sovereignty as the foundation for appropriate moral behavior. First, the Corinthians must not take their brothers and sisters to court since "they will judge the world" (6:2) and "will judge angels" (6:3). Second, the saving realities mediated to them by virtue of their incorporation "in the name of our Lord Jesus Christ and in the Spirit of our God" (6:11) ensures that they *will not* be among those who do not inherit God's kingdom (θεοῦ βασιλείαν οὐ κληρονομήσουσιν, 6:9; οὐκ . . . βασιλείαν θεοῦ κληρονομήσουσιν, 6:10).[63] The close relationship between Messiah and Spirit (see 6:11) enables the Corinthians to inherit God's kingdom, given that they have been joined to the resurrected Messiah's πνεῦμα. Without entering into the complexities of 1 Corinthians 6:12-20 and 15:35-49, it can be seen that Paul's participatory discourse depends upon the premise that the Corinthians participate in Christ because they share the same πνεῦμα, Spirit, that the Messiah received when he was raised from the dead (esp. 6:13; 15:45).[64] By virtue of sharing in Christ's πνεῦμα, the Corinthians are joined to the Lord and assured of sharing in Christ's resurrection (6:14, 17). This is the logic again in 1 Corinthians 12, where Paul argues that the Corinthian church is "the Messiah's body" (12:27) since it shares in the same πνεῦμα that belongs to the Messiah (12:3, 11-13). The apostle sees the Messiah's sharing of his own πνεῦμα as the bond that enables Christ's subjects to share in the king's rule.[65] Thus, Paul's conceptualization of the Corinthians' inheritance of God's kingdom (15:50) and participation in Christ's cosmic rule depends upon having Christ's πνεῦμα (6:9-20; 12:1-31; 15:35-49).

Paul's promises to the Corinthians that they will share in God's kingdom and sovereignty are predicated on the apocalyptic scenario of 15:20-28, a

---

62. See M. David Litwa, *We Are Being Transformed: Deification in Paul's Soteriology*, BZNW (Berlin: de Gruyter, 2012), 186-87.

63. On which, see Mark Forman, *The Politics of Inheritance in Romans*, SNTSMS 148 (Cambridge: Cambridge University Press, 2011), 208-9.

64. See here Martin, *The Corinthian Body*, 174-79; S. K. Stowers, "What Is 'Pauline Participation in Christ'?" in *Redefining First Century Jewish and Christian Identities*, ed. F. E. Udoh (Notre Dame : University of Notre Dame Press, 2008), 357-59.

65. See Hodge, *If Sons, Then Heirs*; Stowers, "What Is 'Pauline Participation in Christ'?"

schema which has been reworked around the resurrection of the Messiah and his return.[66] Paul portrays the Messiah and his battle in cosmic-political language; the Messiah's return, for example, is referred to as a παρουσία, a term that echoes imperial visitations.[67] The term τάγμα, used in 15:23a to describe the distinction between Christ's resurrection and the future resurrection from the dead, was often used to describe the division of troops in an army and suggests that Paul depicts Christ and his people as a messianic army prepared to do battle.[68] In addition, the fact that the victorious Messiah would be accompanied by his subjects—namely, "those who belong to Christ" (οἱ τοῦ Χριστοῦ, 15:23)—was a well-known *topos* in early Judaism and the New Testament.[69] Finally, the Messiah's primary activity is one of triumph by means of destroying all cosmic-political powers (15:24). Paul's description of Christ's victory resonates strongly with Daniel's Son of Man figure who receives from God a kingdom, a rule, and an authority that results in the subjection of God's enemies (cf. Dan 7:13–14, esp. 7:27).[70] The Messiah's defeat of these enemies coincides with his "handing over the kingdom to the God and Father" (1 Cor 15:24a), which is ultimately for the purpose "that God might be all in all" (15:28b). These statements resonate with Israel's royal depictions of the Messiah who rules for God on his behalf.[71]

While 1 Corinthians 15:20–28 is suffused with echoes of Genesis 1–3, military vocabulary, and Daniel's Son of Man figure, the logic that underwrites Christ's entrance into cosmic and universal lordship over his enemies is Jesus's Davidic messiahship: Christ is the one who shares in divine kingship as the enthroned Lord who rules and defeats God's enemies (δεῖ γὰρ αὐτὸν βασιλεύειν ἄχρι οὗ θῇ πάντας τοὺς ἐχθροὺς ὑπὸ τοὺς πόδας αὐτοῦ, LXX Ps 109:1 in 1 Cor 15:25). And as the one who subdues these political-cosmic enemies, the foremost of which is "death" (15:24, 26), he shares in and embodies Adam's

---

66. Richard B. Hays, *1 Corinthians*, Interpretation (Louisville: Westminster John Knox, 1997), 264.

67. BDAG 629–30.

68. See, for only a few examples, Letter of Aristeas 26; Josephus, *Ant.*, 20, 122; 1 Clement 37:1–3; 40:1. See also Hays, *1 Corinthians*, 264–65; BDAG 802–803.

69. Martinus C. de Boer, *The Defeat of Death: Apocalyptic Eschatology in 1 Corinthians 15 and Romans 5*, JSNTSup 22 (Sheffield: JSOT Press, 1988), 200–202; J. Christiaan Beker, *Paul the Apostle: The Triumph of God in Life and Thought* (Philadelphia: Fortress, 1980).

70. See Novenson, *Christ among the Messiahs*, 143–44; cf. James A. Waddell, *The Messiah: A Comparative Study of the Enochic Son of Man and the Pauline Kyrios*, Jewish and Christian Texts Series 10 (London: T&T Clark, 2011), 154–56.

71. Novenson, *Christ among the Messiahs*, 144, rightly notes that here Christ serves the purposes "of the ultimate kingship of God" and that "Christ is God's delegate, whose job it is to subdue all of the hostile powers that oppose God in the present evil age."

vocation to have universal dominion over creation (πάντα γὰρ ὑπέταξεν ὑπὸ τοὺς πόδας αὐτοῦ, Ps 8:7 in 1 Cor 15:27a).[72] Given that Jesus is the Davidic Messiah, Novenson notes, "Paul appeals to psalms of David as if they are straightforwardly about Christ, as for him they are." [73] This allows Paul to weave together, as N. T. Wright has suggested, "the theme of kingship, of messianic rule, from Psalm 110 and Daniel, in order to emphasize that the future bodily resurrection of all the Messiah's people is guaranteed because Jesus fulfills the roles through which, according to the promises, the world is to be brought under the saving rule of its creator God."[74]

Paul's statements that "through a man came death" (1 Cor 15:21b) and "in Adam all die" (15:22a) speak to Adam's failure to extend God's righteous dominion over creation and, instead, to his unleashing of a death-dealing rule over creation by God's enemies. The hope that one from Adam's seed would crush the head of the serpent (Gen 3:15) is reworked in Israel's royal traditions into an expectation for a Davidic deliverer that would conquer Israel's cosmic-mythical enemies by crushing them underneath the king's feet.[75] The enemies will bow down and "lick the dust" (LXX Ps 71:9); they will be subjected "under [his] feet" (LXX Ps 109:1; cf Ps 8:6; 2 Sam 23:39). Likewise, the head of the dragon will be "crushed" (LXX Ps 73:13–14), and the serpent will be "trampled underfoot" (LXX Ps 90:13).[76] Significantly, the two texts which appear to have been the most strongly influenced by Genesis 3:15 are Psalm 8 and LXX Psalm 109. In the former, God is described as having placed "all things under his feet" (Ps 8:6). And in LXX Psalm 109:1, God declares to the one sharing his throne: "I will make your enemies a stool for your feet." As we have seen, Paul's promise to the Romans that God will "crush Satan under your feet" (ὑπὸ τοὺς πόδας ὑμῶν) grants humanity a share in defeating God's enemies by deploying Israel's messianic traditions of the defeat of evil through God's Messiah (Rom 16:20; Gen 3:15; Ps 8:7; LXX Ps 109:1). And here in 1 Corinthians 15:27–28 the

---

72. On Jesus's Davidic messiahship as standing behind the apocalyptic scenario of 1 Cor 15:20–28, see Novenson, *Christ among the Messiahs*, 143–46. The echoes of Israel's Scriptures are set out clearly by N. T. Wright, *The Resurrection of the Son of God*, vol. 3 of *Christian Origins and the Question of God* (Minneapolis: Fortress, 2003), 333–38.

73. Novenson, *Christ among the Messiahs*, 146.

74. Wright, *The Resurrection*, 335.

75. On the role of Gen 3:15 in the royal ideology of the psalmist, see T. Desmond Alexander, "Royal Expectations in Genesis to Kings: Their Importance for Biblical Theology," *TynBul* 49, no. 2 (1998): 191–212.; W. Wifall, "Gen 3:15—A Protevangelium?," *CBQ* 36 (1974): 361–65.

76. It is not unlikely that the widespread hope in later Jewish texts for Israel's enemies to be crushed underfoot is also dependent upon speculation on Gen 3:15. For example, see 1 En. 10:4, 11–12; 13:1–2; Testament of Moses 10:1; 1QS 3:18; 4:18–23.

six occurrences of words related to ὑποτάσσω show Christ's messianic identity clearly as the one who, as humanity's representative, subjects all of creation to himself, and as the one who, invested by God with a share in his rule, brings all of creation into submission to God so that he might reign supreme (15:28b). The six occurrences of forms of ὑποτάσσω, which is derived from the word τάγμα (15:23), suggest that the subjection of the Son to the Father restores the order of creation that was lost in Adam. Thus, Paul insists on the priority of the Father over the Son in the eschatological drama. The Son is the Father's agent who works for the Father's ultimate exaltation and glory (15:28).[77]

Paul's statement that the last enemy that will be defeated is death explicitly calls the reader back, both conceptually and linguistically, to Adam, the one through whom death attained its dominion (15:21). Death is portrayed as the cosmic enemy of the Messiah and his people, a sign of Adam's corruption of creation. Death is also portrayed as exercising a cosmic dominion over humanity (15:24–26), and this suggests that Paul's (negative) participatory statement that "*in Adam* all die" (15:22a) speaks to Adam's kingly role as humanity's failed representative. The destruction of Adam's death-dealing dominion takes place through the Messiah's resurrection from the dead (15:20–21), an event that inaugurates the Messiah's royal enthronement to a position of divine power (15:25–27). This suggests that Paul's christological participatory statements—"through a man is the resurrection from the dead" (15:21b) and "in the Messiah all will be made alive" (15:22b)—along with the earlier promises to share in Christ's sovereignty (3:21–23; 4:8–9; 6:2–3, 9–11), should be understood as conceptualizing union with Christ as participation in his royal narrative and identity, particularly in his cosmic triumph over his enemies, his establishment of God's kingdom, and his resurrection life and victory over death. Those who are in Christ and participate in his resurrection life (15:21–22) are also those who inherit the kingdom of God (15:50).[78] In portraying believers as rulers over "all things" (3:21–23) who "inherit the kingdom of God" (6:9–11; 15:50), Paul conceptualizes union with Christ as participating in the Davidic Messiah's cosmic rule, triumph, and judgment.[79]

77. Robin Scroggs, "Paul: Myth Remaker. The Refashioning of Early Ecclesial Traditions," in *Pauline Conversations in Context: Essays in Honor of Calvin J. Roetzel*, ed. Janice Capel Anderson, Philip Sellew, and Claudia Setzer, JSNTSup 221 (Sheffield: Sheffield Academic Press, 2002), 98.

78. On the relationship between 1 Cor 15:50 and 15:23–25, see Forman, *The Politics of Inheritance*, 209.

79. See the helpful study of Frederick David Carr, "Beginning at the End: The Kingdom of God in 1 Corinthians," *CBQ* 81 (2019): 449–69, who concludes: "Paul presents the king-

Philippians

One of the primary purposes of Philippians 2:6–11 is to set forth the royal pattern which all of Christ's people must follow if they would benefit from and share in his rule. The logic of Philippians trades on the notion that Christ's subjects benefit from his rule if they manifest the same royal virtues Christ himself displayed.[80] The church confesses Christ alone as their ruler, for he is "Lord Jesus the Messiah" (2:11). As we have seen, the Messiah has entered into his heavenly lordship, received the divine name, and been exalted above every other power (2:9–11) not through any lust for power or for the conferral of divine honors and benefits. Christ has, rather, redefined true power, authority, and rule through his obedient acceptance of public humiliation in service to God and to others. Thus, to "walk worthily of the gospel of Christ" (1:27a) will involve taking on the same royal virtues Christ exemplified on his way to entering into universal sovereignty over the world (e.g., the links between 2:1–5 and 2:6–11). Given Christ's royal pattern of obedience to God even in the face of lost status, suffering, and a humiliating death, Christ's people must also be willing to embrace the key virtues exemplified by their king—suffering (1:29–30; 2:17, 30), humiliation, other-regard, and loss of status (2:1–4; 2:20–21) —if they hope to share in the benefits of his rule. Paul's rejection of conferred high status (3:2–7) is of one piece with his desire to "participate in [Christ's] sufferings [and] to be conformed to his death" (3:10; cf. 2:6–8), for this embrace of suffering and humiliation is the necessary prerequisite for sharing in Christ's resurrection life (3:10a, 11).[81]

The political vocabulary and echoes of the Christ hymn in Philippians 3:20–21 show the salvific and beneficial consequences of Christ's rule. Christ is characterized in specifically royal terms as "savior" (σωτῆρα, 3:20) and "Lord Jesus the Messiah" (κύριον Ἰησοῦν Χριστόν, 3:20; cf. 2:11).[82] His exaltation

---

dom of God to the Corinthians as a future incorporation into God's rule, which they can obtain through participation in Christ's present reign, and which manifests as the power that both grounds and governs their corporate existence" (469).

80. Oakes, *Philippians*, 201–2.

81. On the relationship between Phil 3:10 and Phil 2:6–11, see Morna D. Hooker, *From Adam to Christ: Essays on Paul* (Cambridge: Cambridge University Press, 1990), 21. On the relationship between Phil 2:6–11 and Phil 3:20–21, see Ben C. Blackwell, *Christosis: Pauline Soteriology in Light of Deification in Irenaeus and Cyril of Alexandria*, WUNT 2.314 (Tübingen: Mohr Siebeck, 2011), 208.

82. On *Savior* as a term for Hellenistic kings and Roman emperors, see Fee, *Pauline Christology*, 402.

to a position of glory has brought into existence "a heavenly citizenship" (τὸ πολίτευμα ἐν οὐρανοῖς, 3:20; cf. 1:27) and "his body of glory" (3:21).[83] Paul's depiction of a heavenly citizenship, his use of the titles "Messiah," "Lord," and "Savior," and his allusion to Psalm 8:7 and the subjection of all things to his rule portray Christ as holding supreme power and authority.

When Christ returns, an event for which the church anxiously awaits, his people will experience a "transformation" of "our body of humiliation" (τὸ σῶμα τῆς ταπεινώσεως, 3:21a)—language that echoes Christ's own bodily experience of death (σχήματι εὑρεθεὶς ὡς ἄνθρωπος ἐταπείνωσεν ἑαυτόν, 2:7–8).[84] This transformation will result in sharing in Christ's resurrection, that is, "conformation to [Christ's] body of glory" (σύμμορφον τῷ σώματι τῆς δόξης αὐτοῦ, 3:21b; 3:10–11). Christ effects this transformation for those who belong to this heavenly citizenship "by the power that enables him to subject all things to himself" (κατὰ τὴν ἐνέργειαν τοῦ δύνασθαι αὐτὸν καὶ ὑποτάξαι αὐτῷ τὰ πάντα, 3:21c). Paul's allusion to Psalm 8:7 (which echoes Gen 1:26–28) depicts Christ as entering by his own agency into the royal dominion over creation and the glory and honor intended for Adam.[85] Paul's use of the language of "glory" refers, as Goranson Jacob has rightly argued, to "the honor or power associated with the [Messiah's] status of authority and sovereignty."[86] Christ's entrance into a position of cosmic supremacy and universal sovereignty over "all things" is the event depicted in Philippians 2:9, where God "highly exalts" him and gives him the name above "all names," and it is that event which enables Christ to share his resurrection life with his people (3:21b). Thus, those in the Messiah are promised a glorious sharing in the Messiah's cosmic rule. As Morna Hooker states, "In these verses, then, the meaning of Christ's exaltation is worked out for the believer: in Christ the Christian shares in the reversal of status which took place when God raised him."[87] The way in which Christ effects this bodily transformation for his people is by the power and lordship that

83. On which, see Andrew T. Lincoln, *Paradise Now and Not Yet: Studies in the Role of the Heavenly Dimension in Paul's Thought with Special Reference to His Eschatology*, SNTSMS 43 (Cambridge: Cambridge University Press, 1991), 97–100; Pheme Perkins, "Philippians: Theology for the Heavenly Politeuma," in *Thessalonians, Philippians, Galatians, Philippians*, vol. 1 of *Pauline Theology*, ed. Jouette M. Bassler (Minneapolis: Fortress, 1991), 89–104.

84. Fee, *Pauline Christology*, 403.

85. On the allusion to Ps 8:7 in Phil 3:21b, see N. T. Wright, *Paul and the Faithfulness of God*, vol. 4 of *Christian Origins and the Question of God* (Minneapolis: Fortress, 2013), 1292–93.

86. Haley Goranson Jacob, *Conformed to the Image of His Son: Reconsidering Paul's Theology of Glory in Romans* (Downers Grove, IL: InterVarsity Press, 2018), 145.

87. Hooker, *From Adam to Christ*, 21.

was conferred upon him at his own exaltation. In other words, the subjection of "all things" to the powerful lordship of Messiah Jesus (2:9–11; 3:21b) enables Christ to have the power to share his glorious resurrection body with his people so that they will be fit for participating in this heavenly citizenship.

Romans 5–8

Romans 5–8 is the fullest expression of Paul's participatory soteriology that can be found in his letters.[88] This section of Romans is filled with the language of kingship played out in a cosmic manner. For example, Adam and Christ both share in dominions (5:12–21), Sin and Death are over*lords* (6:9, 12, 14), humanity awaits either judgment or vindication (8:1, 33–34), humanity is liberated through sharing in Christ's regal-filial status (8:15, 29), and echoes of enthronement to lordship through resurrection abound (8:9–17, 33–34).[89] As Ernst Käsemann has said: "[Humanity's] life is from the beginning a stake in the confrontation between God and the principalities of the world. In other words, it mirrors the cosmic contention for the lordship of the world and is its concretion."[90] Humanity either shares in the identity and resulting consequences of Adam or Christ—both of whom are portrayed in Romans 5:12–21 as kings that represent dominions which exert lordship over humanity. Paul sees these figures and their actions as having apocalyptic consequences for humanity: humanity either shares in sin, ethically incapacitated flesh, death, and judgment, *or* righteousness, moral transformation, resurrection, and life.[91]

88. Romans 5–8 is given a privileged position for understanding Paul's theology in Campbell, *The Deliverance of God*; William Wrede, *Paul*, trans. E. Lummis (London: Green & Hull, Elson, 1907), 74–154; Albert Schweitzer, *The Mysticism of Paul the Apostle*, trans. William Montgomery (1931; Baltimore: The Johns Hopkins University Press, 1998), esp. 101–40. See the essays throughout Beverly Roberts Gaventa, ed., *Apocalyptic Paul: Cosmos and Anthropos in Romans 5–8* (Waco, TX: Baylor University Press, 2013).

89. See here the helpful reflections by Douglas A. Campbell, "The Story of Jesus in Romans and Galatians," in *Narrative Dynamics in Paul: A Critical Assessment*, ed. Bruce W. Longenecker (Louisville: Westminster John Knox, 2002), 116, who has shown that underlying Rom 8 is "a story of ascent through resurrection to glorification and heavenly enthronement."

90. Ernst Käsemann, "On the Subject of Primitive Christian Apocalyptic," in *New Testament Questions of Today*, trans. W. J. Montague (Philadelphia: Fortress, 1969), 136.

91. By "cosmic" I mean that the consequences of these figures' actions are universally determinative of all of human and worldly existence. For more on this, see Martinus C. de Boer, "Paul's Mythologizing Program in Romans 5–8," in *Apocalyptic Paul: Cosmos and Anthropos in Romans 5–8*, ed. Beverly Roberts Gaventa (Waco, TX: Baylor University Press, 2013), 1–20.

I suggest however, that Paul has taken the compact confession of Romans 1:3–4, examined in the previous section on "Messiah and Gospel," and reworked it throughout his letter in such a way that the christological narrative is programmatic for the identity of the Messiah and provides the christological foundation for humanity's union with Christ as articulated in Romans 5–8. That is to say, Romans 5–8 is essentially a cosmic development and application of the soteriological significance of Christ's messianic identity as set forth in 1:3–4. Thus, the messianic identity of Christ as seed of David who shares in human flesh, his installation as God's powerful Son, his resurrection from the dead, his resurrected state as marked by God's Spirit, and his enthronement to a position of lordship over the nations are taken up by Paul in Romans 5–8 and are reworked as the royal events in which humanity participates. In order for humanity to be saved out of the situation of death, sin, and enslavement to hostile cosmic powers and to share in divine sonship, resurrection, and the Spirit, it is necessary that Israel's Messiah share in these realities and, so to speak, open up the way for humanity to experience them by virtue of participating in his own royal identity and narrative. As the one who simultaneously shares in God's kingship as his Son *and* represents Israel and shares in its fleshly existence, the Messiah is uniquely positioned to share God's rule and its benefits with humanity.[92]

Romans 5:1–11 functions as a transition between 1:18–4:25 and 5:12–8:39 and so provides an introduction to Romans 5–8.[93] Here Paul speaks in distinctly political and royal terms of the Messiah's deliverance of humanity from evil powers: Messiah Jesus provides "peace with God" (5:1); Messiah Jesus gives "access" to this grace (5:2); and the Son's death reconciles humanity to God even while it is still at enmity with God (5:10–11).[94] The way in which God's Son, Messiah Jesus, rescues humanity is spelled out in 5:12–8:39, where Paul maps the liberating realities of 1:3–4 onto Christ's people. Paul's depiction of humanity's sharing in Christ's soteriological narrative corresponds to the two trajectories of the Messiah's own narrative set forth in 1:3–4.

To begin with, humanity's situation, including that of Israel, is marked by enslavement to hostile cosmic powers, and all of these apocalyptic powers

---

92. See also Wright, *Paul and the Faithfulness of God*, 1012.

93. On the function of Rom 5:1–11 as marking a transition into the themes of Rom 5:12–8:39, see especially Douglas J. Moo, *The Epistle to the Romans*, NICNT (Grand Rapids: Eerdmans, 1996), 292–95. Also, see Nils A. Dahl, "Two Notes on Romans 5," *ST* 5 (1952): 37–48.

94. On reconciliation as political language used to describe the cessation of hostilities between those at war, see Cilliers Breytenbach, *Versöhnung: Eine Studie zur paulinische Soteriologie* (Neukirchen-Vluyn: Neukirchener Verlag, 1989).

are introduced in the Adam-Christ antithesis in Romans 5:12–21. This is the negative counterpoint to participation in Christ, and it is important to recognize that it, too, is conceptualized with explicitly kingly language as humanity shares in Adam's dominion.[95] Adam, like Israel's kings, was seen as sharing God's dominion over creation precisely as humanity's representative.[96] Thus, it is no surprise that Paul characterizes Adam in two complementary ways: first, Adam is the prototypical *human* (e.g., 5:12); second, he is a *royal figure* who, by virtue of his act of disobedience, participates in a tyrannical dominion of death and sin (e.g., ἐβασίλευσεν ὁ θάνατος, 5:14; ὁ θάνατος ἐβασίλευσεν διὰ τοῦ ἑνός, 5:17; ἐβασίλευσεν ἡ ἁμαρτία ἐν τῷ θανάτῳ, 5:21).[97] Adam's humanity and primal kingship allow Paul to invoke "Adam as the one who unleashed a worldwide reign of sin and death."[98] Apart from Christ's liberating work, these evil overlords exert their dominion by taking root in the very flesh of unredeemed humanity and thereby bring death and judgment; ergo Paul's warning: "do not let sin <u>rule</u> in your mortal body" (Μὴ οὖν <u>βασιλευέτω</u> ἡ ἁμαρτία ἐν τῷ θνητῷ ὑμῶν σώματι, 6:12). Paul repeatedly uses regal and military language, more specifically the language used to describe a powerful enslaving tyrant, to speak of the "kingly reign" (βασιλεύω, 5:13, 17, 21; 6:12), "lordship" (κυριεύω, 6:6, 9, 14), "enslavement" (δοῦλος and δουλόω, 6:15–22), and "waging of war and imprisonment" (7:23) of the powers of sin and death.[99]

The "I" of Romans 7 witnesses to the incapacitated state of the fleshly human body as it is, in spite of its best intentions, imprisoned by the sin that has taken residence within and which produces death (esp. 7:17–24).[100] Sin, in fact,

---

95. Numerous Jewish texts portray Adam as a ruler. For example, 2 En. 30:12; 31:3; Wis 9:1–3; 10:1–2; Sir 17:1–4; Jub. 2:13–15. See further John R. Levison, *Portraits of Adam in Early Judaism: From Sirach to 2 Baruch*, JSPSup 1 (Sheffield: JSOT Press, 1988).

96. Bernard F. Batto, "The Divine Sovereign: The Image of God in the Priestly Creation Account," in *David and Zion: Biblical Studies in Honor of J. J. M. Roberts*, ed. Bernard Batto and Kathryn L. Roberts (Winona Lake, IN: Eisenbrauns, 2004), 143–86; also, J. Richard Middleton, *The Liberating Image: The Imago Dei in Genesis 1* (Grand Rapids: Brazos, 2005), 93–184.

97. See Robert C. Tannehill, *Dying and Rising with Christ: A Study in Pauline Theology*, BZNW (Berlin: de Gruyter, 1967), 14.

98. Kirk, *Unlocking Romans*, 105; also, Constantine R. Campbell, *Paul and Union with Christ: An Exegetical and Theological Study* (Grand Rapids: Zondervan, 2015), 345.

99. Sensitive to Paul's military language of conflict is Beverly Roberts Gaventa, "Neither Height Nor Depth: Discerning the Cosmology of Romans," *SJT* 64 (2011): 265–78, esp. 270–73.

100. On Rom 7:7–25 and its retrospective (from the standpoint of the Christ event) depiction of one under the Sinai covenant, see Joshua W. Jipp, "Educating the Divided Soul in Paul and Plato: Reading Romans 7:7–25 and Plato's Republic," in *Paul: Jew, Greek, and*

took God's good commandment and used it as "a base of operations" to wage its war (7:8, 11).[101] Here the power of sin successfully and strategically wages battle against humanity by taking advantage of the weakness of human flesh:

> I see another law in my members that is waging war against the law of my mind and is imprisoning me by the law of sin which is in my members. Wretched human that I am, who will rescue me from this body of death. (7:23–24)

It is humanity's Adamic embodied existence that allows the dominion of sin and death to exercise its tyrannical power in a manner that is internal to the body: "I am fleshly and I have been sold to the power of sin" (7:14b). And this accounts for the flurry of references to Adamic bodily existence as *intrinsically* morally incapacitated due to sin dwelling within the body (7:17, 18, 20, 21). Sin's dwelling in human flesh results in a situation where humanity is enslaved to sin, a situation that results in death—and for this reason Paul describes humanity with political language as God's "enemies" (5:10; 8:8).[102]

In order to participate in Christ's glorious resurrection and sonship, clearly humanity will have to first be rescued from the dominion and lordship of sin and death. Further, this rescue must render ineffective the power of these overlords by confronting their ability to make allies with weak, incapacitated, fleshly existence. And at this point it bears reminding that God's own Son, as we have seen, has shared in this situation by virtue of his having human flesh (Rom 1:3). As a descendant from the seed of David and as Israel's royal representative, the Messiah's participation in the human plight is portrayed by Paul as absolutely necessary to fulfill his royal task. And we have seen that this sharing in human flesh results in the predictable consequence of God's Son being found among "the corpses" (1:4). Paul unpacks the soteriological significance of this messianic confession (1:3) in Romans 8:3, when he speaks of "God sending his own Son (τὸν ἑαυτοῦ υἱόν) in the likeness of sinful flesh (ἐν ὁμοιώματι σαρκὸς ἁμαρτίας)"—namely, the very anthropological condition of

---

Roman, ed. Stanley E. Porter, Pauline Studies 5 (Leiden: Brill, 2008), 231–57; see also, D. J. Moo, "Israel and Paul in Romans 7.7–12," *NTS* 32 (1986): 122–35; Emma Wasserman, "The Death of the Soul in Romans 7: Revisiting Paul's Anthropology in Light of Hellenistic Moral Psychology," *JBL* 126 (2007): 793–816.

101. The term is often used in contexts of making war. See Gaventa, "Neither Height Nor Depth," 272, who points to Polybius, *Histories* 3.69; Philo, *Against Flaccus* 47; Dionysius of Halicarnassus, *Roman Antiquities* 5.5.3; 6.25.3.

102. Tannehill, *Dying and Rising with Christ*, 15–16.

humanity that Paul has so negatively detailed in 7:14–25 (cf. 7:14b).[103] As Richard Bell suggests, Paul is concerned here with "the sending of Christ into the area of human existence, and part of the very structure of existence is sin."[104] The similarities between Romans 1:3 and 8:3 are clear enough, but now, in light of Paul's depiction of fleshly humanity in Romans 5–8, the reader can see that the way in which God rescues humanity from the cosmic overlords is precisely through this bodily flesh of his messianic Son. The messianic Son shares in "sinful flesh" so that he can identify with the bodily existence of enslaved humanity and present himself as "a sin offering" (περὶ ἁμαρτίας),[105] so that he can "execute sin in his flesh" (κατέκρινεν τὴν ἁμαρτίαν ἐν τῇ σαρκί, 8:3b).[106] As a sin offering, the Son is humanity's representative who *identifies* completely with human existence and whose body undergoes the judgment and sentence of death.[107] As humanity's representative, in him our sinful Adamic flesh is destroyed and condemned.[108]

A similar set of ideas is presented in Romans 6:3–11, where Paul continues from 5:12–21 the contrast between two dominions. Here humanity is liberated from death and sin by virtue of being "conformed to the likeness of his death" (6:5a; cf. 6:3, 4). What does it mean to say that humanity shares in Christ's death, and how does sharing in Christ's death liberate humanity from Sin and Death? Paul allusively answers these questions when he refers to the crucifixion of our old humanity (ὁ παλαιὸς ἡμῶν ἄνθρωπος συνεσταυρώθη) and the "destruction of the body of sin" (τὸ σῶμα τῆς ἁμαρτίας, 6:6). This body of sin is the same "body of death" (7:24) and the same "sinful flesh" (8:3) shared by the first man, Adam (5:12), and all of humanity that belongs to his dominion. That the "old

---

103. Those who recognize the similarity between Paul's language for the son in Rom 1:3 and Rom 8:3 include Campbell, "The Story of Jesus," 104; Fatehi, *The Spirit's Relation*, 258–59. On the echo of 7:14 in 8:3, see Fee, *Pauline Christology*, 247.

104. Richard H. Bell, "Sacrifice and Christology in Paul," *JTS* 53 (2002): 6. Again, see Branick, "The Sinful Flesh."

105. The prepositional phrase περὶ ἁμαρτίας is frequently used to refer to the sin offering in the LXX (e.g., throughout Lev 17). See Wright, *The Climax of the Covenant*, 200–225.

106. The phrase "in his flesh" is almost certainly a reference to the Messiah's human flesh that has absorbed sin and its attendant condemnation. So also Bell, "Sacrifice and Christology," 8.

107. On the significance of the one making the sacrifice *identifying with* (rather than purely substitutionary) the fate of the sacrifice in the OT cult, see Hartmut Gese, *Essays on Biblical Theology*, trans. Keith Crim (Minneapolis: Augsburg, 1981), 93–116. With respect to Paul, see Bell, "Sacrifice and Christology," 1–27.

108. Bell, "Sacrifice and Christology," 5, is thereby right to note that Rom 8:3 provides the answer and solution to the problem articulated in Rom 7:7–25.

humanity" and "the body of sin" are crucified and done away with by Christ's crucifixion suggests that the Messiah takes the cosmic powers of Adam's dominion onto himself in his crucified body.[109] Thus, because of Christ's sharing in Adamic humanity and submission to crucifixion, Paul can speak of death having once exerted lordship over Christ (6:9). These considerations further suggest that the identity of the one mentioned in 6:7 ("for *the one who has died* has been justified from sin," ὁ γὰρ ἀποθανὼν δεδικαίωται ἀπὸ τῆς ἁμαρτίας) is, in the first instance, Christ, whose death brings freedom and release from Sin for all who share in his death. Christ is subjected to everything that characterizes the old dominion, including death (6:9; 7:4; 8:3), the law (7:4), sin (6:10; 8:3), and sufferings (8:17). Again, humanity's weak fleshly, bodily existence is "crucified" (6:6a), "destroyed" (6:6b), and "condemned" (8:3) by the only one who can function as humanity's representative—namely, God's Son "born according to David's seed from the flesh" (1:3). As a result, Paul describes the ethical consequences of Christ's liberation in decidedly cosmic-political terms: (1) "do not let sin rule in your mortal bodies" (6:12); "sin does not exert its lordship over you" (6:14a); "do not present your bodily members as weapons of unrighteousness to sin . . . but present your members as weapons of righteousness to God" (6:13); "you have been enslaved to righteousness" (6:18; cf. 6:20).[110]

Christ's crucifixion not only enables humanity to be freed from the tyrannical reign of Sin and Death, but his installation as God's resurrected Son who now has God's πνεῦμα functions as the catalyst for inaugurating his messianic reign over his people. The soteriological logic and grammar of Romans 5–8 depends upon: (1) the confession of Rom 1:4, that is, the narrative of the Messiah's resurrection and enthronement to a position of lordship over his people, the cosmos, and his enemies;[111] and (2) the way in which Jesus's messianic, royal identity uniquely enables him, as the one sharing in God's rule and πνεῦμα, to extend divine realities to humanity as their royal representative. Every aspect of the Son's royal enthronement in Romans 1:4 has participatory consequences, as Paul conceptualizes humanity's salvation as participating in the events of Christ's rule—namely, his sonship, resurrection life, reception of the Spirit, and cosmic inheritance.

Paul's claim in Romans 8 that those who belong to Christ are now "God's sons" (υἱοὶ θεοῦ, 8:14; cf. 8:15–17, 19, 21, 23, 29–30) is the result of their participation in the messianic sonship of the one who was "installed as God's Son in

---

109. See Kirk, *Unlocking Romans*, 111; Tannehill, *Dying and Rising with Christ*, 27–28.
110. See Gaventa, "Neither Height Nor Depth," 271.
111. I am persuaded by Campbell's argument in "The Story of Jesus," 97–124, that underlying Rom 8 is a narrative about the Son.

power" (1:4).[112] Again, Paul's ability to make this argument depends, in part, upon the Israelite royal ideology that sets forth the Davidic king as simultaneously sharing in God's kingship and Spirit and as the one who uniquely represented Israel. The king, as we have seen, thereby receives the divine promise: "I will be a father to him, and he will be a son to me" (2 Sam 7:14), and the appropriateness of activating this royal ideology is confirmed by Paul's allusions to LXX Psalm 88 in Romans 8:15 and 8:29. In LXX Psalm 88 the Davidic king is referred to as God's firstborn son (πρωτότοκον, Ps 88:28) who, during his royal enthronement, cries out to Yahweh: "you are my Father, my God, and the Rock of my salvation" (88:27).[113] The king's acclamation "encapsulates the powerful covenantal relationship now established between the new king and the God of the nation that is expressed in terms of immediate kinship."[114] In Romans 8:15 Paul roots humanity's divine sonship in the Messiah's enthronement as depicted in LXX Psalm 88: "you have not received a spirit of slavery leading again to fear, but you have received a Spirit of adoption, by which we are crying out, 'Abba Father' (ἀλλ᾽ ἐλάβετε πνεῦμα υἱοθεσίας ἐν ᾧ κράζομεν, αββα ὁ πατήρ)!" Given that the cry "Abba Father" calls to mind memories of Jesus's experience of sonship during his earthly ministry (Mark 14:36),[115] the allusion to the king's cry of filial relationship to God during his enthronement in LXX Psalm 88, and the fact that Christ is portrayed as humanity's elder brother and prototype (esp. Rom 8:29), humanity's crying out "Abba Father!" is a participation in the Messiah's experience of sonship.[116] Paul makes the relationship between the Messiah's sonship and humanity's adoptive sonship explicit in Galatians 4:6, where it is "the Spirit *of the Son*" that inspires one to cry "Abba Father."[117] Christ's people belong to him and his royal family,

---

112. Rightly Scott, *Adoption as Sons of God*, 244–45; Michael Peppard, *The Son of God in the Roman World: Divine Sonship in Its Social and Political Context* (Oxford: Oxford University Press, 2011), 138–40; Blackwell, *Christosis*, 162; Hodge, *If Sons, Then Heirs*, 70.

113. Similarly, see Scott, *Adoption as Sons of God*, 259–62.

114. Campbell, "The Story of Jesus," 116.

115. Despite overreaching at points, Joachim Jeremias in *The Prayers of Jesus* (London: SCM, 1967), 11–65, has shown that the term "Abba" demonstrates Jesus's filial relationship with God and that the early church saw Jesus's address of God as "Abba" as memorable and distinctive. See also, Fee, *Pauline Christology*, 217–20.

116. See Moo, *The Epistle to the Romans*, 502; Volker Rabens, *The Holy Spirit and Ethics in Paul: Transformation and Empowering for Religious-Ethical Life*, 2nd ed. (Minneapolis: Fortress, 2014), 226–27.

117. Fatehi, *The Spirit's Relation to the Risen Lord*, 216, argues that "by 'the Spirit of his Son' Paul means the Spirit *in its capacity of mediating the risen Son's active presence and power*" (italics his).

then, precisely because they have the same πνεῦμα as Christ.[118] The intimately relational covenantal cry of God's fatherhood forms a contrast between the benevolent and loving rule of Christ (see esp. Rom 8:35, 37–39) and the "fear" and "slavery" that marks the tyrannical rule of sin and death over Adamic humanity. Thus, whereas adoption in the ancient world may or may not be marked by deep familial affection, Paul's emphasis on "the Messiah's love" (8:35, 37) and "God's love which is in Messiah Jesus our Lord" (8:39b; cf. 5:5), among numerous other factors, suggests that covenantal love and intimacy are key components of humanity's adoptive sonship. The transition from υἱοί (8:14) to τέκνα (8:16–17), Grant Macaskill thinks, may even suggest "a reality that surpasses the bare legal concept of adoption and emphasizes instead familial intimacy and possibly even familial likeness."[119]

Further tightening the link between humanity's divine sonship as a participation in the Son of God's sonship is Romans 8:29, where Paul speaks of God's action with respect to believers as: "he predestined [them] to be conformed to the image of his Son, so that he might be the firstborn among many brothers."[120] The language of election, image, son, and firstborn son are at home within messianic discourse, and especially in light of LXX Psalm 88, function, in part, to designate Christ as highly exalted by God and elected to share in his sovereign rule.[121] But Christ's sovereign rule and sonship is shared with his family, and the lexical similarity between προορίζω (believers' predestination to sonship, Rom 8:29, 30) and ὁρίζω (the installation of God's Son, 1:4), further indicates that God's election of humanity to sonship is derivative from God's installation of Christ as God's Son in 1:4. Further, Christ's exalted status as God's firstborn Son, where he is placed above all other kings (Rom 8:29; LXX Ps 88:26), assures Christ's "many brothers and sisters" that his royal identity and narrative is being (and will be) shared with them.[122] And this makes good sense of the statement that believers are being "conformed to the image of his Son" as well as the σύν- prefixes throughout Romans 5–8 that describe the shared destiny between the Son and his siblings (e.g., 8:16, 17).

We have seen that humanity's adoption and participation in the Messiah's

118. Hodge, *If Sons, Then Heirs*, 75.

119. Grant Macaskill, *Union with Christ in the New Testament* (Oxford: Oxford University Press, 2013), 240.

120. See further Reidar Aasgaard, *'My Beloved Brothers and Sisters!': Christian Siblingship in Paul*, JSNTSup 265 (London: T&T Clark, 2004).

121. See my earlier discussion of Col 1:15–20 and Ps 89.

122. See Mark Forman, *The Politics of Inheritance*, 118–19; Aasgard, *'My Beloved Brothers and Sisters!'*, 142–43.

own sonship is due to receiving "the Spirit of adoption" (8:15). Just as God installed his Son to a position of rule by the "Spirit of holiness" (1:4), so also believers receive their adoptive sonship through the agency of the same Spirit who creates the Father-son relation between God and Christ's people (cf. Gal 4:6). Paul thereby implies that Israel's promises of sonship for God's installed king (2 Sam 7:12–14; Ps 2:7; LXX Ps 88:26–27) are extended to the Messiah's people by virtue of the Spirit. Whereas Israel's Scriptures portrayed God's gift of the Spirit as establishing the king as holy, sacrosanct, and the locus of God's presence, so now Messiah Jesus shares the royal gift of the Spirit with all his people. Thus, those who share in the Messiah's sonship receive the same Spirit and are described as "in the Spirit" (Rom 8:9a), and this is why Paul, even within the same breath, refers to the "Spirit of God (8:9a) as "the Spirit of the Messiah" (8:9b).[123] Just as the Spirit enabled the Son to move from a state marked by weak, corruptible, and dead flesh into resurrection existence (1:3–4), so now by virtue of sharing Christ's Spirit (8:9) believers move from the dominion of flesh to that of the Spirit.[124] By virtue of his resurrection from the dead, the powerful Messiah is marked out as the locus for the Spirit—that is, the resurrected Messiah has become a "life-giving Spirit" (1 Cor 15:45; cf. Rom 1:4). Again, it is the Spirit that raises the Messiah from the dead, and it is this same Spirit "that raised the Messiah from the dead who will give life to your mortal bodies" (8:11b; cf. 1:4; 4:24–25). Sharing the Messiah's πνεῦμα is the defining marker that one *belongs* to, or even is *part of*, the Messiah's people (8:9b; cf. 1 Cor 15:23). "If the Messiah is in you" (Rom 8:10a), then one can be assured that just as the Spirit gave resurrection life to the Messiah's dead body, a body which had taken on sinful human flesh (Rom 1:3; 7:4–5; 8:3), so, too, will the same Spirit give life to the dead sin-ridden bodies that have the Messiah's Spirit dwelling within them (8:10–11). Paul conceptualizes this reality as a transition from the dominion marked by "the death of the body because of sin" (τὸ μὲν σῶμα νεκρὸν διὰ ἁμαρτίαν, 8:10a) to the Messiah's dominion that is marked by "the Spirit of life because of righteousness" (τὸ δὲ πνεῦμα ζωὴ διὰ δικαιοσύνην, 8:10b). Whereas the Messiah has *already* experienced the Spirit's work of resurrection to life (1:4; 4:24–25; 5:17–18; 8:11), humanity waits for the revelation of the glory of God (5:5; 8:18b), anticipates the "revelation of the sons of God" (8:19), and looks forward to the "freedom of glory for God's children"

---

123. On the risen Christ's presence and activity among his people through indwelling of the Spirit, see Fatehi, *The Spirit's Relation*, 213–15. See further, Fee, *Pauline Christology*, 269–70.

124. See Stowers, "What Is 'Pauline Participation in Christ'?", 362.

(8:21). The Spirit's present work assures believers of their sonship (8:15–16) and inspires a "groaning" for the manifestation of this adoption—namely, "the redemption of our bodies" (8:23b).[125]

The Spirit's role in resurrecting the Messiah from the dead results in the frequent refrain that the Spirit produces "life" (Rom 8:2, 6, 10, 11, 13). And this is in marked contrast to Adam's dominion in 5:12–21, a situation where death rules humanity by means of sin, and judgment is the attendant result from sin (see esp. 5:14–17; 6:23). Returning to 5:12–21, we can see that Paul sees the Spirit's life-giving resurrection of the Messiah as the event that has brought into existence a messianic dominion where Christ's people share in his reign, namely, in his resurrected life. So, Christ's people "will reign in life" (ἐν ζωῇ βασιλεύσουσιν, 5:17); in contrast to the judgment (εἰς κατάρκιμα, 5:16, 18) that results from Adam's sin, those within Christ's domain experience "the justification which is life" (εἰς δικαίωσιν ζωῆς, 5:18) and the reign of grace "through righteousness for eternal life" (διὰ δικαιοσύνης εἰς ζωὴν αἰώνιον, 5:21; cf. 6:9).[126]

In the preceding chapter we examined how Paul speaks of the Messiah as the ruler over the nations and the eschatological cosmos in Romans 8. This renewed cosmos is the inheritance of the Messiah and his people (see the allusion to Ps 2:7–8 in Rom 1:5). But Paul also conceptualizes the Lord's enthroned rule and inheritance as something that is shared with his people. Paul conceptualizes this shared inheritance as the Messiah's enablement of his people to participate in his cosmic rule over a restored creation. God's intention for humanity to reign over creation as his vicegerents (Gen 1:26–28; Ps 8:4–6), an intention that was corrupted by Adam's unleashing of a dominion of sin, death, and corruption of the cosmos (Rom 5:12–21), is brought to fruition through the Messiah's cosmic rule and his extension of this rule to his people.[127] Paul's reasoning stems from Christ's sharing his Spirit-empowered, resurrected sonship with his people; thus, if humanity shares in this sonship, then they, too, must be "heirs of God, that is co-heirs with the Messiah, if indeed we suffer together with him so that we may also be glorified together with him" (κληρονόμοι μὲν θεοῦ, συγκληρονόμοι δὲ Χριστοῦ, εἴπερ συμπάσχομεν ἵνα καὶ συνδοξασθῶμεν, 8:17b). Given that the Messiah suffered and died before his resurrection and

---

125. On the eschatological aspect of adoption, see Blackwell, *Christosis*, 147–48; Macaskill, *Union with Christ*, 241.

126. On the overlap between "righteousness" and "life" in Romans, see Morna D. Hooker, "Raised for Our Acquittal (Rom. 4,25)," in *Resurrection in the New Testament: Festschrift J. Lambrecht*, ed. R. Bieringer et al., BETL 165 (Leuven: Leuven University Press, 2002), 323–41.

127. See also Forman, *The Politics of Inheritance*, 117–18.

glorification (4:24; 5:6–8; 6:3–4, 8–9; 7:4; 8:11, 34; 10:9; 14:9, 15; 15:3), Christians follow the same narrative pattern as they share in the sufferings (8:17–18) and creational bondage (8:20–23) that marks Adam's dominion.[128] The references to believers' future "glorification" (8:17), the coming "glory that will be revealed for us" (8:18), and "the freedom of glory for God's children" (8:21b) is precisely "the pristine glory meant for Adam, eschatologically restored to redeemed humanity"[129] by virtue of the resurrected and enthroned Messiah's new bodily existence (cf. "the image of his son," 8:29).

This inheritance is universal in scope and is something that is shared with the Son (cf. 8:17)—how will God not also "freely give to us *with him all things*" (σὺν αὐτῷ τὰ πάντα ἡμῖν χαρίσεται, 8:32b)? Paul makes a similar statement in 1 Cor 3:21–23, where he tells the Corinthians, "all things are yours" (3:21b). The Corinthians' sovereign rule provides a fitting parallel to Romans 8:32b, given that: (1) their rule is explicitly connected to their sharing in Christ's rule (3:23), and (2) their rule is cosmic and eschatological in scope (εἴτε κόσμος εἴτε ζωὴ εἴτε θάνατος, εἴτε ἐνεστῶτα εἴτε μέλλοντα, πάντα ὑμῶν, 1 Cor 3:22b). Thus, God's "giving us *all things* with him" in Romans 8:32 almost certainly includes all of the cosmic powers in 8:31–39 which threaten to "separate" (8:35, 39) Christ's people from his loving rule over them. As sharers in Christ's cosmic rule, these powers are impotent to "stand against us" (8:31b), to "bring a charge against us" (8:33), to "condemn" (8:34), or to "separate us from Christ's love" (8:35, 39).[130] Paul's allusions to Christ's cosmic and universal sovereignty with the term πρωτότοκον in Romans 8:29 (LXX Ps 88:26—"I will make him the firstborn, the highest of the kings of the earth") and to LXX Psalm 109:1 in Romans 8:34 (where the resurrected Messiah is seated at God's right hand, interceding for humanity) suggest that the "all things" in 8:32 and the "inheritance together with Christ" include a share in Christ's reign over the cosmic enemies of the old dominion.[131] In fact, 8:33–34 presents the resurrected and

---

128. On the overlap of the ages in Rom 8:18–30, see Blackwell, *Christosis*, 152–57.

129. Edward Adams, "Paul's Story of God and Creation," in *Narrative Dynamics in Paul*, ed. Bruce W. Longenecker (Louisville: Westminster John Knox, 2002), 29. See also Ben C. Blackwell, "Immortal Glory and the Problem of Death in Romans 3:23," *JSNT* 32 (2010); 285–308. Though Paul speaks of Adam as "a type of the coming one" (Rom 5:14b), Christ is the image of God after which Adam is patterned.

130. For a powerful theological reflection on how Christ's kingship assures humanity of its eschatological victory, see Philip G. Ziegler, "The Love of God Is a Sovereign Thing: The Witness of Romans 8:31–39 and the Royal Office of Jesus Christ," in *Apocalyptic Paul: Cosmos and Anthropos in Romans 5–8*, ed. Beverly Roberts Gaventa (Waco, TX: Baylor University Press, 2013), 111–30.

131. Scott, *Adoption as Sons of God*, 249–54.

enthroned Messiah as granting judicial protection over his people from his and their enemies.[132] The Messiah's enthronement to a position of power (8:34; cf. 1:4) ensures that there is simply no aspect of creation, no cosmic power belonging to Adam's dominion, that can return the people of the Messiah to their former enslavement to the reign of sin and death.[133]

Paul's promise that the "God of peace will soon crush Satan under your feet" (16:20; cf. Ps 8:7; Gen 3:15) is relevant in that God enables humanity to participate in his eschatological triumph over evil.[134] The believers' cosmic rule over these enemies is, again, dependent upon the christological narrative of the resurrected Messiah, for to have lordship over suffering (Rom 8:35), the rulers and powers of the old age (8:38), death (8:36, 38), and Satan (16:20) depends upon sharing the destiny and inheritance of the resurrected, enthroned Lord (8:34; cf. 8:29).[135] Thus, over all of these markers and powers of the old age, "we abundantly conquer through the one who has loved us" (8:37). Christ's people are the ones who conquer, but this victory takes place by their participation in the Messiah's triumph.

CONCLUSION

My argument should not be understood as an attempt to provide a comprehensive framework for *all* of Paul's participatory soteriology. Meals, baptism, and marriage, for example, are all significant practices and metaphors which communicate Paul's understanding of the union between the Messiah and his people. However, I have argued that Paul's understanding of Jesus as a messianic and kingly figure, predicated upon Jesus's Davidic messiahship, provides the logic for Paul's participatory soteriology. The messianic king is uniquely situated as the one who can mediate God's salvation to the people. The abundance of messianic royal discourse that is used to conceptualize Paul's grammar of union with Christ confirms, in my opinion, the likelihood that

132. See Eskola, *Messiah and Throne*, 186; cf. Kirk, *Unlocking Romans*, 153–54.

133. See Ziegler, "The Love of God Is a Sovereign Thing," 122–26.

134. Michael J. Thate, "Paul at the Ball: *Ecclesia Victor* and the Cosmic Defeat of Personified Evil in Romans 16:20," in *Paul's World*, ed. Stanley Porter, Pauline Studies 4 (Leiden: Brill, 2007), 151–69.

135. Forman, *The Politics of Inheritance*, 119, in commenting on Rom 8:29 and Christ's status as firstborn among a large family, states: "This suggests that in the process of being conformed to Christ believers become 'brothers and sisters' of God's Son, a relationship which means the people of God participate in Christ's reign over creation."

Jesus's identity as Israel's Davidic Messiah, as seen in relation to his particular narrative as one who suffered and died in obedience to God, was raised to life, and enthroned at God's right hand by the Spirit, contributed to Paul's creative conceptualizing of Christ's people inhabiting and sharing in the identity and narrative of Jesus the Messiah. In the next chapter, I suggest that my argument is confirmed through the witness of Ephesians, Colossians, and 2 Timothy.

CHAPTER 7

Participating in the Rule of the Messianic King (Part II)

Ephesians, Colossians, and 2 Timothy

In the preceding chapter I examined Romans, Philippians, and 1 Corinthians and argued that the grammar and logic of Paul's participatory soteriology is seen in Paul's creative reflection upon Jesus's identity and narrative as the messianic king who shares his saving kingship and its rule with his people. In this chapter I examine the same messianic theme in Ephesians and Colossians (two of the so-called disputed Pauline letters).[1] I examine these two Pauline letters together for a few reasons. First, while I think there are good arguments for affirming Pauline authorship, I have no interest in trying to sway anyone's opinions on the matter here; if one so inclines to view these letters as pseudonymous, I trust most will still regard these letters as providing significant evidence for the importance of messianism as a context for interpreting Paul (or his early interpreters).[2] Second, all interpreters agree that Ephesians and Colossians overlap in terms of their themes, argumentation, and mode

---

1. This chapter is a reworking and revision of arguments I have made in separate places. I am grateful for the permissions from Mohr Siebeck and Fortress to reproduce these arguments here in this form. The earlier version for my section on Ephesians can be found in Joshua W. Jipp, "Sharing in the Heavenly Rule of Christ the King: Paul's Royal Participatory Soteriology in Ephesians," in *"In Christ" in Paul: Explorations in Paul's Theological Vision of Participation*, ed. Michael J. Thate et al. (Tübingen: Mohr Siebeck. 2014), 251–75. The argument from Colossians can be found in Joshua W. Jipp, *Christ Is King: Paul's Royal Ideology* (Minneapolis: Fortress, 2015), 100–127, 142–45.

2. I maintain Pauline authorship for Ephesians, but even if it is pseudonymous, all scholars agree that it was written shortly after Paul's death within the sphere of Paul's missionary network and by someone of the Pauline school. Even on these assumptions, the author would provide invaluable evidence for the roots and use of "Paul's" participatory soteriology. For those accepting Pauline authorship of both Ephesians and Colossians, see Luke Timothy Johnson, *The Writings of the New Testament: An Interpretation* (Minneapolis: Fortress, 1999),

of discourse; it makes good organizational sense, then, to read these letters together. Third, one of my arguments in the previous chapter on Paul was that his participatory soteriology originated out of his creative transformation of notions of the messianic king as uniquely positioned to share in God's kingship and as the embodied representative of his people; I argue here that Ephesians and Colossians (and more briefly, 2 Timothy) function as significant witnesses to the importance of Paul's engagement of notions of messianic kingship to his participatory soteriology.

Again, we will see that these texts provide significant testimony to Paul's understanding of the narrative of Messiah Jesus and his mapping of the same narrative identity onto the Messiah's people. Paul conceptualizes the relationship between Christ and his people as the relationship between king and subjects, with the Messiah's people, however, sharing in the rule and the benefits of the resurrected enthroned Messiah's heavenly rule. As participants in the Messiah's lordship, the king's subjects share in the benefits of his royal rule, foremost of which are: participation in the Messiah's election, participation in the Messiah's assembly where he nourishes and gives gifts to his people, and participating in the Messiah's establishment of ethnic peace and reconciliation.

EPHESIANS

To find evidence for Paul's participatory soteriology in Ephesians, we will look at (1) Paul's use of the word Χριστός as an honorific for Jesus; (2) Paul's rereading of Israel's royal ideology to make a case for the church's participation in the Messiah's rule; and (3) how the people's share in the Messiah's rule is the foundation for their participation in his royal benefits, election, body, reconciliation, and peace.

Χριστός as a Royal Figure

Paul's letter to the Ephesians is dominated by a figure referred to as Χριστός who acts and rules on God's behalf.[3] Though some have argued that Paul's use of the articular ὁ Χριστός indicates that Paul refers to this figure as Israel's Messiah (e.g., Eph 1:10; 1:20; 2:5; 4:20), grammatical arguments

---

393–95, 407–12; N. T. Wright, *Paul and the Faithfulness of God*, vol. 4 of *Christian Origins and the Question of God* (Minneapolis: Fortress, 2013), 56–61.

3. There are forty-six occurrences in Ephesians.

regarding the presence or absence of the article and their indication of Χρι-στός as an honorific or, alternatively, a proper name have proved uncon-vincing one way or the other.[4] Rather, the meaning of Χριστός can best be determined by specific contextual features such as the literary role of the Christ figure, influence from Israel's Scriptures on the use of the term, and confessional statements.[5]

We see, first, that "the Christ" is spoken of as, along with God, having his own kingdom (Eph 5:5b), a kingdom that is marked, here described with what is likely an early hymnic fragment, by the Messiah's bestowal of resurrection light upon the dead (5:14).[6] Second, in significant portions of his argument Paul develops his articulation of the Messiah's activity through marked quo-tations and allusions to Israel's scriptural royal ideology. Thus, the Messiah's resurrection and enthronement by God is understood through the lens of Psalms 8 and 110 (Eph 1:20–23), the Messiah's defeat of his hostile enemies through Psalm 2 and Daniel 7 (Eph 1:21; 2:1–3), the Messiah's establishment of peace for his people through Isaiah (Isa 9:5–6; 52:7; 59:17; Eph 2:14–18), and the Messiah's giving of gifts to his people with the help of Psalm 68 (Eph 4:7–11). Paul's deployment of these royal texts from Israel's Scriptures to refer to "the Christ" in Ephesians suggests Paul uses Χριστός to mean "Messiah."

The third contextual feature is worth developing with a bit more detail. In ancient Israel the king was installed by means of anointing such that he received the title and office of "Messiah," an office that marked him out "not merely [as] 'the Messiah' but 'the Messiah of Yahweh.'"[7] Tryggve Mettinger notes that the term "'Messiah' denotes the king as very definitely set apart from

---

4. See the discussion in Julien Smith, *Christ the Ideal King: Cultural Context, Rhetorical Strategy, and the Power of Divine Monarchy in Ephesians*, WUNT 2.313 (Tübingen: Mohr Siebeck, 2011), 76–82.

5. M. de Jonge, "The Use of the Word 'Anointed' in the Time of Jesus," *NovT* 8 (1966): 147.

6. The hymn begins with the quotation formula διὸ λέγει: "wake up you sleeper, and rise up from the dead, and the Messiah will shine light upon you" (ἔγειρε, ὁ καθεύδων, καὶ ἀνάστα ἐκ τῶν νεκρῶν, καὶ ἐπιφαύσει σοι ὁ Χριστός). The hymnic fragment appears to provide evidence for the early Christian belief that ὁ Χριστός, as the first to be raised from the dead, shines his light upon the dead who are in a state of darkness (Eph 5:8) thereby communicating resurrection and light (cf. 1 Cor 15:20–22). As the first to be raised from the dead, the Messiah is able to shine resurrection light upon the dead, thereby bringing them into a realm of "light in the Lord" (Eph 5:8b) and procuring for them "an inheritance in the kingdom of the Messiah and God" (5:5b).

7. Aubrey R. Johnson, *Sacral Kingship in Ancient Israel* (Cardiff: University of Wales Press, 1967), 14–15, points to Judg 9:7–21; 1 Sam 16:1–13; 2 Sam 2:1–7; 5:1–5; 1 Kgs 1:28–40; 2 Kgs 9:1–13; 11:4–20.

the rest of the people, since it signifies his status *as linked with God and thus inviolable*" (italics mine).[8] As God's own son, Israelite royal ideology viewed the Lord's Messiah as invested with God's authority and power to rule (Ps 2:6–9; 89:26–28; 110:1–4; cf. 2 Sam 7:12–14).[9] It was this relationship between king and God that enabled the anointed Messiah to operate as a channel for God's Spirit (1 Sam 16:13; Isa 11:1–2; 61:1–3; Pss. Sol. 17:22, 37; 18:5–7), to share in and represent God's rule (e.g., Ps 89:20–37), and to shepherd God's people with righteousness and peace (Ps 72:1–3; Ezek 34; Pss. Sol. 17:32). The king's participation in God's rule was thought to result in the bestowal of God's gifts to his people, foremost of which included righteousness, rule over one's enemies, and internal peace and prosperity.[10] The investiture of Israel's anointed king with God's authority and rule was not unique to Israel, but is an element of royal ideology that characterizes ancient Near Eastern and Hellenistic-Roman notions of kingship.[11] The important point here, for our purposes, is that the royal figure is the subordinated vicegerent of God whose job it is to rule and act on God's behalf by bestowing divine benefits to his subjects.[12] He is the royal agent who shares in God's rule and acts as the channel through whom God acts.

When we turn to Ephesians we encounter a figure consistently referred to as Χριστός who is subordinated to the plans, purposes, and acts of God. In almost every instance, when Paul speaks of God as the acting subject he portrays God acting by the channel of the Messiah.[13] God's acting through the Messiah is often indicated through the use of the phrase ἐν Χριστῷ and related prepositional constructions; one frequently finds the pattern of God as the subject of a verbal idea that is put into effect "in/by Christ."[14] The syn-

---

8. Tryggve N. D. Mettinger, *King and Messiah: The Civil and Sacral Legitimation of the Israelite Kings*, ConBOT 8 (Lund: Gleerup, 1976), 199.

9. John H. Eaton, *Kingship and the Psalms*, SBT 32 (London: SCM, 1976), 146–49. Sigmund Mowinckel, *The Psalms in Israel's Worship*, rev. ed., trans. D. R. Ap-Thomas, 2 vols. (Grand Rapids: Eerdmans, 2004), 1:51.

10. For justice and righteousness, see Ps 72:1–4a; Isa 11:4–5; Pss. Sol. 17:32. For defeat over one's enemies, see Gen 49:10–12; Num 24:17–19; Pss 72:4b, 8–11; 2 Bar. 39–40, 70–72. For peace and prosperity, see Pss 72:15–16; 132:15; 144:11–14; Isa 11:6–9.

11. On this, see the excellent and comprehensive study of J. Rufus Fears, *PRINCEPS A DIIS ELECTUS: The Divine Election of the Emperor as Political Concept at Rome* (Rome: American Academy at Rome, 1977).

12. See Smith, *Christ the Ideal King*, 175.

13. This has been argued by Smith, *Christ the Ideal King*, 185–95.

14. Scholars frequently describe this as "God does or gives X for his people in/by the Messiah." See Smith, *Christ the Ideal King*, 183; Constantine R. Campbell, *Paul and Union*

tactical sense of many of these "in Christ" prepositional phrases is, on first blush, instrumental,[15] though I suggest a locative or participatory sense is also likely for most of these phrases. For example, "God has forgiven you in/by the Messiah" (ὁ θεὸς ἐν Χριστῷ ἐχαρίσατο ὑμῖν, Eph 4:32).[16] God the Father has blessed "us with every spiritual blessing in the heavenly places in/by the Messiah (ἐν τοῖς ἐπουρανίος ἐν Χριστῷ, 1:3; cf. 1:4). God will sum up all of his cosmic purposes on heaven and earth "in/by the Messiah" (ἐν τῷ Χριστῷ, 1:10). God demonstrated his great power "in/by the Messiah" (ἣν ἐνέργησεν ἐν τῷ Χριστῷ) by seating the Messiah at God's right hand (1:20). Believers are God's workmanship "created in/by Messiah Jesus" (κτισθέντες ἐν Χριστῷ Ἰησοῦ) for good works that God has ordained (2:10).

The Messiah is, then, as John Allan has argued, God's agent "through whom God works his will, elects, redeems, forgives, blesses, imparts new life, builds up his church."[17] Allan accurately recognizes the use of ἐν Χριστῷ and its correlates to mark out the Messiah as the agent of God who accomplishes his purposes; however, Allan is wrong to deny that the "in Messiah" formula often has a locative sense, and thereby participatory connotations, in many of these constructions, for Paul clearly uses the formula to refer to believers as sharing in the identity of the Messiah.[18] The Messiah's heavenly exaltation (1:20-23), for example, is the basis for the church's co-resurrection and co-exaltation "in the heavenly places in Messiah Jesus" (2:6b).[19] The Messiah's resurrection is the foundation for God's act of "making [the church] alive together *with Christ*" (συνεζωοποίησεν τῷ Χριστῷ, 2:5b). So when Paul begins his epistle by blessing God for granting the church "every spiritual blessing in the heavenly places in/by the Messiah" (ἐν τοῖς ἐπουρανίοις ἐν Χριστῷ, 1:3), it is likely that ἐν Χριστῷ has both an instrumental (i.e., the Messiah as the agent of these blessings) and local sense (i.e., the church shares in

---

with Christ: An Exegetical and Theological Study (Grand Rapids: Zondervan, 2015), 94; Cf. Te-Li Lau, *The Politics of Peace: Ephesians, Dio Chrysostom, and the Confucian* Four Books, NovTSup 133 (Leiden: Brill, 2010), 53-54.

15. John A. Allan, "The 'In Christ' Formula in Ephesians," *NTS* 5 (1958-59): 54-62.

16. For an example of trying to convey the instrumental and locative force of the preposition in 4:32, see Lau, *The Politics of Peace*, 53-54: "God forgave you through Christ and brought you into Christ."

17. Allan, "The 'In Christ' Formula," 59.

18. Allan, "The 'In Christ' Formula," 59. Lau, *The Politics of Peace*, 52-57, is nearer to the mark in arguing that "in Christ" is "not a formula with a single meaning" (p. 52) and that the prepositional phrase often carries both instrumental and locative connotations.

19. See here Thomas G. Allen, "Exaltation and Solidarity with Christ: Ephesians 1:20 and 2:6," *JSNT* 28 (1986): 103-20.

the identity of the Messiah). The σύν- prefixes, which indicate association between Messiah and his people, further suggest that the ἐν prepositional phrases do not exclude a locative force.[20] Believers, then, are not only the recipients of God's actions *by means of the Messiah* but they are also said to share with the Messiah in his identity and rule. How can one account for Paul's diverse employment of the ἐν Χριστῷ formula and its use to connote both the Messiah's agency for the sake of his people *and* the people's location with, or participation in, the Messiah? Might it be that the formula retains both connotations precisely because when God acts *by means of* the Messiah, God acts to *incorporate the people into* the identity and rule of the Messiah (cf. 5:5)? That is, the way in which God rules, saves, and forgives is by the agency of the Messiah in whose rule they participate. Since the Messiah is the agent of salvation *and* the location where salvation is found, I suggest we retain both instrumental and locative connotations of ἐν Χριστῷ.[21] Thus, if the ἐν Χριστῷ formula has both connotations, then God, for example, gives resurrection life to his people *by means of the Messiah*—that is, *by enabling them to share in the Messiah's resurrection life* (2:5-6).[22] God forgives his people ἐν Χριστῷ, that is, by Christ and by incorporating them into his rule.

Participating in the Rule of the Resurrected, Enthroned King in Ephesians

Having established that within Ephesians Χριστός is God's royal vicegerent who acts on God's behalf to bring his subjects within the sphere of his rule, we are now in a position to see that Paul's participatory soteriological discourse is constructed such that the church shares in the Messiah's rule and its benefits. What is true of the king and his rule is applied to the king's subjects such that the church shares in the messianic king's rule over the evil powers and thereby participates in all of the benefits of the king's rule. Paul develops his participatory soteriology through a creative and innovative rereading of Israel's royal ideology through the lens of its fulfillment in God's resurrection and heavenly enthronement of the Messiah.

The central contention of my argument is that Paul develops his participatory soteriology by rereading Israel's royal-messianic ideology, particularly

20. Further locative senses of the formula can be found in Eph 1:1, 4, 13; 2:15; 3:11; 4:21.
21. Similarly, see Ernest Best, *One Body in Christ: A Study in the Relationship of the Church to Christ in the Epistles of the Apostle Paul* (London: SPCK, 1955), 5. Cf. C. F. D. Moule, *The Origin of Christology* (Cambridge: Cambridge University Press, 1977), 54–56, 62.
22. Best, *One Body in Christ*, 29.

(but not exclusively) Psalm 110, such that the Messiah's people not only benefit from, but also participate in the Messiah's resurrection from the dead, enthronement and rule over his enemies, and heavenly-cosmic blessings. Paul's participatory metaphors and language thereby declares that what has happened to the Messiah in his resurrection and enthronement is true, by participation, of the Messiah's people.[23]

Israelite royal ideology, and particularly Psalm 110, supplies the narrative movement and categories for God's resurrection and enthronement of the Messiah in Ephesians 1:20–23.[24] Though assumed in Paul's retelling of the event, the Messiah is under opposition from hostile political-cosmic powers (Eph 1:21) not unlike the anointed figure in Psalm 2, and they have managed to bring about the Messiah's death (Eph 1:20a). That the "rulers of this age" (1 Cor 2:8) are, at least indirectly, responsible for the death of the Messiah is something Paul's readers are familiar with from his other epistles (cf. 1 Cor 2:8; 15:24–25). So, too, the Messiah's people were formerly in a state of death as they were beholden to their transgressions and sins (Eph 2:1, 5). Those responsible for humanity's state of "death" are the same political enemies of the Messiah (cf. Eph 1:21)—namely, the hostile rulers of "the age of this world" (2:2) and "the ruler of the authority of the air" (2:2). Given Paul's direct citation of Psalms 110:1 (Eph 1:20) and 8:7 (Eph 1:22), it is likely that the enemies of God and his anointed are understood by Paul through the lens of the Psalms' portrait of opposition to the anointed (Pss 2:2–3; 110:2–3; cf. Dan 7:27).[25]

God responds, however, to the enemies of his Messiah by demonstrating his great power "at work in the Messiah by raising him from the dead" (Eph 1:20a). God not only raises the Messiah but also, echoing the language of Psalm 110:1, "seats him at his right hand, that is, in the heavenly places" (Eph 1:20b).[26] The opposition against the Messiah is thereby overcome, as it is in Psalm 2,

---

23. M. David Litwa, *We Are Being Transformed: Deification in Paul's Soteriology*, BZNW (Berlin: de Gruyter, 2012), 182.

24. This is articulated by Douglas A. Campbell, "The Story of Jesus in Romans and Galatians," in *Narrative Dynamics in Paul: A Critical Assessment*, ed. Bruce W. Longenecker (Louisville: Westminster John Knox, 2002), 116; cf. Timo Eskola, *Messiah and the Throne: Jewish Merkabah Mysticism and Early Christian Exaltation Discourse*, WUNT 2.142 (Tübingen: Mohr Siebeck, 2001), 158–204.

25. See also, Matthew V. Novenson, *Christ among the Messiahs: Christ Language in Paul and Messiah Language in Ancient Judaism* (Oxford: Oxford University Press, 2012), 144–45.

26. Timothy G. Gombis, "Ephesians 2 as a Narrative of Divine Warfare," *JSNT* 26 (2004): 408–9, argues that Paul "echoes the movement of the entire psalm, especially the manner in which the conquering activity of God and Christ in Eph. 2 reflects the subjecting activity of Yahweh and his appointed king in Ps. 110."

by God's act of giving resurrection life to his anointed and sharing his heavenly throne with his vicegerent.[27] The resurrected, enthroned Messiah, having taken his royal seat at God's right hand, now receives the subjection of all things underneath his feet (Eph 1:22a; cf. Ps 8:7). God's enthronement of his king is cosmic in scope in that the Messiah is exalted over every imaginable heavenly power, that is, "above all rule, authority, power, lord, and every name that is named, not only in this age but also in the coming age" (Eph 1:21). These rulers over which the Messiah now reigns are the same hostile rulers of "the age of this world" (2:2), such as "the ruler of the authority of the air" (2:2), that have held humanity in a state of death and bondage to sin (2:1, 5). The Messiah's enthronement over the evil powers results in the salvation and rescue of the king's subjects (2:5, 8; 5:23).

But Paul sees the resurrection and enthronement of the Messiah as having more than positive and prosperous implications for the Messiah's subjects; those who are "in Messiah Jesus" (ἐν Χριστῷ Ἰησοῦ, Eph 2:6b, 7b) participate in the Messiah's resurrection and enthronement. Thus, God has "made them alive together with the Messiah" (συνεζωοποίησεν τῷ Χριστῷ, 2:5), "raised them together" (συνήγειρεν), and "seated them together in the heavenly places in Messiah Jesus" (συνεκάθισεν ἐν τοῖς ἐπουρανίοις ἐν Χριστῷ Ἰησοῦ, 2:6). The three σύν- prefixed compound verbs in Ephesians 2:5-6 recall Paul's use of Psalm 110 in Ephesians 1:20-23,[28] but here he applies the royal notion of resurrection and enthronement to all who are in Messiah Jesus, thereby royalizing the king's subjects.[29] As God rescued his Messiah "from the dead" (Eph 1:20a) and "seated him at his right hand in the heavenly places" (1:20b), so he has rescued the Messiah's subjects from "death" (2:1, 5) and seated them with him "in the heavenly places—namely, in Messiah Jesus" (2:5b). The locative force of the preceding prepositional phrases should not be missed as they indicate the messianic-royal realm where believers now rule—in the heavenly

---

27. On the early church's interpretation of Jesus's resurrection as his royal enthronement, see Lidija Novakovic, *Raised from the Dead according to the Scripture: The Role of Israel's Scripture in the Early Christian Interpretations of Jesus' Resurrection*, Jewish and Christian Texts Series 12 (London: T&T Clark, 2012), 133-46.

28. The three σύν- prefixed verbs stress the relational solidarity between the Messiah and his people. So Allen, "Exaltation and Solidarity with Christ," 105; Campbell, *Paul and Union with Christ*, 232-33. On the significance of the relationship between 1:20-23 and 2:5-6, see Andrew T. Lincoln, "A Re-examination of 'the Heavenlies' in Ephesians," *NTS* 19 (1972-1973): 472-74.

29. Gombis, "Ephesians 2 as a Narrative," 410-11; Markus Barth, *Ephesians 1-3*, AYB 34A (New Haven: Yale University Press, 1974), 164-65.

realm with the Messiah himself.[30] The Messiah's resurrection life and heavenly rule are now realities that the Messiah's people participate in by virtue of their incorporation into Messiah Jesus and his rule. That is, the royal promises made to the king in Israel's Psalter, particularly the promises of resurrection and enthronement, now belong both to the Messiah and his people.

The peoples' sharing in the Messiah's resurrection and enthronement is the foundation for their active participation in the Messiah's triumph over the evil powers as they do battle against the powers of evil (Eph 6:10–20). When Paul says "be empowered in the Lord and by the might of his strength" (ἐνδυναμοῦσθε ἐν κυρίῳ καὶ ἐν τῷ κράτει τῆς ἰσχύος αὐτοῦ, 6:10), it is difficult to determine whether the prepositional phrases "in the Lord" and "in the strength of his might" refer to God's strength or the Messiah's. Yet, based on Paul's previous mention of power language, I suggest Paul is referring to God's powerful agency that has been climactically displayed in his resurrection of the Messiah. So in Ephesians 1:19–20 he has prayed that the saints might know "the surpassing greatness of [God's] power for us who believe, which is according to the mighty power of his strength *which he worked when he raised the Messiah from the dead and seated him at his right hand*." Thus, Paul's language of divine power is inextricably tied to God's mighty act of raising and enthroning his Son to his right hand. When Paul prays to this powerful God (3:20a) as the one who works his will for his people "according to the power which is at work within us" (3:20b), based on the parallel with 1:19–20, Paul is declaring that God's resurrection power is intrinsic to the life of the church. Thus, by virtue of its union with the resurrected, enthroned Messiah (1:20–23; 2:5–6), the church is strengthened with God's resurrection power to do battle against its enemies. There is no need, however, for the church to triumph over its enemies—simply a need to resist them (6:11, 13), given that they are the same enemies the Messiah has already defeated (6:12). They are the same "rulers" (6:12; cf. 1:21), "authorities" (6:12; cf. 1:21; 2:2b), and "cosmic powers of this darkness" (6:12; 2:1) that the Messiah subjected to his rule when he was enthroned "in the heavenly places" (1:20b), thereby ending their evil dominion "in the heavenly places" (6:12b).

Participating in the Benefits of the Messiah's Rule

The people's share in the rule of God's resurrected and enthroned Messiah is the foundation for their participation in the royal benefits of his rule. As Israel's

---

30. Allen, "Exaltation and Solidarity with Christ," 106.

Psalter held forth the hope that God's enthronement of his king would lead to peace and prosperity for Israel, so the people's participation in the enthroned king's rule enables them to share in the benefits of the Messiah's rule. At least three benefits for the Messiah's people are taken up in Ephesians as ways of articulating the people's participation in the Messiah's rule.

Participating in the Messiah's Election

God's election of his people to adoptive sonship is founded upon their participation in God's election of his royal Son. We have seen that in Israelite royal ideology God's election of the king involves the adoption of him as his son (Pss 2:7; 89:25–27; 1 Sam 16:1–13; 1 Chr 17:13–14).[31] As God's anointed, the king is imbued with the rule, authority, and Spirit of God (1 Sam 10:6–11; 11:6–7; 16:13; Pss 2:2; 89:21–22, 27–28). Foundational here is God's promise in 2 Samuel 7, where God chooses to establish the house of David to rule over Israel thereby creating the Father-son relationship between God and David: "I will be a Father to him, and he will be a son to me" (2 Sam 7:14a).[32] Thus, one of the honorifics for God's enthroned king is his "elect" or "chosen one" (e.g., LXX Pss 88:4, 20). This royal context between God/Father and king/son is the appropriate context for understanding Paul's election language in Ephesians 1:3–14, where the Messiah's people participate in the Son's election.

Within Ephesians 1:3–14 Paul speaks of the Messiah as God the Father's elected Son in whose election the church shares by participation.[33] Thus, Paul declares that "God the Father's (1:3; cf. 1:2) electing grace bestowed upon the adoptive sons "is gifted to us in the beloved" (ἐν τῷ ἠγαπημένῳ, 1:6). The Father's bestowal of electing love upon his Son (1:6) is the foundation for God's choosing the church "in love" (1:4b) and "by means of Messiah Jesus" (1:5).[34]

31. Mowinckel, *The Psalms in Israel's Worship*, 1:53–55, 64–65; J. Randall Short, *The Surprising Election and Confirmation of King David*, HTS 63 (Cambridge: Harvard University Press, 2010), 129–92.

32. On Israel's king as God's son, see Gerald Cooke, "The Israelite King as Son of God," *ZAW* 73 (1961): 202–25; Mettinger, *King and Messiah*, 259–68; Eaton, *Kingship and the Psalms*, 146–49; James M. Scott, *Adoption as Sons of God: An Exegetical Investigation into the Background of ΥΙΟΘΕΣΙΑ in the Pauline Corpus*, WUNT 2.48 (Tübingen: Mohr Siebeck, 1992), 88–117.

33. There are forty occurrences of "Father" as language for God in the Pauline corpus and eight of them occur in Ephesians. This is rightly emphasized by Trevor J. Burke, *Adopted into God's Family: Exploring a Pauline Metaphor*, NSBT 22 (Downers Grove, IL: InterVarsity Press, 2006), 74–75.

34. I am taking ἐν ἀγάπῃ as modifying προορίσας in 1:5.

Some significant witnesses (D*, F, G) even read "is gifted to us *in his beloved Son* (ἐν τῷ ἠγαπημένῳ υἱῷ αὐτοῦ)," a reading that makes explicit the relationship between the Messiah's sonship and the adoptive sonship of his people.[35] This statement may allude to David's response to God's electing love demonstrated in God's bestowal of sonship upon David: "what is my house that you have loved me in this way?" (2 Sam 7:18).[36] The allusion to Israelite royal ideology is further established by the parallel in Collosians 1:13, where Paul speaks of God's redemptive purposes as centering upon τοῦ υἱοῦ τῆς ἀγάπης αὐτοῦ ("his beloved Son," 1:13b).[37] The relationship between God "the Father" (τῷ πατρί, Col 1:12) and "the Son of his love" echoes Psalm 2:6–8 and 2 Samuel 7:12–14, where the king is spoken of as God's son. Thus, Paul's description of the Messiah as "the beloved one" recalls God's election of him as his chosen Son. Paul speaks explicitly of God's election of the Messiah when he refers to God's "kind choice that he set forth in him" (Eph 1:9) to provide reconciliation of all things in him (1:10). Just as the Messiah's accomplishment of reconciliation is according to the Father's "kind choice" (1:9b), so is God's election of his people to sonship through the Messiah "according to the kind choice of his will" (1:5b). The language of "kind choice/pleasure" (εὐδοκ-) is also used to describe God's election of David: "My brothers were handsome and tall, but the Lord did not choose them" (οὐκ εὐδόκησεν ἐν αὐτοῖς); God's rescue of David is the result of his electing delight in the king (ὅτι εὐδόκησεν ἐν ἐμοί, 2 Sam 22:20).[38]

Thus, God "elects us *in him*" (ἐξελέξατο ἡμᾶς ἐν αὐτῷ, Eph 1:4a); God "foreordains us for adoption *through Messiah Jesus*" (1:5a); God's electing adoption of his people is a manifestation of "his grace which he gifted to us *in the beloved*" (1:6b); "we have been called *in him* having been fore-ordained" (ἐν ᾧ καὶ ἐκληρώθημεν προορισθέντος, 1:11). Leslie Allen has argued that many of the occurrences of (προ)ὀρίζω in the NT reflect Psalm 2:7 and God's "decree" to elect the king as his son.[39] So, in Romans 1:4 Paul,

35. Michael Peppard, *The Son of God in the Roman World: Divine Sonship in Its Social and Political Context* (Oxford: Oxford University Press, 2011), 112, makes the intriguing suggestion that Eph 1:4–6 alludes to Mark 1:11 and the Father's declaration of Jesus as his chosen Son.

36. Cf. 1 Chr 17:16: ὅτι ἠγάπησάς με ἕως αἰῶνος. See also the song of Moses in LXX Deut 33:5a, in which Moses prophesies of a time when there "will be a ruler in the beloved one" (ἔσται ἐν τῷ ἠγαπημένῳ ἄρχων).

37. Christopher A. Beetham, *Echoes of Scripture in the Letter to the Colossians*, BibInt 96 (Leiden: Brill, 2008), 97–112.

38. See also Peppard, *The Son of God*, 106–12.

39. Leslie C. Allen, "The Old Testament Background of (προ)ὀρίζειν in the New Testament," *NTS* 17 (1970): 104–8. This is not, however, borne out by the witness of the Septua-

in interaction with Psalm 2, declares that Jesus was "destined as God's Son" (τοῦ ὁρισθέντος υἱοῦ θεοῦ) by his resurrection from the dead. Much of the (προ)ὁρίζω language in the NT, in fact, occurs in contexts where the Messiah is enthroned in power to rule and judge (ὁ ὡρισμένος ὑπὸ τοῦ θεοῦ κριτὴς ζώντων καὶ νεκρῶν, Acts 10:42; κρίνειν τὴν οἰκουμένην ἐν δικαιοσύνῃ, ἐν ἀνδρὶ ᾧ ὥρισεν, 17:31; cf. Rom 8:29; 1 Cor 2:7). Thus, Paul's application of election language to the church (Eph 1:4, 5, 11) whereby it shares in adoptive sonship (1:5) and "every spiritual blessing" (1:3) through participation in the Messiah is (in part) the result of Paul's distinctive application of Psalm 2 to the peoples' share in the Messiah's election.

Paul articulates the foundation for the people's election to share in the Messiah's sonship, however, in Ephesians 1:3, where he gives it as an example (1:4) of God's blessings for those who are "in the heavenly places, in the Messiah" (1:3b). Both prepositional phrases refer to the location of the Messiah's people—namely, "in heaven with the Messiah," and provide the ground for God's bestowal to them of "every spiritual blessing" (1:3). The people's participation in the Messiah's heavenly enthronement (see esp. 1:20 and 2:6) establishes their election to sonship, a blessing that has been given to them "in the heavenly places in the Messiah" (1:3b).[40] The Father's love for his beloved and elect Son (1:6) is the same love (2:4) that stands behind God's decision to extend the Messiah's rule to his people (2:5-6).[41]

Participating in the Messiah's Body

Paul conceptualizes the church's participation in the Messiah's heavenly rule through the royal imagery of "head" and "body."[42] As Constantine Campbell notes, "If the church is Christ's body, of which he is head, the metaphor must convey connotations of union [i.e., with Christ]."[43] But these "connotations of union" are precisely that of participating in the king's lordship, given that God

---

gint which reads πρόσταγμα κυρίου (Ps 2:7a LXX), and it depends upon a possible earlier rendering of חק with (προ)ὁρίζω.

40. See Lincoln, "A Re-examination of 'the Heavenlies,'" 471, who states that the blessings of 1:3-14 "are to be found both ἐν τοῖς ἐπουρανίοις and ἐν Χριστῷ, the latter phrase signifying that believers partake of the benefits because they are incorporated into the ascended Christ as their representative who is himself in the heavenlies."

41. Allen, "Exaltation and Solidarity with Christ," 109-12.

42. There are many complex issues related to this metaphor into which we cannot enter. See the sage treatment Moule, *The Origin of Christology*, 69-89.

43. Campbell, *Paul and Union with Christ*, 268.

makes the Messiah "head over all things" by means of his royal enthronement and by the fact that the metaphor is frequently deployed in royal contexts. And this should not be an entirely surprising claim given the frequent depiction of the commonwealth as body politic.[44]

The first occurrence of the metaphor is in Ephesians 1:22–23, where God's enthronement of his Son to a position of cosmic rule is the prior event that enables God's "subjection of all things underneath his feet" (1:22a). The statement is a quotation of Psalm 8:7 (LXX), a psalm that celebrates God's gift of dominion over creation to Adam/humanity as his royal vicegerent(s). Thus, God's heavenly enthronement of the Messiah enables him to enter into the task given to Adam— namely, the subjugation of "all things" (πάντα). It is God's enthronement of his Messiah that results in God "appoint[ing] him [i.e., the Messiah] to be head over all things for the church" (αὐτὸν ἔδωκεν κεφαλὴν ὑπὲρ πάντα τῇ ἐκκλησίᾳ, Eph 1:22b)[45] and establishes the church as the Messiah's body (1:23a).[46]

Both the context of the metaphor and its primary conceptual field of discourse indicate that, for Paul, to speak of the Messiah as head is to portray him as *ruler* and to speak of the church as his body is to portray it as *ruled*. Paul's use of ἡ κεφαλή has spawned an enormous amount of literature, but for my purposes it is enough to demonstrate how the metaphor of "the head" can be, and here is, language that stresses Christ's regal authority over his assembly. For example, in 2 Samuel 22 David praises God for providing "salvation for his king and steadfast love for his anointed" (LXX 2 Sam 22:51a). David sings: "you kept me as the head over the nations (κεφαλὴν ἐθνῶν); people whom I had not known served me" (22:44; cf. also Philo's *Life of Moses* 2.30). Paul's metaphor finds an obvious parallel with imperial panegyrists who exalt Caesar as head and ruler of his imperial body. In *On Mercy*, Seneca repeatedly refers to Nero as the "head" and "mind" over the body of the empire and as the one who stabilizes the empire and unites his people: "the whole body (*corpus*) is the servant of the mind" and "the vast multitude of men surrounds one man as though he were its mind, ruled by his spirit, guided by his reason" (1.3.5);

---

44. See, for example, Plato, *Republic* 8.556e; Livy 2.32.12–33.1; Dionysius of Halicarnassus, *Roman Antiquities* 6.83.2; Aristotle, *Politics* 3.6.4; Dio Chrysostom, *Oration* 33.16; 34.10–20; Aelius Aristides, *Oration* 24.38–39. Also see Dale B. Martin, *The Corinthian Body* (New Haven: Yale University Press, 1995), 38–47.

45. Barth, *Ephesians 1–3*, 157–58, notes that within political contexts the verb frequently has the sense of "to appoint" or "to install" (cf. 1 Sam 8:5–6; Lev 17:11; Num 14:4; Isa 42:6; Eph 4:11).

46. I understand τῇ ἐκκλησίᾳ here as signifying that the Messiah's enthronement is the event that creates his corporate solidarity with the church (cf. 2:5–6).

the emperor is "the bond by which the commonwealth is united, the breath of life which these many thousands draw," for the empire would be prey were the "mind of the empire to be withdrawn" (1.4.1).[47] For Seneca, the function of the head (emperor)/body (empire) metaphor is to stress the remarkable connection between the ruler and the ruled such that Nero will care for and not harm his own body.

Given that Paul's head/body metaphor is found within a context dominated by royal language, it is almost certain that Paul's employment of the metaphor in Ephesians 1:22–23 portrays the Messiah as the cosmic ruler of the universe.[48] But the church as the Messiah's body does not sit passively under the rule of its head; rather, Paul claims that the church shares in the Messiah's rule by extending his dominion in all places. Such a claim is both the essence and function of the church—to fill the created world with the presence of its king. This is the force of Paul's claim that the church is "the fullness *of the one filling* all things in all places" (τὸ πλήρωμα τοῦ τὰ πάντα ἐν πᾶσιν πληρουμένου, 1:23b). The language of πλήρωμα frequently has connotations of God's glorious dominion, often associated with creation and/or temple, in both the Greek Old Testament (e.g., Pss 23:1; 49:12; 88:12; Isa 6:1–3; Jer 23:24) and in Paul (Col 1:19; 2:9–10), and its employment here speaks of the worldwide dominion of the Messiah ("the head") extended by means of the church ("his body"). The Messiah fills his body with his presence, thereby establishing a deep union between Christ and church that is extended, by means of the body, to "all things in all places."[49]

Paul portrays Christ, the head, as a beneficent king who rules his body by bestowing to it health, nourishment, peace, and salvation.[50] As the victorious heavenly king who "fills all things" (Eph 4:10), the Messiah gives gifts to his church "for the edification of the Messiah's body" (4:12b). In his role as "the head, the Messiah" (ἡ κεφαλή, Χριστός) is the source of nourishment for the body and the enabler of its growth (4:15–16). Christ's rule over the body (ὁ Χριστὸς κεφαλὴ τῆς ἐκκλησίας, 5:22b) is manifested not in tyrannical rule but, rather, in his role as "Savior of the body" (5:22c), further defined as self-giving love, service and nourishment (5:25, 29). As a good king's legislation and character was thought to have produced domestic concord, so the portrayal

47. Cf. Harry Maier, "A Sly Civility: Colossians and Empire," *JSNT* 27 (205): 335n29. See also, Michelle V. Lee, *Paul, the Stoics, and the Body of Christ*, SNTSMS 37 (Cambridge: Cambridge University Press, 2006), 35–39.

48. Smith, *Christ the Ideal King*, 218.

49. Similarly, see Lau, *The Politics of Peace*, 58–59.

50. Both notions of sovereignty and the nourishing union between head and body are emphasized by Best, *One Body in Christ*, 146–48.

of the loving messianic king has as its goal the production of peaceful and harmonious households and assemblies that reflect the rule of their king.

Participating in the Messiah's Reconciliation and Peace

Those who are united with the Messiah also participate in the Messiah's reconciled, peaceful body politic, a sacred assembly where the Messiah's peaceful reconciliation, accomplished through his death, has eradicated all ethnic dissension (Eph 2:11–22).[51] One of the most foundational and widely recognized tasks of any ancient king was the creation of a peaceful body politic.[52] In his *Precepts of Statecraft*, Plutarch says that "peace, liberty, plenty, abundance of men, and concord are the greatest blessings that cities can enjoy," and therefore a primary responsibility of the ruler is to "instill concord and friendship in those who dwell together with him and to remove strifes, discords, and all enmity" (*Moralia* 824D). Thus, the language of (making) peace, reconciliation, and communal harmony are frequently spoken of as a necessity for successful kings and rulers.[53] The successful king usually brought about this peace and harmony through the violent pacification of the king's enemies. J. Rufus Fears refers to this aspect of royal ideology as "the theology of victory."[54] Peace through pacification or reconciliation of one's enemies was often situated in a cosmic context where the peace and harmony was thought to be a gift of the gods.[55] Thus, forms of καταλάσσω and διαλάσσω are frequently used in royal

51. See especially the work of Lau, *The Politics of Peace*, 81–97.

52. This often took the form of reconciliation and peace through military pacification. See Philip de Souza, "*Parta victoriis pax*: Roman Emperors as Peacemakers," in *War and Peace in Ancient and Medieval History*, ed. Philip de Souza and John France (Cambridge: Cambridge University Press, 2008), 76–106.

53. Augustus's *Res Gestae* boasts of his "making of peace on land and sea" (εἰρηνευομένης . . . πάσης γῆς τε καὶ θαλάσσης, 13.1; cf. θάλασσα[ν] [εἰ]ρήνευσα-, 25.1; ἐν εἰρήνῃ κατέστησα, 26.2; εἰρηνεύεσθαι πεπόηκα, 26.3). For text and translation, see Alison E. Cooley, *Res Gestae Divi Augusti: Text, Translation, and Commentary* (Cambridge: Cambridge University Press, 2009). Philo of Alexandria summarizes Augustus's accomplishments in this way (*Embassy to Gaius* 145–47): "This is he who exterminated wars both of the open kind and of the covert which are brought about by the raids of brigands. This is he who cleared the sea of pirate ships and filled it with merchant vessels. This is he who reclaimed every state to liberty, who led disorder into order (ὁ τὴν ἀταξίαν εἰς τάξιν ἀγαγών) and brought gentle manners and harmony to all unsociable and brutish nations, who enlarged Hellas by many a new Hellas and Hellenized the outside world, in its most important regions—the guardian of peace (ὁ εἰρηνοφύλαξ)."

54. Fears, *PRINCEPS A DIIS ELECTUS*, 45–46.

55. For example, see Pliny, *Panegyricus* 4.4; 5.6–9; Calpurnius Siculus, *Eclogue* 4.142–46.

and diplomatic contexts to indicate a leader's pacification of enemies thereby resulting in peace and harmony.[56] Andrew Wallace-Hadrill summarizes it succinctly when he states that the king's legitimacy to rule over a people depends upon his "power to conquer, to save, to bring harmony and stability, and to distribute benefits."[57] This depiction of the king's legitimacy to rule conforms nicely with Paul's narration of the Messiah's activity in Ephesians 1:20–2:22. Paul has portrayed the Messiah's powerful conquering of his enemies (1:20–23), his act of rescuing his subjects (2:1–8), and now proceeds to demonstrate how those in the Messiah benefit by sharing in his establishment of a sacred assembly that is marked by the king's peace.

Paul engages in ethnic stereotyping as a means of highlighting the state of ethnic discord between Jew and gentile as he refers to the *former* (Eph 2:11) animosity between the "gentiles in the flesh" (2:11a)—namely, "those called the foreskinned" (2:11a) and "the so-called circumcision in the flesh with human hands" (2:11b). The former state of the gentiles was one of alienation from Israel's *politeia*, as they are excluded outsiders (ξένοι, 2:12) from God's covenants and have no knowledge of God (2:12). They are "far off," both from God and the covenantal blessings of Israel (2:13a; 2:18). Furthermore, there is a "dividing wall" (2:14) that separates the two groups and perpetuates their enmity and hostility toward one another.

Thus, it is no surprise that Paul portrays the Messiah as an ideal king who eradicates the ethnic hostility between Jew and gentile and transforms the two groups into one peaceful body. What is remarkable, however, is that the messianic king conquers and kills the "hostility" between Jew and gentile, not through the usual weapons of political warfare, but by means of his bloody death on the cross: "but now in Messiah Jesus, you who were far off have been brought near by the Messiah's blood" (2:13). Paul speaks of the Messiah as a conquering king who defeats and destroys the social enmity: he "destroys . . . the enmity in his flesh" (2:14); "he tears down (καταργήσας) the law with its decrees and commands" (2:15a); "he reconciles (ἀποκαταλλάξῃ) both groups into one body for God through the cross" (2:16a); and "he kills the enmity by [the cross]" (ἀποκτείνας τὴν ἔχθραν ἐν αὐτῷ, 2:16). Paul's language of the Messiah as "destroying," "tearing down," "reconciling," and "killing" conforms well with depictions of conquering kings who pacify and reconcile through violence, as we have seen, and yet Paul transforms this trope by declaring that

56. For example, See Dio Cassius 1.5.6; 5.18.9; 41.35.3; 46.1.3; 48.10.2; 48.20.1.
57. Andrew Wallace-Hadrill, "The Emperor and His Virtues," *Historia* 30 (1981): 316.

the Messiah has created a new people by absorbing their enmity and hostility in his flesh, that is, through his bloody death on a cross.

Paul is emphatic that the result of the Messiah's death is the accomplishment of peace between Jew and gentile thereby creating a unified body politic. And his portrait of the Messiah as a peaceful king echoes Isaiah's peaceful depiction of the Davidic king and God's eschatological kingdom (Isa 9:5–6; 52:7; 57:19).[58] Peter Stuhlmacher has argued that within these verses, "the author offers a Christological exegesis of Isa 9:5–6; 52:7; and 57:19" based on the catchword of "peace."[59] In Isaiah 9:5–6 (LXX) God declares that through his royal Davidic son he will "bring peace upon the rulers, peace and health to him" and that "his peace has no boundary." Paul sees the enthroned Messiah as the Isaianic agent who "heralds the announcement of peace" (Isa 52:7).[60] Likewise, Paul speaks of the Messiah as an agent of peace: "he is our peace" (Eph 2:14); he "makes peace" (2:15b); he "comes and proclaims the good news of peace to you who are far and peace to those who are near" (2:17). This latter statement is almost certainly an allusion to Isaiah 57:19, where the Lord declares "peace, peace, to the far and the near."

The result of the Messiah's establishment of peace is the eradication of the social "enmity" between Jew and gentile (Eph 2:14b, 16b) and the creation of "one new people" (2:15), that is, a peaceful unified "single body" (2:16).[61] Thus, the defining marker of this new community is no longer ethnic or religious but is rather union with the messianic king. Those who belong to this peaceful new corporate body are singularly defined by their participation "in Messiah Jesus" (ἐν Χριστῷ Ἰησοῦ, 2:13; ἐν αὐτῷ, 2:15; ἐν ᾧ, 2:21; ἐν ᾧ, 2:22).[62] Paul uses a variety of political metaphors to portray the Messiah's peaceful and harmonious corporate community: (1) it is a community of people transformed from "strangers and outsiders" into "fellow citizens with the saints" (2:19); (2) "God's own household" (2:19); and, (3) a "sacred temple in the Lord" (2:21) having

---

58. Smith, *Christ the Ideal King*, 211, provides further references for the Davidic king as an agent of peace in Jewish thought (see Pss. Sol. 17:24, 35; 1QSb V, 20–29; 4Q285 5 1–6; 4Q161 8–10 III, 18–25).

59. Peter Stuhlmacher, *Reconciliation, Law, & Righteousness: Essays in Biblical Theology* (Philadelphia: Fortress, 1986), 187.

60. Stuhlmacher, *Reconciliation, Law, & Righteousness*, 187–88.

61. It is possible to understand "one body," however, as a reference to the Messiah's bodily death rather than a corporate entity. See, however, Col 3:15; Ignatius, *To the Smyrnaeans* 1.2; Moule, *The Origin of Christology*, 77.

62. The prefixed compound participle and verb also convey union between the believer and Messiah Jesus (συναρμολογουμένη, 2:21; συνοικοδομεῖσθε, 2:22).

"Messiah Jesus himself as the cornerstone" (2:20b). Thus, those who are in the Messiah share in his rule as they benefit from his act of reconciliation that has eradicated ethnic dissension and results in a peaceful, harmonious, sacred community belonging to the Messiah.

But not only does the Messiah *establish* a unified peaceful community, he also provides gifts to its members that enable them to actively share in "the edification the Messiah's body" (4:12) for the establishment of "the unity of faith" (4:13).[63] The language of the Messiah's gift-giving is redolent in 4:7–11: "to each one of us the gift has been given according to the measure of the Messiah's gift" (ἑνὶ δὲ ἑκάστῳ ἡμῶν ἐδόθη ἡ χάρις κατὰ τὸ μέτρον τῆς δωρεᾶς τοῦ Χριστοῦ, 4:7); "he gave gifts to people" (ἔδωκεν δόματα τοῖς ἀνθρώποις, 4:8b); and "he has gifted to some" (αὐτὸς ἔδωκεν τούς, 4:11a).[64] The Messiah's giving of gifts to his people is predicated upon his defeat of the evil powers by his heavenly enthronement. Paul quotes Psalm 68:19, the details of which need not concern us here, to explain (διό, Eph 4:8a) the ground of the Messiah's giving of gifts to his people: "when he rose up on high he took captivity captive" (ἀναβὰς εἰς ὕψος ᾐχμαλώτευσεν αἰχμαλωσίαν, 4:8a). Note that this is followed by another statement about the bestowal of gifts upon humanity (4:8b). Though Paul does not define "he took captivity captive," it is almost surely a reference to the Messiah's triumph over the evil powers based upon Paul's elaboration of the meaning of ἀναβὰς εἰς ὕψος as the Messiah's ascension "above all the heavens" (4:10). The reference to the Messiah's descent to the lower regions of the earth (4:9b), then, is likely a reference to the Messiah's death. We have seen that preceding God's seating the Messiah at his right hand, the event enabling him to rule his enemies is God's resurrection of the Messiah "from the dead" (1:20), and in 2:13–16 Paul will speak of the Messiah's death as the surprising means whereby the Messiah triumphs over the hostility that divides Jew and gentile.[65] Therefore, the Messiah's resurrection and exaltation over his enemies enables him to give gifts to his people that produce peace, harmony, and growth within the community (4:11–16).[66]

---

63. On the good king as giver of gifts and as benefactor, see Klaus Bringmann, "The King as Benefactor: Some Remarks on Ideal Kingship in the Age of Hellenism," in *Images and Ideologies: Self-definition in the Hellenistic World*, ed. Anthony Bulloch et al., Hellenistic Culture and Society 12 (Berkeley: University of California Press, 1993), 7–24.

64. Smith, *Christ the Ideal King*, 217–21.

65. See also Timothy G. Gombis, "Cosmic Lordship and Divine Gift-Giving: Psalm 68 in Ephesians 4:8," *NovT* 47 (2005): 377–78.

66. Moule, *The Origin of Christology*, 78.

COLOSSIANS

To establish the texture of Paul's participatory soteriology in Colossians, we will look at (1) how the Christ hymn enables the Colossians to participate in the Messiah's rule; (2) Paul's use of royal honorifics to expand on the nature of the Messiah's kingly dominion and rule; (3) how the Messiah rules and rescues his people; and (4) how the Colossians can participate in the Messiah's rule.

Praising the Messiah as Cosmic Creator and Ruler in Colossians 1:13–20

I have argued in detail elsewhere that the Christ hymn in Colossians 1:15–20 should be situated within the widespread practice of praise of kings, messiahs, and emperors. Kings were often assimilated to, even identified with, gods and thereby treated as worthy of divine praises. Likewise, at least some Jews praised past kings and the hoped-for coming king through hymns—most notably in poetic seams in the Pentateuch and in the Psalms. Within the hymnic praises to the kings, one often finds the following three reasons for praising the king: (1) the king is the vicegerent of a god; (2) the king is God's representative who rules over and sustains the created universe and/or empire; and (3) the king is a benefactor who has bestowed gifts of peace upon his subjects. All three reasons for praise are paralleled in the Colossian Christ hymn. That is to say, Paul takes over the linguistic and conceptual resources of ancient royal discourse in order to portray Christ as the unique and supreme ruler of the universe.

The Colossian Christ hymn uses conventional royal language to describe Christ as messianic king—though it does so to make the point that Christ alone is ruler. However, Paul transforms and develops the ancient kingship discourse such that his royal claims about Christ go beyond claims made by, or on behalf of, all other rulers. The hymn is most radical, for instance, in its assertion that Christ not only rules the cosmos but is the preexistent creator of the entirety of the cosmos, its claim that Christ is the first to have undergone resurrection from the dead and subsequent exaltation to God's right hand, and its subversion of the royal trope of peace and reconciliation through military pacification by alternatively depicting reconciliation and peacemaking through the bloody death of the king at the hands of his opponents. Paul's hymn to Christ the King uses the tools of royal propaganda precisely to counter any other competing claim to rule and power over the Colossian assembly. The hymn counters the church's preoccupation with other powers, seen now as lesser and insignificant authorities created by Christ the King, as it enables them to participate in the true king's rule. Paul's hymn draws the audience into joining their voices with him such that they bestow divine honors—namely worship—upon the sole king and ruler of the universe and are thereby socialized into a symbolic world where they share in the reign of the king who is lord over every power and authority.[67] Paul is able, subsequently, to use the language of the hymn throughout the rest of the epistle to show the Colossians that they already participate in the true king's rule, thereby countering every other competing ruler to whom the Colossians might be enticed to give honors and worship.

The Messianic King Is God's Son and Image

We have had occasion to see the importance of the relationship between God and his elected Davidic king (e.g., Pss 2, 72, 89, 110). Likewise, Paul's encomium to the Messiah in Colossians uses royal honorifics to describe the hymn's subject as God's unique king who participates in his rule as his sole royal representative. The antecedent of the relative pronoun in 1:15a (ὅς) and all the pronouns that follow is "the Son of his love" (1:13b). This Son is unambiguously portrayed as a royal figure, as he has his own kingdom (βασιλείαν) where his rescued subjects reside as ones who have been "delivered from the dominion of darkness" (v. 13).[68] Like a good king, the royal Son has liberated his subjects from evil—"the dominion of darkness" (1:13) and "sins" (1:14).

The relationship between "the Father" (1:12) and "the Son of his love" echoes Israel's royal ideology whereby the king is God's son. More specifically, the language echoes Nathan's oracle to the house of David: "I will be a Father to him, and he will be a son to me" (2 Sam 7:14a).[69] Increasing the resonances of the echo of 2 Samuel 7 in Paul's honorific "the Son of his love" is the reverber-

---

67. Wayne A. Meeks, *The Origins of Christian Morality: The First Two Centuries* (New Haven: Yale University Press, 1993), 98–99, rightly notes the important role of the hymns in Col 1 and Phil 2 in "shaping the communities' Christology and shaping the communities themselves."

68. We have frequently seen that one of the primary responsibilities of the good king was to deliver and rescue his people from their enemies. See the suggestive comments by Stefan Schreiber, *Gesalbter und König: Titel and Konzeptionen der königlichen Gesalbtenerwartung in früjüdischen und urchristlichen Schriften*, BZNW 105 (Berlin: de Gruyter, 2000), 421–22.

69. For more detail, see Beetham, *Echoes of Scripture*, 97–112; David W. Pao, *Colossians and Philemon*, Exegetical Commentary on the New Testament (Grand Rapids: Zondervan, 2012), 76–77.

ation of David's statement: "what is my house that *you have loved me* in this way?" (2 Sam 7:18).

As is well known, numerous later Israelite texts continue to set forth Israel's king as God's son who rules in God's stead.[70] Thus, in Psalm 2, in response to "the kings of the earth and the rulers" (2:2a) who plot "against the lord and against his anointed one/Messiah" (2:2b), God installs his messianic king to rule: "the Lord said to me, 'You are my son, today I have begotten you'" (2:7). The portrait is of a rebellious group of rulers and authorities who are pacified by God's royal son who is enthroned to reign over them. The enthronement decree (2:7) unpacks the Davidic figure's status as one who has been established "king by him" (2:6a). God promises to give the king "the nations as your inheritance" (2:8). The Davidic king participates as gift in the rule of God his Father, and is commissioned to rule on God's behalf. Again, in Psalm 88 the king is "exalted above all the kings of the earth" (v. 29) as a result of his divine sonship (v. 28). The Israelite king as God's son who rules in God's stead as a gift fits nicely with Paul's language where "the beloved Son" is *the authorized agent through whom* God accomplishes deliverance, redemption, and release from sins (1:13-14).[71] Thus, Paul sets the encomium in an explicitly royal messianic context and prepares the audience for the hymn's expansion on the nature of the king's dominion and rule.

Paul describes the Son of God with another royal honorific—namely, "the image of the invisible God" (ὅς ἐστιν εἰκὼν τοῦ θεοῦ ἀοράτου, 1:15a). In both Jewish and pagan contexts, rulers are spoken of as images of the gods. As living images of the gods, the kings rule and maintain cosmic harmony in the god's stead. To give just a few examples: The Ptolemaic king Philopator is referred to as εἰκὼν τοῦ Διός, while Ptolemy V is spoken of as εἰκὼν ζῶσα τοῦ Διός.[72] In *To an Uneducated Ruler*, Plutarch says, "the ruler is the image of God who orders all things" (ἄρχων δ' εἰκὼν θεοῦ τοῦ πάντα κοσμοῦντος, *Moralia* 780d). The ruler's divine image consists of the fact that "rulers serve god for the care and preservation of men" (780d-e).

---

70. For example, 1 Chr 17; Jer 33:14-22; Zech 6:12-13; Pss. Sol. 17. See William M. Schniedewind, *Society and the Promise to David: The Reception History of 2 Samuel 7:1-17* (Oxford: Oxford University Press, 1999); Sam Janse, *"You Are My Son": The Reception History of Psalm 2 in Early Judaism and the Early Church* (Leuven: Peeters, 2009), 51-75.

71. That the royal son of God is entirely dependent upon God in Ps 2 is rightly emphasized by Jamie A. Grant, *The King as Exemplar: The Function of Deuteronomy's Kingship Law in the Shaping of the Book of Psalms*, AcBib 17 (Atlanta: Society of Biblical Literature, 2004), 58-60.

72. See BDAG 282 (s.v. εἰκών).

But the primary context for understanding the Son as "the image of the invisible God" is the figure of Adam who was made "according to the image of God" (κατ᾽ εἰκόνα θεοῦ, Gen 1:27). Without entering into a detailed discussion of what this entails, one would not go astray by noting Adam's commission to rule and have dominion. As created in God's image, Adam is to "rule" over all of creation (Gen 1:26). All of creation is to be the dominion for humanity as it is commanded to "increase and multiply and fill the earth, and have dominion over it and rule over . . . all creation" (Gen 1:28). Royal motifs are evident as the author uses the language of dominion, rule, and lordship and even commands "the image of God" to expand dominion over all creation. Psalm 8 confirms this, for here humanity is created to have dominion over God's creation (Ps 8:4-8). Therefore, whatever the "image of God" might mean, it is clearly related in a representative way to the God that it images and to the creation over which it rules and has dominion.[73] Gerhard von Rad rightly states, "God set man in the world as the sign of his own sovereign authority, in order that man should uphold and enforce his—God's—claims as lord."[74] Adam is commissioned to "subdue" (κατακυριεύσατε / כבשה) and "rule" (ἄρχετε / רדו) over the earth as God's sovereign representative (Gen 1:28), maintaining and expanding the divine order of God's creation. These words are consistently used throughout the Hebrew Scriptures to denote the authority and power of royal figures.[75] Significantly, the words frequently occur in eschatological contexts that look forward to an ideal messianic king who will rule God's kingdom.[76] It is hard to escape the conclusion that Adam, as God's image, is the context for some later messianic praises where similar commands of "rule" are given to a coming Israelite king (Num 24:17-19; Ps 72:8-11). For example, in Psalm 110 the king at the right hand of God is commanded—"Rule!" (רדה)—with linguistic echoes of Genesis 1. Adam is God's royal ruler, imbued as God's chosen kingly son, who is commissioned to act as God's sovereign, subduing and ruling the earth for God.[77]

---

73. Phyllis A. Bird, " 'Male and Female He Created Them': Gen 1:27b in the Context of the Priestly Account of Creation," *HTR* 74 (1981): 137-38. J. Richard Middleton, *The Liberating Image: The Imago Dei in Genesis 1* (Grand Rapids: Brazos, 2005).

74. Gerhard von Rad, *The Theology of Israel's Historical Traditions*, vol. 1 of *Old Testament Theology* (New York: Harper and Row, 1962), 146.

75. For example, see 1 Kgs 5:4, 30; 9:23; 2 Chr 8:10.

76. Note the insightful discussion of Stephen G. Dempster, *Dominion and Dynasty: A Biblical Theology of the Hebrew Bible*, NSBT 15 (Downers Grove, IL: InterVarsity Press, 2003), 59-60.

77. That Adam was believed to have been God's prototypical king is also a theme in

Situating εἰκὼν τοῦ θεοῦ ἀοράτου in a royal context should occasion no surprise to the student of Paul given that when Adam is named in his epistles he appears in explicitly royal contexts (cf. Rom 5:12–21; 1 Cor 15:20–28). In Romans 5:12–21 the language of "rule" and "dominion" are spoken of in relation to Adam and Christ. And in 1 Corinthians 15:20–28 Adam is spoken of in antithesis to Christ who "hands the kingdom over to God the Father" (v. 24), pacifies God's enemies (vv. 24b–27), and who is the subject of the royal Psalms 8 and 110. And as Sean McDonough has noted, when Paul uses the word εἰκὼν it almost always echoes Adam and the creation narrative of Genesis 1 (e.g., Rom 8:29; 1 Cor 11:7; 15:49; 2 Cor 3:18; 4:4; Col 3:10).[78] The simple point here is that when Paul names "the beloved Son" as εἰκὼν τοῦ θεοῦ ἀοράτου he taps into royal language, language that emphasizes God's election of the Messiah to rule as his messianic king over all of creation.

The Messianic King Creates and Rules the Cosmos

To that of "his beloved Son" and "the image of the invisible God" Paul adds a third royal honorific: he is "the firstborn over all creation" (πρωτότοκος πάσης κτίσεως, 1:15b). In Israel the firstborn son held a special place within the family, as he was endowed with the father's inheritance, entrusted with his father's authority, and given a royal and priestly role within the family.[79] Jacob declares to Reuben: "you are my firstborn, my strength and the *beginning* of my children" (πρωτότοκος μου σύ ἰσχύς καὶ ἀρχὴ τέκνων μου, LXX Gen 49:3).[80] The Deuteronomist's statute protecting the inheritance of the firstborn, likewise, refers to him as the *beginning* of his father's children (οὗτός ἐστιν ἀρχὴ τέκνων

Jewish traditions (Sir 49:16; Jub. 2:14; 4 Ezra 6:53–59; 2 En. 30:12; Philo, *Creation* 136–50). Cf. Robin Scroggs, *The Last Adam: A Study in Pauline Theology* (Philadelphia: Fortress, 1966), 25.

78. Sean M. McDonough, *Christ as Creator: Origins of a New Testament Doctrine* (Oxford: Oxford University Press, 2009), 90.

79. See especially, e.g., Gen 25:25–34; 49:3; Deut 21:15–17.

80. The Targums expand on the meaning: "Reuben, you are my first-born, my might, and the beginning of my strength. For you it would have been fitting to take three parts—the birthright, the priesthood, and royalty" (Gen 49:3, Tg. Onq.). "Reuben, you are my first-born . . . you would have been worthy of the birthright, the dignity of the priesthood and the kingship. But because you sinned, my son, the birthright was given to Joseph, the kingship to Judah, and the priesthood to Levi" (Gen 49:3, Tg. Ps.-J.). Quoted from Scott W. Hahn, *Kinship by Covenant: A Canonical Approach to the Fulfillment of God's Saving Promises*, AYBRL (New Haven: Yale University Press, 2009), 137.

αὐτοῦ, Deut 21:17b).[81] Given its associations with representation of one's father, royal privilege, and inheritance, πρωτότοκος is often used as an honorific as it is, for example, with Israel (Exod 4:22; Jer 38:9). But most important for understanding Paul's description of Christ as "firstborn over all creation" is the psalmist's reference to God's covenant with David: "I will make him the firstborn, the highest of the kings of the earth" (κἀγὼ πρωτότοκον θήσομαι αὐτόν, ὑψηλὸν παρὰ τοῖς βασιλεῦσιν τῆς γῆς, LXX Ps 88:28). That this royal psalm is the primary context for Paul's statement is confirmed by the psalm's preceding verse which refers to the relationship between God and the king as that of Father and son: "He will cry to me, 'You are my Father, my God, and the Rock of my salvation!'" (Ps 88:27; cf. Col 1:13b).[82] We have seen that as the most exalted of the kings of the earth, as God's own firstborn son, the Davidic ruler is given the gift of sharing in God's cosmic rule over all of creation. The Father's throne and the king's throne are *both* founded upon God's steadfast love (Ps 88:15, 29–30; cf. 44:5–7). The Father thus sets the king's "hand on the sea, and his right hand on the rivers" (Ps 88:24; cf. vv. 10–12). And as the most exalted of the kings of the earth, Yahweh promises to defeat the enemies of the king (LXX Ps 88:23a; 88:24a; cf. Ps 2:1–8).

Paul radicalizes the royal-messianic ideology by extending Christ's dominion over creation into an assertion that the firstborn Son actually is the one "in whom all things have been created" (1:16a), and the one "through whom and for whom all things have been created" (1:16c). That is, as the most "exalted of all the kings of the earth" (Ps 88:28), God's royal Son not only rules but even creates the lesser rulers, that is, the "thrones and lords and rulers and dominions" (Col. 1:16).[83] Regardless of the exact identity of the lesser rulers, the language used to describe them is political (cf. Eph. 1:21; cf. Rev 2:13; 13:2). That Christ's creative activity derives from his royal rule is again seen by the fact

---

81. On which, see Jon D. Levenson, *The Death and Resurrection of the Beloved Son: The Transformation of Child Sacrifice in Judaism and Christianity* (New Haven: Yale University Press, 1993), 59–60.

82. Many include LXX Ps 88:28 as one text among many for understanding Col 1:15, but very few unpack its meaning. See, however, McDonough, *Christ as Creator*, 89–92; John Anthony Dunne, "The Regal Status of Christ in the Colossian 'Christ-Hymn': A Re-evaluation of the Influence of Wisdom Traditions," *TJ* 32.1 (Spring 2011): 13–14.

83. See also the royal use of πρωτότοκος for Christ in Rev 1:5 (ὁ πρωτότοκος τῶν νεκρῶν καὶ ἄρχων τῶν βασιλέων τῆς γῆς). Also, the term is employed in Heb 1:6 in a context where Davidic messianism abounds (e.g., Ps 2:8 in 1:2; Ps 2:7 in 1:5; 2 Sam 7:14 in 1:5b; Ps 44:7 in 1:8; Ps 109:1 in 1:13).

that the lesser rulers in Colossians 1:16 are the same "rulers and authorities" who are publicly shamed and led in an imperial triumph in Christ (2:15b).

We have seen that the relationship between God and his elected king results in some incredibly exalted language, such that the king shares God's throne, is referred to as God or divine, and receives divine honors. And if LXX Psalm 88 is the context for Colossians 1:15b–16, then, Paul can be seen as making the claim that God's anointed Son not only rules creation but has been given from his Father the cosmic inheritance of creating all things, and the act of creation is preeminently a *kingly* task in the ancient Near East.[84] If God delegates all earthly rule and authority to his anointed one who is to maintain cosmic harmony and order as "the strength of his Father," as the royal psalms indicate (Pss 2:6–8; 44; 72; 110:1–3), then it may be that Paul is simply, yet incredibly, extending "the purview of the Messiah's authority to include primal creation."[85]

Paul's claim that the royal subject of his encomia "is before all things" (Col 1:17a), a statement that may refer to both the preexistence and preeminence of the Son, can again be situated within honors bestowed upon Israel's kings. There are at least two royal psalms that allow for the possibility of an early interpretation of the figure as a preexistent, coming, messianic king.[86] In LXX Psalm 109, Yahweh speaks of the king as: "from the womb, *before* the morning star I begat you" (ἐκ γαστρὸς πρὸ ἑωσφόρου ἐξεγέννησά σε, 109:3b). Similarly, in LXX Psalm 71, the translator translates 72:17, "his name endures *before the sun*" (שמש לפני) with πρὸ τοῦ ἡλίου and thereby creates the possibility for a temporal reading: "his name endures *before [the creation of] the sun*" (LXX Ps 71:17b).[87] While the context does not demand an interpretation that results in a preexistent Messiah, the use of the pronoun πρό makes it possible. The preexistence of the messiah's name is further attested in 1 Enoch 48:2–3: "the Son of Man was named in the presence of the Lord of Spirits, and his *name before* the Chief of Days; and *before the sun* and the signs were created, *before* the stars of the heavens were made, his name was named *before* the Lord of

---

84. Middleton, *The Liberating Image*, 65–74.

85. McDonough, *Christ as Creator*, 67.

86. Justin Martyr read both Pss 72:17 and 109:3 as witnessing to a preexistent messiah (see *Dialogue with Trypho* 45.4 and 76.7). On the preexistence of the Messiah, see William Horbury, *Jewish Messianism and the Cult of Christ* (London: SCM, 1998), 94–99.

87. Joachim Schaper, *Eschatology in the Greek Psalter*, WUNT 2.76 (Tübingen: Mohr Siebeck, 1995), 93–107. See also Adela Yarbro Collins and John J. Collins, *King and Messiah as Son of God: Divine, Human, and Angelic Messianic Figures in Biblical and Related Literature* (Grand Rapids: Eerdmans, 2008), 58.

the Spirits."[88] Following upon the heels of Paul's claim that Christ rules and creates the cosmos, is the assertion that even the king's existence precedes, and is supreme over, the cosmos.

The statement that "all things are held together in him" (Col 1:17b)—αὐτῷ standing in for the one termed Son of God, image of God, and firstborn over all creation, respectively—reflects the notion of the king as stabilizer of the cosmos. The theme that the king stabilizes the cosmos by establishing divine harmony upon earth is a common *topos* within the Davidic psalms and imperial panegyrics. As noted earlier, Psalms 2, 45, 72, 89, and 110 depict the Davidic king as Yahweh's authorized, deputized ruler who stabilizes the created order on God's behalf. Commenting on Psalm 89, Jon Levenson speaks of God's gift of mastery over creation to the king: "It is now the Davidic throne that guarantees cosmic stability.... David is YHWH's vicar on Earth."[89] One finds a similar dynamic in non-Jewish praise of good kings and emperors for procuring peace and harmony on earth. In his *Panegyricus* for Trajan, Pliny declares the "Father of the universe rules all with a nod of his head" and can now devote himself to heaven's concerns "since he has given you to us to fill his role with regard to the entire human race" (80.5). Plutarch says "the ruler is the image of God *who orders all things*" (780e). Praise of Augustus's rule also often centered upon his production of cosmic stability and order. Philo, for example, refers to Augustus as "the Caesar who calmed the torrential storms on every side, who healed the pestilences common to Greeks and barbarians . . . who led disorder into order and brought gentle manners and harmony to all unsociable and brutish nations" (*Embassy to Gaius* 145–47).[90]

The Messianic King Rules and Rescues His People

Paul's statement that Christ "is the head of the body—the assembly" (αὐτός ἐστιν ἡ κεφαλὴ τοῦ σώματος τῆς ἐκκλησίας, Col 1:18a) portrays Christ as the heavenly enthroned ruler over his body politic much as Caesar or David was spoken of as the head of the empire/Israel. Paul's use of ἡ κεφαλή stresses

---

88. See the discussion in Aquila H. I. Lee, *From Messiah to Preexistent Son: Jesus' Self-Consciousness and Early Christian Exegesis of Messianic Psalms*, WUNT 2.192 (Tübingen: Mohr Siebeck, 2005), 109.

89. Jon D. Levenson, *Creation and the Persistence of Evil: The Jewish Drama of Divine Omnipotence* (Princeton: Princeton University Press, 1995), 22–23. McDonough, *Christ as Creator*, 46–64.

90. See further, Clifford Ando, *Imperial Ideology and Provincial Loyalty in the Roman Empire* (Berkeley: University of California Press, 2000), 389.

Christ's regal authority over his assembly. And this should not be an entirely surprising claim, given that Greco-Roman authors often refer to the commonwealth or the empire as the body politic.[91]

The regal nature of the metaphor cannot be doubted in the parallel text of Ephesians 1:20–23, where Paul refers to Christ as "head over all things with respect to the church" (1:22b). Here the context is one in which God, through raising the Messiah from the dead and "seating him at his right hand in the heavenly realm" (1:20), places Christ "above every rule, authority, power, and lord" (Eph 1:21a). Through his royal enthronement of the Messiah, God "has placed all things underneath his feet" (1:22a; cf. LXX Ps 8:7).[92] Paul's reliance upon the language of the royal LXX Psalm 8 and Psalm 109 to speak of Christ as the heavenly κεφαλή makes it obvious that the metaphor stresses the king's authority and rule over his commonwealth. The same is true for the metaphor in Colossians 2:10, where Paul speaks again of Christ as "the head over every rule and authority" (ἡ κεφαλὴ πάσης ἀρχῆς καὶ ἐξουσίας) in a context that emphasizes the rulers' subjection to Christ.

While the Hebrew term for "ruler" (שׂר) is not *usually* rendered by the Septuagint translators as κεφαλή, there are plenty of instances where its occurrence does have royal, preeminent connotations; we have noted a few examples of these in our discussion of Ephesians 1:20–23.[93] The most important example is David's hymn where he celebrates God's "salvation for his king and steadfast love for his anointed" (μεγαλύνων σωτηρίας βασιλέως αὐτοῦ καὶ ποιῶν ἔλεος τῷ χριστῷ αὐτοῦ, LXX 2 Sam 22:51a). David sings: "you kept me as the head of the nations (φυλάξεις με εἰς κεφαλὴν ἐθνῶν); people whom I had not known served me" (22:44). In our discussion of Ephesians we also noted that Paul's statement finds an obvious parallel with imperial panegyrists who exalt Caesar as head and ruler of his imperial body.[94] We have seen that in his *On Mercy* Seneca repeatedly refers to the young Nero as the "head" and "mind" over the body of the empire and as the one who stabilizes the empire and unites his people together. For Seneca, the function of the head (emperor)/body (empire)

---

91. See, for example, Plato, *Republic* 8.556e; Livy 2.32.12–33.1; Dionysius of Halicarnassus, *Roman Antiquities* 6.83.2; Aristotle, *Politics* 3.6.4; Dio Chrysostom, *Orations* 33.16; 34.10–20; Aelius Aristides, *Oration* 24.38–39. Also see Martin, *The Corinthian Body*, 38–47; and Margaret M. Mitchell, *Paul and the Rhetoric of Reconciliation: An Exegetical Investigation of the Language and Composition of 1 Corinthians* (Louisville: Westminster John Knox, 1991), 157–64.

92. Rightly noted by Dunne, "The Regal Status of Christ," 14.

93. See, for example, Judg 10:18; 11:11; LXX 1 Kgs 20:12; Isa 7:8–9; 11:10–11; LXX Jer 38:7.

94. On the head as the *ruling* part of the body, see Plato, *Timaeus* 44d.

metaphor is to stress the remarkable and real connection between the ruler and the ruled such that emperor will care for and not harm his own body. Just as the "church" is the body of the head (Col 1:18a), so Seneca speaks of "the commonwealth as though it were a part of himself" (i.e., the king; 1.13.4). It may be of relevance to note here that the king as "mind" and "head" has connotations of both ruler and source of the body's health which illuminates Paul's application of κεφαλή to Christ who both rules the church (Col 1:18a; 2:10) and provides health and nourishment to the body (Col 2:19).[95]

Paul's statement in 1:18 that Christ is the ἀρχή may either indicate that he is supreme in terms of rank and hence "ruler," or that he is supreme in temporal terms as "the beginning" of creation.[96] Both readings can find plausible justification within the hymn. Paul has just stressed Christ's preeminence and rule over creation in verses 15b–17, where Christ has been depicted not only as ruler but even creator of all things, and in the next line Paul will celebrate Christ as the first to rise from the dead (1:18c). What needs to be appreciated, however, is that the semantic range of ἀρχή includes both temporal primacy ("beginning") and status/rank primacy ("ruler").[97] The Priene Letter, for example, refers to the birthday of Augustus as "equivalent to the beginning of all things" (τῶν πάντων ἀρχῆι) and "the beginning of the breath of life" (ἀρχὴν τοῦ βίου καὶ τῆς ζωῆς). For this reason, one finds this language applied to rulers to stress their preeminence—sometimes in terms of rank and status and sometimes in terms of source, origin, and temporal priority. Thus, each of the poetic praises placed at the seams of the LXX Pentateuch refer to the coming king as ἀρχή (Gen 49:10; Num 23:21; Deut 33:5).[98] See, for example, the royal use of ἀρχή to refer to Israel's coming king in LXX Isaiah 9:5–6a:

> Because a child was born for us, a son was given to us, *whose sovereignty* (ἡ ἀρχή) was upon his shoulder, and his name shall be called "messenger of great counsel," for I will bring peace upon the rulers (τοὺς ἄρχοντας), peace and health to him. His sovereignty (ἡ ἀρχὴ αὐτοῦ) is great, and his peace has no boundary upon the throne of David and his kingdom.

95. Maier, "Sly Civility," 338.

96. Those who translate ἀρχή as "beginning" include Dunn and O'Brien. Those who see ἀρχή as referring to Christ's status as "ruler" include Dunne, "The Regal Status of Christ," 15.

97. So Clinton E. Arnold, *The Colossian Syncretism: The Interface between Christianity and Folk Belief at Colossae* (Grand Rapids: Baker, 1996), 260–61.

98. For other instances in the LXX where ἀρχή refers to a king or ruler, see LXX Deut 17:20; Dan 2:37; 7:27; Amos 6:7.

That ἀρχή can emphasize both temporal and status preeminence is also seen in the linkage between Israel's firstborn son as temporally first (hence, "the beginning of my sons") and as the ruler to whom the rights, privileges, and bulk of inheritance belongs (e.g., Gen 49:3; Deut 21:17; cf. above on Col 1:15b). Thus, given that Paul's next statement refers to Christ as "the firstborn from the dead" (1:18c), one may justifiably conclude that as the resurrected and enthroned Messiah, Christ is both preeminent as ruler *and* the beginning of the resurrection from the dead.[99]

In Paul's description of Christ as "firstborn from the dead" (πρωτότοκος ἐκ τῶν νεκρῶν), the messianic context of Col 1:12–13 strongly suggests an activation of LXX Ps 88:26 as an echo in which the royal Davidic "firstborn" is promised to be "exalted above the kings of the earth."[100] Here the Father's enthronement of his royal firstborn will secure eternally both his offspring and his throne as the firstborn's inheritance from his Father (Ps 88:30). Yet all of the promises made to the Davidic king in Psalm 88:20–38 are undone in verses 39–51, where the psalmist accuses the Father of reneging on his promises and abandoning the Davidic king to death and defeat (88:39–44): "you have exalted the right hand of his foes" (88:42a) and "you have cut short the days of his youth" (88:45a). Thus, the firstborn son, promised enthronement over all the kings of the earth, faces the situation of death and an end to his offspring. For Paul it is the resurrection of the firstborn Son from death that enables the Davidic son to take his rightful place as exalted king and secures the continuing offspring of the Messiah.

The Father's royal enthronement of his firstborn over "the kings of the earth" fits nicely with Paul's description of Christ as "the head of every ruler and dominion" (ὅς ἐστιν ἡ κεφαλὴ πάσης ἀρχῆς καὶ ἐξουσίας, Col 2:10b).[101] And given the repeated association between the resurrection and enthronement of the Messiah found throughout various NT compositions (e.g., Acts 2:22–36; 13:33–37; Rom 1:3–4; Eph 1:20–23; Heb 1:5–13)—an association made possible not least by the Psalter (e.g., Ps 2:7 in Rom 1:4; Pss 8 and 109 in 1 Cor 15:23–28)—it seems likely that Paul speaks of Jesus as "firstborn from the dead" in order to refer to his messianic enthronement.[102] Thus, being "firstborn from

99. Cf. Rev 1:5. Dunne, "The Regal Status of Christ," 15–16, opts for "ruler" based on the associations with royal enthronement in the phrase "the firstborn from the dead."

100. Note the repeated use of the future tense throughout Ps 88:20–38.

101. McDonough, *Christ as Creator*, 184, suggests that it is precisely this "messianic triumph over the nations [that has] been read back into the original creation and been given cosmic scope."

102. On the Messiah's resurrection as royal enthronement in 1 Cor 15:23–28, see N. T.

the dead" results in the Davidic Messiah's kingship over (new) creation, just as it does in Hebrews 1:6 and Revelation 1:5. But it is not only the exalted *throne* that the firstborn receives in his resurrection; rather, as the firstborn Son he has the royal rights of primogeniture with respect to his church, and, as the *first* to be raised from the dead, he thereby secures the resurrection of his offspring—thus fulfilling God's promise to secure the anointed one's offspring forever (LXX Ps 88:30; cf. 1 Cor 15:20–23; Rom 8:29).[103] The messianic king is the first one to experience resurrection, but his enthronement secures the certainty that his offspring will follow his path.[104]

Christ's status as "firstborn from the dead" results in his preeminence over everything, hence Paul's use of the purpose clause, "in order that he may be first in everything" (ἵνα γένηται ἐν πᾶσιν αὐτὸς πρωτεύων, 1:18d), to interpret his title as "firstborn from the dead" (πρωτότοκος ἐκ τῶν νεκρῶν), thereby further confirming it as a royal honorific. He is "firstborn from the dead" *so that* he might be preeminent over everything, or, in other words, resurrection qualifies him to be the universal ruler of creation and new creation. The language of preeminence and first-ness is conventional for epideictic speeches, including hymns and prayers (especially to gods), and marked off heroic humans or gods as unique and their actions as unparalleled.[105] In the OT, in addition to YHWH, the kings of Israel are the ones who most frequently receive acclamations of uniqueness and incomparability: "no other king shall compare to you" (Solomon: 1 Kgs 3:13; 10:23); "there was no one like him among the kings of Judah, either after him nor those who were before him" (Hezekiah: 2 Kgs 18:5); "before him there was no king like him . . . nor did any like him arise after him" (Josiah: 2 Kgs 23:25).[106] Forms of πρωτευ- are also often attached to prominent Romans seeking to establish themselves as first and unique. Plutarch notes that Caesar's admirers tell him that everyone desires "to have him as first man (πρωτεύσειν)" (*Life of Caesar* 6.4). Caesar is reported to have

---

Wright, *The Resurrection of the Son of God*, vol. 3 of *Christian Origins and the Question of God* (Minneapolis: Fortress, 2003), 333–38; Dunne, "The Regal Status of Christ," 13.

103. Similarly, Gordon D. Fee, *Pauline Christology: An Exegetical-Theological Study* (Peabody, MA: Hendrickson, 2007), 307.

104. See Novakovic, *Raised from the Dead*, 152–53.

105. For example, Aristotle states: "One should also use many kinds of amplification, for example if the subject is the only one, or the first (πρῶτος), or one of a few, or the one who most has done something" (*Rhetoric* 2.7.2). Cf. Quintilian, *Inst.* 3.7.16; Aelius Theon, *Progymnasmata*, 9.35–38. See further Jerome H. Neyrey, "'First,' 'Only,' 'One of a Few,' and 'No One Else': The Rhetoric of Uniqueness and the Doxologies in 1 Timothy," *Bib* 86 (2005): 59–87.

106. See Gary N. Knoppers, "'There Was None Like Him': Incomparability in the Book of Kings," *CBQ* 54 (1992): 411–31.

said in response to "struggles for preeminence" (περὶ πρωτείων, 11.2) witnessed in a barbarian village: "I would rather be first here (εἶναι μᾶλλον πρῶτος) than second in Rome" (11.3). Above we saw Philo speak of Augustus as "the first and the greatest (πρῶτος καὶ μέγιστος)" (*Embassy to Gaius* 149).

In Colossians 1:19, "all the fullness" (πᾶν τὸ πλήρωμα) is likely the subject of "was pleased to dwell" (εὐδόκησεν . . . κατοικῆσαι), and this statement explains both why Christ has preeminence in everything (v. 18d) *and* gives the ground for Christ's reconciling work in verse 20—Christ the King can provide cosmic reconciliation precisely because God has invested him with "all the fullness." The LXX often uses the language of τὸ πλήρωμα in contexts emphasizing God's dominion and authority over all of creation. To give just two examples: "the earth *and its fullness* (τὸ πλήρωμα αὐτῆς) is the Lord's, the world and all those who live in it" (LXX Ps 23:1); and "to you are the heavens, and to you is the earth, the world and its fullness (τὸ πλήρωμα αὐτῆς) you founded" (LXX Ps 88:12).[107] We remember from discussions of LXX Psalm 88 that the Father gifts the royal son with his dominion over creation. So to speak of Christ as embodying "all the fullness" of the Father marks him out as God's deputized agent who rules over the cosmos (Col 1:20).[108] But, secondly, in Israel's royal traditions the language of "fullness" often has semantic overlap with divine "glory." So, to give just one example, in Isaiah's vision of the Lord, he sees the Lord's temple "full of his glory" (πλήρης ὁ οἶκος τῆς δόξης αὐτοῦ, Isa 6:1) and all of "the earth filled with his glory" (πλήρης πᾶσα ἡ γῆ τῆς δόξης αὐτοῦ, 6:3; cf. 2 Chr 7:1-6).[109] Israel's traditions often mark God, God's royal representative, and the temple as marked by "fullness" and "glory" (e.g., Sir 47:11; 49:12; 3 Macc 2:9; 1QM xii 6-11; 4QFlor 1-7, 10-13; Pss. Sol. 17:30-32). This semantic overlap between "fullness" and "glory" continues in Colossians, where Christ is spoken of as related to both the divine fullness (Col 1:19; 2:9) and the divine glory (1:27; 3:4). Paul's declarartion that all of God's fullness inhabits the Messiah would resonate with these royal traditions that speak of the both the Messiah and temple as sharing in God's divine fullness and glory.

Further, if Colossians 1:19 functions, at least in part, as the ground for Paul's

---

107. For more examples, see LXX Ps 49:12; Jer 23:24.

108. Similarly, Suzanne Watts Henderson in "God's Fullness in Bodily Form: Christ and Church in Colossians," *ExpTim* 118 (2007): 172, notes: "When the hymn speaks of 'all the fullness that dwells in him' (Col 1:19), the term confers upon Christ the full extent of authority over 'things visible and invisible, whether thrones or dominions or rulers or powers' (Col 1:16)."

109. See also Grant Mackaskill, *Union with Christ in the New Testament* (Oxford: Oxford University Press, 2013), 149-52.

acclamation of Christ as the royal agent who accomplishes cosmic peace and reconciliation of all things (1:20), then it may be worthwhile to note that εὐδο-κέω is frequently used in the LXX to describe God's election.[110] For example, 1 Maccabees 14:41 narrates the Jews' "choice (εὐδόκησαν) of Simon to be their ruler and priest forever until a trustworthy prophet should arise." In LXX Psalm 67:17, God elects (εὐδόκησεν ὁ θεός) Zion as his exalted mountain in opposition to all other mountains (cf. 2 Macc 14:35). In LXX Psalm 151, the text speaks in the voice of David: "My brothers were handsome and tall, but the Lord did not choose them" (οὐκ εὐδόκησεν ἐν αὐτοῖς, 151:5). God's rescue of David is the result of God's election of the king (ὅτι εὐδόκησεν ἐν ἐμοί, 2 Sam 22:20). Thus, a plausible interpretation of Colossians 1:19 would be one that stressed God's election of the Messiah as his supreme vicegerent and God's decision to share all of his divine fullness with his anointed one. It is precisely YHWH's election of his Davidic king that leads to the most exalted claims on behalf of the king. God's election of David results in his receiving of worship (1 Chr 29:16–26). LXX Psalm 44 refers to God's anointed as *God* (44:7). And LXX Psalm 109 depicts another royal agent sharing YHWH's throne (109:1–3). Thus, the incredible claim that God elected to share all of his fullness ἐν αὐτῷ (the antecedent still being τοῦ υἱοῦ τῆς ἀγάπης αὐτοῦ in Col 1:13b) arises out of royal ideology.

In Colossians 1:20, Paul celebrates God's accomplishment of reconciliation of all things to himself (ἀποκαταλλάξαι τὰ πάντα εἰς αὐτόν) through his royal vicegerent (δι᾽ αὐτοῦ). Here Paul finally draws attention to Christ's great work of accomplishing universal reconciliation by means of "making peace through the blood of the cross" (εἰρηνοποιήσας διὰ τοῦ αἵματος τοῦ σταυροῦ αὐτοῦ). Paul again emphasizes that this reconciling peace is accomplished "through him"[111] and is cosmic in scope, for it encompasses "things on earth and things in heaven."

While there are a host of ancient royal virtues and traits of the good king, the single most significant component of a king's legitimacy was military victory (i.e., conquest and expansion, or pacification and defeat of one's enemies), which resulted in peace and concord.[112] Arguably the single most important

---

110. Here I follow Peppard, *The Son of God*, 106–12; cf. Adela Yarbro Collins, "The Worship of Jesus and the Imperial Cult," in *The Jewish Roots of Christological Monotheism: Papers from the St. Andrews Conference on the Historical Origins of the Worship of Jesus*, ed. Carey C. Newman et al., Supplements to the Journal for the Study of Judaism 63 (Leiden: Brill, 1999), 249–51.

111. The manuscript evidence is strongly split between the presence of the prepositional phrase (P46, Sinaiaticus, A, C, D1, K, P, Ψ) and its omission (e.g., B, D*, F, G, I, L).

112. Andrew Wallace-Hadrill, "The Emperor and his Virtues," 316, has demonstrated

trait of the good king was this production of peace and harmony through defeat and pacification of the empire's enemies. J. Rufus Fears refers to this aspect of royal ideology as "the theology of victory": "Conquest and expansion of his kingdom's frontiers were the duty of the true king, and the gods of the commonwealth aided his martial enterprises, leading his armed host into battle."[113] Peace through pacification or reconciliation of one's enemies was often situated in a cosmic context and spoken of as something that brought peace and harmony to the cosmos (or "land and sea") and was given as a gift of the gods.[114] Thus, forms of καταλάσσω and διαλάσσω are frequently used in royal and/or diplomatic contexts to indicate a leader's reconciliation or pacification of enemies thereby resulting in peace and cosmic harmony.[115]

Military victory was both the source and the ground for the kingship of Alexander and his Hellenistic successors, and this played an enormous role in legitimating the rule of Julius Caesar and Augustus.[116] The author of 1 Maccabees begins his work by characterizing Alexander's kingship as the result of his military exploits and conquests into new territories (1:3–9).[117] The first paragraphs of Augustus's *Res Gestae* boast of his command of the army "by means of which I set the state free from the slavery imposed by the conspirators" (1.1). Military exploits (2.1; 3.1; 21:1–3; 30.1), triumphs celebrating Augustus's victories (ἐθριάμβευσα, 4.1), and the "making of peace on land and sea" (εἰρηνευομένης . . . πάσης γῆς τε καὶ θαλάσσης, 13.1; cf. θάλασσα[ν] [εἰ]ρήνευσα-, 25.1; εἰρήνη κατέστησα, 26.2; θαλάσσης εἰρηνεύεσθαι πεπόηκα, 26.3) litter the list of his accomplishments.[118] Through Augustus's ending of the civil war and his victories over foreign powers, "peace has been brought back again" and his entire reign can be characterized as "the pacification of the world through his victories" (Velleius Paterculus, *Roman History* 2.89).[119] Tacitus, with critical

---

that there was no such established canon of royal virtues, but rather what demonstrates his legitimacy to rule is "the power to conquer, to save, to bring harmony and stability, and to distribute benefits." See also de Souza, "*Parta victoriis pax,*" 76–106.

113. Fears, *PRINCEPS A DIIS ELECTUS*, 45–46; Ando, *Imperial Ideology*, 49–70.

114. For example, see Pliny, *Panegyricus*; Calpurnius Siculus, *Eclogue* 4.142–46.

115. For example, see Anthony Bash, *Ambassadors for Christ: An Exploration of Ambassadorial Language in the New Testament*, WUNT 2.92 (Tübingen: Mohr Siebeck, 1997), 29–32.

116. For Alexander and his successors, see M. M. Austin, "Hellenistic Kings, War and the Economy," *CQ* 36 (1986): 450–66.

117. See Anathea E. Portier-Young, *Apocalypse against Empire: Theologies of Resistance in Early Judaism* (Grand Rapids: Eerdmans, 2011), 49–55.

118. See de Souza, "*Parta victoriis pax,*" 80–81.

119. See de Souza, "*Parta victoriis pax,*" 82–83.

irony, suggests that Augustus was able to increase his royal powers precisely through his provision of "the blandishments of peace" (*Annals* 1.2).[120]

Peace and harmony through pacification led to the poets' consistent depiction of the emperors' reigns as resulting in fertility and abundance—that is, as symbolizing the "divinely ordained product of the natural order of the universe."[121] For example, as an honor for his pacification of Spain and Gaul, a military expedition that lasted over three years, "the senate decreed that an altar of the Augustan Peace should be consecrated next to the Campus Martius in honor of my [Augustus's] return" (*Res Gestae* 12.2). The *Ara Pacis* is related to the decision to shut the gates of the Temple of Janus, a symbolic act celebrating peace and the absence of war, and thereby the altar is "linked with the concept that peace is the result of military victories which secure the *imperium Romanum* on land and sea."[122] Similarly, the Sebasteion in Aphrodisias celebrates peace through pacification as it personifies foreign nations as subjugated women underneath the rule of the Roman emperor.[123]

Thus, the statement that Christ has produced cosmic harmony ("the things on earth and the things in heaven") through his act of reconciling "all things" and bringing peace is of one accord with ancient royal notions of a theology of victory.[124] That Paul portrays Christ according to this piece of kingship ideology is confirmed by Paul's fuller depiction of Christ's pacification of the "rulers and authorities" in Colossians 2:15. Christ, like a Roman general or emperor, first pacifies his enemies by "stripping" (ἀπεκδυσάμενος) them of their authority and then celebrates a triumph over the rebellious rulers (θριαμβεύσας αὐτούς).[125] The celebration of a triumph was a hotly pursued honor

120. See Paul Zanker, *The Power of Images in the Age of Augustus*, trans. Alan Shapiro (Ann Arbor: University of Michigan Press, 1990), 187. See also Tacitus's scathing critique of imperial "peace": "They ransack the world, and afterwards, when all the land has been laid waste by their pillaging, they scour the sea. . . . They plunder, they murder, they rape, in the name of their so-called empire. And where they have made a desert, they call it peace" (*Agricola* 30).

121. J. Rufus Fears, "The Theology of Victory at Rome: Approaches and Problems," *ANRW* 17 2:810.

122. Karl Galinsky, *Augustan Culture: An Interpretive Introduction* (Princeton: Princeton University Press, 1996), 141.

123. See Laura Salah Nasrallah, *Christian Responses to Roman Art and Architecture: The Second-Century Church Amid the Spaces of Empire* (Cambridge: Cambridge University Press, 2010), 76–83; Stefan Weinstock, "*Pax* and the 'Ara Pacis,'" *JRS* 50 (1960): 44–58; Galinsky, *Augustan Culture*, 141–64.

124. This point is established convincingly and in detail by Maier, "Sly Civility," 329–40.

125. That the participles should be read sequentially rather than synonymously, see

by generals and emperors, and it is well documented that those victors who celebrated the triumph were seen as receiving divine honors and in some manner a manifestation of Jupiter (e.g., Livy 10.7.10; 5.23.25; Suetonius, *Augustus* 94; Pliny, *Natural History* 33.111; 35.157; Plutarch, *Camillus* 7).[126] Again, powerful benefactions elicited divine honors, and so, by portraying Christ as celebrating a triumph for his mighty victory over the powers, Paul indicates that Christ the King is worthy of receiving divine glory. This imperial pacification of the rebellious rulers (Col 2:15) is, in fact, presupposed by the celebration of the cosmic harmony in the hymn (1:20).[127] All of creation is in a state of cosmic peace and harmony through the work of God's king who has pacified every rebellious authority. That the harmony on earth now mimics and matches the heavenly harmony of God through the elected king's pacification of the rebels is an imperial commonplace. What cannot be paralleled in any ancient kingship document is the means whereby Christ enacted this pacification—"through the blood of his cross" (1:20; cf. ἐν αὐτῷ, 2:15). The royal victory and conquest of the evil powers occurs not through violent wars but through the king's death. Reconciliation and peacemaking through a king who surrenders himself to give his own body to a shameful and bloody death is precisely the royal act that results in the ultimate defeat and disgrace of the royal pretenders (2:14–15).

Participating in the Messiah's Rule in Colossians

Paul helps the Colossians understand how they can particpate in the Messiah's rule through praising the Messiah, creating a new community and sharing the Messiah's victory over rebellious cosmic powers.

Praising the Messianic King

Paul draws upon the claims of Colossians 1:15–20 throughout the rest of the epistle in order to construct a distinct symbolic universe for the audience to inhabit,[128]

Scott J. Hafemann, *Suffering and the Spirit: An Exegetical Study of 2 Corinthians 2:14–3:3 within the Context of the Corinthian Correspondence* (Tübingen: Mohr Siebeck, 1986), 33–34. On the Roman triumph, see Mary Beard, *The Roman Triumph* (Cambridge: The Belknap Press of Harvard University Press, 2007).

126. On the relationship between divine honors and the granting of imperial triumphs, see Beard, *The Roman Triumph*, 233–34; H. S. Versnel, *Triumphus: An Inquiry into the Origin, Development and Meaning of the Roman Triumph* (Leiden: Brill, 1970), 1.

127. Maier, "Sly Civility," 332.

128. For example, Walter T. Wilson, *The Hope of Glory: Education and Exhortation in*

and one which counters any fascination with lesser powers and authorities (e.g., Col 2:6–8, 16–23).[129] That Paul's hymn in honor of Christ is given a central place in the construction of the church's symbolic universe seems undeniable and possibly even supported by Paul's command to have "the word about the Messiah" (ὁ λόγος τοῦ Χριστοῦ) dwell within them *by means of* teaching and instructing one another through psalms, hymns, and spiritual songs (3:16). Given that Paul has echoed the Christ hymn throughout the epistle, it seems highly likely that he is exhorting the Colossians to sing the royal encomium, an act that socializes them into a symbolic universe where Christ the King reigns supremely as creator, ruler, and restorer of the entire cosmos.[130] This socialization into the worldview where Christ the King reigns supreme will make any concern with other spiritual powers or addition of ritual and practice entirely unnecessary (see 2:16–19). But Paul presents the Colossians not only as benefiting from Christ's rule but also as sharing in numerous aspects of Christ's rule. That is to say, Paul's claim that the Colossians were "transferred into the kingdom of [God's] beloved Son" (1:13b) is conceptualized through enabling the church to share in the royal rule depicted in Colossians 1:15–20. In what follows, I note briefly the relationship between the King and his people in order to draw attention to their participation in the King's reign.

Participating in the Messiah's Creation of New Community

As Christ is "the image of the invisible God" (1:15a), so is the new humanity in the process of being renewed "according to the image of the one creating it [i.e., the new humanity]" (κατ᾽ εἰκόνα τοῦ κτίσαντος αὐτόν, 3:10b). Haley

---

the Epistle to the Colossians, NovTSup 88 (Leiden: Brill, 1997), 183–218; Wayne A. Meeks, "'To Walk Worthily of the Lord': Moral Formation in the Pauline School Exemplified by the Letter to the Colossians," in *Hermes and Athena: Biblical Exegesis and Philosophical Theology,* ed. Eleonore Stump and Thomas P. Flint (Notre Dame: University of Notre Dame Press, 1993), 37–58, esp. 42–43; Stephen E. Fowl, *The Story of Christ in the Ethics of Paul: An Analysis of the Function of the Hymnic Material in the Pauline Corpus,* JSNTSup (Sheffield: Sheffield Academic Press, 1990), 123–54; Adam Copenhaver, "Echoes of a Hymn in a Letter of Paul: The Rhetorical Function of the Christ-Hymn in the Letter to the Colossians," *JSPL* 4 (2014): 235–55.

129. On the situation in Colossae and its relationship to their concern with cosmic powers and authorities, see Ian Smith, *Heavenly Perspective: A Study of the Apostle Paul's Response to a Jewish Mystical Movement at Colossae,* LNTS 326 (London: T&T Clark, 2006); Arnold, *The Colossian Syncretism.*

130. See also Leonard Thompson, "Hymns in Early Christian Worship," *ATR* 55 (1973): 458–72.

Jacob states the connection between 1:15 and 3:10 well: "In their solidarity as redeemed humanity, believers are patterned on the image of the Creator, the image that is Christ—the firstborn of creation and the firstborn of the dead. . . . [B]elievers participate in the Son's kingdom through taking off or disarming their 'old man' loyalties and putting on those of Christ."[131] Further, since "all things" (1:17) are stabilized and held together in Christ (1:17), and given that Christ is supreme in all things (1:17), Paul can apply Christ's cosmic rule to stabilize and unify his people: "Christ is all things and in all [people]" (ἀλλὰ τὰ πάντα καὶ ἐν πᾶσιν Χριστός, 3:11b). Thus, the foundation for a unified new humanity undivided by ethnic, socioeconomic, or religious distinctions is one component of Christ's stabilization and unification of the cosmos (3:10–11). As the Messiah is God's elected one (1:19), so Paul now refers to the Colossians as God's elected, beloved, and holy people (3:12). The "head of the body," that is, Christ's reign over his people, rules not for his own benefit but for the nourishment, growth, and good of his body (2:19). This body is a community of unity, peace, and love (3:12–15). Paul's conceptualization of the relationship between Christ and his people as the head with respect to its body stresses the remarkable connection between the ruler and the ruled and suggests that Christ will care, nourish, and do no harm to his own body.

Participating in the Messiah's Victorious Enthronement

Since Christ is the "firstborn over all creation" (1:15b) and the creator of everything in heaven and on the earth (1:16), Paul can also posit that the Messiah "is the head over every ruler and dominion" (2:10b). But Paul also conceptualizes the Colossians as sharing in his messianic victory over the powers. Given that the Colossians "have been filled in him" (ἐστὲ ἐν αὐτῷ πεπληρωμένοι, 2:10a), the Colossians are able to share in Christ's victory over the rebellious cosmic powers. Furthermore, this divine "filling" in the Messiah is grounded in the fact that "all the fullness chose to dwell in him" (1:19). Given the Colossians' share in the Messiah's rule, they are no longer under attack from these hostile powers who sought to enslave them under their wicked rule (2:14–15). In fact, the Colossians are included in the Messiah's act of reconciling the cosmos to God. Paul situates God's reconciliation of the Colossians to himself through Christ (1:21–22) within the cosmic work of Christ's reconciling activity (1:20).

---

131. Haley Goranson Jacob, *Conformed to the Image of His Son: Reconsidering Paul's Theology of Glory in Romans* (Downers Grove, IL: InterVarsity Press, 2018), 164.

The Colossians comprise those "who were formerly alienated and enemies" (1:21) and in need of God's reconciliation through the self-giving death of the Messiah (1:22). As a result of Christ's accomplishment of divine reconciliation and his "making peace" (1:20), the Colossians can share in the Messiah's peace (ἡ εἰρήνη τοῦ Χριστοῦ, 3:15a).

We have seen that Christ is exalted—supreme as "the firstborn over all creation" (1:15b; cf. LXX Ps 88:28: "I will make him the firstborn son, highly exalted above the kings of the earth") and "the firstborn from the dead" (1:18b). The Colossians share in Christ's supremacy by way of sharing in his resurrection and heavenly exaltation: "you have been raised together in him" (ἐν ᾧ καὶ συνηγέρθητε, 2:12); "he gave you life together with him" (συνεζωοποίησεν ὑμᾶς σὺν αὐτῷ, 2:13b); "if you have been raised together with the Messiah (συνηγέρθητε τῷ Χριστῷ), seek the things above, where the Messiah is, seated at God's right hand" (ὁ Χριστός ἐστιν ἐν δεξιᾷ τοῦ θεοῦ καθήμενος, 3:1b; cf. LXX Ps 109:1). Their participation in the Messiah's resurrection and enthronement is the basis for the assurance that they will share in the Messiah's glory when he returns (Col 3:4).[132]

Paul's conceptualizing of the Colossians as sharing in the cosmic work of Christ's rule could be expanded in much more detail, but these links between Colossians 1:15–20 and the rest of the letter prove the point that one of the functions of the encomium to Christ is to socialize the church into a realm where Christ is supreme over every competitor. By singing "the word about the Messiah" (3:16) and by reflecting upon their own participation in every aspect of the beneficent King, the church is thereby grounded into a reality that makes all competitors of Christ's rule simply irrelevant.

2 Timothy

Perhaps somewhat surprisingly, Paul's Second Letter to Timothy preserves a testimony depicting Jesus as the messianic Davidic king who saves his people precisely by enabling them to share in his rule. The presumed setting for the letter, something of a last will and testament, is Paul's imprisonment, and one of his agendas in the letter is to counter any shame or embarrassment that Timothy and other Christians might have due to Paul's chains (see 2 Tim 1:8,

---

132. On which, see Christopher Rowland, "Apocalyptic Visions and the Exaltation of Christ in the Letter to the Colossians," *JSNT* 19 (1983): 73–83.

12, 16). Paul's claim in 1:12 that he suffers all things because of his appointment as a herald of the gospel (see 1:10b–11), and his affirmation that he is unashamed of his sufferings and imprisonment (1:12), suggest that Timothy's shame is a result of Paul's incarceration. Instead, Paul declares that he is both unashamed and is confident in God's power to protect him from eschatological shame in the day of judgment (1:12b); Paul exhorts Timothy to encourage others to have the same confidence (1:13–14). He also exhorts Timothy to continue in what he has learned from Paul, to pass it on to others as one who is "a good soldier of Messiah Jesus" (2:3).

The basis of Paul's confidence is expressed in 2:8–13 and centers upon Jesus's messianic identity and the promise of sharing in his messianic rule. Given my lengthy argument up to this point, I will be brief. Michael David Marossy notes: "In 2:8–13, Paul shifts to the terminology and logic of kingship discourse to describe Jesus as not only the ultimate example of endurance amongst suffering, but as the resurrected and living Davidic messiah-king, whose faithfulness to believers allows them to participate in the salvific reign of his victory over death."[133] Let me unpack Marossy's argument with three propositions. First, Paul reminds Timothy of the gospel and its saving implications: "Remember Messiah Jesus, raised from the dead, from the seed of David, according to my gospel" (2:8). This is a remarkably similar statement to Romans 1:3–4, where Paul argued that his gospel is expressed in the proclamation of Jesus as the messianic Son of David whose resurrection functioned to install him as God's vindicated and enthroned king. Given the context of 2 Timothy, here Paul emphasizes the second stage of Romans 1:3–4—namely, resurrection as a means of countering potential shame at Paul's sufferings and imprisonment. Second, Paul argues that his suffering is a result of his commitment to the gospel he proclaims, and that his faithfulness in the midst of his incarceration is a participation in the Messiah's sufferings (2:9–11). Third, those who faithfully share in the sufferings of the Messiah have the hope of sharing in the Messiah's resurrection life and reigning together with the Messiah. "The saying is trustworthy: For if we die together with him, we will also live with him; if we endure, we will also reign together with him" (εἰ γὰρ συναπεθάνομεν, καὶ συζήσομεν, εἰ ὑπομένομεν, καὶ συμβασιλεύσομεν, 2:11–12a). The σύν- prefixes serve to emphasize Paul's creative application of the saving events of the messianic king's

---

133. I have benefited greatly from the entire argument here of Michael David Marossy, "The Rule of the Resurrected Messiah: Kingship Discourse in 2 Timothy 2:8–13," *CBQ* 82 (2020); 84–100.

narrative to his people—namely, death, resurrection life, and enthronement. The language is remarkably similar to Paul's statement in Romans 6:8—"if we have died with the Messiah, we believe that we will also live together with him." Paul concludes with the promise that the resurrected messianic king has the power to protect and safeguard those who remain faithful to Messiah Jesus, *for the risen Christ himself is faithful* even when humans are faithless (2:12b–13; cf. 1:10–12).[134] This is stated well by David Downs and Benjamin Lappenga: "To the extent that those in Christ *have died* and *will live* and *reign* with him, the risen and exalted Christ will remain faithful to them, for his faithfulness to those who participate in his own cruciform, resurrected, and kingly existence is actually faithfulness to himself."[135] Christ's resurrection power is the very ground of Paul's confidence that he and his people will experience "salvation" and "eternal glory" (2:10b).[136] As the "Righteous Judge," Jesus is the faithful one who is able to give the "the crown of righteousness" both to Paul and "to all those who love his appearing (τὴν ἐπιφάνειαν)" (2 Tim 4:8).

Conclusion

I have argued that Paul develops his participatory discourse within Ephesians, Colossians, and 2 Timothy through a creative and innovative reinterpretation of royal ideology and reflections upon Israel's ideal and messianic king. The narrative of the Messiah, who he is and what he does, can be situated neatly against this framework: election to sonship, defeat of one's enemies, resurrection, enthronement/exaltation, the creation of a harmonious and peaceful body politic, the giving of gifts to one's subjects, and of course, the honorific "Messiah" itself, all point to Israel's messianic ideology as the framework for Paul's understanding of Jesus as Messiah. Paul has taken the major step, however, in describing the subjects of the Messiah as not simply benefiting from the Messiah's rule but as *sharing in his rule by virtue of their union with the Messiah*. This framework allows us to account for the four models articulated by Richard Hays for conceptualizing Paul's participatory soteriology. Those in Christ: (1) belong to a family by virtue of their participation in the Messiah's

134. So David J. Downs and Benjamin J. Lappenga, *The Faithfulness of the Risen Christ: Pistis and the Exalted Lord in Paul* (Waco, TX: Baylor University Press, 2019), 4–10.

135. Downs and Lappenga, *The Faithfulness of the Risen Christ*, 9.

136. Marossy, "The Rule of the Resurrected Messiah," 96.

sonship; (2) share in the Messiah's political/military victory precisely by virtue of the Davidic Messiah's defeat of his and his peoples' political enemies; (3) participate in the church/assembly as the relation between ruler (head) and ruled (body); and (4) participate in the story of Christ by sharing in the messianic royal events of death, resurrection, and heavenly enthronement.

CHAPTER 8

The Suffering and Enthronement of the Messianic Son of God as Foundation for Humanity's Salvation

Hebrews and 1 Peter

This chapter takes a look at the messianic logic and texture of three more NT compositions, namely, Hebrews, 1 Peter, and very briefly the Letter of James.

THE EPISTLE TO THE HEBREWS

The unique and primary contribution the Epistle to the Hebrews has made to early Christology is its portrait of Jesus as the incarnate and now exalted high priest who has offered the perfect and final sacrifice for sins in God's heavenly tabernacle (e.g., 2:17–18; 4:14–16; 7:24–28; 10:12–14). Jesus's high priestly role so dominates the symbolic world of Hebrews that it may threaten to completely overshadow other images, functions, or titles the author may have drawn upon in his Christology.[1] But it should be remembered that the Scriptures of Israel (and somewhat famously select scrolls from Qumran) speak of two anointed agents—both an eschatological king and high priest (e.g., Zech 3:8; 6:12–13; Jer 33:14–26; 4Q161; 4Q285; 1QSb; CD 7:18–21).[2] Thus, even if Jesus's priestly

---

1. See here especially Eric F. Mason, *"You Are a Priest Forever": Second Temple Jewish Messianism and the Priestly Christology of the Epistle to the Hebrews*, STDJ 74 (Leiden: Brill, 2008).

2. On the relationship between the Davidic Messiah and the eschatological high priest, I have benefited from Bernardo Cho, *Royal Messianism and the Jerusalem Priesthood in the Gospel of Mark*, LNTS 607 (London: T&T Clark, 2019), 25–51. Cho makes a strong argument that the Scrolls by no means minimize the importance of the Davidic Messiah, but that rather "the primary thrust of the messianism of the Scrolls is to affirm the sect as the true Zadokites, whom the king would finally legitimise" (p. 51). See further James C. VanderKam,

identity predominates in Hebrews, one should by no means neglect that he is also the Davidic Messiah. The author does, after all, use the title Χριστός with respect to Christ's high priestly role (e.g., 9:11, 14, 24, 28; 10:10).[3] The author also provides evidence for the very early association we have already witnessed in Paul and Luke between "Messiah" and his sufferings and death (e.g., 5:5; 9:14, 28; cf. Luke 24:25–26, 44–45; Rom 5:6–8; 1 Cor 15:1–3). And yet, I want to argue that Hebrews also manifests a robust and creative messianic Son of God Christology, one that is both foundational for the author's depiction of how Christ accomplishes humanity's salvation and the prior grounds for the author's priestly Christology.[4] In fact, the author begins his argument with a hymnic celebration of the Father's declaration of Jesus's divine sonship and his royal enthronement into the heavenly world (1:4–14). The scriptural texts that the author applies to the Son of God "affirm the divine and Davidic messianic identities of the Son."[5] The Son of God's heavenly enthronement is the foundation for how humanity's salvation is accomplished. It is also the means whereby God secures his promises for all humanity (2:5–18), and the foundation for his argument that Jesus is humanity's high priest (5:5–6; 7:1–28).

"Messianism in the Scrolls," in *The Community of the Renewed Covenant: The Notre Dame Symposium on the Dead Sea Scrolls,* ed. Eugene Ulrich and James C. VanderKam (Notre Dame: University of Notre Dame Press, 1994), 211–34.

3. On the meaning of "Messiah" in Hebrews, see Craig L. Blomberg, "Messiah in the New Testament," in *Israel's Messiah in the Bible and the Dead Sea Scrolls,* ed. Richard S. Hess and M. Daniel Carroll (Grand Rapids: Baker Academic, 2003), 133–34; Cynthia Long Westfall, "Messianic Themes of Temple, Enthronement, and Victory in Hebrews and the General Epistles," in *The Messiah in the Old and New Testaments*, ed. Stanley E. Porter (Grand Rapids: Eerdmans, 2007), 217–19.

4. Contra Crispin Fletcher-Louis, *Christological Origins: The Emerging Consensus and Beyond,* vol. 1 of *Jesus Monotheism* (Eugene, OR: Cascade, 2015), 216: "Insofar as Hebrews' Christology is a fully divine one, there is no evidence that it is indebted to a Jewish royal messianic hope." This is an odd and confusing statement as it seems to suppose that a "fully divine Christology" cannot coexist with Jewish messianic hope, despite the fact that Hebrews begins its argument by systematically applying messianic scriptural texts and titles to the Son of God (e.g., Ps 2:7; 45:6; 89:28; 110:1). Better here is the recent work of Madison N. Pierce, *Divine Discourse in the Epistle to the Hebrews: The Recontextualization of Spoken Quotations of Scripture,* SNTSMS (Cambridge, Cambridge University Press, 2020), esp. chs. 1 and 2. Pierce shows how the author reinterprets messianic texts which were originally spoken to and about a Davidic king and applies them to the divine Son of God. See also Timo Eskola, *Messiah and the Throne: Jewish Merkabah Mysticism and Early Christian Exaltation Discourse,* WUNT 2.142 (Tübingen: Mohr Siebeck, 2001), 206–7.

5. See Eric F. Mason, "Heavenly Revelation in the Epistle to the Hebrews," in *The Jewish Apocalyptic Tradition and the Shaping of New Testament Thought*, ed. Benjamin E. Reynolds and Loren T. Stuckenbruck (Minneapolis: Fortress, 2017), 288–89.

Finally, the Son of God's enthronement establishes the narrative goal or pattern which God's faithful children follow (12:1–4; 12:18–29). Stated simply, Jesus is portrayed as the messianic Son of God who shares in God's sovereign lordship and accomplishes humanity's salvation as its perfected ideal representative.[6]

The Son of God's Enthronement into His Heavenly Kingdom—1:5–14

The author's argument begins with a depiction of the Father uttering words of celebration upon the Son of God's enthronement and entrance into the heavenly world. In 1:5 the author subordinates the role of the angels by placing direct speech from the LXX on the Father's lips: "You are my Son, today I have begotten you," and again, "I will be a Father to him, and he will be a Son to me."[7] It is of utmost significance to note that the primary metaphor which the author uses to refer to Jesus is familial—namely, sonship. The climactic moment of the scene in the scriptural catena is the Father's declaration of Jesus's sonship as he enters into God's throne room. Having referred to the Son as the appointed "heir of all things" (1:2b) and the Son's purification for sins in 1:3b, the author develops the most important theme of the exordium wherein he claims that Jesus "has taken his seat at the right hand of the Majesty on high" (ἐκάθισεν ἐν δεξιᾷ τῆς μεγαλωσύνης ἐν ὑψηλοῖς, 1:3).[8] This allusion to LXX Psalm 109.1, which is the final text quoted in the catena (Heb 1:13; see also Heb 8:1; 10.12–13; and 12.2), sets the theme for the rest of 1:5–14 as the catena centers upon the Son's enthronement and entrance into the Father's heavenly throne room.[9] Having taken his seat at the Father's right hand, Jesus subsequently "inherited a more excellent name than them" (1:4b). While the similarity of this text to Philippians 2:9–11 makes it tempting to assume that the unspecified

6. See here the helpful analysis by Ole Jakob Filtvedt, *The Identity of God's People and the Paradox of Hebrews*, WUNT 2.400 (Tübingen: Mohr Siebeck, 2015), 54–82.

7. That the angel-Christ contrast functions within the author's contrast between the old and new covenants is argued for fruitfully by Kenneth L. Schenk, "A Celebration of the Enthroned Son," *JBL* 123 (2001): 482–84; John P. Meier, "Symmetry and Theology in the Old Testament Citations of Heb.1:5–14," *Bib* 66 (1985): 504–33; L. D. Hurst, "The Christology of Hebrews 1 and 2," in *The Glory of Christ in the New Testament: Studies in Christology in Memory of George Bradford Caird*, ed. L. D. Hurst and N. T. Wright (Oxford: Clarendon, 1987), 156.

8. On the reference to the Son as God's appointed heir of all things (1:2) as a messianic allusion to Ps 2:8, see Filtvedt, *The Identity of God's People*, 56.

9. See the illuminating discussion of Ps 110:1 in Hebrews by Harold W. Attridge, "The Psalms in Hebrews," in *The Psalms in the New Testament*, ed. Steve Moyise and Maarten J. J. Menken, The New Testament and the Scriptures of Israel (London: T&T Clark, 2004), 197–99.

name is "Lord," the inheritance of the name surely must be that of "Son given the father/sonship language of 1.5 and the fact that the author begins his sermon by using the metaphor of son in 1.2."[10] The reader is, therefore, reminded of the fact that the author has just previously claimed that God appointed this Son "heir of all things" (1:2). This reality of the Son being described both as "heir of all things" (1:2) and as inheriting the name Son (1:4) is not insignificant for humanity, for in 1:14 the author claims that the angels are ministers for "those who are about to inherit salvation." While the precise relationship between the Son's inheritance and humanity's inheritance is left ambiguous at this point in the author's argument, the readers are, nevertheless, given a subtle indication that Jesus's inheritance of sonship will have soteriological ramifications for humanity.

Second, the two LXX citations in 1:5, which are from Psalm 2:7 and 2 Samuel 7:14, respectively, demand that the reader view the catena of chapter 1 as depicting and celebrating the enthronement of the Son to the heavenly realm. Both Psalm 2:7 and 2 Samuel 7:14 are royal pronouncements which speak of a Davidic son who enters into kingly rule on behalf of God's people. The tradition history of the use of these verses within the NT and their Septuagintal context confirms that they should be read within Hebrews as referring to the Son's resurrection/exaltation (cf. Mark 1:11; Acts 4:25–27; 13:33; Rom 1:3–4). It is significant, for example, that Psalm 2 refers to a king whom God sets over Zion (Ps 2:6; cf. Heb 12:22–23) who obtains the world as his inheritance (Ps 2:8). And likewise, 2 Samuel 7 depicts God's chosen king as his son, a kingly son who is promised an eternal rule and throne (7:13, 16). More important, however, is the fact that the immediate context suggests a scene of enthronement as it declares: "he sat down at the right of the majesty in the heavens" (1:3). And the next verse refers to him "becoming so much better than the angels" (1:4). Thus, it makes good sense to read these verses as depicting Jesus's exaltation to the heavenly realm where he inherits the royal name "Son." This reading is confirmed by the

---

10. So Scott D. Mackie, "Confession of the Son of God in Hebrews," *NTS* 53 (2007): 116–17; James W. Thompson, "The Structure and Purpose of the Catena in Heb 1:5–13," *CBQ* 38 (1976): 355; Richard Bauckham, "Monotheism and Christology in Hebrews 1," in *Early Jewish and Christian Monotheism*, ed. Loren T. Stuckenbruck and Wendy E. S. North (London: T&T Clark, 2004), 175, argues that the one who already exists as the Son inherits the divine name, the tetragrammaton, on parallels with Phil 2:9. Bauckham is clearly concerned to deny the claim that Jesus became the Son of God at his resurrection or exaltation. See also Richard Bauckham, "The Divinity of Jesus Christ in the Epistle to the Hebrews," in *The Epistle to the Hebrews and Christian Theology*, ed. Richard Bauckham et al. (Grand Rapids: Eerdmans, 2009), 15–36, esp. 21–22.

author's final citation of the catena in 1:13 where he again invokes LXX Psalm 109:1: "Sit at my right hand, until I make your enemies a footstool for your feet." Psalm 109:1 LXX is, of course, the classic prooftext depicting the royal Son's exaltation to the right hand of the Father's throne;[11] it establishes a relationship between Zion and God's heavenly throne room, as the exalted heavenly figure is said to rule "from Zion." The frequency with which these royal-messianic texts (Pss 2, LXX 109, and 2 Sam 7) are quoted and alluded to within the NT makes it necessary to emphasize that the author uses these texts in order to portray the remarkable reality of the Son's entrance into the life and power of God. The unstated but obvious premise is that the Son has been resurrected and is now alive in a more real, transcendent, and powerful existence.[12]

The confluence of these themes, namely the Father-Son relationship and the Son's inheritance of, and entrance into, the heavenly realm of the Father, is continued throughout the chapter. Hebrews 1:6 dramatically depicts the Son's exaltation and entrance into the heavenly world: "and again, when he leads forth the firstborn Son into the world, he says, 'Let all the angels of God worship him'" (ὅταν δὲ πάλιν εἰσαγάγῃ τὸν πρωτότοκον εἰς τὴν οἰκουμένην, λέγει, καὶ προσκυνησάτωσαν αὐτῷ πάντες ἄγγελοι θεοῦ).[13] With respect to 1:6a, many interpreters claim that οἰκουμένη should be read as referring to the earthly material world, and that the verse, therefore, depicts the Son's birth—the incarnation.[14] This interpretation must, however, be rejected. First, the

11. For detailed analyses of the Septuagintal context, tradition-history, and use of Ps 110:1 in the NT, see David M. Hay, *Glory at the Right Hand: Psalm 110 in Early Christianity*, SBLMS 18 (Nashville: Abingdon, 1973); Martin Hengel, "'Sit at My Right Hand!': The Enthronement of Christ at the Right Hand of God and Psalm 110:1," in *Studies in Early Christology* (Edinburgh: T&T Clark, 1995), 119–225.

12. That Hebrews assumes the resurrection of Jesus as necessary for its entire argument is shown convincingly by David M. Moffitt, "'If Another Priest Arises': Jesus' Resurrection and the High Priestly Christology of Hebrews," in *The Cloud of Witnesses*, ed. Richard Bauckham et al. (London: T&T Clark, 2008), 68–79. Also see Gareth E. Cockerill, "The Better Resurrection (Heb. 11:35): A Key to the Structure and Rhetorical Purpose of Hebrews 11," *TynBul* 51 (2000): 215–34. One should not accept, therefore, the common sentiment articulated here by Georg Strecker, *Theology of the New Testament*, trans. M. Eugene Boring (Louisville: Westminster John Knox; Berlin: Walter de Gruyter, 2000), 609: "The Letter to the Hebrews does not know the idea of the rising or resurrection of Jesus from the dead."

13. See here, Filtvedt, *The Identity of God's People*, 57–58.

14. Those who read this text in connection with Luke's account of Jesus's baptism include: *Hebrews: A Commentary on the Epistle to the Hebrews,* Hermeneia (Minneapolis: Fortress, 1989), 55–56; H. W. Bateman, *Early Jewish Hermeneutics and Hebrews 1:5–13* (New York: Lang, 1997), 222. Those who have seen the verse as referring to Jesus's second coming include: William L. Lane, *Hebrews 1–8*, WBC 47A (Grand Rapids: Zondervan, 1991), 27;

author's only other use of the term οἰκουμένη occurs in 2:5, where he states that it is the "world which is to come," which is the topic under discussion.[15] Here in 2:5 it is stated that this "world to come" was not subjected to angels, the premise being that it was, rather, subjected to the Son (the fuller argument being made in 2:5–9).[16] It makes abundant sense, therefore, to view 1:5–14 as the author's description of the Son's entrance into this heavenly reality. After all, the author has described in 1:5–14: (1) the Son's exaltation above all of his enemies (1:13); (2) his eternal and virtuous rule (1:10–12); (3) his sharing of God's eternal throne (1:8–9); and (4) his inheritance of the name "Son" (1:4–5). Thus, "the subjection of the inhabited world" of which the author speaks in 2:5 must refer in some measure to these elements.[17] Secondly, given that the author has just described the Son's exaltation to the Father's right hand in 1:3–5, it is logical to interpret 1:6 as continuing this theme. While one could argue that πάλιν functions adverbially, the author frequently uses it to connect various quotations (additionally, see 2:13 and 10:30).[18] The familial title of τὸν πρωτότοκον indicates that 1:6 is the third of three explicit sonship citations. While the language of "the firstborn son" is abundant throughout the LXX, its usage in Psalm 88:28, where it refers to Israel's coming Davidic king, is especially pertinent.[19] In this Psalm the son cries out: "You are my Father, my God" (LXX Ps 88:27), and in the Father's act of appointing the Davidide as his "firstborn son" the Father makes him "exalted above all those who rule the earth" (ὑψηλὸν παρὰ τοῖς βασιλεῦσιν τῆς γῆς, 88:28). In doing so, the Father

---

O. Michel, *Der Brief an die Hebräer* (Göttingen: Vandenhoek & Ruprecht, 1984), 113; David Peterson, *Hebrews and Perfection: An Examination of the Concept of Perfection in the Epistle to the Hebrews*, SNTSMS 47 (Cambridge: Cambridge University Press, 1982), 214; Ernst Käsemann, *The Wandering People of God: An Investigation of the Letter to the Hebrews* (Minneapolis: Augsburg, 1984), 100–112.

15. Schenk, "A Celebration of the Enthroned Son," 478; Ardel B. Caneday, "The Eschatological World Already Subjected to the Son: The Οἰκουμένη of Hebrews 1.6 and the Son's Enthronement," in *The Cloud of Witnesses*, ed. Richard Bauckham et al. (London: T&T Clark, 2008), 30–36; Pierce, *Divine Discourse*, ch. 1.

16. While the οἰκουμένη is still a future hope from the perspective of humanity, it is a present reality for the Son. So, David A. deSilva, *Perseverance in Gratitude: A Socio-rhetorical Commentary on the Epistle to the Hebrews* (Grand Rapids: Eerdmans, 2000), 97.

17. See here the convincing argument that οἰκουμένη refers to the heavenly world and the Son's heavenly enthronement by David M. Moffitt, *Atonement and the Logic of Resurrection in the Epistle to the Hebrews*, NovTSup 141 (Leiden: Brill, 2011), 53–69.

18. So Caneday, "The Eschatological World," 32.

19. Those who see an allusion to LXX Ps 88 in 1:6 include Luke Timothy Johnson, *Hebrews A Commentary*, NTL (Louisville: Westminster John Knox, 2006), 78–79; Bauckham, "Monotheism and Christology," 178–79.

makes the Son's throne to endure forever and ever (εἰς τὸν αἰῶνα τοῦ αἰῶνος . . . τὸν θρόνον αὐτοῦ, 88:30; note the linguistic similarities with the Son's throne in Heb 1:8). Thus, Hebrews 1:6 further continues the celebration of 1:4–5 as it depicts the Father leading his royal firstborn Son into the heavenly realm and commanding the angels to worship this firstborn Son.

Hebrews 1:7–12 continues the celebration of the enthroned Son by comparing the eternal and virtuous character of his throne and rule with the fleeting and perishing order of the material world with which the author surprisingly connects the angels. In 1:7 the author refers to God as making the angels as "winds" or "spirits" (πνεύματα) and "flames of fire." The angels are, in other words, associated with the sensual material world.[20] The reference to the angels as "his ministering servants" confirms this as it looks forward to the author's claim in 1:14 that the angels are "ministering spirits" whose role is to ensure humanity's salvation.[21] Reference to the angels as "winds" and "flames of fire" likely evokes a connection between the angels and the Sinai theophany (Exod 3:2; 14:19; 19:9, 16–19; cf. Acts 7:30).[22] That an association with Sinai as physical and material is intended by the author is evident from 12:18, a text we will examine in more detail shortly, where the author associates Sinai with such things as fire and wind (12:18b). The reference to the angels as "ministers" in both 1:7 and 1:14 may suggest their function to be that of cultic service whereby they perform cultic worship in the heavenly throne room (2 Bar. 21:6; 4 Ezra 8:20–22).[23] In contrast to the angels who are God's servants and are associated with Sinai, note that when the Son is enthroned to the heavenly realm he becomes a sharer of God's eternal throne and is even addressed as "God": "and to the Son, 'your throne O God is forever and ever'" (ὁ θρόνος σου ὁ θεὸς εἰς τὸν αἰῶνα τοῦ αἰῶνος, 1:8a).[24] The Son not only enters into the sphere of God but also becomes one who shares in the eternal rule and reign of God which, as 1:8b–9 declares, is characterized by the virtues of integrity, righteousness, and a hatred of lawlessness. While

---

20. See here the helpful discussion by Kenneth L. Schenk, *Cosmology and Eschatology in Hebrews: The Settings of the Sacrifice*, SNTSMS 143 (Cambridge: Cambridge University Press, 2007), 122–32.

21. See Schenk, "A Celebration of the Enthroned Son," 474.

22. So also Thompson, "The Structure and Purpose of the Catena," 357–58.

23. Bauckham, "Monotheism and Christology," 179.

24. See Attridge, "The Psalms in Hebrews," 202. On the author's understanding of the Spirit of God speaking through David to the Son, see Matthew W. Bates, *The Birth of the Trinity: Jesus, God, and Spirit in New Testament and Early Christian Interpretations of the Old Testament* (Oxford: Oxford University Press, 2015), 163–65.

the created order associated with the angels will disappear and is even now disappearing, the Son's throne and rule will last forever (1:10–12). The author quotes LXX Psalm 101:26–28 in order to establish the Son's rule over all of creation, including the angels (1:10), something hinted at already in 1:3, where the author claimed that the Son was active in creation. The heavens and the earth will perish and be rolled up like a garment, but the Son's years will never come to an end (1:11–12). Whereas the angels are associated with the transience of the created world (1:7), the enthroned Son's share in the Father's throne ensures that his years will never cease (1:12b).

The Enthronement of the Son of God and the Salvation of Humanity

In light of our examination of Hebrews 1:5–14, three points should be kept in mind as we continue our exploration of the author's Christology of the Son of God and its relationship to the salvation of God's people. First, the significance of the filial language should not be underestimated. The author has chosen to begin his argument with a catena of scriptural quotations which is dominated by the relationship between the Father and the Davidic Son of God. The first and second of the LXX quotations in Hebrews (1:5) are proclamations of Jesus's sonship directly proceeding from the Father's mouth. It is precisely because Jesus is the Son of God that he can share in his Father's sovereignty. Second, the catena of Septuagintal quotations focuses upon celebrating Jesus's inheritance of the name "Son" as he is enthroned upon his Father's throne and enters into the heavenly realm. The author systematically applies royal-messianic texts to the Son and does so in a way that emphasizes this rule as not the earthly rule of the kingdom of the Son of David, but the cosmic reign of the one who has entered into God's own life.[25] Third, the author contrasts the rule of the Son, which is characterized by eternality, with that of the angels, who are associated with the temporal and even dying created order. I suggest that these three claims function as the indispensable and foundational premises for the author's Christology and articulation of how the Son of God accomplishes humanity's salvation. Let's take a briefer look at a handful of texts where the author's messianic Son of God Christology functions as the foundation for his arguments.

25. Bauckham, "Monotheism and Christology," 178.

The Enthroned Son of God Leads His Siblings to Glory—2:5–13

In Hebrews 2:5–9 the author turns from the reign of the exalted Son to humanity's failure to attain the state of glory and rule which God had promised it in Psalm 8:5–7. The quotation of Psalm 8 ends with the promise "you have subjected all things under their [i.e., humanity's] feet" (πάντα ὑπέταξας ὑποκάτω τῶν ποδῶν αὐτοῦ, Heb 2:8a); attentive readers will recognize that the author has, just a mere half-dozen verses before, claimed that God has placed all of the Son's enemies under his feet (ἕως ἂν θῶ τοὺς ἐχθρούς σου ὑποπόδιον τῶν ποδῶν σου, 1:13b).[26] The Son has entered into God's heavenly world (1:6), but humanity's hope of inheriting this world (2:5) has been frustrated. The link with the celebration of Hebrews 1 suggests that the Son has experienced the fulfillment of God's promise to humanity. From humanity's present standpoint, however, God's promise to Adam looks to have been thwarted, as "we do not yet see all things subjected to him" (2:8b). The Son has, however, entered into the promise of Psalm 8 as the author describes him as "having been crowned with glory and honor" (δόξῃ καὶ τιμῇ ἐστεφανωμένον, 2:9b), a direct reference to the promise made in Psalm 8 (δόξῃ καὶ τιμῇ ἐστεφάνωσας αὐτόν, 2:7b). Thus, the argument here depends entirely upon the assumption that the Son has already entered into God's rule—exactly that which we have seen in Hebrews 1:5–14.

The Son's entrance into God's heavenly rule is, however, beneficial for humanity, for it is precisely the Son's obedient suffering and subsequent exaltation which accomplishes humanity's salvation. In 2:10 the author makes the bold claim that it was fitting for God "in leading many sons to glory to perfect the pioneer of their salvation through sufferings" (πολλοὺς υἱοὺς δόξαν ἀγαγόντα τὸν ἀρχηγὸν τῆς σωτηρίας αὐτῶν διὰ παθημάτων τελειῶσαι). It is essential to note the parallel between God *leading* (εἰσαγάγῃ) *the firstborn Son* into the heavenly world in 1:6 and God *leading the many sons into glory* (2:10). In each instance, God is the subject who leads his children into a state of perfection. This immediately helps one make sense of Jesus's title in 2:10 as τὸν ἀρχηγόν. Its connotations of source, initiator, and pioneer result from the fact that as "the firstborn Son" Jesus has proleptically entered into God's rule and heavenly realm in advance of, and on behalf of, "the many sons." The author's choice of

---

26. For an incisive critique of exclusively christological interpretations of Ps 8:4–6 in Heb 2:5–9, see Craig L. Blomberg, "'But We See Jesus': The Relationship between the Son of Man in Hebrews 2.6 and 2.9 and the Implications for English Translations," in *The Cloud of Witnesses*, ed. Richard Bauckham et al. (London: T&T Clark, 2008), 88–99.

"firstborn Son" further functions as a means of identifying Jesus as the head of a family, the elder brother as it were, of God's children. As Marc Cortez notes: "Jesus is not merely the first resurrected human, but he is also the one who establishes through the resurrection a new order of being in which others can now participate."[27] Thus, as the Father proclaims that Jesus is his Son (1:5), so the Son directly affirms humanity as his fellow siblings (2:11–13).[28] The author again engages in a messianic reading of Psalm 22:22 (LXX Ps 21:23) in his placing the words of the Davidic king upon the lips of Jesus: "I will proclaim your name to my siblings, in the midst of the assembly I will sing to you" (2:12). The incarnate Son of God thus testifies to his own praise of the Father who has rescued him and does so in the company of his own brothers and sisters, who will presumably follow the same pattern of the Son.[29] His participation in their humanity ensures their salvation and their reconciliation with the Father (Heb 2:14–18). This is the foundation for the author's claims that his audience "has become participants with the Messiah" (μέτοχοι γὰρ τοῦ Χριστοῦ, 3:14a). This echoes the author's previous description of the audience as "participants in a heavenly calling" (κλήσεως ἐπουρανίου μέτοχοι, 3:1).[30] The audience is so closely bound together with the destiny of the incarnate and heavenly enthroned Messiah that the author, like Paul, can speak of the people as incorporated into, and sharing together, the heavenly perfection of the Messiah provided that they remain faithful (3:2, 6b, 14b).[31] Finally, we must note that the manner in which humanity is led to glory is accomplished through Jesus being perfected through sufferings" (2:10b). The statement is similar to that of 2:9b, where we saw Jesus "crowned with glory and honor because of the suffering of death" (διὰ τὸ πάθημα τοῦ θανάτου). In 2:9, sufferings are the means whereby the Son is "crowned with glory and honor," whereas in 2:10, sufferings are the means through which the Son is "perfected." Thus, while the language of "perfection" has a wide semantic range within Hebrews, here its parallel with 2:9 strongly connotes the sense of exaltation.[32]

---

27. Marc Cortez, *Resourcing Theological Anthropology: A Constructive Account of Humanity in the Light of Christ* (Grand Rapids: Zondervan, 2017), 137.

28. On the significance of Jesus's public declaration of his identification with humanity, see Mackie, "Confession of the Son," 114–29.

29. See further, Bates, *The Birth of the Trinity*, 138–40.

30. See further Filtvedt, *The Identity of God's People*, 79–80.

31. Johnson, *Hebrews*, 118; Blomberg, "Messiah in the New Testament," 133.

32. On the religious background of this language, see deSilva, *Perseverance in Gratitude*, 194–204. On the relationship between the author's language of "perfection" and resurrection, see Moffitt, *Atonement and the Logic*, 198–200.

The Enthroned Son of God Is Humanity's Perfect High Priest—5:5-10 and 7:1-28

Its novel characterization of Jesus as humanity's high priest is perhaps the most well known aspect of the Christology and soteriology of the book of Hebrews. What is not as often recognized, however, is the author's clear indication that his priestly Christology is built upon the presumption that Jesus is the Davidic messianic Son of God.[33] The author is clear that Jesus's priestly status is of another order than the Levitical priesthood, and he plainly admits that Jesus belongs not to the tribe of Levi, but to the tribe of Judah (7:14; cf. 8:4; Num 18:1-7). Jesus's priesthood is based not on the Levitical order of priests, but "according to the order of Melchizedek" (5:6b, 10b). What is central to my argument here is the rarely noted fact that the author's argument for Jesus's Melchizedekian priesthood is based on the audience's acceptance of the prior claim, made in Hebrews 1:5-14, that Jesus is God's royal and heavenly enthroned Son.[34] After claiming in 5:4 that no high priest takes the honor on his own initiative, but, rather, is called by God, the author suggests analogically that the same process took place with Jesus's appointment to high priest. Just as the Father spoke the words of Psalm 2:7 to Jesus, namely, "'You are my Son, today I have begotten you'" (5:5b), so also Jesus receives his high priesthood from the one speaking the words of Psalm 110:4 (LXX 109:4) to him: "You are a priest forever according to the order of Melchizedek" (5:6). It is important to note that the author intentionally draws the reader back to the royal celebration of the enthroned Son by quoting Psalm 2:7, one of the central texts quoted in the opening catena to celebrate the Son's exaltation (1:5).[35] The author's innovation here is to draw upon the common early Christian strategy of applying texts such as Psalm 2:7 (Heb 1:5) and Psalm 110:1 (Heb 1:13), which depict the Son's exaltation, as the foundation for extending the claim that the Father has also spoken the words of Psalm 110:4 to the Son.[36] Thus, it is not an exaggeration to say that the author's high priestly Christology is founded upon the Son of God's entrance into the heavenly kingdom. The author of Hebrews consistently portrays an intrinsic connection between the Son of God's heavenly enthronement (Ps 110:1) and his subsequent priestly offer of himself as

33. Rightly, see Mackie, "Confession of the Son," 126.

34. See here especially Moffitt, *Atonement and the Logic*, 200–207.

35. Johnson, *Hebrews*, 144, rightly notes that the author's quotation of Ps 2:7 "triggers the hearers' memory of the words of God that certified Jesus as the very Son who had been enthroned at God's right hand (Heb 1:3–4)."

36. So deSilva, *Perseverance in Gratitude*, 188–89.

humanity's sacrifice and perpetual priesthood (Ps 110:4). Thus, the traditional early Christian invocation of Psalm 110:1 as depicting the Son's heavenly royal enthronement is the necessary presupposition of the author's high priestly Christology (1:3; 4:14; 8:1; 10:12).[37]

What are the characteristics of this Melchizedekian priesthood?[38] Returning to Hebrews 5, we see that the Son's "having been perfected" (τελειωθείς, 5:9) is parallel to God's "designating (προσαγορευθείς) him . . . a priest according to the order of Melchizedek" (5:10). Thus, it is only after the Son has been perfected, that is, enters into God's heavenly throne room, that he becomes a high priest according to the order of Melchizedek.[39] Why is it that God's act of "perfecting" the Son is parallel to God's "designating" him as an eternal priest? I suggest that it is precisely the key attribute of the Melchizedekian priest, namely "the power of an indestructible life" (7:16), which is parallel to God's act of perfecting the Son. The author fastens upon the words of Psalm 110:4, "you are a priest *forever*" (5:6; 7:17; 7:21), and it is precisely this quality of the Son's eternality which qualifies him to be the Melchizedekian priest. In Hebrews 5 we see the author claim that the Son prayed to "the one able to save him out of death" and that "he was heard because of his piety" (5:7). That the Son "was heard" by God must be taken to indicate that the Son was saved "out of death." Given the fact, however, that the author has made the point that the Son "tasted death for everyone" (2:9b), attained perfection through sufferings (2:10), and defeated death through his own death (2:14), the author cannot mean that Jesus was spared from the experience of death. Since Jesus was not saved from this experience, in order for the author's claim that God "heard him" to have any meaningful substance, it must refer to something that happened to Jesus after he died.[40] Jesus, then, does not avoid death but overcomes it through God's act of resurrection/exaltation.[41] This emphasis on life and eternality in opposition to death and temporality is the primary trait of the Melchizedekian

---

37. So Eskola, *Messiah and the Throne*, 207: "Exaltation Christology is not a minor aspect in the letter, but the main foundation on which the whole train of thought has been constructed."

38. On the author's development of ideas regarding Jesus's high priestly ministry in connection with Jewish views of the high priest as merciful, compassionate, pious, and sympathetic, see William Horbury, "The Aaronic Priesthood in the Epistle to the Hebrews," in *Messianism among Jews and Christians: Biblical and Historical Studies*, 2nd ed. (London: T&T Clark, 2016), 260–85.

39. See here Kenneth L. Schenk, "Keeping His Appointment: Creation and Enthronement in Hebrews," *JSNT* 66 (1997): 96.

40. So Moffitt, "'If Another Priest Arises!,'" 71.

41. So Johnson, *Hebrews*, 146–47.

priesthood and is confirmed throughout Hebrews 7. Thus, Melchizedek is like the Son due to his "having no end of life" (7:3), being testified to as "living" (7:8), and having "the power of an indestructible life" (7:16). Whereas many Levites have been high priests (due to their deaths, 7:23), Jesus holds the priesthood perpetually because "he remains forever" (7:24; cf. Ps 110:4) and he "always lives to intercede on [humanity's] behalf" (7:25b). The author's final statement that God's oath (i.e., Ps 110:4) appoints as high priest "a son made perfect forever" (υἱὸν εἰς τὸν αἰῶνα τετελειωμένον, 7:28) strongly echoes the event in 5:7–10.[42] The relationship between these texts suggests that the Son's perfection refers to the event where he was raised from the dead and entered into the enduring quality of God's life—something depicted in Hebrews 1:10–12 (LXX Ps 101:26–28), where the Father declares to the Son of God that his throne "is forever" (1:8), that creation will perish but "you will remain" (1:11), and "your years will not be erased" (1:12).[43] Stated simply, Martin Hengel writes: "The effectiveness of Jesus as the priestly intercessor and advocate is not only a consequence of his atoning death, but also the expression of his participation in the dominion of God, which he gained through 'sitting at the right hand.'"[44]

Exhortations to Join the Perfected and Enthroned Son of God— 12:1–3 and 12:18–25

Near the end of the discursive argument, the author twice exhorts his audience to persevere in their faith so that they will join the enthroned Son of God in his heavenly perfected state. Both of these hortatory arguments, in Hebrews 12:1–3 and 12:18–24, also depend upon the opening salvo of 1:5–14 and the saving event of the Son of God's heavenly enthronement. In 12:1–3 the author's command to finish the race depends upon the audience granting both the claim that Jesus has entered into God's own life (Heb 1:5–13) and that he, as the firstborn Son (1:6), is their elder human brother (Heb 2:10–14). Specifically, the runners are to "look away to Jesus, the author and perfecter of the faith" (ἀφορῶντες εἰς τὸν τῆς πίστεως ἀρχηγὸν καὶ τελειωτὴν Ἰησοῦν).[45] The injunction commands them to look ahead to Jesus, who has already finished

---

42. See here Marie E. Isaacs, *Sacred Space: An Approach to the Theology of Hebrews*, JSNTSup 73 (Sheffield: JSOT Press, 1992), 153–54.

43. See also Bauckham, "The Divinity of Jesus Christ," 31.

44. Martin Hengel, "'Sit at My Right Hand!,'" 146.

45. On Jesus as a model or prototype of faith and faithfulness in Hebrews, see Christopher A. Richardson, *Pioneer and Perfecter of Faith: Jesus' Faith as the Climax of Israel's History in the Epistle to the Hebrews*, WUNT 2.286 (Tübingen: Mohr Siebeck, 2012).

the race—the same contest in which they are now competing (10:32–33). The mentioning of the proper name "Jesus" emphasizes the Son of God's human nature and thereby his solidarity with humanity (cf. 2:5–18; 5:7–9). The description of Jesus as both ἀρχηγόν and τελειωτήν carries the connotations of the originator/beginner and finisher.[46] That Jesus is the "originator/beginner" of humanity's faith recalls 2:10, where the author declared that God "perfected the ἀρχηγόν of their salvation through sufferings." Jesus is the originator of both "faith" (12:2) and "salvation" (2:10) in that he is the first one, and thereby humanity's prototype, to have entered into God's promises for humanity.

Likewise, Jesus is the τελειωτήν of faith in that he brings to completion the faith of the Old Testament heroes—a faith which had yet to attain perfection and inherit the promises (11:39–40). Already we have seen this language of perfection applied to Jesus. In 2:10 God perfects Jesus through sufferings; in 5:9 Jesus is perfected through his learning obedience through what he suffered; and in 7:28 the author speaks of a Son made perfect forever on the basis of his entrance into a resurrected life. I suggest that in 12:2 these same resonances are at work. Jesus has, through endurance and fidelity to God, finished the race and thereby entered into a perfect form of existence. The author indicates as much in 12:2b, where he says of Jesus that "for the joy set before him (ὅς ἀντὶ τῆς προκειμένης αὐτῷ χαρᾶς), he endured the cross, while thinking lightly of the shame, and has taken his seat at the right hand of the throne of God (ἐν δεξιᾷ τε τοῦ θρόνου τοῦ θεοῦ κεκάθικεν)." The author again holds up Jesus's endurance of suffering as a model for his audience (2:10, 14; 4:15; 5:7–9). While it is possible to translate the preposition ἀντί as "instead of," it makes much better sense to read it as "for" and as indicating the reason for which Jesus endured the cross (cf. 12:16).[47] The joy which Jesus enters into is described in 12:2b with the familiar words of Psalm 110:1: "he has taken his seat (κεκάθικεν) at the right hand of the throne of God." The author foregrounds Jesus's exaltation through his use of the perfect tense and further emphasizes the event and continuing state of Jesus's exaltation. The joy that was set before the earthly Jesus was, therefore, his promised exaltation to the right hand of God—a promised state into which he has now entered. When the author calls upon the audience to consider (12:3) and fix their gaze (12:2) upon this one who endured such hardship, he sets before their eyes the perfected Son who has

46. So Dennis Hamm, "Faith in the Epistle to the Hebrews: The Jesus Factor," *CBQ* 56 (1990): 286–87.

47. See especially N. Clayton Croy, *Endurance in Suffering: Hebrews 12:1–3 in Its Rhetorical, Religious, and Philosophical Context*, SNTSMS 98 (Cambridge: Cambridge University Press, 1998), 177–86.

entered into God's life. And because he is the "author and perfecter of faith," Jesus's experience functions as the paradigm for humanity's narrative. The joy which Jesus has entered into, depicted so powerfully in Hebrews 1:5–14, is the goal which lies before the audience.

The significance of the Son of God's enthronement for the entire sermon becomes more evident when one compares it with the author's final argument in 12:18–29, a passage which contains many of the same themes. As in 1:5–2:4, the author initially establishes the superiority of the Son and the heavenly Jerusalem (1:5–14; 12:18–24), then warns his audience not to ignore this superior revelation (2:1–4; 12:25–29). There seems to be, in fact, something of an *inclusio* between Hebrews 1:5–14 and 12:18–29. The author begins his composition by celebrating the firstborn Son's inheritance and entrance into the heavenly realm, he concludes by celebrating the proleptic inheritance of the firstborn sons as they enter into the heavenly Jerusalem. Whereas the catena celebrates the eternal and unchanging reign of the Son's kingdom in contrast to the transience of the material world, the author concludes his argument with a contrast between the unshakeable heavenly "city of the living God" (12:22) and the created order, which will come to an end (12:26–27). While this insight is significant in establishing the importance of the themes found in Hebrews 1:5–14, only a few comments need to be made here in order to make this point.

First, as the Son's rule is contrasted with the material creation which will perish and fade away (1:10–12), so is the assembly of the sons in heaven contrasted with the sensual phenomena of the Sinai event. This is vividly captured in the author's statement: "for you have not come to a place which can be touched and a burning fire and to darkness and gloom and a whirlwind" (12:18; cf. 1:7). The author's strategy of associating the angels as the mediators of the Sinai covenant in 2:2–3 is reused again here, as the author now associates the Sinai theophany with the sensual and temporal (12:18–19). The author warns that the entire created order, to which the Sinai covenant belongs, will be destroyed, for as God has promised: "Still once more I will shake not only the earth but even the heaven" (12:26b). The author interprets this quote from Haggai 2:6 to mean that in a little while God will "remove the things that are shaken as things that have been made, so that what is not shaken may remain" (12:27b). Again, the warning corresponds quite directly to the first chapter, where the Son's throne is referred to as eternal, unending, and unchanging (1:8, 12), but the created order is said to be destined for destruction (1:10), is in the process of being made old (1:11), and is being rolled up like a garment (1:12).

Second, the author makes the important claim that his audience has now come to "Mount Zion, the city of the living God, the heavenly Jerusalem"

(Σιὼν ὄρει καὶ πόλει θεοῦ ζῶντος, Ἰερουσαλὴμ ἐπουρανίῳ, 12:22a). The mention of Mount Zion evokes the royal Davidic dynasty and kingdom, perhaps most emphatically associated with such texts as 2 Samuel 7, Psalms 2, 89, and 110—all of which appear in some sense in Hebrews 1:5–14 in order to portray the Son's entrance into his heavenly kingdom and reign (respectively: Heb 1:5b, 5a, 6a, and 13b).[48] The author's key move here, a move common to early Christian exegesis, is to associate the fulfillment of these promises, namely, of an everlasting royal Davidic kingdom associated with God's kingly rule, with Jesus Christ's resurrection and exaltation.[49] This "city of the living God" (12.22) which is "the heavenly Jerusalem" is the goal of the pilgrimage of both the ancients and the audience.[50] The former, we are told, made no remembrance of their earthly homeland, for they were looking for the better heavenly city which God had prepared for them (11:14–16). The same goal is held out for the audience, as we will see later, as they run toward the exalted Son (12:1–2).

Third, the occurrence of the phrase "the assembly of firstborn sons enrolled in the heavens" (ἐκκλησίᾳ πρωτοτόκων ἀπογεγραμμένων ἐν οὐρανοῖς, 12:23) should also remind the audience of the mention of Jesus in 1:6 as "the firstborn Son" (τὸν πρωτότοκον). What is remarkable here is that the author begins his composition with the depiction of the royal firstborn Son's entrance into the heavenly world and concludes it with the claim that heaven is now enrolled or registered with firstborn sons. Somehow humanity inherits the role and title of firstborn children of God from the firstborn Son of God.[51] Thus, the author sets forth the Son of God's exaltation and heavenly enthronement (depicted in 1:5–14) as the foundation and cause for the entrance of many more sons into the heavenly Jerusalem (12:18–24). Finally, note that these firstborn sons in heaven are referred to as "spirits of the righteous ones perfected" (πνεύμασιν δικαίων τετελειωμένων, 12:23b). This final occurrence of "perfection" language indicates that humanity has now fully attained the promise for which it was created, and proleptically indicates the goal of humanity.[52] Whatever the precise connotations of "perfection" in Hebrews, humanity's entry into God's heavenly presence where Christ has already gone (4:14; 6:19–20; 7:26; 8:1) is surely essential to our understanding.

48. This point is noted by Johnson, *Hebrews*, 330–31.

49. On which, see Donald Juel, *Messianic Exegesis: Christological Interpretation of the Old Testament in Early Christianity* (Philadelphia: Fortress, 1988), 59–88, 135–50.

50. On the heavenly Jerusalem, see Gal 4:22–31; Rev 21:1–22:5; 4 Ezra 7:26; 8:52; 10:26–27; 13:36; 2 Bar. 4:1–7; 1 En. 14:8–25.

51. Attridge, *Hebrews*, 375; deSilva, *Perseverance in Gratitude*, 467.

52. Johnson, *Hebrews*, 332–33; Schenk, *Cosmology and Eschatology*, 179.

1 PETER

The Epistle of 1 Peter is addressed to gentile believers in Jesus who have abandoned the worship of their native cults and gods, a situation 1 Peter describes as their "foolish lifestyle passed down from their ancestors" (1:18).[53] This abandonment of their former gods and lifestyle and turn to the God of Israel and Messiah Jesus has led to a social situation of hostility and rejection from their neighbors, family, and former friends—hence, Peter's important description of them as sojourners, strangers, and people of the diaspora (1:1; 2:11).[54] One of the author's primary goals is to encourage and strengthen his audience's fidelity to God and the Messiah in the midst of their suffering, lest they turn back to their former pagan worship and practices. To this end, the author employs a consistent strategy of mapping their identity and experiences upon that of the Messiah who faithfully suffered in his obedience to God and endured the shame of rejection before he entered into a glorious victory and enthronement to the right hand of the Father. This is one way, among others, that the author transforms his audience's social experiences of shame and dishonor before humans into honor and privilege before God.[55] The eschatology of 1 Peter is decidedly oriented toward the future in that it calls the audience to recognize that they are participating in the destiny of the Messiah—sharing in the sufferings of the Messiah *now* and sharing in the glory and honor of their resurrection with the Messiah *later*.[56] The letter contains a rich Christology and a significant (though often underappreciated) articulation of the audience's participation in the Messiah. The author refers to Jesus as Χριστός twenty-two times, and while we lack a reference to the Messiah's Davidic descent or sonship (as seen, e.g., in Rom 1:3–4; 2 Tim 2:8), the author's use of messianic motifs and scenarios such as the Messiah's death and resurrection, the Messiah as a temple builder, the identification between the Messiah and his followers, and the Messiah's enthronement and victory over the powers, suggests Peter's

---

53. While it is disputed, I agree with the majority of scholars, who see the audience of 1 Peter as consisting of gentiles (see, for example, 1:14, 18; 2:9–10; 3:6).

54. On the diasporic identity of the audience of 1 Peter, see Shively T. J. Smith, *Strangers to Family: Diaspora and 1 Peter's Invention of God's Household* (Waco, TX: Baylor University Press, 2016).

55. See especially John H. Elliott, "Disgraced Yet Graced: The Gospel according to 1 Peter in the Key of Honor and Shame," *BTB* 25 (1995): 166–78.

56. This is not to deny the presence of realized eschatology in 1 Peter, only to note that the author's conception of the salvation of his audience is primarily oriented toward the future return of the Messiah (e.g., 1:3–9).

Christology is a further example of early Christian reflection upon Jesus as the Messiah.[57] Given that 1 Peter draws upon a variety of early Christian traditions, many of which we have seen already in our study, our examination of 1 Peter's messianism can be brief.[58]

The Suffering, Resurrection, and Victory of the Messiah

In an attempt to encourage the audience of his letter as honored recipients of God's climactic revelatory activity, the author states that long ago Israel's prophets had engaged in diligent inquiries and searches as to the timing and person that "the Spirit of the Messiah (τὸ . . . πνεῦμα Χριστοῦ) within them was testifying to in advance regarding the sufferings destined for the Messiah and the glories that would follow (τὰ εἰς Χριστὸν παθήματα καὶ τὰς μετὰ ταῦτα δόξας)" (1:11).[59] We have seen repeatedly throughout our study that God's Spirit is associated intimately with the Davidic messianic king and often proceeds from the resurrected and enthroned Messiah (e.g., Isa 11:2–4; and note the allusion to Isa 11:2 in 1 Pet 4:14). Here it is remarkable that Peter can speak of Israel's prophets anticipating the coming of Jesus by means of the revelatory work of the "Spirit of the Messiah." There is much that is fascinating and challenging within the author's argument in 1:10–12 regarding the role of these prophets, but his primary agenda is to exalt the recipients of his letter by reminding them that, despite their inability to see Jesus with their own eyes (1:8), the Messiah's coming has placed them in a privileged position within salvation history, even one that "angels desire to examine" (1:12b). The reference here to prophets testifying in advance about a Messiah who suffers and then experiences glories (i.e., resurrection/exaltation) is one that we have seen throughout our study, perhaps most clearly in the words of the risen Jesus in Luke 24:25–26, 44–49. Thus, 1 Peter operates with a traditional early Christian understanding of the pattern or narrative of the Messiah. One sees it again, for example, in 1 Peter 1:21, where the author speaks of God as "the one who raised Christ (Χριστοῦ, 1:19) from the dead and gave glory to him" (τὸν ἐγείραντα

57. See Westfall, "Messianic Themes of Temple," 222–24.

58. See, for example, David G. Horrell, "The Product of a Petrine Circle? A Reassessment of the Origin and Character of 1 Peter," *JSNT* 86 (2002): 29–60.

59. On 1 Peter's belief that the Christ, by means of the Spirit, was present with the Old Testament prophets and its implications for the letter's appropriation of Israel's Scriptures, see Paul J. Achtemeier, "Suffering Servant and Suffering Christ in 1 Peter," in *The Future of Christology: Essays in Honor of Leander E. Keck*, ed. Abraham J. Malherbe and Wayne A. Meeks (Minneapolis: Fortress, 1993), 176–88.

αὐτὸν ἐκ νεκρῶν καὶ δόξαν αὐτῷ δόντα). One sees the pattern in Peter's reference to Christ as one who was "rejected by humans, on the one hand, but on the other hand is chosen and precious in the sight of God" (ὑπὸ ἀνθρώπον μὲν ἀποδεδοκιμασμένον, παρὰ δὲ θεῷ ἐκλεκτὸν ἔντιμον, 2:4). Whatever one makes of the challenging description of Christ preaching to the spirits in prison and the reference to the flood of Noah (3:18–19), it is also clear that Peter frames these verses with the pattern of the Messiah's sufferings (3:18) and Messiah's resurrection and victorious heavenly enthronement (3:21b–22).

Can we discern more specifically which prophetic texts from Israel's Scriptures testify to this pattern of a suffering and then glorified Messiah? Peter's first direct reference to the Messiah and Israel's Scriptures is in 2:4–10 where he applies three biblical "stone" texts, namely, Isaiah 28:16, Psalm 118:22, and Isaiah 8:14, to "Messiah Jesus" (1 Pet 2:5b).[60] We have seen the importance of the royal Psalm 118 in the Synoptic Gospels, where Jesus himself is presented as drawing upon Psalm 118 to describe his entrance into Jerusalem as the messianic king who will be rejected by Israel's leaders but vindicated by God (e.g., Luke 13:31–35; 19:28–44; 20:8–18; Acts 4:4–12). Along with Psalm 118, Isaiah 8:14 also addresses the house of David (see Isa 7–9), and Isaiah 28:16 activates Davidic echoes with its reference to Zion. The author's description of Christ as the "*living* stone" (2:4) and one who is "chosen and precious in the sight of God" (2:4b, 6b) further enacts the messianic scenario of the Christ's resurrection. Further, we have already had occasion to note the frequent association between the Messiah and the temple, sometimes even portraying the messianic king as the eschatological temple builder (e.g., 2 Sam 7:12–14; Zech 6:12–13; 1 En. 90:28–29; Pss. Sol. 17). Peter's portrayal of the Messiah as the foundation stone of the eschatological, spiritual temple may represent his creative expansion of this early Christian tradition (e.g., Mark 11–12; John 14:1–4; Eph 1:20–23; 2:19–22).

We see, secondly, that Peter systematically applies Isaiah 53 to the narrative of the Messiah as the innocent and righteous one who was rejected, suffered, and died on the cross in order to save his people (1 Pet 2:21–25).[61] Whether Isaiah 53 should be understood within its original context as a royal messianic text is disputed, though it seems clear that the Isaianic servant functions as a

---

60. See further Sue Woan, "The Psalms in 1 Peter," in *The Psalms in the New Testament*, ed. Steve Moyise and M. J. J. Menken, The New Testament and the Scriptures of Israel. (London: T&T Clark, 2004), 215–19.

61. On the importance of Isaiah 53 and the Isaianic Servant for 1 Peter, see Patrick Egan, *Ecclesiology and the Scriptural Narrative of 1 Peter* (Eugene, OR: Pickwick, 2016).

representative or symbolic embodiment of Israel.[62] And the servant of Isaiah 53 is connected to an eschatological Davidic hope in Isaiah 55:3: "I will make an eternal covenant with you, my faithful love promised to David" (cf. Acts 13:34b).[63] Here we can simply note that Peter refers to the subject of Isaiah 53 as the Messiah: "For you have been called for this purpose, because even the Messiah suffered for you" (ὅτι καὶ Χριστὸς ἔπαθεν ὑπὲρ ὑμῶν, 1 Pet 2:21a). The Messiah followed the prophetic scriptural precedent in not responding with threats and treachery to his enemies (Isa 53:9 in 1 Pet 2:22), in bearing his peoples' sins in his body on the cross (Isa 53:4, 12 in 1 Pet 2:24a), in providing healing for his people by means of his wounds (Isa 53:5 in 1 Pet 2:24b), and in rescuing his lost sheep who had wandered astray (Isa 53:6 in 1 Pet 2:25). Peter's reading of Isaiah 53 as a messianic text enables him to highlight both the way in which the Messiah's representative and substitutionary death saves his people and the way in which Peter is able to uphold the Messiah's faithfulness in the midst of suffering as an example to imitate for his audience.[64] Finally, we see that in 3:18-22 Peter again refers to "the Messiah [who] once for all suffered for sins" (3:18a), speaks of God's salvation as taking place "by means of the resurrection of Jesus Christ" (3:21b), and then refers to the resurrected Messiah as the one "who has gone into heaven at the right hand of God, with the angels, the authorities, and the powers in submission to him" (ὅς ἐστιν ἐν δεξιᾷ τοῦ θεοῦ πορευθεὶς εἰς οὐρανὸν ὑποταγέντων αὐτῷ ἀγγέλων καὶ ἐξουσιῶν καὶ δυνάμεων, 3:22). Attentive readers will have no trouble recognizing Peter's association of Psalm 110:1 and Psalm 8:4-6 in speaking of the Messiah's resurrection and ascension into heaven together with his victory over the cosmic powers.[65] Similar uses of Psalm 110:1 ("the right hand of God") and Psalm

62. On the complexities of Isa 53 and its tradition history, see Bernd Janowski and Peter Stuhlmacher, eds., *The Suffering Servant: Isaiah 53 in Jewish and Christian Sources* (Grand Rapids: Eerdmans, 2004).

63. On the Isaianic Servant's association with Davidic kingship language, see Daniel I. Block, "My Servant David: Ancient Israel's Vision of the Messiah," in *Israel's Messiah in the Bible and the Dead Sea Scrolls*, ed. Richard S. Hess and M. Daniel Carroll (Grand Rapids: Baker Academic, 2003), 36-49.

64. This is stated nicely by Grant Macaskill, *Union with Christ in the New Testament* (Oxford: Oxford University press, 2013), 276: "The messianic dimension of Isaiah 53 is important: it allows Peter to identify the representative role of the Messiah within the covenant, but his language suggests a participation in his death that is more than formal, indicating the destruction of one reality and the beginning of another."

65. For a helpful study of the relationship between the Messiah's resurrection and its relationship to the difficult statements in 3:19-21, see Cynthia Long Westfall, "The Relationship between the Resurrection, the Proclamation to the Spirits in Prison, and Baptismal Regen-

8:4–6 ("submission/subjection") are common to Hebrews 1–2; Romans 8:34; 1 Corinthians 15:25–27; and Ephesians 1:20–23, all of which draw upon these texts to speak of the cosmic authority and power of the victorious messianic king enthroned in heaven.[66]

Participating in the Messiah's Sufferings and Glories

One of the primary ways the author speaks of God's accomplishment of the audience's salvation is by their participation in the messianic narrative of faithfulness in the midst of suffering and steadfast hope in the resurrection when Christ returns in glory. While many have recognized Peter's obvious call to his audience to imitate Christ, only recently have more scholars recognized that the call to imitate is grounded in the author's portrayal of his audience's union with Christ, that is, their participation in the Messiah's sufferings and glory.[67]

This suffering/glory dynamic is articulated immediately in 1 Peter 1:3–7, where the author blesses God for accomplishing the audience's "new birth into a living hope" (ἀναγεννήσας ἡμᾶς εἰς ἐλπίδα ζῶσαν, 1:3). This *living* hope is grounded in God's act of resurrecting the Messiah from the dead. In particular, it is the Messiah's resurrection (δι' ἀναστάσεως Ἰησοῦ Χριστοῦ, 1:3) that provides the audience with confidence that they have a "pure, enduring, and imperishable inheritance which is being protected for you in heaven" (1:4). While the audience has experienced this new birth now, the author sees the Messiah's resurrection as the ground for the audience's hope in a future salvation, that is, a "salvation ready to be revealed in the last day" (1:5b). This provides the motivation for the audience *now* to continue to direct their loyalty and love to Jesus even in the midst of challenges and sufferings (1:6–8). But Peter speaks also of the risen Messiah as the agent who secures the audience's eschatological inheritance. For example, in 1:20b–21, Peter states: "This was done for you, who through Christ (δι' αὐτοῦ) are faithful to the God who

---

eration: 1 Peter 3:19–22," in *Resurrection*, ed. Stanley E. Porter et al., JSNTSup 186 (Sheffield: Sheffield Academic Press, 1999), 106–35; see also Macaskill, *Union with Christ*, 277–78.

66. On which, see Martin Hengel, *Between Jesus and Paul: Studies in the Earliest History of Christianity*, trans. John Bowden (Philadelphia: Fortress, 1983), 85–88; Lidija Novakovic, *Raised from the Dead according to Scripture: The Role of Israel's Scripture in the Early Christian Interpretations of Jesus' Resurrection*, Jewish and Christian Texts Series 12 (London: T&T Clark, 2012), 159–60.

67. See here especially Sean Christensen, "Reborn Participants in Christ: Recovering the Importance of Union with Christ in 1 Peter," *JETS* 61 (2018): 339–54.

raised him from the dead and gave glory to him (τὸν ἐγείραντα αὐτὸν εκ νεκρῶν καὶ δόξαν αὐτῷ δόντα), so that your faith and hope might be in God." The prepositional phrase indicates that in some way the risen Messiah is the agent or mediator who works to secure his peoples' faithfulness to God. And, again, we see that God is defined as the one who resurrects the Messiah from the dead, and it is this activity that functions as the object of hope for the audience. Peter shares the early Christian belief that God's resurrection of the Messiah is his enthronement to a position of cosmic rule and authority. Thus, after Christ had suffered, he "was put to death in the flesh, and he was made alive in the Spirit (θανατωθεὶς μὲν σαρκὶ, ζῳοποιηθεὶς δὲ πνεύματι, 3:18b; cf. 1 Tim 3:16). Likewise, one sees that Peter can speak of his audience as "living stones" who are coming to *the* "living stone" and a "spiritual house" precisely because their identity and worship are derivative from the resurrected ministry of Christ who is at the right hand of God (2:4–5) The author's application of this cultic imagery to his audience derives from the identity and location of the exalted Christ who reigns at God's right hand.[68] Peter speaks of the community as a "holy priesthood" and in 2:9 as a "royal priesthood," who "offer spiritual sacrifices which are accepted to God *through Jesus Christ*" (2:5b) who is the one now located at God's right hand in heaven (3:22).

We will not explore the extraordinarily difficult statements about Christ's preaching to the imprisoned spirits except to note that Peter depicts Christ here as a cosmic judge whose death to sin and powerful enthronement qualifies him to function as such (also 4:1, 5–6). At any rate, Peter's claim that Jesus was "put to death in the flesh, and made alive in the Spirit" (3:18) is not unlike Paul's articulation of the gospel in Romans 1:3–4, where Christ is spoken of as the Son of David according to the flesh, and the risen, enthroned, and powerful Son of God according to the Spirit. The Messiah's powerful resurrection life in the Spirit is the ground for Peter's argument that it is "by means of the resurrection of Jesus Christ" (3:21b) that the audience is assured of their salvation. As with 1:3, so here Peter emphasizes "the participation of the believer in the resurrection of Christ as a basis for salvation."[69] In fact, the audience's present (already) participation in the Messiah's resurrection is the logic that undergirds Peter's vivid description of the community as a spiritual temple. Christ is the rejected, but now vindicated, *living* cornerstone (λίθον ζῶντα,

---

68. I have learned much here from Max Botner, "You are a Spiritual House: Misunderstanding a Metaphor and the Question of Supersessionism in 1 Peter" (unpublished manuscript, 2019).

69. Christensen, "Reborn Participants in Christ," 345.

2:4) of the temple upon which the Christians are built as "living stones" (λίθοι ζῶντες, 2:5).[70] That their current honorable status before God is anticipatory of their eschatological sharing in Christ's resurrection life is seen in Peter's earlier claim that his audience has a "living hope through the resurrection of Jesus Christ from the dead" (1:3b). Both the Messiah and his people are living stones, rejected by unbelievers but precious and chosen in the sight of God. Grant Macaskill rightly notes that "these images are participatory in nature: the church shares in both the status and privileges of the Messiah, but also in his experience of suffering."[71]

Peter's belief that the Messiah must suffer (and has suffered already) and that this sets the pattern for the Messiah's people is seen clearly in 1 Peter 4:12–5:1.[72] The audience of the epistle should not be surprised at trials and fiery ordeals that come upon them (4:12), but instead they should "rejoice, just as you share in the Messiah's sufferings (κοινωνεῖτε τοῖς παθήμασιν), so that you may also have incredible joy at the revelation of his glory" (4:13). Peter's use of the term κοινωνέω suggests more than just analogical similarity between the Messiah's experiences and theirs, but rather, as Macaskill states, "consciousness of participation in a foundational event that gives significance and moral shape to the believer's own experience of suffering."[73] Peter further encourages his audience by noting that their faithful suffering, particularly when they are "reviled because of the name of the Messiah" (εἰ ὀνειδίζεσθε ἐν ὀνόματι Χριστοῦ, 4:14a), is a demonstration that "the Spirit of glory and Spirit of God rests upon you" (4:14b). Peter here alludes to the messianic oracle of Isaiah 11, where Isaiah anticipates a coming Davidic king who will accomplish justice and righteousness for God's people with the help of "the Lord's Spirit [who] will rest on him" (Isa 11:2a). In a context marked by explicit references to Jesus as the Messiah (4:13, 14a, 16a), this messianic allusion to Isaiah 11 should be read in light of 1 Peter 1:10–12 and Peter's claim that "the Spirit of the Messiah" was testifying ahead of time about the coming sufferings and later glories that were destined for the Messiah. While Peter does not expand upon this in detail, there is clearly a present aspect to the audience's participation

70. So Christensen, "Reborn Participants in Christ," 352.

71. Macaskill, *Union with Christ*, 160.

72. That the sufferings of the Messiah and his people should be understood within the apocalyptic framework and motif of "the messianic woes/tribulation" has been argued effectively by Mark Dubis, *Messianic Woes in 1 Peter: Suffering and Eschatology in 1 Peter 4:12–19*, StBibLit 33 (New York: Lang, 2002). Peter's argument that believers share in Christ's sufferings is shared with Paul's letters as well (e.g., Rom 8:16–17; Phil 3:10–11; Col 1:24).

73. Macaskill, *Union with Christ*, 279.

in the glories of the Messiah granted by means of sharing the same Spirit of the Messiah.[74] Peter's audience is encouraged that they too, like the Messiah, have the Spirit of God resting upon them if they faithfully suffer in obedience to Christ.[75]

But this encouragement and joy in the face of suffering stems not only from a recognition that they are sharing in the sufferings of the Messiah; it is also dependent upon a recognition that they will have incredible joy at the revelation of the Messiah's glory (4:13b). This is why Peter exhorts them to be unashamed if they suffer "as a Christian"—perhaps better, "as a Messianist" (ὡς Χριστιανός, 4:16).[76] Almost certainly, the term Χριστιανός is a slur coined by outsiders who are hostile to Peter's audience (cf. Acts 11:26), but Peter instead reverses the shame and stigma, calling his audience to "give glory to God as you bear this name" (δοξαζέτω δὲ τὸν θεὸν ἐν τῷ ὀνόματι τούτῳ, 4:16b).[77] This is a restatement of Peter's encouragement in 4:14 that they are blessed if they suffer because of "the name of the Messiah" and not from one's bad behavior (e.g., 2:18–20; 4:15). Following in the steps of the Messiah will involve a non-violent, nonretaliatory response (2:21–25). This is what it means, for Peter, to rightly and honorably bear the name of the Messiah, or Christian.[78] Peter himself grounds his exhortation to the elders in his identity as one who is "a witness of the Messiah's sufferings (τῶν τοῦ Χριστοῦ παθημάτων) and a participant (κοινωνός) in the glory that is about to be revealed" (5:1b).[79] To this end, Peter connects his "participation" in these future glories with his audience's identity as those who are "in Christ" when he draws his letter to a close with a promise that "the God of grace who has called you into his eternal glory in the Messiah (ἐν Χριστῷ) will, after you have suffered for a little while, restore, establish, strengthen, and ground you" (5:10). The language and theology is clearly reminiscent of Paul's participatory soteriology, which grounds humanity's identity and salvation in the narrative pattern of the Messiah.

74. Christensen, "Reborn Participants in Christ," 349.

75. This is stated nicely by Karen Jobes, 1 Peter, BECNT (Grand Rapids: Baker Academic, 2005), 288.

76. See the excellent discussion here by David G. Horrell, "The Label Χριστιανός: 1 Peter 4:16 and the Formation of Christian Identity," JBL 126 (2007): 361–81.

77. I am reading this as the original reading instead of μέρει. See further, Horrell, "The Label Χριστιανός," 368.

78. Horrell, "The Label Χριστιανός," 380, states that "the author of 1 Peter insists that the label is no shame but instead a source of honor, even and especially when it leads to suffering, precisely because it represents a sharing in Christ's sufferings (4:13), a following in his footsteps."

79. See further Christensen, "Reborn Participants in Christ," 348–49.

A Short Note on the Epistle of James

The Epistle of James may appear to contain little to work with for evidence of a messianic Christology. After all, the letter only refers to Jesus as "Christ" on two occasions, and in contexts that do not clearly emphasize his messianic identity (Ἰησοῦ Χριστοῦ, 1:1; 2:1). Furthermore, many of the messianic scriptural texts, honorifics and designations, motifs, and scenarios which we have seen on display in other NT compositions are absent in James. And yet, there are at least two motifs which suggest that one important strand of James's letter is indeed indebted to Jewish messianism. First, Christ is depicted as an eschatological judge who will return to both vindicate his people and enact judgment against his enemies. Throughout the epistle, Jesus is the exalted κύριος who is able to answer prayer, heal, and especially return as ultimate judge (on Jesus as Lord, see 1:1; 2:1; 5:7–8, 14–15).[80] The motif is signaled immediately in James 1:1, where the audience is identified as "the twelve tribes who are in the Diaspora." The language of Messiah in connection with the twelve tribes of Israel calls to mind numerous Jewish messianic texts which anticipate a Davidic king ruling over Israel after the wicked enemies of God's people have been defeated and destroyed (e.g., 1QM; Pss. Sol. 17; 4 Ezra 12–13; also Acts 1:15–26).[81] And throughout the letter, James speaks of an eschatological promise for the righteous, who will be "exalted" and will receive "the crown of life" (James 1:9–12). These are the ones who are poor in the world but who have been divinely elected as "heirs of the kingdom promised to those who love [God]" (2:6). Alternatively, the wealthy wicked will face judgment and destruction since they oppress and persecute the righteous, give themselves over to pleasure and luxury, and defraud their laborers (e.g., 2:1–6; 5:1–6). The day of judgment will result in exaltation for the righteous poor and judgment for the wicked (4:9–10). Judgment will take place at the "coming of the Lord" (ἕως τῆς παρουσίας τοῦ κυρίου, 5:7a; ἡ παρουσία τοῦ κυρίου ἤγγικεν, 5:8b)—a clear reference to Christ's eschatological return for vindication and judgment (see also 2:12–13; 4:11–12).[82] The reference to the righteous judge "standing at the door" (James 5:9) almost certainly alludes to remembrances of Jesus's

---

80. See especially Richard Bauckham, "Messianic Jewish Identity in James," in *Muted Voices of the New Testament: Readings in the Catholic Epistles and Hebrews*, ed. Katherine M. Hockey, Madison N. Pierce, and Francis Watson, LNTS 587 (London T&T Clark, 2018), 101–20.

81. See here especially Matt Jackson-McCabe, "The Messiah Jesus in the Mythic World of James," *JBL* 122 (2003): 715–23.

82. Again, Jackson-McCabe, "The Messiah Jesus," 726–27.

eschatological forecasting of his own impending return as the Son of Man (Mark 13:26–29; Rev 3:20).

Second, James also refers to Leviticus 19:18 ("you shall love your neighbor as yourself") as the "royal law" (νόμον τελεῖτε βασιλικόν, Jas 2:8a) which his audience must "fulfill." Just as our study of Paul revealed the association between the law of the Messiah, Leviticus 19:18, and the teachings of Jesus (see again 1 Cor 8:1–11:1; Gal 5:13–6:2; Rom 13:8–15:13), so many of James's exhortations draw upon Jesus's sayings as interpretations of Leviticus 19 (e.g., on impartiality and not favoring the rich, see Lev 19:15 and Luke 6:20–26 in Jas 2:1–7).[83] The law of loving your neighbor is, as Luke Timothy Johnson notes, "characterized as βασιλικός . . . because it is the 'law of the kingdom' . . . first enunciated by Jesus (cf. Matt 19:19; 22:39; Mark 12:31; Luke 10:27; Rom 13:9; Gal 5:14)."[84] Those who obey this "royal law" are precisely those who are the "heirs of the kingdom" (κληρονόμους τῆς βασιλείας, 2:5). James's exhortation to receive "the implanted word (τὸν ἔμφυτον λόγον) which is able to save your souls" (1:21b) likely refers to divine enablement to embody the Torah within one's very being (cf. 1:25; 2:8).[85] Divine empowerment in obeying the Torah in combination with the theme of Jesus as the supreme teacher of the royal law (2:8–9) calls to mind, albeit more allusively, Paul's references to the law of Christ in Galatians 5:13–14, 6:2 and 1 Corinthians 9:21–22.

Conclusion

My study of Hebrews and 1 Peter has not argued that the depiction of Christ as the messianic king is the singular (or even most important) theme of these compositions. But both texts work out their broader argument and develop their so-called Christology in dependence upon common early Christian traditions regarding Jesus as the suffering and enthroned Davidic king. The high priestly Christology of Hebrews, for example, is worked out explicitly on the basis of the author's prior assumption that Jesus is the messianic king who has faithfully suffered in obedience to God and in solidarity with humanity and has entered into God's heavenly rule and power. If Psalm 110:1 speaks truth

---

83. I am deeply indebted here to Luke Timothy Johnson, "The Use of Leviticus 19 in the Letter of James," in *Brother of Jesus, Friend of God: Studies in the Letter of James* (Grand Rapids: Eerdmans, 2004), 123–35.

84. Johnson, "The Use of Leviticus 19," 134.

85. Interpretation of the short phrase is challenging. See further Scot McKnight, *The Letter of James*, NICNT (Grand Rapids: Eerdmans, 2011), 143–44.

about Christ's royal enthronement (e.g., Heb 1:13), then surely the author argues that Psalm 110:4 speaks truthfully with respect to the same person's high priestly role (throughout Heb 5:5–6; 7:1–28). The Christology of 1 Peter presents nothing that is truly surprising, but rather offers a Christology of Jesus as the faithful, suffering, enthroned, and victorious Messiah (1 Pet 1:10–12, 21; 2:21–25; 3:18–22). Both Hebrews and 1 Peter use the language of Χριστός in relation to messianic motifs and scenarios, depicting God's agent as faithful and obedient to God in the midst of suffering, the ruler over his people and firstborn among his siblings, the builder or foundation of the eschatological temple, and the resurrected and enthroned advocate for his people. Both texts continue to read Israel's Scriptures, particularly the Psalter, as providing evidence for the vocation and destiny of the Messiah. And both texts portray the Messiah and his people in the closest possible relationship with one another. Whether one speaks of this as union with Christ or participating in the Messiah's life, pattern, and destiny, both Hebrews and 1 Peter develop their soteriology by means of reflecting upon the messianic Son of God who both shares in God's sovereign lordship and accomplishes humanity's salvation as its ideal representative.

CHAPTER 9

Sharing in the Battle of the Triumphant Lamb

The Book of Revelation

At the center of John's Apocalypse is the question of power and authority. Who rules the world? What are the instruments or means whereby this rule is enforced? More specifically, the book centers upon a conflict between the rule of God and the Lamb versus the rule of Satan and his powers. This cosmic conflict is in the process of being played out as a contest among the churches in Roman Asia and centers upon whether the churches will give their worship and allegiance to the true rulers of the world or the idolatrous Roman imperial powers.[1] The Apocalypse communicates its message through a complex web of symbols which give the audience a transcendent hermeneutical lens for their own domestic and social situation.[2] John thereby creates an alternative vision which will help the churches—namely, Christ's kingdom—disentangle

---

1. There are many helpful studies which insightfully situated the Apocalypse within its Roman imperial context. See here, for example, Jörg Frey, "The Relevance of the Roman Imperial Cult for the Book of Revelation: Exegetical and Hermeneutical Reflections on the Relation between the Seven Letters and the Visionary Main Part of the Book," in *The New Testament and Early Christian Literature in Greco-Roman Context: Studies in Honor of David E. Aune*, ed. John Fotopoulos (Leiden: Brill, 2006), 231–55. At a more popular level, see for example, Elisabeth Schüssler Fiorenza, *Revelation: Vision of a Just World* (Minneapolis: Fortress, 1991); David A. deSilva, *Unholy Allegiances: Heeding Revelation's Warning* (Peabody, MA: Hendrickson, 2013).

2. My approach to the symbolism in the Apocalypse is in line with the methodological discussions in G. K. Beale, *The Book of Revelation*, NIGTC (Grand Rapids: Eerdmans, 1999), 50–69; Richard Bauckham, *The Theology of the Book of Revelation* (Cambridge: Cambridge University Press, 1993), 17–22. At a more popular level, also helpful is Justin Jeffcoat Schedtler, "The Beast or the Lamb in the Apocalypse to John: Will the Real Emperor Please Stand Up?" in *Apocalypses in Context: Apocalyptic Currents through History*, ed. Kelly J. Murphy and Justin Jeffcoat Schedtler (Minneapolis: Fortress, 2016), 143–60.

themselves and their allegiances from the corrupting influence of the Roman imperial power, economics, and cult and strengthen their exclusive allegiance to God and the Lamb.[3]

Foremost among John's symbols and images are those associated with imperial power and authority, but John engages in a reading of Jewish messianic scriptures and traditions as a means of countering standard imperial notions of power, rule, and authority. More specifically, I will argue that John engages in a creative exegesis of Jewish messianic scriptural texts and images in light of his understanding of Jesus of Nazareth's soteriological narrative of suffering, death, resurrection, and heavenly enthronement. Foremost among these messianic oracles, psalms, and images are Genesis 49:8–12; Numbers 24:17; Isaiah 11:1–10; Psalm 2; Psalm 89; and Psalm 110. Thus, John does not so much reject traditional Jewish messianic expectations of a conquering Davidic ruler who would establish God's kingdom; rather, he engages in a powerful and creative appropriation of kingship, rule, means or weapons of warfare, and sovereign authority in light of the death, resurrection, and enthronement of Jesus Christ. In what follows I will: (1) note the programmatic role of messianism and kingship for the Christology of Revelation (esp. in Rev 1), after which (2) I will take an extended look at the way in which the hymns and worship of Christ flow from the recognition that he is the singular anointed king who reigns with God (Rev 4–5), as well as (3) the significance of the theme of the messianic war and battle which pervades both the Christology and vision of salvation in Revelation.

Messiah and Kingship in Revelation 1

Of all the writings in the New Testament, it is the book of Revelation that is most dominated by political, martial, and royal imagery. Jesus is referred to frequently as king, lord, and messiah. Antagonists to his kingship and rule are referred to as "the kings of the earth." The call to conquer or be victorious is the consistent exhortation given by the risen Jesus to the seven churches in chapters 2 and 3, and this makes good sense in light of the author's frequent use of warfare as a means of expressing cosmic conflict. John's primary conceptualization of the audience of the Apocalypse is that they are Christ's kingdom

3. This is stated well by Gregory M. Barnhill, "Seeing Christ through Hearing the Apocalypse: An Exploration of John's Use of *Ekphrasis* in Revelation 1 and 19," *JSNT* 39 (2017): 236: "As poetic, apocalyptic rhetoric, Revelation seeks through apocalyptic visions to persuade its hearers to embrace both a critical distance from Roman imperial ideology as well as a commitment to the vision of Jesus as Lord over against the deceitful powers of Empire."

(βασιλεία, 1:5–6; 5:9–10). And most agree that Rome's imperial propaganda is (at least part of) the focus of the author's critique (esp. in chapters 13, 17–18). Twice the author recounts songs of triumphant victory where the angels in heaven sing the praises of God and his anointed Messiah. In the next section we will examine the rhetorical function of John's messianic Christology as it pertains to the churches in Asia, but here we can simply note that John's Apocalypse has as its overarching goal the hope of encouraging followers of Jesus to remain loyal in their allegiance to Jesus by exposing the fleetingly temporal, idolatrous, and death-dealing nature of imperial power. Revelation 1 alerts us to three significant themes that will pervade our study of messianic kingship in Revelation.

Jesus Is the Davidic Messiah

A bedrock assumption of the Apocalypse is that Jesus is the Davidic Messiah. John refers to Jesus as Messiah on seven occasions (three times with the personal name Jesus, 1:1, 2, 5; four times as an honorific, 11:15; 12:10; 20:4, 6). In the latter references, the titular use of Χριστός to refer to Jesus as God's anointed king is obvious: "The kingdom of the world has become the kingdom of our Lord and his Messiah (καὶ τοῦ χριστοῦ αὐτοῦ), and he will rule forever and ever" (11:15b); "Now the salvation and power and kingdom of our God and the authority of his Messiah (τοῦ χριστοῦ αὐτοῦ) have come" (12:10a). In Revelation 20:4 and 6 the author speaks of those who have suffered faithfully ruling "with the Messiah" in the millennial kingdom. To these four unambiguous references to Jesus as a kingly messiah should be added the descriptions of Jesus as "the Lion from the tribe of Judah" (5:5), "the Root of David" (5:5; 22:16), and "the one who has the key of David" (3:7). These Davidic messianic honorifics for Jesus Christ and John's messianic exegesis of Israel's Scriptures play a critical role in the construction of his Christology.[4] John also presents Jesus as the powerful one "like a Son of Man" (Rev 1:13a) described in Daniel 7 who shares God's throne and is endowed with the authority to procure the saints as the people of his kingdom (e.g., Rev 1:6–7, 13; cf. Dan 7:13, 27).[5] The

---

4. Throughout this chapter we will see John's messianic exegesis on full display in his reading and appropriation of Gen 49:8–12; Num 24:17; Pss 2, 89, 110; and Isa 11.

5. On the messianic associations of the Danielic Son of Man in the Similitudes of Enoch, 4 Ezra, and 2 Bar., see John J. Collins, *The Scepter and the Star: The Messiahs of the Dead Sea Scrolls and Other Ancient Literature* (New York: Doubleday, 1995), 173–94. In Dan 7, 1 En. 37–71, and 4 Ezra the Son of Man is an anointed figure who takes on explicitly royal functions.

symbolism and scriptural traditions of "the one like a Son of Man" in Revelation 1:13–17 is multifaceted as John weaves together imagery, for example, from Daniel (Dan 7:9 and 10:6 in Rev 1:14–15a), Ezekiel (Ezek 1:24, 26 in Rev 1:13, 16a), and Isaiah (Isa 49:2 and 11:4 in Rev 1:16) to present Christ as God's singular eschatological judge.[6]

Messianic Exegesis—Psalm 89

We see in 1:1–8 how John engages in messianic exegesis of Israel's Scriptures and traditions, specifically with Psalm 89, to establish his messianic Christology. While the cluster of references in 1:1–8 to Ἰησοῦ Χριστοῦ may at first blush seem to speak of Χριστός as simply a second name, the context within which the references occur are dominated by allusions to Messiah Jesus's powerful kingship. The opening phrase "the revelation of Messiah Jesus" (Ἀποκάλυψις Ἰησοῦ Χριστοῦ) indicates that Jesus is both the agent and the object of the apocalypse.[7] John receives this revelation and is tasked with giving testimony to "the word of God and the testimony of Messiah Jesus (τὴν μαρτυρίαν Ἰησοῦ Χριστοῦ) which he has seen" (1:2b). And in 1:5 John's bestowal of grace and peace to the seven churches in Asia comes from "Messiah Jesus, the faithful witness, the firstborn from the dead, and the ruler over the kings of the earth" (καὶ ἀπὸ Ἰησοῦ Χριστοῦ, ὁ μάρτυς, ὁ πιστός, ὁ πρωτότοκος τῶν νεκρῶν καὶ ὁ ἄρχων τῶν βασιλέων τῆς γῆς, 1:5a). Psalm 89, a messianic psalm which takes up the promises and hopes of the Davidic covenant (2 Sam 7; 1 Chr 17), stands as the backdrop for each of these titles. The psalmist laments how exile and the absence of a king over Israel on David's throne seems to have thrown God's promises to David into question. He remembers God's election of David (89:20), his promises to defeat David's enemies (89:21–23), his gift of faithfulness and love (89:24–25), and his promise to exalt him high above every other rule: "I will set his hand on the sea. I will put his hand over the rivers. He will cry to me: 'You are my Father, my God and the helper for my salvation.' And so I will make him the firstborn, highly exalted above all the kings of the earth" (κἀγὼ πρωτότοκον θήσομαι αὐτόν, ὑψηλὸν παρὰ τοῖς βασιλεῦσιν τῆς γῆς 89:25–27). The psalmist expresses further confidence that God's faithful promises to give David an everlasting dynasty and throne will be "securely

6. See further Thomas B. Slater, *Christ and Community: A Socio-historical Study of the Christology of Revelation*, JSNTSup 178 (Sheffield: Sheffield Academic Press, 1999), 95–107.

7. There are good reasons for seeing this phrase as expressing *both* Jesus as the source/subject of the apocalypse and Jesus as the object of the book. See further Beale, *Revelation*, 183.

established, like the moon, forever; and a faithful witness (καὶ ὁ μάρτυς ἐν οὐρανῷ πιστός) in the heaven" (LXX Ps 88:38; 89:38).[8]

We will return to these titles for Jesus in due course, but here we can make two broad points about John's use of Psalm 89 in Revelation 1:5a. First, and most obviously, John's use of the language of Psalm 89 to speak of "Messiah Jesus" indicates in programmatic fashion that at least one plank of the author's Christology is a "Christianized" form of Jewish messianism.[9] Second, John reads Psalm 89 through the lens of the faithful suffering and obedience, death and resurrection, and royal enthronement of Jesus of Nazareth. John's description of Jesus as "the faithful witness" alludes to his faithful endurance and commitment to God and truth even in the face of persecution leading to suffering and death. Followers of Jesus are also often spoken of as holding fast to the truthful testimony of Jesus and enduring in the face of persecution and opposition, which will often lead to suffering and death for them (e.g., 11:3–10; 12:11, 17). John's designation of Jesus as God's "firstborn" highlights the intimacy and closest association between God and the Messiah. In Psalm 89 God gives the Davidic king the gift of sharing in God's rule over creation and declares that both the Father's and the Davidic king's thrones are founded upon God's faithful love (Ps 89:14, 28–29). God promises his Davidic ruler, as the most exalted of the kings of the earth, defeat of the enemies of his Messiah (Ps 89:22–23; cf. Ps 2:1–8). Thus, Jesus is "the ruler over the kingdoms of the earth" (1:5). Not unlike the rest of the witness of the NT writings, John sees both the Messiah's status as firstborn son and his current position of exalted and powerful ruler over "the kings of the earth" as originating from God's act of resurrecting Jesus from the dead. Thus, the powerful, regal, and priestly one like a "Son of Man," described in 1:13–17, declares: "I am the first and the last, and *the living one*. I was dead, but look! Now I am alive forever and ever. And I have the keys of death and Hades" (1:17b–18). As the resurrected and enthroned messianic king, Jesus is "Lord over lords and King over kings" (κύριος κυρίων ἐστὶν καὶ βασιλεὺς βασιλέων, 17:14; cf. 19:16) who secures God's eschatological triumph over the kings and rulers of the earth (e.g., 16:14; 19:19). Thus, the second point is stated well by Beale, who in commenting on the significance of Psalm 89 in

---

8. See Paul Spilsbury, "The Apocalypse," in *Redemption and Resistance: The Messianic Hopes of Jews and Christians in Antiquity*, ed. Markus Bockmuehl and James Carleton Paget (London: T&T Clark, 2007), 140.

9. See the comments on the relationship between Ps 89 and John's understanding of the death and resurrection of Jesus by Steve Moyise, "The Psalms in the Book of Revelation," in *The Psalms in the New Testament*, ed. Steve Moyise and Maarten J. J. Menken, The New Testament and the Scriptures of Israel (London: T&T Clark, 2004), 236–37.

Revelation 1:5 notes: "John views Jesus as the ideal Davidic king on an escalated eschatological level, whose death and resurrection have resulted in his eternal kingship and the kingship of his 'beloved' children."[10]

Worship and Divine Honors for Benefaction

Revelation is filled with hymns, acclamations, and songs of praise to God as well as to Christ (the Lamb), who is also frequently the recipient of worship and divine honors throughout the Apocalypse. We will see this in much more detail in the next section, but following upon the heels of John's reference to Jesus as "the firstborn from the dead and the ruler over the kings of the earth" is the acclamation or ascription of eternal glory and power to the messianic king (1:5b–6). Christ is praised for two reasons. First, this messianic king's sovereignty is manifested in his love and rescue of his subjects from their sins "by means of his blood" (1:5b). We will have good reasons to interpret the messianic king's sacrificial and loving death as his ultimate gift or benefaction for his people, and this elicits worship and praise of both God and Messiah Jesus. Second, the king's death is the ultimate grounds for the establishment of a people who are both "a kingdom (ἐποίησεν ἡμᾶς βασιλείαν), and priests to his God and Father" (1:6a; cf. Exod 19:5–6). It is not surprising to find kings securing their kingdoms through military warfare and violence, but procuring a kingdom and a people by means of one's bloody death is a surprising reversal of cultural expectations for royal power. The death of Jesus thereby establishes the churches of John's Apocalypse as his own kingdom and as "an alternative to the earthly rule of kings and emperors."[11] What it means that the Messiah's death has created a people who are kings and priests will be fleshed out in the following sections.

PRAISING THE CONQUERING SLAUGHTERED LAMB
IN REVELATION 4 AND 5

In his first heavenly vision, John receives an invitation to "come up here" into heaven, where he is able to see the heavenly throne room (4:1). The vision is dominated by the throne. The noun θρόνος is repeated fourteen times (4:2

10. Beale, *Revelation*, 191.

11. Steven J. Friesen, *Imperial Cults and the Apocalypse of John: Reading Revelation in the Ruins* (Oxford: Oxford University Press, 2001), 181.

[2X], 3, 4 [3X], 5 [2X], 6 [3X], 9, 10 [2X]). John sees that the one who is seated on the throne is the recipient of worship from twenty-four elders (4:4) and four living creatures (4:6b–8a; cf. Isa 6:1–3). The twenty-four elders wear "golden crowns on their head" (4:4), and the elders vacate their thrones and "throw down their crowns" when they worship the one seated on the throne (4:10). This performance functions as a powerful image of subordination and complete recognition that the one who is seated on the throne is singularly worthy of worship and honor.[12] The content of their praise and thanksgiving centers upon a recognition of God's perfect holiness and creative power: "Holy, holy, holy is the Lord God Almighty, who was and is and is to come" (4:8b); "You are worthy (ἄξιος εἶ), our Lord and God, to receive glory and honor and power, because you created all things, and by your will they exist and were created" (4:11). The literary form of the praise offered by the elders and living creatures are hymns or acclamations that were a prevalent form of communicating gratitude to emperors and rulers in the first century.[13] Thus, despite never mentioning explicitly Rome or its imperial propaganda, John's visions of heavenly worship in chapters 4–5 are motivated, in part (and as we will see in more detail), to powerfully critique Rome's imperial, economic, and militaristic pretenses.

God is praised here as a *worthy* benefactor, deserving of divine worship and gratitude; this is rooted in his power as the creator of all things. The vision presents a remarkable display of God's cosmic and transcendent power and holiness, and in itself presents a significant critique of Roman imperial propaganda which portrayed the emperors and their gods as divine benefactors. But there is nothing in Revelation 4 that could not have been written by a non-messianic Jewish apocalypse such as 4 Ezra, 2 Baruch, or 1 Enoch. What is surprising is that John's throne room vision does not conclude with the singular God of Israel receiving worship; rather, John sees a second figure receiving praise and thanksgiving from the twenty-four elders and living creatures (5:6, 8–9a). And, remarkably, he is praised in similar terms as the God of Israel and with three short hymns after he takes the unopened scroll.[14] It is worth setting out the three hymns in full:

12. On this, see Gregory M. Stevenson, "Conceptual Background to the Golden Crown Imagery in the Apocalypse of John (4:4, 10; 14:14)," *JBL* 114 (1995): 257–72, esp., 268–69.

13. See David Seal, "Shouting in the Apocalypse: The Influence of First-Century Acclamations on the Praise Utterances in Revelation 4:8 and 11," *JETS* 51 (2008): 350.

14. For an important evaluation of the role of the hymns in the Apocalypse, see Justin Jeffcoat Schedtler, *A Heavenly Chorus: The Dramatic Function of Revelation's Hymns*, WUNT 2.381 (Tübingen: Mohr Siebeck, 2014).

And they sang a new song, saying: "Worthy are you (ἄξιος εἶ) to take the scroll and open its seals, because you were slain and have purchased by your own blood for God people from every tribe and tongue and people and nation. And you have made them to be a kingdom and priests for our God and they will reign on the earth." (Rev 5:9–10)

Worthy is (ἄξιος ἐστιν) the slain Lamb to receive power and wealth and wisdom and strength and honor and glory and blessing. (Rev 5:12)

To the one seated on the throne and to the Lamb, blessing and honor and glory and strength forever and ever. (Rev 5:13)

The importance of these hymns for the entire argument of Revelation should not be underestimated, for they provide a critical lens for making sense of the book's Christology of a victorious king who establishes his kingdom of a worldwide people through his sacrificial death.

Worshipping the Lamb

First, it is a striking fact that the Lamb is a *second* figure, along with the transcendent divine figure on the throne in 4:2–13, who receives worship, praise, and acclamations alongside of and in the same way as the figure in chapter 4.[15] Both God in chapter 4 and the Lamb in chapter 5 receive "glory, honor, and power (τὴν δόξαν καὶ τὴν τιμὴν καὶ τὴν δύναμιν)"—terms often used to express gratitude in exchange for royal benefactions (4:11; cf. 5:12b; 5:13).[16] In addition to Revelation 4–5, the Lamb receives praise from the great crowd who "stand before the throne and before the Lamb, wearing white robes and holding palm branches in their hands. They cried out with a loud voice: 'Salvation to our God who sits on the throne and to the Lamb'" (7:9b–10). And in 15:1–4 John sees a group of victorious saints singing "the song of Moses, God's servant, and the song of the Lamb."

---

15. See especially Justin Jeffcoat Schedtler, "Praising Christ the King: Royal Discourse and Ideology in Revelation 5," *NovT* 60 (2018): 163; Richard Bauckham, *The Climax of Prophecy: Studies on the Book of Revelation* (London: T&T Clark, 1993), 137–38.

16. See Seal, "Shouting in the Apocalypse," 350.

THE MESSIANIC TESTIMONY OF THE NEW TESTAMENT

The Conquering Davidic King

But, second, while the content of the praise and thanksgiving offered to God and the Lamb are remarkably similar, the hymns speak of different reasons for their respective worthiness, rooting the Lamb's "worthiness" in the gift of his sacrificial death. Whereas God is "worthy" (4:11) to receive praise for his creation of all things, the Lamb's worthiness (5:9, 12) is due to his sacrificial act of voluntarily dying, thereby creating a royal and priestly people for God. The language of "you are worthy" evokes connotations of military generals and emperors who establish their kingdoms through successful military warfare. In fact, while there are a host of virtues that the good king was supposed to embody, the single most important one was military victory. J. Rufus Fears refers to this as "the theology of victory": "Conquest and expansion of his kingdom's frontiers were the duty of the true king, and the gods of the commonwealth aided his martial enterprises, leading his armed host into battle."[17] As the last part of Fears's comment states, the king was viewed as the vicegerent or agent of the gods and thus his conquest and military victory was in service to the gods and a tangible enactment of their gifts of peace and harmony to their people.[18]

Surprisingly, however, the Lamb's death is spoken of as a military victory. In the beginning verses of chapter 5 John sees "a scroll in the right hand of the one seated on the throne" (5:1). An angel shouts: "Who is *worthy* (τίς ἄξιος) to open the scroll and break its seals?" (5:2b). John weeps profusely when in all of heaven, earth, and under the earth "no one worthy (οὐδεὶς ἄξιος) was found to open the scroll or to look into it" (5:4). This has the function of preparing the reader to accept that whoever is able to open the scroll—he *alone* is worthy of worship. The martial imagery is evoked when one of the elders tells John to stop weeping: "Behold, the Lion from the tribe of Judah, the Root of David has conquered (ἰδοὺ ἐνίκησεν ὁ λέων ὁ ἐκ τῆς φυλῆς Ἰούδα, ἡ ῥίζα Δαυίδ) so that he can open the scroll and its seven seals" (5:5). The title "Lion of Judah" stems from the messianic oracle of Genesis 49:8–12 (specifically, Gen 49:9), which in itself is an oracle of poetic praise offered to a coming king who is worthy to receive royal honors for his worldwide dominion. In LXX Genesis 49:8–12, the poetic prophecy pertains to "the end of days" (49:1b) when a royal

---

17. J. Rufus Fears, "*PRINCEPS A DIIS ELECTUS: The Divine Election of the Emperor as Political Concept at Rome* (Rome: American Academy at Rome, 1977), 45–46.

18. I have written on this in more detail in my *Christ Is King: Paul's Royal Ideology* (Minneapolis: Fortress, 2015), 122–27.

descendant from Judah will receive the praise and obeisance of his eleven brothers and his own sons (49:8). He will be praised for his military victories and defeat of God's enemies, which will result in the deliverance of Israel and Eden-like peace and fertility for his kingdom (vv. 8, 9b, 11–12).[19] Throughout the OT the lion often functions as a symbol for a military hero or warrior (e.g., 2 Sam 17:10; Isa 31:4; 38:13; Ezek 19:1–6; 22:25–27).[20] The title "Root of David" comes from Isaiah 11:1–5 (specifically, Isa 11:1; cf. 11:10), where Isaiah forecasts a coming Davidic king who will be marked by the Spirit of God (Isa 11:2), will execute justice and righteousness for God's people (11:3–4a), and will "strike the violent with the rod of his mouth; by the breath of his lips he will kill the wicked" (11:4b). The oracle of Isaiah 11:1–10 was a significant text for Jewish messianic reflection upon a coming Spirit-empowered Davidic Messiah who would enact justice for God's people and judge/conquer the enemies of Israel (e.g., Pss. Sol. 17:21–47; 1 En. 48:10–49:4; 62:2; 1QSb 5:24; cf. Rom 15:9–12).[21] Thus, when John hears the angel's proclamation that the Lion of Judah, the Root of David, has conquered and been victorious, this would certainly activate expectations for a Jewish messianic king who will conquer, defeat, and destroy God's enemies. Richard Bauckham states the point clearly: "There seems little doubt that Revelation 5:5 strongly and deliberately evokes the image of the Messiah as a new David who wins a military victory over the enemies of Israel."[22]

The Sacrificial, Nonviolent Conquering King

Third, the image of a Davidic conquering warrior undergoes radical revision when John sees "a Lamb, standing as if it had been slain" (ἀρνίον ἑστηκὸς ὡς ἐσφαγμένον, Rev 5:6). The "slain Lamb" is probably a tensive symbol that functions to recall such sacrificial lambs like that of the Jewish Passover (Exod 12), the lamb led to the slaughter in Isaiah 53, and more broadly the lambs sacri-

---

19. On the messianic significance of Gen 49:8–12, see Joseph Blenkinsopp, "The Oracle of Judah and the Messianic Entry," *JBL* 80 (1961); 55–64; T. Desmond Alexander, "Messianic Ideology in Genesis," in *The Lord's Anointed: Interpretation of Old Testament Messianic Texts*, ed. Philip E. Satterthwaite et al. (Grand Rapids: Baker, 1995), 32–37; William Horbury, *Jewish Messianism and the Cult of Christ* (London: SCM, 1998), 127–32.

20. Loren L. Johns, *The Lamb Christology of the Apocalypse of John: An Investigation into Its Origins and Rhetorical Force*, WUNT 2.167 (Tübingen: Mohr Siebeck, 2003), 165.

21. See Matthew V. Novenson, *Christ among the Messiahs: Christ Language in Paul and Messiah Language in Ancient Judaism* (Oxford: Oxford University Press, 2012), 59–60.

22. Bauckham, *The Climax of Prophecy*, 215.

ficed under the cultic traditions and laws of the Torah (e.g., Exod 29:38–41; Num 28:1–10).[23] Jesus is the conquering, triumphant Davidic Messiah, but this military battle and act of conquering has taken place through the highly paradoxical sacrificial death of Jesus the slaughtered Lamb. Thus, the popular ancient Mediterranean kingship ideology, congruent with strands of Jewish messianism, which saw the legitimation of the king's rule in his powerful and violent act of military success, is subverted through Jesus's victory "by means of his blood" (5:9).[24] Davidic messianism is not rejected, but is rather reinterpreted such that conquest and kingdom come by way of the bloody sacrifice of the Lamb. This is obviously a remarkable redefinition of power and sovereignty. Again, Bauckham states the dynamic clearly: Jesus has "won a victory, but by sacrifice, not military conflict, and he has delivered God's people, but they are from all nations, not only Jews."[25] That the Messiah's death is an act of saving deliverance for the Jewish people *and* the nations is evident in that the hymns proclaim Jesus's death has purchased a people for God "from every tribe, tongue, people, and nation" (5:9b). The *death* of the messianic king—instead of the conventional notion of military success through violence—is the basis for Christ's purchase of a people for his βασιλεία (1:5–6; 5:9–10).

Hymns and Acclamations for the Messianic King

Fourth, the hymns offer evidence that the worship of Jesus is understood within the logic of divine honors in exchange for benefaction.[26] Composing and singing hymns for kings and rulers was a widespread practice throughout antiquity, and it was one important way people bestowed honors upon their rulers. These hymnic honors are given in response to the belief that the king is the visible agent of God (or the gods), who rules the world or their kingdom

23. See further Johns, *The Lamb Christology*, 108–49; Friesen, *Imperial Cults*, 198–200. Timo Eskola, *Messiah and the Throne: Jewish Merkabah Mysticism and Early Christian Exaltation Discourse*, WUNT 2.142 (Tübingen: Mohr Siebeck, 2001), 213–14, claims that it "is obvious that the Lamb appearing here is the apocalyptic ram" and that "the character of the Lamb expresses the idea of messianic kingship." He does not mention the fact that John refers to the Lamb as *slaughtered*, something the hymns emphasize as well (5:9, 12).

24. Similar subversive notions are found in Paul's declaration that Messiah Jesus has reconciled his enemies to himself and led them in a festal triumph by means of his blood and the cross (Col 1:20; 2:14–15). See Jipp, *Christ Is King*, 126–27.

25. Bauckham, *The Climax of Prophecy*, 215.

26. See here in more detail Ittai Gradel, *Emperor Worship and Roman Religion*, Oxford Classical Monographs (Oxford: Clarendon, 2002); S. R. F. Price, *Rituals and Power: The Roman Imperial Cult in Asia Minor* (Cambridge: Cambridge University Press, 1984).

and gives benefactions to his people. The praise is a way of giving divine honors to a ruler who has granted gifts to his subjects. The king is often portrayed as God's elected earthly representative who shares the divine throne and is, therefore, worthy of receiving divine praise, honors, and hymns. While this practice is extremely popular in Greek and Roman texts, one can find some evidence for it in Israel's Scriptures as well (Ps 44; cf. 1 Chr 29:20, 25).[27] I suggest, however, that the audience of Revelation, written as it is to the churches in Asia (Rev 1:4, 11), would have been deeply aware of this practice given the prevalence of hymns and acclamations offered to the Roman emperor. David Aune has adduced numerous parallels, in fact, between the worship practices in the throne room in Revelation 4–5 and the ceremonies of the Roman imperial cult, thereby suggesting that the former was a parody of the latter.[28] These include the hymns and acclamations, the presence of other royal figures wearing crowns and offering them to the king/emperor, a throne room with gold, and honorific titles which express or imply divinity. The effect of these parallels, which John has heightened and even given cosmic significance, suggests that "the sovereignty of God and the Lamb have been elevated so far above all pretensions and claims of earthly rulers that the latter, upon comparison, become only pale, even diabolical imitations of the transcendent majesty of the King of kings and Lord of lords."[29] Further, the refrain of the hymns that only the Lord God Almighty, along with the Lamb, are worthy of praise has as its "implicit claim that the Roman Emperor was *not* holy and was entirely *unworthy* to receive these honors."[30] This contrast between the rightful rule and worship of God and the Lamb over and against the imperial powers provides an important lens for the interpretation of the entire book.

For John, it is Jesus's sacrificial and saving death, his act of procuring a priestly and royal people for God (5:9–10), which justifies the bestowal of divine praise upon the Lamb, as he is the singular and unique vicegerent of God. Whereas praise to God is rooted in his holiness and creative activity (4:11), chapter 5 emphasizes that the Lamb's worthiness to receive praise (5:2, 4, 9, 11) is rooted in the giving of his own life unto death.[31] Whereas kings

27. I have presented the ancient texts recounting the hymnic praise of rulers in detail in Jipp, *Christ Is King*, 81–100; see also Jeffcoat Schedtler, "Praising Christ the King," 169–78.

28. David E. Aune, "The Influence of Roman Imperial Court Ceremonial on the Apocalypse of John," *Papers of the Chicago Society for Biblical Research* 28 (1983): 5–26.

29. Aune, "The Influence of Roman Imperial Court," 22.

30. Jeffcoat Schedtler, "The Beast or the Lamb," 151.

31. This is not to set up a false dichotomy between ontology and function. Christ's

and emperors were universally understood to receive their kingdoms through military violence, the Lion from the tribe of Judah, the Root of David, subverts this script as he acquires his kingdom and conquers through his bloody cross. The frequent acclamations, hymns, and songs that pervade the Apocalypse and are offered to the Messiah express the conviction that he alone is the divine agent of God who has offered his own life and blood as the singular *saving gift* that creates a new people as his kingdom.

SHARING IN THE LAMB'S TRIUMPHANT VICTORY AND MESSIANIC KINGDOM

We have seen that the Davidic messianic expectations for a successful military ruler to rescue his people and judge God's enemies are not repudiated but are instead taken up by John and reworked around the Messiah's death, resurrection, and royal enthronement. John's vision of the conquering, slain Lamb who has purchased a kingdom of people for himself by his own blood sets the pattern for how the Messiah's people emerge victorious in their battle against the powerful forces arrayed against them. In other words, the Apocalypse conceptualizes its audience as active participants in the messianic battle against Satan and his powers.

A Call to Conquer and a Promise to Share in the Rule of the Messiah—Revelation 2–3

The Lion-Lamb has already emerged victorious in this messianic war by his faithfulness unto death and his ensuing resurrection from the dead whereby he is now exalted as the true "ruler over the kings of the earth" (1:5b). Thus, Christ's present position as the powerful one "like a Son of Man" (cf. Dan 7:9–14) who rules, judges, and protects his churches is rooted in his identity as, in his own words, "the one who is living, I was dead and behold I am alive forever and I have the keys of death and Hades" (1:18).[32] This messianic Son of Man is the one who addresses his people in Revelation 2–3, the seven churches in Asia Minor, and exhorts them to engage in active participation in

---

preexistence is likely implied in the description of him as the Word of God in Rev 19:13 (cf. John 1:1–2, 14). So Jeffcoat Schedtler, "Praising Christ the King," 178–79.

32. See here G. K. Beale, *John's Use of the Old Testament in Revelation*, JSNTSup 166 (Sheffield: Sheffield Academic Press, 1998), 255–59.

his messianic battle. As those who belong to Christ's kingdom, they represent an "alternative sovereignty" to Roman imperial power and are called to resist its idolatry.[33] Let me summarize and synthesize the living Christ's exhortations and promises to his people.

First, in each of the seven letters, the Son of Man, that is the risen Christ, calls upon his people to "conquer" or "to be victorious" (ὁ νικῶν, 2:7, 11, 17, 26; 3:5, 12, 21).[34] The call to the churches to conquer draws upon the language of military warfare, but of course at play here is the same reworking of Davidic messianic symbolism evident in the depiction of Jesus as the Lion of the tribe of Judah, the Root of David who "conquered" (ἐνίκησεν, 5:5) by means of his bloody, sacrificial death (5:6). Thus, the churches are called to participate in the messianic war *in the same way* as their messianic king.

Second, this means that the churches are called to actively participate in the messianic war, not by taking up arms or engaging in violent rebellion, but simply through their endurance, obedience, commitment to the truth, and singular loyalty to God and the Messiah. For some of the churches, this call to participate in Christ's messianic battle is expressed through encouragement and for some (i.e., most) through repentance. For example, the risen Christ says to the church in Pergamum in response to the opposition they are receiving from imperial elites (aka "the throne of Satan"): "you have not denied your loyalty to me" (οὐκ ἠρνήσω τὴν πίστιν μου, 2:13; cf. also 2:19).[35] This statement interprets and expands upon Christ's affirmation that "you are holding fast to my name" (κρατεῖς τὸ ὄνομά μου, 2:13). A concrete example of holding fast to Jesus's name and not denying loyalty toward him is Antipas "my witness, my faithful one (ὁ μάρτυς μου ὁ πιστός), who was killed in your presence" (2:13b). The description of Antipas indicates that his identity and actions are rooted in and replicate the pattern of "Jesus Christ—the faithful witness" (1:5a; cf. 3:14).[36] Throughout the letters, the risen Christ exhorts his churches to pro-

33. Again, Friesen, *Imperial Cults*, 181.

34. For a helpful study of the letters in chapters 2–3, see John M. Court, *Myth and History in the Book of Revelation* (Atlanta: John Knox Press, 1979), 20–41.

35. I translate μου here as an objective genitive and τὴν πίστιν as "loyalty" given the emphasis in the context upon endurance, witness, and faithfulness in the face of opposition. See further the important work on the language of "faith" by Teresa Morgan, *Roman Faith and Christian Faith: Pistis and Fides in the Early Roman Empire and Early Churches* (Oxford: Oxford University Press, 2015), "That relationality is central to concepts whose foundational and most common meanings are trust, trustworthiness, and faithfulness, and among whose more specialized meanings are good faith, assurance, pledge, and anything that is entrusted, needs no demonstration" (444).

36. On πίστις language in Revelation as having the connotations of "loyalty, faithfulness,

vide the appropriate response to Christ's benefaction—namely, by continuing to demonstrate endurance and loyalty to Jesus (2:3, 19; 3:3, 9–10), to remain faithful in the face of persecution and suffering (2:10), and to hold fast to the truth by rejecting false teaching that would compromise their loyalty to Jesus (2:6, 9, 14–16, 20–24; 3:1, 17).[37]

Third, one of the primary promises Christ offers to his victorious people is sharing in his messianic kingdom. Some of these promises center upon the hope and expectation that Christ's royal people will participate in the garden-like city of the new Jerusalem. Thus, those who are victorious will "eat from the tree of life which is in God's paradise" (2:7); they will "not be harmed by the second death" (2:11); and they "will be pillars in the temple of my God," receiving "the name of my God and the name of the city of my God, the new Jerusalem that comes down out of heaven from my God. I will also write on them my own new name" (3:12). These promises anticipate the final vision, where the new Jerusalem from heaven is a paradise with both the water and tree of life, and draws deeply upon the garden of Eden and temple imagery (e.g., Rev 22:1–2). Here the ultimate fulfillment of God's promises to King David's descendants will come to pass as they inherit God's promises of divine presence, peace, and rule in the new creation as God "will be God to them, and [they] will be his son" (21:6b; cf. 2 Sam 7:14). Furthermore, these promises of sharing Christ's messianic rule in the new Jerusalem "invite the readers to participate in the eschatological war which is described in the central part of the book . . . and so gain their place in the new Jerusalem."[38]

Two of the promises, in particular, concern us here as they center upon sharing in Christ's messianic rule and authority. For example, to the church in Thyatira Christ makes this promise: "To the one who conquers and who keeps my works until the end, I will give to him authority over the nations and he will rule the nations with an iron rod and smash them like clay pottery—just as I received from my Father, so I will also give to him the morning star" (2:26–28). Somewhat surprisingly, Jesus reproduces an almost exact quotation of Psalm 2:9 (LXX) in verse 27, a psalm which in its original context speaks of God's gift of sovereign authority and rule over the nations *to the messianic son of God* (Ps 2:7). The heavenly vision of the cosmic battle between the woman and the

---

and sacrificial witness" see Nijay K. Gupta, *Paul and the Language of Faith* (Grand Rapids: Eerdmans, 2020), 92.

37. Non-material returns of thanksgiving and loyalty are often the appropriate response to the gifts of benefactors. Though he does not discuss the book of Revelation, see especially Thomas Blanton IV, *A Spiritual Economy: Gift Exchange in the Letters of Paul of Tarsus* (New Haven: Yale University Press, 2017).

38. Bauckham, *The Climax of Prophecy*, 213.

beast in Revelation 12 draws upon the messianic promise of Psalm 2:9 when it speaks of the woman's son, "who will rule all the nations with an iron rod" (Rev 12:5). Christ's second promise to give the church "the morning star" (τὸν ἀστέρα τὸν πρωινόν, 2:28b) is also rooted in Davidic messianism, as the image of the star draws upon LXX Numbers 24:15–20, where a coming messianic king is prophesied and is described as a "rising star" (Num 24:17) who will "destroy" the nations (24:18) and will receive the nations as his own "inheritance" (24:19; cf. Ps 2:8). That this promise is rooted in Jesus's Davidic messianic identity is further established by Jesus's self-description, which draws upon the messianic oracles of Numbers 24:17 and Isaiah 11:1–10: "I am the Root and descendant of David, the bright morning star" (Rev 22:16). Thus, Jesus's promise to give the church in Thyatira "the bright morning star" is almost certainly, as with the use of Psalm 2:9 in Revelation 2:27, another promise to the church of sharing in Christ's messianic rule.[39] Thus, the promise to the church of rule and authority over the rebellious kings and rulers of the earth is rooted in and derivative of what Christ himself has received from the Father (Rev 2:28a).

There is a participatory logic here that undergirds the Messiah's sharing of his benefits with the kingdom of his people which is also on display in Revelation 3:21. To the church in Laodicea, Christ gives the promise of sharing in his own rule and even sitting on his throne: "To the one who conquers I will give to him to sit with me on my throne, just as even I have conquered and I have taken my seat with my Father on his throne" (ὁ νικῶν δώσω αὐτῷ καθίσαι μετ' ἐμοῦ ἐν τῷ θρόνῳ μου, ὡς κἀγὼ ἐνίκησα καὶ ἐκάθισα μετὰ τοῦ πατρός μου ἐν τῷ θρόνῳ αὐτοῦ, Rev 3:21). There are a number of remarkable aspects of Christ's promise. First, it is already surprising to find the Davidic Messiah sharing God's throne as a result of his victory through his sacrificial death in 5:5–6, but here Christ's people are promised to actively share in Christ's rule by sitting on the Father's throne with the Christ. Second, similar to the author's application of Psalm 2:9 to Christ's *people* in Revelation 2:27, so here it would seem as though the author is extending the application of texts such as Psalm 110:1, which refer to God sharing his throne with his Davidic son, to *the people of the Messiah*.[40]

The Messiah's Army—Revelation 7:4–17

In our brief foray into Christ's letters to the seven churches, we have seen that the Messiah's people are called to an active engagement in this military battle, but it is not one of violent revolt and resistance; it is, rather, one that involves

39. See also, Beale, *Revelation*, 268–69.
40. See further Eskola, *Messiah and the Throne*, 211–12.

the rejection of false teaching, endurance, a commitment to truth, and loyalty to the one who sits on the throne and to the Lamb.[41] The letters have hinted that standing behind the deceptive false teaching and threats to compromise one's allegiance to Christ are Satan and his powers (e.g., 2:13).[42] As a means of exhorting the churches to continue in their loyalty to Jesus and resist the powerful but deceptive influence of Satan and his powers, John offers visions of the saints' role as the messianic army and other dramatis personae involved in the cosmic battle.

In Revelation 7 John has a vision where he hears that the number of the servants of God who have been sealed are 144,000 (Rev. 7:3-4).[43] Following in list form, then, is a military census whereby 12,000 people from each tribe of the children of Israel are gathered together (7:5-8). At the head of the list is "the tribe of Judah" (7:5a; cf. 5:5). The literary form of Revelation 7:4-8 is clear— this is a military census, not unlike what one finds in Israel's Scriptures and traditions (e.g., Num 1:1-3; 26:1-4; 1 Chr 27:1-15; 1QM 1:1-3). But they are also described repeatedly as "those who have been sealed" (τῶν ἐσφραγισμένων, 7:4a; also 7:3, 5, 8), indicating that they are divinely protected and that they belong to God (cf. Rev 14:1). But just as the first image of the "Lion of the tribe of Judah, the Root of David" (5:5) was reinterpreted by the image of the standing slain Lamb (5:6), so also the image of the 144,000 is reinterpreted by the vision of "the great crowd which no one is able to number, from every nation and tribe and people and tongue, standing before the throne and before the Lamb, clothed in white and with palm branches in their hands" (7:9). In other words, just as the slain Lamb's death purchased for God a people from "every tribe and tongue and people and nation" (5:9b), so here the Messiah's army is actually an innumerable multitude of people of every ethnicity and nation. The reference to their "white robes" indicates that they share in Christ's purity and holiness (e.g., Rev 1:14) and fulfills Christ's promise to the churches that the faithful will "walk with me in white clothes" (3:4-5; cf. 2:17). The waving of palm branches likely signifies the celebration of the messianic army's military

41. On the use of holy war traditions in Revelation, see Adela Yarbro Collins, "The Political Perspective of the Revelation to John," *JBL* 96 (1977): 241-56. She uses the language of "passive resistance" to describe the role of the audience, by which she means trusting in God to provide vindication rather than active warfare and violence.

42. On John's perception of the churches' situation as one of potential complacency and temptation to compromise with political powers, see Adela Yarbro Collins, *Crisis and Catharsis: The Power of the Apocalypse* (Philadelphia: Westminster, 1984), 84-109.

43. For my understanding of the theme of the messianic holy war in Revelation, I acknowledge my debt to Bauckham, *The Climax of Prophecy*, 210-37.

victory (1 Macc 13:51; 2 Macc 10:7) and recalls the same image in the Fourth Gospel of a crowd waving palm branches as they celebrate "the King of Israel" as he enters into Jerusalem for his own ironic victory and royal enthronement (John 12:12–16).[44] They sing a song celebrating their military victory and it is, unsurprisingly after our examination of chapters 4 and 5, directed to both God and the Messiah: "Salvation belongs to our God who is seated on the throne and to the Lamb" (7:10). Their successful victory, the act of conquering, is explicitly interpreted when one of the worshipping elders declares to John: "These are those who have come out of the great tribulation, and they have washed their robes and have made them clean *by the blood of the Lamb*" (ἐν τῷ αἵματι τοῦ ἀρνίου, 7:13).[45] We have seen that Christ's kingship, the basis for his sharing the throne with God, and his act of procuring a kingdom of people for himself are rooted in the offering of his blood (1:5–6; 5:5–6, 9–10), and here in 7:4–17 is the basis for the Messiah's army's victory. The messianic army likewise accomplishes its victory by no other means than through its active allegiance to the Lamb even if it leads to death. The vision concludes with an eschatological vision of the Davidic shepherd and Lamb enacting his perfect rule over his people (7:15–17).[46] Those who "fight" successfully in the Messiah's army spend their days worshipping God and receiving the messianic blessings of the Lamb, "who will shepherd them and will lead them to springs of living water" (7:15–17; Isa 49:9; Ezek 34:23; Ps 23:1–2).

Messianic Exegesis of Psalm 2: Triumph over the Messiah's Enemies—Revelation 12:1–14:5

Chapters 12–14 center upon the Messiah's triumph over Satan and his powers, as well as a call to the saints to overcome satanic violence and opposition by maintaining their loyalty to the Lamb. This is not the place for a detailed engagement with these visions; here I only want to highlight their appropriation of Jewish messianic motifs and Scriptures to describe Christ's and his people's victory. In the vision recounted in 14:1–5, John sees the 144,000 standing together with the Lamb on Mount Zion (14:1). The image of the messianic Lamb, with his military army, standing on Mount Zion activates

44. See Beale, *Revelation*, 428.

45. This is stated well by Bauckham, *The Climax of Prophecy*, 226: "[T]he ascription of victory not only to God but also to the Lamb (7:10) prepares for the revelation that it is a victory *of the same kind* as the Lamb's (cf. 5:6): those whom the Lamb's sacrificial death has ransomed from all nations (5:9) share in his victory through *martyrdom*."

46. See Friesen, *Imperial Cults*, 200.

Psalm 2 once again, one of John's favorite OT texts.[47] Psalm 2 is repeatedly used throughout Revelation to depict the sovereign authority of the Messiah/ Lamb *and his people* over and against their enemies; this makes good sense as a cosmic-apocalyptic appropriation of the psalm where God's response to the hostile kings of the earth is to subject them to the Davidic son of God who has been installed as God's king on Mount Zion (Ps 2:1–6).[48] In fact, the frequent references in Revelation to "the kings of the earth" (οἱ βασιλεῖς τῆς γῆς, 6:15; also 1:5; 17:2, 9, 12, 18; 18:3, 9; 19:19; 21:24; sometimes just "kings," e.g., Rev 9:11; 10:11; 16:12; 17:12) stems from Psalm 2:1, where "the kings of the earth take their stand and the rulers gather together against the Lord and his Messiah" (Ps 2:2). While there is some dispute about the eschatological conversion of the kings (see Rev 21:24), they are most frequently associated with cosmic powers such as the beast and its armies (Rev 19:19) and the great harlot who utters blasphemies and makes war against the saints (17:18). Their proper response is to worship and give allegiance to Christ as the superior and singular ruler over the kings, as is called for in Psalm 2:10–12, but primarily they resist Christ's rule due to their deception by the dragon and the beast (e.g., 17:7–14; cf. 13:3–4).[49] They are those, in the words of Joel Marcus, who "set themselves against Yahweh and his anointed one, not entirely on their own initiative, but as the exponents of a world-embracing kingship opposed to that of God."[50] Returning to the vision in Revelation 14:1–4, the Messiah's army reigns together with him from Mount Zion, singing songs of worship before the throne (14:3). They are described as those who have not defiled themselves and have remained virgins, understood here not as a literal reference to sexual renunciation so much as a refusal to engage in the fornication described in the letters as idolatrous interactions with teachings that compromise one's loyalty to the Lamb (Rev 2:14, 20).

In other words, the Messiah's chaste army on Mount Zion is composed of those who have successfully resisted the deception and threats of Satan and his powers. This is not the place to engage in a full-scale exegesis of the visions of the dragon (ch. 12) and the beasts from the sea and the land (ch. 13), along with

47. See Bauckham, *The Climax of Prophecy*, 229–32.
48. That Psalm 2 had already undergone reinterpretation in a cosmic direction in some Jewish texts (e.g., 4QFlor 1:18–19) is noted by Joel Marcus, *The Way of the Lord: Christological Exegesis of the Old Testament in the Gospel of Mark* (Louisville: Westminster John Knox, 1992), 61–62.
49. So Friesen, *Imperial Cults*, 182–83.
50. Marcus, *The Way of the Lord*, 62.

their complex scriptural and ancient Near Eastern contexts.[51] I simply make two points. First, John continues to draw upon Psalm 2 in his portrait of the cosmic war between the dragon/beasts and God and the Messiah. The dragon (symbolizing Satan) is at war with the woman (symbolizing the covenant people of God).[52] He knows that God's plan is to accomplish his purposes through his messianic king, the son of God with whom he has promised to share his authority and rule as a means of establishing his rule over the unruly nations and peoples of the earth (Ps 2:1-9). John activates this Psalm, especially verses 8 and 9, when he notes that the dragon is prepared to devour the child of the woman (Rev 12:4), the child who "is to rule all the nations with an iron rod" (ὃς μέλλει ποιμαίνειν πάντα τὰ ἔθνη ἐν ῥάβδῳ σιδηρᾷ, Rev 12:5b; cf. Ps 2:9; Rev 2:27).[53] The image here is of the messianic king putting a complete end to all violent opposition to his and God's rule. But when the "child is snatched away to God and to his throne (πρὸς τὸν θρόνον αὐτοῦ)" (12:5c), a reference to God resurrecting and enthroning his Son (cf. Rev 5:5-6), the dragon directs his anger at the rest of the offspring of the woman—namely, "those who keep God's commands and hold fast to the witness of Jesus" (12:17).[54] The dragon's war against the people of God and the Messiah is waged through the sea beast who is an ironic and deceptive parody of the Lion-Lamb, the true king. Like the Messiah who receives authority and power from Yahweh, so the dragon enacts his own version of Psalm 2:6-9 as he gives to the beast "his power, throne, and great authority" (τὴν δύναμιν αὐτοῦ καὶ τὸν θρόνον αὐτοῦ καὶ ἐξουσίαν μεγάλην, 13:2b).[55] His ability to make war against the saints is the result of his reception of "authority over every tribe, people, language, and nation" (ἐδόθη αὐτῷ ἐξουσία ἐπὶ πᾶσαν φυλὴν καὶ λαὸν καὶ γλῶσσαν καὶ ἔθνος, 13:7b). The beast mimics and parodies the true royal rule and power of the Lion-Lamb as he wears royal diadems on his horns (13:1b), receives authority and a throne from the dragon (13:2), has one of his seven heads apparently

---

51. See here especially Adela Yarbro Collins, *The Combat Myth in the Book of Revelation*, Harvard Dissertations in Religion 9 (Missoula, MT: Scholars Press, 1976).

52. My understanding of the symbolism in Rev 12:1-2 follows Bauckham, *The Climax of Prophecy*, 185-98.

53. So Moyise, "The Psalms in the Book of Revelation," 234; M. de Jonge, "The Use of the Expression ὁ Χριστός in the Apocalypse of John," in *L'Apocalypse johannique et l'Apocalyptique dans le Nouveau Testament* (Gembloux, Belgium: Louvain, 1980), 271-72.

54. Bauckham, *The Climax of Prophecy*, 186: "The defeat of the Dragon (12:7-9) is doubtless the same event as the victory of the Lamb (5:5-6), and both are to be historically located in the death and resurrection of Jesus Christ." See further Court, *Myth and History*, 106-21.

55. See also Spilsbury, "The Apocalypse," 144.

slain but then healed (13:3), and receives worship and the acclamation: "Who is like the beast, and who can fight against it?" (13:4; cf. 13:8). By the deception and royal pretensions of the beast, the dragon successfully deceives the nations and the inhabitants of the earth. Standing behind the imagery of the beast and its power is almost certainly the military strength of the Roman Empire and its persecution of the saints (so 13:7; cf. this theme in 2:8–11; 2:12–17; 6:9–11; 7:9–17). When the dragon and the beast are finally defeated, John once again draws upon the language of Psalm 2 in the victory songs to depict the ultimate fulfillment of God's plan to rule the cosmos through his messianic king (11:15–19; 12:10–12). When the seventh trumpet is blown, loud voices in heaven declare: "The kingdom of the world has become the kingdom of our Lord and his Messiah (ἐγένετο ἡ βασιλεία τοῦ κόσμου τοῦ κυρίου ἡμῶν καὶ τοῦ χριστοῦ αὐτοῦ), and he will rule (βασιλεύσει) forever and ever" (11:15b). Upon this celebratory proclamation, further praise is given to God by the twenty-four elders for his powerful act of enforcing his rule against "the nations who raged (τὰ ἔθνη ὠργίσθησαν; cf. Ps. 2:1)" (11:17b–18). The references to "the Lord and his Messiah" and "the nations raging" stem from Psalm 2:1–2, and the victory song declares that the opposition to God and the Christ has finally been overcome through the messianic kingdom.[56] Likewise, the victory song in 12:10 celebrates with similar language: "Now the salvation and power and kingdom of our God and the authority of his Messiah have come (ἡ ἐξουσία τοῦ χριστοῦ αὐτοῦ)" (12:10a). The references to God's *kingdom* and the Messiah's *authority* make good sense in light of Psalm 2 and Israel's royal ideology of God enacting his kingdom through his messianic king. In both 11:15 and 12:10 one finds obvious references to Χριστός as a title or royal honorific to speak of Jesus as the David King who ushers in God's eschatological kingdom.

Second, the successful waging of war against the evil powers by the church is highly paradoxical in that their victory comes through their witness to and participation in the Messiah's death. The reader is prepared for this, however, not least by the recent vision of the two witnesses in chapter 11, where John states: "when they complete their testimony, the beast which comes up from the abyss will make war with them and he will conquer (νικήσει) them and will kill them" (11:7). That the death of the witnesses follows the precedent of the death of Jesus "the faithful witness" (1:5; 3:14) is made explicit by the note that their martyrdom occurs in the place "where also their Lord was crucified" (11:8), and it is no surprise that the witnesses are also publicly vindicated and enthroned

---

56. See here Moyise, "The Psalms in the Book of Revelation," 232–33; Marcus, *The Way of the Lord*, 65.

into heaven (11:11–12). In the words of Bauckham: "So it is the witness of Jesus himself that the witnesses continue, and their death is a participation in the blood of the Lamb."[57] Likewise, when the dragon is defeated, those in heaven celebrate that the saints "have conquered [the dragon] because of the blood of the Lamb (αὐτοὶ ἐνίκησαν αὐτὸν διὰ τὸ αἷμα τοῦ ἀρνίου) and the word of their testimony and they did not love their own lives to the point of death" (12:11). The triumphant victory of the saints, then, takes place not through violent revolt but through following the pattern of the slain Lamb's faithful testimony even to the point of death. Thus, the visions of chapters 12–14 continue to call the audience to engage in the same active resistance against Satan and the evil powers as were set forth in the letters (chs. 2–3).[58] Thus, the vision of the sea beast in 13:1–10 concludes with the exhortation: "here then is a call for endurance and faithfulness on the part of the saints" (ἡ ὑπομονὴ καὶ πίστις τῶν ἁγίων, 13:10). Similarly, after the vision of an angel announcing God's judgment upon those who worship the beast, John notes: "This calls for the endurance of the saints, for those who keep God's commands and their faithfulness toward Jesus" (τὴν πίστιν Ἰησοῦ, 14:12). The people of the Messiah, then, continue the messianic war as they bear witness to the truth, hold fast in their allegiance and faithfulness to Jesus, and give their lives even to the point of death.

Sharing in the Messiah's Final Victory—19:11–21

In the visions of eschatological judgment and salvation, John narrates Christ's final battle over his enemies where Christ's victory takes the form of the public revelation of his truthfulness as the true king of the cosmos. The vision is a remarkably vivid picture of Christ as a victorious king, and the image encourages loyalty and faithfulness to Christ in the midst of temptations to compromise as it portrays a gruesome end for the wicked oppressors.[59] The depiction of a king riding a horse, wearing diadems, and an army following him likely calls to mind the Roman triumph.[60] This public revelation of Christ as God's rightful ruler is emphasized in the twofold description of him as

57. Bauckham, *The Theology of the Book of Revelation*, 85.

58. On the relationship between the visions and the letters to the seven churches, where the visions are seen as radicalizing and giving a transcendent depiction of the churches' negotiation of Roman imperial rule, see Frey, "The Relevance of the Roman Imperial Cult," 246–47.

59. See especially Barnhill, "Seeing Christ through Hearing the Apocalypse," 251–52.

60. See further David E. Aune, *Revelation 17–22*, WBC 52C (Grand Rapids: Zondervan, 1998), 1051.

"the Lord of lords and the King of kings" (κύριος κυρίων ἐστὶν καὶ βασιλεὺς βασιλέων, 17:14b; cf. 19:16b).[61] John presents this scene as the public display that Christ is God's true king, to whom he has entrusted the responsibility for divine judgment (e.g., God is the judge in 15:3; 16:5; 19:2).[62] John's narration of the Messiah's victory takes the form not of violent slaughter of his rebels but of a public validation that he alone is the true and rightful judge. The judicial aspect of Christ's victory is emphasized in almost every christological image and descriptor in 19:11–21. Thus, in John's vision, he sees one riding on a white horse who is called "Faithful and True" (πιστὸς καὶ ἀληθινός, 19:11), and this is an obvious reference to his initial description of Christ as "the faithful and true witness, the ruler over God's creation" (3:14), and "the faithful witness" and "ruler over the kings of the earth" (1:5–6). References to the Messiah's justice and right to engage in judgment through his truthful words abound in Revelation 19:11–16. John notes that the rider engages in warfare "with justice" (ἐν δικαιοσύνῃ, 19:11b; cf. Ps 72:1–3). He is "the Word of God" (ὁ λόγος τοῦ θεοῦ, 19:13b). John draws once again upon the messianic oracle of Isaiah 11 and the messianic Psalm 2 in his description of Christ having a "sharp sword coming out of his mouth that he will use to strike down the nations, and he will rule them with an iron rod" (19:15a; cf. Isa 11:4; Ps 2:9).[63] Thus, Christ's victory does not deviate from or overturn what we have seen to be John's consistent narration of the Messiah's "triumph" in 5:5–6 and the nature of the messianic warfare throughout the Apocalypse.[64] In other words, the final messianic battle is a nonviolent but *real* judgment of Christ against his enemies by means of a public declaration that Christ alone is the true and rightful ruler of the cosmos. While not self-evident to all readers, this interpretation is further confirmed by the reference to the rider's clothes as "dyed with blood" (βεβαμμένον αἵματι, 19:13), which, I suggest, is best taken as a reference to the rider's sacrificial blood (and perhaps also the blood of the martyrs, see 6:9–10; 16:6; 17:6; 18:24; 19:2), which has functioned throughout the Apocalypse as the ironic and paradoxical means whereby Christ has conquered and won his victory (5:5–6) and the means whereby his messianic army successfully participates in Christ's

61. On Dan 4:37 (LXX) as the background for this title and its implications for Revelation see G. K. Beale, "The Origin of the Title 'King of Kings and Lord of Lords' in Revelation 17.14," *NTS* 31 (1985): 618–20.

62. See Slater, *Christ and Community*, 209.

63. Cf. Pss. Sol. 17:24, which speaks of the Davidic king as one who will "shatter all of their material possession with a rod of iron, and will destroy the lawless nations by the word of his mouth." On the messianic imagery in 19:15, see Slater, *Christ and Community*, 226–27.

64. See Friesen, *Imperial Cults*, 189–91.

victory (e.g., 12:11–12).[65] Thus, John's vision of the rider's eschatological defeat of his enemies proceeds from the conviction that God has resurrected and enthroned the Messiah, the only one who faithfully obeyed God even to the point of a bloody death, whereby Christ both received a kingdom of people and has taken his rightful place on the throne with God. The Messiah's final victory is a public revelation of this reality that he alone is the "King of kings and Lord of lords" (19:16b). John is clear, furthermore, that Christ's judgment of his enemies is a salvific necessity since it vindicates his people from their oppressors and persecutors (19:17–12; cf. 6:9–11; 12:17). Christ's righteous rule cannot coexist with the deceptive, oppressive parodies of his rule propagated by the kings of the earth, the beast, and the false prophet (19:17–21). Furthermore, Christ's kingdom cannot coexist with power and authority perpetuated through the use of violence.

Finally, I note once again that John portrays Christ's people not only as subjects of the messianic king but also as participants in Christ's war and his reign in fulfillment of the promises he made to the seven churches (see esp. Rev 2:26–28; 3:21).[66] The "soldiers in heaven" (i.e., the army of God's faithful) are *following* (ἠκολούθει αὐτῷ) the rider on the horse, suggesting that they share in the king's rule and victory (19:14a). The language is reminiscent of 14:4, which describes the saints as those who "follow (οἱ ἀκολουθοῦντες) the Lamb wherever he goes."[67] Nevertheless, it must be emphasized that those following the rider on the white horse do not engage in active battle or warfare, and this draws attention to both Christ's agency and the call upon the saints to embody endurance and faithfulness as a means of active resistance (cf. 17:14).[68] Further-

---

65. The scriptural context of the imagery in Isa 63:1–6 and the reference to the "fierce winepress of the wrath of the Almighty God" in Rev 19:16 has suggested to many that the blood-stained garments refers to the blood of Christ's opponents. John's consistently surprising re-interpretation of images of warfare, conquering, and blood in light of the death of Jesus, however, makes this view unlikely. See here M. Eugene Boring, *Revelation*, Interpretation (Louisville: John Knox Press, 1989), 196: "Yet, though not all of his interpreters have remembered, John has not forgotten the definitive picture of the nature of Christ's conquest already given in 5:1–14. The death by which he conquers is his own, the once-for-all offering of his life on the cross. John uses all of the traditional messianic imagery, but he consistently asks the hearer-reader to interpret the Lion as the Lamb, as he himself does, even in this bloody scene."

66. On the union of Christology and royal rule, see also Slater, *Christ and Community*, 219–20.

67. For a balanced discussion here, see Grant R. Osborne, *Revelation*, BECNT (Grand Rapids: Baker Academic, 2002), 684.

68. On this point, see further Collins, "The Political Perspective," 247–48.

more, the images used to depict the messianic king's identity are also found as promises to the churches as rewards for maintaining one's witness to Jesus. In other words, both Christ and the faithful wear white robes symbolizing faithfulness and vindication (19:11, 14; cf. 3:4–5; 19:7–8); Christ wears many crowns, crowns he has promised to his saints who endure (19:12; cf. 2:10; 3:11); Christ has a special name inscribed upon himself, a name he promises to share with his people (19:12; cf. 2:17; 3:12; 14:1); and he enacts the messianic authority of Psalm 2 in his rule over the nations, a promise he extends to those who keep his works to the end (19:15; cf. 2:26–27).[69] The complexities of John's discussion of the millennial reign of Christ prevent discussion of Revelation 20, but here I simply note that in John's depiction of the vindication of the martyrs and faithful saints (e.g., 6:9–11), he speaks twice of them reigning together with "the Messiah" (ἔζησαν καὶ ἐβασίλευσαν μετὰ τοῦ Χριστοῦ, 20:4; cf. v. 6).

Conclusion

Davidic messianism plays a critical role in the Christology, soteriology, and eschatology of the Apocalypse. Jesus is "the Messiah" (11:15–19; 12:10–12; 20:4–6), the Lion from the tribe of Judah and the Root of David (5:5–6), the bright morning star (2:28; 22:16), and the one who has the key of David (3:7). John's messianic exegesis is on display in his application of messianic oracles from the Torah (Gen 49:8–12; Num 24:15–20), Davidic psalms (Pss 2, 89, and 110), and the prophetic oracle of Isaiah 11. John embraces Jesus's identity as the Davidic Messiah who rules the nations, has a victorious triumph, receives a kingdom through his superior benefaction, and is enthroned to a position of cosmic rule and authority over all creation. As a result, he is worthy to receive divine honors in the form of hymns and acclamations that are reserved only for the one God who sits on the throne (5:1–13; 7:9–10; 15:1–3). But, as we have seen throughout this study, the Messiah's triumph, his rule, and his superior benefaction come by means of his faithful witness and allegiance to God in the face of evil even unto the point of his own bloody death. Davidic messianism is embraced and the Messiah does indeed conquer and establish his kingdom, but he does so by means of the cross and a rejection of violence and the typical trappings of power and domination. Those who belong to Christ's kingdom follow the same pattern of their messianic king as they reject vio-

---

69. See further de Jonge, "The Use of the Expression ὁ Χριστός," 274–78; Spilsbury, "The Apocalypse," 145.

lence but engage in active resistance through rejecting idolatrous allegiances with Rome's economy, military, and cult and by holding fast and enduring in their testimony and loyalty to God and the Lamb who sits on the throne. These followers of Jesus are promised not only to find a place as subjects in the messianic kingdom but to actively participate in the Messiah's kingdom, his authority and rule over the nations, and to sit on his very throne (2:26–28; 3:20–21; 19:11–16; 20:4–6).

Part Two

The MESSIANIC THEOLOGY *of the* NEW TESTAMENT

CHAPTER 10

Scripture

Messianic Exegesis and Christology

The preceding chapters have argued, by way of a reading of the primary compositions of the New Testament, that Jesus's messianic identity is both the presupposition for and content of New Testament theology. While each author engages messianic texts, traditions, and motifs in their own creative and unique way, the result, I suggest, is that Jesus's messianic kingship functions as a root metaphor or basic assumption for reading the New Testament in a way that other important images do not. Thus, while by no means wanting to minimize the christological portraits of Jesus as wise teacher, prophet, healer, or priest I do not think they can account for the breadth of NT Christology in the way Jesus's messianic kingship can. And while a fully orbed dogmatic theology would, of course, need to be more comprehensive, in the following chapters I want to explore in a more synthetic way how some fundamental features of dogmatic theology are inextricably dependent upon the application of messianic language to Jesus of Nazareth. Again, the reader is invited to engage the following theological loci—Scripture, Christology, soteriology, sanctification, ecclesiology, and eschatology—not under the auspices of messianism as the *singular* governing framework but as inextricably dependent upon the confession that (and creative expansion thereof) Jesus is God's messianic king.

The NT writings demonstrate that the earliest Christians articulated their conviction that Jesus was *the* Davidic Messiah through a profound (and dialectical) reading and exegesis of Israel's Scriptures in light of the life and vocation of Jesus of Nazareth.[1] Of course, no one anticipated (at least in an unambiguous manner) that the Messiah of Israel would be rejected by his own people,

---

1. So Donald Juel, *Messianic Exegesis: Christological Interpretation of the Old Testament in Early Christianity* (Philadelphia: Fortress, 1992), 1.

be tortured, and die a shameful death on a Roman cross. But their surprising experiences of Jesus as one resurrected from the dead and powerfully alive led them to an equally new and surprising reading of Israel's Scriptures. The early Christians developed their messianic reading of Israel's Scriptures under their convictions that the crucified and resurrected Jesus was the Davidic Messiah and that their Scriptures foretold of their recent and surprising experiences.[2]

LITERARY FORMS AND MESSIANIC EXEGESIS IN THE NEW TESTAMENT

The NT writings witness to a variety of literary forms employed to express their conviction that this particular person—Jesus of Nazareth—is God's Davidic Messiah and even the subject matter of the Hebrew Scriptures. We have seen evidence, first, that the NT writings express their conviction that Jesus is the Messiah through something like proto-creeds and confessions. Thus, common performative utterances such as "Jesus [is] the Messiah" (e.g., Acts 9:22; 17:3; 18:5) and "Jesus [is] the Lord" (Acts 2:36) are expressed throughout the NT writings both with frequency and unadorned with explanations of their meaning. Perhaps more importantly, if, as seems likely, Paul's statements in Romans 1:2–4 and 1 Corinthians 15:3–11 can be taken as representative of shared early Christian tradition, then this provides important evidence that shared assumptions between Paul and his communities focused on: (1) Jesus's messianic identity as the Χριστός (1 Cor 15:3; Rom 1:1, 4) and God's Son "from the seed of David" (Rom 1:3); (2) Jesus's narrative, centered upon his saving death, resurrection, and enthronement to God's right hand (1 Cor 15:3b–5; Rom 1:4); and (3) Jesus's identity and narrative as having taken place "according to the Scriptures" (κατὰ τὰς γραφάς, 1 Cor 15:3b, 4b) and "pre-promised through [God's] prophets in the holy scriptures" (Rom 1:2).[3] One finds similar confessional testimony to Jesus's Davidic identity in 2 Timothy 2:8—"Remember Jesus Christ raised from the dead, from the seed of David, according to my gospel."

Second, we have seen that the earliest Christians demonstrated their messianic convictions and reading of the Scriptures of Israel through their com-

2. On the significance and generative function of the earliest Christians' experience of the resurrected Messiah Jesus, see Luke Timothy Johnson, *Religious Experience in Earliest Christianity: A Missing Dimension in New Testament Studies* (Minneapolis: Fortress, 1998).

3. See here further, Matthew W. Bates, *The Hermeneutics of the Apostolic Proclamation: The Center of Paul's Method of Scriptural Interpretation* (Waco, TX: Baylor University Press, 2012), 59–106.

position of hymns, acclamations, and poetic praise in honor of the Messiah.[4] The NT provides significant evidence that the early Christians practiced what Paul commanded—namely, to "sing psalms and hymns and spiritual songs among yourselves, singing and making melody in your hearts *to the Lord*" (Eph 5:19; cf. 1 Cor 14:26; Acts 16:25; Jas 5:13). The first two chapters of Luke's Gospel have a liturgical feel as Mary (Luke 1:46–55), Zechariah (1:67–79), the angels in heaven (2:14), and Simeon (2:28–32) sing hymns praising God for his faithfulness to Israel in granting them a messianic deliverer. The hymns of the characters in Luke's Gospel take as their starting point the promise the angel Gabriel makes to Mary, which draws upon the language of 2 Samuel 7:12–14 and is also the first narratorial description of the identity of Mary's son: "he will be great and he will be called a Son of the Most High and the Lord God will give to him the throne of David his father, and he will rule (βασιλεύσει) over the house of Jacob forever and his kingdom will have no end" (Luke 1:32–33). Thus, as we have seen, throughout Luke's infancy narrative there are a variety of scriptural texts and titles which speak to Jesus's messianic identity: a horn of salvation in the house of David (1:69–70), a mighty warrior (1:71, 75), a Branch from on high (1:78), a Savior (2:11; cf. 1:71; 2:30–32), and "the Messiah the Lord" (2:11; cf. 2:26). The christological hymns of Philippians 2 and Colossians 1 both celebrate Christ's royal identity as "Messiah Jesus" (Phil 2:5) and as God's "beloved Son" (Col 1:13b). And, as I have argued in detail, both hymns apply well-known messianic and kingly descriptors to the Messiah: he is the image and form of God (Phil 2:6; Col 1:15), possesses a kingdom (Col 1:13), and is resurrected and enthroned in heaven (Phil 2:9–11; Col 1:18). Both christological hymns draw portions of their language from the Septuagintal Psalter, specifically, psalms which portray God sharing his throne and authority over creation with his anointed firstborn son (LXX Ps 88; Col 1:15, 18), inviting another lord to share his throne and sit at his right hand (LXX Ps 109; Phil 2:9–11), and giving the anointed son the rule over the nations (Ps 2; Col 1:13). Thus, these hymns to Christ may have developed within the early assemblies, where worshippers of Jesus sang both biblical psalms and new hymnic compositions in honor of Christ the messianic king, the royal figure who liberates and saves God's people, shares God's throne, and receives divine

4. See especially Martin Hengel, "The Song about Christ in Earliest Worship," in *Studies in Early Christology* (Edinburgh: T&T Clark, 1995), 227–91; Margaret Daly-Denton, "Singing Hymns to Christ as to a God (Cf. Pliny *Epistles* X, 96)," in *The Jewish Roots of Christological Monotheism: Papers from the St. Andrews Conference on the Historical Origins of the Worship of Jesus*, ed. Carey C. Newman et al., Supplements to the Journal for the Study of Judaism 63 (Leiden: Brill, 1999), 277–92.

honors and worship.[5] Further, the author of Hebrews, after his exordium (Heb 1:1–3), offers a celebratory paean to the messianic king upon his enthronement and entrance into heaven (Heb 1:4–14). And this hymnic celebration not only depicts a messianic event (i.e., royal enthronement), it also draws upon a plethora of common early Christian prooftexts to speak of Jesus's Davidic messianic identity (e.g., Ps 2:7; 2 Sam 7:14; Ps 89:28; Ps 110:1). We have seen that in the book of Revelation, the heavenly assembly sings a new song to the Davidic Lion-Lamb who shares God's throne (Rev 5:5–14).

Third, we have seen that the passion narratives in the Gospels display the use of "typological narrativization" as a means of narrating and interpreting Jesus's final days in Jerusalem, especially his sufferings and death, as messianic events.[6] In other words, the Gospel authors draw upon biblical messianic scriptural categories, concepts, type scenes, and quotations to interpret Jesus's surprising final days in Jerusalem and to present Jesus as God's messianic king.[7] Thus, the Synoptic Gospels take head-on the difficult question of whether Jesus is or *is not* the anticipated Davidic son (e.g., Mark 10:46, 52), but often through the use of Davidic psalms which portray the king as a righteous, suffering king. And this creates a highly paradoxical and ironic depiction of Jesus's kingship. We have seen, for example, that Matthew's account of Jesus's prayer in Gethsemane and ensuing arrest has been typologically modeled on David's sufferings and trials during Absalom's revolt (Matt 26:36–56 in 2 Sam 13–18).[8] The Synoptic account of Jesus's so-called triumphal entry portrays Jesus as a messianic ruler making his rightful entrance into Jerusalem—the city of David—and to the temple (Gen 49:11 and Zech 9:9); but whereas the crowds acclaim him as the blessed one "coming in the name of the Lord" from Psalm 118:25, Jesus will also draw upon lines from the same Psalm to declare that he is the rejected and vindicated cornerstone (Ps 118:22 in Mark 12:10–11; also Luke 13:31–35; 19:28–44; 20:13, 17–18). Each one of the Gospel writers makes their characterization of Jesus as the *suffering* Messiah clear, as we have seen repeatedly, through their consistent invoking of the Davidic psalms to portray

5. Similarly, William Horbury, *Jewish Messianism and the Cult of Christ* (London: SCM, 1998), 112, 150; see also Daly-Denton, "Singing Hymns to Christ."

6. See especially Anthony Le Donne, *The Historiographical Jesus: Memory, Typology, and the Son of David* (Waco, TX: Baylor University Press, 2009), 59.

7. Mark Goodacre, "Scripturalization in Mark's Crucifixion Narrative," in *The Trial and Death of Jesus: Essays on the Passion Narrative in Mark*, ed. Geert van Oyen and Tom Shepherd (Leuven: Peeters, 2006), 40.

8. Nathan C. Johnson, "The Passion according to David: Matthew's Arrest Narrative, the Absalom Revolt, and Militant Messianism," *CBQ* 80 (2018): 247–72.

Jesus as faithful to God amid his sufferings and confidently trusting God for his vindication. By way of reminder, and with no attempt to be comprehensive, Jesus prays the words of David's lament in his trials in the garden (Ps 41:6, 12; 42:5; Mark 14:34); Jesus's persecutors play the role of the enemies of the Davidic king (Ps 22:7, 18 and Luke 23:34b; Ps 69:21 and Luke 23:36 and John 19:28–29; Ps 69:9; John 2:18); and the Psalter provides his expectation for resurrection and enthronement (Ps 110:1 and Mark 14:51–52; Ps 31:5 and Luke 23:46).

Fourth, one also sees messianic reading of Old Testament texts in the practice of exegetical argumentation, for example, in the Jesus of the Synoptics and the apostle Paul. We have seen the Markan Jesus present his own riddling exegetical conundrum to the scribes when he appeals to David's declaration of another lord enthroned next to Yahweh in Psalm 110:1 and then asks: "How can the scribes say that the Messiah is the son of David?" (Mark 12:36). Paul engages in a complex messianic interpretation of the patriarchal narratives of Genesis in Galatians 3, where he declares that God's promises were made to Abraham and to Abraham's *singular seed* (Gal 3:16). Paul's declaration that Abraham's seed "is the Messiah" derives, in part, from his understanding of a link between the Abrahamic covenant and God's promise to David in 2 Samuel 7:12–14: "I will raise up your seed after you; he will come from your loins, and I will prepare his kingdom" (2 Sam 7:12). In John 7 we have seen that the Feast of Tabernacles provides the occasion for the crowd to engage in some messianic speculation regarding whether Jesus's origins (John 7:26–27), performance of miraculous signs (7:31), and Galilean birth (7:40–42) conform to messianic scriptural precedent.

Fifth, the book of Acts uses the literary form of speeches to interpret recent events in Jerusalem as God's fulfillment of his promises to Israel to raise up a final righteous king to rule forever over his people. Thus, Peter interprets Judas's betrayal of Jesus and apostasy from the twelve with language from the Psalter originally used to portray David's enemies (Ps 69:25 and 109:8 in Acts 1:20; cf. Ps 2:1–2 in Acts 4:29–30). The Psalter is almost always near at hand when Peter interprets Jesus's resurrection from the dead as a royal enthronement (Ps 17:6; 16:8–11; 132:11; 110:1 in Acts 2:22–36; Ps 118:22 in Acts 4:11). Paul's sermon in the synagogue in Pisidian Antioch invokes Psalm 2:7 (13:33), Psalm 16:10 (13:35), and Isaiah 55:3 (13:34b) to declare that God's election of Israel has found its significance in God's salvific blessings for his people through the resurrected, enthroned Davidic Messiah. And James draws upon Amos 9:11 to declare that God has restored and rebuilt the fallen tent of David (15:16–17).

Sixth, we have seen the literary convention of intrapersonal dialogue between God and the Messiah in a handful of places.[9] In Romans 15:3 Paul presents "the Messiah" (ὁ Χριστός) praying David's words from Psalm 69 to God: "the insults of those insulting you have fallen on me" (cf. Ps 69:9).[10] A few verses later in Romans 15:7–13, Paul places messianic Scripture in the mouth of the Messiah who, as "the root of Jesse" and "the one rising up to rule over the nations" (Isa 11:10 in Rom 15:12a), gives praise and testimony to God for the salvation of the gentiles (also, Ps 17:50; Deut 32:43; Ps 117:1). We have already mentioned the celebration of the Son's entrance into the heavenly world in Hebrews 1:5–14, but here it is worth noting that the Father is the one depicted as speaking these words of honor on behalf of the messianic Son; and the Son responds to the Father by confessing the Father's name singing hymns to him in Hebrews 2:12–13 (using the language of Ps 21:23 and Isa 8:7–18).

To this list, we might add the literary forms of the Fourth Gospel's stories of quests for the Messiah (John 1:19–51), Matthew's messianic genealogy (Matt 1:1–17) and formulaic fulfillment of Israel's Scriptures (Matt 1:18–2:23), and the apocalyptic messianic scenario of Christ's eschatological conquering of his enemies (1 Cor 15:20–28; Rev 12).

THE MESSIANIC LOGIC OF NEW TESTAMENT EXEGESIS

The messianic exegetical readings of the NT authors testify to their conviction that Jesus of Nazareth is *the singular* Davidic Messiah and that his life and vocation have climactically brought the Davidic kingdom to its fulfillment and restoration. The messianic conviction that Jesus is the Messiah of Israel, resurrected from the dead and enthroned at God's right hand, results in a powerful messianic reading of Israel's Scriptures such that these texts anticipate the particular identity and vocation of Messiah Jesus as the inaugurator of God's kingdom.

Messiah Jesus and the Reconstitution of the Davidic Kingdom

As the promised messianic Son of David, he is the one who has ended Israel's exile, the singular Davidic king who will rule eternally over God's people

---

9. See in much more detail, Matthew W. Bates *The Birth of the Trinity: Jesus, God, and Spirit in New Testament and Early Christian Interpretations of the Old Testament* (Oxford: Oxford University Press, 2015). Essential reading here is also the work of Madison N. Pierce, *Divine Discourse in the Epistle to the Hebrews: The Recontextualization of Spoken Quotations of Scripture*, SNTSMS (Cambridge: Cambridge University Press, 2020).

10. See Bates, *The Hermeneutics of the Apostolic Proclamation*, 240–55.

(Matt 1:1, 17)[11] and the Davidic shepherd-king anticipated by Israel's prophets who establishes his just and compassionate reign over Israel (Matt 2:6). For Luke, Jesus is the one who inaugurates Israel's consolation and restoration as he receives the Father's promises of David's everlasting throne and kingdom, by which he will reign over "the house of Jacob forever" (Luke 1:32–33; cf. 2 Sam 7:12–14; Pss 2:7; 89:27–38; 132:11–12). Luke narrates the fulfillment of God's promise to David in the book of Acts in Peter's Pentecost speech, where Jesus as the Davidic Son is resurrected from the dead and enthroned in heaven as Messiah and Lord (Acts 2:30–36; cf. Ps 110:1). Likewise, Paul in Pisidian Antioch establishes that the Davidic kingdom has been reconstituted as the result of God's resurrection and enthronement of his Davidic king (Acts 13:23, 32–37). And James, as we have seen, declares that God's actions through the Messiah have led to the rebuilding of David's fallen tent (Acts 15:16–17). While the Gospels of Mark and John are more ambiguous, both texts engage Israel's Scriptures with the assumption that Jesus is God's Davidic king. In Mark's Gospel, as we have seen, Mark draws upon Psalms 2 (Mark 1:9–11), 110 (Mark 12:35–37; 14:61–62), and 118 (Mark 12:10–11), and these psalms convey Jesus to not only be the Davidic messianic Son of God but they also bespeak a future vindication and rule for Jesus. In John, Jesus is the Spirit-anointed Son of God (John 1:32–34) of Isaiah 11 whose inauguration of the messianic kingdom results in the bringing of the new and abundant wine (John 2:1–11; Gen 49:9–12; Amos 9:11–15), the sanctifying and cleansing water (3:5–6; Ezek 36:23–27), and the eschatological temple (John 2:12–21; 2 Sam 7:12–14; Zech 3:8–10; 6:12–13). For Paul the gospel is centered upon the resurrection of the offspring of David and his installation in heaven as the powerful Son of God (Rom 1:1–4; cf. 1 Cor 15:3–7; 2 Tim 2:8). Paul's frequent application of Davidic psalms to articulate the identity and activity of Jesus only makes sense on the assumption that he is the Davidic Messiah and, therefore, his resurrection and royal enthronement establish him as the apocalyptic messianic king (e.g., Pss 8 and 110 in 1 Cor 15:20–28). We have seen that Hebrews 1 draws upon 2 Samuel 7 and Psalms 2, 89, and 110 to depict Christ's royal enthronement and entrance into his heavenly kingdom. For Revelation he is "Messiah Jesus, the faithful witness, the firstborn from the dead, and the ruler over the kings of the earth" (Rev 1:5; Ps 89:21–27). Jesus is the conquering "Lion from the tribe of Judah, the Root of David" (Rev 5:5), and as the powerful, resurrected, and enthroned

---

11. On the hermeneutics of Matthew's messianic exegesis, see Patrick R. Schreiner, *Matthew, Disciple and Scribe: The First Gospel and Its Portrait of Jesus* (Grand Rapids: Baker Academic, 2019).

messianic ruler he is "Lord over lords and King over kings" (17:14; cf. 19:16) who establishes his rule over every other earthly king and ruler (e.g., 16:14; 19:19). In particular, Revelation draws upon Psalm 2 to depict Jesus as the one to whom God has entrusted divine power and authority to rule (Rev 2:28–29; 12:1–5). The apocalyptic hope is geared toward the eschatological messianic kingdom for Revelation: "The kingdom of the world has become the kingdom of our Lord and his Messiah, and he will rule forever and ever" (11:15b); "Now the salvation and power and kingdom of our God and the authority of his Messiah have come" (12:10a).

Reframing Messianic Scripture around the Crucified Jesus of Nazareth

As many have demonstrated with ease, there are a variety of Jewish and Old Testament texts which bespeak of a variety of different kinds of messiahs, and attempting to amalgamate them into one coherent unified doctrine is not advisable.[12] There is no singular self-evident meaning of "messiah" or "son of David." Rather, there are Jewish and early Christian messiah texts which draw upon scriptural language about an anointed royal figure from the line of David; thus, there is often great variety in how these literary messiah figures are presented, but, in the words of Matthew Novenson, "the Jewish Scriptures provided the pool of shared linguistic resources for them all."[13] This is exactly what we have seen in detail throughout this study. While I do think convincing arguments can be made that the establishment of God's kingdom through a righteous king is one of the centerpieces of Israel's Scriptures,[14] that the Psalter has been constructed and edited so as to have a royal, messianic shape,[15] that the editing of the Pentateuch also has a royal and eschatological plot line

12. See, for example, Jacob Neusner, William Scott Green, and Ernest Frerichs, eds., *Judaisms and Their Messiahs at the Turn of the Christian Era* (Cambridge: Cambridge University Press, 1987).

13. Matthew V. Novenson, *Christ among the Messiahs: Christ Language in Paul and Messiah Language in Ancient Judaism* (Oxford: Oxford University Press, 2012), 62.

14. Though controversial, I think the following demonstrate that this thesis is at least one significant thread to the Old Testament: John Bright, *The Kingdom of God: The Biblical Concept and Its Meaning for the Church* (Nashville: Abingdon, 1953); Stephen Dempster, *Dominion and Dynasty: A Biblical Theology for the Hebrew Bible*, NSBT 15 (Downers Grove, IL: InterVarsity Press, 2003).

15. Gerald H. Wilson, *The Editing of the Hebrew Psalter*, SBLDS 76 (Chico, CA: Scholars Press, 1985); also Joachim Schaper, *Eschatology in the Greek Psalter*, WUNT 2.76 (Tübingen: Mohr Siebeck, 1995).

based, in part, on the poetic praises of a coming king who will rule Israel and the nations (LXX Gen 49:8–12; Num 23–24; Deut 32:1–5),[16] and that the prophets obviously engage in eschatological anticipation and hope for a Davidic shepherd-king (e.g., Isa 9:6–7; 11:1–10; Jer 23:1–5; Mic 5), the messianic identity and vocation of Jesus cannot be comprehended *prospectively* apart from Jesus's own (re-)definition and declaration of its meaning. The NT writings provide further evidence that while some anticipated a coming messianic figure from the line of David, there was no widespread agreement upon his exact origins and vocation. The NT texts also indicate quite clearly that the meaning of Davidic messiahship is not one singular idea or doctrine and cannot be taken as an assumed given but, rather, is something that is ambiguous and, for the NT authors, must be interpreted and given its meaning only through the particular life and experiences of Jesus of Nazareth.

Thus, the NT writings are unified in presenting Jesus as indeed the Davidic Messiah, God's anointed King of Israel; but the texts demonstrate that this title and vocation is capable of being deeply misunderstood if it is not understood *retrospectively*, that is, in light of Jesus's reframing of its meaning.[17] For example, we have seen that the book of Revelation affirms that Jesus is "the Christ" (Rev 11:15; 12:10; 20:4, 6) who has his own kingdom (1:5–6; 5:9–10). And the invocation of messianic texts such as Genesis 49 ("the Lion of Judah," Rev 5:5) and Isaiah 11 ("the Root of David," Rev 5:5) present him as a conquering Davidic military figure. But these messianic texts, and indeed the entirety of Revelation, are only rightly interpreted when they are seen through the prism of the crucified Christ, that is, the slain Lamb (5:6, 9). We have seen that Jesus in the Gospel of Mark is deeply suspicious of those human characters who confess him to be the Messiah or Son of God (1:24–25; 3:11–12; 5:7–9; 8:27–31; 9:7–9), and Jesus never applies the language to himself in a direct and unambiguous manner. And yet there are numerous factors that suggest one of Mark's purposes was to narrate Jesus's surprising and paradoxical identity as God's anointed messianic king. There is, then, a tension between Mark's articulation of Jesus's messianic identity and many contemporary traditional understandings of Jewish messianism. Here I quote again Daniel Kirk: "Like the term 'Christ' itself, Davidic messiahship is not a sufficient category for interpreting Jesus' ministry. It needs reframing and reinterpretation by Jesus'

---

16. Horbury, *Jewish Messianism*, 46–51.

17. On the NT writers (here Gospel authors) as retrospective interpreters of the Old Testament, see Richard B. Hays, *Echoes of Scripture in the Gospels* (Waco, TX: Baylor University Press, 2016), 4–5.

own ministry."[18] One of the ways in which Mark does this, as we have seen, is through the application of Davidic lament psalms where the righteous king suffers in confident hope and expectation that his Father will vindicate and enthrone him. Similarly, we have seen that John's Gospel begins with quest stories that stoke messianic fervor (John 1:19–51), invoke messianic themes as critical to Jesus's identity (e.g., Spirit, temple, shepherd), is infused with characters engaging in messianic speculation (e.g., 4:25–29; 7:28–44; 9:22), characterizes Jesus as a king with his own kingdom (3:3–5; chs. 18–19), and declares its purpose as centering upon convincing the readers that Jesus is the Messiah (20:30–31). But just as Mark's Gospel demonstrates a concern that its readers interpret messianic categories according to Jesus's identity and vocation, so also John's Gospel presents a surprising interpretation of Jesus the Messiah as one whose kingship and enthronement is revealed in crucifixion (e.g., 8:28; 12:31–32) and whose filial relationship with the Father demands seeing him as coequal with his Father (e.g., John 1:1–3; 5:19–47).

Messianic Exegesis in the Second Century

Making sense of Jesus's messianic identity and vocation through messianic exegesis did not stop with the NT writings but continued to provide a significant resource in the second century (and well beyond), as I demonstrate here through a brief look at Justin Martyr's *First Apology* and Irenaeus's *Against Heresies*. Both Justin and Irenaeus demonstrate similarities with the reading practices of some of the NT writings and they develop their own creative messianic interpretations of the Old Testament.

In Justin Martyr's *First Apology* (approx. 150–155 CE), specifically chapters 32–52, he presents what Oskar Skarsaune calls a "creed-like enumeration of Jesus' messianic career" through a detailed messianic reading of Israel's Scriptures.[19] Skarsaune makes a strong argument that Justin's messianic reading is derived, at least in part, from an earlier christological "kerygma source" based on significant parallels with *The Kerygma of Peter*.[20] A brief summary of Justin's understanding of Jesus's messianic identity and vocation, to be expanded upon in chapters 32–52 with his messianic reading of Israel's Scriptures, is set forth in 31:7:

18. J. R. Daniel Kirk, *A Man Attested by God: The Human Jesus of the Synoptic Gospels* (Grand Rapids: Eerdmans, 2016), 497.

19. See here Oskar Skarsaune, "Jewish Christian Sources Used by Justin Martyr and Other Greek and Latin Fathers," in *Jewish Believers in Jesus: The Early Centuries* (Peabody, MA: Hendrickson, 2007), 381.

20. Skarsaune, "Jewish Christian Sources," 381.

Well then, in the rolls of the prophets we found our Lord Jesus Christ, pro-claimed ahead of time as drawing near, being born of a virgin, and growing to manhood, and healing every disease and every illness, and raising the dead, and being resented and not acknowledged, and being crucified, and dying and rising again, and going to the heavens, and being, and being called, the Son of God, and we found certain people sent by him to every race of people to proclaim these things, and that it was people from the gentiles rather who believed in him.[21]

Justin suggests, then, that the basic plot line for "the Lord Jesus Christ" is found in Israel's prophets and centers upon their foretelling the following major events: incarnation, virgin birth, growth to adulthood, healing ministry, sufferings and rejection, crucifixion, resurrection and ascension, the confession that Jesus is the Son of God, and the succession mission to the gentiles through his apostles. I will not attempt to be exhaustive here, but it should be noted that Justin sees this summary of Jesus's life and vocation as conforming to well known messianic scriptural prooftexts. Thus, Justin draws upon Genesis 49:10-11, Numbers 24:17, and Isaiah 11:1 to speak of Messiah Jesus as a powerful ruler, a Davidic king from the tribe of Judah (*1 Apol.* 32). The Messiah's virgin birth is foretold by Isaiah 7:14 and Micah 5:1. The Messiah speaks and inspires the words of the psalmist regarding his sufferings, specifically Psalm 22: "They pierced my hands and feet and cast lots for my clothing" (Ps 22:17, 19; *1 Apol.* 35.5).[22] Justin's reading of Psalm 22 is remarkably similar to Peter's messianic exegesis in Acts 2:30-36: "And David, the king and prophet who said this [i.e., Ps 22], suffered none of these things" (*1 Apol.* 35.6). Justin thus reads all of Psalm 22 as spoken by the preincarnate Christ.[23] The Messiah's heavenly reign after his crucifixion is foretold by David in Psalm 2 (*1 Apol.* 41), and God's intention to enthrone Messiah Jesus to his right hand during the apostolic mission is foretold in Psalm 110:1 (*1 Apol.* 45). Again, Justin comments on his messianic reading of the Psalter: "David spoke the foregoing texts [i.e., the Davidic psalms] fifteen hundred years before Christ became a human being and was crucified, and none of those who lived before David caused rejoicing among the nations on being crucified, and neither did any of those who lived after him. But in our time, Jesus Christ, after being crucified and dying, rose

21. I am using the translation of Denis Minns and Paul Parvis, eds., *Justin, Philosopher and Martyr: Apologies* (Oxford: Oxford University Press, 2009).

22. In addition to Ps 22, Justin draws upon Isa 50:6-8; 65:2 and Zech 9:9 in *1 Apol.* 35, 38, as well as Isa 53 in *1 Apol.* 50-51.

23. See Bates, *The Birth of the Trinity*, 133-34.

and reigned, ascending into heaven" (*1 Apol.* 42). More could be said here, but my intention is simply to illustrate that messianic exegesis of Israel's Scriptures continued to function as a necessary means of articulating the basic identity, vocation, and plot line of Jesus's messianic significance.

Irenaeus, too, uses the language of anointing to draw together God the Father, Jesus, and the Holy Spirit into a unified economy of salvation for humanity.[24] Thus, Irenaeus invokes Psalm 45:6: "Thy throne, O God, is forever and ever; the scepter of thy kingdom is a right scepter. Thou hast loved righteousness, and hated iniquity; therefore God, thy God, hath anointed Thee." Irenaeus suggests that it is the Spirit who refers to both characters as God— "both him who is anointed as Son, and him who does anoint, that is, the Father" (*Haer.* 3.6.1). Irenaeus is concerned here to establish that the Spirit names both the Father and his Son as truly God. In his *Demonstration of Apostolic Preaching* Irenaeus quotes the same psalm and suggests that the Son receives "the oil of anointing" from the Father, which he defines as "the Spirit by whom he is the anointed" (*Epid.* 47). Irenaeus later reflects upon the potentially problematic baptismal scene where the Spirit of God descends upon Jesus. But Irenaeus here argues that what is depicted is "the Word of God, who is the Savior of all, and the ruler of heaven and earth, who is Jesus . . . [and] was anointed by the Spirit from the Father was made Jesus Christ" (*Haer.* 3.9.3).[25] The Son is anointed here not with oil but with the Holy Spirit which comes from the Father. Irenaeus invokes Isaiah 11:1–4 which foretells of a ruler from the line of David whose rule will be empowered by the Spirit of God which rests upon him. Irenaeus further draws upon Isaiah 61:1, quoted by Jesus in Luke 4:18–19, to speak of "the reason why [Jesus] was anointed"—namely, God's Spirit anointed Jesus to proclaim the gospel and provide salvation for the poor and brokenhearted. Irenaeus's economy of salvation is evident in his use of anointing language, for the Spirit of God has anointed Jesus the Word of God *and* true human from the line of David, and has "anointed him to preach the gospel to the lowly." This anointing was for no other purpose than the accomplishing of humanity's salvation: "the Spirit of God did descend upon him, the Spirit of him who had promised by the prophets that he would anoint him, so that we, receiving from the abundance of his unction, might be saved." Irenaeus reflects upon the naming of Jesus as the Anointed and gives a

---

24. See further Joshua W. Jipp, "Messiah Christology in Paul and Irenaeus," in *Paul and Irenaeus* (London: T&T Clark, forthcoming).

25. All of the following quotations from Irenaeus in this paragraph are from *Haer.* (*Against Heresies*) 3.9.3.

twofold reason which corresponds to Christ as both divine and human: first, he is Christ because it is "through him that the Father anointed and adorned all things" (*Epid.* 53); second, he is Christ "because in his coming as man, he was anointed by the Spirit of God his Father, as he himself says of himself, by Isaiah, 'The Spirit of the Lord is upon me, because he has anointed me, to bring good news to the poor'" (Isa 61:1; Luke 4:18). Thus, Irenaeus's language is constrained by the language of the Scriptures and by Paul's (and indeed the rest of the apostolic testimony) understanding of Jesus as the anointed Messiah, but for Irenaeus this anointing of Jesus further establishes Jesus's identity as both truly God and truly human.

Like the NT authors, Irenaeus reads Israel's Scriptures through a messianic paradigm. For example, Irenaeus invokes Judah's prediction of a coming ruler who will rule the nations from Genesis 49:8–12 (*Epid.* 57) as well as Balaam's prophecy from Numbers 24:17 ("a star shall come out of Jacob, a ruler shall arise in Israel," *Haer.* 3.9.2; *Epid.* 58). As we have seen already, like Paul, he quotes Isaiah 11:1–4 to proclaim a messianic ruler who, coming from the seed of Jesse, will rule righteously because he is endowed with the Father's Holy Spirit (*Haer.* 3.9.3; *Epid.* 30, 59–60). Irenaeus invokes the psalms of David as a means of explaining the preexistence of the Messiah (Pss 71:17; 109:3 LXX; *Epid.* 43).[26] Irenaeus continues the early Christian tradition of drawing upon Psalm 110:1 (and Ps 2:7), but his emphasis is primarily upon the way in which the Father's address to his Son *as Lord* demonstrates that both the Father and Son are truly God (*Haer.* 3.6.1; 3.10.5). Jesus's Davidic ancestry is significant for Irenaeus because it ensures that Jesus's flesh is truly human flesh: the prophets announced that "his flesh would blossom from the seed of David, that he would be, according to the flesh, son of David, who was the son of Abraham, through a long succession" (*Epid.* 30).[27] But Jesus's Davidic sonship is interpreted by Irenaeus also as a fulfillment of God's promises to David—namely, that God would give David a son who would rule Israel forever (2 Sam 7:12–13; Ps 132:11). "And this King is Christ, the Son of God become the Son of man, that is, become the fruit from the Virgin, who was of the seed of David" (*Epid.* 36; cf. *Haer.* 3.9.2 and 3.16.2 both quoting Ps 132:11). Thus, Psalm 110:1 is used both to affirm Jesus's human Davidic ancestry *and* that he is truly God. Again,

---

26. See here also Horbury, *Jewish Messianism*, 94–96; Adela Yarbro Collins and John J. Collins, *King and Messiah as Son of God: Divine, Human, and Angelic Messianic Figures in Biblical and Related Literature* (Grand Rapids: Eerdmans, 2008), 55–58.

27. On Irenaeus's reading of Israel's Scriptures in this section of *The Demonstration of the Apostolic Preaching*, see Nathan MacDonald, "Israel and the Old Testament Story in Irenaeus's Presentation of the Rule of Faith," *JTI* 3 (2009), 290–94.

Irenaeus in quoting Psalm 110:1 comments: "He who is the son of the Highest, the same is himself also the Son of David. And David, knowing by the Spirit the dispensation of the advent of this Person, by which he is supreme over all the living and dead, confessed him as Lord, sitting on the right hand of the Most High Father" (*Haer.* 3.16.3).[28]

CONCLUSION

I have tried to draw many of the scriptural threads from the preceding chapters together here to advance my claim that the confession "Jesus is the Messiah" is the starting point for the early Christian interpretation of the Scriptures of Israel.[29] This conclusion is witnessed to by a diverse array of literary forms and expressions, including: confessions, hymns, scriptural types and quotations, exegetical argumentation, speeches, and intrapersonal dramatic dialogue. And while the NT draws upon a host of biblical texts to articulate Jesus's identity and mission, the repeated and consistent appeal to certain texts was dependent upon the conviction that Jesus was God's incarnate, crucified, risen, and enthroned Davidic Messiah (esp. Gen 49:8–12; Num 24:17; Pss 2, 89, 110, 132; Isa 11). The retrospective messianic reading of the OT held together in paradoxical fashion the affirmation that Jesus was God's true messianic king and inaugurator of God's kingdom *and* that Davidic kingship was revealed not through naked power and force but through the embodiment of faithful and righteous suffering.

28. On Irenaeus's (and that of other early Christian authors) practice of reading Ps 110 as David reporting the speech of God the Father as addressing the Son, see Bates, *The Birth of the Trinity*, 67–71.

29. So Juel, *Messianic Exegesis*, 171–73.

CHAPTER 11

Christology

The Messianic Identity and Vocation of Jesus

In this chapter I argue, first, that the New Testament texts, despite a significant diversity of literary forms and perspectives, are unified in their portrayal of Jesus's identity and major narratival events as messianic. That is to say, one of the unifying threads of the NT is a messianic Christology that centers upon six major activities of Messiah Jesus: (1) incarnation and birth; (2) baptismal anointing; (3) proclamation and inauguration of God's kingdom; (4) suffering and crucifixion; (5) resurrection and enthronement; and (6) royal reign over all the nations. The NT texts articulate this sixfold pattern as something I refer to as *the messianic events of King Jesus* through activating messianic-royal scenarios and motifs, application of messianic, royal Scripture, and honorific messianic naming of Jesus's identity.[1] Of course, this is not to say that this six-fold pattern is present in every text or even that the pattern is present in all its particularities in every text; however, I suggest that the NT consistently portrays Jesus's major activities and vocation as messianic acts. And, once again, while I readily affirm that the NT authors also draw upon priestly, prophetic, and other images to construct their Christology, it seems to me that Jesus's messianic identity deserves pride of place in terms of an organizing center for his life and ministry. Second, while I am not so bold (or naïve—I hope) as to advance here a full-blown historical and exegetical argument regarding the development of early divine Christology, I will also argue that Jewish messianism

---

1. While his work does not thematize Jesus's messianic identity as a starting point, I have been influenced by Thomas G. Weinandy, *Jesus Becoming Jesus: A Theological Interpretation of the Synoptic Gospels* (Washington DC: The Catholic University of America Press, 2018). He argues that the major events of the Synoptic Gospels portray Jesus enacting his very identity, expressed in the meaning of his name—"YHWH saves." Jesus's acts are simultaneously the acts of the human Jesus and those of the triune God.

and the conviction that Jesus was the singular anointed messianic king played a necessary and critical role in the early Christian worship of Jesus and belief that he was uniquely related to the God of Israel.

The Incarnation and Birth of the Messiah

The NT authors' depiction of the incarnation and birth of Jesus as a messianic event emphasizes God as one who is making good on his faithfulness to bring about his promises to David, heighten readers' expectations for Jesus's identity and vocation as messianic king of Israel and the nations, and portend the preexistent Son of God's humble solidarity with humanity and assumption of Adamic flesh. Whereas Mark's Gospel famously includes no description of Jesus's birth and instead emphasizes his baptism as the moment of his messianic anointing (Mark 1:9–11), the infancy narratives of both Matthew and Luke lace their descriptions of Jesus's birth with descriptors of Jesus's messianic identity and typological narratives alluding to important events from the history of Israel that mark Jesus out as Israel's messianic king. Thus, in Matthew's Gospel Jesus is "David's son" (Matt 1:1), the Messiah (1:16, 17), and has the royal Judah as his ancestor (1:6). The Messiah is the one who conclusively ends Israel's exile and the period of protracted absence of a Davidic king to rule Israel (1:16–17). Jesus is ironically referred to as the promised messianic shepherd-king, born in Bethlehem (2:5–6). Jesus is referred to not only as "the child" (2:11, 13) but also as "the King of the Jews" (2:2) whose birth threatens King Herod (2:7–9). Jesus is the referent of the messianic anticipation of Israel's prophets (e.g., Isa 7:14 in 1:23; Mic 5:3 in 2:5–6). King Jesus is the recipient of the gifts of the rulers of the nations (Ps 45:7–9; 72:15; Isa 60:1–17 in Matt 2:1–12). Luke's Gospel, too, stresses Jesus's Davidic ancestry, emphasizing Joseph's Davidic descent (Luke 1:27) and Jesus's birth in Bethlehem, "the city of David" (2:4, 11). The angel Gabriel explicitly tells Mary that her son is the promised Davidic Messiah who will sit on "the throne of his father David and will rule over the house of Jacob forever and his kingdom will have no end" (Luke 1:32–33). And so, likewise, Zechariah praises God for his faithfulness, through the birth of Jesus, to the promises made to the house of David (1:69–70); the angels declare that the content of their gospel proclamation centers upon the birth of Jesus—"the Savior who is the Messiah the Lord" (2:10–11; cf. 2:25–26). John's Gospel knows also of the messianic tradition of the Messiah's birth in the village of Bethlehem (John 7:42), though not much is made of it. I have argued that Jesus's fleshly Davidic descent ("born from the seed of David according to the flesh," Rom 1:3) is of importance for Paul's letter to the Romans (cf. also Rom 15:8; 2 Tim 2:8) in that: (1) God's faithfulness to his promises are tied up in the promises he made to David and his descendants (2 Sam 7:12–14; 1 Chr 17:11–14; Ps 18:50–52), and (2) Jesus's messiahship is deeply connected to Paul's argument regarding the Son's assumption of sinful human flesh—that is, Christ's real solidarity with Adamic humanity (e.g., Rom 8:3). Paul's descriptions of Jesus as in "the form of God" (Phil 2:6) and "the image of the invisible God" (Col 1:15a) speak of the preincarnate Messiah as a kingly figure who exists, rules, and even creates with and alongside of the God of Israel. Paul's reference to Jesus as God's *Son* should not be understood as anything other than his creative articulation of Jesus's messianic identity; he frequently uses the term to speak of the Son's identification with fleshly human existence (Rom 8:3; Gal 4:4; cf. Phil 2:7). Drawing on God's promise in Psalm 2:9, Revelation 12:5 speaks of the woman (Israel) giving birth to a male child, the messianic ruler given the authority to rule and shepherd the nations. And, as we have seen, intra-divine dialogue between the Father and messianic Son (i.e., prosopological exegesis), situated as it is before Jesus's birth, also makes the preincarnate Christ the speaker of messianic Scriptures (e.g., see Ps 22:22 and Isa 8:17–18 in Heb 2:11–13).

The Anointing of the Messiah

We have seen that Israel's royal ideology spoke of the Messiah as shorthand for "the *Lord's* Messiah," and that it was the act of anointing the king which marked him out as having a unique relationship with God (e.g., 1 Sam. 2:10, 35; 24:7–11; 26:9–16; Ps 89:21–29). As such, the anointed king was often portrayed as holy and sacrosanct due to his bearing God's Spirit (e.g., 1 Sam 10:1–13; 16:1–13), and prophetic texts sometimes spoke of God's coming Messiah as one who would have God's Spirit in a remarkable way (Isa 11:1–10; 61:1–4; Pss Sol. 17:22, 37; 18:5–7).[2] God's anointed messianic ruler, and the prophetic hope for a perfectly righteous anointed king, will establish God's kingdom on his behalf.

All four canonical Gospels speak of Jesus's baptism as the event where he receives God's messianic anointing and receives the Spirit.[3] And this Spirit-anointing designates and empowers Jesus for his messianic kingly mission. Jesus's baptism, thus, is the event that publicly marks him out as bearing a

---

2. Joshua W. Jipp, *Christ Is King: Paul's Royal Ideology* (Minneapolis: Fortress, 2015), 151–53.

3. On the kingly identity and vocation of Jesus as prefigured in the Synoptics' baptism account, see Weinandy, *Jesus Becoming Jesus*, 97–98.

ather-Son relationship with the God of Israel, as God speaks the Psalm 2:7 to Jesus: "You are my beloved Son, I am well pleased in you" (Mark 1:10–11; cf. Matt 3:17; Luke 3:22).[4] John's Gospel draws upon the messianic oracle of Isaiah 11:1–10 as it has the Baptist testifying of his vision of the descending dove which "rests" upon Jesus, thereby indicating that Jesus is the Spirit-anointed Messiah who will share God's Spirit with others (John 1:32–34). One of Luke's unique contributions to the event of Jesus's Spirit-anointed baptism is his scene where Jesus declares to his fellow Nazarenes, using the language of Isaiah 61:1–4, that he is God's Spirit-anointed proclaimer and enactor of God's gospel (Luke 4:18–19). Jesus's messianic anointing, however, is one which foreshadows the full revelation and manifestation of Jesus's kingship in his sufferings and faithfulness unto death on a Roman cross (see again the connections between Mark 1:9–11 and Mark 15:35–39). Furthermore, the Synoptic literary relation between Jesus's baptism and ensuing temptation scene, shows that Jesus's messiahship, his divine sonship, will be revealed not in bare use of power and authority or in personal and selfish aggrandizement, but rather in humility, suffering, and complete obedience to his Father (Matt 4:1–13; Luke 4:1–13; Mark 1:12–13). I have argued that Matthew's account of Jesus's baptism suggests that Jesus's messianic vocation is to fully identify with sinful Israel's plight as he receives John's baptism, which symbolizes Israel's repentance for forgiveness of sins (Matt 3:1–2, 6, 11; cf. 3:15 with 1:21). Thus, there are good reasons for seeing Jesus's messianic baptismal anointing as an act that is taken *for humanity*, an act whereby Christ identifies and enacts his solidarity with those he has come to rescue and save. We have also seen that Paul, in Romans 1:4, speaks of God's installation or designation of Jesus as the powerful resurrected Son of God. As a result, the resurrected and enthroned Son of God is marked in a powerful way by the "Spirit of holiness," thereby granting him the power to give life and resurrection (Rom 8:9–11), enact familial relations between God, himself, and those in Christ (8:14–17), and produce moral and mental transformation in his people (7:5–6; 8:5–8). As Messiah, Jesus is God's Anointed One, so Paul can speak of persons in Christ sharing in Jesus's messianic anointing such that they share in his messianic identity and vocation (2 Cor 1:21–22). In Ephesians 1:3–14, Paul speaks of Christ as God's elected and beloved Son *in and through whom* believers are also God's elected sons and daughters. While Paul does not provide us

---

4. I agree that the Markan scene portrays God's election of Jesus as the Son of God but do not think this is best understood in an adoptionist sense. See here Michael Peppard, *The Son of God in the Roman World: Divine Sonship in Its Social and Political Context* (Oxford: Oxford University Press, 2011). For a response to Peppard, see Michael F. Bird, *Jesus the Eternal Son: Answering Adoptionist Christology* (Grand Rapids: Eerdmans, 2017), 64–81.

with explicit indications that he knew of Jesus's baptism by John the Baptist, he does speak of baptism with Christ—in his suffering, death, and resurrection—as the means of believers' participation in Christ's messianic identity and narrative (esp. Rom 6:1–11; cf. Gal 3:28; Col 2:11–15).

The Kingdom of the Messiah

It is no surprise, then, that immediately after God anoints Jesus as his Spirit-empowered Messiah, Jesus's first act is to proclaim "the gospel of God" (Mark 1:14) and "the kingdom of God" (1:15). The Synoptic Gospels repeatedly speak of Jesus's fundamental task as the proclamation and enactment of God's kingdom and gospel. Matthew uses repeated references to Jesus as one who proclaimed "the gospel of the kingdom" as a structural marker in chapters 5–9 (4:23; 9:35; cf. 4:17). In Luke's Gospel, Jesus declares that God has sent him to proclaim good news of God's kingdom (4:43). In the Fourth Gospel, Jesus receives the acclamation that he is Israel's King (John 1:49; 12:13), proclaims God's kingdom to Nicodemus (John 3:3–5), and declares that he has his own nonworldly kingdom (18:36–37). Matthew Bates nicely states the close connection between God's gospel and kingdom in the Gospels: "[G]iven that Jesus's most characteristic teaching was the gospel of the nearness/arrival of the kingdom of God, and granted that this was typically understood to entail a turning of the ages such that God's reign was actualized through a Davidic king, then whenever Jesus put himself forward through word or action as the Davidic Messiah, he was preaching and effecting the gospel."[5] And the gospel of God's kingdom, in the canonical Fourfold Gospel, centers upon God's actions in the life and events of Messiah Jesus (i.e., precisely the messianic events we are examining here). I won't belabor the point in any detail, but we have seen that Paul's gospel also centers upon the story of the Messiah's Davidic descent and incarnation, faithfulness and obedience to God, death on the cross, and resurrection and enthronement (Rom 1:1–5; 1 Cor 15:1–11; 2 Tim 2:8; cf. Rom 10:9–10; Gal 4:4–7; Phil 2:6–11). One of the primary motifs of the book of Revelation is its depiction of the Davidic Messiah (Rev 11:15; 12:10)—the Lion of Judah and the Root of Jesse (5:5)—who sacrificially and nonviolently conquers Satan and his powers and thereby procures and establishes a people who *are* God's kingdom (1:5–6; 5:9–10).

---

5. Matthew W. Bates, *Salvation by Allegiance Alone: Rethinking Faith, Works, and the Gospel of Jesus the King* (Grand Rapids: Baker Academic, 2017), 50. On Jesus's kingship in the Gospels, see Scot McKnight, *The King Jesus Gospel: The Original Good News Revisited* (Grand Rapids: Zondervan, 2011).

We have seen that the NT authors understand the earthly life of Jesus to have inaugurated or foreshadowed God's kingdom in the following ways. First, just as God's Messiah and good king was understood to be a lover of God's Torah and supremely wise, so the NT depicts Messiah Jesus as the perfect interpreter and embodiment of God's Torah. Matthew and Luke present Jesus as one who rightly interprets God's Torah from the standpoint of mercy, justice, and love (Matt 12:1–14; 22:34–40; 23:23; Luke 11:42). Jesus is the eschatological manifestation of God's will and perfect righteousness (Matt 3:15; 5:20). Paul's phrase "the law of Christ" (Gal 6:2; 1 Cor 9:21–22; cf. Rom 15:1–7) is coined to express how the Messiah's loving and cruciform death embodies the Torah's demand for self-sacrifice and love of neighbor. Second, the Gospels understand Jesus's messianic kingship and inauguration of God's kingdom as centering upon Jesus as God's singular messianic shepherd who leads and shepherds God's flock with compassion, justice, and mercy (Matt 2:6; 9:27–31; 26:26–32; John 10; cf. Jer 23:1–5; Ezek 34:23; Mic 5:1–3). For the Synoptic Gospels, and of course especially Luke-Acts, Jesus's compassion and mercy are highlighted through his table fellowship and extension of hospitality to the vulnerable, marginalized, and outcast (e.g., Luke 5:27–32; 7:36–50; 15:1–2; 19:1–10). That God's kingdom is one of justice, peace, and joy is expressed in these shared meals between the Messiah and his people, and thereby Jesus's meals often function as an opportunity to reveal his messianic identity (e.g., Luke 9:11–27; 22:14–30; 24:28–35). Third, the NT writings portray God's kingdom as inaugurated through Jesus's destruction and scattering of Satan and his demons. While the Messiah's defeat of evil is emphasized in a variety of NT texts, Mark's Gospel especially establishes Jesus's messianic identity as on display in his authority over the demons and his plundering of Satan's kingdom (Mark 1:23–28; 3:10–11, 23–30; 5:7; cf. Luke 10:9–11; 1 Cor 15:23–28; 2 Thess 2:1–8). Fourth, and relatedly, the Gospels and Acts see God's kingdom as on display through Jesus's healings (as well as those of his disciples) as they express God's merciful compassion for his scattered and afflicted people (Matt 10:5–9; 12:15–21; Luke 4:18:19, 31–37; 9:1–6; 10:1–13; 13:10–17; Acts 2:22; 3:1–10; 14:8–10). Fifth, Paul argues that Christ's obedience to his Father has inaugurated a kingdom of people who have been established in justice, peace, and life (Rom 5:12–21; 6:12–23; cf. Phil 2:7–8). Sixth, we may include here John's portrait of Jesus's messianic identity as consisting in signs which reveal divine glory (e.g., 2:1–12; 4:25–29; 11:25–27), something not unlike the Synoptic accounts of Jesus's transfiguration where his divine sonship and messianic identity, power, and kingdom are proleptically revealed to the disciples after the messianic confession of Peter (Mark 8:27–33 and 9:2–9).

The Death of the Messiah

Almost every NT composition has argued that rather than disconfirming it, Jesus's faithful sufferings and death by crucifixion is at the heart of God's kingdom and Jesus's messianic kingship. Luke's account of the resurrected Jesus's speech—"'did you not know that it was necessary that the Messiah must suffer and enter into [God's] glory,' and beginning from Moses and from all the prophets he explained to them all the things written in the Scriptures concerning him" (Luke 24:26–27; cf. 24:44–49)—is typical for a variety of NT writings which indicate that Israel's Scriptures anticipated the sufferings of the Messiah. For Paul it is of "first importance" that the Christian tradition declares that "the Messiah died for our sins according to the Scriptures" (1 Cor 15:3). In Matthew's Gospel, Jesus's death is the means whereby he, as Israel's Davidic ruler, saves his people from their sins and ransoms Israel from slavery (Matt 1:21; 20:28; 26:28). We have seen in the preceding chapter ("Scripture: Messianic Exegesis and Christology") that the NT consistently appropriates the Psalter, specifically the Davidic psalms which portend a righteous king who suffers at the hands of the wicked, as a means of explaining the death of the Messiah. One finds this dynamic, and in abundance, in the passion narratives of all four Gospels, the apostolic speeches in Acts, throughout the letters of Paul, Hebrews, 1 Peter, and Revelation. We have also seen that the Markan Jesus does not reject the title of "Messiah" but is rather, one might say, suspicious of whether humans appropriately understand that the Messiah and his kingdom are defined by means of his suffering and cross. Thus, one can confess that Jesus is the Messiah and do so in a way that embodies the worldly patterns of Satan and "the thoughts of humans" (Mark 8:33)—so long as Messiah and cross are understood as antithetically related (Mark 8:34–9:1). So for Mark's Gospel, as well as Matthew's and Luke's, the mock royal enthronement of Jesus by the soldiers (Mark 15:1–25), the placard "The King of the Jews" (15:26), and the confession of Jesus as "the Son of God" (15:36–39) speak the soberest truth—God's kingdom and the revelation of Jesus as messianic king come by means of Jesus's death on the cross. Similarly, for John's Gospel it is the cross that reveals Jesus's glorification and enthronement as king of Israel (John 8:28; 12:1–16; 12:31–34). In Revelation, Jesus's means of military warfare and conquering is ironically through his martyrdom, a saving death that has purchased for himself a people from all nations (Rev 1:5–6; 5:5–12; 7:13–17; 19:11–13).

The Resurrection and Enthronement of the Messiah

Just as David was God's elected king even while King Saul was alive but only entered into his role as King of Israel upon Saul's death (1 Sam 15–2 Sam 5), so it is only at the Davidic Messiah's resurrection and heavenly enthronement to God's right hand that Jesus, as the incarnate, crucified, true human, is installed as messianic king. The NT writings consistently interpret God's resurrection of Jesus from the dead as the act whereby God vindicates Jesus of Nazareth as his anointed Messiah, positions him to a place of powerful rule over his people and the cosmos, and enacts his defeat and dethroning of Satan and his powers (e.g., Rom 1:4; 1 Cor 15:43–45; Eph 1:20–2:6). As the resurrected and enthroned Messiah, his establishment to a place of cosmic rule is the event that demonstrates him to be both "Lord" and "Messiah" (e.g., Phil 2:9–11; Acts 2:36). The NT's frequent application of Psalm 110:1 implies that the risen Jesus is currently sitting in a position of power in heaven as he reigns until all enemies are put under his feet (e.g., 1 Cor 15:25–28; Heb 1:13; 1 Pet 3:18–22; cf. Col 2:14–15; Rev 19:11–21). He is, therefore, the judge of heaven and earth and all people (e.g., Matt 23:32–39; 25:31–46; 2 Cor 5:9–10; 1 Pet 3:18, 22; 4:1–6; Rev 1:13–17). As such, Christ is "the firstborn from the dead and the ruler of the kings of the earth" (Rev 1:5a). As the firstborn from the dead, he is worthy to receive "first place in all things" (Col 1:18) and to receive worship from the angels (Heb 1:6). Even now God's perfected Son, the enthroned messianic king, is serving as God's high priest in heaven and interceding for his people (Heb 4:14–16; 7:23–28; 8:1–6; 9:11–28). While the Synoptic Gospels emphasize and give pride of place to narrating the necessity of the Messiah's death in their passion narratives, they are also emphatic that Jesus's death is meaningful and salvific because of God's resurrection of Christ from the dead. For example, invoking Psalm 118:22 anticipates Jesus's resurrection as the means whereby he becomes the new chief cornerstone of his messianic community (e.g., Mark 11:22–25; 12:10–11; Luke 20:8–18; Acts 4:10–11). The Synoptic Gospels often express Jesus's bringing the kingdom to its fulfillment when he is resurrected and enthroned as the heavenly king and Son of Man (e.g., Matt 19:28; Mark 10:35–40). His resurrection is the event whereby he unleashes salvation and blessings for his people (Acts 3:18–26; 13:32–37). The NT texts frequently speak of Christ's resurrection and heavenly ascension as the origin of the event whereby the Holy Spirit is poured out upon God's people (e.g., John 16:8–15; 20:21–23; Acts 2:1–36; Rom 1:3–4; 1 Cor 15:44–45).

The Gentile Nations as the Inheritance of the Messiah

If Christ is the messianic king enthroned in heaven, that is to say, the ruler of the cosmos, then it makes sense that the messianic mission would be for all the nations and not simply Israel. And many scriptural texts and traditions anticipate that God's restoration of Israel will have as its consequence the extension of salvation to the nations and their recognition that the God of Israel is the one true God (e.g., Isa 2:1–4; 66:17–24), and some of these texts even anticipate the nations of the earth, along with their rulers, recognizing and submitting to Israel's Davidic king (e.g., Ps 45:7–9; 72:8–15; Isa 60:1–6). We have seen that even the poetic seams in the Torah anticipate an eschatological ruler who receives the nations as his inheritance (Gen 49:8–12; Num 24:17–18). The Psalter is filled with oracles that the coming Davidic king will establish a righteous rule over the entire cosmos and the foreign nations will come to worship the king (e.g., Pss 72:1–18; 89:1–28). In Psalm 2, God promises to give his enthroned messianic king the nations as his inheritance (Ps 2:6–8; cf. 18:39–45).

The NT often portrays Christ's resurrection and ascension as having as its consequence the mission to the gentile nations as a means of procuring the Messiah's inheritance. We have seen in Matthew's Gospel, for example, that the magi from the east give gifts and even worship to "the child" who is "the King of Jews" (Matt 2:2, 8, 11). After the full revelation of Jesus's kingship, by means of the cross and resurrection, the risen Son of Man commissions his disciples to teach and make disciples of all the nations (Matt 28:16–20). In Luke's Gospel, Simeon's seeing "the Lord's Messiah" causes him to declare that Jesus is salvation for "all peoples" and "a light of revelation to the nations and glory for your people Israel" (2:27, 30, 31b–32). In Acts 15 we have seen that James appeals to Amos 9:11–12 to settle the argument that gentiles are included within God's people now that God has rebuilt and restored "the fallen tent of David" (see Acts 15:16–18). In other words, God has provided salvation for Israel through the Davidic king, and this event unleashes God's salvific blessings to *also* go to the gentiles. Similarly, John's Gospel portrays Jesus's death and subsequent "lifting up" as the event which both unifies the scattered people of God and draws *all people* to Jesus (John 11:51–52; 12:31–32). Christ's kingship is universal in scope for Revelation as Christ is "the Lord over lords and King over Kings" (Rev 17:14; cf. 19:16). Likewise, Paul's commitment to take the gospel to the gentiles is rooted in his conviction that they, along with the restored cosmos, are his rightful inheritance (Rom 1:5; 4:13; 8:17–25; 15:8–13; Gal 3:14–19).

CHRIST THE MESSIANIC KING AND THE ORIGINS OF CHRISTOLOGY

My second thesis is that Jesus Christ's identity as Israel's messianic king plays a significant role in the early Christian conception of Jesus as divine and as worthy of receiving worship alongside the God of Israel. That is to say, Israel's Scriptures with their depiction of God electing, anointing, and sharing his throne and glory with his covenanted Davidic king is indispensable for understanding the early Christian belief that Jesus of Nazareth, as God's messianic king, was singularly worthy of receiving worship due to his unique relationship to the God of Israel. This is not to say that there is an obvious and straight line from Israel's royal ideology to early Christian Christology; I only intend to make the more limited and yet still, in my view, important claim that Israel's royal ideology and Jewish messianism is a critical and indispensable context for the NT's exalted claims about Jesus of Nazareth.

While it was once fashionable to provide an evolutionary historical explanation for the gradual rise of early Christian belief in Jesus's divinity as something that could only arise in a pagan/gentile context where it was common to worship many gods and even heroes or emperors, the past thirty years or so has witnessed an increased recognition that the worship of Jesus and belief in him as divine occurred within Jewish monotheism.[6] Thus, Larry Hurtado has argued that Jesus received worship and devotion along with an exclusive allegiance to God the Father resulting in what he calls a "binitarian" shape of Christian devotion/worship.[7] Crispin Fletcher-Louis even speaks of a "new emerging consensus" that sees belief in Jesus as divine as emerging very early, within a Jewish monotheistic context, and as binitarian/dyadic in character.[8] Perhaps the most influential argument for positing belief in Christ's divine identity as arising within a strict Jewish monotheistic framework is that of Richard Bauckham.[9] Bauckham has argued that God's identity is revealed

6. The classic work here is, of course, Wilhelm Bousset, *Kyrios Christos: A History of the Belief in Christ from the Beginnings of Christianity to Irenaeus*, trans. John E. Steely (Nashville: Abingdon, 1970). For a creative rearticulation of the older history of religions consensus, however, see Maurice Casey, *From Jewish Prophet to Gentile God: The Origins and Development of New Testament Christology* (Louisville: Westminster John Knox, 1991).

7. See especially Larry W. Hurtado, *Lord Jesus Christ: Devotion to Jesus in Earliest Christianity* (Grand Rapids: Eerdmans, 2003); Larry W. Hurtado, *How on Earth Did Jesus Become a God? Historical Questions about Earliest Devotion to Jesus* (Grand Rapids: Eerdmans, 2005).

8. Crispin Fletcher-Louis, *Christological Origins: The Emerging Consensus and Beyond*, vol. 1 of *Jesus Monotheism* (Eugene, OR: Cascade, 2015), 3–30.

9. Richard J. Bauckham, *Jesus and the God of Israel: God Crucified and Other Studies on the New Testament's Christology of Divine Identity* (Grand Rapids: Eerdmans, 2008).

through his being the sole creator and ruler of the world, as the singular re-cipient of the divine name, and as the sole recipient of worship. Bauckham uses the language of "divine identity" to speak of the one who creates, rules, and receives worship. There is a complete divide, then, between God the creator and all that he has created.

> The point is that both of these features of the divine identity [i.e., creator and sovereign ruler] define an absolute distinction between God and all other reality. He alone is Creator; all else is created by him. He alone is su-preme Ruler; all else is subject to his will. Even the most exalted of creatures is created and subject to God, while God is uncreated and subject to none.[10]

Many scholars have been convinced by Bauckham's argument for a strict and absolute divide between Yahweh's divine identity that excludes all else from sharing in the so-called divine identity.[11] The NT texts repeatedly speak of Christ as performing divine activities which are reserved only for the God of Israel (e.g., creating, ruling, judging, receiving worship) and this suggests that the "earliest christology was already the highest Christology."[12] While I am in large agreement with Bauckham, I suggest, however, that three very significant caveats need to be made concerning (1) the personal relation between Christ and the God of Israel; (2) God's freedom and ability to share his identity and functions with those he elects; and (3) the role of Israelite royal ideology and Jewish messianism in the origins of NT Christology.

Divine Personal Relationships

First, some have rightly, in my view, argued that rather than speak of divine *identity* and Christ as *identified* with the God of Israel, the biblical texts sup-port a Christology of divine *persons*.[13] To give just one example, Wesley Hill

---

10. Bauckham, *Jesus and the God of Israel*, 154.

11. For example, Bird, *Jesus the Eternal Son*; Richard B. Hays, *Echoes of Scripture in the Gospels* (Waco, TX: Baylor University Press, 2016); Chris Tilling, *Paul's Divine Christology*, WUNT 2.323 (Tübingen: Mohr Siebeck, 2012); N. T. Wright, *Paul and the Faithfulness of God*, vol. 4 of *Christian Origins and the Question of God* (Minneapolis: Fortress, 2013).

12. Bauckham, "Paul's Christology of Divine Identity," in *Jesus and the God of Israel*, 184.

13. This argument has been made with respect to the Father, Son, and Spirit engaging in intra-divine dialogue with one another. See here Matthew W. Bates *The Birth of the Trinity: Jesus, God, and Spirit in New Testament and Early Christian Interpretations of the*

argues that the God of Israel and Jesus the Son *are who they are* only in relation to one another. God is, for example, the God who sent his Son (e.g., Rom 8:3; Gal 4:4) and the God who raised Jesus from the dead (Rom 4:24). Thus, "by his act of giving and raising Jesus . . . God defines himself as a distinct person, in such a way that the relation is internal to the self-definition."[14] God differentiates himself from the Son in his actions of sending, raising, granting the name above all names, and enthroning him to his right hand, but within this differentiation is a mutuality between the Father and the Son such that "God is not who God is as 'father' without Jesus and Jesus is not who he is as the raised and exalted one without God."[15] Thus, instead of starting with God and trying to figure out how to include Jesus and the Spirit within the so-called divine identity, it makes better sense to see Father, Son, and Spirit as relational persons who are all "equally primal, mutually determinative, relationally constituted."[16] James Dunn has more significant disagreements with Bauckham's thesis than Hill, but he, too, is concerned that the language of sharing in the divine identity fails to do "justice to the history of Jesus and to the diverse roles attributed to Jesus that are distinguished from God's."[17] That is to say, there are some things which are true for Jesus but are not true for the Father and vice versa. In other words, Dunn is concerned that the appropriate differentiation between God and Jesus is upheld such that Jesus is not directly equated with or identified as God the Father.

God's Election of Individuals to Share in His Rule

Secondly, I suggest that Bauckham's treatment of Jewish monotheism is too exclusive and that his account of both monotheism and NT Christology works with categories that are "too neat and self-contained" and ultimately fails to account for impressive analogies in Jewish literature where other figures do actually engage in cosmic rule, share God's throne, and receive worship.[18] I men-

---

Old Testament (Oxford: Oxford University Press, 2015) and also Bates, *The Hermeneutics of Apostolic Proclamation: The Center of Paul's Method of Scriptural Interpretation* (Waco, TX: Baylor University Press, 2012).

14. Wesley Hill, *Paul and the Trinity: Persons, Relations, and the Pauline Letters* (Grand Rapids: Eerdmans, 2015), 74.

15. Hill, *Paul and the Trinity*, 133.

16. Hill, *Paul and the Trinity*, 168.

17. James D. G. Dunn, *Did the First Christians Worship Jesus? The New Testament Evidence* (Louisville: Westminster John Knox, 2011), 142–43.

18. Andrew Chester, "High Christology—Whence, When and Why?," *EC* 2.1 (2011): 41.

tion three works here as helpfully representing my concerns. The first work is
J. R. Daniel Kirk's study of the Christology of the Synoptic Gospels—*A Man
Attested by God*. Here Kirk provides an abundance of examples wherein Israel's
Scriptures and Jewish literature are filled with "idealized humans" (his term
for non-angelic and non-preexistent persons) who are granted a share in God's
rule and work. Thus, Genesis 1–2 (and more Jewish traditions) depict Adam
as sharing in God's sovereign rule and, in some texts, even receiving worship;
Philo speaks of Moses as both god and king in his *Life of Moses*; and Ezekiel
the Tragedian portrays Moses as enthroned to heaven and ruling the world
for God on his throne. According to the Chronicler, the Davidic king receives
worship with Yahweh; he is referred to as God by the psalmist (Ps 45) and rules
over the created order (Ps 89); and Daniel's Son of Man figure rules the world
on God's behalf (Dan 7:13–27). The Synoptic Gospels draw upon the traditions
of these idealized humans to portray Jesus as sharing in God's rule. Kirk makes
an important distinction between using the language of being identified with
God and being identified as God. In his words: "Idealized human figures are
identified with God in various ways in early Judaism, including sharing in
God's sovereignty and receiving worship. This shows us that being identified
with God is not the same as being identified *as* God."[19] The Jewish literature
presents all kinds of human figures who participate in "the divine identity,
without any sense that this puts pressure on the inherent identity of God, demanding its reconfiguration."[20] In my view, Kirk has helpfully problematized
Bauckham's emphasis on monotheism as so strict as to exclude figures from
sharing in God's rule. Kirk's project raises important questions but does not
answer *how* the early Christians came to see Jesus as preexistent, sharing in
God's *creation at the beginning*, and the singular human who shares God's rule
and throne and receives worship. Kirk says that the "exalted place occupied by
idealized humans makes it difficult to even articulate what would be entailed
in the appearance of a divine being who causes us to reimagine the inherent
identity of Israel's God."[21] And yet this is exactly what happened. God is now
identified by his relation to Jesus (and vice versa).

Similar concerns are raised by Crispin Fletcher-Louis in his first volume
of *Jesus Monotheism*, where he argues for a more inclusive monotheism.

See throughout, Andrew Chester, *Messiah and Exaltation: Jewish Messianic and Visionary
Traditions and New Testament Christology*, WUNT 207 (Tübingen: Mohr Siebeck, 1991).

19. J. R. Daniel Kirk, *A Man Attested by God: The Human Jesus of the Synoptic Gospels*
(Grand Rapids: Eerdmans, 2016), 174.

20. Kirk, *A Man Attested by God*, 174.

21. Kirk, *A Man Attested by God*, 570.

Fletcher-Louis also points to Jewish texts that portray righteous humans who are described with divine language, who are deified by God, who share God's throne, and who receive worship.[22] He examines in detail 1 Enoch 37–71, Jewish messianism, and the Life of Adam and Eve and suggests that while these texts obviously cannot fully explain the origins of NT Christology, they do function as precedents that show "that parts of that full pattern were anticipated in ways that can help explain, as one or more set of factors and forces, the appearance of Christ devotion and 'Christological monotheism.'"[23] Fletcher-Louis notes that Bauckham has simply asserted rather than provided evidence for his belief that God cannot share his own identity with another person or place; instead, Fletcher-Louis suggests that it is precisely because God is transcendent, free, sovereign, and distinguished from created reality *"that God is able to enter into and take on the nature and identity of that reality, even on occasion, taking that reality up into his very own self."*[24] In other words, God has "a shareable divine identity," and this sharing of his divine identity reflects "God's original intention for humanity from the beginning."[25] Thus, contrary to what some have assumed, God's sharing of his identity is his sovereign prerogative, and Jewish monotheism is not compromised simply because it is not strictly exclusive.[26]

Jewish Messianism and the Origins of New Testament Christology

If the NT writings often depict a Jewish monotheism that allows for God's ability to freely elect and thereby share his divine identity with other humans, then

22. Fletcher-Louis, *Christological Origins*, 299–305.

23. Fletcher-Louis, *Christological Origins*, 132.

24. Fletcher-Louis, *Christological Origins*, 306, 310. Also valuable here is Matthew J. Lynch, *Monotheism and Institutions in the Book of Chronicles: Temple, Priesthood, and Kingship in Post-exilic Perspective*, FAT 2.64 (Tübingen Mohr Siebeck, 2014). Lynch notes that Yahweh's unique supremacy is revealed in his bond with his people through Israel's primary institutions of temple, priesthood, and monarchy—*institutions which embody the presence and power of Yahweh.*

25. Fletcher-Louis, *Christological Origins*, 312.

26. Kirk and Fletcher-Louis are by no means the only ones who have pushed against an exclusionary understanding of Jewish monotheism. Another recent example, David Litwa, notes that a host of biblical texts emphasize aspects of God that cannot be shared with humans (see, for example, Num 23:19 LXX; Isa 31:3; Hos 11:9), but that these only pertain to *certain qualities* and that in fact the Greek Scriptures present "a God willing to share his divine glory and universal sovereignty—two aspects of his divine identity." M. David Litwa, *We Are Being Transformed: Deification in Paul's Soteriology*, BZNW (Berlin: de Gruyter, 2012), 86–87, 116. See also the critique of Hurtado and Bauckham's exclusive monotheism by Peppard, *The Son of God*, 11–26.

there is no a priori reason why we should reject the possibility that early Christian Christology developed, in *part*, through reflections upon Jesus's identity as Israel's singular messianic king. Numerous recent works have pointed to the significance of Jewish messianism and ancient kingship ideology as a critical context for understanding a variety of the NT claims about Messiah Jesus.[27] William Horbury, for example, has argued that it is Jesus's *messianic* identity that best explains the early origins of the Christian worship of Christ.[28] His primary argument is that "messianism is then likely to have been a major factor in creating the cult of Christ among Christians and their corresponding christological affirmations."[29] Kirk also makes a significant contribution to the view that the origin of NT Christology is situated within Jewish messianism. He summarizes his conclusions on kings and rulers within early Judaism:

> The kings are God's sons, those who are enthroned at God's right hand. At times, they are even depicted as sitting on God's own throne, for the purpose of enacting God's reign on earth. This reign is far-reaching, inasmuch as it is an expression of God's own reign over all the chaotic forces that threaten creation, human life in general, and Israel in particular. . . . [T]he biblical Israelite tradition depicts Israel's kings in precisely the ways

27. For just a sampling, see Matthew V. Novenson, *Christ among the Messiahs: Christ Language in Paul and Messiah Language in Ancient Judaism* (Oxford: Oxford University Press, 2012); Adela Yarbro Collins and John J. Collins, *King and Messiah as Son of God: Divine, Human, and Angelic Messianic Figures in Biblical and Related Literature* (Grand Rapids: Eerdmans, 2008); Paula Fredriksen, *Paul: The Pagans' Apostle* (New Haven: Yale University Press, 2017), 131–66; Julien Smith, *Christ the Ideal King: Cultural Context, Rhetorical Strategy, and the Power of Divine Monarchy in Ephesians*, WUNT 2.313 (Tübingen: Mohr Siebeck, 2011).

28. William Horbury, *Jewish Messianism and the Cult of Christ* (London: SCM, 1998), 3. In my view, Horbury's controversial (and probably untenable) claims about both the coherence and prevalence of Jewish messianism has unfortunately resulted in the neglect of his specific argument regarding the origins of NT Christology. See here the sage methodological alternatives in Matthew V. Novenson, *The Grammar of Messianism: An Ancient Jewish Political Idiom and Its Users* (Oxford: Oxford University Press, 2017), 120–24. On the coherence and prevalence of Jewish Messianism, see the balanced study of Stefan Schreiber, *Gesalbter und König: Titel and Konzeptionen der königlichen Gesalbtenerwartung in früjüdischen und unchristlichen Schriften*, BZNW 105 (Berlin: de Gruyter, 2000).

29. William Horbury, "Jewish Messianism and Early Christology," in *Contours of Christology in the New Testament*, ed. Richard N. Longenecker (Grand Rapids: Eerdmans, 2005), 22.

that some New Testament scholars have argued to be signals that a being is none other than God.[30]

Within Israel's Scriptures, God's election of Israel's messianic king to participate in his rule, activity, and divine glory functions as a significant framework for the NT's depiction of Jesus Christ's identity and activities. Israel's Scriptures often depict God electing, anointing, and exalting the Davidic king such that he participates in God's kingship as his earthly ruler. The king *is*, then, simply a human who has, through God's election, been called to participate in God's divine kingship.[31] For example, Israel's Scriptures declare that the king shares in God's kingship when it states that the Davidic king: sits on God's throne (1 Chr 29:23; LXX Ps 44:6; Pss. Sol. 17:30–32); shares in Yahweh's rule (LXX Pss 2; 89); receives divine honors (1 Chr 29:20); is enthroned to God's right hand (Ps 110; cf. Ps 2:6–8); shares in God's royal glory (Pss 3:4; LXX 20:7–8; LXX 44:4; LXX 61:9); and receives the honorifics of "Yahweh's anointed" (1 Sam 16:6; 24:7, 11; 26:9, 11; 2 Sam 19:22; LXX Pss 17:51; 88:39, 52; 131:10), "Lord" (LXX Ps 109:1), "son of God" (LXX Pss 2:7; 109:3; cf. 2 Sam 7:12–14), and God's "firstborn son" (LXX Ps 88:27).

The NT writings we have examined present us with a figure spoken of as "Lord," "Messiah," "firstborn Son," and "Son of God." This figure is spoken of as *elected* by Yahweh. He is exalted to God's right hand, shares in God's rule, and is marked out as sharing in and bestowing God's *pneuma*. And he receives divine honors and worship. Furthermore, the NT authors repeatedly indicate that they are drawing upon Israel's Psalter as one conceptual resource for explaining the identity of Messiah Jesus. The Synoptic Gospels' portrait of Jesus as sharing in God's rule over the world, exerting authority over the sea, enthroned next to God, and having intimate knowledge of the Father are best interpreted within Israelite royal ideology.[32] The Pauline Christ hymns in Philippians 2:6–11 and Colossians 1:15–20, as we have seen, present the Messiah as God's singular vicegerent who shares in God's rule and authority and reveals true rule and power by giving his life on the cross. The resonances of the Septuagintal royal psalms in these hymns suggest that the Christ hymns may have developed in the Christian assemblies where worshippers of Jesus sang both biblical psalms and new hymnic compositions in honor of Christ, the messianic king who liberates and saves God's people, shares God's throne, and

---

30. Kirk, *A Man Attested by God*, 109–10.

31. I have argued this in more detail in Jipp, *Christ Is King*, 150–60.

32. So Kirk, *A Man Attested by God*, 259.

receives divine honors and worship. These biblical psalms, echoed throughout the Christ hymns, depict God sharing the divine throne and divine authority over creation with the anointed firstborn son (Ps 89; Col 1:15, 18), inviting another lord to share his throne and sit at his right hand (Ps 110:1; Phil 2:9–11), and giving the anointed son the rule over the nations (Ps 2; Col 1:13).

If creation is a hallmark of divine activity, then there are good reasons for supposing that Christ's role as creator was posited as an extension of his rule as God's messiah. Sean McDonough has advanced a powerful argument that claims such as the one found in Colossians 1:16—namely, that Christ is the creator of all things—stem from Jesus's messianic status. In his words, "Jesus' role in creation emerged within a messianic matrix of reflection. Creation marks the beginning of his messianic dominion; he rules the world he made."[33] As Yahweh's anointed one, Christ is entrusted with the task of ruling on God's behalf; the Father, therefore, grants Jesus the task of sharing in the creation of the universe. McDonough notes that all of the NT texts which depict Jesus as creator "focus on the theme of messianic lordship."[34] In fact, it seems highly likely that the Davidic Psalm 89 (LXX Ps 88) is the context for the hymn's claims that Jesus is "firstborn over all creation" and the one who has created all things (1:15b–16). McDonough is right, then, to claim that Paul is extending "the purview of the Messiah's authority to include primal creation."[35]

The Gospel of John gives testimony to the belief that God's coming messiah would have an eternal kingdom and rule based on specific Davidic oracles (John 11:25–27; 12:31–34; Gen 49:8–12; 2 Sam 7:12–17; Ps 89:28–29, 35–37). And it is precisely as God's enthroned messianic king, paradoxically by means of the cross, that Jesus receives divine glory and honors (John 12:23–29; 13:31–32; 17:1–5). We have seen that the author of Hebrews uses Davidic kingship language to speak of the eternal Son (Heb 1:1–3) as God's Son (Heb 1:5; Ps 2:7; 2 Sam 7:14), who receives worship from God's angels (Heb 1:6), is referred to as "God" and shares God's throne (Heb 1:8–10; Ps 45:7), and sits at God's right hand (Heb 1:13; Ps 110:1). In the book of Revelation, the one sharing God's throne and receiving worship and divine honors (Rev 5:5–13) is the kingly Messiah—namely, "the Lion from the tribe of Judah" (5:5; Gen 49:8–12), "the Root of David" (5:5; Isa 11:1–10). We have seen Revelation frequently use Psalm 2 to

33. Sean M. McDonough, *Christ as Creator: Origins of a New Testament Doctrine* (Oxford: Oxford University Press, 2009), 65.

34. McDonough, *Christ as Creator*, 68.

35. McDonough, *Christ as Creator*, 67. See further, Jipp, *Christ Is King*, 107–10; J. R. Daniel Kirk and Stephen L. Young, "'I Will Set His Hand to the Sea'; Psalm 88:26 LXX and Christology in Mark," *JBL* 133 (2014): 333–40.

portray Christ as God's anointed ruler who shares his throne and rules over the rebellious rulers of the earth (e.g., Rev 12:5–17; 19:11–16).

Conclusion

In this chapter I have briefly argued for two theses. First, Jesus's life, vocation, and acts have a narratival unity grounded in the NT's conviction that Jesus is the Messiah of Israel. While NT texts engage an array of metaphors, images, and titles to depict the significance of Jesus, I have suggested that Jesus's life is construed in terms of his messianic identity and activities in terms of his birth and incarnation, anointing and baptism, proclamation of God's kingdom, sacrificial death on the cross, resurrection and enthronement, and ongoing rule over the gentile nations. Secondly, I have suggested, and by no means fully argued, that the NT's highly exalted claims about Jesus's unique relationship to the God of Israel, as one who shares God's throne and who receives divine honors and worship are illuminated, in part, as creative reflections upon Jesus as God's singular and unique Davidic king. More nuances regarding the relationship between Jewish messianism and NT Christology are necessary than what can be offered here. I am not suggesting that Jewish messianism is the *singular* feature that explains NT Christology or, to use the language of James Charlesworth, that "Jewish messianology . . . flow[s] majestically into Christian Christology."[36] There is no perfect conceptual antecedent here that explains the origins of the worship of the Messiah alongside the God of Israel. And yet, surely, or so it would seem to me, one of the conclusions of our examination of the NT texts is that Jesus's royal, messianic identity played a significant and indispensable role in the origins of early Christology. It strikes me as eminently plausible that the earliest Christians reflected deeply upon the identity, resurrection, and redemptive work of Messiah Jesus in light of the kinds of claims made for Israel's kings, especially as found in the Psalter.[37]

---

36. To be clear, Charlesworth is arguing *against* this view. See J. H. Charlesworth, "From Jewish Messianology to Christian Christology: Some Caveats and Perspectives," in *Judaisms and Their Messiahs at the Turn of the Christian Era*, ed. Jacob Neusner et al. (Cambridge: Cambridge University Press, 1987), 255.

37. Jipp, *Christ Is King*, 136.

CHAPTER 12

Soteriology

Participating in the Saving Reign of the Messiah

The NT texts are emphatic that Messiah Jesus saves his people and that he does so in fulfillment of God's scriptural promises to establish his saving kingdom over his people. But how does God save his people through his messianic king? While different texts emphasize different aspects of the life of the Son of God, their unified witness is that it is the entire life and narrative of the Lord's Messiah that is necessary for humanity's salvation. In other words, the Messiah's incarnation, life, death, resurrection, and session at the right hand of the Father function as the means whereby God saves his people and establishes his kingdom for his people. While Paul especially witnesses to a participatory soteriology whereby humans are saved by virtue of being conjoined to the Messiah, I have argued that the theme (conceptualized by me often as sharing in Christ's reign or kingdom) is present throughout the NT. I have argued that royal messianism best explains the NT's articulation of the narrative of Messiah Jesus and the NT's mapping of the same narrative identity onto the Messiah's people. Many of the NT texts conceptualize the relationship between Christ and his people as the relationship between king and subjects, with the Messiah's people, however, sharing in the resurrected, enthroned Messiah's heavenly rule. As participants in the Messiah's lordship, the king's subjects share in the benefits of his ongoing rule.

When the question is asked—how does Jesus save people?—it is easy to extract short propositional statements from the NT in order to give a clear and simple answer. This often takes the form of "Believe in Jesus and you will be saved" (e.g., Acts 16:31; John 9; Rom 4:4-5; 10:9-10). What is asked to be believed in is usually conceived of as something like the saving substitutionary death of Jesus for the sins of a wicked humanity. There is much here to affirm. The NT texts emphatically hold up Jesus's death as the saving event and as something that only Jesus, God's sinless Messiah, was able to accomplish. This is a historical event which the NT texts repeatedly speak of as having happened *for* humanity (e.g., John 11:50–51; 15:13; Rom 5:6–8; Gal 3:13; 1 Cor 15:3–5). And the NT texts absolutely call for humans to believe and make confessions regarding Jesus and his death. But I want to argue that the NT texts witness to a more robust account of how Christ accomplishes salvation and one that considers *the entire narrative shape of his messianic life*—the messianic narrative just examined in the previous chapter. In other words, it is Christ's messianic life and narrative which establishes his saving reign over his people. And this saving reign is something that, by virtue of Christ's incarnation and solidarity with humanity, his people actively share and participate in. There is an unrepeatable historical pastness to the saving events and life of Jesus, but the NT also witnesses to an active, dynamic, and ongoing reign of Christ given that he is the resurrected and enthroned king in heaven who continues to rule over his people by means of his Spirit. In what follows, I examine how the messianic narrative of the Son of God, particularly his incarnation, death, resurrection, and heavenly enthronement function to establish Christ's saving kingdom over his people.

The Saving Necessity of the Messiah's Incarnation and Spirit-Anointing

We have seen that one of the bedrock convictions of the NT authors is that the messianic king is the designated representative of the people of God.[1] I have argued that within Israel's royal ideology, God's election of the Davidic king entails adopting him as the son of God. This is classically expressed in 2 Samuel 7, where God chooses the house of David to rule over Israel, thereby creating the Father-son relationship between God and David: "I will be a Father to him, and he will be a son to me" (2 Sam 7:14a). Thus, the king is God's chosen and elected one. The king both participates in divine kingship and represents God's people. Oliver O'Donovan notes this dual relationship of the messianic king: "he represented Yhwh's rule to the people, ensuring their obedience, and he represented the people to Yhwh, ensuring his constant favour."[2] The representative nature of the Davidic king is seen, for example, in the depiction

---

1. I have written on this in more detail in Joshua W. Jipp, *Christ Is King: Paul's Royal Ideology* (Minneapolis: Fortress, 2015), 160–65.

2. Oliver O'Donovan, *The Desire of the Nations: Rediscovering the Roots of Political Theology* (Cambridge: Cambridge University Press, 1996), 61.

of the king as God's shepherd over Israel (e.g., 2 Sam 5:2; 7:7). Israel's royal representative is responsible for feeding, guiding, and protecting God's flock. Further, many of God's promises to Abraham and Israel become mediated through God's covenantal relationship with the dynasty of David. Whereas God had gifted the nation of Israel with the honored status of "my firstborn son" (Exod 4:22), now God creates a covenantal Father-son relationship with the Davidic king (2 Sam 7:13a; Pss 2:7; 89:26–28). I suggest that the Jewish messianic depiction of the king as the human representative of God's people is one of the sources that enabled the early Christians to speak of Messiah Jesus as the incarnation of the son of God. I am not arguing that Jesus's Davidic descent as the messianic king of Israel is *the* singular historical-religious analogue here, but we will see that the NT writers and early church fathers draw upon messianic texts in order to affirm Christ's full humanity as a necessity for how Christ accomplishes the salvation of his people.

Christ is the true human, the faithful and obedient Israelite, who fully identifies with the sinful humans he came to save. This is grounded, in part, in the belief that Jesus, the Messiah, is humanity's embodied representative and provides the necessary basis for our participation in his saving reign. Paul frequently applies messianic-kingly titles to Jesus which emphasize his role as simultaneously one who shares in God's divine kingship *and* as the true human who stands in full solidarity with humanity. Thus, the Christ hymn in Philippians 2 speaks of the preexistent Messiah Jesus (Phil 2:5) as the one who was "in the form of God" (2:6) and entered fully into the human condition (2:7–8). The "beloved Son" (Col 1:13) is the one who is "the image of the invisible God" (1:15a) and the "firstborn over all of creation" (1:15b). We have seen that Paul speaks of believers in Christ as those who share in the Messiah's election in Ephesians 1:3–14. I have argued that Paul's reference to Christ as "the firstborn Son" and his claim that those who are in Christ are sons of God (e.g., Rom 8:29; cf. 8:14–15) derive, in part, from Paul's conviction that Christ plays the role of the exalted firstborn Davidic king of Psalm 89. God's sending of the Messiah to be born as a human is the prior condition upon which humanity's adoption to sonship is based (Gal 4:4–7). The Fourth Gospel's Christology begins, as we have seen, with the plethora of titles applied to Jesus by John the Baptist and the disciples, and these titles emphasize his unique role as both God's *and* humanity's representative; as such, he is the Lamb of God (John 1:29), the Christ (1:41), the King of Israel (1:49), the Son of God (1:49), and the Son of Man (1:51). Jesus is confessed as the messianic Son of God who has come into the world from the Father (John 1:32–34; 4:25–27; 11:25–27).

We have seen that the early chapters of the Gospel of Matthew depict Jesus

347

as the messianic king of Israel who is born, albeit through the agency of God's Holy Spirit, into the sinful history of the people of Israel, and that includes the sinful history of the Davidic kings of Judah (Matt 1:1–17). In his mission to save his people from their sins (1:21), Jesus the Messiah submits to John the Baptist's baptism, a symbol which enacts the peoples' repentance for the forgiveness of sins (3:13–17). The Spirit-anointed Son of God, thus, identifies with the plight of his people as their representative and offers the righteousness and obedience to God the Father that Adam and Israel did not (4:1–11). The apostolic claims that God's Son was sent "in the likeness of sinful flesh" (Rom 8:3; cf. Gal 4:4–7), that Messiah Jesus was the obedient and righteous one (Rom 5:18–19; Phil 2:8), and that Jesus shared in flesh and blood in order to proclaim God's name among his fellow siblings (Heb 2:12–14) can be seen as commentary upon the Gospels' narratival representation of the Messiah's solidarity with his people. God the Father's anointing of Jesus by the Spirit, narrated in all four Gospels (Matt 3:13–17; Mark 1:9–11; Luke 3:21–22; John 1:32–34), can be seen, then, as a vicarious act for humanity whereby the Messiah receives the Spirit, not simply for himself, but rather as the Messiah who represents humanity. Stated in explicitly theological terms: the Son receives the Spirit upon his human nature and thereby preserves it to human nature through his obedience to the Father so that the Spirit might again take root in humanity. John Calvin states this well: "[H]e is called the Christ of God, because 'the Spirit of the Lord' rested upon him; 'The Spirit of wisdom and understanding, the Spirit of counsel and might, the Spirit of knowledge and of the fear of the Lord' (Isaiah xi. 9). . . . For, as has been said, he was not enriched privately for himself, but that he might refresh the parched and hungry with his abundance."[3] Jesus is anointed by the Spirit of God, empowered for service and mission, and is thereby able to share the divine benefits, fullness, and gifts with his people (cf. John 3:33–34; 7:37–39; 20:21–23; 1 Cor 15:44–45; Eph 1:20–2:6; 4:7–15). The messianic Son of God enacts complete solidarity with his sinful people, is anointed by God's Spirit, and is thereby at once both the giver of the Spirit and its representative recipient. What Marc Cortez states regarding the soteriological necessity of Jesus's humanity in Hebrews summarizes well my overall claim: "[T]he eternal Son became fully human to the extent that he experienced the same temptation, suffering, and death that we associate with the fallen condition, and that this was necessary for him to bring humanity to its intended telos."[4]

3. John Calvin, *Institutes of the Christian Religion*, trans. Henry Beveridge (Grand Rapids: Eerdmans, 1989), 429. The quote comes from *Institutes*, II, xv, 5.

4. Marc Cortez, *Resourcing Theological Anthropology: A Constructive Account of Humanity in the Light of Christ* (Grand Rapids: Zondervan, 2017), 152.

In what follows, I want to illustrate, albeit all too briefly, that significant church fathers continued to engage the NT's so-called Messiah Christology in their articulation of the saving significance of the incarnation of the Son of God and his anointing by the Holy Spirit. One of the classic patristic dictums goes along the lines of "that which has not been assumed has not been redeemed."[5] The church fathers see with particular clarity the NT's witness to the soteriological necessity of Jesus's true humanity and his solidarity with humanity. Not only Jesus's divinity but also his full humanity is necessary for humanity's adoption to sonship and bodily resurrection.

Cyril of Alexandria and the Spirit-Anointing of the Messiah

With respect to Jesus's baptismal anointing as the Spirit-endowed Messiah, for example, I note Cyril of Alexandria's exegesis. Cyril begins his Scholia on the Incarnation with a summary of the narrative of the Christ, which will occupy his scriptural interpretation throughout his work.[6] Cyril explains that the title "Christ" does not denote an essence or quality but rather refers to an anointing for kingship, something Israel's "christs" foreshadowed of the Christ (cf. Ps 104.15; Hab 3.13; Isa 45.1). The Son of God was anointed as humanity's representative, just as Israel's kings were representative of Israel, to effect liberation for humanity from sin's dominion, which had reigned as a result of Adam's trespass (Rom 5:14).[7] Given humanity's sin and marring of the divine image, the Son of God takes on sinful human flesh and renders perfect human obedience to God. Cyril frequently draws upon Jesus's Spirit-anointing at his baptism as humanity's representative. I will focus my comments on Cyril's interpretation of Jesus's Spirit-anointing in John 1:32–34.[8] Cyril emphasizes that unlike the kings of Israel, when Jesus receives the Spirit, the Spirit of God *remains* upon Jesus. The Son of God receives the Spirit upon himself and

5. For the prevalence of this theme in the early church fathers, see Hans Urs von Balthasar, *The Action*, vol. 4 of *Theo-Drama: Theological Dramatic Theory*, trans. Graham Harrison (San Francisco: Ignatius Press, 1994), 244–54. See further Kathryn Tanner, *Christ the Key* (Cambridge: Cambridge University Press, 2010), esp. 1–57.

6. I am using the translation of the Scholia provided in John A. McGuckin, *St. Cyril of Alexandria: The Christological Controversy*, VCSup (Leiden: Brill, 1994), 294–335.

7. The first and second Adams play a significant role in Cyril's soteriology and the baptism of Christ. See further Ben C. Blackwell, *Christosis: Pauline Soteriology in Light of Deification in Irenaeus and Cyril of Alexandria*, WUNT 2.314 (Tübingen: Mohr Siebeck, 2011), 77–78.

8. Quotations are from *In Joannis Evangelium*, ed. P. E. Pusey (Oxford: Clarendon, 1872), 2:174–90.

thereby preserves the Spirit of God to human nature through his obedience to the Father so that the Spirit might again take root in humanity. The Son is thereby at once both the giver of the Spirit and its representative recipient. Jesus's baptism is thus emphasized by Cyril as the decisive event within salvation history, for it is here that the image of God is restored and the Spirit returns to transform and sanctify human nature.[9] Cyril notes that transformation of human nature is not completed, however, until Jesus's resurrection, when he anoints his disciples with the Spirit (John 20:22-23). Cyril summarizes the salvific nature of Jesus's anointing in his Scholia on the Incarnation, interpreting the event with the messianic oracle of Isaiah 11: "The Son was thus anointed in human fashion like us . . . for our sake . . . and in him the nature of man was made radiant so that it now became worthy to participate in the Holy Spirit. No longer was the Spirit absent from that nature, as in former times, but now he loved to dwell within it. And so it is written: 'The Spirit came down upon the Messiah and rested on him' [cf. Isa 11:2]" (S1, p. 295). It is remarkable how frequently in his exposition of Jesus's baptism Cyril quotes or alludes to Pauline texts which emphasize the human nature of Christ. Pauline phrases such as "he humbled himself" (Phil 2:8), "the form of a servant" (Phil 2:7), "for us/our sakes," "in the likeness of human flesh" (Rom 8:3), and "for our sakes became poor" (2 Cor 8:9) pepper his exegesis, emphasizing the soteriological benefits accrued through the incarnation.

The Davidic Descent of the Son of God and the Incarnation

Many of the church fathers draw upon Paul's description of Jesus as the Son of David in Romans 1:3-4 in order to emphasize Jesus's real humanity. Ignatius of Antioch, for example, invokes Jesus's Davidic descent (alluding to Rom 1:3-4) on at least five occasions in his letters in order to establish Jesus's full humanity. In *To the Ephesians* 18.2 Ignatius states that Jesus was "conceived by Mary according to God's economy, both from the seed of David and the Holy Spirit."[10] Ignatius's invocation of Jesus's Davidic descent here is immediately tied to the virgin birth and the reality of Christ's humanity (19.1-3).[11] It is Ig-

---

9. On theosis in Cyril see, Daniel A. Keating, *The Appropriation of Divine Life in Cyril of Alexandria* (Oxford: Oxford University Press, 2004), 144-90.

10. References to Ignatius's writings are my own translations from Michael W. Holmes, ed., *The Apostolic Fathers: Greek Texts and English Translations* (Grand Rapids: Baker Academic, 1999).

11. It does not seem farfetched to claim that, in Ignatius, one finds already the nascent beginnings of the doctrinal formulation of the communication of idioms. See Thomas G.

natius's hope, in fact, that he will be able to visit the Ephesians so as to explain more fully the "divine economy" of Christ (20.1) who "was from the family of David according to the flesh, both Son of Man and Son of God" (20.2). Romans 1:3 is invoked by Ignatius precisely to emphasize the real humanity of this "new man Jesus Christ" and how his humanity *and* deity are necessary for humanity's salvation. Ignatius introduces an important theme that will appear in later letters—namely, the necessity of Jesus's participation in human nature for establishing the future resurrection of believers (see Ignatius, *To the Trallians* 9.1–2). The Son of God's incarnation, evidenced in his Davidic descent and birth from Mary, *and* his bodily resurrection ensures that the Father "in the same way will likewise also raise us up *in Christ Jesus* who believe in him, apart from whom we have no true life" (Ign. *Trall.* 9.2).[12] Thus far Ignatius has used Romans 1:3–4 only to focus on Jesus's humanity. Finally, in *To the Smyrnaeans* 1.1 Ignatius alludes to both verse 3 and verse 4 in his claim that Jesus Christ "is truly of the family of David with respect to human descent, [and] Son of God with respect to the will and power." There is here an emphasis on both halves of Romans 1:3–4, but we see that Ignatius fastens on these verses to support two aspects of Jesus's identity—namely, his real humanity and his identity as God's Son.

Origen also fastens on Jesus's Davidic descent in Romans 1:3 as evidence for the real humanity of Christ. With Origen, however, there is a marked concern to emphasize Christ's preexistence; thus, Origen claims that Jesus's birth from the seed of David is confirmation that Christ "became that which previously he was not" (*Commentary on the Epistle to the Romans* 1.5.1).[13] Jesus's prior existence was "according to the Spirit," meaning, for Origen, that there was never a time when the Son was not. Thus, Paul's words in 1:4 do not mark a real change in the life of the Son of God, for in fact Origen sees the phrase "the Son of God in power according to the Spirit of holiness" as simply an affirmation of what the Son substantially is in his essence. (1.5.2). Much of Origen's exegesis of Romans 1:3–4 is occupied with the question of whether the Son's

---

Weinandy, "The Apostolic Christology of Ignatius of Antioch: The Road to Chalcedon," in *Trajectories through the New Testament and the Apostolic Fathers*, ed. Andrew F. Gregory and Christopher M. Tuckett (Oxford: Clarendon, 2005), 71–84.

12. The participatory soteriology of Ignatius of Antioch and its relationship to Paul's epistle is explored well by David J. Downs, "The Pauline Concept of Union with Christ in Ignatius of Antioch," in *The Apostolic Fathers and Paul*, ed. Todd D. Still and David E. Wilhite (London: T&T Clark, 2017), 143–61.

13. I am using the translation of Thomas P. Scheck, *Origen: Commentary on the Epistle to the Romans Books 1–5* (Washington, DC: The Catholic University of America Press, 2001).

soul is generated from the seed of David or from the spirit of holiness (1.5.2–3). While this issue need not concern us here, it is important to note that Origen's insistence is upon the Son's real assumption of flesh for the sake of humanity's salvation.[14] There is an inseparable unity between the two natures of the Son, such that "everything that is of the flesh is attributed to the Word" (1.6.2). It is the humanity of the Son which allows him to be the *firstborn* from the dead of other participants (cf. Col 1:18; Rev 1:5). For Origen, the Son's humanity allows the rest of humanity to participate in the Son's own life and the future resurrection from the dead (1.6.2–3).

Irenaeus also makes much of Jesus's Davidic descent in order to expand upon Paul's concept of adoption as an image of humanity's salvation. Irenaeus quotes both Romans 1:3 and Romans 9:5 to establish that the Son of God was born "of the seed of David according to the flesh" and is descended from Israel's forefathers as "the Christ according to the flesh" (*Haer.* 3.16.3). Irenaeus draws upon Galatians 4:4–5 to further indicate that in this way God has fulfilled the promises made to David—namely, through sending the Messiah "who was of the seed of David according to his birth from Mary" and was the very same "Son of God made the Son of Man."[15] The Son of God's incarnation whereby he takes human flesh from the line of David is absolutely necessary for Irenaeus, since it is "through him that we may receive the adoption," that is, "humanity sustaining and receiving and embracing the Son of God" (*Haer.* 3.16.3). Irenaeus repeatedly draws these Pauline texts together with statements from Luke's Gospel which proclaim that the Messiah comes from the house of David and that this Messiah will rule over the house of Jacob forever (Luke 1:31–35; 1:68–69; 2:1–11; *Haer.* 3.9.2; 3.10.1–3; 3.16.3; *Epid.* 36–37). Again, invoking Romans 1:3–4 and Galatians 4:4, Irenaeus affirms why the Son of God's Davidic ancestry is so crucial to humanity's salvation as adopted sons: "For if he did not receive the substance of flesh from a human being, he neither was made man nor the Son of man; and if he was not made what we were, he did no great thing in what he suffered and endured" (*Haer.* 3.22.1).[16] Or again: "It was for this end that the Word of God was made man, and he who was the Son of God became the Son of man, that man, having been taken into

---

14. One can see this in Origen's homily on Luke 1:67–76, where Rom 1:3 is invoked as necessary for humanity's deliverance from their spiritual enemies. See the entirety of his Tenth Homily in *Origen: Homilies on Luke, Fragments of Luke*, trans. Joseph T. Lienhard (Washington, DC: The Catholic University of America Press, 1996).

15. Helpful here is Blackwell, *Christosis*, 48–50.

16. See further Matthew W. Bates, "A Christology of Incarnation and Enthronement: Romans 1:3–4 as Unified, Nonadoptionist, and Nonconciliatory," *CBQ* 77 (2015): 118–20.

the Word, and receiving the adoption, might become the son of God" (*Haer.* 3.19.1). It would take my argument too far afield to engage in any detail Irenaeus's frequent quotation of Psalm 82 to show how the Father and Son work to accomplish adoption for the church, but this psalm is often combined with Pauline notions of adoption to sonship. For example, Irenaeus quotes from Romans 8:15 to prove that believers in Christ "have received the grace of the 'adoption by which we cry, Abba Father'" (*Haer.* 3.6.1). And again, in *Haer.* 4.4.1 Irenaeus refers to those who believe in God and believe in Jesus as the Messiah and the true Son of God with Pauline resonances as "those who have received the Spirit of adoption." Kathryn Tanner states the saving necessity of Christ's incarnation well in the summary of her examination of the early church fathers' teachings: "Christ's own life provides not just the pattern of a new human way of life for our imitation, but the cause of that pattern in us, by way of the uniting of humanity and divinity in him. The second person of the trinity not only shows forth the true image in human form by becoming incarnate but makes us like that image by uniting human nature thereby with the very incomprehensibility of the divine life."[17]

The Saving Necessity of the Messiah's Death

While the NT texts articulate Christ's saving significance on the cross in a variety of ways, they cohere in their depiction of the Messiah's establishment of his kingdom reign through his saving death on the cross. So, Jeremy Treat: "The kingdom is the ultimate goal of the cross, and the cross is the means by which the kingdom comes."[18] Christ's kingship and his kingdom are revealed and established by means of the cross. Christ's obedience to the Father unto death on the cross is the messianic king's supreme benefaction for his people, a gift which stems from the Messiah's unrelenting mercy, compassion, and love. The Messiah's death functions as the ransom payment which rescues and liberates his people from sin and the power of the evil one. The consequences of the death are neither abstract nor are they merely forensic; rather, the death of the messianic king is one that effects a transformative liberation from one kingdom into another.

17. Tanner, *Christ the Key*, 57.
18. Jeremy R. Treat, "Exaltation in and through Humiliation: Rethinking the States of Christ," in *Christology Ancient and Modern: Explorations in Constructive Dogmatics* (Grand Rapids: Zondervan, 2013), 114.

The Cross and Divine Revelation

The NT texts consistently identified Christ's humble obedience to the Father, faithfulness amid sufferings, and death on the Roman cross as both constituent of Jesus's messianic identity and as an act of divine revelation. The earliest Christian writings are emphatic that God is revealed and known through the Father's messianic Son, and central to the life and narrative of the Messiah is his loving and sacrificial death on the cross. We have seen that the early Christian practice of reading the royal psalms as anticipating the obedience and sufferings of the messianic king pervades the NT writings. Jesus's messiahship is seen, therefore, as not merely compatible with his sufferings and death; rather, his faithfulness unto death is actually at the center of his messianic identity. While some have argued that the Gospel of Mark is ambivalent regarding Davidic messiahship as a framework for understanding the identity of Jesus, I have argued that Mark is, instead, deeply suspicious of characters and readers who interpret messiahship within a framework of military might and power. Mark's middle section, in fact, is patterned through a threefold repetition of Jesus's declaration that the Son of Man must suffer (Mark 8:31; 9:31; 10:32–34), the disciples' misunderstanding of Jesus's identity (8:32–33; 9:33–34; 10:35–41), and Jesus's further correction (8:34–9:1; 9:35–50; 10:42–45). In other words, Mark's "way" section seems to be intended to correct Peter's (and the reader's) difficulty in seeing that Jesus's messianic royal identity is revealed in humble obedience, suffering, and crucifixion. Jesus is not portrayed as a Davidic military war hero, but is rather a Davidic righteous sufferer who prays the psalms of lament amid his sufferings (e.g., Pss 42:6, 12; 43:5 in Mark 14:32–44). All four Gospels depict Jesus's crucifixion as an ironic enthronement of the King of Israel. Within the passion narratives, Jesus is repeatedly referred to as king and messiah, as having his own kingdom, as receiving mock worship from the Roman soldiers, and wearing a purple robe and crown of thorns. I have already quoted Joel Marcus, who rightly argues that the Gospels counter the mock enthronement of Jesus as king with their own intentional irony as they seek to lead the reader to the conclusion that Jesus's kingship is indeed revealed precisely in his crucifixion.[19] The climax of this theme, of course, occurs when the Roman centurion identifies the crucified Jesus as God's Son (Matt 27:54; Mark 15:39; cf. Luke 23:47). The Gospel of John, too, depicts Jesus's glorification and enthronement as taking place through his crucifixion (John 3:14–15; 8:28; 12:33). Jesus's enthronement upon the cross is the event whereby

19. Joel Marcus, "Crucifixion as Parodic Exaltation," *JBL* 125 (2006): 73–87.

the one great exorcism occurs and Satan is cast out (John 12:31–33; 16:33); the cross is also the climactic moment whereby Jesus's divine identity is revealed (8:28; 13:19). Jesus's kingship is a reign of truth whereby Jesus reveals the love and identity of the Father to the people through his humiliation and sacrificial love on the cross. We have seen that Paul connects "Messiah" and "crucifixion" in a surprising way in 1 Corinthians 1:23, where he declares that he preaches "a crucified Messiah." Paul's preaching of the crucified Messiah is, he argues, the supreme revelation of God's power, strength, and wisdom (1 Cor 1:18–25). Within Revelation, Jesus's messianic identity as the conquering Lion from the tribe of Judah is revealed by means of the sacrificial image of a slaughtered Lamb seated on the divine throne (Rev 5:5–6). And so, throughout the Apocalypse, the ironical pattern set by the crucified Messiah of conquering through faithful suffering even unto death is followed by the Messiah's army (e.g., Rev 7:9–17). There is remarkable emphasis, especially within Paul and John, upon the Messiah's death revealing the extraordinary love of God and Christ. Paul's paean in Romans 8:31–39 celebrates the depths and strength of the revelation of God's love in Christ for his people. Paul celebrates the Messiah quite simply as "the one who loved us and gave himself up for us" (Gal 2:20) and proclaims that "the Messiah's love controls us" (2 Cor 5:14–15).[20]

The Cross and the Kingdom of God

The Messiah's death on the cross is also the apocalyptic and redemptive event whereby Jesus rescues a sinful people and liberates them from sin and the powers of the evil one.[21] Within Matthew's Gospel, we have seen that both Jesus and John the Baptist proclaim the arrival of the kingdom of heaven (e.g., 3:2; 4:17, 23; 9:35). Messiah Jesus is the one sinless king born into a history of sinful Davidic rulers (1:1–17) but who stands in solidarity with his people, draws Israel's exile to an end, and offers his very life as a means of paying the ransom price to rescue his people from their sins (Matt 1:21; 3:13–17; 20:28; 26:28). Jesus's messianic kingship is qualified through his role as the Passover sacrificial Lamb of God whose gift purchases a people for his kingdom (e.g., Luke 22:24–30; John 1:29, 36; Rev 5:5–12). Christ's death on the cross is an outworking of his incarnation in that it expresses Jesus's complete solidarity with

20. On Paul's emotional devotion to Christ, see Larry W. Hurtado, "Paul's Messianic Christology," in *Paul the Jew: Rereading the Apostle as a Figure of Second Temple Judaism*, ed. Gabriele Boccaccini and Carlos A. Segovia (Minneapolis: Fortress, 2016), 115–16.

21. See also the excellent study of Jeremy R. Treat, *The Crucified King: Atonement and Kingdom in Biblical and Systematic Theology* (Grand Rapids: Zondervan, 2014).

sinful humanity and his bearing the full burden of Adam's sinful condition (Rom 8:3; Gal 4:4–5). The Messiah's death on the cross is the event that thereby destroys the old sinful humanity, whereby the Messiah's people experience freedom and liberation from the powers of sin and death (Rom 6:3–7; Gal 2:20; Col 2:11–13). We have seen that the Gospels depict Jesus as the lamenting David who both maintains faithfulness to God in the midst of his sufferings and who agonizes over his bearing the weight of sin's condemnation (so Matt 27:46; Mark 14:32–42; cf. Heb 2:8–9; 5:7–9). Thus, Christ not only assumes humanity's sinful Adamic flesh in the incarnation; on the cross "he assumed our condemnation that we might be saved from it."[22] Thus, Christ, as a merciful and good king, gives his own life and is "made sin," thereby accomplishing *humanity's* reconciliation to God and leading to peace (2 Cor 5:15–21; Col 1:20–22; cf. Eph 2:14–18).

Jesus's life, climaxing with his death, embodies one of the premier characteristics of the good king—namely, mercy, compassion, and love for his people. And this is often exemplified in Matthew in the characterization of Jesus as the good shepherd who leads his people with justice and mercy and gathers together the scattered and distressed flock of God (e.g., Matt 9:35–36; 10:1–13; 26:26–32). Jesus is the truly good ruler who uses his power and authority not to benefit himself or for personal aggrandizement but rather dies as a "ransom for the many" (Mark 10:45). So, John's Jesus draws upon the image of "the good shepherd" to contrast his leadership over the people against the illegitimate rulers who are bandits and thieves (John 10:1–16). Life, peace, abundance, and the gathering of the scattered flock into one people is given to the people of God through the loving death of the good shepherd (John 10:9–18). Paul also associates Christ's death and "the blood of the cross" as the means whereby God the Father rescues a people from the evil rulers and authorities and transfers his people into "the kingdom of his beloved Son" (Col 1:13–14). Christ's death is the outworking and extension, then, of his messianic attack upon and victory over the demonic powers of darkness in his earthly ministry (e.g., Mark 1:16–45; 3:23–30).[23] Christ's death liberates people from *both* their sins *and* the evil powers (Col 2:14–15). Within Romans 5–8, Christ's obedience and death rescue his people from the dominion of sin and death and thereby transfer them into a kingdom marked by holiness and righteousness.[24] Treat states this

22. Thomas G. Weinandy, *Does God Suffer?* (Notre Dame: University of Notre Dame Press, 2000), 219.

23. See here Thomas F. Torrance, "The Kingdom of Christ and Evil," in *Incarnation: The Person and Life of Christ* (Downers Grove, IL: InterVarsity Press, 2008), 235–56.

24. On Christ's death functioning as an apocalyptic rescue of humanity from evil over-

well when he notes that Christ dethrones "the unrightful king of the fallen creation . . . primarily at the cross, where Jesus fulfills the core promises of the kingdom; namely, victory over Satan (Dan 2:44; Col 2:15), the forgiveness of sins (Isa 40:2; Eph 1:7), and a new exodus (Isa 52:12; Mark 1:2–3)."[25]

Christ's crucified body ("the blood of the Messiah," Eph 2:13b) is the means whereby he establishes a new people marked by peace and unity (Eph 2:11–18; cf. Rom 15:1–13). While Hebrews emphasizes God's enthronement of the messianic Son to his right hand, it is only through the Son's suffering and death that Jesus is able to perfect his people, lead them to glory, and break the power of the evil one (e.g., Heb 2:5–18). In Revelation, the messianic king's death is the royal benefaction by which Christ purchases a royal, priestly kingdom of people for himself (Rev 1:5–6; 5:9–12). The kingdom of God and his Messiah is established ironically through the very blood of the sacrificed messianic king (Rev 12:10–11). Thus, in this highly paradoxical way, Christ "the faithful witness" conquers Satan and exposes his dominion as based on deception and falsehood (Rev 12:9–10; cf. 3:14).

The Saving Necessity of the Messiah's Resurrection and Enthronement

In the summary of his analysis of Jesus's resurrection and ascension to heaven, Matthew Levering notes that "Jesus's passage always has in view our participation in it. The Son of God undertook his paschal journey for our sake."[26] Similarly, John Calvin speaks of Christ's exalted kingship: "[H]e reigns more for us than for himself."[27] Jesus's messianic narrative and identity, then, undertaken as it is in solidarity with Adamic humanity and for its sake, is itself saving as his incarnation, death, resurrection, and enthronement accomplish and enact his saving rule and kingdom over his people. Irenaeus's soteriology articulates clearly the way in which the messianic life of Jesus, particularly his incarnation (see above) and ascension, is saving. Thus, Irenaeus argues, for example, that

lords, see Philip G. Zeigler, *Militant Grace: The Apocalyptic Turn and the Future of Christian Theology* (Grand Rapids: Baker Academic, 2018), 53–70.

25. Treat, "Exaltation in and through Humiliation," 99.

26. Matthew Levering, *Jesus and the Demise of Death: Resurrection, Afterlife, and the Fate of the Christian* (Waco, TX: Baylor University Press, 2012), 63. See also Gerrit Scott Dawson, *Jesus Ascended: The Meaning of Christ's Continuing Incarnation* (London: T&T Clark, 2004), 7.

27. Calvin, *Institutes*, II, xv, 4.

Jesus ascended into heaven in order to "offer and commend to his Father that human nature which had been found, making in his own person the first-fruits of the resurrection of man" (*Haer.* 3.19.3). The eternal Son of God joins himself to our humanity and in his ascension takes "our history with him into the age to come."[28] As Michael Horton notes, what has happened to Jesus in his ascension "will happen to those who are united to him." And this further results in Christ opening up "a space within our history for the descent of the Spirit who brings the powers of the age to come into this present age."[29]

Participating in the Kingdom and Rule of the Enthroned Messiah

We have seen an abundance of NT texts which claim that God's resurrection of Jesus from the dead and his subsequent heavenly ascension is the pinnacle of Jesus's messianic kingship and the means whereby Jesus is enthroned to the right hand of the Father.[30] Jesus's establishment of the kingdom of God as the resurrected and enthroned Messiah is a soteriological necessity, as it establishes the messianic pattern and eschatological passage for the Messiah's people. As Douglas Farrow has stated: "Jesus's destiny is our destiny; . . . in reaching our destiny, he has reached it not only for himself but also for us."[31]

The NT frequently conceptualizes Christ's relationship with his people as the relationship between king and subjects, with the king's subjects sharing in the dynamic reign and receiving the royal benefits of the resurrected, enthroned Messiah's rule. One helpful step in this direction has been taken by Matthew Bates in his *Salvation by Allegiance Alone*, who rightly emphasizes the NT depiction of Jesus as messianic king and the soteriological necessity of his royal enthronement to the right hand of the Father. Thus, Bates speaks of Jesus as the one who "*is* actively ruling" the cosmos, "serving in heaven as the great high priest," and who has a "dynamic rule as he serves as king of heaven and earth at the right hand of God the Father while his enemies are being subdued."[32] I, too, have argued that the NT texts repeatedly emphasize Jesus's

28. Michael Horton, "Atonement and Ascension," in *Locating Atonement: Explorations in Constructive Dogmatics*, ed. Oliver D. Crisp and Fred Sanders (Grand Rapids: Zondervan, 2015), 234.

29. Horton, "Atonement and Ascension," 235.

30. See further Douglas Farrow, *Ascension Theology* (London: T&T Clark, 2011), 2–14.

31. Farrow, *Ascension Theology*, 10.

32. Matthew W. Bates, *Salvation by Allegiance Alone: Rethinking Faith, Works, and the Gospel of Jesus the King* (Grand Rapids: Baker Academic, 2017), 67–68. Also arguing that Jesus's ascension is the pinnacle and climactic point of Christ's accomplishment of human-

ascension and enthronement as the incarnate, crucified Jesus's full entrance into and establishment of his kingship, and this kingship and its benefits are held out as saving promise and reward for his people.

In the Synoptic Gospels, Jesus promises his disciples that they will receive eschatological life and will participate in the glorious kingdom of the Messiah *provided* they bear their own crosses and follow Jesus (e.g., Matt 16:24–28). Peter and the Twelve are exhorted to remain faithful in following Jesus, for when the "Son of Man sits on his glorious throne" so will they share in ruling and judging the people of God (Matt 19:28). When James and John make known their desire to share in Jesus's messianic kingdom by sitting at the right and left hand of Jesus in his glory (Mark 10:37), Jesus does not reject their belief that he (and they) will rule in the messianic kingdom. We have seen that within Mark's Gospel Jesus connects his kingship and messiahship with his life of obedience, suffering, and crucifixion. And within Mark 10:35–45, as I have noted, there are an abundance of allusions to Daniel 7 and the eternal dominion and kingdom of the Son of Man. John and James are right, then, that a promise of sharing in the glorious kingdom of the Messiah is held out for them, but sharing in Jesus's glory is contingent upon bearing their own crosses (cf. Mark 8:34–9:1). In the Gospel of Luke, Jesus is explicit that he is gifting his own kingdom to the disciples and that they will sit on their own thrones and rule God's people (Luke 22:28–30). We have seen that this conferral scene looks backward to Gabriel's promise that God would fulfill his promises made to David through Jesus who would eternally rule over God's people (Luke 1:31–35). The scene also looks forward, however, to the entire book of Acts, where the presence of the Spirit of the risen and enthroned Messiah empowers the mission of the disciples who spread the salvific blessings of the Davidic messianic kingdom (e.g., Acts 3–5; 13:17–41).

In John's Gospel it is Jesus's messianic role as the enthroned and anointed giver of the Holy Spirit which enables his people to continue the mission of the Father and the Son. And this mission is one of enjoying and sharing in God's life. John's well-known theme of inaugurated eschatology (with emphasis on the "now" or "already") makes a major contribution to the saving necessity of Christ's resurrection and enthronement, as Christ's people are currently able to share in his resurrection life (esp. John 5:24–30). The experiential quality of this life is equated for John's Jesus with entering into the very kingdom of God (John 3:1–18). Jesus's glorification is the basis for his conquest over the ruler

---

ity's salvation is Douglas Farrow, *Ascension and Ecclesia: On the Significance of the Doctrine of the Ascension for Ecclesiology and Christian Cosmology* (Grand Rapids: Eerdmans, 1999).

of this world (12:33), and Christ's victory is what enables his disciples to share in Christ's peace, joy, and triumph (see John 14:27; 15:11; 16:33).[33] Sharing in Christ's kingship, thus, entails participating in a dynamic mission of offering liberation, forgiveness of sins, and conviction to the world. The risen Christ's present reign over his people is mediated through the Spirit which empowers Christ's people to do the "greater works" (14:12) in continuing Jesus's ministry of teaching, judgment, and salvation.

I have argued at length through detailed examinations of large portions of his letters that Paul conceptualizes participation in and with Christ as sharing in the life, rule, and benefits of Christ the messianic king (e.g., Rom 5–8, 1 Cor 15; Eph; Phil 2–3; Col 1:15–20; 2:9–3:4; and 2 Tim 2:8–13). In Romans 5–8 Paul conceptualizes this as Christ's people rescued from the kingdom of sin and death mediated through Adam and transferred to a kingdom marked by obedience, righteousness, and life. Throughout his letters, Christ's people share in (or are given the eschatological promise of sharing in) the Messiah's election as God's Son through adoption (Rom 8:14–17; Eph 1:3–14), resurrection and life (Rom 6:3–6; 8:9–11; Eph 2:1–6; Phil 3:20–21; Col 2:12–13), royal enthronement (Eph 2:6; Col 3:1–4; 2 Tim 2:8–13), and defeat of and protection from the evil powers (Col 2:9–10, 14–15). Further, Christ's people receive the benefits of the Messiah's kingdom as they share in his peace (Rom 8:15–16; Eph 2:14–18; Col 3:15–16) and love (Rom 5:3–5; 8:31–39) and as they experience liberation from the power of sin, unrighteousness, and death (Rom 5:15–19; 6:7, 14–23). First Peter similarly articulates a narrative of the Messiah as one who suffered, died, was raised, and was endowed with glory when he was enthroned to God's right hand (1 Pet 1:10–11, 21; 3:18–22) as the foundation for the promise made to the churches that they, too, will share in resurrection and enthronement, provided they remain faithful amid their trials and sufferings (e.g., 2:4–10; 3:21; 4:13–16; 5:1–2).

Similarly, the author of Hebrews begins his literary masterpiece with a dramatic depiction of the Son of God's heavenly enthronement whereby he enters into God's presence and is "perfected" as the resurrected Davidic Son of God (Heb 1:3–14). As we have seen, the incarnate Son of God's exaltation provides the foundation for the salvation of the Messiah's fellow siblings (Heb 2:12–13). Jesus is the Son of God who himself has been "perfected" and who has "perfected the faith," indicating that he is the prototype for his people who has already entered into God's life and promises (2:10; 5:7–9; 7:28; 12:1–3). Jesus's

---

33. See Carlos Raúl Sosa Siliezar, *Savior of the World: A Theology of the Universal Gospel* (Waco, TX: Baylor University Press, 2019), 106.

royal enthronement to heaven further provides the eschatological goal which his people follow as they anticipate celebrating and worshipping God in the heavenly Mount Zion (Heb 12:1–3 and 12:18–29).

We have seen that Revelation, too, depicts churches as participating in the paradoxical military victory of the slaughtered, but victorious, Lamb (Rev 5:5–9). They hold fast to their faithfulness in Jesus by enduring and not compromising their witness and worship (2:13, 19; 3:3, 9–10). Jesus explicitly promises his faithful church a share in his own royal and messianic authority, provided they remain faithful. This is stated most explicitly to the church in Laodicea, to whom Jesus promises that those who conquer will share Jesus's throne (3:21). But sharing in Jesus's messianic kingship is also seen in a variety of passages where the faithful believers are portrayed as the army of the Messiah who engage in active resistance by holding fast to their faith, resisting the deception and falsehood of the imperial elites, and even willingly accepting martyrdom (e.g., 7:3–17; 14:1–5; 19:11–16). The Gospel of John shows Jesus also as one whose kingship is revealed in his paradoxical conquering of the evil one through the cross (John 12:31–33; 16:33). His enthronement through the cross is the means whereby the kingdom is established, all people are drawn to him, and the life of the age to come is given to his people (3:3–21; 12:33–34).

Christ the King's Present Rule over His People

The NT texts are emphatic that the resurrected and enthroned messianic king continues to rule over his people as the one who loves, sustains, empowers, and provides gifts to his people. Here are a variety of ways the risen and enthroned Christ establishes his kingdom and rules over his people.

First, Christ the enthroned messianic king is endowed with judicial authority over the living and the dead and actively protects his people from threats to their salvation (cf. Acts 10:42). Calvin states the implications of Christ's kingship well: "Therefore, as often as we hear that Christ is armed with eternal power, let us learn that the perpetuity of the Church is thus effectually secured; that amid the turbulent agitations by which it is constantly harassed, and the grievous and fearful commotions which threaten innumerable disasters, it still remains safe."[34] Christ's sovereign rule over his people is, in the words of Philip Ziegler, "A Lordship of Love."[35] In Romans 8 Paul says that the enthroned Christ is the eschatological judge, as "the one who has died and much more has

---

34. Calvin, *Institutes*, II, xv, 3.
35. Ziegler, *Militant Grace*, 48–49.

been raised, who is at the right hand of God and who intercedes on our behalf" (8:34). Christ's intercession, motivated out of "the love of the Messiah" (8:35), safeguards and protects his people from threats to their salvation (see also Heb 7:24–28). Despite the church's present experience of suffering with Christ, there is nothing that can separate Christ's people from God's love. Those who are in Christ Jesus need not fear condemnation or a guilty verdict on the last day due to Christ's execution of sin in his incarnate flesh (Rom 8:1–3). One of the rhetorical functions of Romans 8 is to counter eschatological anxiety for believers at the judgment, and this is rooted in both the love and power of Christ the King. The Messiah's enthronement to a position of power (8:34; cf. 1:4) ensures that there is simply no aspect of creation, no cosmic power belonging to Adam's dominion, that can return Christ's people to their former enslavement to the reign of sin and death.[36]

Paul argues similarly in Colossians. Those joined together with Christ are given assurance that their eschatological destiny is safe with God. God has resurrected his Messiah and seated him at God's right hand above every ruler and power (Col 2:10b). Those who belong to the Messiah "have been hidden with the Messiah in God" (Col 3:3b). Therefore, no heavenly or earthly power can separate us from Christ's benevolent rule. Christians need not endlessly worry about their salvation. This is why Paul later says, "Let the peace of the Messiah rule in your hearts" (Col 3:15a), for Christ has already reconciled them to God, thereby "making peace through the blood of his cross" (Col 1:20a). Levering notes that Christ's position at the right hand of the Father expresses the exalted Jesus's "judiciary power and his intercession for us, which he accomplishes as king and priest of the people of God. Sitting at the right hand of the Father signals Jesus's authority and power to establish his people in righteousness and to bring us to share in the divine life."[37] One sees the exalted Christ's judicial authority portrayed narratively in Acts, where Christ the enthroned, heavenly king provides protection from the church's enemies who seek to destroy the church. The enemies of the Messiah often find that they meet a difficult death as they "fight against God" (e.g., Judas in Acts 1:15–26; Ananias and Sapphira in 5:1–11; Herod in 12:20–23). The heavenly Messiah answers the prayers of his people by sending forth his Spirit to empower them for mission even in the face of opposition (Acts 4:23–31) and vindicates and receives into glory those who suffer and die in faithfulness to him (7:55–60).

36. Jipp, *Christ Is King*, 196.
37. Levering, *Jesus and the Demise of Death*, 60.

Second, the enthroned Christ sends forth his Spirit into the heart of believers. There is the closest relationship in the NT between Christ's resurrection/ enthronement and the gift of the Spirit. Thomas Weinandy comments upon the soteriological significance of the relationship between Jesus's resurrection and the sending of the Spirit:

> As risen, Jesus is now fully empowered to save all who come to him in faith by uniting them to himself within the communion of the Holy Spirit, thus making them children of his Father. Being transfigured into the likeness of the risen Jesus through the indwelling Spirit, his disciples and all the faithful are thus united to Jesus in a new manner, for they now share in his risen humanity, and in so doing Jesus continues to be intimately present to them.[38]

In Acts, Peter's speech declares that the Spirit of God is poured out upon God's people *from* the risen and enthroned, heavenly Messiah (Acts 2:30–36). The Spirit creates a community of believers who have implemented Jesus's teachings (2:41–47; 4:32–37; 5:12–16). Further, the Spirit of the enthroned Messiah empowers the church for mission (Acts 2:1–13; 10:34–48). In Acts 1:4–8 it is the risen Jesus who associates the sending of his Spirit, which will empower the disciples in their missionary task, with the kingdom (Acts 1:3b, 6). In John's Gospel, the Spirit-anointed Messiah (1:32–34; cf. Isa 11:1–4) shares the Spirit of God without measure with his people upon his own glorification and exaltation (e.g., John 7:37–39). Jesus's Spirit-empowered revelatory teaching leads his people into sanctification, truth, and freedom (4:24–26; 8:21–47; 12:48–49; 17:17–18). In Paul, God "sends the Spirit *of his Son* into our hearts, whereby we cry out 'Abba Father'" (Gal 4:6). This Spirit testifies that the people of Christ are the objects of God's love as his children; therefore, again, the ongoing work of Christ through the Spirit counters fear and anxiety (Gal 4:7; Rom 8:15; cf. 1 Pet 4:13–16). Further, it is the Spirit of the risen Christ who enables and empowers one to give an appropriate response to Christ, as the Spirit transforms us into Christ's image (2 Cor 3:18) and provides the ability to destroy the sinful deeds of the body (Rom 8:13).[39]

Third, the risen Messiah gives gifts to his people. Paul, for example, in

---

38. Thomas G. Weinandy, *Jesus Becoming Jesus: A Theological Interpretation of the Synoptic Gospels* (Washington DC: Catholic University of America Press, 2018), 436.

39. Again, Weinandy, *Jesus Becoming Jesus*, 440, states this well: "Having bestowed upon Jesus, his incarnate Son, the Spirit of Sonship, the Father has given him the proper capacity to send forth that Spirit which properly belongs to the Father, but which he has bestowed fully upon Jesus as his Son. . . . By sending the Holy Spirit upon his disciples and all the

Ephesians 4:7–16 speaks of Christ, the head, as a gift-giving king who rules over his body by giving it health, nourishment, peace, and salvation. As the victorious heavenly king who "fills all things" (Eph 4:10), the Messiah gives gifts to his church "for the edification of the Messiah's body" (4:12b). The ascended Christ is the one who gives "spiritual gifts" to the church for its edification and sustenance. In his role as "the head, the Messiah," he is the source of nourishment for the body and the enabler of its growth (4:15–16). This union with Christ has the further result of protecting Christ's people from error, deception, and false teaching (4:13–16). In Acts, the apostles interpret the healing of the lame man as an example of how the active and "glorified" (Acts 3:12–13) Jesus continues his healing ministry (cf. Luke 5:17–26). Peter refers to the "times of refreshment from the face of the Lord" (Acts 3:20) which stem from the glorified messiah in heaven (3:21) who gives signs of his favor, presence, and healing to those who turn to him. As the king "exalted to the right hand" of the Father, Jesus sends forth repentance and forgiveness of sins to the repentant (5:30–31; cf. 4:10).

Fourth, the risen Messiah continues to meet his people through the Lord's Supper. Paul refers to this meal as expressing our "fellowship with the blood of Christ" and "our fellowship with the body of Christ" (1 Cor 10:16).[40] Paul assumes Christ is present as the host of the meal in 11:23–26. We have seen that God's joyous presence, symbolized through the messianic banquet, is made known through Jesus's hospitality and table fellowship meals in Luke-Acts. And the revelation of Jesus's messianic identity and ongoing presence with his people through the sharing of food (so Luke 9:11–17; 22:24–30; 24:38–35; Acts 1–5) indicates that Jesus continues to reveal his presence through the early Christian meals. Calvin expresses the ongoing relationship between the risen Messiah and his people by means of the Lord's Supper well when he says:

> For though he has taken his flesh away from us, and in the body has ascended into heaven, yet he sits at the right hand of the Father—that is, he reigns in the Father's power and majesty and glory. This Kingdom is neither bounded by location in space nor circumscribed by any limits. Thus, Christ is not prevented from exerting his power wherever he pleases, in heaven and on earth. He shows his presence in power and strength, is always among

---

faithful, Jesus, the Father's Son, will unite them to himself and so, in union with him, will come into living Spirit-filled communion with his Father."

40. On the ascended Jesus's real presence in the Eucharist, see Farrow, *Ascension Theology*, 64–87.

his own people, and breathes his life upon them, and lives in them, sustaining them, strengthening, quickening, keeping them unharmed, as if he were present in the body. In short, he feeds his people with his own body, the communion of which he bestows upon them by the power of his Spirit. In this manner, the body and blood of Christ are shown to us in the Sacrament.[41]

Julie Canlis has argued that Calvin's teaching on the Lord's Supper moves away from disputes over substance and instead emphasizes "the true nature of participation."[42] Christ's people are able to participate in Christ's ongoing and real presence by means of the Spirit when they share in the Lord's Supper.[43]

Fifth, and finally, the risen Christ actively secures the church's ongoing allegiance to himself by means of giving them exhortations and warnings to persevere. We have seen, for example, that Revelation begins with the powerful resurrected Christ walking among his churches and offering both words of encouragement and exhortation, primarily for the purpose of making sure that these churches hold fast to the "*faith* of/to the Messiah" (2:13, 19; 13:10; 14:12). Paul exhorts his congregations to persevere and encourages them that the risen "Lord" provides the power to continue in obedience to God until the day of judgment (Rom 14:4–5). On occasion, however, Paul warns his churches that the risen Christ can also be present in judgment against those who sin egregiously against him (e.g., 1 Cor 5:3–5; 10:18–22).[44] In Hebrews the warning passages are not given from the mouth of the risen Messiah but rather from the preacher himself, but the author does hold up the ascended Messiah as the one who not only sets the paradigm of perseverance for his followers but promises to aid his brothers and sisters in the race set before them—providing help in response to their prayers and interceding for them (so Heb 2:16–18; 4:14–16; 7:25–26). Again, Calvin makes clear Christ's ongoing role in enabling his people to persevere: "so Christ also enriches his people with all things necessary to the eternal salvation of their souls, and fortifies them with courage

---

41. Calvin, *Institutes*, IV, xvii, 18. Quoted from Dawson, *Jesus Ascended*, 46. For a plea to Protestants to recover the real presence of Christ within the Lord's Supper, see Hans Boersma, *Heavenly Participation: The Weaving of a Sacramental Tapestry* (Grand Rapids: Eerdmans, 2011), 103–19.

42. Julie Canlis, *Calvin's Ladder: A Spiritual Theology of Ascent and Ascension* (Grand Rapids: Eerdmans, 2010), 159.

43. Canlis, *Calvin's Ladder*, 159–64.

44. See further, Chris Tilling, *Paul's Divine Christology*, WUNT 2.323 (Tübingen: Mohr Siebeck, 2012), 137–54.

to stand unassailable by all the attacks of spiritual foes. . . . [C]ontented with this, that our King will never abandon us, but will supply our necessities until our warfare is ended, and we are called to triumph: such being the nature of his kingdom, that he communicates to us whatever he received of his Father. Since then he arms and equips us by his power, adorns us with splendor and magnificence, enriches us with wealth, we here find most abundant cause of glorying, and also are inspired with boldness, so that we can contend intrepidly with devil, sin, and death."[45]

CONCLUSION

The incarnate, crucified, and enthroned Christ continues to relate to his people. Christ the King powerfully protects his people; he sends forth the powerful and transformative Spirit of God upon his people; he gives gifts to his people for the edification, unity, and protection of his church; he meets his people through the sacrament of the Lord's Supper; and he speaks words of exhortation and warning to encourage endurance and perseverance.

45. Calvin, *Institutes*, II, xv, 4.

CHAPTER 13

Sanctification and Ecclesiology

Living as Citizens under the Reign of the Messiah

In the previous chapter I argued that the NT testifies to a soteriology that is a necessary entailment of the entire narrative and identity of Jesus's messianic life. The Messiah's life, death, resurrection, and ascension are the means whereby God enacts his saving reign over his people. In this chapter, I suggest that the inauguration of the Messiah's saving rule results in the creation of a people composed of Jews and gentiles who, through the empowering work of the Spirit and through their participatory fellowship with the Messiah, replicate the character of the Messiah and actively participate in his activity and mission. More concretely, the Messiah's people replicate his character as they embody, for example, the faith(fulness), obedience, love, and righteousness of the Messiah in concrete ecclesial practices. The Messiah's people share in his activity and mission as they proclaim the reign of God, make disciples among all the nations, heal the sick, forgive and reconcile, and dispense mercy and compassion to those within the community.

THE MESSIAH AND HIS PEOPLE

In the concluding reflections to his Christology of the Synoptic Gospels, J. R. Daniel Kirk makes an important observation that goes a long way in encapsulating my primary argument in this chapter:

> What Jesus does as son of God, Human One, and Lord of creation becomes the defining set of features of the community he gathers around himself. The content and quality of his life become the content and quality of the lives of his followers. . . . As Christ and Lord and son of God, Jesus inaugu-

rates the reign of God on the earth in such a way that it becomes possible for others to share in the work that he is doing. Others can be part of the family of God and exercise authority on the earth because Jesus does so first.[1]

The inauguration of Christ's saving reign through his messianic life establishes the saving relationship between the Messiah and his people, but it also provides the pattern for the character and activity for the church. In our study we have seen that there is the closest relationship between the Messiah and his people, a relationship that is often expressed through notions of participation and fellowship.

Paul's favorite phrase, "in Christ," often expresses both the agency of the Messiah who acts to accomplish God's purposes *and* the realm or location where Christ's people live and exist. In other words, to speak of believers as "in Christ" indicates most basically that the church is relationally and ontologically related to the Messiah and shares in his identity (e.g., Gal 2:20; 3:28–29; Eph 1:20–23; Col 2:9–15). The NT texts frequently refer to Christ with the language of election as "the beloved" or "beloved Son" as the foundation for the church's election as loved by God (see Mark 1:11; 9:7; Eph 1:4–6; Col 1:13; Rom 1:7; Col 3:12; as a Septuagintal messianic designation, see Deut 32:15; Ps 2:6–7; Isa 44:3).[2] One of the primary images used by Paul to describe those who are "in Christ" and the relationship between Christ and his people is that of the body and the head, and I have argued in detail that this image is often articulated in the context of royal discourse. Paul thinks of those who are "in Christ" as defined by relationship to Christ's own person or body. And this means that, for Paul, persons are further defined in their relation to one another. Paul's language here is relational, participatory, and ontological. Persons-in-Christ together are the "Messiah's body" (σῶμα Χριστοῦ, 1 Cor 12:27). This relation is established by means of the community's shared experience of the Spirit of the Messiah (1 Cor 12:2–3, 12–13). Just as a human body is composed of many different body parts and organs, Paul says "so it is the same with the Messiah" (οὕτως καὶ ὁ Χριστός, 12:12b). Paul's discourse pushes beyond his world's contemporary metaphorical use of the state or commonwealth as a corporate body to something that is an ontological reality for Paul.[3] In other words, the

1. J. R. Daniel Kirk, *A Man Attested by God: The Human Jesus of the Synoptic Gospels* (Grand Rapids: Eerdmans, 2016), 575–76.

2. See here William Horbury, "Septuagintal and New Testament Conceptions of the Church," in *Messianism among Jews and Christians: Biblical and Historical Studies*, 2nd ed. (London: T&T Clark, 2016), 301–2.

3. On the use of the body metaphor to speak of the state and commonwealth in Greco-

corporate gathering of persons in Christ *actually are* Christ's body. They are related to Christ since they have his πνεῦμα. And, as a result, the assembly is not only divinely related to Christ, its individual members are also related to one another, not simply by shared cognitive beliefs or by individual member-ship in a voluntary association, but by means of their relation to Christ.[4] We have seen that in his letters to the Ephesians and the Colossians, Paul speaks of the relationship between the Messiah and his people through the language of "head" and "body" (e.g., Eph 1:20–23; Col 2:9–10). While Paul employs this language to speak of the Messiah as the resurrected-enthroned cosmic king who rules his people, he also emphasizes that the church—as the body of the Messiah—shares in his rule by seeking to extend the knowledge of his kingship in all places (so Eph 1:23). The church is nourished by and grown through its life-sustaining relationship with the Messiah who loves, serves, and cares for the body (Eph. 4:15–16; 5:25–26, 29). Paul can even say that Christ, the messi-anic "head," is "filling up" his people through their relationship (Col 2:9–10). Christ's relationship with his people is marked by the gift of his sacrificial death whereby he has saved the body (Eph 5:22).

We have had occasion to note that all four Gospels speak of Christ as the messianic shepherd who establishes a beneficent and merciful rule over his flock. Jesus's role as the Davidic shepherd often functions as a critique of the current religious leaders who, from the standpoint of the Gospel texts, are exploiting, harming, and ignoring their responsibilities in their care for the people of Israel. In contrast, Jesus's shepherding ministry is one that is marked by mercy, compassion, nourishment, and peace (e.g., Matt 9:35–36; 10:5–6; John 10:9–10). The shepherd's love for his sheep extends even to the point of laying down his life in order to save and rescue them (Matt 26:29–32; John 10:11–18). And as a result, the shepherd's compassion unto the point of death draws the lost sheep into his fold (Matt 10:6; 15:24; Luke 15:3–7; John 10:16).

The NT writings also often portray a relational participation between the Messiah and his people through the image of the church as the eschatological temple built upon Christ—the rejected and now vindicated cornerstone of the temple. This image is not exclusively royal-messianic, and yet many of the NT texts employ Davidic psalms and messianic motifs in their image of the

---

Roman discourse, see Dale B. Martin, *The Corinthian Body* (New Haven: Yale University Press, 1995), 38–68; Margaret M. Mitchell, *Paul and the Rhetoric of Reconciliation: An Exeget-ical Investigation of the Language and Composition of 1 Corinthians* (Louisville: Westminster John Knox, 1991), 157–64.

4. This is stated well by Grant Macaskill, "Autism Spectrum Disorders and the New Testament: Preliminary Reflections," *Journal of Disability and Religion* 22 (2018): 29.

church as an eschatological temple and the Messiah as temple builder. For example, the Synoptic Gospels have Jesus quoting Psalm 118:22 ("the stone the builders rejected has become the chief cornerstone") in such a way that it simultaneously critiques the human building project of Israel's leaders even as it anticipates Jesus's disciples as constituting the eschatological temple built upon Jesus, the new cornerstone of the temple (e.g., Mark 12:10–11; Luke 13:31–35; 19:28–44; 20:17–19; Acts 4:8–12). Within the context of Psalm 118, it is the king making his way to Jerusalem who is "the stone" rejected by men but precious and vindicated in the sight of God. We have seen that John's Gospel also depicts Jesus's resurrected body as the very tabernacle and temple of God (John 1:14, 51). He is also the builder and agent of the eschatological temple as he raises his crucified, rejected body from the dead (2:16–18; 14:1–4). And it is from his crucified and glorified body that he dispenses the living water and the Holy Spirit to his followers (4:11–15; 7:37–39; 20:19–23). The epistolary literature of the NT continues to speak of Jesus as the cornerstone of the eschatological temple, perhaps most expansively in 1 Peter 2:4–10, where "Messiah Jesus" is the subject of three "stone texts" (Isa 8:14; 28:16; Ps 118:22). Here again Christ is the stone rejected by humans but resurrected and vindicated by God; he is the cornerstone for the "spiritual house" and the "living stones" which constitute the broader church (1 Pet 2:5). This temple is further established as God's sacred temple due to the presence of the Spirit of the Messiah which rests upon Christ's people (cf. 1 Pet 1:10–11; 2:5; 3:18; 4:14). To summarize, Christ is the rejected but now resurrected living cornerstone of the eschatological temple (1 Pet 2:4), upon which the Messiah's people are being built as "living stones," enlivened by the very Spirit of Christ, into a "spiritual house" (2:5). Paul makes a very similar claim in Ephesians, where he employs the same temple imagery of Christ "the chief cornerstone" (2:20b) upon whom the "foundation" of the apostles and prophets is constructed (2:20a). This is the foundation for the "holy temple" which includes all of Christ's people. Paul's conviction that those who are in Christ receive the very same Spirit of Christ in their bodies functions as the basis for his claim that the church is the sacred temple of God (Eph 2:18, 22; 1 Cor 3:16; 6:19).

My study has also highlighted Jesus's surprising messiahship as the foundation for a community composed of both Jews and gentiles. Jesus is not a generic "human" Savior; rather, he is the Messiah of Israel, the one whose lineage and descent belongs squarely *within and for* God's covenant people of Israel (Matt 1:1–17; Rom 9:4–5). Thus, Jesus is indeed, according to the NT texts, the Messiah *of Israel*. He is the Davidic Shepherd-King of Israel (e.g., Matt 2:6; 10:5–6; 15:24; 26:31; Luke 15:1–7; 19:10; John 10:1–18); the one born as "the King of the Jews" (Matt 2:2, 8, 11); "the Messiah of the Lord" who will bring salvation to the gentiles and glory to Israel (Luke 2:25–30); the messianic ruler in the line of David (Matt 1:1; 9:27; 21:9, 15; Mark 10:47–48; Rom 1:3; 15:9–12; 2 Tim 2:8); the Lion from the tribe of Judah, and the Root of David (Rev 5:5–6; 22:16). As a result, and as we have seen repeatedly, the salvation of the gentiles is contingent upon the Messiah's prior blessing and restoration of Israel. The conviction that Jesus is the Messiah and Savior of Israel was, of course, and still is, a highly contested and controversial claim. The belief that the Messiah's life, death, and resurrection are the climax of Israel's history results in a remarkable reevaluation and new understanding of Israel's primary identity markers. For example, Paul is emphatic that God has elected Israel as his people, that the Torah is good and holy, that gentiles are sinners "by birth," and that circumcision is good and divinely ordained (e.g., 3:1–2; Rom 9:4–5; 11:28–32; Gal 2:15). But Paul's conviction that Jesus is the Messiah of Israel and the nations, and his belief that only the Messiah's death and resurrection can liberate Jews and gentiles from sin and death results in his conviction that only Jesus the Messiah can save Jews and gentiles.[5] Similarly, Acts makes the strongest connection between the hope of Israel, which includes the reconstitution of the Davidic kingdom, and the resurrection of Jesus the Messiah from the dead (Luke 1:31–35; Acts 13:32–37; 15:13–14; 26:6–8). This messianic interpretation of Israel's history and identity markers, as evidenced in the NT writings, results in a complex and paradoxical situation whereby God's faithfulness to his people is on display in Messiah Jesus but is resulting in an uncomfortable and contested reevaluation of the meaning of Israelite identity/ethnicity, Torah observance, and temple/cultic practices.

On the one hand, I would suggest that the NT texts do not provide evidence for the beliefs that the Torah is abrogated, that Israel's election is nullified, or that Judaism was replaced with Christianity. The Jewish people are not held up as exemplars of failed Torah observance, for legalism or hypocritical judgment of others, or for national pride. The NT authors do not critique or call upon fellow Jewish people to reject or abandon their ancestral heritage. The NT texts I have studied stand as witnesses against extreme supersessionist forms of Christian theology that have dispensed with the ongoing significance of God's election of Israel, which view Christianity or the church as replacing Judaism, and which denigrate Judaism as particularistic and now superseded by the

---

5. I have written more on this in "Is the Apostle Paul the Father of Anti-Judaism? Engaging John Gager's *Who Made Early Christianity?*," *HBT* 39 (2017): 83–92.

universal gospel of Paul.[6] On the other hand, one cannot ignore the historical consequences of the NT's unrelenting reinterpretation of Israel's history and hope through the lens of a crucified, resurrected, heavenly enthroned messianic ruler of the world. The NT authors' foundational commitment to Jesus as the risen Messiah results in a totalizing and hegemonic appropriation of Israel's ancestral heritage, customs, and Scriptures.

The Church's Life under the Reign of the Messiah

One of the primary ways in which the NT calls for the church to progress in its holiness and sanctification is through embodying the very character and activity of its messianic king. One might say that discipleship flows from Christology, and the church's imitation of the Messiah is rooted in its participation in the Messiah's establishing of his saving kingdom. Again, my comments here are by no means exhaustive but they do, I hope, draw together some of the most significant threads of my exegetical engagements in order to demonstrate that the NT conceptualizes the life of the church as embodying and participating in the character and life of the Messiah. Here are four concrete examples.

Embodying the Character of the Messiah

What is often referred to as sanctification in Christian theology is for the New Testament texts, in many ways, conformity to the character of the Messiah. Just as Christ's very life and narrative inaugurate the saving reign of God, so also does Christ's character establish the pattern and quality of the lives of his disciples. Sanctification and discipleship flow from Christology. Allow me to draw together a few of the primary themes that have pervaded my study in order to establish this point.

First, disciples share in the sufferings of the Messiah. In the Synoptic Gospels Jesus uses the language of cross-bearing to describe how his followers participate in his sufferings (e.g., Matt 16:24–27; Mark 8:34–9:1; Luke 9:23–27).

6. See, however, the attempt by many now to reckon with Christian theology's supersessionist past and to chart a better way forward. For example, Willie James Jennings, *The Christian Imagination: Theology and the Origins of Race* (New Haven: Yale University Press, 2010); Robert W. Jenson, "Toward a Christian Theology of Israel," *Pro Ecclesia* 9 (2000): 43–56; R. Kendall Soulen, *The God of Israel and Christian Theology* (Minneapolis: Fortress, 1996); R. Kendall Soulen, *The Divine Name(s) and the Holy Trinity: Distinguishing the Voices* (Louisville: Westminster John Knox, 2011).

For the author of Hebrews, discipleship is a journey toward the enthroned messianic king who, through his obedience and faithfulness to God even in the midst of suffering, has been perfected and has thereby entered into God's glory (so Heb 2:10–14; 5:7–9; 7:25–29; 11:1–12:3). Just as the Messiah triumphs through his sufferings and faithful testimony even in the face of his persecutors in Revelation (Rev 1:5–6; 5:5–6), so do his followers embody faithful endurance and truthful testimony in their sufferings (Rev 2:3, 9–10; 12:11–17; 20:4–6). The text of 1 Peter programmatically asserts that the OT prophets anticipated, by means of the Spirit of the Messiah, that the Messiah would suffer before his glories (1 Pet 1:10–12). And this pattern of the Messiah's suffering provides the precedent for the audience, who share in the messianic tribulations and sufferings (1 Pet 2:21–25; 4:12–19). The apostle Paul everywhere articulates that sharing in the sufferings of the Messiah is a necessary component of discipleship for those who will be conformed to the image of the Son of God—so much so, in fact, that Paul sees his ministry as embodying the sufferings, death, and resurrection power of the Messiah (e.g., Rom 8:17; 2 Cor 4:7–15; 11:23–12:10; 2 Tim 2:11–13).

Second, disciples embody the character of Christ when they intentionally renounce and sacrifice their status, power, and rights in order to serve and love their fellow brothers and sisters. Taking up Christ's cross is exemplified through narratives which emphasize embracing service and humility as well as renouncing status, power, and privilege (Matt 20:26–27; Mark 9:35; 10:35–45). Paul speaks of Christ's renunciation of status and privilege, that is, his downward mobility, as providing a necessary pattern of humility for those living in Christ's kingdom (e.g., Phil 2:6–8; 3:2–11). This takes a variety of forms in the NT through extreme generosity and the sharing of economic resources. For example, Paul's multifaceted appeals to the Corinthian churches to participate in the famine relief collection are rooted in the character of Christ, that is, "the one who, even though he was rich, became poor for your sakes so that you might become rich by his poverty" (2 Cor 8:9). Economic generosity for those who are experiencing suffering and need, then, is rooted in God's gift in Christ (see 2 Cor 8:1, 4, 6–9; 9:10–15). In the Gospel of Luke, Jesus's teaching at the Last Supper holds him up as a model of service and renunciation of power in his own table fellowship (Luke 22:24–30), and this provides a model for the early Christian church to use their meals and economic resources as an opportunity to generously care for all of their members (so Acts 2:42–47; 4:32–37). The Gospels witness to true discipleship—giving up one's comfort, security, and wealth as a means of serving and loving one another (e.g., Matt 19:16–30; Luke 14:12–24; 16:19–31).

Third, Christ's people are called to follow his example by implementing practices of peace, forgiveness, and reconciliation. We have seen that Matthew's Gospel conceptualizes the death of the Messiah as paying a debt/ransom for the sins of God's people (e.g., Matt 1:21; 20:28; 26:28). Those who have experienced this ransom must respond by forgiving, reconciling, and canceling the debts of fellow disciples who have wronged them (6:12–15; 18:18–19; 18:21–35). The church forgives the little ones in God's flock who sin and is called upon to do everything possible to restore and reconcile the lost sheep who go astray (18:10–20). Likewise, Paul argues that Christ's death on the cross has established peace between those peoples formerly at enmity with one another and, as a result, the body of Christ implements the Messiah's activity through forgiving and reconciling with one another (Eph 2:11–18). Christ's peace, in other words, has a tangible outworking in a peaceful and unified people (Eph 2:14, 15, 17).

Fourth, and most importantly, just as the Messiah has done all things out of love for his people, so disciples are called upon to engage in concrete actions of love for one another. We have seen that Jesus interprets the Torah as a witness to God's love for his people and, therefore, is rightly read when it elicits concrete displays of mercy and compassion for God's people (Matt 22:34–40). All of God's Torah is good and holy, but one's hermeneutical starting point must be the weightier matters of the law—namely, justice, mercy, and faithfulness (Matt 23:23; Luke 11:37–44). A right understanding of God's law will lead to tangible displays of hospitality and justice, economic generosity, and love of both neighbor and even enemy (Luke 6:27–36; 10:25–37; 16:19–31). Thus, Jesus's ministry as *the* true and good Davidic shepherd who has the right to rule over his people is rooted in his messianic deeds which, through exorcisms, healings, teachings, and provisions of food, extend his rule of mercy and compassion over his people (e.g., Matt 9:27–31; 9:35–10:13; 11:2–6; 12:15–21; John 10:11–18). Jesus's kingly and messianic identity is revealed in his sacrificial offering of his own life, an act which displays both the Father's and the Son of God's love for his people (esp. John 12:27–36; 13:11–19).[7] And this display of divine love is the ground for Jesus's exhortations that his disciples enact the same love toward each other (John 13:1–20; 13:31–35; 15:12–14). I have argued that Paul also witnesses to a reading of the Torah as something which primarily calls

---

7. On this theme, see Francis J. Moloney, *Love in the Gospel of John: An Exegetical, Theological, and Literary Study* (Grand Rapids: Baker Academic, 2013); Carlos Raul Sosa Siliezar, *Savior of the World: A Theology of the Universal Gospel* (Waco, TX: Baylor University Press, 2019), 104–5.

forth the love of neighbor. Paul connects "the law of the Messiah" and the call to bear one another's burdens (Gal 6:2) with his earlier claim that the Torah has been brought to its completion in the command to "love your neighbor as yourself" (Gal 5:14). And the climactic display of loving one's neighbor has been embodied in the Messiah who "loved us and gave himself up for us" (Gal 2:20). Similarly, being under the Messiah's law in 1 Corinthians 9:21 almost certainly means something to the effect of foregoing one's rights, enacting other-regarding love at all costs, and willingly renouncing perceived rights for the good of one's fellow brothers and sisters in Christ (1 Cor 8:11–13; 10:19–22). Christ's love of his own neighbors and his extension of hospitality climaxing in his willing embrace of death on the cross stands for Paul as the messianic example for the church's love and hospitality (Rom 15:1–12). This other-regarding love flows from an understanding that God's wisdom, power, and love have been revealed in the crucified Messiah (1 Cor 1:18–2:5). Those who have "the mind of the Messiah" are able to think and act in ways that express this other-regarding love (1 Cor 2:16; Rom 15:6; Phil 2:5). In addition to Paul's understanding of the character of the Messiah as mediated through his cruciform death, his invocation of Leviticus 19:18 as the primary command which summarizes the Torah also attests to the influence of Jesus's teachings regarding the Torah as calling forth love, mercy, and compassion for God's people.

Pistis/Faith toward the Messiah

One of the primary marks of the people of the Messiah, witnessed to in almost all of the NT texts, is the mark of faith or perhaps, we might say, allegiance. In his *Salvation by Allegiance Alone*, Matthew Bates has argued that the best macro-term for understanding *pistis* (most commonly translated as "faith") is allegiance, given that the right response to the singular enthroned messianic king is allegiance rather than simply belief.[8] And Bates is absolutely right that there are significant instances where the contemporary connotations of "faith" do not do justice to the ways in which the NT texts often associate forms of *pistis* with obedience, loyalty, and an entire way of life oriented around Messiah Jesus. One of the central insights of Teresa Morgan's comprehensive study of the meaning of *pistis* language in the Roman Empire and early Christianity is that faith is "first and foremost, neither a body of beliefs nor a function of the

---

8. Matthew W. Bates, *Salvation by Allegiance Alone: Rethinking Faith, Works, and the Gospel of Jesus the King* (Grand Rapids: Baker Academic, 2017).

heart or mind, but a relationship which creates community."[9] Morgan shows how the language of *pistis* is constantly used in contexts that describe how faith initiates and sustains relationships. The frequent use of faith language in relational contexts means that one cannot so easily disentangle faith as propositional content (belief), from trust in and loyalty toward the object of one's *pistis*.

Paul's exhortation to the Philippian jailer, for example, calls for a faith toward Jesus that will result in a radical reorientation of life: "Believe (πίστευ-σον) in the Lord Jesus and you and your household will be saved" (Acts 16:31). Enacting *pistis* here involves recognizing that Jesus alone is "Lord," and this recognition contains within it a simultaneous rejection of the jailer's worship and piety toward his pagan gods. In other words, a way of life is contained within his newfound *pistis* in the Lord Jesus—a way of life that includes but is not limited to "acceptance of truth" but is better expressed by something stronger—namely, allegiance or loyalty to the Lord Jesus. First Peter further witnesses to a use of *pistis* that certainly includes mental assent and belief, but Peter's focus is primarily upon a Christocentric *way of life* that endures even in the midst of threats, sufferings, and challenges. Peter speaks of *pistis* as something that is tested by fire and is able to stand at the return of Jesus Christ with the result that they receive the "goal of their *pistis*—namely, the salvation of your souls" (1 Pet 1:7, 9). These threats and challenges to their *pistis* are almost certainly the societal pressure to return to their former gods, family and friendship relationships, and way of life (cf. 1 Pet 1:18). Within the Gospel of John, the appropriate response to Jesus is also faith or belief that he is the Messiah, the very Son of God, and this faith is a living and relational stance toward Jesus that comes by way of divine revelation (e.g., John 4:15–29; 11:25–27; 20:30–31). We have also seen the book of Revelation's portrait of the

---

9. Teresa Morgan, *Roman Faith and Christian Faith: Pistis and Fides in the Early Roman Empire and Early Churches* (Oxford: Oxford University Press, 2015), 14. See her following summary of her study: "That relationality is central to concepts whose foundational and most common meanings are trust, trustworthiness, and faithfulness, and among whose more specialized meanings are good faith, assurance, pledge, and anything that is entrusted, needs no demonstration. In studies of *pistis/fides* by classicists, as we have noted, relationality has always been central and uncontroversial. Among theologians and NT scholars, approaches to *pistis/fides* have been strongly influenced by Augustine's taxonomy of *fides* as *fides quae* and *fides qua*, and have tended to focus on either the propositional content of *pistis/fides* or the interiority of that 'faith by which the believer believes.' I have argued in the earlier chapters that the propositional content of *pistis*, though always implicit in its relationality and not infrequently articulated or alluded to, is not usually its main focus in the NT" (444).

risen Christ who calls the church to embody faith and resist the idolatry of the Roman Empire. For example, the risen Christ speaks to the church in Pergamum in response to the opposition they are receiving from imperial elites (a.k.a. "the throne of Satan"): "you have not denied faith in me" (ἠρνήσω τὴν πίστιν μου, 2:13; cf. also 2:19). This statement interprets and expands upon his affirmation that "you are holding fast to my name." A concrete example of holding fast to Jesus's name and not denying faith toward him is Antipas "my witness, my faithful one, who was killed in your presence" (2:13b). The vision in chapter 13 of the evil beast that rages against and even conquers God's saints concludes with the exhortation: "here then is a call for endurance and *pistis* on behalf of the saints" (ἡ ὑπομονὴ καὶ πίστις τῶν ἁγίων, 13:10). Similarly, after a vision where an angel announces God's judgment upon those who worship the beast, John notes: "This calls for the endurance of the saints, for those who keep God's commands and their *pistis* toward Jesus (καὶ τὴν πίστιν Ἰησοῦ)" (14:12). Stated simply, John's call for *pistis* toward Jesus is a call to remain loyal in their worship of the true Lord even in the face of opposition, suffering, and persecution.

But I want to suggest here that the risen and living Christ is present and active even within our enactment of *pistis* toward him.[10] In other words, human *pistis* is inherently *participatory*, and it is "Christ's faithfulness toward humanity—the abiding, justifying, mission-empowering trustworthiness of the risen and exalted Lord for those united to him—that allows humans to place their trust in him."[11] Just as the Christian's sharing in "the mind of Christ" requires that Christ himself had a mind (1 Cor 2:16; Phil 2:5–11; cf. Rom 15:1–7), and just as the Christian's act of loving her neighbor is grounded in Christ's act of loving his neighbor (Gal 2:20; 5:5–6; 5:13–14), so, too, the Christian's enactment of *pistis* is rooted in our relational union with the risen Christ. Separating our *pistis* from our relational participation with the Messiah leads to critical distortions of the gospel—often resulting in a minimalistic role for the Spirit and a failure to recognize the presence of the risen Christ as acting subject in our enactment of *pistis*.[12] In Galatians 2:15–21, the "I" of which Paul speaks is a transformed

10. For a similar argument regarding the activity of the risen Christ, see the very fine and stimulating work of David J. Downs and Benjamin J. Lappenga, *The Faithfulness of the Risen Christ: Pistis and the Exalted Lord in Paul* (Waco, TX: Baylor University Press, 2019).

11. Downs and Lappenga, *The Faithfulness of the Risen Christ*, 155.

12. See further Douglas A. Campbell, "Participation and Faith in Paul," in *"In Christ" in Paul: Explorations in Paul's Theology of Union and Participation*, ed. Michael J. Thate et al. (Grand Rapids: Eerdmans, 2018), 57–58; David M. Hay, "Paul's Understanding of Faith as Participation," in *Paul and His Theology*, ed. Stanley E. Porter (Leiden: Brill, 2006), 45–76.

individual whose agency and identity is interconnected with the living Christ who dwells within the "I" who lives "in/by *pistis*" (2:20b). There is an overlap, then, between the "I" and the living Christ such that, to use the language of Susan Eastman, "the believer as indwelt by Christ is structured by trust that is extrinsically sourced, as well as directed to Christ."[13] In Galatians 3:15–29 the *identification* of the coming of *pistis* with the coming of *Christ* and the coming of *the seed* indicates that, however we understand the *pistis Christou* phrases, we cannot avoid a participatory understanding of *pistis* and one that thereby guards against speaking of *pistis* as something that we do apart from the active presence of the risen Christ.[14] So also in Hebrews, the participatory nature of *pistis* is evident in that Christ, as the paradigmatic exemplar of the true human, is held up as the one who is both in solidarity with his fellow human siblings (2:14–17) and as the one who has enacted *pistis* and thereby entered into God's heavenly life (12:1–2; cf. 3:1–6).[15] Throughout Hebrews, Jesus is the one who is the perfect exemplar of faith toward God. Marc Cortez rightly comments on Hebrews: "[Faith] is the true mode of human existence. However, no one besides Jesus has truly exemplified the life of faith. . . . Jesus is both the paradigmatic instantiation of true humanity but also the one who prepares the way for others to participate in this new way of being."[16]

Practices Which Express the Church's Relationship with the Messiah and One Another

Given the participatory and relational connection between the Messiah and his people, the NT witnesses to a variety of practices that express both the church's ontological relationship with the Messiah and its relationships with one another. In particular the early Christian practices of friendship, the Lord's Supper, baptism, and communal worship ritualize this vertical and horizontal relationship.

13. Susan Grove Eastman, *Paul and the Person: Reframing Paul's Anthropology* (Grand Rapids: Eerdmans, 2017), 161.

14. See further the participatory nature of *pistis* in 2 Cor 4:7–15; Eph 3:16–19; and Phil 3:7–11. Important here is the recent work of Jeanette Hagen Pifer, *Faith as Participation: An Exegetical Study of Some Key Pauline Texts*, WUNT 2.486 (Tübingen: Mohr-Siebeck, 2019).

15. Stephen Chester has argued recently that this participatory understanding of *pistis* is characteristic of Calvin's and Luther's reading of Paul, where "present in faith is the living person of Christ." See Stephen Chester, *Reading Paul with the Reformers: Reconciling Old and New Perspectives* (Grand Rapids: Eerdmans, 2017), 199.

16. Marc Cortez, *Resourcing Theological Anthropology: A Constructive Account of Humanity in the Light of Christ* (Grand Rapids: Zondervan, 2017), 142.

Singing Hymns to Christ the King

Pliny the Younger's famous letter to Trajan provides important evidence that the early Christians worshipped Jesus through singing "a hymn to Christ, as to a god" (*Letters to Trajan* 10.96). Pliny's statement can be corroborated through the NT texts. Paul, for example, exhorts his congregations to "sing psalms and hymns and spiritual songs among yourselves, singing and making melody in your hearts *to the Lord*" (Eph 5:19; cf. 1 Cor 14:26). The NT texts are filled with royal acclamations to Christ, including: "Jesus is Lord" (e.g., 1 Cor 12:2–3; Phil 2:10–11) and "Blessed is he who comes in the name of the Lord" (e.g., Luke 19:38). I have suggested that Paul's command to the Colossians to "let the word about the Messiah dwell in you richly, teaching and instructing one another wisely, with psalms, hymns, and spiritual songs" (Col 3:16) may include the expectation that they will sing the hymn to Christ, the messianic ruler, in Colossians 1:15–20. Martin Hengel, among others, has argued that the hymns and acclamations to Christ were probably spontaneous expressions of worship stemming from the early Christians' experience of the Spirit and the enthroned Lord in their assemblies.[17] We have seen that Paul applies exalted messianic language to the enthroned Messiah as his hymns center upon the Messiah's incarnation, humility, death, resurrection, and exaltation to a position of powerful rule (Phil 2:6–11; Col 1:15–20; cf. Eph 1:20–23; 1 Tim 3:16). Paul may even expect the church to join their voices together with the enthroned Messiah who sings songs of rejoicing to God the Father in praise for the gentiles who have turned to God (Rom 15:9b–12). The book of Hebrews begins with a hymnic and poetic celebration of the Son's royal enthronement into heaven (Heb 1:4–13) and depicts Christ as one who sings hymns of celebration to God in the assembly with his people (Heb 2:11–13). The book of Revelation is filled with hymns which declare thanksgiving and glory to Christ, the true king, who has purchased a kingdom for himself through his own sacrificial death (Rev 5:5–14). As a result, the church sings "the song of the Lamb" to the sacrificial Lamb of God (e.g., Rev 15:3; cf. 7:9–17; 11:15–18). The early Christian church's practice of singing hymns and uttering acclamations in praise to Christ functioned to both celebrate the presence of the living Messiah in their communities and to remind them of the ground of their common identity

---

17. Martin Hengel, *Between Jesus and Paul: Studies in the Earliest History of Christianity*, trans. John Bowden (Philadelphia: Fortress, 1983), 81. Similarly, see Adela Yarbro Collins, "The Psalms and the Origins of Christology," in *Psalms in Community: Jewish and Christian Textual, Liturgical, and Artistic Traditions*, ed. Harold W. Attridge and Margot E. Fassler (Atlanta: Society of Biblical Literature, 2003), 113–23.

as those who live and participate in the Messiah's saving reign. The hymns, thanksgiving, and worship offered to Christ enable the church to confess that Jesus is their singular ruler who has been invested with cosmic rule, divine authority, and the power to liberate and save.

Friendship in Christ

Another way the NT authors strategically seek to help their audience understand their relation to others in Christ is through the practice of friendship. In the Messiah, God has extended divine friendship and welcome to those who were formerly enemies and transformed them into friends (e.g., Rom 5:9–10; 15:7–8). Luke's Jesus is revealed as God's Messiah when he acts as the divine host of the messianic banquet, sharing an abundance of food with the hungry (Luke 9:11–17) and extending hospitality and table fellowship to those alienated from the kingdom of God (Luke 5:27–32; 7:36–50; 15:1–2; 19:1–10). We have seen that these meals act as an opportunity for the lost, broken, poor, and lonely to experience God's transformative and reconciling presence in the person of Messiah Jesus. This shared experience of "divine friendship" has as its necessary correlation the creation of a horizontal community of friends, as seen most powerfully in the book of Acts. Luke's language used to describe the early church as having "fellowship" with one another (Acts 2:42), sharing "all things in common" (2:44; 4:32b), and having "one heart and soul" (4:32) resonates powerfully with ancient philosophical descriptions of friendship.[18] And this demonstrates that this community is a new family or community of friends who has implemented Jesus's teachings on generosity, hospitality, and embrace. Luke's theme of table fellowship and hospitality is remarkable in that he has expanded friendship to include all people, both rich and poor, men and women, patrons and clients, Jews and gentiles, and so forth. The church's practice of sharing meals, then, celebrates their common friendship with one another *and* their friendship with the Messiah, whose life was constantly marked by table fellowship and who taught them to "remember" him through their shared meals (Luke 22:24–30; 24:28–35).

Paul also draws upon and reconfigures the philosophical theme of friendship into the language of spiritual kinship such that true friendship is elevated

---

18. See Alan C. Mitchell, "The Social Function of Friendship in Acts 2:44–47 and 4:32–37," *JBL* 111 (1992): 255–72; Douglas A. Hume, *The Early Christian Community: A Narrative Analysis of Acts 2:41–47 and 4:32–35*, WUNT 2.298 (Tübingen: Mohr Siebeck, 2011).

to "a way of speaking about the bonds between Christian siblings."[19] Paul's attempt to create churches that embody God's friendship in Christ is seen most clearly in his letter to the Philippians.[20] Here Paul draws upon the theme of friendship in order to form the church into a community of friends patterned on Christ's model of humility and self-abasement (Phil 2:5–8). Paul wants to find them standing firm "in *one spirit and with one soul,* working together for the faith of the gospel" (1:27). The assembly is to implement the pattern of moral and practical reasoning seen in Christ that enables them to "think the same way, have the same love, share the same soul, and think together on one goal" (Phil 2:2). And this unity of thinking is predicated upon the pattern of other-regarding love that has been embodied in Jesus (Phil 2:5). Paul sets forth his friends Timothy and Epaphroditus, who do not strive to satisfy their own self-interests but rather set their minds on pleasing Christ, Paul, and the Philippians (2:19–30; cf. 3:2–17; 4:2). The participatory and ontological grounding of Christian friendship is stated well by Stephen Fowl: "Christian friends do not really choose each other. We are called into friendship with each other because of our common friendship in Christ."[21] Given that family metaphors were a common way of describing fictive kinship in the ancient world, Paul's conceptualization of the church as "friends in Christ" is of one piece with his frequent use of family metaphors for God, Christ, and the assemblies.[22] Paul consistently refers to his churches as fellow brothers and sisters of one another (1 Cor 1:11, 26; 2:1; 3:1; 2 Cor 2:12–13; Gal 4:12–20; Phil 2:25; 1 Thess 2:17–3:8) and as sons or children of God (Gal 3:26; 4:5–7). He refers to Jesus as "God's Son" (Col 1:13; Rom 8:9–17, 29; Col 1:15, 18) and to God as "Father" (Rom 1:7; 6:4; 8:15; 15:6).[23] Paul's "family language" is not illustrative but is, rather, real and participatory. In other words, Paul's family language encapsulates the partic-

19. Wesley Hill, *Spiritual Friendship: Finding Love in the Church as a Celibate Gay Christian* (Grand Rapids: Brazos, 2015), 60.

20. I rely here on the work of L. Michael White, "Morality between Two Worlds: A Paradigm of Friendship in Philippians," in *Greeks, Romans, and Christians,* ed. David L. Balch, Everett Fergusson, and Wayne A. Meeks (Minneapolis: Fortress, 1990), 201–15; Wayne Meeks, "The Man from Heaven in Paul's Letter to the Philippians," in *The Future of Early Christianity: Essays in Honor of Helmut Koester,* ed. Birger Pearson (Minneapolis: Fortress, 1991), 329–36; John T. Fitzgerald, "Paul and Friendship," in *Paul in the Greco-Roman World: A Handbook,* ed. J. Paul Sampley (Harrisburg, PA: Trinity Press International, 2003), 319–43.

21. Stephen E. Fowl, *Philippians,* THNTC (Grand Rapids: Eerdmans, 2005), 216.

22. See Wayne A. Meeks, *The First Urban Christians: The Social World of the Apostle Paul* (New Haven: Yale University Press, 1983), 85–94.

23. See here Joseph H. Hellerman, *When the Church Was a Family: Recapturing Jesus' Vision for Authentic Christian Community* (Nashville: B&H, 2009), 76–96.

ular Christian narrative in which persons in Christ participate—namely, that the *Father* of Jesus Christ sends forth his *firstborn Son* who saves a community of brothers and sisters.

The Lord's Supper and Baptism

The NT texts also portray the Messiah's people as "ritually performing" their value as divine gift and not a personal achievement. In other words, human worth and value is not something achieved but is, rather, something that is given by God apart from any prior attempts to make oneself a fitting or worthy recipient.[24] The ancient Mediterranean world, of which the NT texts are a part, had a particular way of calculating human worth and value, and this value was often organized in terms of an honor/shame dynamic. This code for pursuing human worth and value traded upon competition, ambition, and love for honor. We can see this clearly in Paul's letters where he consistently calls upon believers to enact a new economy on the basis of Christ's incongruous gift, that is, a new framework for ascribing worth and value for persons in Christ.[25] This shocking transformation of human value in light of the gift of Christ is seen in a powerful way in Paul's autobiographical statement in Philippians 3:4–11, where he makes the remarkable claim that his ethnicity, ancestry, Torah-observance, *paideia*, and religious zeal are "loss" (κέρδη, 3:7; ζημίαν, 3:8; σκύβαλα, 3:8) in light of knowing *Christ*, being found *in Christ*, and sharing in Christ's death and resurrection (cf. 1 Cor 1:26–28). Paul's autobiographical statement is a declaration that he has rejected his former competitive quests for status that would bring him communal recognition and that this path of pursuing meaning is nothing but "human excrement" (Phil 3:8) in light of God's gift in Christ. In Paul's world social identities usually come in binaries and are marked by obvious hierarchical freight. So, Jew/gentile, patron/client, free/slave, Greek/barbarian, male/female, citizen/foreigner provide the fundamental structures for understanding human identity, value, and social worth.[26] While Paul does not erase a person's social identities—people are still male and female, Jew and gentile, free and slave—he deeply relativizes their

---

24. The divine gift is, for Paul, radically incongruous. See John M. G. Barclay, *Paul and the Gift*, (Grand Rapids: Eerdmans, 2015), 72–73.

25. With respect especially to the exchange of resources, see Stephen C. Barton, "Money Matters: Economic Relations and the Transformation of Value in Early Christianity," in *Engaging Economics: New Testament Scenarios and Early Christian Reception*, ed. Bruce W. Longenecker and Kelly D. Liebengood (Grand Rapids: Eerdmans, 2009), 37–59.

26. See especially, J. Louis Martyn, "Apocalyptic Antinomies," and "Christ and the El-

value in terms of divine value.[27] Paul tried to live out his commitments to a new humanity that did not eradicate, but severely qualified, social identity. We see that not only men but also women, not only the free but also slaves, not only Jews but also pagans participated in his planting of churches and were encouraged to participate freely in the common gathering of the Christian assemblies. This vision stands in marked contrast to what is often seen in our church life: namely, ethnic and cultural sameness, men refusing to share their power with women in leadership, and aversion and fear of difference as a potential polluting or destabilizing of the church. When our social identities are valued above our shared identity in Christ, then inevitably those with less power—usually ethnic minorities, women, the poor, or marginalized—are relegated to a position of subservience within the church.

The two most significant ritual practices in Paul's assemblies—baptism and the Lord's Supper—create a common group identity of christological value for everyone regardless of the individual's particular social identities.[28] We have seen in the Synoptic Gospels (particularly in our examination of Mark) and in Paul that baptism initiates a participation into the Messiah's death and resurrection and is a prerequisite for sharing in the Messiah's kingdom (e.g., Mark 10:35–45; Rom 6:3–11; Eph 5:26). This participation in Christ's death is the means whereby the church is transferred from the powers of sin and darkness and made to share in Christ's saving kingdom. Thus, Paul's baptismal formulae assert that for those who are "in Messiah Jesus" (Gal 3:28), who have been baptized into "one body" and have "drunk from one Spirit" (1 Cor 12:13), and who are now "clothed with the new humanity" of Christ (Col 3:10–11; cf. 2:11–13) ethnic, economic, and gender identities are no longer the basis for ascriptions of human value and worth. The ritual of baptism symbolizes and expresses the believer's union with the Messiah and the receipt of his Spirit (Rom 6:3–11; 1 Cor 12:11–13). This is stated well by Isaac Augustine Morales: "Union with Christ and union with other believers are of a piece precisely because the former is ordered, at least in part, to the latter (Gal 3:27–28; 1 Cor 12:13). Baptism thus initiates a life patterned on Christ's own death and res-

---

ements of the Cosmos," in *Theological Issues in the Letters of Paul* (Nashville: Abingdon, 1997), 111–40.

27. See here David G. Horrell, *Solidarity and Difference: A Contemporary Reading of Paul's Ethics*, 2nd ed. (London: T&T Clark, 2015), 136–42; J. Brian Tucker, *"Remain in Your Calling": Paul and the Continuation of Social Identities in 1 Corinthians* (Eugene, OR: Pickwick, 2011).

28. On baptism and the Lord's Supper as the rituals in Pauline Christianity, see Meeks, *The First Urban Christians*, 150–62.

urrection (cf. Rom 8:17) that empowers and obligates the baptized to live out the holiness that builds up the body of Christ (1 Cor 12:25), and will one day fully bloom to eternal life (Rom 6:22–23)."[29]

Similarly, the Lord's Supper and the shared common meals of the Pauline Christians express their conviction that Christ is present among them as the singular host of the meal, and that they are feasting with and upon the Lord Jesus Christ who has graciously given his body and blood as the food and drink (1 Cor 11:23–26; "fellowship" with Christ, see 1 Cor 10:16–18).[30] When the common meal is used, however, as an opportunity to privilege patrons over clients, the wealthy over the poor, then this false evaluation of human worth makes that meal "so fundamentally at odds with the gospel that the meal ceases to be the Lord's Supper at all (1 Cor 11:20)."[31] Thus, the Lord's Supper and early Christian meals provide opportunities for the Messiah's body to enact the grounds of their identity through other-regarding love, gift, and hospitality (see also 1 Cor 8:7–13; Rom 14–15).[32]

The early Christian rituals of baptism and the Lord's Supper were necessary reminders that their identity in Christ was a divine gift and not something achieved through performance. Paul's world often connected (multiple) ritual initiations with enhanced status elevation, esoteric knowledge, and divine power. Numerous initiations into religious cults were often seen as leading to "greater knowledge, dignity, and status within the cult. [In other words], Ritual imprinting was toward the politics of perfection."[33] Thus, Paul addresses a variety of situations where churches are tempted to pursue religious rituals or

29. Isaac Augustine Morales, "Baptism and Union with Christ," in *"In Christ" in Paul: Explorations in Paul's Theological Vision of Participation*, ed. Michael J. Thate et al. (Tübingen: Mohr Siebeck. 2014), 176.

30. It was common belief that the gods were present in the cultic meals of their worshippers. See Dennis E. Smith, *From Symposium to Eucharist: The Banquet in the Early Christian World* (Minneapolis: Fortress, 2003).

31. Macaskill, "Autism Spectrum Disorders," 24.

32. Barclay, *Paul and the Gift*, 509: "Paul thus calls for a way of life recalibrated in disregard of whatever ethnic, social, or individual characteristics had previously constituted the believers' cultural or symbolic capital, whatever had formed their grounds for distinctive or superior value." And again, Barclay, *Paul and the Gift*, 515: "For Paul, the gift (or 'welcome') of Christ, because it neither matched nor reinforced preexistent norms or values, has put all other value systems into question. The only salient values for believers are those that arise from the good news, what is true 'in the Lord Jesus' (14:14) and what accords with 'the kingdom of God' (14:17)."

33. Luke Timothy Johnson, *Religious Experience in Earliest Christianity: A Missing Dimension in New Testament Studies* (Minneapolis: Fortress, 1998), 89.

powerful displays as a means of bolstering their religious identity: for example, some are tempted to engage in ascetic practices for the purpose of heavenly ascents (Col 2:16–19; cf. 2 Cor 12:1–13); some are tempted to undergo adult male circumcision as a means of curbing their base passions (Rom 2:25–29; Gal 5:2–12; 6:11–16; cf. Col 2:11); some churches are seeking to enhance their status through connection to powerful charismatic Christian orators (1 Cor 1:10–4:21); and some individuals seek upward mobility through the public display of higher-status gifts such as ecstatic speech (1 Cor 12–14).[34] The church's regular ritual practices of baptism and the Lord's Supper publicly display the meaning of the Christ narrative as a transformative gift, given without respect to any human criterion, and as the ground for corporate belonging of *all* persons-in-Christ.[35] The practices thereby stand against attempts to base the worth of persons in Christ upon individual competition and achievement, or our social identities.

The Church Participates in the Mission of the Messiah

Finally, the church's mission stems from God's royal enthronement of the Messiah to a position of heavenly rule. In other words, Jesus's universal kingship has as its corollary the extension and proclamation of his kingdom to all peoples. Paul understands his mission to bring about "the obedience of faith among all the gentiles for the sake of [Jesus Christ's] name" as fulfilling God's promise from Psalm 2 to give his royal king all of the nations as his messianic inheritance (Rom 1:5; cf. Ps 2:6–8; Gen 49:8–12; Isa 11:1–13). And this flows from Paul's conviction that the Messiah has been resurrected, endowed with God's Spirit, and exalted as the singular Lord of the world (Rom 1:3–4). We have seen that the discursive argument of Romans not only begins but also concludes with Paul's proclamation that Messiah Jesus is reigning as king over

---

34. On the quest for higher status in the Corinthian assembly, see throughout Martin, *The Corinthian Body*. On competitive quests for status and honor in Corinth, see George H. van Kooten, "Paul versus the Sophists: Outward Performance and Rhetorical Competition within the Christian Community at Corinth," in *Paul's Anthropology in Context: The Image of God, Assimilation to God, and Tripartite Man in Ancient Judaism, Ancient Philosophy and Early Christianity*, WUNT 232 (Tübingen: Mohr Siebeck, 2008), 245–68.

35. Horrell, *Solidarity and Difference*, 121: "Both rituals, baptism and Lord's supper, at least as Paul interprets them, communicate and reinforce a world-view in which the death and resurrection of Christ are the central events in a cosmic story . . . and at the same time convey as the central theme of the Christian ethos the notion of a solidarity in Christ that transcends former distinctions."

both Jews and gentiles (so also Rom 15:7–13). And so, one of Paul's agendas in Romans is to seek tangible support from the Roman Christians for Paul's mission to continue securing the Messiah's inheritance even as Paul seeks to move westward and proclaim Christ in Spain (see Rom 15:14–24). Paul reads Israel's Scriptures, and especially the patriarchal narratives in Genesis, as testifying to God's promise to Abraham and his messianic seed that they would have the entire world as their inheritance (so Rom 4:13; Gal 3:14–22). And while the fulfillment of the promise is currently underway through the extension of the gospel to the gentiles, Paul anticipates the inheritance finding its consummation in the eschatologically restored creation (Rom 8:18–25).

The Synoptic Gospels also depict the church as sharing in the Messiah's mission to proclaim and enact God's kingdom, both in his earthly mission and after his resurrection. We have seen that Matthew's Gospel frequently draws upon the messianic image of Jesus as God's Davidic shepherd who compassionately gathers the lost sheep through his meals, teaching, exorcisms, and healings. Notably, this messianic ministry of caring for the "distressed and harassed" flock of God is passed on to the disciples, who engage in the very same activities of the Messiah—namely, healings, proclaiming the kingdom, sharing hospitality, and exorcisms for Israel's lost sheep (see esp. Matt 9:35–10:13). Jesus's famous parable of the sheep and the goats seems to presume a context where followers of Jesus are engaging in an itinerant mission of proclaiming the kingdom and enacting the gospel through works of mercy, and God's people are exhorted to continue Jesus's ministry of compassion and hospitality for "the least of these my brothers and sisters" (Matt 25:31–46). Matthew, Luke, and John all have distinct scenes where Jesus commissions his disciples to share in his risen authority and power to extend the gospel to all peoples. Matthew's "Great Commission" depicts Jesus in a position of power and authority as the risen Son of Man and enthroned Davidic messianic king who commands his disciples to continue making disciples, baptizing, and teaching (Matt 28:16–20). In Luke's Gospel Jesus makes the remarkable claim that just as God gave him a kingdom, so he is now entrusting the disciples with *his own kingdom* as they now have the power to rule over God's people through eating and drinking at Christ's table (Luke 22:29–30). And, as we have seen, the book of Acts narrates the fulfillment of this promise as the disciples receive the Spirit from the Messiah and extend the saving blessings of the Messiah precisely through their common meals (Acts 1:4; 2:42–47; 4:32–37). In Acts it is the risen and enthroned Messiah who pours his Spirit upon his people, thereby gifting them with his powerful presence to continue proclaiming and enacting the kingdom of God (see Luke 24:47–49; Acts 1:7–8; 2:30–36). In

John's Gospel we have seen that the risen Jesus imparts his own Spirit as the empowering presence which will enable his disciples to continue his ministry of love, forgiveness, and teaching (John 20:19–23).

CONCLUSION

As the true human and representative of the people of God, the life, character, and activity of Jesus provides the pattern and paradigm for living as citizens in God's reign. The NT texts provide exhortations to follow and imitate the character of the Messiah, but this is rooted in their conception of the church as ontologically and relationally united to the Messiah. We have seen that the texts portray this union between Christ and the church through such images as the church as the body of Christ, the eschatological temple, the flock of God, and simply being "in Christ." Furthermore, the risen and enthroned Messiah provides his Spirit as a means of both establishing this relationship and providing the empowerment to the church to continue his activities and mission. While I have not attempted to provide an exhaustive portrait, I have argued that the relationship between the Messiah and his people manifests itself in the church embodying the character of Jesus, continuing to display faith and allegiance toward the risen Messiah, and continuing the concrete practices of worship, friendship, baptism, and the Lord's Supper.

CHAPTER 14

Politics, Power, and Eschatology

Christians as Subjects of a Good and Righteous King

One of the primary expectations of Israel's king is that he will both establish himself as a lover of justice and righteousness and will enact a kingdom of justice for his people in service to God.[1] The Davidic king "is an agent whom God ordains and empowers primarily to promote justice and righteousness."[2] The king's commitment to social justice derives from God who is consistently portrayed as one who loves and reigns by justice and righteousness, and who, therefore, provides liberation for his people and renders truthful verdicts for the oppressed. While David and the kings of Judah are expected to enact God's justice and righteousness (e.g., 2 Sam 8:15; 1 Kgs 10:9; Jer 22:3–5), they are most frequently implicated in acts that result in injustice, thereby failing to live up to God's expectations (Isa 59:14–18; Ezek 18:4–21; Zech 7:8–14).[3] And this lack of royal justice gives rise to prophetic expectations for a coming king who will fully embody God's righteousness. For example, Jeremiah proclaims a coming day when God will "raise up for David a righteous Branch and he will reign as king and deal wisely, and he will execute justice and righteousness in the land" (Jer 23:5). Isaiah looks forward to a Davidic king who will judge the poor and the meek with perfect righteousness, so much so in fact that "righ-

---

1. See especially Moshe Weinfeld, *Social Justice in Ancient Israel and in the Ancient Near East* (Minneapolis: Fortress, 1995); Keith W. Whitelam, *The Just King: Monarchical Judicial Authority in Ancient Israel*, JSOTSup 12 (Sheffield: Sheffield Academic Press, 1979).

2. Andrew T. Abernethy, *The Book of Isaiah and God's Kingdom: A Thematic-Theological Approach*, NSBT 40 (Downers Grove, IL: InterVarsity Press, 2016), 121. Abernethy's comment is a specific summary of his exegetical findings from Isa 1–39.

3. This is not to deny that many of the prophetic texts can be plausibly interpreted as referring to historical existing rulers. However, and at minimum, from the standpoint of the NT it is Jesus the messianic Son of David who is their full and final referent.

teousness will be the belt around his waist and faithfulness the belt around his loins" (Isa 11:1–5); this Davidic king will be "a judge who seeks justice and timely righteousness" (Isa 16:5; also Isa 32:1). The psalmist consistently associates God's justice with the king's justice, and in Psalm 72 we find a prayer that God would give his justice and righteousness to the king and king's son to usher in a period of peace, freedom, and flourishing (Ps 72:1–15, 11–14). Throughout the Psalter and the Prophets, God's people are called upon to take refuge in their righteous king and to trust in God's righteousness despite the fact that they are often experiencing violence, oppression, and slander from the wicked (e.g., LXX Pss 9:22–39; 34:23–28; Isa 51:4–8).[4] God's enactment of justice, it is expected, will take place through his messianic ruler defeating and subjugating his enemies—precisely those who are oppressing the righteous. The close association between the eschatological messianic age and perfect righteousness functions as a means of encouraging the righteous to hope in God (e.g., Isa 45:8, 22–25; 59:14–21; 61:1–11; Mal 4:1–4). Many more texts could be adduced to establish the central task of Israel's king and messiah as consisting of establishing God's justice for his people, and the way in which the failure of Israel's kings resulted in, we might say, eschatological hope that God would one day raise up a truly just king to usher in a period of peace and prosperity for God's people.[5]

From the early Christian vantage point of Jesus as the Messiah, these scriptural promises of God sending a just messianic king who will establish his people in a righteous kingdom and defeat their enemies provides a helpful framework for understanding much of the NT teaching pertaining to politics and eschatology. More specifically, I suggest that the NT texts portray Christ as *the singular* righteous king who is deserving of ultimate allegiance and worship and who provides a refuge for God's people in a hostile and unredeemed world. This conviction is the starting point for how the subjects of the messianic king conduct their relationships with worldly powers and institutions, and for the hopeful expectation that Christ will bring about a restored cosmos where his resurrected faithful saints will rule with him. Stated differently, Jesus's messianic kingship of truth and justice exposes the pretense of the unjust and corrupt rule of worldly powers, thereby calling the Messiah's people to embody practices that are oriented toward peace, justice, and a refusal to

---

4. See the helpful study by Jerome F. D. Creach, *The Destiny of the Righteous in the Psalms* (St. Louis: Chalice, 2008).

5. I have cataloged and discussed many of these texts in Joshua W. Jipp, *Christ Is King: Paul's Royal Ideology* (Minneapolis: Fortress, 2015), 221–33.

compromise with powers that threaten one's allegiance to Christ the King. Those who remain firm in their allegiance to Christ the King are promised the eschatological reward of participating in the Messiah's glorious rule.

CHRIST'S KINGSHIP AND THE KINGDOMS OF THIS WORLD

One of the central themes I have highlighted in my study of the messianic language of the NT is the conflict between Jesus's kingship and the other powers, kings, and kingdoms of this world. Most frequently the conflict is predicated upon the radically countercultural understanding of power revealed in Jesus's kingship. Robert Sherman rightly notes that "the single most telling point one may make about the kingdom that Christ proclaims and inaugurates is that it displays none of the characteristics typically associated with worldly kingdoms. Indeed, it turns such characteristics upside down."[6] Christ's countercultural kingship and use of power is expressed beautifully in *The Epistle to Diognetus* 7.3–4: "But perhaps [God] sent him, as a man might suppose, to rule by tyranny, fear, and terror. Certainly not! On the contrary, he sent him in gentleness and meekness, as a king might send his son who is a king; he sent him as God; he sent him as a man to men. When he sent him, he did so as one who saves by persuasions, not compulsion, for compulsion is no attribute of God." Christ's messianic kingship thereby exposes the limited and often counterfeit nature of human claims to power and sovereignty. Thus, while the NT writings consistently depict Jesus and his disciples as faithful, good citizens who are not seeking revolt or rebellion against the governments and institutions of this world, they nevertheless portray Jesus's kingship and kingdom as representing an ultimate threat and challenge to their rule.

The Gospels carry on an ongoing comparison between Jesus's kingship and the flawed, oppressive, and violent rule enacted by human rulers. Herod, Pilate, and others entrusted with imperial authority and rule are exposed, therefore, as fraudulent counterfeits of Jesus who embodies true kingship.[7] Satan's temptations of Jesus trade upon an attempt to convince Jesus to use his messianic status, authority, and power to serve himself (Matt 4:1–11). In other words, Satan's tests of Jesus attempt to convince him to use power and authority in

---

6. Robert Sherman, *King, Priest, and Prophet: A Trinitarian Theology of Atonement* (London: T&T Clark, 2004), 143.

7. With respect to the contrast between King Herod and Jesus the true King, see Deirde J. Good, *Jesus the Meek King* (Harrisburg, PA: Trinity Press International, 1999), 82–90.

exactly the same self-serving way as do other tyrannical characters who dot the landscape of the Gospels. And, of course, as we have seen repeatedly, Jesus enacts God's kingdom through the merciful and compassionate displays of healings, table fellowship and hospitality, teaching, exorcisms, and feeding the hungry. In other words, he enacts his kingship and uses his power not for self-aggrandizement but for service to his subjects. We have seen that in Matthew's Gospel, "King" Herod (Matt 2:1, 3, 9) embodies the core characteristics of the tyrant who is emotionally unstable in his rage, engages in collusion and deception, and is wickedly violent against the vulnerable (Matt 2:1–15). There is more than a hint of irony, then, in Matthew's dual reference to Jesus as "King" and "child" (2:2–4). Herod's deception, violence, and use of power for self-serving ends stands in contrast to Jesus the shepherd-king who obeys God the Father, is characterized by humility and gentleness, and wields his power for merciful and compassionate ends. We have also seen Mark's skilled comparison of two types of royal benefactions and banquets, which typify the character of Herod Antipas and Jesus. Again, Antipas displays the marks of the tyrant and is foolishly tricked into using his royal power for violence against the righteous (i.e., John the Baptist; Mark 6:14–29). Antipas finds his place in the story of Mark as one of those whom Jesus describes as wielding his royal power and authority to his own benefit, rather than in service to his subjects (Mark 10:42–43). Jesus's benefactions and gifts for his people, in marked contrast to that of Antipas, stem from his deep compassion for the lost sheep and reveal a remarkable power and authority used in service for the weak and small. In a way that challenges all human authorities and powers, Jesus claims that his kingship is revealed in his voluntary embodiment of slavery for the sake of serving and rescuing his people, even to the point of voluntarily laying down his life (Mark 10:44–45). Jesus's display of his messianic power and authority through slavery, sacrifice, and voluntary death characterizes him as a counter-imperial ruler and offers a powerful critique of worldly notions of human rule and kingship. John's Gospel applies the common ruling imagery of shepherding to Jesus to show that he is the good and just king. He is singularly qualified to rule over God's people since his life displays compassion, mercy, protection, and life for the people of God. Unlike the other teachers and rulers who exploit and profit off of God's flock, Jesus's voluntary laying down of his own life functions as the means whereby he rescues and saves the people of God (John 10:9–18). Jesus's kingship is of a completely different kind than the normal kings and kingdoms of this world, as Jesus made clear both in his refusal to be exalted as king by the crowds (John 6:14–15) and in his declaration to Pilate: "My kingdom is not from this world; if my kingdom were of this world, my servants would fight so that I would not be handed over to the Jews. But now my kingdom is not from this place" (John 18:36). While Pilate's authority, dependent as it was on the workings of imperial Rome and the emperor, hinged upon violence, force, and brute power, Jesus's kingship and glory is manifested in his obedience to the Father and display of love in his sacrificial death on the cross.[8] Jesus's kingship is revealed in his establishment of a reign of truth which has revealed the Father and the divine love that is capable of drawing all people to God, rather than the violence and force of imperial Rome.

Kavin Rowe has shown how the Acts of the Apostles depicts the early Christian movement as presenting a destabilizing threat to the political and religious authorities as their leaders proclaim that there is another king—namely, Jesus—and by doing so are disloyal to Caesar and have turned the world upside down (Acts 17:6–7). There is truth in this statement given that Luke-Acts has declared there to be one singular king, Messiah Jesus, who has been gifted with an everlasting kingdom (Luke 1:31–35; Acts 2:30–36; 13:32–37).[9] As many have noted, Luke's infancy narrative not only depicts Jesus programmatically as the messianic king but also suggests that his kingship critiques and surpasses that of the Roman emperor. Jesus's kingship will result in the scattering of the proud and the tearing down of the powerful from their positions of rule (Luke 1:51–52; cf. 1:68–79). Jesus is both Savior and the true bringer of peace (Luke 2:1–11). And the protagonists of Acts do indeed give singular allegiance to Jesus the King, yet they have no interest in a political coup against Rome but, rather, are aiming toward the creation of a new culture and way of life that is directly antithetical to the predominant displays of power, authority, and worship in Greco-Roman religion and culture.[10] While Luke does not engage in outright critique of the Roman Empire, it is no longer tenable to suggest that Acts presents the Roman Empire in a positive light as a means of political apologetic given the many instances where imperial authorities are portrayed in a negative manner.[11] The book of Acts establishes that the messianic King

8. See further Sigurd Grindheim, *Living in the Kingdom of God: A Biblical Theology for the Life of the Church* (Grand Rapids: Baker Academic, 2018), 137–39.

9. See here especially C. Kavin Rowe, *World Upside Down: Reading Acts in the Graeco-Roman Age* (Oxford: Oxford University Press, 2009), 91–102.

10. Rowe's argument thereby has significant consequences for how one thinks of the relationship between Christianity and the Roman Empire in Acts. See especially, Matthew Skinner, "Who Speaks for or against Rome? Acts in Relation to Empire," in *Reading Acts in the Discourse of Masculinity and Politics*, LNTS 559 (London: T&T Clark, 2017), 107–25.

11. In addition to Rowe, *World Upside Down*, ch. 3, see Kazuhiko Yamazaki-Ransom, *The Roman Empire in Luke's Narrative*, LNTS 404 (London: T&T Clark, 2010).

Jesus alone has true claim to kingship. Herod (Acts 12), Simon Magus (Acts 8), Simon bar-Jesus (Acts 13), and the spirit in the manic slave girl (Acts 16) are all false pretenders. And so, the claim that the Christians are proclaiming "another king" and that allegiance to this king is "turning the world upside down" (Acts 17:6–7) is right. If Jesus is king, then he alone is the singular ruler. Stated differently, if Jesus is king, then Caesar, Herod, Zeus, Hermes, and miracle-workers like Simon Magus and Elymas are not. The contrast between Christ's kingship and that of the royal pretenders in Acts "reminds us," in the words of John Calvin, "that however numerous and powerful the enemies who conspire to assault the Church, they are not possessors of strength sufficient to prevail against the immortal decree by which [God] appointed his Son eternal King. Whence it follows that the devil, with the whole power of the world, can never possibly destroy the Church, which is founded on the eternal throne of Christ."[12] It is for this reason that the proclamation of Jesus as king results in remarkable conversions but also produces rejection, conflict, and division in the empire. Rowe argues that the conviction that Jesus alone is king results in the necessary practices, within Acts, of confessing Jesus as Lord of all, world-wide mission, and Christian assembly. [13]

Paul is decidedly less interested in naming specific historical powers, rulers, and governors as are the Gospels and the book of Acts, and yet he provides further important testimony to the NT's paradoxical and surprising understanding of how Christ's kingship reveals and establishes God's power. There is perhaps no better summary of this dynamic than Paul's statement that "we proclaim a crucified Messiah, who is a stumbling block to the Jews and is foolishness to the gentiles, but to those who are called, to both Jews and Greeks, the Messiah is the power of God and the wisdom of God" (1 Cor 1:23–24). Paul consistently speaks of Christ's death on the cross as the power of God in that it, along with God's resurrection of Christ from the dead, is the event whereby Christ's people are rescued from the powers of the evil one. We have seen that in Romans, Paul mythologizes the powers and authorities in his conceptualization of them as the acting agents of sin, death, and unrighteousness. They have exerted a dominion of unrighteousness over humanity, and this reign is characterized by violence and deception (Rom 3:9–18). The Messiah, who alone is God's righteous king (see Rom 1:17; 5:15–21), creates and establishes a new kingdom and dominion characterized by righteousness and peace for his

---

12. John Calvin, *Institutes of the Christian Religion*, trans. Henry Beveridge (Grand Rapids: Eerdmans, 1989), 428.

13. Rowe, *World Upside Down*, 103–35.

people (throughout Rom 5–8, esp. 5:12–21 and 6:12–23). But Christ's provision of freedom from the kingdom of sin and death comes about not through military violence or deception but, ironically, through his obedience and death (Rom 5:15–19; 6:3–8; 7:4–6). As a result, Christ's judicial task consists in his promise to protect his citizens from all threats or accusations of judgment from their enemies (Rom 8:1–2, 31–39). Similarly, in Ephesians, Paul posits Christ's death, resurrection, and enthronement as the means whereby his people are rescued from the evil dominion of death that is wielded by the rulers, powers, authorities, and dominions of this age (Eph 1:20–2:6). In his letter to the church in Colossae, Paul argues that it is Christ's death on the cross that has publicly humiliated and disarmed the powers and authorities (Col 2:14–15).

Finally, I will only briefly remind the reader of how Revelation sets forth a paradoxical notion of victory and conquering over the powers of the evil one. Revelation employs the theme of a messianic war to encourage God's people to actively resist Satan and his wielding of power, violence, and deception through the idolatrous pretenses of Rome. God's people conquer and triumph insofar as they follow the pattern set by the messianic Lamb who triumphed and was exalted to share God's throne precisely through his sacrificial death and martyrdom (esp. Rev 5:5–6). The victory of the Lamb critiques and exposes the popular notion of a king's legitimation coming by way of military success and pacification of one's enemies through violent force. Instead of taking a kingdom by military violence, the messianic Lamb procures a kingdom for himself through his unfailing faithfulness and testimony to truth, which results in his death (1:5–6; 5:9–10). So, likewise, the churches are exhorted to follow their messianic king in conquering as well, but this conquering takes the form of rejection of the idolatry of Rome, endurance and allegiance to the risen Christ, and faithfulness and truth (chs. 2–3). The visions of the rest of the Apocalypse depict God's people following the Lamb in his war by continuing to bear witness to the truth even as this results in persecution and martyrdom.

Thus, throughout the NT writings, we see a new form of power on display in Christ's kingship. First, the power of Christ is revealed through his ability to do what any good king must do—namely, procure a kingdom for himself; yet Christ's accomplishment of the salvation and liberation of his subjects takes place through his voluntary sacrifice and death on a Roman cross. Second, Christ's power is revealed in that this saving event is the very means whereby the historical kings and tyrants, as well as the powers of darkness which stand behind them, are disarmed and exposed as fraudulent counterfeits to Christ's reign of truth and righteousness. Third, Christ's kingship witnesses to a form of power that is counterintuitive—a power revealed in love, suffering, sacrifice, and truth-telling. This stands against the constant temptation to use power to inflict oppression and force upon others. Kings and kingdoms who engage in deception, manipulation, and violence to accomplish their agendas are exposed as wicked opponents of Christ's reign. Fourth, the NT's depiction of Christ and power stands as a call to Christ's disciples to follow their messianic ruler by embodying his same stance toward the powers and kingdoms of this world.

Christ, the Church, and Power

How the church is called upon to live as subjects of Christ's kingship when this world is ruled and administered through human kingdoms, rulers, and governments is a remarkably large and complicated topic. And here I can only make a few suggestions based upon our NT theology of Christ's messianic kingship and kingdom. As with much that I have suggested in this book, my argument is illustrative rather than comprehensive.

Of utmost importance here is the recognition that those who claim to follow Christ fully embrace their primary identity as citizens of the kingdom of God and subjects of Christ's kingship. The church's ultimate citizenship is with Christ in heaven and, therefore, exclusive allegiance and loyalty belongs only to him (Phil 3:20–21).[14] Given that the church's singular allegiance belongs to Christ and not any government or ruler of this world, the NT writings often speak of Christians as strangers, aliens, and sojourners (e.g., Heb 11). As a result, while the NT consistently encourages and exhorts the church to be good citizens and non-rebellious subjects (e.g., Rom 13:1–7; 1 Tim 2:1–2; 1 Pet 2:13–17), the church's singular fidelity to Christ the king means that there will be inevitable conflict with human institutions and governments. The church's singular acknowledgment of Christ as king is why 1 Peter portrays the church as having a diasporic identity, as their embrace of Christ's kingship has resulted in tangible forms of social, cultural, economic, and religious alienation from society (again, see 1 Pet 1:1–2; 1:17; 2:11; 4:3–6, 12–19). Followers of Christ are not looking to dethrone Caesar, nor do they look for ways to instigate active revolt and rebellion through refusing to pay taxes or taking up arms against their enemies, but the disciples certainly do proclaim "another king" (Acts 17:6–7; Rom 1:1–5). And this results in a way of life that is often in conflict with and

---

14. See here David Crump, *I Pledge Allegiance: A Believer's Guide to Kingdom Citizenship in 21st-Century America* (Grand Rapids: Eerdmans, 2018), 49.

threatening to the powers and kingdoms of this earth.[15] Allegiance to Christ as king means, of course, that his subjects cannot simultaneously worship Christ and participate in the worship of, and sacrifices offered to, other deities (so Acts 14:8–20; 19:23–41; 1 Pet 1:17). And yet we have seen that Satan's power is wielded in ways that are deceitful and manipulative, as he works in ways that tempt Christ's people to subtly compromise their exclusive allegiance to Christ (esp. Rev 12–13; cf. Matt 4:1–11; Luke 22–23). And this is why, I suggest, John's Gospel and Revelation emphasize the importance of speaking and holding fast to *truthful testimony* (e.g., 1 John 4:2–3; Rev 12:11, 17). In what follows, I offer three important practices for the church to embody Christ's paradoxical relationship to power.

Economic Practices

First, allegiance to Christ the king results in new economic practices. This should be no surprise given that Jesus consistently proclaims that the poor, the meek, and those who are persecuted will inherit the kingdom of God (e.g., Matt 5:3–12; Luke 6:20–26). Christ's kingship consistently relativizes and critiques the typical this-worldly assumptions about who are worthy subjects of Christ's rule based on their wealth and status.[16] And this gives rise to new considerations regarding economic practices. In Luke's Gospel, Jesus argues that one cannot serve both God and money (Luke 16:13–15).[17] Wealth is personified as a power that tempts and deceives people into giving it their ultimate priority and love (cf. 1 Tim 6:6–19). Thus, one of the primary responses to Christ's enthronement to a position of powerful rule over his church in the book of Acts is that of the Jerusalem church selling their possessions and distributing them "to everyone who had need" (2:45), with the result that there were none who had any need in their community (4:34).[18] Barnabas functions as a representative model for these early Christians who, in spite of having some land wealth, reject the normal systems of reciprocity and benefaction by selling their land

---

15. John Howard Yoder, *The Politics of Jesus: Vicit Agnus Noster*, 2nd ed. (Grand Rapids: Eerdmans, 1994), 53: "No such slicing can avoid his call to an ethic marked by the cross, a cross identified as the punishment of a man who threatens society by creating a new kind of community leading a radically new kind of life."

16. See Sherman, *King, Priest, and Prophet*, 143–44.

17. See especially Luke Timothy Johnson, *Sharing Possessions: What Faith Demands*, 2nd ed. (Grand Rapids: Eerdmans, 2011).

18. I have written on the NT's teaching on economics in more detail in Joshua W. Jipp, *Saved by Faith and Hospitality* (Grand Rapids: Eerdmans, 2017), ch. 6.

and using their resources for the mutual economic benefit of the church. And this is in fulfillment of Jesus's commission to them to share in his kingdom and rule over Israel through food and drink (Luke 22:28–30). Jesus explicitly demands that their table practices and their forms of hospitality and sharing must not look like the normal practices of kings, lords, and the powerful who use their wealth for power and exploitation (Luke 22:25). Standard hospitality and meal practices were often used as opportunities for increasing status and power, but Jesus declares, "Not so for you!" (22:26). Instead, meals must be a place where rule is manifested by conducting oneself as "the youngest" and "one who serves [food]" (22:26b). Thus, when Jesus asks, "who is greater, the one reclining or the one serving?" (22:27a), he alludes to their dispute over who was the greatest (22:24) and reminds them: "I have been in your midst as one who serves" (22:27b).

Similarly, the book of James makes a stark contrast between friendship with God and friendship with the world (Jas 4:4). Those who are friends of God engage in countercultural economic practices. James blames an uncritical participation in the normal workings of the ancient economy and court system for the consequence of inequality and exploitation of the poor. Rather than exalt the virtues of the wealthy landowners, James sees the pursuit of luxury, wealth, and status as the greed, envy, and thirsty desire for acquisition that results in violence and oppression (4:1–2).[19] The wealthy landowners are responsible for living in luxury (5:2–3, 5), storing up treasures and wealth for their own consumption (5:3), exploiting and withholding just payment from those laboring in their fields (5:4), and oppressing the righteous (5:6). Thus, James condemns one of the primary features of the ancient economy for the way in which it enables the rich to accumulate wealth and capital at the expense of the poor. In addition, he criticizes the wealthy for using the surplus for their wasteful and luxurious lifestyles. James argues that "resources are distributed unequally in society because landowners exploit workers, because the rich manipulate the justice system, and because the rich squander their immoral gains on self-indulgence."[20] In Revelation 17–18 the seer celebrates the destruction of "the whore of Babylon" (Rev 18:2)—namely, the Roman imperial economic system that is controlled by Satan himself. Rome's economic system is castigated for:

19. On the theme of greed and envy, see Luke Timothy Johnson, "James 3:13–4:10 and the Τοπος περὶ φθόνου," *NovT* 25 (1983): 327–47.

20. Steven J. Friesen, "Injustice or God's Will? Early Christian Explanations of Poverty," in *Wealth and Poverty in Early Church and Society*, ed. Susan R. Holman, Holy Cross Studies in Patristic Theology and History (Grand Rapids: Baker Academic, 2008), 26.

(1) extravagant luxury and consumptive greed (18:3, 7, 9, 11–14);[21] (2) benefiting the local and imperial elites at the expense of the majority (18:15–19); (3) the exploitation involved in human slavery as it trades and imports "bodies, that is human lives" (18:13); (4) the idolatry of worshipping wealth (18:7); and (5) violently killing the righteous and those who criticize Rome's economic, political, and military idolatry (18:20–24). The harlot's boast—"I sit as a queen; I am not a widow, and I will never see grief" (18:7b)—gives voice to the economy's idolatrous self-divinization and belief that luxury, consumption, and acquisition, even at the expense of the good of others, will fulfill one's deepest desires. The author's exhortation is radical—withdraw completely from the economic injustices of the entire economy: "Come out of her, my people, so that you will not share in her sins or receive any of her plagues" (18:4). The Seer calls for a total withdrawal from the idolatry and evil of the Roman economic system, even if it should mean martyrdom or financial deprivation, since God will destroy the whore of Babylon and vindicate the righteous.[22]

Forgiveness, Peacemaking, and Rejection of Violence

Second, citizens of Christ's kingdom will reject the use of violence, brute force, and coercion in all areas of life. The Synoptic Gospels' scene of Christ's so-called triumphal entry stands as a reminder that Jesus's kingship is predicated upon humility and peace instead of power through violence (esp. Mark 11:1–11). One of the things Mark is doing here is saying: "Do you really want Jesus to be your king?" The crowds and even the disciples had a false understanding of what it meant for Jesus to be the Messiah (see Mark 10:35–41). The scene poses stark questions to its readers: Do you really want a crucified king, or a king who crucifies his enemies? Do you want an enemy-loving king—a king who forgives his crucifiers and demands that his disciples forgive their enemies? Do you really want a king who embraces and loves strangers, or a king who clearly differentiates, excludes, and divides the "good" from the "bad," the "moral" from the "immoral," the citizen from the outsider?

The center point of Mark's Gospel is when Jesus asks Peter: "Who do you say that I am?" Peter says: "You are the Messiah" (8:27–30). But when Jesus goes on to teach the disciples that messiahship entails humility, sacrifice, service,

---

21. On this, see especially Richard Bauckham, "The Economic Critique of Rome in Revelation 18," in *Images of Empire*, ed. Loveday Alexander, JSOTSup 12 (Sheffield: Sheffield Academic Press, 1991), 47–90.

22. Friesen, "Injustice or God's Will?," 23.

love—all culminating in his rejection and crucifixion on a Roman cross—Peter rebukes Jesus, saying "God forbid the Messiah should do such a thing!" And Jesus says to Peter, "Get behind me, Satan. You are not thinking God's thoughts but rather man's thoughts" (8:31–33). Peter is doing exactly what Satan did earlier, tempting Jesus to be a *spectacular* Messiah, tempting Jesus to pursue self-advancement through power, tempting Jesus to be a Messiah who pursues honor and glory and the exaltation of his own tribe (1:12–13).[23] In other words, Peter can say Jesus is the Messiah and at the same time be so completely wrong and misguided that he is embodying the intentions of Satan. One can say, "Blessed is he who comes in the name of the Lord" (Mark 11:9a), wave palms branches (11:7–8), and sing, "Hosanna in the highest" (11:10), but be worshipping a false messiah. The crowds and even the disciples on more than a few occasions have a selfish, self-centered faith that longs for a kingdom that will exalt them at the expense of their enemies, give them power, and satisfy their own personal hopes and dreams. The same kind of selfish and fake faith in a fake Jesus can exist today, when motives for being a Christian are that it looks good in society or that it will raise one's status in the community. Fake faith in a fake Jesus exists when we think that being a Christian is part of what it means to be a good American; good Americans are Christians and, therefore, being a Christian is wrapped up in patriotism and flag-waving and in so-called American values of hard work, self-reliance, and achievement. Jesus's messianic kingship, as articulated by the Gospels, stands as a constant reminder that Jesus's kingship is revealed in suffering, humility, sacrifice, peacemaking, and the utter rejection of violence.

Followers of Christ will, instead, seek to implement practices of peacemaking, forgiveness, and nonretaliation in situations of conflict. That Christ's disciples are called to reject violence and retaliation is, of course, deeply rooted in both Christ's teaching and his practices. Luke's Jesus, in fact, is portrayed as an agent of peacemaking. His messianic task, according to Zechariah, consists in "giving light to those who sit in darkness and in the shadow of death, and to guide our feet in the way of peace" (Luke 1:79). Throughout his messianic ministry, Jesus offers peace upon those who welcome him (e.g., Luke 2:14, 38; 7:50; 8:48; 10:5–8). Jerusalem's rejection of him as their messianic visitor results in Jesus's lamentation: "If only you had recognized on this day, even you, the things which make for peace" (Luke 19:42). Throughout the Gospels, Jesus

---

23. Timothy Gombis, "1 Maccabees and Mark 11:1–11: A Subversive Entry into Jerusalem," in *Reading Mark in Context: Jesus and Second Temple Judaism*, ed. Ben Blackwell et al. (Grand Rapids: Zondervan, 2018), 174–81.

is remembered as one who denied his followers the option of responding to their enemies or persecutors with vengeance and retribution and, instead, calls them to love their enemies (Matt 5:38–48; Luke 6:27–36; 10:25–37; cf. 9:51–56).[24] Jesus's teaching is directly in line with his refusal to take Satan's offer of the gift of worldly power over the kingdoms of the earth (Matt 4:1–11). Jesus embodies his teaching as he makes his way into Jerusalem as the messianic king but overturns any anticipation that his kingship will be revealed through violence and force (esp. Matt 26:51–54; Mark 10:35–45; Luke 22:37–38; John 18:36). The Gospels' lacing of the passion narrative with Davidic psalms works to depict Jesus as the righteous and faithful sufferer who entrusts his cause and hope for vindication to God (e.g., Mark 14:32–44; Luke 23:34–49; cf. Rom 15:3; Heb 5:7–9).[25] John's passion narrative, as we have seen, centers upon Jesus's surprising identity as a king, but the text is emphatic that Jesus is not an earthly king who wields authority through violence but, rather, the messianic king sent from heaven (18:33–38). And this king manifests his reign in both love for his disciples and, in the words of Michael Gorman, "by forsaking violence and taking up the cross that draws all kinds of people, even enemies, to the Crucified One."[26]

Thus, disciples of Jesus do not engage in violence or retribution against their enemies; rather, they commit to canceling and forgiving the debts of others (Matt 6:12–14; 18:21–35). Just as Jesus commissions his disciples to teaching everything he commanded them, so the church practices and teaches others to follow his commitment to peace and rejection of vengeance against his enemies (Matt 28:18–20). Paul exhorts the Christians in Rome to reject rebellion and revolt against the civil authorities tasked by God to provide order and even wrath against lawbreakers (Rom 13:1–7); he prefaces this call to submission with a command to Christians to reject vengeance and violence against their enemies and to seek to bless and do good to those persecuting them (Rom 12:19–21).[27] Similarly, 1 Peter expects followers of Christ will follow "in his

24. See especially Richard B. Hays, *The Moral Vision of the New Testament: A Contemporary Introduction to New Testament Ethics* (San Francisco: HarperSanFrancisco, 1997), 319–29.

25. Nicholas Perrin, *The Kingdom of God: A Biblical Theology* (Grand Rapids: Zondervan, 2019), 179: "Jesus's assumption of the throne through suffering unto death confirms the kingdom's arrival and offers a model for his disciples to follow."

26. In much more detail, see Michael J. Gorman, "John's Implicit Ethic of Enemy–Love," in *Johannine Ethics: The Moral World of the Gospel and Epistles of John*, ed. Sherri Brown and Christopher W. Skinner (Minneapolis: Fortress, 2017), 149.

27. See here John Howard Yoder, "Let Every Soul Be Subject: Romans 13 and the Authority of the State," in *The Politics of Jesus*, 193–211.

footsteps" in doing good and rejecting retaliation and violence when they encounter unjust suffering and persecution (e.g., 1 Pet 2:18–25; 4:12–19). We have seen that Paul expects the body of Christ to be characterized by peace, most emphatically in Ephesians, a place where alienation, divisions, and hostility are done away with through Christ's reconciling death (Eph 2:11–18; cf. Col 3:15–16). And this is rooted in how God has treated his enemies—namely, through accomplishing peace and reconciliation through the gift of Christ's death (e.g., Rom 5:1–11; Col 1:20–22). Jesus's paradoxical display of power through rejection of violence and retribution is perhaps most evident in Revelation, where Christ's army actively shares in his battle not through the use of military violence and warfare but instead through endurance, truth-telling, and faith—practices that often lead to their suffering and martyrdom (e.g., Rev 6:9–11; 7:9–17; 14:1–5). The messianic army conquers "the power of evil through 'the blood of the Lamb and by the word of their testimony' (Rev 12:11), not through recourse to violence."[28]

Solidarity with the Weak and Vulnerable

Third, allegiance to Christ's paradoxical embodiment of power results in a commitment to protect and stand in solidarity with the most vulnerable, marginalized, and oppressed in society. We have seen repeatedly that Christ's power is revealed in the very midst of weakness and suffering. God reveals himself and inaugurates his kingdom not through the powerful, strong, and wise, but rather, through his suffering, obedient, and humble messianic Son. Kings, tyrants, and human governments, however, have the power and propensity to inflict pain, suffering, violence, and exclusion upon the weakest and most vulnerable within society. The early Christians themselves experienced this dynamic, of course, as their allegiance to Christ often brought them into conflict with the governing rulers. Again, I note that the Gospels display Christ's royal shepherding ministry, his interpretation of Torah, and his call to imitate the shape of his own messianic life as involving a rejection of power and status for the sake of compassionately caring for and serving the weak and vulnerable (e.g., Matt 9:35–36; 18:1–35; Mark 8:34–38). Christ's teaching and life, then, often deconstruct our notions of power, masculinity, and normalcy as privileged goods. And Christ is often portrayed as acting and working within situations of human vulnerability. This theme is perhaps most emphatically

28. Hays, *The Moral Vision of the New Testament*, 332.

declared by Paul's surprising claims that God's power is revealed in the cross of Christ and in his bodily suffering: "I will most gladly boast all the more about my weaknesses, so that Christ's power may reside in me. So I take pleasure in weaknesses, insults, hardships, persecutions, and in difficulties, for the sake of Christ. For when I am weak, then I am strong" (2 Cor 12:9–10). But the theme is present in the Lukan writings as well; for example, in Jesus's experience of his deepest moments of suffering and vulnerability, he forgives his executioners (Luke 23:34), enacts salvation for one of the criminals on the cross (23:39–43), and entrusts himself to his Father with his last breath (23:46).

And the consistent witness of Jesus's inauguration of God's reign through his healing of the sick and weak and scattering of the demons who prevent human health and flourishing testifies to the necessity of the church's protection and care for the vulnerable (e.g., Luke 4:34–41; 8:26–39; 13:10–17; Acts 3:1–10; 14:8–10). Jesus's healings are a form of release and welcome that liberates humans from bondage and oppression, restores them to proper physical and social engagement, and flows from Jesus's compassion for human suffering and vulnerability. Those who seek to continue the healing ministry of Jesus, then, will "stand with those whose lives or whose flourishing are threatened and to withstand the disorders that threaten them, however we explain those disorders."[29] The church's care for the sick continued in the early centuries of the church's existence, and this was rooted in Jesus's attention to the weak and vulnerable. Amanda Porterfield states this well: "[C]are for the sick was a distinctive and remarkable characteristic of early Christian missionary outreach. Early Christians nursed the sick to emulate the healing ministry of Jesus, to express their faith in the ongoing healing power of Christ, and to distinguish Christian heroism in the face of sickness and death from pagan fear."[30] The church's indiscriminate concern for the poor was one of the major factors that led to the creation of institutions such as "poorhouses" that supported widows, the sick, and the poor, as well as hospitals, which were "in origin and conception, a distinctively Christian institution, rooted in Christian concepts of charity and philanthropy."[31] Those who live as subjects of Christ, then, will

29. Allen Verhey, *Remembering Jesus: Christian Community, Scripture, and the Moral Life* (Grand Rapids: Eerdmans, 2002), 101.

30. Amanda Porterfield, *Healing in the History of Christianity* (Oxford: Oxford University Press, 2005), 47.

31. Gary B. Ferngren, *Medicine & Health Care in Early Christianity* (Baltimore, MD: The Johns Hopkins University Press, 2009), 124. Very helpful here is Willard M. Swartley, *Health, Healing and the Church's Mission: Biblical Perspectives and Moral Priorities* (Downers Grove, IL: InterVarsity Press, 2012).

stand against governments, rulers, and those in power who would seek to act against the stigmatized, stereotyped, and vulnerable.

Ruling with Christ in His Kingdom

We have seen that Christ's establishment of the kingdom of God has resulted in the defeat and disarming of the powers of Satan. In Mark's Gospel, Jesus is the "stronger one" who binds the "strong man" (i.e., Satan), scatters demons with an unparalleled authority and power, and overthrows Satan's kingdom (esp. Mark 1:16–45; 3:23–30). Jesus's victorious enthronement and glorification in John's Gospel results in the singular exorcism of "the ruler of the world," whose reign of deception and violence is broken by Christ's reign of truth (John 12:31–32; cf. 14:30–31; 16:8–11). Those tyrants, evil powers, and enemies of God's kingdom who seek to destroy the people of God typically find a grisly death by the superior power of Christ's disciples (e.g., Acts 1:15–26; 12:20–25; cf. 9:1–19). Paul, among other NT texts, consistently draws upon Christ's messianic and judicial authority to proclaim the resurrected and exalted Christ as the one who has defeated and broken the power of the authorities and rulers (e.g., Rom 5:12–21; 8:31–39; Eph 1:20–23; 6:10–20; Col 2:14–15; 1 Pet 3:18–22).

And yet, there is obviously a further hope and expectation that Christ's kingdom will be consummated, fully established, and that God's resurrected and vindicated faithful saints will share in the Messiah's inheritance and rule together with him. This will involve God's final defeat of his enemies where he will publicly exalt Christ as the world's only true and rightful king (Phil 2:10–11; Rev 17:14; 19:16) and the enemies of death, sin, and Satan will be fully defeated and placed under Christ's sovereign authority (1 Cor 15:25–27; 2 Thess 1–2; Rev 19:11–22:5). One of my primary arguments in this book has been to highlight the centrality of the NT's theme of Christ's people actively participating in the Messiah's kingly rule. And so, the texts anticipate the consummation of God's purposes as culminating in the unhindered and joyful reign of God's people together with the Messiah. Matthew Bates has stated this well: "[F]inal salvation is not primarily about the individual soul going to heaven, but about embodied *transformation* as the individual participates alongside others in the holistic restoration of the entire cosmos. . . . Allegiance entails an invitation to rule alongside him and is the foundation for transformation into his image."[32]

32. Matthew W. Bates, *Salvation by Allegiance Alone: Rethinking Faith, Works, and the Gospel of Jesus the King* (Grand Rapids: Baker Academic, 2017), 131.

Thus, Christ's people are promised to receive the Messiah's final inheritance of a renewed and restored cosmos where they will reign with Christ (Rom 8:18–25; cf. 4:13; Gal 3:15–29). The argument of Hebrews ends with a celebratory vision of God, the angels, the Messiah, and the church of the firstborn children all together at Mount Zion joyfully celebrating and praising God in worship (Heb 12:18–29). Christ's people now fully share in the glory originally intended for humanity (Heb 2:5–18; 1 Pet 1:6–7, 11–12). And the risen Christ's promises to his churches that they will reign together with him in his kingdom, even sharing his throne, if they remain faithful (esp. Rev 2:26–28; 3:21), come to fruition as they share together with him in his final battle (Rev 19:11–21)—the result of which is their reigning together with the Messiah (Rev. 20:4, 6) and sharing in the restored new heavens and earth (Rev 21:1–22:5). Those who share in Christ's sovereignty will do so as those who have been fully vindicated and have thereby received resurrected bodies (e.g., Matt 16:25–27; Rom 6:3–5; 1 Cor 15:20–58; Phil 3:20–21).

CONCLUSION

The Scriptural promise for God to rule the world through a righteous, just, and peace-loving messianic king is ultimately fulfilled in the surprising manner of the King's death and resurrection. This results in an ethic whereby God's people entrust themselves and their causes to God and not to the violent coercive methods of the human kings, kingdoms, and governments of this world. Forgiveness, the rejection of violence, non-oppressive economic practices, peace-making and reconciliation, and solidarity with the vulnerable and marginalized may often have the appearance of weakness, but they are the appropriate practices for Christ's people engaging matters of power in this world. Those who resist evil and actively pursue truth-telling, loyalty to Christ, and hope are promised the eschatological reward of vindication whereby, with their resurrected bodies, they will rule in Christ's kingdom where the powers of Satan, Sin, and Death have all been subjected to Christ's messianic kingship.

Acknowledgments

Portions of some of my previous publications on the New Testament's depiction of Christ as messianic ruler are contained and woven into this manuscript. I offer my gratitude to Fortress Press, T&T Clark, Mohr-Siebeck, and *New Testament Studies* for allowing me to use portions of previously published work in this manuscript.

Chapter 2 contains a portion of "Messiah Language and Gospel Writing." Pages 126–44 in *Writing the Gospels: A Dialogue with Francis Watson*. Edited by Catherine Sider Hamilton. LNTS 606. London/New York: T&T Clark, 2019.

Chapter 3 has a few sections from "'For David Did Not Ascend into Heaven . . .' (Acts 2:34a): Reprogramming Royal Psalms to Proclaim the Enthroned-in-Heaven King." Pages 41–59 in *Ascent into Heaven in Luke-Acts: New Explorations of Luke's Narrative Hinge*. Edited by David K. Bryan and David W. Pao Minneapolis: Fortress, 2016.

Chapters 5–7 contain elements from *Christ Is King: Paul's Royal Ideology*, Minneapolis: Fortress, 2015, and "Sharing in the Heavenly Rule of Christ the King: Paul's Royal Participatory Soteriology in Ephesians." Pages 261–75 in *"In Christ" in Paul: Explorations in Paul's Theological Vision of Participation*. Edited by Michael J. Thate, Kevin J. Vanhoozer, and Constantine R. Campbell. Tübingen: Mohr-Siebeck. 2014.

Chapter 8 draws upon "The Son's Entrance into the Heavenly World: The Soteriological Necessity of the Scriptural Catena in Hebrews 1:5–14." *NTS* 56 (2010): 557–75.

Many people have helped me to think carefully about the ideas in this book. Those who deserve much gratitude are my students at Trinity Evangelical Divinity School—especially those from the seminars Pauline Christology, New Testament Theology, and Messianism and the Origins of Christology. Thanks also to friends and scholars who read and gave careful feedback on the work. There are more than what I can remember, but at the forefront of my mind are Madison Pierce, David Luy, David Pao, Steve Bryan, Jonathan Pennington, Drew Strait, Matt Bates, Chris Skinner, and Justin Jeffcoat Schedtler. Thanks also to TEDS student Tyler Carrera for reading the manuscript and making editorial improvements. I look forward to "working together" with you in the future. Thank you to Lauren Januzik. Thank you also to Jennifer Guo and Geoff Ng for the massive help with preparing the indexes! I'm beyond fortunate to have had your assistance, but I'm even more grateful for my friendship with both of you. I'm excited to see how your gifts—in scholarship, teaching, and caring for people—will continue to grow and be put to great use. To more wing nights in the future (thanks for BOGO BW3's)! Thanks also to Jeff Tweedy and Jason Isbell for making music that enabled me to keep writing when my energy was lacking. I am grateful for Michael Thomson for encouraging this project; thanks also to Trevor Thompson of Eerdmans who went far above and beyond in his assistance and his commitment to this book! Thank you also to my wonderful family for their constant support and love: Amber, Josiah, Lukas, Sapna, and Buxton. I would like to dedicate this book to my students at Trinity Evangelical Divinity School. Thank you for your hard work, your passion for the scriptural texts, and for your hard work to make me a better teacher and scholar. The joy and satisfaction that I find in my vocation is the direct result of your passion to know and live out the theological vision of our scriptures.

Bibliography

Aasgaard, Reidar. *'My Beloved Brothers and Sisters!': Christian Siblingship in Paul.* JSNTSup 265. London: T&T Clark, 2004.

Abernethy, Andrew T. *The Book of Isaiah and God's Kingdom: A Thematic-Theological Approach.* NSBT 40. Downers Grove, IL: InterVarsity Press, 2016.

Achtemeier, Paul J. "And He Followed Him: Miracles and Discipleship in Mark 10:46–52." *Semeia* 11 (1978): 126–30.

———. "Suffering Servant and Suffering Christ in 1 Peter." Pages 176–88 in *The Future of Christology: Essays in Honor of Leander E. Keck.* Edited by Abraham J. Malherbe and Wayne A. Meeks. Minneapolis: Fortress, 1993.

Adams, Edward. "Paul's Story of God and Creation." Pages 19–43 in *Narrative Dynamics in Paul.* Edited by Bruce W. Longenecker. Louisville: Westminster John Knox, 2002.

Agamben, Giorgio. *The Time That Remains: A Commentary on the Letter to the Romans.* Translated by Patricia Dailey. Stanford: Stanford University Press, 2005.

Ahearne-Kroll, Stephen P. *The Psalms of Lament in Mark's Passion: Jesus' Davidic Suffering.* SNTSMS 142. Cambridge: Cambridge University Press, 2007.

Alexander, T. Desmond. "Messianic Ideology in Genesis." Pages 19–39 in *The Lord's Anointed: Interpretation of Old Testament Messianic Texts.* Edited by Philip E. Satterthwaite et al. Grand Rapids: Baker, 1995.

———. "Royal Expectations in Genesis to Kings: Their Importance for Biblical Theology." *TynBul* 49.2 (1998): 191–212.

Allan, John A. "The 'In Christ' Formula in Ephesians." *NTS* 5 (1958–59): 54–62.

Allen, Leslie C. "The Old Testament Background of (προ)ὁρίζειν in the New Testament." *NTS* 17 (1970): 104–108.

Allen, Thomas G. "Exaltation and Solidarity with Christ: Ephesians 1:20 and 2:6." *JSNT* 28 (1986): 103–20.

Allison, Dale C., Jr. *Constructing Jesus: Memory, Imagination, and History.* Grand Rapids: Baker Academic, 2010.

———. "The Embodiment of God's Will: Jesus in Matthew." Pages 117–32 in *Seeking* the Identity of Jesus: A Pilgrimage. Edited by Beverly Roberts Gaventa and Richard B. Hays. Grand Rapids: Eerdmans, 2008.

———. "The Magi's Angel (Matt. 2:2, 9–10)." Pages 17–41 in Studies in Matthew: Interpretation Past and Present. Grand Rapids: Baker Academic, 2005.

———. The New Moses: A Matthean Typology. Eugene, OR: Wipf & Stock, 2013. First published 1993 by Fortress (Minneapolis).

———. The Sermon on the Mount: Inspiring the Moral Imagination. New York: Crossroad, 1999.

———. "Structure, Biographical Impulse, and the Imitatio Christi." Pages 135–55 in Studies in Matthew: Interpretation Past and Present. Grand Rapids: Baker Academic, 2005.

Anderson, Gary A. Sin: A History. New Haven: Yale University Press, 2009.

Anderson, Kevin L. "But God Raised Him from the Dead": The Theology of Jesus's Resurrection in Luke-Acts. Eugene, OR: Wipf & Stock, 2007.

Ando, Clifford. Imperial Ideology and Provincial Loyalty in the Roman Empire. Berkeley: University of California Press, 2000.

Arnold, Clinton E. The Colossian Syncretism: The Interface between Christianity and Folk Belief at Colossae. Grand Rapids: Baker, 1996.

Ashton, John. Understanding the Fourth Gospel. 2nd ed. Oxford: Clarendon, 2007.

Attridge, Harold W. Hebrews: A Commentary on the Epistle to the Hebrews. Hermeneia. Minneapolis: Fortress, 1989.

———. "The Psalms in Hebrews." Pages 197–212 in The Psalms in the New Testament. Edited by Steve Moyise and Maarten J. J. Menken. The New Testament and the Scriptures of Israel. London: T&T Clark, 2004.

Aune, David E. "The Influence of Roman Imperial Court Ceremonial on the Apocalypse of John." Papers of the Chicago Society for Biblical Research 28 (1983): 5–26.

———. Revelation 17–22. WBC 52C. Grand Rapids: Zondervan, 1998.

Austin, M. M. "Hellenistic Kings, War and the Economy." CQ 36 (1986): 450–66.

Badiou, Alain. Saint Paul: The Foundation of Universalism. Stanford: Stanford University Press, 2003.

Balthasar, Hans Urs von. The Action. Vol. 4 of Theo-Drama: Theological Dramatic Theory. Translated by Graham Harrison. San Francisco: Ignatius Press, 1994.

Barber, Michael Patrick. "Jesus as the Davidic Temple Builder and Peter's Priestly Role in Matthew 16:16–19." JBL 132 (2013): 935–53.

Barclay, John. Obeying the Truth: Paul's Ethics in Galatians. SNTW. Edinburgh: T&T Clark, 1988.

———. Paul and the Gift. Grand Rapids: Eerdmans, 2015.

Barnhill, Gregory M. "Seeing Christ through Hearing the Apocalypse: An Exploration of John's Use of *Ekphrasis* in Revelation 1 and 19." *JSNT* 39 (2017): 235–57.

Barth, Markus. *Ephesians 1–3*. AYB 34A. New Haven: Yale University Press, 1974.

Barton, Stephen C. "Money Matters: Economic Relations and the Transformation of Value in Early Christianity." Pages 37–59 in *Engaging Economics: New Testament Scenarios and Early Christian Reception*. Edited by Bruce W. Longenecker and Kelly D. Liebengood. Grand Rapids: Eerdmans, 2009.

Bash, Anthony. *Ambassadors for Christ: An Exploration of Ambassadorial Language in the New Testament*. WUNT 2.92. Tübingen: Mohr Siebeck, 1997.

Bateman, H. W. *Early Jewish Hermeneutics and Hebrews 1:5–13*. New York: Lang, 1997.

Bates, Matthew W. *The Birth of the Trinity: Jesus, God, and Spirit in New Testament and Early Christian Interpretations of the Old Testament*. Oxford: Oxford University Press, 2015.

———. "A Christology of Incarnation and Enthronement: Romans 1:3–4 as Unified, Nonadoptionist, and Nonconciliatory." *CBQ* 77 (2015): 107–27.

———. *The Hermeneutics of the Apostolic Proclamation: The Center of Paul's Method of Scriptural Interpretation*. Waco, TX: Baylor University Press, 2012.

———. *Salvation by Allegiance Alone: Rethinking Faith, Works, and the Gospel of Jesus the King*. Grand Rapids: Baker Academic, 2017.

Batto, Bernard F. "The Divine Sovereign: The Image of God in the Priestly Creation Account." Pages 143–86 in *David and Zion: Biblical Studies in Honor of J. J. M. Roberts*. Edited by Bernard Batto and Kathryn L. Roberts. Winona Lake, IN: Eisenbrauns, 2004.

Bauckham, Richard. *The Climax of Prophecy: Studies on the Book of Revelation*. London: T&T Clark, 1993.

———. "The Divinity of Jesus Christ in the Epistle to the Hebrews." Pages 15–36 in *The Epistle to the Hebrews and Christian Theology*. Edited by Richard Bauckham et al. Grand Rapids: Eerdmans, 2009.

———. "The Economic Critique of Rome in Revelation 18." Pages 47–90 in *Images of Empire*. Edited by Loveday Alexander. JSOTSup 12. Sheffield: Sheffield Academic Press, 1991.

———. *Gospel of Glory: Major Themes in Johannine Theology*. Grand Rapids: Baker Academic, 2015.

———. "The Holiness of Jesus and His Disciples in the Gospel of John." Pages 253–70 in *The Testimony of the Beloved Disciple: Narrative, History, and Theology in the Gospel of John*. Grand Rapids: Baker Academic, 2007.

———. *Jesus and the God of Israel: God Crucified and Other Studies on the New Testament's Christology of Divine Identity*. Grand Rapids: Eerdmans, 2008.

———. "Jewish Messianism according to the Gospel of John." Pages 207–38 in *The Testimony of the Beloved Disciple: Narrative, History, and Theology in the Gospel of John*. Grand Rapids: Baker Academic, 2007.

———. "Messianic Jewish Identity in James." Pages 101–20 in *Muted Voices of the New Testament: Readings in the Catholic Epistles and Hebrews*. Edited by Katherine M. Hockey, Madison N. Pierce, and Francis Watson. LNTS 587. London T&T Clark, 2018.

———. "Monotheism and Christology in Hebrews 1." Pages 167–85 in *Early Jewish and Christian Monotheism*. Edited by Loren T. Stuckenbruck and Wendy E. S. North. London: T&T Clark, 2004.

———. *The Theology of the Book of Revelation*. Cambridge: Cambridge University Press, 1993.

———. "The Worship of Jesus in Philippians 2:9–11." Pages 128–39 in *Where Christology Began*. Edited by Ralph P. Martin and Brian Dodd. Louisville: Westminster John Knox, 1998.

Bauer, David R. "The Kingship of Jesus in the Matthean Infancy Narrative: A Literary Analysis." *CBQ* 57 (1995): 306–23.

Bauer, Walter, Frederick W. Danker, William F. Arndt, and F. Wilbur Gingrich. *Greek-English Lexicon of the New Testament and Other Early Christian Literature*. 3rd ed. Chicago: University of Chicago Press, 2000.

Baxter, Wayne. *Israel's Only Shepherd: Matthew's Shepherd Motif and His Social Setting*. LNTS 457. London: T&T Clark, 2012.

Beale, G. K. *The Book of Revelation*. NIGTC. Grand Rapids: Eerdmans, 1999.

———. *John's Use of the Old Testament in Revelation*. JSNTSup 166. Sheffield: Sheffield Academic Press, 1998.

———. "The Origin of the Title 'King of Kings and Lord of Lords' in Revelation 17.14." *NTS* 31 (1985): 618–20.

Beard, Mary. *The Roman Triumph*. Cambridge: The Belknap Press of Harvard University Press, 2007.

Beaton, Richard. *Isaiah's Christ in Matthew's Gospel*. SNTSMS 123. Cambridge: Cambridge University Press, 2002.

———. "Messiah and Justice: A Key to Matthew's Use of Isaiah 42.1–4." *JSNT* 75 (1999): 5–23.

Beetham, Christopher A. *Echoes of Scripture in the Letter to the Colossians*. BibInt 96. Leiden: Brill, 2008.

Beker, J. Christiaan. *Paul the Apostle: The Triumph of God in Life and Thought*. Philadelphia: Fortress, 1980.

Bell, Richard H. "Sacrifice and Christology in Paul." *JTS* 53 (2002): 1–27.

Belleville, Linda L. "Christology, Greco-Roman Religious Piety, and the Pseud-onymity of the Pastoral Epistles." Pages 221–43 in *Paul and Pseudepigra-phy*. Edited by Stanley E. Porter and Gregory P. Fewster. Pauline Studies 8. Leiden: Brill, 2013.

Bennema, Cornelis. "Spirit-Baptism in the Fourth Gospel: A Messianic Reading of John 1,33." *Biblica* 84 (2003): 35–60.

———. "The Sword of the Messiah and the Concept of Liberation in the Fourth Gospel." *Biblica* 86 (2005): 35–58.

Beskow, Per. *Rex Gloriae: The Kingship of Christ in the Early Church*. Translated by Eric J. Sharpe. Eugene, OR: Wipf & Stock, 2014. First published 1962 by Almqvist & Wiksells (Uppsala).

Best, Ernest. *One Body in Christ: A Study in the Relationship of the Church to Christ in the Epistles of the Apostle Paul*. London: SPCK, 1955.

Betz, Hans Dieter. *Galatians*. Hermeneia. Philadelphia: Fortress, 1979.

Bird, Michael F. *Jesus Is the Christ: The Messianic Testimony of the Gospels*. Downers Grove, IL: InterVarsity Press, 2012.

———. *Jesus the Eternal Son: Answering Adoptionist Christology*. Grand Rapids: Eerdmans, 2017.

Bird, Phyllis A. "'Male and Female He Created Them': Gen 1:27b in the Context of the Priestly Account of Creation." *HTR* 74 (1981): 129–59.

Blackwell, Ben C. *Christosis: Pauline Soteriology in Light of Deification in Irenaeus and Cyril of Alexandria*. WUNT 2.314. Tübingen: Mohr Siebeck, 2011.

———. "Immortal Glory and the Problem of Death in Romans 3:23." *JSNT* 32 (2010): 285–308.

Blanton, Thomas, IV. "Saved by Obedience: Matthew 1:21 in Light of Jesus's Teach-ing on the Torah." *JBL* 132 (2013): 393–413.

———. *A Spiritual Economy: Gift Exchange in the Letters of Paul of Tarsus*. New Haven: Yale University Press, 2017.

Blanton, Ward, and Hent de Vries, eds. *Paul and the Philosophers*. New York: Ford-ham University Press, 2013.

Blenkinsopp, Joseph. *David Remembered: Kingship and National Identity in An-cient Israel*. Grand Rapids: Eerdmans, 2013.

———. "The Oracle of Judah and the Messianic Entry." *JBL* 80 (1961): 55–64.

Block, Daniel I. "My Servant David: Ancient Israel's Vision of the Messiah." Pages 17–56 in *Israel's Messiah in the Bible and the Dead Sea Scrolls*. Edited by Rich-ard S. Hess and M. Daniel Carroll. Grand Rapids: Baker Academic, 2003.

Blomberg, Craig L. "'But We See Jesus': The Relationship between the Son of Man in Hebrews 2.6 and 2.9 and the Implications for English Translations." Pages

88–99 in *The Cloud of Witnesses*. Edited by Richard Bauckham et al. London: T&T Clark, 2008.

———. "Messiah in the New Testament." Pages 111–41 in *Israel's Messiah in the Bible and the Dead Sea Scrolls*. Edited by Richard S. Hess and M. Daniel Carroll. Grand Rapids: Baker Academic, 2003.

———. *A New Testament Theology*. Waco, TX: Baylor University Press, 2018.

Bock, Darrell L. *Proclamation from Prophecy and Pattern: Lucan Old Testament Christology*. JSNTSup 12. Sheffield: JSOT Press, 1987.

Bockmuehl, Markus. "'The Form of God' (Phil. 2:6): Variations on a Theme of Jewish Mysticism." *JTS* 48 (1997): 1–23.

Boer, Martinus C. de. *The Defeat of Death: Apocalyptic Eschatology in 1 Corinthians 15 and Romans 5*. JSNTSup 22. Sheffield: JSOT Press, 1988.

———. "Paul's Mythologizing Program in Romans 5–8." Pages 1–20 in *Apocalyptic Paul: Cosmos and Anthropos in Romans 5–8*. Edited by Beverly Roberts Gaventa. Waco, TX: Baylor University Press, 2013.

Boers, Hendrikus. *What Is New Testament Theology: The Rise of Criticism and the Problem of a Theology of the New Testament*. Philadelphia: Fortress, 1979.

Boersma, Hans. *Heavenly Participation: The Weaving of a Sacramental Tapestry*. Grand Rapids: Eerdmans, 2011.

Boismard, Marie Emile. "Constitué Fils de Dieu (Rom. 1.4)." *RB* 60 (1953): 5–17.

Bond, Helen K. *Pontius Pilate in History and Interpretation*. SNTSMS 100. Cambridge: Cambridge University Press, 1998.

Boring, M. Eugene. *Revelation*. Interpretation. Louisville: John Knox Press, 1989.

Bornhäuser, K. *Jesus Imperator Mundi (Phil 3,17–1 und 2,5–12)*. Gütersloh: Bertelsmann, 1938.

———. "Zum Verständnis von Philipper 2,5–11." *NKZ* 44 (1033): 428–34.

Botner, Max. "The Messiah Is 'the Holy One': ὁ ἅγιος τοῦ θεοῦ as a Messianic Title in Mark 1:24." *JBL* 136 (2017): 417–33.

_____. "You Are a Spiritual House: Misunderstanding Metaphor and the Question of Supersessionism in 1 Peter." Unpublished Paper, 2019.

Bousset, Wilhelm. *Kyrios Christos: A History of the Belief in Christ from the Beginnings of Christianity to Irenaeus*. Translated by John E. Steely. Nashville: Abingdon, 1970.

Branick, Vincent P. "The Sinful Flesh of the Son of God (Rom 8:3): A Key Image of Pauline Theology." *CBQ* 47 (1985): 246–62.

Breytenbach, Cilliers. *Versöhnung: Eine Studie zur paulinische Soteriologie*. Neukirchen-Vluyn: Neukirchener Verlag, 1989.

Bright, John. *The Kingdom of God: The Biblical Concept and Its Meaning for the Church*. Nashville: Abingdon, 1953.

Bringmann, Klaus. "The King as Benefactor: Some Remarks on Ideal Kingship in the Age of Hellenism." Pages 7–24 in *Images and Ideologies: Self-definition in the Hellenistic World*. Edited by Anthony Bulloch et al. Hellenistic Culture and Society 12. Berkeley: University of California Press, 1993.

Brown, Raymond. *The Birth of the Messiah: A Commentary on the Infancy Narratives in the Gospels of Matthew and Luke*. AYBRL. New Haven: Yale University Press, 1999.

Bruce, F. F. *Commentary on the Book of Acts*. Grand Rapids: Eerdmans, 1970.

Bryan, Steven M. "Consumed by Zeal: John's Use of Psalm 69:9 and the Action in the Temple." *BBR* 21 (2011): 479–94.

———. "The End of Exile: The Reception of Jeremiah's Prediction of a Seventy-Year Exile." *JBL* 137 (2018): 107–26.

———. "The Eschatological Temple in John 14." *BBR* 15 (2005): 187–98.

Bultmann, Rudolf. *Theology of the New Testament*. 2 vols. New York: Scribner's Sons, 1951.

Burge, Gary M. *The Anointed Community: The Holy Spirit in Johannine Tradition*. Grand Rapids: Eerdmans, 1987.

Burke, Trevor J. *Adopted into God's Family: Exploring a Pauline Metaphor*. NSBT 22. Downers Grove, IL: InterVarsity Press, 2006.

Butticaz, Simon David. *L'identité de l'Eglise dans les Actes des apôtres: De la restauration d'Israël à la conquête universelle*. BZNW 174. Berlin: de Gruyter, 2011.

Byrne, Brendan. "Living Out the Righteousness of God: The Contribution of Rom 6:1–8:13 to an Understanding of Paul's Ethical Presuppositions." *CBQ* 43 (1981): 557–81.

Caird, G. B. "The Glory of God in the Fourth Gospel: An Exercise in Biblical Semantics." *NTS* 15 (1968/69): 265–77.

Calvin, John. *Institutes of the Christian Religion*. Translated by Henry Beveridge. Grand Rapids: Eerdmans, 1989.

Campbell, Douglas A. "2 Corinthians 4:13: Evidence in Paul That Christ Believes." *JBL* 128 (2009): 337–56.

———. *The Deliverance of God: An Apocalyptic Rereading of Justification in Paul*. Grand Rapids: Eerdmans, 2009.

———. "Participation and Faith in Paul." Pages 37–60 in *"In Christ" in Paul: Explorations in Paul's Theology of Union and Participation*. Edited by Michael J. Thate et al. Grand Rapids: Eerdmans, 2018. First published 2014 by Mohr Siebeck (Tübingen).

———. "The Story of Jesus in Romans and Galatians." Pages 97–124 in *Narrative Dynamics in Paul: A Critical Assessment*. Edited by Bruce W. Longenecker. Louisville: Westminster John Knox, 2002.

Campbell, Constantine R. *Paul and Union with Christ: An Exegetical and Theological Study*. Grand Rapids: Zondervan, 2015.

Caneday, Ardel B. "The Eschatological World Already Subjected to the Son: The Οἰκουμένη of Hebrews 1.6 and the Son's Enthronement." Pages 28–39 in *The Cloud of Witnesses*. Edited by Richard Bauckham et al. London: T&T Clark, 2008.

Canlis, Julie. *Calvin's Ladder: A Spiritual Theology of Ascent and Ascension*. Grand Rapids: Eerdmans, 2010.

Carlson, Stephen C. "The Davidic Key for Counting the Generations in Matthew 1:17." *CBQ* 76 (2014): 665–83.

Carr, Frederick David. "Beginning at the End: The Kingdom of God in 1 Corinthians." *CBQ* 81 (2019): 449–69.

Carroll, John T. "Luke's Crucifixion Scene." Pages 108–24 in *Reimagining the Death of the Lukan Jesus*. Edited by Dennis D. Sylva. Athenäums Monografien, Theologie 73. Frankfurt am Main: Anton Hain, 1990.

Carson, D. A. "The Purpose of the Fourth Gospel: John 20:30–31 Reconsidered." *JBL* 108 (1987): 639–51.

———. "Syntactical Text-Critical Observations on John 20:30–31: One More Round on the Purpose of the Fourth Gospel." *JBL* 124 (2005): 693–714.

Carter, Warren. *John and Empire: Initial Explorations*. London: T&T Clark, 2008.

———. "Pilate and Jesus: Roman Justice All Washed Up (Matt 27:11–26)." Pages 145–68 in *Matthew and Empire: Initial Explorations*. Harrisburg, PA: Trinity Press International, 2001.

Casey, Maurice. *From Jewish Prophet to Gentile God: The Origins and Development of New Testament Christology*. Louisville: Westminster John Knox, 1991.

Centrone, Bruno. "Platonism and Pythagoreanism in the Early Empire." Pages 567–75 in *The Cambridge History of Greek and Roman Political Thought*. Edited by Christopher Rowe and Malcolm Schofield. Cambridge: Cambridge University Press, 2005.

Chae, Young S. *Jesus as the Eschatological Davidic Shepherd: Studies in the Old Testament, Second Temple Judaism, and in the Gospel of Matthew*. WUNT 2.216. Tübingen: Mohr Siebeck, 2006.

Charlesworth, James H. "From Jewish Messianology to Christian Christology: Some Caveats and Perspectives." Pages 225–64 in *Judaisms and Their Messiahs at the Turn of the Christian Era*. Edited by Jacob Neusner, William S. Green, and Ernest Frerichs. Cambridge: Cambridge University Press, 1987.

Charlesworth, James H., William Scott Green, and Ernest Frerichs, eds. *Judaisms and Their Messiahs at the Turn of the Christian Era*. Cambridge: Cambridge University Press, 1987.

Charlesworth, M. P. "The Virtues of a Roman Emperor: Propaganda and the Creation of Belief." *Proceedings of the British Academy* 23 (1937): 105–33.

Chester, Andrew. "Christ of Paul." Pages 109–21 in *Redemption and Resistance: The Messianic Hopes of Jews and Christians in Antiquity*. Edited by Markus Bockmuehl and James Carleton Paget. London: T&T Clark, 2008.

———. "High Christology—Whence, When and Why?" *EC* 2.1 (2011): 22–50

———. "The 'Law of Christ' and the 'Law of the Spirit.'" Pages 537–601 in *Messiah and Exaltation: Jewish Messianic and Visionary Traditions and New Testament Christology*. Tübingen: Mohr Siebeck, 2007.

———. *Messiah and Exaltation: Jewish Messianic and Visionary Traditions and New Testament Christology*. WUNT 207. Tübingen: Mohr Siebeck, 1991.

Chester, Stephen. *Reading Paul with the Reformers: Reconciling Old and New Perspectives*. Grand Rapids: Eerdmans, 2017.

Cho, Bernardo. *Royal Messianism and the Jerusalem Priesthood in the Gospel of Mark*. LNTS 607. London: T&T Clark, 2019.

Christensen, Sean. "Reborn Participants in Christ: Recovering the Importance of Union with Christ in 1 Peter." *JETS* 61 (2018): 339–54.

Cockerill, Gareth E. "The Better Resurrection (Heb. 11:35): A Key to the Structure and Rhetorical Purpose of Hebrews 11." *TynBul* 51 (2000): 215–34.

Collins, Adela Yarbro. *The Combat Myth in the Book of Revelation*. Harvard Dissertations in Religion 9. Missoula, MT: Scholars Press, 1976.

———. *Crisis and Catharsis: The Power of the Apocalypse*. Philadelphia: Westminster, 1984.

———. "Mark and His Readers: The Son of God among Greeks and Romans." *HTR* 93 (2000): 85–100.

———. "The Political Perspective of the Revelation to John." *JBL* 96 (1977): 241–56.

———. "The Psalms and the Origins of Christology." Pages 113–24 in *Psalms in Community: Jewish and Christian Textual, Liturgical, and Artistic Traditions*. Edited by Harold W. Attridge and Margot E. Fassler. Atlanta: Society of Biblical Literature, 2003.

———. "The Worship of Jesus and the Imperial Cult." Pages 234–57 in *The Jewish Roots of Christological Monotheism: Papers from the St. Andrews Conference on the Historical Origins of the Worship of Jesus*. Edited by Carey C. Newman et al. SSJJ 63; Leiden: Brill, 1999.

———. "The Significance of Mark 10:45 among Gentile Christians." *HTR* 90 (1997): 371–82.

Collins, Adela Yarbro, and John J. Collins. *King and Messiah as Son of God: Divine, Human, and Angelic Messianic Figures in Biblical and Related Literature.* Grand Rapids: Eerdmans, 2008.

Collins, John J. *The Scepter and the Star: The Messiahs of the Dead Sea Scrolls and Other Ancient Literature.* New York: Doubleday, 1995.

Coloe, Mary L. *Dwelling in the Household of God: Johannine Ecclesiology and Spirituality.* Collegeville, MN: Liturgical Press, 2007.

———. *God Dwells with Us: Temple Symbolism in the Fourth Gospel.* Collegeville, MN: Liturgical Press, 2001.

Cooke, Gerald. "The Israelite King as Son of God." *ZAW* 73 (1961): 202–25.

Cooley, Alison E. *Res Gestae Divi Augusti: Text, Translation, and Commentary.* Cambridge: Cambridge University Press, 2009.

Copenhaver, Adam. "Echoes of a Hymn in a Letter of Paul: The Rhetorical Function of the Christ-Hymn in the Letter to the Colossians." *JSPL* 4 (2014): 235–55.

Cortez, Marc. *Resourcing Theological Anthropology: A Constructive Account of Humanity in the Light of Christ.* Grand Rapids: Zondervan, 2017.

Court, John M. *Myth and History in the Book of Revelation.* Atlanta: John Knox Press, 1979.

Cranfield, C. E. B. *Romans 1–8.* ICC. London: T&T Clark, 2004. 58.

Creach, Jerome F. D. *The Destiny of the Righteous in the Psalms.* St. Louis: Chalice, 2008.

Croy, N. Clayton. *Endurance in Suffering: Hebrews 12:1–3 in Its Rhetorical, Religious, and Philosophical Context.* SNTSMS 98. Cambridge: Cambridge University Press, 1998.

Crump, David. *I Pledge Allegiance: A Believer's Guide to Kingdom Citizenship in 21st-Century America.* Grand Rapids: Eerdmans, 2018.

Cullmann, Oscar. "The Kingship of Christ and the Church in the New Testament." Pages 105–37 in *The Early Church: Studies in Early Christian History and Theology.* Edited by A. J. B. Higgins. Philadelphia: Westminster Press, 1956.

Dahl, Nils A. "The Crucified Messiah." Pages 27–47 in *Jesus the Christ: The Historical Origins of a Christological Doctrine.* Edited by Donald H. Juel. Minneapolis: Fortress, 1991.

———. *Jesus the Christ: The Historical Origins of Christological Doctrine.* Minneapolis: Fortress, 1991.

———. *Studies in Paul: Theology for the Early Christian Mission.* Minneapolis: Ausburg, 1977.

———. "The Johannine Church and History." Pages 122–40 in *The Interpretation of John.* Edited by John Ashton. London: T&T Clark, 2000.

———. "The Messiahship of Jesus in Paul." Pages 15–25 in *Jesus the Christ: The Historical Origins of Christological Doctrine*. Edited by Donald H. Juel. Minneapolis: Fortress, 1991.

———. "Two Notes on Romans 5." *ST* 5 (1952): 37–48.

Daly-Denton, Margaret. *David in the Fourth Gospel: The Johannine Reception of the Psalms*. Leiden: Brill, 2000.

———. "Singing Hymns to Christ as to a God (Cf. Pliny EP. X, 96)." Pages 277–92 in *The Jewish Roots of Christological Monotheism: Papers from the St. Andrews Conference on the Historical Origins of the Worship of Jesus*. Edited by Carey C. Newman et al. Supplements to the Journal for the Study of Judaism 63. Leiden: Brill, 1999.

Davies, W. D. *Torah in the Messianic Age and/or the Age to Come*. SBLMS 7. Atlanta: Scholars Press, 1952.

Dawson, Gerrit Scott. *Jesus Ascended: The Meaning of Christ's Continuing Incarnation*. London: T&T Clark, 2004.

Deines, Roland. "Not the Law but the Messiah: Law and Righteousness in the Gospel of Matthew—An Ongoing Debate." Pages 53–84 in *Built upon the Rock: Studies in the Gospel of Matthew*. Edited by Daniel M. Gurtner and John Nolland. Grand Rapids: Eerdmans, 2008.

Dempster, Stephen. *Dominion and Dynasty: A Biblical Theology for the Hebrew Bible*. NSBT 15. Downers Grove, IL: InterVarsity Press, 2003.

Dennis, John A. *Jesus' Death and the Gathering of True Israel: The Johannine Appropriation of Restoration Theology in the Light of John 11.47–52*. WUNT 2.217. Tübingen: Mohr Siebeck, 2006.

deSilva, David A. *Perseverance in Gratitude: A Socio-rhetorical Commentary on the Epistle to the Hebrews*. Grand Rapids: Eerdmans, 2000.

———. *Unholy Allegiances: Heeding Revelation's Warning*. Peabody, MA: Hendrickson, 2013.

Doble, Peter. "Luke 24.26, 44—Songs of God's Servant: David and His Psalms in Luke-Acts." *JSNT* 28 (2006): 267–83.

———. "The Psalms in Luke-Acts." Pages 83–119 in *The Psalms in the New Testament*. Edited by Steve Moyise and Maarten J. J. Menken. The New Testament and the Scriptures of Israel. London: T&T Clark, 2004.

Dodd, C. H. *The Apostolic Preaching and Its Developments*. New York: Harper & Row, 1964.

———. *The Interpretation of the Fourth Gospel*. Cambridge: Cambridge University Press, 1953.

Donahue, John. "Temple, Trial, and Royal Christology (Mark 14:53–65)." Pages

61–79 in *The Passion in Mark: Studies on Mark 14–16*. Edited by Werner Kelber. Philadelphia: Fortress, 1976.

Downs, David J. "The Pauline Concept of Union with Christ in Ignatius of Antioch." Pages 143–61 in *The Apostolic Fathers and Paul*. Edited by Todd D. Still and David E. Wilhite. London: T&T Clark, 2017.

Downs, David J., and Benjamin J. Lappenga. *The Faithfulness of the Risen Christ: Pistis and the Exalted Lord in Paul*. Waco, TX: Baylor University Press, 2019.

Dubis, Mark. *Messianic Woes in 1 Peter: Suffering and Eschatology in 1 Peter 4:12–19*. StBibLit 33. New York: Lang, 2002.

Duff, Paul Brooks. "The March of the Divine Warrior and the Advent of the Greco-Roman King: Mark's Account of Jesus' Entry into Jerusalem." *JBL* 111 (1992): 55–71.

Duling, Dennis C. "The Eleazar Miracle and Solomon's Magical Wisdom in Flavius Josephus's *Antiquitates Judaicae* 8.42–49." *HTR* 78 (1985): 1–25

———. "The Promises to David and Their Entrance into Christianity: Nailing Down a Likely Hypothesis." *NTS* 20 (1973): 55–77

———. "The Therapeutic Son of David: An Element in Matthew's Christological Apologetic." *NTS* 24 (1977–78): 392–410.

Dunn, James D. G. *Did the First Christians Worship Jesus? The New Testament Evidence*. Louisville: Westminster John Knox, 2011.

Dunne, John Anthony. "The Regal Status of Christ in the Colossian 'Christ-Hymn': A Re-evaluation of the Influence of Wisdom Traditions." *TJ* 32.1 (Spring 2011): 3–18.

Eastman, Susan Grove. *Paul and the Person: Reframing Paul's Anthropology*. Grand Rapids: Eerdmans, 2017.

Eaton, John H. *Kingship and the Psalms*. SBT 32. London: SCM, 1976.

Edwards, James R. "Markan Sandwiches: The Significance of Interpolations in Markan Narratives." *NovT* 31 (1989): 193–216.

Egan, Patrick. *Ecclesiology and the Scriptural Narrative of 1 Peter*. Eugene, OR: Pickwick, 2016.

Ehrman, Bart D. *How Jesus Became God: The Exaltation of a Jewish Preacher from Galilee*. San Francisco: HarperOne, 2014.

Elliott, John H. "Disgraced Yet Graced: The Gospel according to 1 Peter in the Key of Honor and Shame." *BTB* 25 (1995): 166–78.

Elliott, Neil. "Paul and the Politics of Empire." Pages 17–39 in *Paul and Politics: Ekklesia, Israel, Imperium, Interpretation*. Edited by Richard A. Horsley. Harrisburg, PA: Trinity International, 2000.

Eskola, Timo. *Messiah and the Throne: Jewish Merkabah Mysticism and Early Christian Exaltation Discourse*. WUNT 2.142. Tübingen: Mohr Siebeck, 2001.

Eubank, Nathan. *Wages of Cross-Bearing and the Debt of Sin: The Economy of Heaven in Matthew's Gospel*. BZNW 196. Berlin: de Gruyter, 2013.

Fantin, Joseph D. *The Lord of the Entire World: Lord Jesus, a Challenge to Lord Caesar*. Sheffield: Sheffield Phoenix Press, 2011.

Farrow, Douglas. *Ascension and Ecclesia: On the Significance of the Doctrine of the Ascension for Ecclesiology and Christian Cosmology*. Grand Rapids: Eerdmans, 1999.

——. *Ascension Theology*. London: T&T Clark, 2011.

Fatehi, Mehrdad. *The Spirit's Relation to the Risen Lord in Paul: An Examination of Its Christological Implications*. WUNT 2.128. Tübingen: Mohr Siebeck, 2000.

Fears, J. Rufus. *PRINCEPS A DIIS ELECTUS: The Divine Election of the Emperor as Political Concept at Rome*. Rome: American Academy at Rome, 1977.

——. "Theology of Victory at Rome: Approaches and Problems." *ANRW* 17 2:736–826.

Fee, Gordon D. Pauline Christology: An Exegetical-Theological Study. Peabody, MA: Hendrickson, 2007.

Ferngren, Gary B. *Medicine & Health Care in Early Christianity*. Baltimore: The Johns Hopkins University Press, 2009.

Filtvedt, Ole Jakob. *The Identity of God's People and the Paradox of Hebrews*. WUNT 2.400. Tübingen: Mohr Siebeck, 2015.

Fitzgerald, John T. "Paul and Friendship." Pages 319–43 in *Paul in the Greco-Roman World: A Handbook*. Edited by J. Paul Sampley. Harrisburg, PA: Trinity Press International, 2003.

Fitzmyer, Joseph A. *The Acts of the Apostles*. AYB 31. New York: Doubleday, 1998.

——. "David 'Being Therefore a Prophet . . .' (Acts 2:30)." *CBQ* 34 (1972): 332–39.

Fletcher-Louis, Crispin. *Christological Origins: The Emerging Consensus and Beyond*. Vol. 1 of Jesus Monotheism. Eugene, OR: Cascade, 2015.

Forman, Mark. *The Politics of Inheritance in Romans*. SNTSMS 148. Cambridge: Cambridge University Press, 2011.

Fowl, Stephen E. *Philippians*. THNTC. Grand Rapids: Eerdmans, 2005.

——. *The Story of Christ in the Ethics of Paul: An Analysis of the Function of the Hymnic Material in the Pauline Corpus*. JSNTSup. Sheffield: Sheffield Academic Press, 1990.

Fowler, Robert M. *Let the Reader Understand: Reader-Response Criticism and the Gospel of Mark*. Minneapolis: Fortress, 1991.

France, R. T. *The Gospel of Mark*. NIGTC. Grand Rapids: Eerdmans, 2002.

——. *Matthew: Evangelist and Teacher*. Downers Grove, IL: InterVarsity Press, 1995.

Fredriksen, Paula. *Paul: The Pagans' Apostle*. New Haven: Yale University Press, 2017.

Frey, Jörg. *The Glory of the Crucified One: Christology and Theology in the Gospel of John*. Translated by Wayne Coppins and Christoph Heilig. Waco, TX: Baylor University Press, 2018.

———. "The Relevance of the Roman Imperial Cult for the Book of Revelation: Exegetical and Hermeneutical Reflections on the Relation between the Seven Letters and the Visionary Main Part of the Book." Pages 231–55 in *The New Testament and Early Christian Literature in Greco-Roman Context: Studies in Honor of David E. Aune*. Edited by John Fotopoulos. Leiden: Brill, 2006.

Friesen, Steven J. *Imperial Cults and the Apocalypse of John: Reading Revelation in the Ruins*. Oxford: Oxford University Press, 2001.

———. "Injustice or God's Will? Early Christian Explanations of Poverty." Pages 17–36 in *Wealth and Poverty in Early Church and Society*. Edited by Susan R. Holman. Holy Cross Studies in Patristic Theology and History. Grand Rapids: Baker Academic, 2008.

Fuller, Reginald H. *The Foundations of New Testament Christology*. New York: Charles Scribner's Sons, 1965.

Galinsky, Karl. *Augustan Culture: An Interpretive Introduction*. Princeton: Princeton University Press, 1996.

Garlington, Don. "Israel's Triumphant King: Romans 1:5 and the Scriptures of Israel." Pages 173–83 in *Jesus and Paul: Global Perspectives in Honor of James D. G. Dunn for His 70th Birthday*. Edited by B. J. Oropeza, C. K. Robertson, and Douglas C. Mohrmann. LNTS 414. London: T&T Clark, 2010.

———. "The Obedience of Faith in the Letter to the Romans: Part I: The Meaning of ὑπακοὴ πίστεως (Rom 1:5; 16:26)." *WTJ* 52 (1990): 201–24.

———. "The Obedience of Faith in the Letter to the Romans: Part III: The Obedience of Christ and the Obedience of the Christian." *WTJ* 55 (1993): 87–112.

Gathercole, Simon J. "The Heavenly ἀνατολή." *JTS* 56 (2005): 471–88.

Gaventa, Beverly Roberts, ed. *Apocalyptic Paul: Cosmos and Anthropos in Romans 5–8*. Waco, TX: Baylor University Press, 2013.

———. "Neither Height Nor Depth: Discerning the Cosmology of Romans." *SJT* 64 (2011): 265–78.

Gelardini, Gabriella. "The Contest for a Royal Title: Herod versus Jesus in the Gospel according to Mark (6,14–29; 15, 6–15)." *ASE* 28 (2011): 93–106.

Gerbrandt, Gerald Eddie. *Kingship according to the Deuteronomistic History*. SBLDS 87. Atlanta: Scholars Press, 1986.

Gerhardsson, Birger. *The Testing of God's Son (Matt. 4:1–11 & Par): An Analysis of an Early Christian Midrash*. Eugene, OR: Wipf & Stock, 2009.

Gese, Hartmut. *Essays on Biblical Theology.* Translated by Keith Crim. Minneapolis: Augsburg, 1981.

Gombis, Timothy G. "Cosmic Lordship and Divine Gift-Giving: Psalm 68 in Ephesians 4:8." *NovT* 47 (2005): 367–80.

———. "Ephesians 2 as a Narrative of Divine Warfare." *JSNT* 26 (2004): 403–18.

———. "1 Maccabees and Mark 11:1–11: A Subversive Entry into Jerusalem." Pages 174–81 in *Reading Mark in Context: Jesus and Second Temple Judaism.* Edited by Ben Blackwell et al. Grand Rapids: Zondervan, 2018.

Good, Deirdre J. *Jesus the Meek King.* Harrisburg, PA: Trinity Press International, 1999.

Goodacre, Mark. "Scripturalization in Mark's Crucifixion Narrative." Pages 33–47 in *The Trial and Death of Jesus: Essays on the Passion Narrative in Mark.* Edited by Geert van Oyen and Tom Shepherd. Leuven: Peeters, 2006.

Goranson Jacob, Haley. *Conformed to the Image of His Son: Reconsidering Paul's Theology of Glory in Romans.* Downers Grove, IL: InterVarsity Press, 2018.

Gorman, Michael J. *Abide and Go: Missional Theosis in the Gospel of John.* Eugene, OR: Cascade, 2018.

———. *Inhabiting the Cruciform God: Kenosis, Justification, and Theosis in Paul's Narrative Soteriology.* Grand Rapids: Eerdmans, 2009.

———. "John's Implicit Ethic of Enemy-Love." Pages 135–58 in *Johannine Ethics: The Moral World of the Gospel and Epistles of John.* Edited by Sherri Brown and Christopher W. Skinner. Minneapolis: Fortress, 2017.

Gradel, Ittai. *Emperor Worship and Roman Religion.* Oxford Classical Monographs. Oxford: Clarendon, 2002.

Grant, Jamie A. *The King as Exemplar: The Function of Deuteronomy's Kingship Law in the Shaping of the Book of Psalms.* AcBib 17. Atlanta: Society of Biblical Literature, 2004.

Gray, Timothy C. *The Temple in the Gospel of Mark: A Study in Its Narrative Role.* Grand Rapids: Baker Academic, 2010.

Green, Joel B. *The Gospel of Luke.* NIGTC. Grand Rapids: Eerdmans, 1997.

———. "The Problem of a Beginning: Israel's Scriptures in Luke 1–2." *BBR* 4 (1994): 61–85.

Greene, Joseph R. "Jesus as the Heavenly Temple in the Fourth Gospel." *BBR* 28 (2018): 425–46.

Grindheim, Sigurd. *Living in the Kingdom of God: A Biblical Theology for the Life of the Church.* Grand Rapids: Baker Academic, 2018.

Gupta, Nijay K. *Paul and the Language of Faith.* Grand Rapids: Eerdmans, 2020.

Haacker, Klaus. "Das Bekenntnis des Paulus zur Hoffnung Israels." *NTS* 31 (1985): 437–51.

Hafemann, Scott J. *Suffering and the Spirit: An Exegetical Study of 2 Corinthians 2:14–3:3 within the Context of the Corinthian Correspondence*. Tübingen: Mohr Siebeck, 1986

Hahn, Ferdinand. *The Titles of Jesus in Christology: Their History in Early Christianity*. New York: World, 1969.

Hahn, Scott W. *Kinship by Covenant: A Canonical Approach to the Fulfillment of God's Saving Promises*. AYBRL. New Haven: Yale University Press, 2009.

Hamilton, Catherine Sider. "'His Blood Be upon Us': Innocent Blood and the Death of Jesus in Matthew." *CBQ* 70 (2008): 82–100.

Hamm, Dennis. "Faith in the Epistle to the Hebrews: The Jesus Factor." *CBQ* 56 (1990): 270–91.

Harris, Sarah. *The Davidic Shepherd King in the Lukan Narrative*. LNTS 558. London: T&T Clark, 2016.

Hay, David M. *Glory at the Right Hand: Psalm 110 in Early Christianity*. SBLMS 18. Nashville: Abingdon, 1973.

———. "Paul's Understanding of Faith as Participation." Pages 45–76 in *Paul and His Theology*. Edited by Stanley E. Porter. Leiden: Brill, 2006.

Hays, Richard B. "Can Narrative Criticism Recover the Theological Unity of Scripture?" *JTI* 2 (2008): 193–211.

———. "Christ Prays the Psalms: Paul's Use of an Early Christian Convention." Pages 122–36 in *The Future of Christology: Essays in Honor of Leander E. Keck*. Edited by Abraham J. Malherbe and Wayne A. Meeks. Minneapolis: Fortress, 1993.

———. "Christology and Ethics in Galatians: The Law of Christ." *CBQ* 49 (1987): 268–90.

———. "The Conversion of the Imagination: Scripture and Eschatology in 1 Corinthians." *NTS* 45 (1999): 391–412.

———. *1 Corinthians*. Interpretation. Louisville: Westminster John Knox, 1997.

———. *Echoes of Scripture in the Gospels*. Waco, TX: Baylor University Press, 2016.

———. *Echoes of Scripture in the Letters of Paul*. New Haven: Yale University Press, 1989.

———. *The Faith of Jesus Christ: The Narrative Substructure of Galatians 3:1–4:11*. 2nd ed. Grand Rapids: Eerdmans, 2002.

———. *The Moral Vision of the New Testament: A Contemporary Introduction to New Testament Ethics*. San Francisco: HarperSanFrancisco, 1997.

———. "Paul's Use of an Early Christian Convention." Pages 122–36 in *The Future of Christology: Essays in Honor of Leander E. Keck*. Edited by Abraham J. Malherbe and Wayne A. Meeks. Minneapolis: Fortress, 1993.

———. *Reading Backwards: Figural Christology and the Fourfold Gospel Witness.* Waco, TX: Baylor University Press, 2014.

Heath, Jane. "'You Say that I Am a King' (John 18.37)." *JSNT* 34 (2012): 232–53.

Heen, Erik M. "Phil 2:6–11 and Resistance to Local Timocratic Rule: *Isa theō* and the Cult of the Emperor in the East." Pages 125–53 in *Paul and the Roman Imperial Order.* Edited by Richard A. Horsley. Harrisburg, PA: Trinity Press International, 2004.

Heil, John Paul. "The Narrative Strategy and Pragmatics of the Temple Theme in Mark." *CBQ* 59 (1997): 76–100.

Heitmüller, Wilhelm. "Zum Problem Paulus und Jesus." *ZNW* 13 (1912): 320–37.

Hellerman, Joseph H. "ΜΟΡΦΗ ΘΕΟΥ as a Signifier of Social Status in Philippians 2:6." *JETS* 52 (2009): 779–97.

———. *Reconstructing Honor in Roman Philippi: Carmen Christi as Cursus Pudorum.* SNTSMS 132. Cambridge: Cambridge University Press, 2005.

———. *When the Church Was a Family: Recapturing Jesus' Vision for Authentic Christian Community.* Nashville: B&H, 2009.

Henderson, Suzanne Watts. *Christology and Discipleship in the Gospel of Mark.* SNTSMS 135. Cambridge: Cambridge University Press, 2006.

———. "God's Fullness in Bodily Form: Christ and Church in Colossians." *ExpTim* 118 (2007): 169–73.

Hengel, Martin. *Between Jesus and Paul: Studies in the Earliest History of Christianity.* Translated by John Bowden. Philadelphia: Fortress, 1983.

———. "'Christos' in Paul." Pages 65–77 in *Between Jesus and Paul: Studies in the Earliest History of Christianity.* Philadelphia: Fortress, 1983.

———. "Jesus, the Messiah of Israel." Pages 1–72 in *Studies in Early Christology.* Edinburgh: T&T Clark, 1995.

———. *Judaism and Hellenism.* 2 vols. Philadelphia: Fortress, 1974.

———. "The Kingdom of Christ in John." Pages 333–58 in *Studies in Early Christology.* London: T&T Clark, 2004.

———. "'Sit at My Right Hand!': The Enthronement of Christ at the Right Hand of God and Psalm 110:1." Pages 119–225 in *Studies in Early Christology.* Edinburgh: T&T Clark, 1995.

———. "The Song about Christ in Earliest Worship." Pages 227–91 in *Studies in Early Christology.* Edinburgh: T&T Clark, 1995.

———. *Studies in Early Christology.* Edinburgh: T&T Clark, 1995.

Henriksen, Jan-Olav, and Karl Olav Sandnes. *Jesus as Healer: A Gospel for the Body.* Grand Rapids: Eerdmans, 2016.

Hewitt, J. Thomas. "Ancient Messiah Discourse and Paul's Expression ἄχρις οὗ ἔλθῃ τὸ σπέρμα in Galatians 3.19." *NTS* 65 (2019): 398–411.

Hewitt, J. Thomas, and Matthew V. Noveson. "Participationism and Messiah Christology in Paul." Pages 393–416 in *God and the Faithfulness of Paul: A Critical Examination of the Pauline Theology of N. T. Wright*. Edited by Christoph Heileg et al. WUNT 2.413. Tübingen: Mohr Siebeck, 2016.

Hill, Wesley. *Paul and the Trinity: Persons, Relations, and the Pauline Letters*. Grand Rapids: Eerdmans, 2015.

———. *Spiritual Friendship: Finding Love in the Church as a Celibate Gay Christian*. Grand Rapids: Brazos, 2015.

Hodge, Caroline Johnson. *If Sons, Then Heirs: A Study of Kinship and Ethnicity in the Letters of Paul*. Oxford: Oxford University Press, 2007.

Holladay, Carl R. *Acts: A Commentary*. NTL. Louisville: Westminster John Knox, 2016.

Holmes, Michael W., ed. *The Apostolic Fathers: Greek Texts and English Translations*. Grand Rapids: Baker Academic, 1999.

Hood, Jason B. *The Messiah, His Brothers, and the Nations: Matthew 1.1–17*. LNTS 441. London: T&T Clark, 2011.

Hooker, Morna D. *From Adam to Christ: Essays on Paul*. Cambridge: Cambridge University Press, 1990.

———. "Raised for Our Acquittal (Rom 4,25)." Pages 323–41 in *Resurrection in the New Testament: Festschrift J. Lambrecht*. Edited by R. Bieringer et al. BETL 165. Leuven: Leuven University Press, 2002.

Hoover, Roy. "The HARPAGMOS Enigma: A Philological Solution." *HTR* 64 (1971): 95–119.

Horbury, William. "The Aaronic Priesthood in the Epistle to the Hebrews." Pages 260–85 in *Messianism among Jews and Christians: Biblical and Historical Studies*. 2nd ed. London: T&T Clark, 2016.

———. "Antichrist among Jews and Gentiles." Pages 366–86 in *Messianism among Jews and Christians: Biblical and Historical Studies*. 2nd ed. London: T&T Clark, 2016.

———. "Jewish Messianism and Early Christology." Pages 3–24 in *Contours of Christology in the New Testament*. Edited by Richard N. Longenecker. Grand Rapids: Eerdmans, 2005.

———. *Jewish Messianism and the Cult of Christ*. London: SCM, 1998.

———. "The Messianic Associations of 'The Son of Man.'" Pages 153–85 in *Messianism among Jews and Christians: Biblical and Historical Studies*. 2nd ed. London: T&T Clark, 2016.

———. "Messianism in the Old Testament Apocrypha and Pseudepigrapha." Pages 61–90 in *Messianism among Jews and Christians: Biblical and Historical Studies*. 3rd ed. London: T&T Clark, 2016.

———. "Septuagintal and New Testament Conceptions of the Church." Pages 289–307 in *Messianism among Jews and Christians: Biblical and Historical Studies*. 2nd ed. London: T&T Clark, 2016.

———. "The Twelve and the Phylarchs." Pages 186–219 in *Messianism among Jews and Christians: Biblical and Historical Studies*. 2nd ed. London: T&T Clark, 2016.

Horrell, David G. "The Label Χριστιανός: 1 Peter 4:16 and the Formation of Christian Identity." *JBL* 126 (2007): 361–81.

———. "The Product of a Petrine Circle? A Reassessment of the Origin and Character of 1 Peter." *JSNT* 86 (2002): 29–60.

———. *Solidarity and Difference: A Contemporary Reading of Paul's Ethics*. 2nd ed. London: T&T Clark, 2015.

———. "Theological Principle or Christological Praxis? Pauline Ethics in 1 Corinthians 8–11:1." *JSNT* 67 (1997): 83–114.

Horton, Michael. "Atonement and Ascension." Pages 226–50 in *Locating Atonement: Explorations in Constructive Dogmatics*. Edited by Oliver D. Crisp and Fred Sanders. Grand Rapids: Zondervan, 2015.

Hume, Douglas A. *The Early Christian Community: A Narrative Analysis of Acts 2:41–47 and 4:32–35*. WUNT 2.298. Tübingen: Mohr Siebeck, 2011.

Hurst, L. D. "The Christology of Hebrews 1 and 2." Pages 151–64 in *The Glory of Christ in the New Testament: Studies in Christology in Memory of George Bradford Caird*. Edited by L. D. Hurst and N. T. Wright. Oxford: Clarendon, 1987.

Hurtado, Larry W. *How on Earth Did Jesus Become a God? Historical Questions about Earliest Devotion to Jesus*. Grand Rapids: Eerdmans, 2005.

———. *Lord Jesus Christ: Devotion to Jesus in Earliest Christianity*. Grand Rapids: Eerdmans, 2003.

———. "New Testament Christology: A Critique of Bousset's Influence." *TS* 40 (1979): 306–17.

———. "Paul's Messianic Christology." Pages 107–31 in *Paul the Jew: Rereading the Apostle as a Figure of Second Temple Judaism*. Edited by Gabriele Boccaccini and Carlos A. Segovia. Minneapolis: Fortress, 2016.

Isaacs, Marie E. *Sacred Space: An Approach to the Theology of Hebrews*. JSNTSup 73. Sheffield: JSOT Press, 1992.

Jackson-McCabe, Matt. "The Messiah Jesus in the Mythic World of James." *JBL* 122 (2003): 701–30.

Jacob, Haley Goranson. *Conformed to the Image of His Son: Reconsidering Paul's Theology of Glory in Romans*. Downers Grove, IL: InterVarsity Press, 2018.

Janowski, Bernd, and Peter Stuhlmacher, eds. *The Suffering Servant: Isaiah 53 in Jewish and Christian Sources*. Grand Rapids: Eerdmans, 2004.

Janse, Sam. *"You Are My Son": The Reception History of Psalm 2 in Early Judaism and the Early Church*. Leuven: Peeters, 2009.

Jennings, Willie James. *The Christian Imagination: Theology and the Origins of Race*. New Haven: Yale University Press, 2010.

Jenson, Robert W. "Toward a Christian Theology of Israel." *Pro Ecclesia* 9 (2000): 43–56.

Jeremias, Joachim. *The Prayers of Jesus*. London: SCM, 1967.

Jervell, Jacob. *Luke and the People of God: A New Look at Luke-Acts*. Minneapolis: Augsburg, 1972.

Jipp, Joshua W. "Ancient, Modern, and Future Interpretations of Romans 1:3–4: Reception History and Biblical Interpretation." *JTI* 3 (2009): 241–59.

———. *Christ Is King: Paul's Royal Ideology*. Minneapolis: Fortress, 2015.

———. "Educating the Divided Soul in Paul and Plato: Reading Romans 7:7–25 and Plato's Republic." Pages 231–57 in *Paul: Jew, Greek, and Roman*. Edited by Stanley E. Porter. Pauline Studies 5. Leiden: Brill, 2008.

———. "'For David Did Not Ascend into Heaven . . .' (Acts 2:34a): Reprogramming Royal Psalms to Proclaim the Enthroned-in-Heaven King." Pages 41–59 in *Ascent into Heaven in Luke-Acts: New Explorations of Luke's Narrative Hinge*. Edited by David K. Bryan and David W. Pao Minneapolis: Fortress, 2016.

———. "Is the Apostle Paul the Father of Anti-Judaism? Engaging John Gager's *Who Made Early Christianity?*" *HBT* 39 (2017): 83–92.

———. "Luke's Scriptural Suffering Messiah: A Search for Precedent, a Search for Identity." *CBQ* 72 (2010): 255–74.

———. "Messiah Christology in Paul and Irenaeus." In *Paul and Irenaeus*. London: T&T Clark, forthcoming.

———. "Messiah Language and Gospel Writing." Pages 126–44 in *Writing the Gospels: A Dialogue with Francis Watson*. Edited by Catherine Sider Hamilton. LNTS 606. New York: T&T Clark, 2019.

———. "Raymond E. Brown and the Fourth Gospel: Composition and Community." Pages 173–96 in *The Gospel of John in Modern Interpretation*. Edited by Stanley Porter and Ron Fay. Grand Rapids: Kregel, 2018.

———. *Reading Acts*. Cascade Companions. Eugene, OR: Cascade, 2018.

———. "Rereading the Story of Abraham, Isaac, and 'Us' in Romans 4." *JSNT* 32 (2009): 217–42.

———. *Saved by Faith and Hospitality*. Grand Rapids: Eerdmans, 2017.

———. "Sharing in the Heavenly Rule of Christ the King: Paul's Royal Participatory Soteriology in Ephesians." Pages 251–75 in *"In Christ" in Paul: Explorations in Paul's Theological Vision of Participation*. Edited by Michael J. Thate et al. Tübingen: Mohr Siebeck. 2014.

———. "The Son's Entrance into the Heavenly World: The Soteriological Necessity of the Scriptural Catena in Hebrews 1:5–14." *NTS* 56 (2010): 557–75.

Jobes, Karen. *1 Peter*. BECNT. Grand Rapids: Baker Academic, 2005.

Johns, Loren L. *The Lamb Christology of the Apocalypse of John: An Investigation into Its Origins and Rhetorical Force*. WUNT 2.167. Tübingen: Mohr Siebeck, 2003.

Johnson, Aubrey R. *Sacral Kingship in Ancient Israel*. Cardiff: University of Wales Press, 1967.

Johnson, Luke Timothy. *The Acts of the Apostles*. SP 5. Collegeville, MN: Liturgical Press, 1992.

———. "Does a Theology of the Canonical Gospels Make Sense?" Pages 93–108 in *The Nature of New Testament Theology: Essays in Honour of Robert Morgan*. Edited by Christopher Rowland and Christopher Tuckett. Malden, MA: Blackwell, 2006.

———. *Hebrews: A Commentary*. NTL. Louisville: Westminster John Knox, 2006. 78–79;

———. "James 3:13–4:10 and the Topos περὶ φθόνου." *NovT* 25 (1983): 327–47.

———. *Religious Experience in Earliest Christianity: A Missing Dimension in New Testament Studies*. Minneapolis: Fortress, 1998.

———. *Septuagintal Midrash in the Speeches of Acts*. Milwaukee: Marquette University Press, 2002.

———. *Sharing Possessions: What Faith Demands*. 2nd ed. Grand Rapids: Eerdmans, 2011.

———. "The Use of Leviticus 19 in the Letter of James." Pages 123–35 in *Brother of Jesus, Friend of God: Studies in the Letter of James*. Grand Rapids: Eerdmans, 2004.

———. *The Writings of the New Testament: An Interpretation*. Minneapolis: Fortress, 1999.

Johnson, Nathan C. "The Passion according to David: Matthew's Arrest Narrative, the Absalom Revolt, and Militant Messianism." *CBQ* 80 (2018): 247–72.

———. "Romans 1:3–4: Beyond Antithetical Parallelism." *JBL* 136 (2017): 467–90.

Jonge, Marinus de. "The Use of the Expression ὁ Χριστός in the Apocalypse of John." Pages 267–81 in *L'Apocalypse johannique et l'Apocalyptique dans le Nouveau Testament*. Gembloux, Belgium: Louvain, 1980.

———. "The Use of the Word 'Anointed' in the Time of Jesus." *NovT* 8 (1966): 132–48.

Joseph, Alison L. *Portrait of the Kings: The Davidic Prototype in Deuteronomist Poetics*. Minneapolis: Fortress, 2015.

Juel, Donald. *Messianic Exegesis: Christological Interpretation of the Old Testament in Early Christianity*. Philadelphia: Fortress, 1988.

———. "The Origin of Mark's Christology." Pages 449–60 in *The Messiah: Developments in Earliest Judaism and Christianity: The First Princeton Symposium on Judaism and Christian Origins*. Edited by James H. Charlesworth et al. Minneapolis: Fortress, 1992.

———. "The Social Dimensions of Exegesis: The Use of Psalm 16 in Acts 2." *CBQ* 43 (1981): 543–56.

Käsemann, Ernst. "On the Subject of Primitive Christian Apocalyptic." Pages 108–37 in *New Testament Questions of Today*. Translated by W. J. Montague. Philadelphia: Fortress, 1969.

———. *The Wandering People of God: An Investigation of the Letter to the Hebrews*. Minneapolis: Augsburg, 1984.

Keating, Daniel A. *The Appropriation of Divine Life in Cyril of Alexandria*. Oxford: Oxford University Press, 2004.

Keck, Leander E. "Christology of the New Testament: What, Then, Is New Testament Christology?" Pages 185–200 in *Who Do You Say That I Am? Essays on Christology*. Edited by Mark Allan Powell and David R. Bauer. Louisville: Westminster John Knox, 1999.

Kerr, Alan R. *The Temple of Jesus' Body: The Temple Theme in the Gospel of John*. JSNTSup 220. Sheffield: Sheffield Academic Press, 2002.

Kim, Seyoon. "Imitatio Christi (1 Corinthians 11:1): How Paul Imitates Jesus Christ in Dealing with Idol Food." *BBR* 13 (2003): 193–226.

Kinman, Brent. "Parousia, Jesus' 'A-Triumphal' Entry, and the Fate of Jerusalem (Luke 19:28–44)." *JBL* 118 (1999): 279–94.

Kirk, J. R. Daniel. *A Man Attested by God: The Human Jesus of the Synoptic Gospels*. Grand Rapids: Eerdmans, 2016.

———. *Unlocking Romans: Resurrection and the Justification of God*. Grand Rapids: Eerdmans, 2008.

Kirk, J. R. Daniel, and Stephen L. Young. "'I Will Set His Hand to the Sea': Psalm 88:26 LXX and Christology in Mark." *JBL* 133 (2014): 333–40.

Kirschner, Robert. "Imitatio Rabbini." *JSJ* 17 (1986): 70–79.

Knoppers, Gary N. "'There Was None Like Him': Incomparability in the Book of Kings." *CBQ* 54 (1992): 411–31.

Koester, Craig R. *Symbolism in the Fourth Gospel: Meaning, Mystery, Community*. 2nd ed. Minneapolis: Fortress, 2003.

Konradt, Matthias. *Israel, Church, and the Gentiles in the Gospel of Matthew*. Translated by Kathleen Ess. Baylor-Mohr Siebeck Studies in Early Christianity. Waco, TX: Baylor University Press, 2014.

Köstenberger, Andreas J. "Jesus the Good Shepherd Who Will Also Bring Other Sheep (John 10:16): The Old Testament Background of a Familiar Metaphor." *BBR* 12 (2002): 67–96.

Kovacs, Judith L. "'Now Shall the Ruler of This World Be Driven Out': Jesus' Death as Cosmic Battle in John 12:20–36." *JBL* 114 (1995): 227–47.

Kramer, Werner. *Christ, Lord, Son of God.* Studies in Biblical Theology 50. London: SCM, 1966.

Kreitzer, L. Joseph. *Jesus and God in Paul's Eschatology.* JSNTS 19. Sheffield: JSOT Press, 1987.

Ladd, George Eldon. *A Theology of the New Testament.* 2nd ed. Grand Rapids: Eerdmans, 1998.

Lane, William L. *Hebrews 1–8.* WBC 47A. Grand Rapids: Zondervan, 1991.

Lau, Te-Li. *The Politics of Peace: Ephesians, Dio Chrysostom, and the Confucian Four Books.* NovTSup 133. Leiden: Brill, 2010.

LaVerdiere, Eugene. *Dining in the Kingdom of God: The Origins of the Eucharist in the Gospel of Luke.* Chicago: Liturgy Training, 1994.

Le Donne, Anthony. *The Historiographical Jesus: Memory, Typology, and the Son of David.* Waco, TX: Baylor University Press, 2009.

Lee, Aquila H. I. *From Messiah to Preexistent Son: Jesus' Self-Consciousness and Early Christian Exegesis of Messianic Psalms.* WUNT 2.192. Tübingen: Mohr Siebeck, 2005.

Lee, Michelle V. *Paul, the Stoics, and the Body of Christ.* SNTSMS 37. Cambridge: Cambridge University Press, 2006.

Leung, Mavis M. *The Kingship-Cross Interplay in the Gospel of John: Jesus' Death as Corroboration of His Royal Messiahship.* Eugene, OR: Wipf & Stock, 2011.

Levenson, Jon D. *Creation and the Persistence of Evil: The Jewish Drama of Divine Omnipotence.* Princeton: Princeton University Press, 1995.

———. *The Death and Resurrection of the Beloved Son: The Transformation of Child Sacrifice in Judaism and Christianity.* New Haven: Yale University Press, 1993.

Levering, Matthew. *Jesus and the Demise of Death: Resurrection, Afterlife, and the Fate of the Christian.* Waco, TX: Baylor University Press, 2012.

Levison, John R. *Portraits of Adam in Early Judaism: From Sirach to 2 Baruch.* JSPSup 1. Sheffield: JSOT Press, 1988.

Lierman, John. "The Mosaic Pattern of John's Christology." Pages 210–34 in *Challenging Perspectives on the Gospel of John.* Edited by John Lierman. WUNT 2.219. Tübingen: Mohr Siebeck, 2006.

Lincoln, Andrew T. *Paradise Now and Not Yet: Studies in the Role of the Heav-*

enly Dimension in Paul's Thought with Special Reference to His Eschatology.
SNTSMS 43. Cambridge: Cambridge University Press, 1991.

———. "A Re-examination of 'the Heavenlies in Ephesians." NTS 19 (1972–73):
468–83.

———. *Truth on Trial: The Lawsuit Motif in the Fourth Gospel.* Peabody, MA: Hendrickson, 2000.

Litwa, M. David. *IEUS DEUS: The Early Christian Depiction of Jesus as a Mediterranean God.* Minneapolis: Fortress, 2014.

———. *We Are Being Transformed: Deification in Paul's Soteriology.* BZNW. Berlin:
de Gruyter, 2012.

Longenecker, Richard N. *Galatians.* WBC 41. Grand Rapids: Zondervan, 1990.

Luz, Ulrich. *Matthew 1–7: A Commentary.* Translated by Wilhelm C. Linss. Minneapolis: Augsburg, 1989.

Lynch, Matthew J. *Monotheism and Institutions in the Book of Chronicles: Temple, Priesthood, and Kingship in Post-exilic Perspective.* FAT 2.64. Tübingen:
Mohr Siebeck, 2014.

Macaskill, Grant. "Autism Spectrum Disorders and the New Testament: Preliminary Reflections." *Journal of Disability and Religion* 22 (2018): 15–41.

———. *Union with Christ in the New Testament.* Oxford: Oxford University Press,
2013.

MacDonald, Nathan. "Israel and the Old Testament Story in Irenaeus's Presentation of the Rule of Faith." *JTI* 3 (2009): 281–98.

Mackie, Scott D. "Confession of the Son of God in Hebrews." *NTS* 53 (2007):
114–29.

Maier, Harry O. *Picturing Paul in Empire: Imperial Image, Text and Persuasion in Colossians, Ephesians and the Pastoral Letters.* London: Bloomsbury T&T
Clark, 2013.

———. "A Sly Civility: Colossians and Empire." *JSNT* 27 (205): 323–49.

Malbon, Elizabeth Struthers. *Mark's Jesus: Characterization as Narrative Christology.* Waco, TX: Baylor University Press, 2009.

Marcus, Joel. "Crucifixion as Parodic Exaltation." *JBL* 125 (2006): 73–87.

———. *Mark 1–8.* AYB 27. New York: Doubleday, 2000.

———. *Mark 8–16.* AYB 27A. New Haven: Yale University Press, 2009.

———. "'The Time Has Been Fulfilled!' (Mark 1:15)." Pages 49–68 in *Apocalyptic and the New Testament: Essays in Honor of J. Louis Martyn.* Edited by Joel
Marcus and Marion L. Soards. JSNTSup 24. Sheffield: Sheffield Academic
Press, 1989.

———. *The Way of the Lord: Christological Exegesis of the Old Testament in the Gospel of Mark.* Louisville: Westminster John Knox, 1992.

Marossy, Michael. "The Rule of the Resurrected Messiah: Kingship Discourse in 2 Timothy 2:8–13." *CBQ* 82 (2020): 84–100.

Martin, Dale B. *Biblical Truths: The Meaning of Scripture in the Twenty-First Century*. New Haven: Yale University Press, 2017.

———. *The Corinthian Body*. New Haven: Yale University Press, 1995.

———. *Slavery as Salvation: The Metaphor of Slavery in Pauline Christianity*. New Haven: Yale University Press, 1990.

Martyn, J. Louis. "Apocalyptic Antinomies." Pages 111–24 in *Theological Issues in the Letters of Paul*. Nashville: Abingdon, 1997.

———. "Christ and the Elements of the Cosmos." Pages 125–40 in *Theological Issues in the Letters of Paul*. Nashville: Abingdon, 1997.

———. *Galatians*. AYB 33A. New York: Doubleday, 1997.

———. *History and Theology in the Fourth Gospel*. 3rd ed. Louisville: Westminster John Knox, 2003.

Mason, Eric F. "Heavenly Revelation in the Epistle to the Hebrews." Pages 277–91 in *The Jewish Apocalyptic Tradition and the Shaping of New Testament Thought*. Edited by Benjamin E. Reynolds and Loren T. Stuckenbruck. Minneapolis: Fortress, 2017.

———. *"You Are a Priest Forever": Second Temple Jewish Messianism and the Priestly Christology of the Epistle to the Hebrews*. STDJ 74. Leiden: Brill, 2008.

Matera, Frank J. *II Corinthians: A Commentary*. NTL. Louisville: Westminster John Knox, 2003.

———. *The Kingship of Jesus: Composition and Theology in Mark 15*. SBLSDS 66. Chico, CA: Scholars Press, 1982.

Mays, James L. "'In a Vision': The Portrayal of the Messiah in the Psalms." *Ex auditu* 7 (1991):1–8.

———. *The Lord Reigns: A Theological Handbook to the Psalms*. Louisville: Westminster John Knox, 1994.

McBride, S. Dean. "Polity of the Covenant People: The Book of Deuteronomy." *Int* 41 (1987): 229–44.

McCaulley, Esau. *Sharing in the Son's Inheritance: Davidic Messianism and Paul's Worldwide Interpretation of the Abrahamic Land Promise in Galatians*. LNTS 608. London: T&T Clark, 2019.

McDonough, Sean M. *Christ as Creator: Origins of a New Testament Doctrine*. Oxford: Oxford University Press, 2009.

McFague, Sallie. *Models of God: Theology for an Ecological, Nuclear Age*. Philadelphia: Fortress, 1987.

McGrath, James F. "The Gospel of John as Jewish Messianism: Formative Influences and Neglected Avenues in the History of Scholarship." Pages 43–65 in *Reading the Gospel of John's Christology as Jewish Messianism: Royal, Prophetic, and Divine Messiahs.* Edited by Benjamin E. Reynolds and Gabrielle Boccaccini. Ancient Judaism and Early Christianity 106. Leiden: Brill, 2018.

McGuckin, John A. *St. Cyril of Alexandria: The Christological Controversy.* VCSup. Leiden: Brill, 1994.

McKnight, Scot. *The King Jesus Gospel: The Original Good News Revisited.* Grand Rapids: Zondervan, 2011.

———. *The Letter of James.* NICNT. Grand Rapids: Eerdmans, 2011.

McNeil, Brian. "The Quotation at John XII.34." *NovT* 19 (1977): 22–33.

McWhirter, Jocelyn. "Messianic Exegesis in the Fourth Gospel." Pages 124–48 in *Reading the Gospel of John's Christology as Jewish Messianism.* Edited by Benjamin Reynolds and Gabriele Boccaccini. Leiden: Brill, 2018.

Meeks, Wayne A. *The First Urban Christians: The Social World of the Apostle Paul.* New Haven: Yale University Press, 1983.

———. "The Man from Heaven in Paul's Letter to the Philippians." Pages 329–36 in *The Future of Early Christianity: Essays in Honor of Helmut Koester.* Edited by Birger Pearson. Minneapolis: Fortress, 1991.

———. "Moses as God and King." Pages 354–71 in *Religions in Antiquity.* Edited by Jacob Neusner. Leiden: Brill, 1968.

———. *The Origins of Christian Morality: The First Two Centuries.* New Haven: Yale University Press, 1993.

———. *The Prophet-King: Moses Traditions and the Johannine Christology.* NovTSup 14. Leiden: Brill, 1967.

———. "'To Walk Worthily of the Lord': Moral Formation in the Pauline School Exemplified by the Letter to the Colossians." Pages 37–58 in *Hermes and Athena: Biblical Exegesis and Philosophical Theology.* Edited by Eleonore Stump and Thomas P. Flint. Notre Dame: University of Notre Dame Press, 1993.

Meier, John P. "From Elijah-Like Prophet to Royal Davidic Messiah." Pages 45–83 in *Jesus: A Colloquium in the Holy Land.* Edited by Doris Donnelly. London: Continuum, 2001.

———. "Symmetry and Theology in the Old Testament Citations of Heb. 1:5–14." *Bib* 66 (1985): 504–33.

Menn, Esther Marie. *Judah and Tamar (Genesis 38) in Ancient Jewish Exegesis: Studies in Literary Form and Hermeneutics.* Supplements to the Journal for the Study of Judaism 51. Leiden: Brill, 1997.

Mettinger, Tryggve N. D. *King and Messiah: The Civil and Sacral Legitimation of the Israelite Kings.* ConBOT 8. Lund: Gleerup, 1976.

Michel, O. *Der Brief an die Hebräer.* Göttingen: Vandenhoek & Ruprecht, 1984.

Middleton, J. Richard. *The Liberating Image: The Imago Dei in Genesis 1.* Grand Rapids: Brazos, 2005.

Miller, Patrick D. "The Beginning of the Psalter." Pages 83–92 in *The Shape and Shaping of the Psalter*. Edited by J. Clinton McCann. JSOTSup 159. Sheffield: JSOT Press, 1993.

———. "Kingship, Torah Obedience and Prayer." Pages 127–42 in *Neue Wege der Psalmenforschung*. Edited by K. Seybold and E. Zenger. Freiburg: Herder, 1995.

Minns, Denis, and Paul Parvis, eds. *Justin, Philosopher and Martyr: Apologies*. Oxford: Oxford University Press, 2009.

Mitchell, Alan C. "The Social Function of Friendship in Acts 2:44–47 and 4:32–37." *JBL* 111 (1992): 255–72.

Mitchell, Margaret M. *Paul and the Rhetoric of Reconciliation: An Exegetical Investigation of the Language and Composition of 1 Corinthians*. Louisville: Westminster John Knox, 1991.

Miura, Yuzuru. *David in Luke-Acts: His Portrayal in the Light of Early Judaism*. WUNT 2.232. Tübingen: Mohr Siebeck, 2007.

Moffitt, David M. *Atonement and the Logic of Resurrection in the Epistle to the Hebrews*. NovTSup 141. Leiden: Brill, 2011.

———. "'If Another Priest Arises': Jesus' Resurrection and the High Priestly Christology of Hebrews." Pages 68–79 in *The Cloud of Witnesses*. Edited by Richard Bauckham et al. London: T&T Clark, 2008.

Moloney, Francis J. *Love in the Gospel of John: An Exegetical, Theological, and Literary Study*. Grand Rapids: Baker Academic, 2013.

Moo, Douglas J. *The Epistle to the Romans*. NICNT. Grand Rapids: Eerdmans, 1996.

———. "Israel and Paul in Romans 7.7–12." *NTS* 32 (1986): 122–35.

Morales, Isaac Augustine. "Baptism and Union with Christ." Pages 157–79 in *"In Christ" in Paul: Explorations in Paul's Theological Vision of Participation*. Edited by Michael J. Thate et al. Tübingen: Mohr Siebeck. 2014.

Morgan, Teresa. *Roman Faith and Christian Faith: Pistis and Fides in the Early Roman Empire and Early Churches*. Oxford: Oxford University Press, 2015.

Moss, Charlene McAfee. *The Zechariah Tradition and the Gospel of Matthew*. BZNW 156. Berlin: de Gruyter, 2008.

Moule, C. F. D. "Fulfilment Words in the New Testament: Use and Abuse." *NTS* 14 (1967–68): 293–320.

———. *The Origin of Christology*. Cambridge: Cambridge University Press, 1977.

Mowinckel, Sigmund. *He That Cometh: The Messiah Concept in the Old Testament and Later Judaism*. Translated by G. W. Anderson. Grand Rapids: Eerdmans, 2005.

———. *The Psalms in Israel's Worship*. Rev. ed. Translated by D. R. Ap-Thomas. 2 vols. Grand Rapids: Eerdmans, 2004.

Moyise, Steve. "The Psalms in the Book of Revelation." Pages 231–46 in *The Psalms in the New Testament.* Edited by Steve Moyise and Maarten J. J. Menken. The New Testament and the Scriptures of Israel. London: T&T Clark, 2004.

Myers, Alicia D. "Isaiah 42 and the Characterization of Jesus in Matthew 12:17–21." Pages 70–89 in *The Synoptic Gospels*. Vol. 1 of *'What Does the Scripture Say'? Studies in the Function of Scripture in Early Judaism and Christianity*. Edited by Craig A. Evans and H. Daniel Zacharias. London: T&T Clark, 2012.

Nasrallah, Laura Salah. *Christian Responses to Roman Art and Architecture: The Second-Century Church Amid the Spaces of Empire*. Cambridge: Cambridge University Press, 2010.

Neagoe, Alexandru. *The Trial of the Gospel: An Apologetic Reading of Luke's Trial Narratives*. SNTSMS 116. Cambridge: Cambridge University Press, 2002.

Nelson, Richard D. "Josiah in the Book of Joshua." *JBL* 100 (1981): 531–40.

Neusner, Jacob, William Scott Green, and Ernest Frerichs, eds. *Judaisms and Their Messiahs at the Turn of the Christian Era*. Cambridge: Cambridge University Press, 1987.

Neyrey, Jerome H. "'First,' 'Only,' 'One of a Few,' and 'No One Else': The Rhetoric of Uniqueness and the Doxologies in 1 Timothy." *Bib* 86 (2005): 59–87.

Nicholson, Godfrey C. *Death as Departure: The Johannine Descent-Ascent Schema*. SBLDS. Chico, CA: Scholars Press, 1983.

Nicolaci, Marida. "Divine Kingship and Jesus's Identity in Johannine Messianism." Pages 178–202 in *Reading the Gospel of John's Christology as Jewish Messianism: Royal, Prophetic, and Divine Messiahs*. Edited by Benjamin Reynolds and Gabriele Boccaccini. Leiden: Brill, 2018.

Novakovic, Lidija. "Jesus as the Davidic Messiah in Matthew." *HBT* 19 (1997): 148–91.

———. *Messiah, the Healer of the Sick: A Study of Jesus as the Son of David in the Gospel of Matthew*. WUNT 2.170. Tübingen: Mohr Siebeck, 2003.

———. *Raised from the Dead according to Scripture: The Role of Israel's Scripture in the Early Christian Interpretations of Jesus' Resurrection*. Jewish and Christian Texts Series 12. London: T&T Clark, 2012.

Novenson, Matthew V. *Christ among the Messiahs: Christ Language in Paul and Messiah Language in Ancient Judaism*. Oxford: Oxford University Press, 2012.

———. *The Grammar of Messianism: An Ancient Jewish Political Idiom and Its Users*. Oxford: Oxford University Press, 2017.

———. "Jesus the Messiah: Conservativism and Radicalism in Johannine Christology." Pages 109–23 in *Portraits of Jesus in the Gospel of John: A Christological Spectrum*. Edited by Craig Koester. LNTS 589. London: T&T Clark, 2018.

Oakes, Peter. *Philippians: From People to Letter*. SNTSMS 110. Cambridge: Cambridge University Press, 2001.

———. "Re-mapping the Universe: Paul and the Emperor in 1 Thessalonians and Philippians." *JSNT* 27 (2005): 301–22.

O'Donovan, Oliver. *The Desire of the Nations: Rediscovering the Roots of Political Theology*. Cambridge: Cambridge University Press, 1996.

Origen. *Homilies on Luke, Fragments of Luke*. Translated by Joseph T. Lienhard. Washington, DC: The Catholic University of America Press, 1996.

Osborne, Grant R. *Revelation*. BECNT. Grand Rapids: Baker Academic, 2002.

O'Toole, Robert F. "Acts 2:30 and the Davidic Covenant of Pentecost." *JBL* 102 (1983): 245–58.

———. *Acts 26, The Christological Climax of Paul's Defense (Ac 22:1–26:32)*. AnBib 78. Rome: Pontifical Biblical Institutes Press, 1978.

Painter, John. *The Quest for the Messiah: The History, Literature and Theology of the Johannine Community*. 2nd ed. Nashville: Abingdon, 1993.

Pao, David W. *Acts and the Isaianic New Exodus*. WUNT 2.130. Tübingen: Mohr Siebeck, 2000.

———. *Colossians and Philemon. Exegetical Commentary on the New Testament*. Grand Rapids: Zondervan, 2012.

Pennington, Jonathan T. *Heaven and Earth in the Gospel of Matthew*. NovTSup 126. Leiden: Brill, 2007.

———. *The Sermon on the Mount and Human Flourishing: A Theological Commentary*. Grand Rapids: Baker Academic, 2017.

Peppard, Michael. *The Son of God in the Roman World: Divine Sonship in Its Social and Political Context*. Oxford: Oxford University Press, 2011.

Perkins, Pheme. "Philippians: Theology for the Heavenly Politeuma." Pages 89–104 in *Thessalonians, Philippians, Galatians, Philemon*. Vol. 1 of *Pauline Theology*. Edited by Jouette M. Bassler. Minneapolis: Fortress, 1991.

Perrin, Nicholas. *Jesus the Temple*. Grand Rapids: Baker Academic, 2010.

———. *The Kingdom of God: A Biblical Theology*. Grand Rapids: Zondervan, 2019.

Peterson, David. *Hebrews and Perfection: An Examination of the Concept of Perfection in the Epistle to the Hebrews*. SNTSMS 47. Cambridge: Cambridge University Press, 1982.

Pierce, Madison N. *Divine Discourse in the Epistle to the Hebrews: The Recontextualization of Spoken Quotations of Scripture*. SNTSMS. Cambridge: Cambridge University Press, 2020.

Pifer, Jeanette Hagen. *Faith as Participation: An Exegetical Study of Some Key Pauline Texts*. WUNT 2.486. Tübingen: Mohr Siebeck, 2019.

Piotrowski, Nicholas G. "'After the Deportation': Observations in Matthew's Apocalyptic Genealogy." *BBR* 25 (2015): 189–203.

———. *Matthew's New David at the End of Exile: A Socio-rhetorical Study of Scriptural Quotations.* NovTSup 170. Leiden: Brill, 2016.

Pitre, Brant. *Jesus and the Last Supper.* Grand Rapids: Eerdmans, 2015.

Pomykala, Kenneth. *The Davidic Dynasty Tradition in Early Judaism: Its History and Significance for Messianism.* SBLEJL 7. Atlanta: Scholars Press, 1995.

Porter, J. R. "The Succession of Joshua." Pages 102–32 in *Proclamation and Presence: Old Testament Essays in Honour of Gwynne Henton Davies.* Edited by J. R. Porter and J. I. Durham. London: SCM, 1970.

Porterfield, Amanda. *Healing in the History of Christianity.* Oxford: Oxford University Press, 2005.

Portier-Young, Anathea E. *Apocalypse against Empire: Theologies of Resistance in Early Judaism.* Grand Rapids: Eerdmans, 2011.

Price, S. R. F. "Between Man and God." *JRS* (1980): 28–43

———. "Gods and Emperors: The Greek Language of the Roman Imperial Cult." *JHS* 104 (1984): 79–95.

———. *Rituals and Power: The Roman Imperial Cult in Asia Minor.* Cambridge: Cambridge University Press, 1984.

Pusey, P. E., ed. *In Joannis Evangelium.* 2 vols. Oxford: Clarendon, 1872.

Rabens, Volker. *The Holy Spirit and Ethics in Paul: Transformation and Empowering for Religious-Ethical Life.* 2nd ed. Minneapolis: Fortress, 2014.

Rad, Gerhard von. *The Theology of Israel's Historical Traditions.* Vol. 1 of Old Testament Theology. New York: Harper and Row, 1962.

Räisänen, Heikki. *Beyond New Testament Theology: A Story and a Programme.* London: SCM, 1990.

Rajak, Tessa, Sarah Pearce, James Aitken, and Jennifer Dines, eds. *Jewish Perspectives on Hellenistic Rulers.* Berkeley: University of California Press, 2007.

Reinhartz, Adele. "The Lyin' King? Deception and Christology in the Gospel of John." Pages 117–33 in *Johannine Ethics: The Moral Word of the Gospel and Epistles of John.* Edited by Sherri Brown and Christopher W. Skinner. Minneapolis: Fortress, 2018.

Repschinski, Boris. "'For He Will Save His People from Their Sins' (Matthew 1:21): A Christology for Christian Jews." *CBQ* 68 (2006): 248–67.

Rese, Martin. *Alttestamentliche Motive in der Christologie des Lukas.* SZNT 1. Gütersloh: Mohn, 1969.

Reuman, John. *Philippians: A New Translation with Introduction and Commentary.* AYB 33B. New Haven: Yale University Press, 2008.

Reynolds, Benjamin E. *The Apocalyptic Son of Man in the Gospel of John*. WUNT 2.249. Tübingen: Mohr Siebeck, 2008.

———. "The Gospel of John's Christology as Evidence for Early Jewish Messianic Expectations: Challenges and Possibilities." Pages 13–42 in *Reading the Gospel of John's Christology as Jewish Messianism*. Edited by Benjamin Reynolds and Gabriele Boccaccini. Leiden: Brill, 2018.

Richardson, Christopher A. *Pioneer and Perfecter of Faith: Jesus' Faith as the Climax of Israel's History in the Epistle to the Hebrews*. WUNT 2.286. Tübingen: Mohr Siebeck, 2012.

Riedl, Matthias. "Apocalyptic Violence and Revolutionary Action: Thomas Müntzer's *Sermon to the Princes*." Pages 260–96 in *A Companion to the Premodern Apocalypse*. Edited by Michael A. Ryan. Brill's Companions to the Christian Tradition 64. Leiden: Brill, 2016.

Rindge, Matthew S. "Reconfiguring the Akedah and Recasting God: Lament and Divine Abandonment in Mark." *JBL* 130 (2011): 755–74.

Rogers, Trent. "The Great Commission as the Climax of Matthew's Mountain Scenes." *BBR* 22 (2012): 383–98.

Roueche, Charlotte. "Acclamations in the Later Roman Empire: New Evidence from Aphrodisias." *JRS* 74 (1984): 181–99.

Rowe, C. Kavin. *Early Narrative Christology: The Lord in the Gospel of Luke*. Grand Rapids: Baker Academic, 2009.

———. *World Upside Down: Reading Acts in the Graeco-Roman Age*. Oxford: Oxford University Press, 2009.

Rowe, Christopher. "The *Politicus* and Other Dialogues." Pages 254–61 in *The Cambridge History of Greek and Roman Political Thought*. Edited by Christopher Rowe and Malcolm Schofield. Cambridge: Cambridge University Press, 2005.

Rowe, Robert D. *God's Kingdom and God's Son: The Background to Mark's Christology from Concepts of Kingship in the Psalms*. Leiden: Brill, 2002.

Rowland, Christopher. "Apocalyptic Visions and the Exaltation of Christ in the Letter to the Colossians." *JSNT* 19 (1983): 73–83.

Rudolph, David. *A Jew to the Jews: Jewish Contours of Pauline Flexibility in 1 Corinthians 9:19–23*. WUNT 2.304. Tübingen: Mohr Siebeck, 2011.

Runesson, Anders. *Divine Wrath and Salvation in Matthew: The Narrative World of the First Gospel*. Minneapolis: Fortress, 2016.

Sanders, E. P. *Paul, the Law, and the Jewish People*. Minneapolis: Fortress, 1983.

Schaper, Joachim. *Eschatology in the Greek Psalter*. WUNT 2.76. Tübingen: Mohr Siebeck, 1995.

Scheck, Thomas P. *Origen: Commentary on the Epistle to the Romans Books 1–5.* Washington, DC: The Catholic University of America Press, 2001.

Schedtler, Justin Jeffcoat. "The Beast or the Lamb in the Apocalypse to John: Will the Real Emperor Please Stand up?" Pages 143–60 in *Apocalypses in Context: Apocalyptic Currents through History.* Edited by Kelly J. Murphy and Justin Jeffcoat Schedtler. Minneapolis: Fortress, 2016.

———. *A Heavenly Chorus: The Dramatic Function of Revelation's Hymns.* WUNT 2.381. Tübingen: Mohr Siebeck, 2014.

———. *The Last King: Royal Ideologies in the Book of Revelation.* Forthcoming.

———. "Praising Christ the King: Royal Discourse and Ideology in Revelation 5." *NovT* 60 (2018): 162–82.

Schenk, Kenneth L. "A Celebration of the Enthroned Son." *JBL* 123 (2001): 469–85

———. *Cosmology and Eschatology in Hebrews: The Settings of the Sacrifice.* SNTSMS 143. Cambridge: Cambridge University Press, 2007.

———. "Keeping his Appointment: Creation and Enthronement in Hebrews." *JSNT* 66 (1997): 91–117.

Schlatter, Adolf. *Romans: The Righteousness of God.* Peabody, MA: Hendrickson, 1995.

Schmidt, T. E. "Mark 15.16–32: The Crucifixion Narrative and the Roman Triumphal Procession." *NTS* 41 (1995): 1–18.

Schniedewind, William M. *Society and the Promise to David: The Reception History of 2 Samuel 7:1–17.* Oxford: Oxford University Press, 1999.

Schreiber, Stefan. *Gesalbter und König: Titel and Konzeptionen der königlichen Gesalbtenerwartung in früjüdischen und urchristlichen Schriften.* BZNW 105. Berlin: de Gruyter, 2000.

———. "Rätsel um den König: Zur religionsgeschichtlichen Herkunft des König-Titels im Johannesevangelium." Pages 45–70 in *Johannes Aenigmaticus: Studien zum Johannesevangelium für Herbert Leroy.* Biblische Untersuchungen 29. Regensburg: Friedrich Pustet.

Schreiner, Patrick R. *Matthew, Disciple and Scribe: The First Gospel and Its Portrait of Jesus.* Grand Rapids: Baker Academic, 2019.

Schröter, Jens. *Jesus of Nazareth: Jew from Galilee, Savior of the World.* Translated by Wayne Coppins. Waco, TX: Baylor University Press, 2015.

Schüssler Fiorenza, Elisabeth. *Jesus: Miriam's Child, Sophia's Prophet: Critical Issues in Feminist Christology.* 2nd ed. London: T&T Clark, 2015.

———. *Revelation: Vision of a Just World.* Minneapolis: Fortress, 1991.

Schweitzer, Albert. *The Mysticism of Paul the Apostle.* Translated by William Montgomery. 1931. Reprint, Baltimore: The Johns Hopkins University Press, 1998.

Scott, James M. *Adoption as Sons of God: An Exegetical Investigation into the Back-*

ground of ΥΙΟΘΕΣΙΑ in the Pauline Corpus. WUNT 2.48. Tübingen: Mohr Siebeck, 1992.

Scroggs, Robin. *The Last Adam: A Study in Pauline Theology.* Philadelphia: Fortress, 1966.

———. "Paul: Myth Remaker. The Refashioning of Early Ecclesial Traditions." Pages 87–101 in *Pauline Conversations in Context: Essays in Honor of Calvin J. Roetzel.* Edited by Janice Capel Anderson, Philip Sellew, and Claudia Setzer. JSNTSup 221. Sheffield: Sheffield Academic Press, 2002.

Seal, David. "The Background of the Philippians Hymn (2:6–11)." *Journal of Higher Criticism* 1 (1994): 49–72.

———. "Shouting in the Apocalypse: The Influence of First-Century Acclamations on the Praise Utterances in Revelation 4:8 and 11." *JETS* 51 (2008): 339–52.

Shauf, Scott. *The Divine in Acts and in Ancient Historiography.* Minneapolis: Fortress, 2015.

Sherman, Robert. *King, Priest, and Prophet: A Trinitarian Theology of Atonement.* London: T&T Clark, 2004.

Shively, Elizabeth E. *Apocalyptic Imagination in the Gospel of Mark: The Literary and Theological Role of Mark 3:22–30.* BZNW 189. Berlin: de Gruyter, 2012.

Short, J. Randall. *The Surprising Election and Confirmation of King David.* HTS 63. Cambridge: Harvard University Press, 2010.

Siliezar, Carlos Raul Sosa. *Savior of the World: A Theology of the Universal Gospel.* Waco, TX: Baylor University Press, 2019.

Skarsaune, Oskar. "Jewish Christian Sources Used by Justin Martyr and Other Greek and Latin Fathers." Pages 379–416 in *Jewish Believers in Jesus: The Early Centuries.* Peabody, MA: Hendrickson, 2007.

Skinner, Christopher W. "'The Good Shepherd Lays Down His Life for the Sheep' (John 10:11, 15, 17): Questioning the Limits of a Johannine Metaphor." *CBQ* 80 (2018): 97–113.

Skinner, Matthew. "Who Speaks for or against Rome? Acts in Relation to Empire." Pages 107–25 in *Reading Acts in the Discourse of Masculinity and Politics.* LNTS 559. London: T&T Clark, 2017.

Slater, Thomas B. *Christ and Community: A Socio-historical Study of the Christology of Revelation.* JSNTSup 178. Sheffield: Sheffield Academic Press, 1999.

Sleeman, Matthew. *Geography and the Ascensions Narrative in Acts.* SNTSMS 146. Cambridge: Cambridge University Press, 2009.

Smalley, Stephen S. *1, 2, 3 John.* WBC 51. Waco, TX: Word, 1984.

Smith, Dennis E. *From Symposium to Eucharist: The Banquet in the Early Christian World.* Minneapolis: Fortress, 2003.

Smith, Ian. *Heavenly Perspective: A Study of the Apostle Paul's Response to a Jewish Mystical Movement at Colossae*. LNTS 326. London: T&T Clark, 2006.

Smith, Julien. *Christ the Ideal King: Cultural Context, Rhetorical Strategy, and the Power of Divine Monarchy in Ephesians*. WUNT 2.313. Tübingen: Mohr Siebeck, 2011.

Smith, Shively T. J. *Strangers to Family: Diaspora and 1 Peter's Invention of God's Household*. Waco, TX: Baylor University Press, 2016.

Soulen, R. Kendall. *The Divine Name(s) and the Holy Trinity: Distinguishing the Voices*. Louisville: Westminster John Knox, 2011.

———. *The God of Israel and Christian Theology*. Minneapolis: Fortress, 1996.

Southall, David J. *Rediscovering Righteousness in Romans: Personified dikaiosyne within Metaphoric and Narratorial Settings*. WUNT 2.240. Tübingen: Mohr Siebeck, 2008.

Souza, Philip de. "*Parta victoriis pax*: Roman Emperors as Peacemakers." Pages 76–106 in *War and Peace in Ancient and Medieval History*. Edited by Philip de Souza and John France. Cambridge: Cambridge University Press, 2008.

Spilsbury, Paul. "The Apocalypse." Pages 136–46 in *Redemption and Resistance: The Messianic Hopes of Jews and Christians in Antiquity*. Edited by Markus Bockmuehl and James Carleton Paget. London: T&T Clark, 2007.

Stanton, Graham. "Messianism and Christology: Mark, Matthew, Luke and Acts." Pages 237–59 in *Studies in Matthew and Early Christianity*. Edited by Markus Bockmuehl and David Lincicum. WUNT 309. Tübingen: Mohr Siebeck, 2013.

Stegman, Thomas D. "Ἐπίστευσα, διὸ ἐλάλησα (2 Corinthians 4:13): Paul's Christological Reading of Psalm 115:1a LXX." *CBQ* 69 (2007): 725–45.

Stevenson, Gregory M. "Conceptual Background to the Golden Crown Imagery in the Apocalypse of John 4:4, 10; 14:14." *JBL* 114 (1995): 257–72.

Stovell, Beth M. "Son of God as Anointed One? Johannine Davidic Christology and Second Temple Messianism." Pages 151–75 in *Reading the Gospel of John's Christology as Jewish Messianism*. Edited by Benjamin E. Reynolds and Gabriele Boccaccini. Leiden: Brill, 2018.

Stowers, S. K. "What Is 'Pauline Participation in Christ'?" Pages 352–71 in *Redefining First-Century Jewish and Christian Identities*. Edited by F. E. Udoh. Notre Dame: University of Notre Dame Press, 2008.

Strauss, Mark L. *The Davidic Messiah in Luke-Acts: The Promise and Its Fulfillment in Lukan Christology*. JSNTSup 110. Sheffield: Sheffield Academic Press, 1995.

Strecker, Georg. *Theology of the New Testament*. Translated by M. Eugene Boring. Louisville: Westminster John Knox; Berlin: Walter de Gruyter, 2000.

Stuhlmacher, Peter. *Biblical Theology of the New Testament*. Grand Rapids: Eerdmans, 2018.

———. *Reconciliation, Law, & Righteousness: Essays in Biblical Theology*. Philadelphia: Fortress, 1986.

Suggs, M. Jack. *Wisdom, Christology and Law in Matthew's Gospel*. Cambridge, MA: Harvard University Press, 1970.

Swartley, Willard M. *Health, Healing and the Church's Mission: Biblical Perspectives and Moral Priorities*. Downers Grove, IL: InterVarsity Press, 2012.

Tannehill, Robert C. *Dying and Rising with Christ: A Study in Pauline Theology*. BZNW. Berlin: de Gruyter, 1967.

Tanner, Kathryn. *Christ the Key*. Cambridge: Cambridge University Press, 2010.

Taubes, Jacob. *The Political Theology of Paul*. Translated by Dana Hollander. Stanford: Stanford University Press, 2004.

Tellbe, Mikael. *Paul between Synagogue and State: Christians, Jews, and Civic Authorities in 1 Thessalonians, Romans, and Philippians*. Stockholm: Almqvist & Wiksell International, 2001.

Thatcher, Tom. *Greater than Caesar: Christology and Empire in the Fourth Gospel*. Minneapolis: Fortress, 2009.

Thate, Michael J. "Paul at the Ball: *Ecclesia Victor* and the Cosmic Defeat of Personified Evil in Romans 16:20." Pages 151–69 in *Paul's World*. Edited by Stanley Porter. Pauline Studies 4. Leiden: Brill, 2007.

Thiessen, Matthew. "The Many for One or the One for Many: Reading Mark 10:45 in the Roman Empire." *HTR* 109 (2016): 447–66.

———. *Paul and the Gentile Problem*. Oxford: Oxford University Press, 2016.

Thompson, Alan J. *The Acts of the Risen Lord Jesus: Luke's Account of God's Unfolding Plan*. NSBT 27. Downers Grove, IL: InterVarsity Press, 2011.

Thompson, James W. *Moral Formation according to Paul: The Context and Coherence of Pauline Ethics*. Grand Rapids: Baker Academic, 2011.

———. "The Structure and Purpose of the Catena in Heb 1:5–13." *CBQ* 38 (1976): 352–63

Thompson, Leonard. "Hymns in Early Christian Worship." *ATR* 55 (1973): 458–72.

Thompson, Michael. *Clothed with Christ: The Example and Teaching of Jesus in Romans 12.1–15.13*. JSNTSup 59. Sheffield: JSOT Press, 1991.

Thrall, Margaret. *2 Corinthians 1–7*. ICC. London: T&T Clark, 1994.

Tilling, Chris. *Paul's Divine Christology*. WUNT 2.323. Tübingen: Mohr Siebeck, 2012.

Torrance, Thomas F. "The Kingdom of Christ and Evil." Pages 235–56 in *Incarnation: The Person and Life of Christ*. Downers Grove, IL: InterVarsity Press, 2008.

Treat, Jeremy R. *The Crucified King: Atonement and Kingdom in Biblical and Systematic Theology*. Grand Rapids: Zondervan, 2014.

——. "Exaltation in and through Humiliation: Rethinking the States of Christ." Pages 96–114 in *Christology Ancient and Modern: Explorations in Constructive Dogmatics*. Grand Rapids: Zondervan, 2013.

Tucker, J. Brian. *"Remain in Your Calling": Paul and the Continuation of Social Identities in 1 Corinthians*. Eugene, OR: Pickwick, 2011.

VanderKam, James C. "Messianism in the Scrolls." Pages 211–34 in *The Community of the Renewed Covenant: The Notre Dame Symposium on the Dead Sea Scrolls*. Edited by Eugene Ulrich and James C. VanderKam. Notre Dame: University of Notre Dame Press, 1994.

van Kooten, George H. "Paul versus the Sophists: Outward Performance and Rhetorical Competition within the Christian Community at Corinth." Pages 245–68 in *Paul's Anthropology in Context: The Image of God, Assimilation to God, and Tripartite Man in Ancient Judaism, Ancient Philosophy and Early Christianity*. WUNT 232. Tübingen: Mohr Siebeck, 2008.

Vawter, Bruce. "Ezekiel and John." *CBQ* 26 (1964): 450–58.

Verhey, Allen. *Remembering Jesus: Christian Community, Scripture, and the Moral Life*. Grand Rapids: Eerdmans, 2002.

Versnel, H. S. *Triumphus: An Inquiry into the Origin, Development and Meaning of the Roman Triumph*. Leiden: Brill, 1970.

Vollenweider, Samuel. "Der 'Raub' Der Gottgleichheit: Ein Religionsgeschichtlicher Vorschlag zu Phil 2.6(–11)." *NTS* 45 (1999): 413–33.

Waddell, James A. *The Messiah: A Comparative Study of the Enochic Son of Man and the Pauline Kyrios*. Jewish and Christian Texts Series 10. London: T&T Clark, 2011.

Wagner, J. Ross. "Psalm 118 in Luke-Acts: Tracing a Narrative Thread." Pages 154–78 in *Early Christian Interpretation of the Scriptures of Israel: Investigations and Proposals*. Edited by C. A. Evans and J. A. Sanders. SSEJC. Sheffield: Sheffield Academic Press, 1997.

Walker, Donald Dale. *Paul's Offer of Leniency (2 Cor 10:1): Populist Ideology and Rhetoric in a Pauline Letter Fragment*. WUNT 2.152. Tübingen: Mohr Siebeck, 2002.

Wallace-Hadrill, Andrew. "The Emperor and His Virtues." *Historia* 30 (1981): 298–323.

Wasserman, Emma. "The Death of the Soul in Romans 7: Revisiting Paul's Anthropology in Light of Hellenistic Moral Psychology." *JBL* 126 (2007): 793–816.

Wasserman, Tommy. "The 'Son of God' Was in the Beginning (Mark 1:1)." *JTS* 62 (2011): 20–50.

Watson, Francis. *The Fourfold Gospel: A Theological Reading of the New Testament Portraits of Jesus*. Grand Rapids: Baker Academic, 2016.

Watts, Rikki E. *Isaiah's New Exodus in Mark*. Grand Rapids: Baker, 1997.

Weaver, Dorothy Jean. "Rewriting the Messianic Script: Matthew's Account of the Birth of Jesus." Pages 125–36 in *The Irony of Power: The Politics of God within Matthew's Narrative*. Eugene, OR: Pickwick, 2017.

———. "'What Is That to Us? See to It Yourself': Making Atonement and the Matthean Portrait of the Jewish Chief Priests." Pages 66–84 in *The Irony of Power: The Politics of God within Matthew's Narrative*. Eugene, OR: Pickwick, 2017.

Webster, Jane S. *Ingesting Jesus: Eating and Drinking in the Gospel of John*. AcBib 6. Atlanta: Society of Biblical Literature, 2003.

Weinandy, Thomas G. "The Apostolic Christology of Ignatius of Antioch: The Road to Chalcedon." Pages 71–84 in *Trajectories through the New Testament and the Apostolic Fathers*. Edited by Andrew F. Gregory and Christopher M. Tuckett. Clarendon: Oxford University Press, 2005.

———. *Does God Suffer?* Notre Dame: University of Notre Dame Press, 2000.

———. *Jesus Becoming Jesus: A Theological Interpretation of the Synoptic Gospels*. Washington, DC: Catholic University of America Press, 2018.

Weinfeld, Moshe. *Social Justice in Ancient Israel and in the Ancient Near East*. Minneapolis: Fortress, 1995.

Weinstock, Stefan. "*Pax* and the 'Ara Pacis.'" *JRS* 50 (1960): 44–58

Westfall, Cynthia Long. "Messianic Themes of Temple, Enthronement, and Victory in Hebrews and the General Epistles." Pages 210–29 in *The Messiah in the Old and New Testaments*. Edited by Stanley E. Porter. Grand Rapids: Eerdmans, 2007.

———. "The Relationship between the Resurrection, the Proclamation to the Spirits in Prison, and Baptismal Regeneration: 1 Peter 3:19–22." Pages 106–35 in *Resurrection*. Edited by Stanley E. Porter et al. JSNTSup 186. Sheffield: Sheffield Academic Press, 1999.

White, L. Michael. "Morality between Two Worlds: A Paradigm of Friendship in Philippians." Pages 201–15 in *Greeks, Romans, and Christians*. Edited by David L. Balch, Everett Fergusson, and Wayne A. Meeks. Minneapolis: Fortress, 1990.

Whitelam, Keith W. *The Just King: Monarchical Judicial Authority in Ancient Israel*. JSOTSup 12. Sheffield: Sheffield Academic Press, 1979.

Whitsett, Christopher G. "Son of God, Seed of David: Paul's Messianic Exegesis in Romans 1:3–4." *JBL* 119 (2000): 661–81.

Wiarda, Timothy. *Spirit and Word: Dual Testimony in Paul, John and Luke*. LNTS 565. London: T&T Clark, 2017.

Widengren, Geo. "King and Covenant." *Journal of Semitic Studies* 2 (1957): 1–32.

Wifall, W. "Gen 3:15—A Protevangelium?" *CBQ* 36 (1974): 361–65.

Williams, Sam K. *Galatians*. ANTC. Nashville: Abingdon, 1997.

Williamson, H. G. M. "'The Sure Mercies of David': Subjective or Objective Genitive?" *JSS* 23 (1978): 31–49.

Willitts, Joel. "Matthew and Psalms of Solomon's Messianism: A Comparative Study in First-Century Messianology." *BBR* 22 (2012): 27–50.

———. *Matthew's Messianic Shepherd-King: In Search of "The Lost Sheep of the House of Israel."* BZNW 147. Berlin: de Gruyter, 2007.

Wilson, Gerald H. *The Editing of the Hebrew Psalter*. SBLDS 76. Chico, CA: Scholars Press, 1985.

Wilson, Todd A. "The Law of Christ and the Law of Moses: Reflections on a Recent Trend in Interpretation." *CurBS* 5 (2006): 123–44.

Wilson, Walter T. *The Hope of Glory: Education and Exhortation in the Epistle to the Colossians*. NovTSup 88. Leiden: Brill, 1997.

Winn, Adam. *The Purpose of Mark's Gospel: An Early Christian Response to Roman Imperial Propaganda*. WUNT 2.245. Tübingen: Mohr Siebeck, 2008.

———. "Tyrant or Servant: Roman Political Ideology and Mark 10.42–45." *JSNT* 36 (2014): 325–52.

Witherington, Ben, III. *Jesus the Sage: The Pilgrimage of Wisdom*. Minneapolis: Fortress, 1994.

Woan, Sue. "The Psalms in 1 Peter." Pages 213–29 in *The Psalms in the New Testament*. Edited by Steve Moyise and M. J. J. Menken. The New Testament and the Scriptures of Israel. London: T&T Clark, 2004.

Wolter, Michael. *The Gospel according to Luke: Volume 1 (Luke 1–9:50)*. Translated by Wayne Coppins and Christoph Heilig. Waco, TX: Baylor University Press, 2016.

Wrede, William. *Das Messiasgeheimnis in den Evangelien: Zugleich ein Beitrag zum Verständnis des Markusevangeliums*. Göttingen: Vandenhoeck & Ruprecht, 1901.

———. *Paul*. Translated by E. Lummis. London: Green & Hull, Elson, 1907.

———. *The Messianic Secret*. Translated by J. C. C. Grieg. Cambridge: James Clarke, 1971.

———. "The Task and Methods of 'New Testament Theology.'" Pages 68–116 in *The Nature of New Testament Theology: The Contribution of William Wrede and Adolf Schlatter*. Edited by Robert Morgan. Naperville, IL: Alec R. Allenson, 1973.

———. *Über Aufgabe und Methode der sogenannten Neutestamentlichen Theologie*. Göttingen: Vandenhoeck & Ruprecht, 1897.

Wright, N. T. *The Climax of the Covenant: Christ and the Law in Pauline Theology.* Minneapolis: Fortress, 1991.

———. *How God Became King: The Forgotten Story of the Gospels.* San Francisco: HarperOne, 2016.

———. *Jesus and the Victory of God.* Vol. 2 of *Christian Origins and the Question of God.* Minneapolis: Fortress, 1996.

———. "Jesus Christ Is Lord: Philippians 2.5–11." Pages 56–98 in *The Climax of the Covenant: Christ and the Law in Pauline Theology.* Minneapolis: Fortress, 1991.

———. "The Letter to the Romans." Pages 417–18 in vol. 10 of s*The New Interpreter's Bible: A Commentary in Twelve Volumes.* Nashville: Abingdon, 2002.

———. "Messiahship in Galatians?" Pages 3–23 in *Galatians and Christian Theology.* Edited by Mark W. Elliott. Grand Rapids: Eerdmans, 2014.

———. *Paul and the Faithfulness of God.* Vol. 4 of *Christian Origins and the Question of God.* Minneapolis: Fortress, 2013.

———. *The Resurrection of the Son of God.* Vol. 3 of *Christian Origins and the Question of God.* Minneapolis: Fortress, 2003.

Yamazaki-Ransom, Kazuhiko. *The Roman Empire in Luke's Narrative.* LNTS 404. London: T&T Clark, 2010.

Yoder, John Howard. "Let Every Soul Be Subject: Romans 13 and the Authority of the State." Pages 193–211 in *The Politics of Jesus: Vicit Agnus Noster.* 2nd ed. Grand Rapids: Eerdmans, 1994.

———. *The Politics of Jesus: Vicit Agnus Noster.* 2nd ed. Grand Rapids: Eerdmans, 1994.

Young, Frances, and David F. Ford. *Meaning and Truth in 2 Corinthians.* Grand Rapids: Eerdmans, 1987.

Zacharias, H. Daniel. *Matthew's Presentation of the Son of David: Davidic Tradition and Typology in the Gospel of Matthew.* London: T&T Clark, 2016.

Zanker, Paul. *The Power of Images in the Age of Augustus.* Translated by Alan Shapiro. Ann Arbor: University of Michigan Press, 1990.

Zetterholm, Magnus. "Paul and the Missing Messiah." Pages 33–55 in *The Messiah in Early Judaism and Christianity.* Edited by Magnus Zetterholm. Minneapolis: Fortress, 2007.

Ziegler, Philip G. "The Love of God Is a Sovereign Thing: The Witness of Romans 8:31–39 and the Royal Office of Jesus Christ." Pages 111–30 in *Apocalyptic Paul: Cosmos and Anthropos in Romans 5–8.* Edited by Beverly Roberts Gaventa. Waco, TX: Baylor University Press, 2013.

———. *Militant Grace: The Apocalyptic Turn and the Future of Christian Theology.* Grand Rapids: Baker Academic, 2018.

Zwiep, A. W. *Ascension of the Messiah in Lukan Christology.* Leiden: Brill, 1997.

Index of Authors

Index of Subjects

Index of Scripture and Other Ancient Sources

481